THE FUTURE OF POLICING

D1613057

The police service in England and Wales is facing major challenges in its financing, political oversight and reorganisation of its structures. Current economic conditions have created a wholly new environment, whereby cost saving is permitting hitherto unthinkable changes in the style and means of delivery of policing services. In the context of these proposed changes Lord Stevens, formerly Commissioner of the Metropolitan Police Service, was asked to chair an Independent Commission looking into the future of policing. The Commission has a wide-ranging remit and the chapters in this book offer an up-to-date analysis of contemporary problems from the novel perspective of developing a reform agenda to assist the Commission.

Bringing together contributions from both key academic thinkers and police professionals, this book discusses new policing paradigms, lays out a case for an evidence-based practice approach and draws attention to developing areas such as terrorism, public order and hate crime.

Policing is too important to be left to politicians, as the health of a democracy can be judged by the relationship between the police and the public. The aim of this book is to question and present analyses of problems, offer new ideas and propose realistically achievable solutions without being so timid as to preserve the status quo. It will be of interest to both academics and students in the fields of criminology and policing studies, as well as professionals in the policing service, NGOs and local authority organisations.

Jennifer M. Brown is a co-director of the Mannheim Centre for Criminology at the London School of Economics. She is also the deputy chair of the Independent Commission looking at the future of policing in England and Wales. She is a chartered forensic and chartered occupational psychologist and has been an active researcher in the areas of police occupational culture and police decision making in the investigation of serious crime. Professor Brown previously worked as research manager for the Hampshire Constabulary where she undertook pioneering studies of stress among police officers and sex discrimination experienced by female police.

THE FUTURE OF POLICING

Edited by Jennifer M. Brown

Routledge
Taylor & Francis Group

LONDON AND NEW YORK

First published 2014
by Routledge
2 Park Square, Milton Park, Abingdon, Oxon, OX14 4RN

and by Routledge
711 Third Avenue, New York, NY 10017

Routledge is an imprint of the Taylor & Francis Group, an informa business

British Library Cataloguing in Publication Data
A catalogue record for this book is available from the British Library

Library of Congress Cataloging-in-Publication Data
The future of policing / [edited by] Jennifer M. Brown.
pages cm
Includes bibliographical references.
    1. Police—Great Britain. 2. Law enforcement—Great Britain.
    I. Brown, Jennifer, 1948-
    HV8195.A2F88 2014
    363.2'30941—dc23
    2013012117

ISBN: 978-0-415-82162-9 (hbk)
ISBN: 978-0-203-43594-6 (ebk)
ISBN: 978-0-415-71184-5 (pbk)

Typeset in Bembo
by Swales & Willis Ltd, Exeter, Devon

MIX
Paper from
responsible sources
FSC® C013604

CONTENTS

ILLUSTRATIONS

Figures

Tables

Boxes

CONTRIBUTORS

Rachel Armitage has over 15 years' experience in crime prevention and has published extensively on the subject of designing out crime – specifically the UK Secured by Design award scheme. She managed a prestigious Home Office project to update the evidence base on the impact of residential design on crime and recently completed a project to develop Abu Dhabi's planning guidance on crime prevention through environmental design. Rachel co-edited a special edition of *Built Environment* on International Perspectives on Planning for Crime Prevention and has just completed a book for Palgrave Macmillan on the impact of residential design on crime. She was elected president of the Design against Crime Association (DOCA) in 2012.

Matthew Bacon is an early-career researcher who was until recently the lead researcher on a study of the contractual governance of drug users at the University of Manchester. Currently he holds a lectureship in Criminology at the University of Sheffield. Drawing on extensive ethnographic fieldwork carried out in two English police service areas, his PhD thesis provides an insight into the world and work of police detectives and the key formal and informal mechanisms underlying the objectives, processes and techniques of drug investigations.

Adrian Barton is an Associate Professor (Senior Lecturer) in Public Management and Policy, School of Management (Plymouth Business School (Faculty). He, with Nick Johns, has an edited collection entitled *Evaluating the Political Achievement of New Labour Since 1997: Social Policy and Public Trust*, published by Edward Mellen Press in 2009. He has a forthcoming book, also with Nick Johns, on *Policymaking in the Criminal Justice System*, published by Routledge.

Ben Bradford is Career Development Fellow at the Centre for Criminology, University of Oxford. Ben has collaborated with the London Metropolitan Police and the National Policing Improvement Agency on several research projects concerned with improving police understanding of public opinions and priorities.

Jennifer M. Brown is Co-director of the Mannheim Centre for Criminology at the London School of Economics where she is a visiting professor. She is also deputy chair of the Independent Commission into the Future of Policing. Her research interests cover gender equality within the police occupational culture and decision making in serious crime.

Robin Bryant is the Director of the Criminal Justice Practice within the Department of Law and Criminal Justice Studies at Canterbury Christ Church University. His research and knowledge exchange has included cybercrime prevention and homicide investigation. He has worked on a number of projects with the National Police Improvement Agency and CEPOL. He is the editor and author of the popular *Blackstone's Handbook for Policing Students*, which is now in its eighth edition. He is also joint editor of *Investigating Digital Crime* (Wiley & Sons, 2008) and joint author of *Understanding Criminal Investigation* (Wiley & Sons, 2009).

Karen Bullock graduated from the London School of Economics in 1998 with a BSc in Social Policy and Sociology. The following summer she obtained an MSc from the University of Surrey in Social Research Methods. Her PhD is from the Jill Dando Institute of Crime Science at University College London. Karen joined the University of Surrey as a lecturer in 2007. Before that she worked in the research directorate at the Home Office. She primarily conducts research in the fields of policing and crime reduction and her teaching reflects these areas of expertise.

Tom Cockcroft came to work at Canterbury Christ Church University in 2004, having previously been employed as a post-doctoral researcher at the University of Kent. Prior to that, he undertook PhD research, using oral history techniques, to investigate the cultural dynamics of the Metropolitan Police Force between the 1930s and the 1960s. A persistent theme in his academic output has related to the area of police culture and in 2012 he published *Police Culture: Themes and Concepts* with Routledge Publishing.

Adam Crawford is Professor of Criminology and Criminal Justice in the Centre for Criminal Justice Studies at the University of Leeds where he is also Pro-Dean for Research and Innovation in the Faculty of Education, Social Sciences and Law. His research and publications have coalesced around policing, crime prevention, urban (in)security and responses to youth crime and anti-social behaviour. His most recent book (co-edited with Anthea Hucklesby) is *Legitimacy and Compliance in Criminal Justice* (Routledge, 2012). He is also Editor in Chief of the journal *Criminology and Criminal Justice*.

Penny Dick is Reader in Critical and Organisational Psychology at the University of Sheffield. Penny received her PhD, which was concerned with the social construction of gender in police work, from Sheffield University in 2000. Penny's research interests include stress; the management of diversity; identity, resistance and power; and the impact of family-friendly policies on organisations and individuals. Published papers include, 'Bending over backwards? Using a pluralistic framework to explore the management of flexible working in the police service', *British Journal of Management*, 2009, 20, 1, 182–193.

Paul Ekblom gained his PhD in psychology at University College London. As a researcher in the Home Office, Paul worked on diverse crime prevention projects; also horizon-scanning; Design Against Crime; and developing the professional discipline and knowledge management of crime prevention. Paul has worked internationally with EU, Europol and Council of Europe. He is currently Professor of Design Against Crime, University of the Arts London at Central Saint Martins, working on design and evaluation of products, places, systems and communications and practical frameworks for general crime prevention and counter terrorism (for example, see http://5isframework.wordpress.com).

Clive Emsley is Emeritus Professor of History and Senior Research Associate at the Open University. He has held visiting posts at the University of Paris VIII, the universities of Calgary, Alberta, and Christchurch, New Zealand and Griffith, Queensland. Most recently he was a Fellow of the Humanities Research Centre at the Australian University and Visiting Professor of the Australian Centre for Excellence in Policing and Security. He was president of the International Association for the History of Crime and Criminal Justice for ten years. His publications include, *The English Police: A Political and Social History* (2nd edn 1996); *Gendarmes and the State in Nineteenth-Century Europe* (1999); *Crime, Police and Penal Policy: European Experiences 1750–1940* (2007); *The Great British Bobby* (revised edn 2009).

Robin S. Engel is Director of the Institute of Crime Science and Associate Professor of Criminal Justice at the University of Cincinnati in the United States. Her research includes qualitative and quantitative assessments of police behaviour, police supervision and management, policing policies, criminal gangs and violence reduction strategies. She serves as the Principal Investigator for numerous contracts and grants, and provides statistical and policy consulting and expert testimony for international, state and municipal law enforcement agencies in the areas of evidence-based policing, police–academic partnerships, police–race relations and violence reduction.

Jenny Fleming was the first Research Professor and then Director of the Tasmanian Institute of Law Enforcement Studies at the University of Tasmania for six years from 2006. She joined the University of Southampton as Professor of Criminology in 2012 and, with Phil Palmer, is co-director of the Institute of Criminal

Justice Research at the University of Southampton. For the past 15 years, Jenny has worked on a formal and informal basis with police agencies and police associations in Australia, the United Kingdom, Scotland, Canada, the Netherlands, the United States and New Zealand. A strong advocate of participatory action research with the emphasis on practitioner involvement, Jenny is the Editor of *Australasian Policing: A Journal of Professional Practice, Policy and Research* and she is also on the editorial board of *Policing: A Journal of Policy and Practice* (UK).

Nicholas R. Fyfe is the founding director of the Scottish Institute for Policing Research, Fellow of the Scottish Police College and Professor of Human Geography at the University of Dundee. He has acted as a Specialist Advisor to the Scottish Parliament's Justice Committee inquiring into the effective use of police resources (2007) and community policing (2009). His areas of research include witness intimidation, witness protection and missing persons, and his in-depth evaluation of a police witness protection programme was published in a book entitled *Protecting Intimidated Witnesses* (Ashgate). More recently he has focused on issues of police reform and has co-edited (with Jan Terpstra and Pieter Tops) *Centralizing Forces? Comparative Perspectives on Contemporary Police Reform in Northern and Western Europe* (Boom Legal Publishers).

Hugo Gorringe is a Senior Lecturer in Sociology at the University of Edinburgh's School of Social and Political Science. His research interests focus on the interactive dynamics between police and protestors. He has looked at the global protests surrounding the Edinburgh G8 meeting in 2005 and the policing of those protests, in collaboration with Michael Rosie. Since then he has investigated challenges to public order policing in the UK, especially since the G20 in 2009. He and Michael Rosie have written on police–protest dynamics; media coverage of protest and policing; experiments in liaison or dialogue policing; and the 2010 student protests.

John G. D. Grieve is a former National Coordinator for Counter Terrorism (CT) in England and Wales and Commander of the Anti-Terrorist Branch at New Scotland Yard. He was a member of the Independent Monitoring Commission (IMC) during the Northern Ireland peace process. Currently he is Professor Emeritus at London Metropolitan University and Senior Research Fellow at University of Portsmouth.

Samantha Henderson is a doctoral student in the School of Criminal Justice at the University of Cincinnati. She graduated from the Wilfrid Laurier University in 2009 with an Honours BA in Criminology and Contemporary Studies, and a minor in Psychology. She earned an MA in Sociology from the University of Waterloo in 2011. She is a Social Sciences and Humanities Research Council of Canada Doctoral Fellowship award holder. Her research interests include focused deterrence, crime prevention and correctional programming.

Alex Hirschfield directs the Applied Criminology Centre at Huddersfield University. His research interests include situational crime prevention, problem-oriented policing and policy evaluation techniques. He led the evaluation of the Reducing Burglary Initiative (Home Office), the New Deal for Communities Crime Theme (ODPM) and investigated the impact of changes to the Licensing Act ('24 hour drinking') on crime. He has worked with a number of police forces on evaluating crime prevention, including a 10 year involvement in the Safer Merseyside Partnership initiative. He served as Home Office Senior Academic Advisor for Government Office North West for six years and is a Fellow of the Faculty of Public Health.

Mike Hough is Co-Director, Institute for Criminal Policy Research, School of Law, Birkbeck, and University of London. He is currently working on a large EU-funded project, FIDUCIA, looking at the best ways of controlling emerging forms of crime across Europe.

Martin Innes is a Professor in the School of Social Sciences at Cardiff University. He is Director of the Universities' Police Science Institute and Deputy Director (Research) for the School. He has published two books and over 50 scholarly articles and papers. Since 2004 he has been Editor of the journal *Policing and Society* published by Routledge. His research interests include reassurance and neighbourhood policing, the signal crimes perspective and homicide investigations. He has been commissioned by and has advised a large number of national and international policing organisations.

Jonathan Jackson is Senior Lecturer in Research Methodology and member of the Mannheim Centre for Criminology at the London School of Economics. Jon has held recent visiting appointments in the Psychology Departments of John Jay College of Criminal Justice (City University of New York) and New York University.

Anja Johansen joined the University of Dundee's History Programme in 2002 after studying and researching at several European institutions: Copenhagen University, the High School for Social Sciences in Paris, The European University Institute in Florence and Clare Hall, Cambridge. Her research is focused on the relationship between police and the public in France, Germany and Britain during the nineteenth and twentieth centuries. Her current research project is 'Quarrelsome Citizens: Emerging Police Complaints Cultures in London, Paris and Berlin, 1880–1914'.

Nick Johns is Senior Lecturer in Social and Public Policy at Cardiff University, Wales. His research interests lie in 'race' issues, ethnic diversity and welfare, sentencing policy and social welfare. He is co-author of *Trust and Substitutes for Trust: The Case of Britain under New Labour* (New York: Nova Science). He has co-authored, with Adrian Barton, *Policymaking in the Criminal Justice System*, published by Routledge.

Paul Johnson went to Derwentside College in Consett to study for a Higher Education Foundation Course after leaving school at 16 and spending five years working in various jobs (and a few periods of unemployment). From there he went to the University of Durham and graduated in 1997 with a BA in Sociology and Social Policy. He stayed in Durham to complete an MA and then obtained a PhD from the University of Newcastle in 2002. Paul then worked in the School of Applied Social Sciences at Durham from 2002 and joined the Department of Sociology in Surrey in 2006.

Matthew Jones is Senior Lecturer in Policing Studies at Liverpool John Moores University. He teaches across the FDA/BA Policing Studies programmes and is the admissions tutor for the department. Matthew's research is concerned with police diversity, specifically the occupational experiences of police officers from minority social groups. He is also concerned with advancing scholarship relating to social science research methods – particularly mixed, online and participatory research methods relating to policing and subaltern populations.

Gloria Laycock graduated in psychology from University College London in 1968 and completed her PhD at UCL in 1975. She worked in the Home Office for over 30 years in policing and crime prevention. She established and headed the Home Office Police Research Group in 1992. In 1999 she was awarded an International Visiting Fellowship by the United States Department of Justice based in Washington DC. She returned to the UK in April 2001 to become the first Director of the UCL Jill Dando Institute of Crime Science. She is currently Head of the UCL Department of Security and Crime Science and Director of the new £7m EPSRC-funded Doctoral Training Centre in Security Science at UCL.

Ian Loader is Professor of Criminology at the University of Oxford and Professorial Fellow at All Souls College. He is author or co-author of six books, the latest being *Public Criminology?* (2010, Routledge, with R. Sparks) and his writings cover contemporary transformations in policing and security; the intersections between politics, criminology and crime control; and penal politics and culture. Ian was a member of the Commission on English Prisons Today from 2007 to 2009, and now chairs the Research Advisory Group of the Howard League for Penal Reform. He has, since 2006, been co-convener, with the Police Foundation, of the Oxford Policing Policy Forum. Ian is an Associate Fellow of IPPR and is a member of the Independent Commission into the Future of Policing.

Peter K. Manning (PhD, Duke), is the Elmer V.H. and Eileen M. Brooks Chair in the School of Criminology and Criminal Justice at Northeastern University. He has been a Visiting Scholar at Goldsmiths College, the University of Surrey, a

Fellow of Wolfson and Balliol College, Oxford, and a Senior Researcher at the Centre for Socio-Legal Studies, Oxford.

Andrew Millie is Professor of Criminology at Edge Hill University. He is interested in aspects of policing, philosophical criminology, urban criminalisation and anti-social behaviour. He is the author of *Anti-Social Behaviour* (Open University Press, 2009) and editor of the collection *Securing Respect: Behavioural Expectations and Anti-Social Behaviour in the UK* (2009, The Policy Press). Andrew has recently co-edited (with Karen Bullock) a special issue of the journal *Criminology & Criminal Justice* entitled 'Policing in a time of contraction and constraint: Re-imagining the role and function of contemporary policing'.

Aogán Mulcahy is a Senior Lecturer in Sociology at University College Dublin. His main research interests are in the broad area of policing and social change, particularly the dynamics of the police reform process, the role of 'community' within policing debates, and relations between the police and marginalised communities.

Megan O'Neill has recently moved to the University of Dundee. She was formerly a Senior Lecturer in Criminology at the University of Salford in the Centre for Social Research. Her work focuses broadly on issues of police culture, including its expression in partnership work, Neighbourhood Policing, with Police Community Support Officers, the private sector and in football policing. She has written extensively on police occupational culture and explored in particular attitudes towards and experiences of various 'minority' groups within policing.

Samuel Peterson is a doctoral student in the College of Criminal Justice at the University of Cincinnati. He received a BA in psychology and criminology from the University of Northern Iowa and an MS in Criminal Justice from the University of Cincinnati. He is currently a research associate in the Institute of Crime Science where he works on a number of violence reduction projects, including the Cincinnati Initiative to Reduce Violence (CIRV). His current research interests include programme evaluation, gang networks, and life-course criminology and the desistance process.

Jason Roach is Reader in Crime and Policing and Director of the Crime and Policing Group, at the University of Huddersfield. Jason is a chartered psychologist who has previously worked in mental health services and as a crime analyst for the UK Home Office. Jason's current areas of research and publication include: criminal psychology, police decision making, violent crime and homicide, self-selection policing, crime prevention, and criminal investigative practice. Jason continues to act as an advisor to several police forces with regard to the investigation of serious crime and the reviewing of 'cold case homicides'.

Michael Rowe is Professor of Criminology at Northumbria University and Director of the Centre for Offenders and Offending. His research interests have embraced a wide range of issues in relation to racism, ethnicity and criminal justice, as well as in policing and desistance from crime.

Mark Roycroft, now at the University of West London, was a Lecturer in Forensic and Crime Science at Stafford University. He received his doctorate at the University of Surrey on decision making in murder enquiries. He was formerly a police officer, reaching the rank of Detective Chief Inspector in the Metropolitan Police Service. He also had a secondment with the National Policing Improvement Agency. He has published a number of papers on the investigation of murder.

Dan Silverstone has a BSc and PhD from the London School of Economics and is currently a Principal Lecturer and Head of Criminology at London Metropolitan University. His research expertise is in the areas of organised crime, drugs and night time economy and illegal firearms use.

Marisa Silvestri is a Reader in Criminology and Head of the Crime and Criminal Justice Research Group at London South Bank University. Her research interests are focused on the broad areas of gender, policing and criminal justice. In particular she is interested in women in police leadership and the impacts of a gendered criminal justice system. In addition to various articles and reports, she is author of *Women in Charge: Gender, Policing and Leadership* (2002, Willan Press) and co-author (with C. Crowther-Dowey) of *Gender and Crime* (2008, Sage).

David Alan Sklansky is Yosef Osheawich Professor of Law at the University of California, Berkeley, where he teaches and writes about policing, criminal procedure and evidence law. David started his career as a federal prosecutor in Los Angeles.

Peter Sproat is a Lecturer in Policing at the Hamilton Campus of the University of West of Scotland. He teaches modules on policing, transnational crime and international responses, and comparative criminal justice. His research interests include terrorism, counter-terrorist finance, money laundering, asset recovery and the policing of organised crime.

Kevin Stenson is Visiting Professor at the Mannheim Centre for Criminology, the University of Kent and London Metropolitan University. His wide range of research has included studies of police stop and search, fear of crime, and community safety strategies.

Clifford Stott is the Principal Research Fellow of the Security and Justice Research Group and a Visiting Professor to the Business School at the University of Leeds. His research focuses upon the underlying causes, psychology and management of 'riots'. In particular he is interested in the relationships between policing, group interaction, social identity, power and legitimacy in the development of collective conflict. He publishes extensively on these issues and advises governments and police forces internationally.

Nick Tilley is a Professor in the Department of Security and Crime Science, where he is the Director of the UCL Security Science Research Training Centre. He is also Emeritus Professor of Sociology at Nottingham Trent University. He was seconded to the Home Office to undertake research there from 1992–2003. He was an advisor to the Government Office for the East Midlands from 2003 to 2008.

Steve Tong is the Director of Policing in the Department of Law & Criminal Justice at Canterbury Christ Church University. His research interests include police learning and development, professionalisation, criminal investigation, police practice and qualitative research. He has recently published articles in the *Journal of Investigative Psychology and Offender Profiling, Police Journal, Police Practice & Research* and *International Journal of Police Science and Management* and is joint author of *Blackstone's Handbook for Policing* (2013) and *Understanding Criminal Investigation* (Wiley & Sons, 2009).

Louise Westmarland is a Senior Lecturer in Criminology with the Open University. She is currently conducting an extensive survey of police officers' corrupt behaviour and beliefs about their actions and those of their colleagues. Recent publications include: 'Police ethics and integrity: breaking the blue code of silence', *Policing and Society*, Vol. 15, No. 2, 2005, pp. 145–165, and 'Policing Integrity: Britain's Thin Blue Line' in Klockars, C.B., Haberfeld, M. and Kutjnak Ivkovich, S. (2003) *The Contours of Police Integrity*, Thousand Oaks, CA, Sage.

Dominic Wood is Head of the Department for Law & Criminal Justice Studies and the Chair of the Higher Education Forum for Learning and Development in Policing. His research interests include police education, police ethics and police governance and he has published articles in *Police Journal, Police Practice & Research* and *International Journal of Police Science and Management*. He has contributed to all eight editions of *Blackstone's Handbook for Policing*. In 2004 he was a Visiting Professor at Simon Fraser University in Canada.

PREFACE

I am delighted to write a few words to introduce this edited collection about the future of policing. The police service is facing challenges unprecedented in my police career which spans over 40 years. Questions facing the service about its integrity, ethical practices, public disorder, and its relationships with the wider community though are not new. My earliest days as a Metropolitan police officer were marked by the aftermath of the Challoner Enquiry in 1964 which investigated allegations of planted evidence on young protestors and which was crucial in developing thinking about ethical codes of practice. I have long thought registration and professionalisation were the key to making the police service more accountable.

In my time as Chief Constable of Northumbria, I and my colleagues had to get to grips with breakdowns of public order in the Meadowell Estate so I am very attuned to the problems confronting the Metropolitan Police Service when facing the riots in August 2011. I have always looked to the academic community for fresh ideas. James Morgan's research on local delivery of crime prevention initiatives through partnership very much influenced my thinking while at Northumbria when we began an ambitious programme of public consultation to develop our community safety strategy.

I have had the privilege of leading several inquiries including the inquiry into the misuse of secret intercept evidence by the National Criminal Intelligence Service and three into allegations of collusion between loyalist paramilitaries and security services in Northern Ireland. My inclinations in these and the investigation into Princess Diana's death, and inquiries into sports corruption, are the same as my approach to the Independent Police Commission which I am chairing: to go where the evidence takes you.

In early December, 2011 the Labour Party set up the Commission into the future of policing in the 21st century. I have 40 colleagues assisting in the work of the Commission, hearing witness evidence and chairing regional meetings to widen the scope of the public's involvement. I very much wanted to run the Commission as closely as possible to the principles of a Royal Commission and I am grateful to them in helping me to do this.

I am also indebted to the scholars who have contributed to this volume because they, as an academic reference group advising the Commission, have contributed the evidence base to our thinking. They have done so as acts of goodwill and their work illustrates their independence of thought, deep understanding of policing and commitment towards creating a professional police service to serve the people of our country.

Particularly close to my heart is the work in the book discussing the police culture and the importance of a diverse workforce. Surveys that have been undertaken as part of the work of the Commission reveal a disturbing loss of morale and sense of direction from those working within the police service, both officers and support staff. We have talented people who feel frustrated in developing their ideas and are rather beleaguered by the raft of reforms which they have not had a hand in shaping. The Commission has been listening to them and to the ideas in this book. Procedural justice reveals the startlingly simple idea that if managers and supervisors treat their staff fairly, they will sign up to the values of a professional public service and perform well because it is the right thing to do.

The chapters address questions that the Commission has been grappling with: what are the police for, how to make the police accountable, what skills and qualities we want of those working within the police, how do we accommodate the private sector in the delivery of policing? These thoughtful essays have informed the Commission's debates and contributed hugely to the working through of the many strands of evidence we have gathered. I am reminded of some reflections when I undertook some of my own research in the 1990s. There is often a knee jerk reaction to concerns about the police and a desire to try to fix things without asking the basic questions about what reforms are needed and why and the principles that the reforms should adhere to. The contributions in this book have given us the intellectual raw materials to carefully consider both why we need reform and what the grounding principles are.

Jennifer Brown is to be congratulated and commended on getting together a wide range of researchers and thinkers from a variety of backgrounds and disciplines who have so generously contributed their chapters. This is a book which not only assisted the work of the Commission but will also be a valued resource for all of those interested in the health and wellbeing of policing and those working for the service.

Lord Stevens of Kirkwhelpington
2013

ACKNOWLEDGEMENTS

The Independent Police Commission owes a considerable debt to the academic reference group who contributed their papers and worked them into chapters for this edited collection. They are all incredibly busy people with many calls upon their time. There was an amazingly generous response to our call for help. So thank you to Rachel Armitage, Matthew Bacon, Adrian Barton, Ben Bradford, Robin Bryant, Karen Bullock, Tom Cockcroft, Adam Crawford, Penny Dick, Paul Ekblom, Clive Emsley, Robin Engel, Jenny Fleming, Nick Fyfe, Hugo Gorringe, John Grieve, Samantha Henderson, Alex Hirschfield, Mike Hough, Martin Innes, Jonathan Jackson, Anja Johansen, Nick Johns, Paul Johnson, Matthew Jones, Gloria Laycock, Ian Loader, Peter Manning, Andrew Millie, Aogán Mulcahy, Megan O'Neill, Samuel Peterson, Jason Roach, Michael Rowe, Mark Roycroft, Marisa Silvestri, Dan Silverstone, David Sklansky, Pete Sproat, Kevin Stenson, Cliff Stott, Nick Tilley, Steve Tong, Louise Westmarland and Dominic Wood for your endeavours.

Thank you to Nicola Hartley and colleagues from Routledge for your patience and support in getting the book ready for publication.

Jennifer Brown would also like to note her thanks to colleagues from the Mannheim Centre at LSE for their unfailing support, continued interest and timely advice.

INTRODUCTION

Third wave policing reform

Jennifer M. Brown

Introduction

On 6 December 2011 the Right Honourable Yvette Cooper MP, shadow Home Secretary, invited Lord Stevens to chair an Independent Commission into the Future of Policing. Commissions have a long history as a way to enquire into the state of policing. Ever since its inception there has been a cycle of concerns, enquiries and deliberations seeking improvement in the public police service. Indeed, prior to the passing of the Metropolis Police Improvement Act in 1829, Sir Robert Peel observed that there had been eight committees over the preceding 56 years investigating policing arrangements for the capital. When introducing the Bill in a debate in the House of Commons on 15 April 1829, he said

> I think – and it is useless to disguise the fact – that the time is come, when, from the increase in its population, the enlargement of its resources, and the multiplied development of its energies, we may fairly pronounce that the country has outgrown her police institutions, and that the cheapest and safest course will be found to be the introduction of a new mode of protection.

Have we outgrown our present policing institutions? Why do we need another Commission of Enquiry? Well, it has been a long time since we had a Royal Commission on the police. Peel's was the first great reform of the police, establishing a paid professional force whose primary purpose was to prevent crime and maintain order. The second wave of reform was associated with the advent of technology in the form of radios, motorised patrols and the amalgamations into the present 43 separate forces in England and Wales. That was over 60 years ago and we now are on the cusp of another set of significant reforms whose ramifications have yet to be played out. The world in which we live has changed significantly since the last Royal

Commission on the Police sat in 1960–62. Conditions prevailing then included: the growth of affluence; decline in deference; inclination to question authority; glorification of youth culture; civil protest; self-conscious Afro-Caribbean/ Asian identity; changes wrought by new technology; police scandals. The backdrop against which the current Commission sits is austerity rather than affluence. There have been advances in information technology that have given individuals access to the world wide web and changed our mode of social interaction. Other shifts include the means of informal social control. Lost are the park keepers, bus conductors and station porters who were among the sentinels of social order to be replaced by surveillance cameras and CCTV. In 1983 the then Home Secretary issued Circular (HO 114/83) which introduced the vocabulary of economy, efficiency and effectiveness into the police service and extolled the virtues of multi-agency partnerships, regional collaborations and dissemination of innovative practice. What followed was the introduction of New Public Management as a way to induce private sector discipline into public sector organisations, changes in the constitution of Police Authorities and increases in the number of the professionally qualified taking senior roles in the police with portfolios such as finance, computing and personnel management.

Savage (2007) tells us that reform is driven by a process of politicisation of the police, policy disasters, police failures, scandals and corruption and that a combination of legislative changes, imported ideas and home grown initiatives lead to changing police practices. The aftermath of the Leveson inquiry into phone hacking and the media's relationship with the police; various Independent Police Complaints Commission investigations into operational failures, introduction of elected police and crime commissioners would indicate the presence of Savage's cocktail of ingredients.

The police service itself is aware of its own shortcomings. Sir Denis O'Connor, a former chief inspector of Her Majesty's Inspectorate of Constabulary told the House of Commons Home Affairs Committee (2011) in evidence of a 'parent–child' relationship that can pervade the police service and Sir Ronnie Flanagan, another former chief HMI spoke of 'a culture of "risk aversion" which can seriously dilute, or at worst remove, discretion or professional judgement'. Reasons for this over reliance on prescription has been attributed to 'status quo bias' (Harris, 2012) i.e. the sense that movement away from trusted and tried ways of doing things leads to a diminution or loss of what previously had been valued and a narrowing of 'organisational attention' (Brown, 2007) whereby anxiety engendered by a threat to the organisation's integrity will overly concentrate managements on that problem at the expense of other matters.

The present Coalition Government has a speed and scale of police reform in England and Wales indicative of a determination to engineer a revolution in British policing. Whether this is a coherent programme is a matter of debate but Theresa May, the present Home Secretary, has clearly signalled that the objective is to create a leaner, more locally responsive police service whose prime purpose is to focus on cutting crime (May, 2013). The Coalition Government's design is one that seems to narrow the role of policing to deterrent, reactive crime fighting. There has already been a reduction in police numbers – 7 per cent in front line officer numbers across England & Wales – a loss of some 7,000 officers between 2010 and 2012. An overall loss of 30,000 officers is projected by 2014–15. It is likely that further cuts will be made in the next Spending Review. Financial austerity will be part of the restructuring context for policing for the foreseeable future. This effectively rules out spending our way to improved service or performance. We will not only have to be more ingenious but also create an interlocking programme whereby options for change are mutually supportive rather than a dislocated Heath Robinson engine where unintended consequences frustrate forward momentum.

So it is timely to have an Independent Commission into the Future of Policing. The Commission was asked to look at:

1   The challenges for policing in the 21st century – what is the role of the police and what is expected of the police?
2   How to deliver the workforce to best equip the police to cut crime and increase public confidence.
3   The police's relationship with the wider criminal justice system and the agencies of the state.
4   Governance and accountability – how to ensure the police are both held to account but unencumbered by bureaucracy.
5   Striking the right balance between the need for the police service to meet both local and national priorities, and the national structures to support that effort.
6   Management of resources and the efficiencies to be found to get the most out of police spending.

The Commission

The machinery set up by Lord Stevens to undertake the work of reviewing the future of policing in England and Wales is not that of a Royal Commission. It has not the status, powers or resources. However, it has gone about its work in the manner of a Royal Commission by holding witness hearings, conducting attitude surveys and making visits to hear views of those outside London. The Commission has a body of invited participants making up an advisory panel[1] and a reference group of academics. This book presents the papers contributed by those academics whose brief was to present ideas around some key themes to assist the Commission in its deliberations. The themes identified by the Commission are: purpose of policing, legitimacy, delivery, organisation, relationships, the workforce and resourcing.

The Commission will be reporting in due course, which at time of writing, is intended to be October 2013. The purpose of this edited collection is to make the work of the academic reference group publicly available. The papers have fed into the Commission's discussions and formulations and it was felt important that these analyses be transparent. As a collection, it is to be hoped that in addition the contents of this volume will be a useful resource to scholars and practitioners who have an interest in promoting this step change towards a professional model of policing.

It is not the task of the academic reference group to pre-empt the conclusions of the Commission. The work presented here is intended as a companion volume to the Commission's report when published. So there might be some disappointment that there is not a programme of change recommended within these pages. The book is not attempting to provide a broad-based introduction to policing subjects such as can be found in the handbook edited by Tim Newburn (Newburn, 2008) nor is it an historical treatise tracing the development of policy initiatives and previous reform efforts (see Savage, 2007). Rather, readers will find reviews of the relevant literature, analyses of evidence, critical opinion and some speculation but, even more importantly, the outlining of ideas such as procedural justice, and concepts such as the professional project and social identity, which can be applied to new ways of thinking about police and policing. Lessons from other policing jurisdictions, within the UK and also from Australia and the United States are included.

The Commission's report very broadly will be organised under three headings: challenges of contemporary policing; practice of policing; and support for policing. The chapters in this book reflect these headings. As a preliminary, each section has an editor's introduction that briefly outlines the ideas discussed and developed in the chapters, and cross references to other chapters where relevant.

The challenges of contemporary policing

Parts I and II of the book ask some basic questions:

- Where does the modern police service come from?
- What are the limits to the state divesting itself of its policing responsibilities?
- Why do the police matter?
- What are the police for?
- How can we re-invent the office of constable?
- How can we define good policing?

Through these chapters, there is a firm declaration that policing is more than crime fighting and the model to emerge is a tripartite crime control *and* social service *and* order maintenance one. There is not a naive nostalgia for Dixonian omni competence, but there is recognition that the police cannot do everything. The authors vigorously argue that critical aspects of the police's functions in a healthy democracy should not be thrown out with the crime fighting bathwater. Ideas drawn from procedural justice are introduced which, in an over simplification, state that treating people fairly is not only a reasonable thing to do, but also engenders compliance with trusted institutions.

Analysis of successes and failings of the police often turn to the police culture for an explanation. Said to be resistant to change and responsible for discriminatory treatment both within and without the service, it is crucial to understand the dynamics and meaning of this if the police are to be responsive to new ideas. Part II of the book looks at culture through the lenses of race and ethnicity, gender and sexual orientation. An idea that emerges from these chapters is the notion of disruption to the status quo bias as a precursor to reorientate organisational attention towards establishing new ways of working.

The practice of policing

Tangible new ways of working are presented in Parts III and IV. Chapters here take on issues such as the addition of new members to the extended police family as coming from the private sector and academia. Examples are provided of the contribution to be made by these new players and the developing of criteria that manage new relationships. Case studies of neighbourhood policing and crime prevention work show how innovating in these areas of policing can not only reclaim public confidence, but also rehabilitate and enhance the status and prestige of these as specialisms.

The concepts of high and low policing, meaning duties associated with routine locally delivered services and state-level national security, are discussed in the delivery section. Rather than a separation of powers, the case is made uncompromisingly that local and national are intimately connected and embedded in communities. Police security operations that may succeed in the short term, if not carefully conceived, may result in longer term erosion of public confidence. The rapprochement between police and academia is illustrated through the concept of police liaison teams which draws on social psychological principles and policing crowd control tactics to create new ways of managing protest and large events. Lessons from Northern Ireland are drawn upon through a discussion of counter terrorism policing, in juxtaposition with analysis of hate crime as a neat illustration of the complementarity of high and low policing. The relative pros and cons of models of delivering organised crime policing are presented as well as the dangers associated with too close a link between the state's aims and operational policing.

Supporting policing

Given the police service has powers to use force and restrict a citizen's liberty, maintaining the rule of law and abiding by its own precepts is critical in the sustaining of trust and building legitimacy of the police. Satisfaction with the quality of police–public encounters is premised on impartiality and treating people with dignity, yet there is evidence that young people and those from black and ethnic minorities feel a sense of alienation through tactics such as stop and search. While crime rates are dropping, detection rates are variable. So depending on the type of crime a member of the public is a victim of there is a greater or lesser chance of that being detected.

One route to building greater satisfaction, confidence and trust is through the 'professional project' (MacDonald, 1995). This is an occupation's quest to develop a body of knowledge that supports a more systematic approach to its endeavours and a licensing of its practitioners. Part V describes progress made in Australia and America to this end as well as offering ways to achieve this aspiration within England and Wales.

The twin to professionalism is accountability. This involves a discussion of standard setting, regulation and inspection on the one hand and democratic oversight on the other. These are the subjects of Part VI which includes an analysis of the police and crime commissioners.

Two policing remodellings have already taken place within the United Kingdom. Policing in Northern Ireland transformed itself after the Patten Commission and the Sustainable Policing Project team advised the setting up of a national force for Scotland. Reflections on these two great reform projects are also given.

Conclusion

The arguments presented in these pages point to the development of a new model of policing for England and Wales with a mandate to promote as well as maintain order, having a police service with a social purpose that takes the service element seriously and one that prevents as well as detects crime. Underpinning relationships within the police itself and between the police and the public are ideas drawn from procedural justice; treating people fairly and with dignity. Demand for policing will have to be managed but this can be done through triaging the neediest and targeting resources where they will be most effective, which is better done by drawing on an evidence base of what works.

The details of how this may be achieved are a matter for the Commission.

Note

1 A full list of Commissioners is available at http://independentpolicecommission.org.uk/References

References

Brown, J. (2007) From cult of masculinity to smart macho, in M. O'Neill, M. Marks and A.-M. Singh (eds.) *Police Occupational Cultures: New Debates and Directions*. Sociology of Crime, Law and Deviance, Volume 8, Amsterdam: Elsevier, pp. 205–226.

Flanagan, Sir Ronnie (2007) *The Review of Policing: Interim Report*. London: Home Office.

Harris, D. (2012) *Failed Evidence: Why Law Enforcement Resists Science*. New York: New York Press.

House of Commons Home Affairs Committee (2011) *New Policing Landscape*. 14th session 2010/12, Vol. 1 Report. HC 939. Transcript of Sir Denis O'Connor's evidence. London: Stationery Office.

MacDonald, K. (1995) *The Sociology of the Professions*. London: Sage.

May, T. (2013) A singular focus on cutting crime, in P. Neyroud (ed.) *Policing UK 2013: Priorities and Pressure, a Year of Transformation*. London: Witan Media.

Newburn, T. (ed.) (2008) *Handbook of Policing*. Cullompton: Willan.

Savage, S. (2007) *Police Reform: Forces for Change*. Oxford: Oxford University Press.

INTRODUCTION TO PARTS I AND II

Challenges of contemporary policing

Jennifer M. Brown

Introduction

This first section of the book analyses the purposes of the public police, identifies some of the key problem areas, such as aspects of the police culture, and as diagnosed, presents some remedies.

In essence, the chapters take a critical look at the emphasis on the crime-fighting component of policing and argue that, while necessary, this is not a sufficient mandate for the police. There needs to be, in addition, a social mandate which performs reassuring and community strengthening functions. The police also have a symbolic function in terms of representing what is right and presenting a statement about the nation's efforts to secure order and preserve the peace. As Herbert (2006: 81) says, the police are a visible reminder of the state's coercive power representing both 'the majesty and potential tyranny of state authority'. The focus on law enforcement and crime control and its associated police style has its locus in the occupational culture. The contributions in Part II look at the problems this can generate. When police abuse their powers we are doubly disappointed. Like the priest who sins and the bank manager who embezzles, the self-serving or immoral police officer undermines confidence in the people who are meant to protect and serve us.

The questions the first six chapters address include: what are the police for? Why are the police important? What do police do? How do the police focus on the relevant information in today's data-rich world? What is good policing? Ideas from this last question are picked up in the Part II chapters on police culture. These chapters introduce the idea of disruption as a way to confront and change culture. This, in turn, feeds into notions of professionalism (which is dealt with in more detail in Part V).

Several themes are discernible in the chapters in Part I. First there is the developing argument about the originating purposes of the police as protection and prevention and how, in more recent times, this has been truncated by a political focus on reducing crime. The authors, in their different ways, seek to reclaim the expanded version of the policing purpose. Second, collectively the chapters take a time perspective – looking historically, providing a critical contemporary take and developing some ideas about the future – thereby revealing the evolving phases of the model of British policing. Third there is a recognition that the police cannot do everything. Suggestions are made about areas to retreat from and the need to target efforts for those who need interventions most. Finally, authors ask some fundamental questions and contest some prevailing assumptions such as the relationship between crime rates and police action and utilitarian models for why people do and do not commit crime.

The British model of policing has been described in a recent HMIC report as an approachable, impartial and accountable style of policing based on minimum force designed to *win* public consent through tolerance and patience (HMIC, 2009). In the opening chapter, Clive Emsley describes the characteristics of the early Metropolitan Police as being unarmed, non-military, emanating from the people and serving the public impartially regardless of wealth or social standing. He argues this is contested territory. While not in military red, nevertheless police officers wore and still wear uniform. He indicates that from the outset, the protection of life and property were among the chief aims of the police and this did favour the propertied classes with police activity rather more directed at the disorderly, lower classes. A contemporary critique by Brogden and Ellison (2013: 20) claims 'state policing is primarily a practice of enforcing unequal laws within an unequal social order mandate against unequal peoples'. This thesis, that policing was and still is the 'regulation of the lower classes' is picked up by and discussed in Andrew Millie's chapter.

Emsley reminds us of the Peelian principles in which prevention was seen as the paramount function of the police whose success was couched in terms of the absence of crime. The maintenance of order was also enshrined as a Peelian principle. Notwithstanding Emsley's refuting the provenance of the principles, nonetheless they are upheld as a model of democratic policing. A number of scholars, including Robert Reiner, observe that over the last two decades public and political discourse about the role of policing in England and Wales has fundamentally changed. He writes 'two propositions have become axiomatic, a) crime fighting is the central police task and b) the police are central to the control and reduction of crime' (Reiner, 2012: 5). What Reiner argues is that there is a broader social service function of policing. This theme runs through Andrew Millie's chapter as he tries to answer the question: what are the police for? He posits that as well as crime control and order maintenance, the police make a contribution to improving the citizen's quality of life and feelings of safety. He presents an argument that use of the risk paradigm, i.e. intervention to reduce risk, has contributed to the police's role shifting from the preservation of order to the production of order. He reiterates the criticality in times of austerity to retain the triple focus on crime, social service and order-maintenance functions.

Peter K. Manning provides a chronology of the last decades of police reform in England and Wales which, he argues, is illustrative of an increasing political valency. Intervention in standard setting, performance management, regulation, introduction of the market and shifts towards efficiency demonstrate, in his terms, 'the willingness of politicians to take on police' as an institution *of* government (*my emphasis*). The police, he says, are intimately connected to state legitimacy, tradition and social order. 'The police are the visible, everyday any day face of the state to the citizen.'

Martin Innes articulates phases in the reform process in the police. He thinks we are now in a third wave of reform in which the officer is moving from the generalist to more specialist roles, such as neighbourhood policing, response and investigation. This trend is augmented by the information environment and, just as radios transformed policing in earlier decades, IT and mobile technology will transform policing in this decade. Ian Loader in his chapter provides a plausible explanation for why the present Coalition Government's policing reforms for England and Wales are so wide and being carried out with such speed. He suggests that the Government's analysis of the police service is that it lacks incentives to improve performance, is wasteful of public money and is unresponsive to its customers. Financial austerity provides the imperative to make sweeping changes. But, says Loader, the logic of their policies is focused on the police becoming more effective crime fighters. Indeed at the launch of the College of Policing, a Coalition Government innovation, the police minister, Damien Green, stated that the objective of the college was to help the police become better at fighting crime. In his chapter, Loader protests at this concentration on the crime-fighting purpose, rather he describes the police's function as one that also regulates conflict and that the police play a role in repairing trust that has been breached by the harm caused by crime.

Ben Bradford, Jonathan Jackson and Mike Hough pursue the concept of trust and how this speaks to the legitimacy of the police. They dispute the utilitarian notion that people make a risk benefit calculation as a precursor to breaking the law in terms of the possibility of gain against the chances of being caught. They draw upon Tyler's ideas of procedural justice and their starting point is that actually people are inclined to be cooperative and they conform because they think it is the right thing to do. Beginning with this premise, their question is 'Can the police encourage people to do the right thing?' They argue that to be able to do this, the police themselves must do the right thing by respecting the rule of law and following their own rules and procedures. Doing so confers legitimacy to the authority wielded by the police. Then, so their argument goes, how people are treated by the police helps to shape individuals' and, by implication, communities', sense of identity through a sharing of values. This, in turn, contributes to strengthening the connect to society at large.

Martin Innes shows how this may be achieved through a reconfiguring of the role of the constable that occurred in South Wales. He sees the police as harnessing the social capital possessed by communities in order to respond to the needs of people rather than have policing priorities organisationally defined, i.e. a needs-based model rather than a demand-led one. The South Wales model was an experiment in structured community engagement which captured and mapped intelligence and fed this back to the community to aid in interpretation and participation in making choices about how and where to direct activity and resources. This then helps to address the Brogden and Ellison critique, as an evaluation of the initiative showed there to be a broader range of people involved in the public consultation and an extension of the geographic concentration of police activity.

As mentioned above, these chapters draw attention to the idea that the public police have an important symbolic role. Ian Loader and Peter K. Manning talk about the police sending signals about the world being an ordered and safe place. One area playing this role is visible patrol. Andrew Millie discusses this and also mentions the symbolic value of police stations and messages sent out through their closures. In an analysis of the power that the police station invokes, McLaughlin (2008) says

> The Home Office's performance management regime has systematically disassembled the 'structures of feeling' and traditions associated with the Dixonian policing model – this includes the asset stripping of multi-functional 'blue lamp' police stations. At its most simple, the inability of performance management to encapsulate cultural meanings methodologically means that these aspects of public police work are deemed to be not just irrelevant but an obstacle to reform. As a consequence, public legitimacy is degraded as technical capabilities are enhanced.

Manning's chapter anticipates a more detailed discussion about the role of the private sector in the provision of policing (see also chapters by Adam Crawford and Mark Roycroft in Part III). Manning's point is that the public police have specific obligations in that people cannot actually refuse their services and, as recipients of service, do not in reality have choices. That a particular force happens to be rather good at, say, investigating burglaries is of little use to a victim living the other side of the country. He also suggests that there is a conceptual separation, which too often is conflated, between the economic domains of efficiency and effectiveness and the moral which is about service, fairness and justice. This links into the discussion by Bradford and his co-authors who ask the question 'What is good policing?' They suggest three outcomes that measure the success of policing: crime reduction; building strong links with communities and providing reassurance; and being just and fair. Such a triumvirate reinforces the assessment in Millie's chapter. This involves, first, targeting strategies, as described by Innes, where resources are pointed at groups who most need interventions and, second, tackling the police culture which is the subject of the chapters in Part II.

Police culture has been the subject of considerable attention as an analytic and conceptual device which Matthew Bacon takes us through in his chapter. He presents a critical deconstruction of the descriptive and explanatory power attributed to the construct and snakes his way through the 'contested, complicated and contradictory' claims made for its utility. In reviewing the many and various definitions offered, he establishes a consensus which says that police culture, by and large, is taken to mean beliefs and values; taken-for-granted assumptions; and artefacts (language, stories, symbols) that play a role in shaping attitudes and guiding behaviour. He makes several very important points. First, that police culture is not monolithic and that there are differences within the organisation; second, police are reflective of attitudes in broader society; third that what may be said in talk is not necessarily translated into action; and fourth, as people, those working in the police have individual histories, backgrounds and experiences which they bring to bear on the choices they make in accepting or rejecting the cultural paraphernalia that permeates the police service.

Bacon, like the other authors in this section of the book, explains why an understanding of police culture is so important. Dick and colleagues, Rowe, and Jones show that there are problems associated with the experiences of officers and staff on grounds of gender, race and sexual orientation, respectively, which result in discriminatory treatment inimitable to their working in an optimal environment that makes best use of their skills. Further, the attitudes delineated by these authors shown to prevail within the service, are associated with the way in which some officers deal with members of the public in these protected categories (as exemplified in the case of stop and search detailed by Rowe).

As laid out in the Introduction to this book, the Independent Police Commission was asked to address a series of questions. This first section of the book teases out the role that police might play and workforce issues. First, a case is made to reclaim a communitarian role for the police alongside its crime-fighting function. Second, ways to improve both operational effectiveness and managerial fairness through the medium of occupational culture are laid out. Police culture stands accused of creating problem behaviours on the one hand and being a barrier to change on the other. The analysis presented in Part II develops the hint, provided by Manning when he says that the Winsor proposals to reform the police are potentially 'disruptive' in rewarding officers and relabelling what it is to be a 'good' officer, i.e. one who acquires educational qualifications and is physically fit and able to perform their duties. Penny Dick, Marisa Silvestri and Louise Westmarland argue a case for a focus on gender and Matthew Jones for different sexualities in order to permit a degree of disruption in the taken-for-granted ways of doing things and create changes in the reference group who traditionally have been the markers of good officers.

Notions of the good officer derive from occupational culturally acquired knowledge and approbation which, according to Fielding (1994), is a portfolio of 'good arrests' and 'street cred'. Police culture provides resources whereby officers make sense of the world and come to understand how things are done and what is valued. The means by which they do this, as new recruits, are to observe behaviours, be told stories, and to be rewarded or sanctioned as they undertake the practices of the existing members of the organisation. This knowledge is subjective, experiential, commonsense, informal, pragmatic, and recruits are dependent on others to say whether what they are doing is right. In addition, as Westmarland shows in Chapter 29 on ethics, a loyalty develops to those you work with because of your reliance on colleagues for assistance, advice and solidarity.

Bloor and Dawson (1994), in discussing the entry of professional knowledge into an organisation, describe how this is formal, systematic, ethically codified and intended to create autonomous practice in which checking gives way to trust. The professional assumes responsibility for his/her competence and conduct which has an external, objective and certified imprimatur. If police practices, operationally, managerially and interpersonally are to change, then there needs to be a shift from the occupational culture's reference group from whom organisational behaviours are learnt and attitudes transmitted, to a professional reference group such as the newly established College of Policing as the locus of authoritative practice.

Additionally, Penny Dick and her colleagues intimate that the disruption in the taken-for-granted everyday routines may be achieved through a practice-based approach. So, their argument goes, rather than external shocks and major external intervention, practice theory proposes incremental internally generated shifts. Now, they are not saying there is no need for some external drivers of change, but that there are important 'transformational' spaces in which to challenge the taken for granted. For example, focusing on neighbourhood policing, as Megan O'Neill shows in Part III, and Crime Prevention work discussed by Alex Hirschfield and colleagues in Part IV, are sites within policing where the value of doing these differently, gaining positive outcomes, changes the poor status previously attributed to these policing duties.

Another means for changing taken-for-granted assumptions and ways of doing things is through the disruptive potential of 'otherness'. In a world that is skewed by a particular social grouping which, in the case of the police is white, straight men, and adoption of cultural resources which promotes the identity of that group, then those who do not fit that category are cast as 'other'. Being other is to be considered separate and different (Chryssochoou, 2004) whose presence challenges norms and practices. There is a literature (e.g. Fielding, 1994; Cavender and Jurik, 1998) that posits that the presence of women in the police disrupts and undermines links between what is considered 'good' police work and masculine prowess. Thus Dick, Silvestri and Westmarland show how women do policing differently to men, Jones says that lesbian, gay and bisexual police officers can also make a unique contribution because their histories provide them with different resources to bring to police–public interactions, and Rowe argues that the police service has much to gain by recruitment of more ethnic minorities. In this way a greater diversity in styles of interacting, managing and leading, as well as community engagement, becomes available.

If the aspiration then is to move the definitions of good policing and a good officer from the perverse elements of the informal occupational cultural to the domain of the professional then a process is needed to achieve this (which is the subject of discussions presented in Part V). As Ben Bradford and colleagues note, as does Jenny Fleming in her account of the Australian experience and Aogán

Mulcahy in Northern Ireland, this is a slow and difficult process not achieved without setbacks and barriers. Bethan Loftus (2012) draws upon the concept of 'ressentiment' to describe feelings of anger and angst articulated by white, heterosexual males towards the challenges presented to the 'old' police culture and their feelings of loss, injustice and envy which will have to be acknowledged in the change programme.

References

Bloor, G. and Dawson, P. (1994) Understanding professional culture in organizational context. *Organizational Studies*, 15, 275–295.

Brogden, M. and Ellison, G. (2013) *Policing in the Age of Austerity: A Post Colonial Perspective*. London: Routledge.

Cavender, G. and Jurik, N. (1998) Jane Tennison and feminist police procedural. *Violence Against Women*, 4, 10–29.

Chryssochoou, X. (2004) *Cultural Diversity: Its Social Psychology*. Oxford: Blackwells.

Fielding, N. (1994) Cop canteen culture, in T. Newburn and B. Stanko (eds.) *Just the Boys Doing Business: Men, Masculinities and Crime*. London: Routledge.

Her Majesty's Inspectorate of Constabulary (2009) *Adapting to Protest*. London: HMIC.

Herbert, S.C. (2006) Tangled up in blue: conflicting paths to police legitimacy. *Theoretical Criminology*, 10, 481–504.

Loftus, B. (2012) *Police Culture in a Changing World*. Oxford: Clarendon.

McLaughlin, E. (2008) Last one out, turn off the 'blue lamp': the geographical 'placing' of police performance management. *Policing, a Journal of Policy and Practice*, 2, 266–275.

Reiner, R. (2012) *In Praise of Fire-Brigade Policing: Contra Common Sense Conceptions of the Police*. London: Mannheim Centre of Criminology/Howard League.

PART I
Purposes

1

PEEL'S PRINCIPLES, POLICE PRINCIPLES

Clive Emsley

> History is a *necessity*. Individuals, communities, societies could scarcely exist if all knowledge of the past was wiped out. As memory is to the individual, so history is to the community or society. . . . It is a commonplace that we live in a time of rapid and far-reaching cultural change. If we are to make a rational assessment of the extent and significance of this change we have no other recourse than to look to the past: how does present change compare with previous periods of change? If we wish to discuss contemporary morality, we can only do so effectively by making comparisons with past moralities. The very stuff of so many pub conversations is in fact drawn from the past. . . . Actually, much of the stuff of pub conversations is likely to be mythical rather than historical.
>
> *(Marwick, 2001, pp. 31 and 33)*

Introduction

Peel's principles might not be pub chat, or in the context of the police that should perhaps be 'canteen chat', but they have developed a mythical quality. They appear on various websites.[1] They have been cited time after time in text books, and initially, it seems, in text books on policing aimed at students in the United States. But for all that they are called Peel's principles and identified as originating with the Metropolitan Police in 1829, there is no evidence to suggest that they were written in 1829, let alone by Peel, or by either of the first two Commissioners of the Metropolitan Police. Rather, they were given their first significant formulation in the work of Charles Reith, writing more than a hundred years after the first Metropolitan Police constables took to the streets of London, and were subsequently taken up and remoulded in twentieth-century policing textbooks. It is also worth noting that in a series of interviews which I have undertaken with former police officers, several of whom had begun their police careers in the late 1920s and 1930s, while the older men could still quote, verbatim, passages from C.C.H. Moriarty's

Police Law, and while most of them credited Peel with founding the whole idea of modern police, not one of them made any mention of 'Peel's principles'.[2]

Similarly, it has long been noted that many forces in the nineteenth century repeated the well-known statement from the initial instructions to the Metropolitan Police in 1829:

> It should be understood at the outset, that the object to be attained is 'the prevention of crime.' To this great end every effort of the police is to be directed. The security of person and property, the preservation of the public tranquillity, and all the other objects of the police establishment, will thus be better effected than by the detection and punishment of the offender after he has succeeded in committing the crime.
>
> (Times, *25 September 1829*)

But Joanne Klein's current research on Police Instruction Books suggests that while, during the nineteenth century, this formulation was particularly popular in the south of England, forces in the north were more favourable towards the instructions prepared for the Liverpool City Police which listed two 'primary objectives', the first being the 'protection of life and property' and the second being the 'prevention of crime'. The Liverpool instructions also stressed that efficiency could be measured by a decrease in crime and by there being no complaints against police. In 1919 the Desborough Committee recommended that the Home Office prepare an instruction book to help establish uniformity among the 200 or so police forces in England and Wales. In the subsequent discussions the Metropolitan Police made it clear that, while it was prepared to participate in discussions, it considered itself significantly different from all other forces having many distinct and separate tasks, and that in consequence no universal set of instructions could apply to it. Other forces also made pleas for their own, special circumstances and while the Scottish police forces were able to agree on such a book, discussions in inter-war England and Wales, and again during the 1950s, all foundered (Klein, 2010a, 2010b). Once again, aside from the constant repetition of the importance of the 1829 dictum of the centrality of the 'prevention of crime', there appears to have been no mention of Peel's principles.

Peel's principles

The principles, as formulated by Reith, were linked with his firm belief that English/British policing was different from policing on continental Europe. Reith spent some 20 years at the beginning of the twentieth century as a tea and rubber planter in Ceylon (Sri Lanka) and was an officer in the Indian Army during the First World War (Hjellemo, 1977). His beliefs about the contrast between British and continental police institutions were based on a comfortable middle-class Victorian understanding of the world and a general ignorance of the structure of policing in Europe and how it had developed. Furthermore, Reith did little archival research beyond the first 20 years or so of the Metropolitan Police and appears to have assumed a broad consensus in Victorian politics and society. Subsequent Whig historians[3] of the police largely adopted Reith's national and historical perspectives with further assumptions about 'rioters', 'criminals', 'protestors' and even critics of the police as the 'other', essentially individuals who did not behave or think like the ordinary, law-abiding citizen (Robinson, 1979).

Reith presented 'nine principles of police' as a summation of both how the British police evolved and the foundations upon which it is based (Reith, 1943b, pp. 3–4; Reith, 1952, p. 154). But different American textbooks from the 1960s to the 1980s identify nine, ten and twelve principles, often with significant variations; and while some make reference to Reith, others cite Captain W.L. Melville Lee's *A History of Police in England* first published in 1901 but which has no discussion of Peel's principles (Lentz and Chaires, 2007, pp. 72–3). The fullest statement of nine principles and one which makes reference to both Reith and Melville Lee is that contained in P.D. Mayhall's *Police–Community Relations and the Administration of Justice* reproduced as Box 1.1.

BOX 1.1 PEEL'S PRINCIPLES (AS LISTED IN MAYHALL, 1985, PP. 425–6)

1   To prevent crime and disorder, as an alternative to their repression by military force and severity of legal punishment.

2   To recognize always that the power of the police to fulfil their functions and duties is dependent on public approval of their existence, actions and behaviour, and on their ability to secure and maintain public respect.

3   To recognize always that to secure and maintain the respect and approval of the public means also the securing of the willing cooperation of the public in the task of securing observance of the law.

4   To recognize always that the extent to which the cooperation of the public can be secured diminishes, proportionately, the necessity of the use of physical force and compulsion for achieving police objectives.

5   To seek and preserve public favour, not by pandering to public opinion, but by constantly demonstrating absolutely impartial service to law, in complete independence of policy, and without regard to the justice or injustice of the substance of individual laws, by ready offering of individual service and friendship to all members of the public without regard to their wealth or social standing; by ready exercise of courtesy and good humour; and by ready offering of individual sacrifice in protecting and preserving life.

6   To use physical force only when the exercise of persuasion, advice and warning is found to be insufficient to obtain public cooperation to an extent necessary to secure observance of law or restore order; and to use

> only the minimum degree of physical force which is necessary on any particular occasion for achieving a police objective.
>
> 7   To maintain at all times a relationship with the public that gives reality to the historic tradition that the police are the public and that the public are the police; the police being only members of the public who are paid to give full-time attention to duties which are incumbent on every citizen in the interests of community welfare and existence.
>
> 8   To recognize always the need for strict adherence to police-executive functions, and to refrain from even seeming to usurp the power of the judiciary of avenging individuals or the state, and authoritatively judging guilt and punishing the guilty.
>
> 9   To recognize always that the test of police efficiency is the absence of crime and disorder and not the visible evidence of police action in dealing with them.

Generally speaking, and given the emphasis placed on avoiding the use of physical force and maintaining the support of the public, it would be difficult to find a modern, liberal democratic state that did not subscribe to such principles when it came to its policing institutions. Moreover, reading the histories of the policing of such states it becomes clear that significant elements of these principles were present within them from the beginning of modern bureaucratic policing in the late eighteenth and early nineteenth centuries. It is also apparent that some of the principles were more noticed in the breach than in the observance. This is perhaps most noticeable in Principle 9. John Wainwright joined the West Yorkshire Police after war service in the RAF and he recalled learning rapidly that

> [b]obbying was as near to piece-work as the powers-that-be could make it. 'Don't tell me you can walk about for eight hours and not see someone doing *something* you can book 'em for.' That was the standard remark from on high if you didn't make a weekly court appearance, and it was always made on pay-day. . . . Court appearances really were the yardsticks used to measure efficiency.
>
> *(Wainwright, 1987, p. 19)*

Nor is it necessary to be a police institution in a liberal democratic state for at least some of these principles to apply. The *Gestapo* was a tiny institution linked with the detective police of the Third Reich, the *Kriminalpolizei* (or *Kripo*), and the Nazis made tremendous efforts to build on the Weimar Republic's notion of the police officer as a 'friend and helper' and to develop close relations with the public. The *Polizeitag* (or Day of the Police) was held for the first time shortly before Christmas 1934 and annually thereafter. It became so popular that, by 1937, it was no longer a day but a week with parades, bands, charity collections and so forth (Gellately, 2001, pp. 43–5). Karl Daluege, the commander of the beat patrol police of Nazi Germany insisted that his men's authority came from the community (*Volksgemeinschaft*) and that they were the servants of that community (Blood, 2003, p. 100). This, and the Nazi suggestion that the people should not to worry too much about the police sticking rigorously to the law when it came to dealing with 'criminals' and 'enemies of the state' or of the *Volk*, highlights some of the potential problems inherent in the principles; specifically problems that result from ignoring the political and social context of policing, and commentators on that policing.

The nineteenth century: a unique new system?

Modern, bureaucratic police institutions were not exactly new inventions of the early nineteenth century, but they did become more firmly established, better organised and disciplined in that period. It is possible but, in the end, rather pointless to argue about which police force was the 'first'. Some Scottish police historians have claimed that Glasgow beat London; the *sergents de ville* of Paris took to the streets in March 1829, six months before the first constables of the Metropolitan Police started their beats in London. But first or not, the Metropolitan Police rapidly acquired an impressive reputation overseas and by the close of the nineteenth century senior police officers, politicians and a variety of other commentators regularly spoke of the English/British police as 'the best in the world' and hence, by implication, the model for elsewhere.

For the early, traditional police historians such as Reith, the reasons for this reputation lay in the far-sightedness of Peel and the first two commissioners, the soldier, Lt. Col. Charles Rowan, and the Irish barrister, Richard Mayne. While not specifically spelt out, but certainly implicit in Peel's principles, Reith and others saw the unique nature of the English police as resulting from it being non-military, unarmed and non-political. Reith himself insisted that the English police was 'a kin police' which emanated from the people rather than a *Gendarmerie* imposed on the people from above by the state. Each of these supposed unique qualities can be challenged.

Given the eighteenth- and early nineteenth-century 'free-born Englishman's' hostility to a standing army it was essential that any police established in England did not look military. Their tunics were blue, unlike the scarlet of the infantry, and they wore top hats rather than military shakos; yet by the end of the century the police wore high-collared tunics like the army, and the police helmet – especially those into which a spike might be screwed on top for parades and special occasions – closely resembled the infantry helmet. The divisions of the Metropolitan Police were initially called 'companies'. The discipline was ferocious and among the earliest sergeants, inspectors and superintendents were men who had served as NCOs in the army, notably at Waterloo. Such former NCOs commanded police units in clashes with political radicals, Chartists and opponents of the New Poor Law. They might not have carried firearms or edged weapons as a rule, but it is at least arguable that such weapons were not much needed at the close of the 1820s. John Beattie has made a convincing case for a shift to less violent offending in early nineteenth-century London, a shift brought about in part by the old Bow Street Police who, armed to the teeth with all kinds of weaponry, fought successful campaigns against violent footpads and highwaymen (Beattie, 2012). If Beattie is right, then the need for such weaponry scarcely existed in early nineteenth-century London. And even if lethal weaponry was not carried as a rule, when engaged with rioters, the new police were commonly armed with cutlasses, wide-blade curved short swords used by seamen generally when an enemy ship was boarded. A scare about armed burglars during the 1880s led to constables of the Metropolitan Police being asked about whether they wished to carry revolvers; the majority of those asked replied in the affirmative, and an embarrassed Scotland Yard and Home Office found themselves making provision for trusted men on isolated beats to carry such weapons (Emsley, 2009, pp. 157–9).

The question of the extent to which police in Britain were non-political is equally debatable. The free-born Englishman was as suspicious of a police that investigated people's politics as he was of a military-style police. France, the principal opponent in the succession of wars from the accession of William III in 1688 to the final defeat of Napoleon in 1815, was identified as the possessor of both military police – in the shape of the *Maréchaussée* and its successor, created during the Revolution, the *Gendarmerie* – and political police. Napoleon's first minister of police, Joseph Fouché, acquired an unenviable and probably undeserved reputation in Britain, for a sinister political surveillance of the régime's opponents. But any government is going to want information about threats to the security of the state and Britain's advantage during the nineteenth century was that there were so few such threats. The political reformers from the 1830s, through the Chartists and beyond sought inclusion in the parliamentary system; few sought to establish a republic and there was no rival claimant to the throne. On continental Europe, in contrast, there was more political turbulence, and often it was more violent than anything witnessed in mainland Britain. There were many more republicans; in France there were rival claimants to the throne who drew support across different social classes; in Germany and Italy there were those who sought state reorganisation under the banner of unification; and there could be fierce peasant uprisings and banditry. Police in Britain investigated Chartists but, following the scandal of Sergeant William Popay acting as an *agent provocateur* in the early 1830s, this was done with care and sometimes quite openly (Emsley, 2009, pp. 57–9). Special Branch was formed initially to deal with the Fenian threat spreading across the Irish Sea. But by the turn of the century it was engaged with other European police institutions in a conflict against what contemporaries described as 'anarchism' and the Branch often exceeded its legal powers. Robert Anderson, the head of the Metropolitan Police CID, explained to the Home Office in December 1898 that Special Branch did not want additional powers to be granted to bring it more into line with European police forces, since even an extended definition of the Branch's powers might serve to frustrate its officers:

> In recent years the Police have succeeded only by straining the law, or, in plain English, by doing utterly unlawful things, at intervals, to check this conspiracy, & my serious fear is that if new legislation affecting it is passed, Police powers may be thus defined, & our practical powers seriously impaired.
>
> *(Quoted in Porter, 1987, p. 136)*

But then it seems equally probable that Anderson wrote this in the full knowledge that it would have been difficult, if not impossible, for any British government at that time to have provided such statutory powers. At the same time he could have been testing the political water to see how much leeway he could allow the Branch. Some officers in the Branch decided that anarchism, both its violent and pacific political elements, and its enthusiasm for a degree of sexual liberation, were un-English or un-British. As a consequence, while much of the police activity directed at anarchists was unknown to the general public, the ideology itself was seen as a threat to the race – a term freely used at the time. Inspector John Sweeney had no qualms about telling readers of his memoirs how he organised some plea bargaining with the intention of closing down the journal *The Adult* and the Legitimation League, which sought to remove the stigma of bastardy, in the hopes of preventing 'the growth of a Frankenstein monster wrecking the marriage laws of our country, and perhaps carrying off the general respect for all law' (Sweeney, 1904, pp. 189–90).

Any police institution can appear political when called upon to enforce a law on people who regard that law as unjust. Assumptions that British society was based on consensus were rarely clearly articulated, nevertheless they informed the perceptions of British police institutions by politicians, many political commentators, senior police officers and the historians of police such as Reith. From the very beginning of the Metropolitan Police there was a determination that the men should be identifiable and accountable, hence the divisional numbers on a constable's collar and strict instructions that these were never to be obscured. Complaints were acted upon and also, from the beginning, the commissioners kept a close eye on how their men were described in the press and demanded that local commanders provide explanations of any criticisms. Yet in other countries, also, complaints were made and investigated. Anja Johansen's comparative research on the late nineteenth century suggests that the difference between investigations in London and Berlin was that those of the Prussians were rather clumsier and less convincingly conducted (Johansen, 2009, 2011).

Probably the key aspect to the development of nineteenth-century policing in Britain was the political and social environment in which it occurred. Historians of the police, such as Reith, put this down to a consensual society established by British common sense, constitutional excellence and 'the appearance of orderliness and love of public order' that was coincident with the emergence of the police and partly created by them (Reith, 1943a, p. 207; Reith, 1943b). These happy coincidences had ensured that nineteenth-century Britain did not experience the violent political turbulence witnessed on continental Europe. There was violence in Ireland, but Reith and his ilk ignored the parallel development of the Royal Irish Constabulary which was, in many respects, an institution similar to the French *Gendarmerie* and its other clones such as the Italian *Carabinieri*, the Spanish *Guardia Civil*, the Dutch *Marechaussee* and the various German gendarmeries (Emsley, 1999a). This was a line also taken by many nineteenth-century contemporaries, including continental European Liberals who were astonished by the fact that within three years of the Revolutions of 1848 in Europe, London could hold a Great Exhibition at which different social classes rubbed shoulders without trouble. London's Metropolitan Police were given much of the credit for this. It was claimed, for example, that during the exhibition there were only eight cases of pick-pocketing and ten of, mainly petty, pilfering and that all of the stolen property was recovered (Anon. (O'Brien), 1852, p. 21).

Control, public approval and respect

Much of the traditional police history in England focused on the Metropolitan Police of London and implied that it became the model for police institutions elsewhere in the country. The London model of policing, however, was just one of several models that were tried during the 1830s and 1840s. In spite of its paramilitary elements and resemblance to the *Gendarmerie* some counties and larger boroughs looked to the Irish model and selected their senior officers from the Irish Constabulary.

The police administration of London was ultimately under the supervision of the Home Secretary as the police authority and while the Home Secretary generally left policing matters to his commissioner, he did intervene in what appeared to be emergencies (Morris, 2004). The situation of the police in a capital city being ultimately under the direction of a government minister was little different from the state civilian police institutions elsewhere in Europe. Similarly the direction of the police in the provinces was in many ways the responsibility of local politicians (Emsley, 1999b). In the boroughs the police depended upon Watch Committees that were appointed by elected town councils; in the counties there were policing committees of unelected magistrates, followed, from 1888, by Standing Joint Committees (SJCs) made up of equal numbers of magistrates and elected county councillors. The SJCs appear to have given their chief constables considerable freedom regarding decision-making, and much more so than the boroughs. But Borough Watch Committees had greater powers of appointment and discipline over their police and it was possible for a Watch Committee chairman of long standing to have a considerable degree of experience in all matters of policing, and possibly greater experience than a new head constable. In such circumstances, particularly, it was possible for a Watch Committee of local politicians to exert considerable sway over policing policy and practice. This could mean that a faction on the committee might direct the head constable to act in a fashion that he considered undesirable; in Liverpool in the 1890s, for example, the head constable was directed to close brothels, even though he warned, correctly, that this would simply move the problem and waste police time in seeking out new such houses. It could also mean the police being used on behalf of one section of the population against another. In the industrial boom-town of Middlesbrough, for example, 'there is little doubt that the police were seen by many local politicians and local citizens to be key agents in the disciplining of the working classes and especially the "poor Irish".' This disciplining, however, could be mediated by pragmatic considerations on the part of police officers of all ranks (Taylor, 2002, p. 12). But through to the mid-twentieth century, tough areas were deliberately patrolled by tough police officers who knew how to fight; alternatively it was possible for tough areas to be used as punishment beats and/or beats designed to force weak men to resign.

It could be the same in London. The Metropolitan Police in the East End was described by one Oxford graduate working for Canon Barnett's Toynbee Trust as 'like a mercenary force in a strange and alien land'.

> The pretty woman of the West [End] may think highly of [the policeman's] chivalry; but the pretty woman of the East is not so confident of it. There are those among the police who are ready to make obscene remarks to a passing woman, whose position makes it safe. Ask a comely Jewess of Whitechapel.
>
> (Gamon, 1907, pp. 26–7)

Areas regarded as peopled by the residuum were patrolled by tough constables who gained respect because they were as hard or, better still, harder than the local hard men. Moreover, if a man complained of assault by a police officer, few magistrates appear to have found against the officer. At the beginning of the twentieth century one of the London stipendiaries explained to members of a Royal Commission investigating the Metropolitan Police that he had dismissed a case against a constable because 'it was one of those cases in which the man was a notoriously bad character, and the constable had seen him outside a public house where he had no doubt committed an assault the previous day' (*Report of Royal Commission*, 1908, p. 66). The behaviour of neither the stipendiary nor the constable in this account was unique; all of which is a far cry from the principles credited to Peel and assumed by the traditional historians. If Reith was right in asserting that the police were instrumental in helping to create a love of order, it seems that it was often achieved with the swing of the officer's baton, his lead-weighted cape, his boot or his fist.

Facing the future

A set of written principles offer one way, possibly the best way, of informing a workforce of the guidelines for its tasks and what is to be considered as appropriate and decent behaviour in executing those tasks. But any such set of principles and guidelines is going to be affected by contemporary circumstances, contingencies, economic, political and social pressures. Modern politicians and media regularly use the terms 'public' and 'community' when referring to the society that the police serve; yet there are several publics and several communities within any society. Police in Britain, excluding perhaps Ireland, developed during the nine-teenth century in a period of relative political calm and national self-satisfaction. In many respects up until the Second World War it was only the voice of the respect-able, middle-class public/community that was heard with reference to police activ-ity. A deep well of support and sympathy for police officers remains within British society evidenced particularly when individual officers show courage in difficult or life-threatening situations. In September 2012, for example, two women officers responding to a burglary in Manchester were killed in a gun and grenade attack. There was a national outpouring of grief and sympathy; the Chief Constable of Greater Manchester, commenting on the women officers' courage, explained to the media that he had Peel's principles inscribed on glass windows in his headquar-ters – specifically the words 'the police are the public and the public are the police'. However, relying on a mythical model and set of principles without an awareness of the context in which they were developed and the shifting contemporary con-text is risky.

When HM Inspectorate of Constabulary published its inquiry into the polic-ing of the G20 confrontations in London in 2009 it subtitled the report *Nurturing the British Model of Policing*. It is tempting to wonder how the model would have looked had the mobile phones available at the time of the G20 been available at Coldbath Fields in 1832, in the Birmingham Bull Ring in 1839, in Trafalgar Square on Bloody Sunday 1887, in Cable Street in 1936 as well as other confrontations that are less well known, but after which police behaviour and/or orders were severely criticised. Peel and the first commissioners appear to have given serious thought to the clothing and equipment of their men and what this should convey to the public. In the less formal society that emerged after 1945 the military-style tunic gave way to a jacket with a collar and tie, and many officers objected to this. In turn these gave way to tee-shirts and stab-proof vests, and, in public order emer-gencies, to closed helmets, flame-proof overalls and boots. The health and safety of officers require this, but did anyone consider how such developments and how Officer Safety Training, as recently explored by John Buttle (Buttle, 2007), might impact upon relations with different elements of the national community?

The police officer has always had discretion in the way that he or she handles a problem. Sergeants and inspectors checked up on beat patrols, but they were not always around and, at least up until the mid-twentieth century, they would prob-ably not always have disciplined an officer for dealing out rough, tough, summary justice. It was against this backdrop that Reith and others could eulogise the unique nature of 'the best police in the world', its immediate links with the national com-munity and its fair treatment of all. The deferential nature of British society and the perceived consensus running through it, declined in the second half of the twenti-eth century. Together with this decline was a growing awareness of human rights and, at the close of the century, their formal incorporation into law. Such social, political and legal change, together with the new technologies available to citizens, provide a much more rigorous context for the understanding and deployment of policing principles such as those ascribed to Sir Robert Peel.

Notes

1 E.g. http://www.civitas.org.uk/pubs/policeNine.php (accessed 27 March 2012). The Principles on the Civitas website are the same as those listed in Mayhall (1985) and reproduced here in Box 1.1.
2 C.C.H. Moriarty (1877–1958), joined the RIC in 1899 and was appointed Assistant Chief Constable of the Birmingham City Police in 1918 where he made significant contributions to police training and education; he became Chief Constable of Birmingham in 1935. His *Police Law* was first published in 1929 and reached its tenth edition in 1950.
3 The Whig view of history was first identified by Herbert Butterfield during the 1930s. Drawing on his research into the struggle between Whigs and Tories in eighteenth-century England, and how several of the earliest historians had been the descendants of Whig grandees, he described how Whig historians tend to divide historical actors into the friends and enemies of progress (Butterfield, 1931).

Bibliography

Anon. [O'Brien, W.J.] (1852) 'The Police System of London', *Edinburgh Review*, XCVI, pp. 1–33.

Beattie, J.M. (2012) *The First English Detectives: The Bow Street Runners and the Policing of London, 1750–1840*, Oxford: Oxford University Press.

Blood, P. (2003) 'Karl Daluege and the Militarization of the Ordnungspolizei', in G. Oram, ed. *Conflict and Legality: Policing in Mid-Twentieth-Century Europe*, London: Francis Bootle Publishers.

Butterfield, H. (1931) *The Whig Interpretation of History*, London: Bell & Sons.

Buttle, J.W. (2007) 'A Constructive Critique of the Officer Safety Programme used in England and Wales', *Policing and Society*, 17, 2, pp. 164–81.

Emsley, C. (1993) '"Mother, What *Did* Policemen Do When There Weren't Any Motors?" The Law, the Police and the Regulation of Motor Traffic in England, 1900–1939', *Historical Journal*, 36, pp. 357–81.

Emsley, C. (1999a) *Gendarmes and the State in Nineteenth-Century Europe*, Oxford: Oxford University Press.

Emsley, C. (1999b) 'A Typology of Nineteenth-Century Police', *Crime, histoire & sociétés/Crime, history & societies*, 3, 1, pp. 29–44.

Emsley, C. (2009) *The Great British Bobby: A History of British Policing from the 18th Century to the Present*, London: Quercus.

Gamon, H.R.P. (1907) *The London Police Court Today and Tomorrow*, London: J.M. Dent.

Gellately, R. (2001) *Backing Hitler: Consent and Coercion in Nazi Germany*, Oxford: Oxford University Press.

Hjellemo, E.O. (1977) 'A Tribute to an Unusual Historian of Police: Charles Edward Williams Reith (1886–1857)', *Police College Magazine*, 14, 2, pp. 5–8.

Johansen, A. (2009) 'Complain in Vain? The Development of a "Police Complaints Culture" in Wilhelmine Berlin', *Crime, histoire & sociétés/Crime, history & societies*, 13, 2, pp. 119–42.

Johansen, A. (2011) 'Keeping Up Appearances: Police Rhetoric, Public Trust and "Police Scandal" in London and Berlin, 1880–1914', *Crime, histoire & sociétés/Crime, history & societies*, 15, 1, pp. 59–83.

Klein, J. (2010a) 'The Evolution of the Ideal English Constable: Portrayals in Police Instruction Books from the 19th Century to the Present', paper presented at the European Social Science History Conference, Ghent, April 2010.

Klein, J. (2010b) 'England's Futile Efforts to Create a National Police Instruction Book, 1920s–1950s', paper presented at the Social Science History Association, Chicago, November 2010.

Lentz, S.A. and Chaires, R.H. (2007) 'The Invention of Peel's Principles: A Study of Policing "Textbook" History', *Journal of Criminal Justice*, 33, pp. 69–79.

Marwick, A. (2001) *The New Nature of History*, Basingstoke: Palgrave.

Mayhall, P.D. (1985) *Police–Community Relations and the Administration of Justice*, 3rd edn, New York: John Wiley and Sons.

Melville Lee, W.L. (1901) *A History of Police in England*, London: Methuen and Co.

Morris, R.M. (2004) 'The Metropolitan Police and Government 1860–1920', Ph.D., The Open University.

Porter, B. (1987) *The Origins of the Vigilant State: The London Metropolitan Police Special Branch before the First World War*, London: Weidenfeld and Nicolson.

Reith, C. (1943a) 'Preventive Principle of Police', *Journal of Criminal Law and Criminology*, 34, pp. 206–9.

Reith, C. (1943b) *British Police and the Democratic Idea*, Oxford: Oxford University Press.

Reith, C. (1952) *The Blind Eye of History*, London: Faber and Faber.

Report of the Royal Commission upon the Duties of the Metropolitan Police (1908) Cd. 4158.

Robinson, C.D. (1979) 'Ideology as History: A Look at the Way Some English Police Historians Look at the Police', *Police Studies*, 2, pp. 35–49.

Sweeney, J. (1904) *At Scotland Yard*, London: Grant Richards.

Taylor, D. (2002) *Policing the Victorian Town: The Development of the Police in Middlesbrough c.1840–1914*, Basingstoke: Palgrave Macmillan.

Wainwright, J. (1987) *Wainwright's Beat: One Man's Journey with a Police Force*, London: Macmillan.

2

POLICING

Privatizing and changes in the policing web[1]

Peter K. Manning

Introduction

There is now potential for dramatic changes in the configuration of the policing web (Brodeur, 2010). This web includes all those ways in which order is sustained formally. The public police, in particular, are subject to increasingly close governmental scrutiny, and a variety of new efforts have appeared that might alter the sources of payment, conditions of employment and the role and duties of police personnel and staff. Yet, currently, trust in the public police is high, and officially recorded crime (ORC) is declining. This chapter outlines the current climate and rhetoric of police restructuring; the emerging nature of the police mandate; types of policing; and discusses the nature of democratic policing.

The narrative of police reform

Prior to the rise of ACPO and the growth of powerful police unions, the police have always had a political face. This face was seen dramatically in the recent demonstration featuring an estimated 30,000 officers protesting against the 20 per cent cuts in police budgets in May, 2012. These events were but the end of a dramatic series covering almost 50 years.

A narrative including these political matters, encompassing the police and their role in politics, can be constructed, and punctuated by a series of laws and commissions beginning with the Royal Commission of 1962 (see the chapters by Crawford and Loader in this volume). Consider the series of laws. The Police Act of 1964 allowed the police to charge for special services; and this was followed by revision of the judges rules in the PACE Act. With the election of the conservative Thatcher government, police were favoured with raises and with the expectation that they would wage war on crime and win. They were seen as allies in the 1984–85 miners' strikes. However, they lost their favoured status when crime continued to rise (see Reiner, 2010). The Home Office circular requiring efficient use of resources (114/83) and the more direct requirement for the best possible use of resources in the later circular (106/88), set the stage for a more penetrating look into police operations. The Sheehy Report (1993) focused on pay and performance and, in many respects, was a harbinger of the later Winsor Report (2012), the architect of which was the first non-police HMI in recent times. The Police and Magistrates Courts Act of 1994 further broadened the ambit of policing as well as allowing contracting for police officers' time.

The late 1990s also saw New Labour's efforts to set standards and to create a more efficient and regulated public sector. They also attempted to refocus policing on neighbourhood and reassurance policing in their programme (Reiner, 2010, chs 7 and 8). The Criminal Justice and Police Act was followed by the Police Reform Act of 2002 that created the Police and Community Support Officer (PCSO) role and broadened the powers of non-public police in regulatory functions. The Private Security Industry Act of 2001 provided an umbrella for private security regulation. An effort at controlling organized crime was signalled by the 2005 Serious Organized Crime and Police Act. Several new organizations such as the National Police Improvement Agency (NPIA) were established with a brief to improve police training, and police education more generally. They have not found favour with the Coalition Government and were burned along with the once powerful Audit Commission in the bonfire of the quangos. NPIA has morphed into a new Police College, established in February 2013. These laws and organizations shaped the 'police family' over the course of time, adding personnel and functions. The formation of the Coalition Government in 2010 led to the passage of the Police Reform and Social Responsibility Act of 2011 which set in motion the election of Police Commissioners and a new tripartite assemblage for police accountability.

Although the police have fostered the illusion that they are apolitical, and the public have long accepted this proposition, the police in the UK, the focus here, are connected to state legitimacy, tradition, social order, law, morality, national pride and visible state functions. These are political matters. The police are the visible everyday-any day face of the state to the citizen. Recent laws and reform efforts make it painfully difficult, now, to see the police as a non-political organization. What has changed perhaps since the 1962 Royal Commission on Police Report is the willingness of politicians to take on police as an institution of government and to reform and reshape 'policing' broadly considered.[2]

Politics and rhetoric

The change in the economic climate post-2008 raised questions about the costs and extensiveness of public service – a scrutiny begun by New Labour at least ten years earlier. These were first seen as a matter of setting 'standards' of performance: objectives, goals, targets and related auditing practices. The questions of performance were based on context and the conventions of the occupation – in the case of the police, ORC, clearances, 'detections', and other indications of looking after public safety. In due course, post-2008, questions of the costs and role of the police and other social services in the larger market system were raised, as well as a search for new forms of accountability. Proposals included quite radical changes in the role of policing in the context of the market place. Since the formation of the present government, the concern has been to gear the public services into the 'market' or demand for police services without too much regard to criteria, standards or indeed what constitutes this 'market'. The aim has been to reduce the size of the public police force and the costs of public services, and to expand the number and kinds of police functions that might be carried out by staff. This has been achieved by outsourcing previously public police functions, hiring private corporations and/or relying on new hybrid units such as PCSOs.

Changes in the rhetoric

In order to discuss the question of the changing nature of policing functions and who should carry them out, it is necessary to first establish the rhetorical *coup de grâce* carried out in the UK in the last 30 years or so by politicians. They have shaped and defined the *rhetorical framework* within which the discussion of 'policing' is carried out. Politicians, with their ideas simplified for public consumption and amplified by the media, have produced a framework in which:

- The issue of reform of the public police services is now defined in *market terms* in spite of the historical fact that services, being in the collective interest and binding on the collective to support, is not profitable. That is, the marginal utility of such services is insufficient to yield a profit. Or, to put it another way, if private enterprise could make a profit doing it, they would. So, if private agencies undertake it, their profits i.e., costs plus, ostensibly would exceed the current costs of public service.
- The criteria and current rhetoric favour funding alternatives to a public police. This is done by arguing both that public service is inefficient and that the same services can be provided more efficiently by private corporations. Other forms of policing are also suggested to be more efficient. The policing functions, however, are seen as essential.
- Two quite different language games are in conflict. The language game of public service and the language game of profit-making differ. Each game is a context and requires different terms of reference and assessment. On the one hand, concepts such as 'efficiency', 'effectiveness', 'profit', 'costs', and 'value for money', are odd job terms borrowed from macro-economics. They play a role in the profit-making language game. On the other hand, terms such as fairness, justice, equity, and duty, honour and quality belong to a service language game. To mix, confound and combine economic terms such as efficiency with service terms, moral and philosophical terms such as 'equity', and 'legitimacy', is to produce a logical nonsense. To use them together mixes values, practices, attitudes and ideology. The first are problematic terms crudely imported from economics, while

the latter are aesthetic terms drawn from sociology and philosophy. As is argued below, public policing is a service; it is not a business, it is not an industry; if it has a product, it would be 'trust' and its assessment (Manning, 2003, 2010).

- The debate is carried out without precise definition or context. There are no conventional terms that circumscribe precisely notions such as efficiency, effectiveness and value for money in regard to public services in general. In a market context, consumers can withdraw from the particular market, choose other options or products, or refuse to purchase. This assumes a limited and controlled market with knowable, known and variable demand, costs and profits. Policing, like medical care, is characterized by elastic demand and only crudely can be seen as operating in a 'market'. Its costs are indeterminate. These are contentious within the police world and outside it. There is no agreement about the referent of these terms. Absent conventional definitions and auditing practices, using the profit game's terms blurs vision and circumvents imagination.

- Claims are merited more than facts. The claim on the one hand that it is essential to get more officers out of the 'back office' is one aspect of reorganization that suggests increased use of staff rather than sworn or warranted officers. There is no clear definition of front or back office (Brogden and Ellison, 2013: 69–71; citing HMIC), notwithstanding HMIC's attempts. The assumption that if officers are 'on the streets' they are therefore visible. Unfortunately, fighting crime is almost impossible to show in practice. This is ironic as well, given the constant decline in ORC.

- There is little appreciation for the essential character of administration, supervision and management of information systems. Like the army, there is a necessary ratio of office staff to 'front line' that is essential in order to keep records, deal with the public in stations, manage human resources, make and keep budgets and carry out legal and scientific analyses. Whether these functions should be carried out by non-sworn staff, or outsourced is certainly a question.

- The assumption that police are all about crime control and should be evaluated in that context is fallacious and misleading (Loader, this volume). Their functions are many, they are interrelated and they represent many things to their several publics: victims, criminals, the respectable classes, politicians and those at the margins of society by virtue of education, income, citizenship status, or incorrigibility.

These rhetorical moves have created a political context in which the debate about policing is carried out in pseudo-economic terms absent any data to show evidence of the superiority of non-police functionaries in regard to quality, quantity, cost, impact on public trust, and on safety or security.

Police mandate

The public police mandate is the abstract symbolic statement of the efforts of the nation state to secure the safety of its citizens. Each of these facets of reform was, in fact, an effort to reconstitute the public police *mandate*, defined as the dialectic process balancing what the public expects of the police and how the police respond to and manage these demands (Manning, 1977, 2010). An occupation, in effect, has a validated claim to carrying out some named tasks – those denied to others – and to define the proper attitude of those it serves toward that occupation and its practitioners. In each new emphasis upon a facet of policing function, the public police *mandate* has been the base-line against which other modes are judged. That is, people trust and rely on the public police and consider them to be 'the police'. Other forms of policing are back stage or unrecognized. Since the Peel innovation, the state has taken an interest in the well-being of its citizens and this responsibility until now has remained with the public police, and governments have emphasized this fact.

In the English context, and perhaps in an Anglo-American context, the public police are a unique organization. They have a near monopoly on the use of force within the legally defined territory of the state. They apply violence to cope with situational defined exigencies and use this violence, up to and including fatal force, to manage that which might get worse (paraphrase of Bittner, 1970: 46). In effect, the application of force is a very specialized skill to be held in abeyance and used parsimoniously. Bittner likens the central feature of the role, application of force when other means are unavailable or exhausted, to the priest's administration of the mass. It is not the entirety of the role, but that which is its essence. The work, with the core of the potential of applying force, has a very wide mandate that is open-ended and malleable. This violence potential makes them both the ally and a potential threat to the citizens. The constable alone traditionally is seen as having 'original authority' under law. The police as an organization have the only legitimate access to the criminal justice system in practical terms. That is, they possess the traditional power to submit a case to be considered for prosecution. The police have a negotiated obligation to carry out governmental policies and to sustain politically defined order. The police do not have clients for whom they work; they do not have customers, for their obligations are collective and citizens cannot refuse their services nor abandon the obligations to pay for the services on offer. They assess uncertain risks on behalf of the public, but while this is 'craft-work', the job is a bundle of diffuse communicative skills, not easily assessed, and their application is a matter of judgement. Historically, in metaphoric terms, the police do 'dirty work', work that other occupations are not permitted to do, and which the police alone can carry out. This often leads them to target the lower classes and disadvantaged areas, as these are seen as 'disorderly'. In part because of their traditional status as the centre of governmental interfaces with the public, they are in control of enormous amounts of information, both formal and informal. They carry out a low visibility function that is rarely supervised, have a wide variety of choices about whether to intervene, when and how, and their paperwork is rarely transparent. In effect, one must rely on the sensible and reasonable actions of the police to micro manage 'trouble'. Historically, the bases of the paramilitary organization, rigid rules and careful recruitment were to limit the intrusion of kinship, class or gender and to, in effect, reduce temptation structurally (Bordua and Reiss, 1966). These features constitute the mandate of the public police, and their claims to be deserving of public trust and confidence.

The fact is that policing in the UK has long been considered a sacred organization historically connected to the state, morality and justice, and constables are seen as icons of good conduct (Manning, 1977; Reiner, 2010). It has connotations associated with national pride, honour, dignity, respect and consensus. The police communicate about social relations and send messages about what is right, correct and trustworthy as well as what is sanctioned as wrong. They dramatize contingencies and their management. They actively patrol the edges of order on our behalf. The police, unlike Corporate CEOs, serve the citizens (see Forst and Manning, 1999: Table 2.1: 66–67). Importantly in this context, the police traditionally stand outside the rhetoric of the market. There are good and sound reasons for this. Is a priest to be effective? To give value for money? How are the hours he works to be connected to 'morality' or the absence of 'sin'? The priest, the nurse, the teacher, the social worker, and civil servants are acting analogously to the constable. They do not work for money (as correctly stated in the Winsor Report); they are not working for profit; their works cannot be assessed metrically; their value is not monetary because it is, in fact, connected to order and security (Loader, this volume). Furthermore, one might see the police as acting on our behalf, as having a sacrificial function (certainly dramatically illustrated by the over 300 officers who died in Northern Ireland), thus operating under a sacred canopy.

The aim of recently advanced reforms is to penetrate police organization with a modern management, introducing budgeting, deployment, altering the conditions of work as well as what might be called *secularizing and rationalizing* policing and police organizations. The Winsor Report argues the need to reward specialist skills and to monitor them regularly; to focus on skill and performance, not seniority; to monitor health, fitness and disability; to introduce a compulsory severance scheme; and introduce again lateral entry for officers at the inspector and superintendent ranks. This might be called a rational-legal scheme for accountability that is designed to replace a common-law based (Marshall, 1965) quasi-bureaucracy that has developed to insulate officers and sustain the occupational culture of neutral, even-handed service to the public. In many respects, academic observers have seen the occupational culture of the police, generally referring to the culture of the uniformed officer as a negative force. The virtues of a supportive, symbolically unifying and even comforting source of emotional and interpersonal support, have been overlooked. The positive functions of such a culture in the face of adversity and criticism and its vulnerability to radical revisions in the conditions of work have not been widely discussed.

Given this thrust toward rationalization, the impact of governmental policies will differentially impact present types of policing. If there is to be a re-shaping of the configuration or the policing web, some definitions are required.

Definitions and types of policing

Let us step back and consider types of policing, formal and informal. It is well to recall, as Banton argued in the first, now classic, ethnographic work on policing

(1964), informal and local social control is always more important in the control of crime and disorder than formal policing. Formal policing sits in a network of exchanges, controlling actions, sanctioning and punishment carried out in families, churches, neighbourhoods and schools. It is also impossible to sort out the relative contributions to politically defined order of any of the following forms of policing. They are an overlapping set of categories, rather than distinctive and mutually exclusive. They cooperate and are complementary at times and at other times are in conflict and antagonistic.

- *Self-help* (acting directly to avenge wrongs, Black, 1983). This covers modes of informal sanctioning for perceived wrong-doing without the intervention/role of the state as a third-party functionary. In the United States, perhaps more than in the UK, individual citizens carrying weapons, concealed or openly depending on state laws, are a part of policing. They may be deemed necessary for self-protection. As Black correctly notes 'self-help' actions are very often considered crimes by the courts.
- *Secondary social control* occupations (Jones and Newburn, 2002). These are those who regulate and respond to behaviour informally in public and quasi-public spaces. These include such occupations as teachers, priests and clergy, bus and taxi drivers, train and bus conductors, traffic wardens, crossing guards and the like.
- *Informal policing* or, perhaps, 'self-appointed or nominated policing', includes *ad hoc* policing, posses, militias, vigilante groups and other informal, part-time policing individually or collectively without uniform, pay and specific conditions of employment such as neighbourhood patrols. These informal police officers cannot be fired and, thus, their accountability is dubious.
- *Private policing* – paid-for actions in regard to private interests. Usually connected to policing given territories. The point here is that policing with private interests as the mandate only marginally, if at all, serves the public welfare, even when policing quasi-public property. The functions carried out by private police are not only those connected with sustaining order in quasi-public spaces (Forst and Manning, 1999: 103–106).
- *Policing carrying out previously public police functions* – using public funds to pay for agents to carry out functions connected to the public good, e.g. traffic tickets, order-maintenance; regulation that does not entail arrest in excess of 'everyday' citizen powers. This is also called 'outsourcing' on the ground that it reduces costs and functions by contracting. Such policing functions have a mandate in the sense that they are licensed, legitimate and have territorial limitations. They draw also on the mandate of public police by simulating their uniforms, interactional style, the decoration of their vehicles and symbols. In the United States, they carry visible weapons. They may or may not include some arrest powers in private spaces for trespassing.
- *Hybrid policing* – this includes all varieties of policing, i.e. noticing, responding to and, perhaps, sanctioning behaviour. This sort of policing is now included

in the 'police family'. The confusion in regard to legitimacy comes in that these functions can be carried out by police employed privately, police employed and paid by the public or some amalgam of these. This can also include third-party policing and varieties of the police web.

- *Public police*. The police organization includes those who are not warranted or sworn. These can make up as much as 50 per cent of the organization's employees. In addition, the organization can include reserve constables, cadets and part-time officers. The organizational culture includes more than the segmented occupational culture of the police, and the percentage of officers in uniform patrol in the UK has been declining for some years (Home Office, 2012). The range of functions carried out by the public police is diverse and complex (Forst and Manning, 1999: 27–29). It is important to note also that the RCMP in Canada provides contract policing in Canada outside Quebec, Newfoundland and Ontario, that the public police in the Anglo-American world work for private companies routinely, and that there are many circumstances of cooperation between public and private police. This cooperative pattern is, in part, due to the fact that many retired senior police officers have now been employed by security firms or have begun their own.

The most important distinction between types of policing is between the citizen-base, or self-defence and self-help, and formal, legitimate types of policing. The formal and legitimate police types can then be divided into policing done by public police and other formally organized policing. This is because these formally constituted organizations have legal status, a collectively known identity, an exact roster of members, and means by which new members are selected, recruited and trained and by which others are terminated (Caplow, 1964: 1). The point is that these characteristics of organized policing make such organizations accountable collectively and individually. In this sense, by degree of formal accountability and collective obligation, the scale runs from self-help to public policing, and any combination of functions and types, even under the umbrella of public policing, blurs function, responsibility and, ultimately, legitimacy.

Consider now this preliminary definition of democratic public police:

> The public police as an organization in Anglo-American societies, constituted of many diverse agencies, are authoritatively coordinated and legitimate organizations. They stand ready to apply force up to and including fatal force in politically defined territories. They generally proceed by exception rather than policy. They seek to sustain politically defined order and ordering via tracking, surveillance and arrest. As such, they require compliance to command from lower personnel and the citizens.
>
> *(Manning, 2010: 44)*

This definition does not include the role of ideology, which is the hidden canopy that protects public police against periodic charges that they are 'political' or

that they serve special interests. Another aspect of the canopy is surely the traditional operational independence of the Chief Constable. The police are embedded
in a policing culture, public traditions, memories, attitudes, and key events that
reflect further values, beliefs, myths and historical conventions (Loader and Mulcahy, 2003). This culture of policing, in turn, is a facet of the mandate or the ever-
negotiated contract between the institution of policing and the public. Whatever
the police do, as Bittner (1970) points out, is produced in a situation and explained
or accounted for later. The rhetoric justifies in the political arena the idealization
of policing, not its actual practices. The organization and the role might differ and
the democratic police might not always police democratically, and police in non-
democratic states can police democratically. The belief that they do not violate
unstated democratic principles is essential to their survival in a competitive organizational network. They act to punctuate order, but it is not a single order that is
to be produced by such police responses. It is the order suggested by that which
touches off the ordering: 'calling the cops'. Authoritatively coordinated refers to
the fact that the agency is accountable, as are the officers. They can be fired. It
is important to note that compliance and loyalty of officers is problematic. The
authority of the organization to sanction increases the probability of compliance
with orders. The compliance of citizens to request and commands is implicit in
discussions of democratic policing. Tracking and surveillance are increasing. This
will continue to vex those who wish to control the police as their capacity to do
so has vastly increased in the last 30 years. The sanctioning powers, that is, the use
of the criminal sanction and access to the criminal justice system, are an important feature that distinguishes the public from the private police. Private police on
duty are often off-duty public police who can exercise the arrest sanction, so that
the monopoly of control of the arrest sanction is less clear in use than might be
expected, but the limiting factor is that private police cannot per se enter a case into
the criminal justice system: they cannot apply the criminal law to sanction behaviour. The implicit bargain or negotiated order between top command and lower
participants is an often overlooked in the capacity of police to act consistently.
Police are ultimately dependent on citizens' compliance and the organization relies
on loyalty and willingness to act without question on order when required. There
is a tacit contract between the police officer and the organization that is established
at hiring and implies a future obligation and mutual trust. Public police are permitted to proceed by exception rather than rigid and detailed instructions because their
mandate is elastic, negotiated and local in large part. The mandate is the source of
legitimacy and it is a kind of negotiated contract between the several publics they
serve, not a reified 'public', and their own definition of the nature of the work and
its obligations. It therefore expands and contracts over time and changes in public
demands and legal constraints. The mandate in a democracy is fraught with contradictions because of the various expectations of police – service, crime control,
order management, control of traffic and demonstrations – and the shifting scope of
their practices. That is, the police in a democracy are subject to changes in public
opinion, law, political decisions and media, and their elasticity is essential. In part

because of this the democratic police have been most successful when they have convinced the middle class 'respectable public' that their primary role is to control, or at least manage, ORC. In many respects, this is an impossible mandate because of the limits of official modes of crime control. In fact, public trust in the police and maintenance of the public trust is probably the most significant 'product' of democratic police. They assess trustworthiness in others; they monitor sources of distrust, both in groups and individuals; they are a repository of trust by citizens in their symbolic expressive role. It is for this reason that corruption, crime and self-serving actions of police are judged more harshly than the actions of other citizens. These points about the definition of policing are intended to specify the essential nature of the public police functions in a democracy. Let us consider this further.

Ten features of Anglo-American policing

Given this definition and outline of the essential features of democratic policing, there still remain what might be called the constraining functions of democratic policing in any society. By stating the problem in this way, the scope of this discussion can be widened to include problems associated with the transformation of police systems to democratic modes of policing, or the augmentation of policing means by new forms of policing. Here is a list of features (Manning, 2010: 65–66) that can be used to judge public police practices. Public police:

1 are a public entity and are accountable indirectly to the people. Their ability to command compliance is contingent on the trust granted to representatives of the legitimate government and, in Great Britain, in the traditional authority of the monarchy;
2 cannot be guided solely by citizens' demands or requests. These cannot alone guide the organization because its obligations are collective and general, not individual, and the demand is open-ended; service must be and is rationed; callers are not 'customers' or clients because they cannot choose to refuse the 'service' or opt out of paying for it. There is no free market in police services;
3 cannot abandon or eschew their symbolic role as representatives of governance and governing because this is central to the belief in fair practice within a democracy;
4 use violence cautiously and in a limited mannered fashion. By 'mannered' is meant in a predictable, trained and restrained way that is recognizable and signalled well to citizens. Media amplification of incidents serves to confuse viewers and produce periodic crises in large cities;
5 patrol a legally defined political territory, but this is problematic and cannot be restricted in advance to the limits of a legally defined territory. This ambiguity has increased as a result of international police cooperation; concerns about terrorism and its global dimensions and non-national origins; policing under the guise of foreign aid;

6 manage order by restraint: they do not produce it and may undermine or destroy it;

7 are not a neutral political force; they act on behalf of the state in crises;

8 are expected to comply with command and show loyalty in face of danger. These two requirements are essential to consistent, predictable policing, but they are always problematic;

9 are respected because they volunteer when they join, making an implicit or tacit contract to carry out dangerous work, and are given wide tolerance for their actions. They sacrifice themselves at times;

10 using tracking and surveillance of citizens increasingly. The extent of this is largely unknown and unmonitored. These activities are concentrated in lower class areas and on lower class groups, but are certainly not restricted to these areas and groups. The use of Twitter, Facebook and other social media by the police both as data and such community relations modalities are increasing. The very active PSNI on Facebook is but one example.

In summary, these ten points apply poorly to private policing in its various forms in part because of: the absence of accountability; their character as 'hired' rather than as serving in the collective interest; the low visibility of much that is done; their non-neutral role in political ordering (for what police do, see the above definition); the absence of clear territorial and legal constraints on their actions; the confusion of the citizens about the nature of the source of authority, and finally the ambiguity of multiple symbols of authority on uniforms, vehicles and equipment (Lincolnshire). Let us now consider democratic policing more specifically.

Policing in accord with the difference principle

What analytic principles might guide judgement of police practices? It is the practices that should command attention, not the proscription. The most important statement of political philosophy in the past century, and still the classic statement, is made by John Rawls in his *Theory of Justice* (1999; hereafter TJ) and in a condensed version of the argument entitled *Justice as Fairness* (2001; hereafter JF). These works are based on the two fundamental principles of justice. The first claims that all positions in general, and in this case the police, should be available to all on the basis of free and open competition, and the second states that whatever passes for *policy* should be based on the difference principle. The second or the difference principle can be summarized as stating that any implicit or explicit policy affecting extant inequalities should be to the benefit of the least advantaged (JF: 42–43). This is an inference from Rawls. Since it is unlikely that the police can actually reduce inequality and, in fact, they have no obligation to do so, a political philosophy with policing in mind and based on the justice as fairness idea requires some modification. One might argue that the justice as fairness principle in regard to policing should be refocused in a manner consistent with the Hippocratic Oath: *the police should strive to minimize harm.* The form and kind of harm are various and not exclusively physical or material. The working version of this abstraction in regard to policing means that any action, planned, stated or enacted, should not increase inequalities. The role of the constable on the ground in this conception remains open-ended and relies on sensible judgement.

How can this grand working principle be grasped as a set of objectives or guidelines? Expectations of policing are questions of function: if the following principles or rules of thumb are observed, one might expect of (domestic) democratic policing that it function in a manner that is:

- Constrained in dealing with citizens and fair in procedure. These dealings should entail a degree of civility in interactions and in police practices. This excludes under virtually all conditions, torture, mass detentions, 'round ups' based on political beliefs, not behaviours, and lengthy suspensions of habeas corpus for citizens.
- Largely reactive to citizens' complaints – reticent rather than sporadic – and not given to frequent secret proactive interventions, crackdowns, sweeps and militaristic 'operations'.
- Equal in its application of coercion to populations defined spatially and temporally. The level of coercion is based on minimalistic criteria, much as counter insurgency tactics, rather than a mechanistic 'use of force continuum.'
- Fair in hiring, internal evaluation, promotion and demotion, transfers and disciplinary treatment of employees, officers and civilians.
- Competitive in an environment that includes private police, vigilante groups, posses, ad hoc policing under the guise of 'self-help' and revenge. It may include the National Guard and the armed services (army, navy, coast guard and the air force). This implies formal and informal modes of cooperation rather than unified and unrelenting actions.
- Accountable and responsible for their actions individually and organizationally.

Abiding issues

There is a debate about what is good policing and how to accomplish it. Embedded in this debate is a more elusive question: what are the symbolic, sacred and mysterious functions that any police do that reify the state, ourselves and public morality? There is no clear definition of privatization, nor what functions private or public police play in the morality play of modern life. Private policing includes a wide variety of functions (Johnston, 1992) – part- and full-time employees, management, and those on the ground – and the data on their numbers, training, competence and functions are unrewarding. There is no consensus on what a private employee is or how many there are in any given industrialized country – the numbers remain dubious (Brodeur, 2010). There is almost no ethnographic research or systematic case studies of the functions, costs, impacts and realities of private policing (Rigakos, 2002; Hobbes *et al.*, 2003). How can a debate be carried out with no data whatever on the efficacy of private policing? The debate is data-free, and has been cast into the high politics of policing in the UK. The collapse of GS4 in connection with Olympic security does suggest the combination of collective behaviour, the interacting effect of assumptions, beliefs, rumours, gossip, media amplification, and politics on what private policing, outsourcing, and hybrid policing should or can do. The lurch toward privatization, illustrated in the moves of Surrey, Lincolnshire and West Midlands prior to the collapse of the efforts of GS4 to provide security forces for the London Olympics, suggests that these developments are not based on sound factual material and clear reasoning. There is, perhaps, a new questioning of the long-standing belief that public policing alone produces a sense of well-being. In general terms, what is being considered and imagined is a reduction of the role of the state in conflict resolution; in theory acting as a neutral and disinterested actor. In conclusion, the following issues may be of value in shaping discussion.

First, let us consider restructuring that bears on staff functions in public policing because these are one aspect of reducing functions carried out by sworn officers. These include questions of fairness in hiring, disability, firing and promotion.

- Staff and police officers are not paid equally for performing the same functions; Their rewards are quite different in regard to retirement plans, perks of office, disability schemes, transfers and promotion opportunities and long-term career stability (Winsor, 2012).
- There is increasing need for experts, either hired by the organization as employees or as contract labour: specialists in IT/computer repair, maintenance and operation; chemists; ballistic experts; accountants and human resource managers. It is unrealistic to expect the police, as they have in the past, to recruit, train, reward and promote such employees.
- The functional analysis of policing will suggest that many functions do not require police powers, and these will be increasingly carried out by non-sworn employees.

Second, consider a set of questions relating to outsourcing, privatizing and rationalization which bear on the manner of personnel management. These have to do with changes in the traditional 'police family':

- Disability, accidents and illness cost the police more than injuries incurred in dangerous law-enforcement activities, and these are treated as families do – informal modes – by transferring people to low-stress work, or to niches (semi-specialized jobs, not rank designated) that are not demanding; tolerance of illness and days lost by disability. The secularization and rationalization of policing will mean new standards will arise for dealing with the ill and disabled.
- Health and well-being, as a variable empirical fact which contradicts the assumption of equality in the police family, will be more closely assessed.
- If further privatization of police functions goes forward, that is outsourcing functions, producing more hybrid units, and giving contracts to corporate organizations to operate police stations, a number of internal consequences

may occur. These include excessive sickness and disability claims; working to rule and work stoppages; a morale crisis that affects police officers generally. There will also be questions of disloyalty and how to handle unexpected rates of attrition and retirement. These trends will be exacerbated by the reforms in pay, retirement, initial pay, and lateral entry advanced by Winsor.

- There will also be unanticipated and unintended consequences of any radical policy shift.

Third, there could be consequences of the decentralization of knowledge and lack of cooperation among the segments of the police web, public, private and quasi-public. Police are well known for their secrecy (a well-defined necessity indeed for a secret organization that must conceal its investigations, cases to be prosecuted and investigations of government itself) as well as rather chaotic information management systems, record-keeping, and poorly managing new technologies (Manning, 2008).

Fourth, reflect on the need to vet and make contracts made by the police to private organizations. These are skills not possessed by present police organizations in rich abundance or by the current HMI as constituted. While it is true the police outsource many of their IT contracts, this has not been a happy circumstance (Neyroud, n.d.), and it is unlikely that Police Commissioners and their staffs will have such capacity even in the coming years.

Fifth, what of what the economists call 'the agency problem'? How can one control and sanction contractors? What sanctions are available if 'rent-a-cops' fail to perform? Is it responsible for a police organization to contract another organization to carry out its core functions? This is a basket of snakes conjured up by outsourcing and privatization. What of the complex difficulties in sanctioning and renegotiating contracts gone bad, or egregiously violated? These issues have salience and power because designated agents of the police will take on their moral umbrella, simulations of public police uniforms, their sanctity and, to some degree at least, their well-earned public trust.

Sixth, what of the morale problems associated with downsizing, retirement, unequal pay rates, increased inequalities in the public police organization, new modes of severance, lateral entries and fast track promotions? Studies of the morale of officers caught in the process of transition of the RUC to the PSNI and attendant problems have revealed anger, depression, frustration and feelings of betrayal among retirees (Gilbert, 2013).

Seventh, would not increasing private bases for public visible policing produce inequalities in the practice of policing, within police organizations and across the 43 public police constabularies, given differential capacity and willingness of newly elected Police Commissioners to support policing? If this is the case, then inequalities might well increase crime and disorder in disadvantaged areas without the wherewithal to support or acquire more policing services.

In a market-based economy, the powers of models of assessment, algorithms and formal sanctions attached to the presumptive models can have a powerful effect on organizations. The models shape performance in abstract ticking boxes, and meeting 'objectives', while the actual policing practices might not change. As organizations seek to meet expectations, garner rewards and expand if not lose budget lines, they modify the appearance of compliance. Since outsourced contracts are seen as budget reductions, rather than fixed costs, and most policing costs are personnel, the short-term reductions are budget magic. They shift costs to long-term aging of equipment, investment in future projects, and other non-current costs, rather than actual long-term cost reductions (Fox, 2009).

There are some positive points that could emerge from the encouragement of forms of policing other than traditional public policing with its traditional strategies: random patrol (mostly motorized), answering calls for service, and investigating crime. All the past reforms have been narrow, limited and *tactical* in large part – altering the way the 'service is delivered' without alteration of the basic structure of the police organization. It could increase private/public competition for quality of service. Government scrutiny could lead to more rational deployment, pay allocation, e.g. overtime, and especially court time for CID; retirement patterns, e.g. age limits and examination of the interactions between disability, sickness, absenteeism, and retirement. Some of these assume the core functions are public and the augmentation of policing service by other means broadens security. These include the notion that sellers and individual officers can be fired and replaced (however, see above); that they are more sensitive to consumer demands than public police (almost by definition true); that private organizations are more innovative in service delivery and they may provide services more cheaply (support functions such as laboratory and IT functions) based on economies of scale.

Since there are no accepted criteria for judging the quality of police work, even work associated with crime control, there is no easy answer to what are the virtues of the latest efforts at police restructuring. The functions of what is called policing, or the functions of the policing web, are diverse, complex, subtle, nuanced, symbolically loaded and ultimately difficult to grasp, conceptualize and measure. The sense of public duty, training, screening for selection and retention, surely contribute to sustaining that which is valued in public policing. They are also interconnected inextricably such that altering the salience of some function by rewarding one function, e.g. 'crime control' (whatever that connotes), alters the array and ranking of the entire set of organizational functions. As the period under New Labour suggests, working to the numbers, ticking the boxes, and orienting to the visible accounts of the job alter the time and energy available to do the job – wherever that entails being with and serving people. Policing is more than crime control, and it is also more than managing the numbers and satisfying the HMI, because it involves acting out the meanings of security for others. The police perform for us and to us, and their performance is essential to that which we call order, security, and even justice in practice.

Finally, the question of the quality, and perhaps quantity, of policing service is left unanswered in these radical efforts to alter the nature of the public police. Does policing have a precisely defined skill-set? Can this be measured and rewarded systematically? Bittner (1970) suggests that it is systematically applied and constrained violence that is the 'core skill' or competence of police. Or is this core communicative skills? Accessing and using the right software? Physical fitness? How is this core skill learned and cultivated? What is good policing? It is certainly not simple arrests and clearances of crime. How is it done? How can it be trained for? How can it be evaluated and rewarded? It is impossible to reorganize and restructure a public service if there is no definition of the essential and core skills required.

Comment

The narrative of police reform and restructuring has been shaped by the simplified and amplified rhetoric of politicians, and the discussion cast in the language of profit-making and cost reduction in the aid of profits. This rhetorical move has obscured the merits of public democratic policing, and claimed merit when none has been demonstrated. In weighing the merits and demerits of various alterations in the policing web, it is imperative that the public police mandate be made visible and its merits, well demonstrated historically, be dramatized and identified. The merits of a civil, public, accountable and visible uniformed force are an intrinsic part of what is considered good policing. The rationalization of police management can be seen as a meritorious exercise quite apart from the funding of various forms of non-public or semi-public police forces. The ten features of the public police listed above are, for the most part, absent in hybrid police, services outsourced to private security companies, and in short any non-public police. These essential and defining features of the public police, to underscore the argument made here, include: accountability; a mediated and mannered response to citizens' requests; symbolic representation of authority; limited use of violence geared to local standards and expectations; availability in a legitimacy crisis; and in a general sense a representative of public trust. As public agencies, they can be expected to proceed in respect of the 'rules of thumb' that might guide policing by the difference principle. The symbolic role of the police, emphasized elsewhere (Manning, 1977, 2010), is at the heart of the superior virtues of modern democratic policing. That is, by representing the collective will, dramatized and made visible by their uniforms and equipment, and their role as trust assessors for the citizenry, they are a condensed icon of governance. Policing, by its very nature, is not a business to be run for profit. These features cannot be found in the private security world, most significantly because they cannot unequivocally represent legitimate authority; they work for profit; and their very use of the symbols of government pollutes the performance and calls it into question. These are concrete matters of how privatization and outsourcing can alter interpersonal compliance, respect for authority, and trust in the goodwill of those who serve the society. In some sense, it is necessary to ask what are the costs of eroding and contaminating that which is a representation of the collective will, and the confusion attendant to such political moves.

Note

1 2 July 2013. For the Stevens Commission and the volume edited by Jennifer Brown.
2 It should be noted prior to further discussion of changes in the policing web, that there are efforts to reevaluate the police function and rationalize policing in most of Western Europe. Police organizations within Europe, long-established public institutions, vary widely in their capacity to rationalize (fit their procedures to clearly stated objectives or long-term goals) their complex and diverse functions, i.e. providing human services; budgeting; deployment (new rosters in Ireland); purchases; applied technology; hiring, firing and promotion; and other functions. This is partially in the nature of public service organizations, i.e. the question of 'market', 'efficiency', and 'effectiveness', and partially the result of the sacred canopy that has been adroitly fashioned over policing, albeit tattered of late. The present government in the UK is examining these functions more carefully and systematically than any other Western industrialized nation, except perhaps Ireland. The costs of policing have been local issues, not national issues in the United States, in part because the budgets for policing are local, the numbers of federal agents small in comparison to other nations, and crime has been declining for more than twenty years.

References

Banton, M. 1964. The Policeman in the Community. New York: Basic Books.
Bittner, E. 1970. The Functions of the Police in Modern Society. Washington, DC: NIMH.
Black, D. 1983. Crime as Social Control. *American Sociological Review*, 48: 34–45.
Bordua, D. and A.J. Reiss, Jr. 1966. Command, Control and Charisma. *American Journal of Sociology*, 72: 68–72.
Brodeur, Jean P. 2010. The Policing Web. New York: Oxford University Press.
Brogden, M. and G. Ellison. 2013. Policing in an Age of Austerity. London: Routledge.
Caplow, T. 1964. Principles of Organization. New York: Harcourt, Brace.
Forst, B. and P.K. Manning. 1999. Privatization: Two Views. Washington, DC: Georgetown University Press.
Fox, J. 2009. The Myth of the Rational Market. New York: Harper.
Gilbert, P. 2013. Policing Change–Changing Police. Unpublished Ph.D. Glyndwr University, Wrexham, Wales.
Hobbes, R. *et al.* 2003. Bouncers. Oxford: Oxford University Press.
Home Office. 2012. Police Service Strength England and Wales, 2012. London.
Johnston, L. 1992. The Rebirth of Private Policing. London: Routledge.
Jones, T. and T. Newburn. 2002. The Transformation of Policing? *British Journal of Criminology*, 36: 182–198.
Loader, I. and A. Mulcahy. 2003. Policing and the Condition of England. Oxford: Oxford University Press.
Manning, P.K. 1977. Police Work. Cambridge, MA: MIT Press.
Manning, P.K. 2003. Policing Contingencies. Chicago: University of Chicago Press.
Manning, P.K. 2008. The Technology of Policing. New York: New York University Press.
Manning, P.K. 2010. Democratic Policing. Boulder, CO: Paradigm Publishers.
Marshall, G. (1965) Police and Government. London: Methuen.
Neyroud, P. n.d. (unpublished) Privatizing the Police? Working paper.
Rawls, J. 1999. A Theory of Justice. Cambridge, MA: Harvard University Press.
Rawls, J. and E. Kelly. 2001. Justice as Fairness. Cambridge, MA: Harvard University Press.
Reiner, R. 2010. The Politics of the Police. 4th edn. Oxford: Oxford University Press.
Rigakos, G. 2002. The New Parapolice. Toronto: University of Toronto Press.
Winsor, T. 2012. Independent Review of Police Officer and Staff Remuneration and Conditions. Final Report, two volumes. London: HMSO.

3

WHY DO THE POLICE MATTER?

Beyond the myth of crime-fighting

Ian Loader[1]

> I have given you just one objective – to cut crime.
>
> *(Theresa May, July 2011)*

Introduction

The Coalition Government has embarked on a radical overhaul of policing in England and Wales. In the face of great hostility from many inside the police and much scepticism outside of it, the government appears determined to engineer a revolution in British policing. Indeed their determination is such that Ministers sometimes forget to utter the normally obligatory political platitudes about the police 'doing a great job'. The shiny flagship of this reform effort was the introduction in November 2012 of elected Police and Crime Commissioners – a measure that attracts a mix of intense scepticism and public indifference. But alongside Commissioners there exists a flotilla of further significant reform initiatives, the scale and speed of which have left many police officers and police experts aghast (e.g., Blair 2012).

Taking Police and Crime Commissioners as my point of departure, I want in this essay to reconstruct the political logic (or, to use an unfashionable term, ideology) of the Coalition's police reform agenda – my claim being that the dominant meaning of Commissioners can only be fully understood once placed in the context of that wider programme. My argument is that this agenda *does* have an overarching logic and trajectory which has to do with 'freeing' the police from the obstacles that have prevented them from resolutely and effectively fighting crime. I further argue that many of the dangers associated with Police and Crime Commissioners flow from, or are at least amplified by, Commissioners being cast in the mould of crime-fighter. This formulation of the police role is a myth, an emotionally seductive and politically tempting myth, but a myth nonetheless. In the second half of the essay I outline the reasons why this is so and make the case for a more prudent and sociologically grounded answer to the question of why, in a democracy, the police matter. We can, I argue, become better attuned to the dangers of democratizing the police (via Police and Crime Commissioners, or by any other route), as well as better able to grasp the vital importance of doing so, if we apprehend the police role in this wider frame.

Releasing the inner crime-fighter: the political ideology of the Coalition's police reform agenda

On 15 November 2012, an event took place that was both unique in British political history and something of a damp squib. On that day voters in all areas of England & Wales (outside London) went to the polls to elect 41 Police and Crime Commissioners.[2] This was the first time elections had been held for a political office responsible for running a single public service. It was also an opportunity that failed to ignite public interest: turnout across the country averaged 14.7 per cent (Berman *et al.* 2012). There was also evidence of public hostility to the very idea of Police and Crime Commissioners (2.8 per cent of ballot papers were spoilt) and an apparent reluctance among many of those who did vote to permit party politicians to control local policing – Independent candidates were elected in 12 out of 41 force areas, the remaining forces being split between 16 Conservatives and 13 Labour. Despite these 'teething troubles' – and the Electoral Reform Society conducted an enquiry into what went wrong – 41 Police and Crime Commissioners were elected and duly sworn-in to this new political office.[3]

The 41 elected Commissioners will each serve a four-year term. They will be responsible for determining the strategic priorities of their force (to be set out in a police and crime plan) and for setting police budgets. They will have the power to appoint chief constables and hold them to account and can dismiss them without cause – the first time an elected politician has possessed such a power. They are to commission victims' services and, from April 2013, will receive and distribute local community safety budgets. Police and Crime Commissioners seem destined to become powerful actors – even the most powerful actor – on the local policing and crime reduction scene.

Police and Crime Commissioners are, in my judgement, a flawed means of giving institutional effect to three valuable ideas (I turn to the flaws below). Commissioners are, first of all, one answer to the question of how to make the police responsive to the experiences and concerns of the multiple publics that they serve – and hence minimally credible to those in whose name police resources are spent and police power exercised. They give effect, second, to the idea that, in a democracy, the strategic priorities of public services – the police included – should be set by elected politicians not by unelected officials – in the police case chief constables. Commissioners can be seen, third, as one response to the crisis of trust in democratic politics that afflicts contemporary British society – as it does many other modern democracies. Faced with such a crisis of public confidence, and the diminution in the quality of democratic governance that flows from it (Flinders 2012), one can take a conservative course, doing business-as-usual in the same discredited set of political institutions. Or one can innovate and experiment with new ways of engaging disaffected publics in the political process. Police and Crime Commissioners are most generously interpreted as one such experiment in extending and enhancing democracy.

Viewed in this way, the puzzle is why the idea of Police and Crime Commissioners germinated in right-wing think-tanks and was brought into being by the Conservative Party (I am not alone in puzzling over this – it baffles many Conservatives too). A generation ago making the police *democratically* accountable was a progressive cause – a rallying cry of the municipal left of the 1980s (Walker 2000: ch. 3; Loader and Mulcahy 2003: ch. 8). At that time, the Conservative Party stood resolutely alongside chief officers in defence of the then sacred cow of constabulary independence and against the idea of permitting police authorities to set police priorities. How times have changed.[4] But how are we to account for this *volte face* in Conservative thought on policing? How can we best make sense of the political identity of the idea of Police and Crime Commissioners?

To answer this question one has to situate Commissioners among the raft of police reform measures that the Coalition has introduced since 2010 – a package, as I have said, whose ambition and speed easily matches the legislative hyperactivity that marked the Blair years and seem set to usher in what many commentators view as a revolution in British policing. So what is happening? Why so much and so fast and with such apparent disdain for police opinion? What is the political logic and telos of this overall reform programme, and what sense can we make of Police and Crime Commissioners once located in this wider context?

One common interpretation of the Coalition's police agenda is that the government is finally and determinedly bringing to bear on the police a standard neo-liberal critique of public service provision – namely, that state agencies lack incentives to improve performance, are wary of new ideas, wasteful of public money, reward longevity not talent, are unresponsive to customers, and prone to being captured by producers and run in their interests. The Conservatives, it is argued, have come to see the police as the last unreformed public bureaucracy and have eyed an opportunity (in the context of budgets cuts and the imperative to make savings, and the police's diminished standing following the revelations at the Leveson Inquiry) to do something about it. Hence the scale – 'we must grasp this chance to shake-up a complacent, backward-looking public service'. Hence the speed – 'we have a potentially short time window in which to act'. On this view of the government agenda, the Conservatives have set about completing a process that they started with the Sheehy Report in 1993, but which was defeated at the time due to a combination of organized police opposition and the political weakness of the then Conservative administration. There is, in short, unfinished business.

There is something in this view of things, but it only takes us so far. What it fails to illuminate very much is the substance of what the Coalition is proposing and enacting. Police reform in the name of what? What is the end-game? What kind of police force is meant to emerge from this reform process? The answer to these questions is, I think, this: that the government sees itself as *releasing the police's inner crime-fighter*. Inside every police force, it reasons, there is a lean, mean crime-fighting machine struggling to get out. That machine has over recent decades been shackled by an excess of rules, bureaucracy and regulation, by antiquated working practices, by interference from Home Office civil servants, by deferential and anonymous police authorities, and by remote, complacent, liberal-minded chief officers. The task the government has set itself is to 'liberate' the police from these restraints so that it can once again focus on 'just one objective – to cut crime' (May 2011).

Let us, with this thought in mind, briefly consider the main planks of the government's police reform agenda. First, the government has set about cutting national targets and 'wasteful bureaucracy that hampers police operations'. To this end it established a Reducing Bureaucracy Programme Board to streamline recording and related processes across a number of police tasks and give over more decisions to the discretion of officers. Most controversially, it has reduced the reporting requirements for stop and search and removed the national obligation to record 'stop and accounts'. This is all being done in the name of 'freeing officers to fight crime', as the Home Secretary put it. Second, the government commissioned and then broadly welcomed a report by Tom Winsor on police pay and conditions. Winsor took a dim view of present arrangements, describing them as having 'developed a degree of rigidity and a distance from modern management instruments and practices', as well as taking aim at what he claimed was a 'timid and reticent' management culture. His report sets out some radical proposals for both dealing with severe fiscal restraint in the short term and restructuring police working practices to face the challenges of the next 30 years. The key proposals include rewarding specialist skills and high performance rather than length of service, and concentrating pay on front-line officers; developing more robust appraisal systems; routine fitness testing of officers; establishing a compulsory severance scheme; and enabling 'direct entry' to inspector and superintendent levels from outside the police service. Tom Winsor has now – provocatively – been appointed as the next Chief Inspector of Constabulary. The government has, third, been quietly but insistently supportive of the steps that several forces (most controversially, Surrey and the West Midlands) started making towards outsourcing a range of police services and functions to the private sector. These mainly cover what have been termed 'back' and 'middle' office tasks, though they have also included the building and staffing of police stations and managing custody suites. Chief constables have clearly felt moved to travel (further) in this direction as a response to cuts in police budgets – though it is not at all clear who authorized them to do so.[5] But the move is also defended as necessary to enable officers to take their place on the front line, fighting crime. Finally, the government has required police forces to make available local crime statistics for their area. In February 2011, it launched an online crime mapping service (http://www.police.uk/), searchable by postcode, which provides information on recorded crime and neighbourhood policing teams. This was again heralded as bringing greater transparency to policing, 'empowering' individuals and communities with information about crime that would enable them to bring the police to account for their performance in tackling it.[6]

With this raft of measures in mind, we can revisit Police and Crime Commissioners and seek to decipher their dominant meaning. Commissioners represent – in the view of their authors – a shift from central targets to local determination of policing priorities, and from bureaucratic to democratic accountability. Their stated aim is to give local people a direct voice in policing by creating an elected figure that can 'ensure that the police concentrate on the crimes that most affect people's quality of life' (Forsyth 2009). The government has, in this respect, consistently insisted that Police and Crime Commissioners are a vehicle for making the police more effective crime-fighters. It is by no means clear why this should be so. But I think the logic goes something like this: Police and Crime Commissioners are intended to act as a disruptive technology sent to shake up what the government think are cosy and opaque relations between police authorities and chief officers. Their task is to replace complacency and obfuscation with transparency and accountability with a view to requiring chief constables to focus on delivering better performance. Police and Crime Commissioners will, as the former Police and Justice Minister put it, 'be big local figures with a mandate to drive the fight against crime and anti-social behaviour' (Herbert 2010). In the political imagination of its authors, Commissioners are to act either as a constant thorn-in-the-side of chief officers (who can be dismissed if they are deemed ineffective or recalcitrant), or else are to form a dynamic crime-fighting team with the chief – a sort of Bratton-Giuliani British-style. With such arrangements in place, 'Chief constables will be liberated to be crime-fighters rather than government managers, free to run their workforces, and relieved of the burden of politics which they can safely leave to Police and Crime Commissioners' (Herbert 2010).

Beyond fantasy: why the police (and police governance) matter

This bandit-catching conception of the police role has a widespread, but superficial, appeal within the English social imaginary – a common-sense 'obviousness' that seems difficult to gainsay. What else are the police for if it is not to catch criminals and fight crime? But we should be clear that it is a fantasy, one of the 'myths we live by' (Samuel and Thompson 1990). To say this is not to make the absurd claim that the police do not or should not investigate crime or apprehend offenders. Nor is it to deny that the police have an important – if secondary – role among the institutions that prevent crime and foster public security. It is, however, to argue that the idea that the police have 'just one objective – to cut crime' rests on a partial, sociologically illiterate account of what the police do, and a reductive, impoverished conception of why the police matter.

In recent years, Jean-Paul Brodeur (2010) has observed, the question of 'what the police do' has been superseded by the question of 'what works'. This matters,

Brodeur argues, because it has given rise to a social and political (not to mention criminological) forgetting of what has been learned during the past four decades of police research. Such research has, Brodeur reminds us, demonstrated across decades and jurisdictions that a minority of calls to the police concern crime, and that most police time is spent on non-crime related matters (Brodeur 2010: 150–164).[7] The conclusion that Brodeur, standing in a long line of policing scholars (Reiner 2010: ch. 5), draws from this, is that dealing with crime forms but one aspect of an omnibus police role that is better interpreted as having to do with the regulation of social conflict and the management of order, in respect of which the police's unique resource is the capacity, if required, to wield non-negotiable coercive force. The police are, as Egon Bittner once famously quipped, the agency to which individuals turn when 'something-is-happening-that-ought-not-to-be-happening-and-about-which-someone-had-better-do-something-now' (Bittner 1990: 355). Many of the things that 'ought-not-to-be-happening' turn out not to be crime.

An instrumental, crime-cutting conception of policing also has a profoundly limited understanding of what is, arguably, a more basic question: why do the police matter? An important strand of the sociology of policing has shown that what the police symbolize is as, if not more, important than what they actually do (Manning 1977, 2012; Reiner 1992; Loader 1997; Loader and Mulcahy 2003). The police, on this view, matter because of their ongoing capacity to send authoritative signals which sustain or bolster (or chip away at, or sharply undermine) people's sense of the social world as an ordered place, and their feelings of belonging securely within it. The police, Peter Manning (2010) argues, dramatize order, allocate censure and affirm trust in ways that matter deeply to, and speak volumes about, the nature of social relations and the quality of governance within a society. Every police action, or inaction, sends a powerful message to its recipient and to wider audiences about who belongs within a society and about their place (or lack thereof) within its extant social hierarchies. How policing is carried out thus operates as a sensitive and often highly charged indicator of how adequately any society attends to the security and well-being of its members – and, increasingly today, of its denizen non-members. This is why policing so often grabs people's attention and provokes such strong and conflicting emotions. This is why policing matters. It does so in powerful ways that include, but do not reduce to, the question of how effectively the police can control crime.

Two principal lessons can, I think, be drawn from these brief reflections on what the police do and why policing matters. The first is that it matters enormously not just that the police effectively investigate crime, regulate conflict and manage order, but also *how* they go about these tasks. This is the key message to emerge from an impressive body of empirical research on procedural justice conducted in both the USA and the UK over recent years (e.g., Sunshine and Tyler 2003; Hough *et al.* 2010). This research has demonstrated that people's belief in the legitimacy of the police, and motivation to comply with the law for other than instrumental reasons, depends greatly on how fairly they are treated during encounters with the police. It has also been shown that people are generally more concerned with the perceived fairness of such encounters – whether they 'had their say', and were treated with respect, by an officer they believed to be neutral and open-minded (Tyler 2004) – than with their outcomes. Every police–public interaction, Tyler (2012) argues, is a 'teachable moment' – an occasion in which something is necessarily communicated about the law and legal authorities and what they stand for. That 'something' can have fateful (positive or negative) consequences for people's future willingness to trust and cooperate with the police, and for whether they think of the law as worthy of their compliance because it represents moral values which they share.

The research on procedural justice has important consequences for practical police work. Its lessons can, moreover, be implemented during times of severe austerity (respect does not cost money!) and without having to make hard choices about how and to whom to distribute the benefits. Treating people fairly and with regard to their dignity is a public good that can be supplied equally to all (Rosanvallon 2011: 186). It is, however, a good whose benefits are likely to be experienced most intensely by those who feel that their sense of belonging to British society is precarious and cannot be taken for granted. But one might also use the insights of procedural justice as the basis for developing a more capacious and ambitious account of what one might term *civic* policing. By this I mean that we first and foremost understand policing as one means through which members of British society express mutual solidarity and give institutional effect to that solidarity. This means viewing the myriad tasks that police officers undertake to control crime and manage order as being connected – and guided – by the following aspirations: that the police are mobilized as a means of repairing the trust that is breached by criminal harms; that police work needs to be conducted in ways that reinforce people's sense of secure belonging and capacity to live confidently with risk (Loader and Walker 2007), and that the police (indeed, the wider criminal justice system) should undertake their necessary interventions in social life not merely with a view to minimizing the 'damage to civility' (Manning 2010: 20) they might entail (as liberals would have it), but with the aim of leaving victims and communities better off as a result of that intervention.

A second key lesson of the above reflections on what the police do, and why policing matters, is to underscore the importance of putting in place suitable arrangements for subjecting policing to *democratic* governance. To be sure, it is vital that any system of democratic accountability respects the operational independence (or, better, responsibility) of chief constables. It is equally imperative that any such arrangements are coupled with an effective human rights regime and mechanisms of complaint and redress that protect the legitimate entitlements of unpopular minorities and shield them from the dangers of majority rule. But the police should not be counted solely as among the 'fixed' rather than 'moving' parts of the constitution (cf. Chakrabarti 2008). Police forces are public services that allocate scarce resources and decide as between different priorities. They choose to devote more or less of those resources to different neighbourhoods; to burglary, robbery, domestic violence, child protection, human trafficking, or cybercrime; and to different units within the organization – detection, neighbourhood policing, crime prevention, partnership working, and so on. They also now take decisions about whether and to what extent to outsource police tasks. All these decisions have material effects on the lives of citizens. Those citizens thus have a legitimate stake in how these decisions are made and a reasonable expectation of being their authors as well as their addressees. Strategic policing decisions should not be left to selected officials (whether chief constables, or Home Office officials) or elected national politicians.

Police and Crime Commissioners are one possible means of giving people such a voice. But the election every four years of a single individual to determine the priorities of often large police forces moves us only a small way along the path which needs to be travelled. Commissioners are limited in two senses, one often remarked upon, another much less so. The first is that Police and Crime Commissioners are no substitute for mechanisms of continuous public engagement with, and deliberation about, local crime and policing questions.[8] The procedural justice literature again gives us a clue as to why such mechanisms are important: if we are in a realm of scarce resources where not everyone can be a winner, and where (insatiable) public expectations have to be carefully managed, the legitimacy of the decisions taken and the choices made will depend heavily on the capacity of all affected groups to have a meaningful say in how those decisions are made. One might add that such deliberation maximizes the amount of relevant social information that guides decision-making and, to that extent, enhances the likely quality of decisions. In short, democratic *processes* matter – both to the legitimacy and to the quality of policing practices. It therefore remains a progressive challenge to think about – and experiment with – institutional mechanisms by which it is possible to engage professionals, experts and affected publics in the formation of informed, intelligent and publicly intelligible crime and justice policies (Loader and Sparks 2012; see more broadly Smith 2009).

The second limitation concerns the scope of Police and Crime Commissioners and their adequacy to the world we today inhabit. The government is keen to emphasize that they have introduced Police *and Crime* Commissioners with a wide brief to engage themselves in victims, crime reduction and criminal justice services in their area. This is, potentially, to the good. It is less often observed that they are to be *Police* and Crime Commissioners whose oversight and steering responsibilities extend to only one among the agencies that are engaged in *policing*. But it has become commonplace in the policing literature to observe that policing is today a plural activity undertaken by a range of agencies other than the police, notably the private security industry (e.g., Ayling *et al.* 2010). Moreover, that industry not only supplies personnel to watch over shopping malls, office complexes, sports stadia, etc., as well as those services that have been outsourced by the police, it also produces and supplies a large range of security and surveillance technology. Our democratic and regulatory imagination has not kept pace with these developments on the ground, and we continue to think in capsules about police accountability on the one hand, and separately, if at all, about the regulation of private security on the other. This, too, presents a challenge for progressive thinking in this field, the challenge being to extend the democratic considerations that have been applied more extensively to the police in recent years to the governance of private security – both to its people and to the development and deployment of its technologies (Brodeur 2010: 308). This lies well beyond the ambit of Police and Crime Commissioners. It is also presently nowhere close to the radar screen of those who vie for office with contemporary British politics.

Conclusion: Police and Crime Commissioners and after

Many of the risks to the 'British police tradition' (Chakrabarti 2008; Blair 2012) that critics fear will follow the introduction of Police and Crime Commissioners flow from, or are magnified by, the coupling of Commissioners with a crime-fighting model of policing. The more a Police and Crime Commissioner thinks that his or her job is to get the police to catch and lock up criminals, the more likely they are to tread on the operational toes of chief officers, or to scold or sack them for failing to drive down crime. The more Commissioners understand themselves to be 'big local figures with a mandate to drive the fight against crime and anti-social behaviour' the less likely they are to foster inclusive public debate about local crime and security problems. Instead, the temptation will loom large to disregard the views of, or even actively target, unpopular minorities (Muslims, travellers, foreign nationals, disaffected youth, and so on) and to play fast and loose with civil liberties and the rule of law. Finally, of course, the more they ask to be judged as Commissioners solely by their (or the police's) success or failure in reducing crime, the more they will be creating a petard from which they may be hoist at the 2016 elections.

There is a real prospect that Commissioners will act in just these ways over the next four years – at least in some places. But other possibilities also remain open. Police and Crime Commissioners are best interpreted not as a crime reduction measure, but as a piece of constitutional reform, a radical recalibration of the relationship between citizens and a key public service – the police. By interpreting Commissioners this way (and taking seriously the Coalition Government's stated aim of handing control of policing from the centre to the local), one is reminded that the success or failure, indeed the very shape, of this democratic experiment lies largely beyond the control of its Conservative authors. In fact, the impact of Commissioners on the ground is clearly going to depend not only on how Independents perform, but on the programme that the 13 Labour Police and Crime Commissioners develop over the next four years (Loader and Muir 2011). In this context, two tasks lie ahead. The first is to labour on the ground to support the work of Commissioners who are willing to use the office and its powers to give practical effect to a more civic, deliberative conception of policing – to Commissioners who respect police operational independence, run an office for public engagement, improve the transparency and public responsiveness of their force, hard-wire social justice considerations into the work of the police, work with other agencies to develop holistic crime prevention, are open to (but not slaves of) evidence about what works, and take seriously the trans-local elements of crime and policing. But it is important to do all this, second, while remaining alive to the possibility that Police and Crime Commissioners are not the only, and may not be the best, way of giving institutional effect to what should rightly remain a left-liberal cause: democratizing policing. We still need to think hard about the best model for electing politicians to set strategic priorities for the police and hold them to account, and about how to supplement (and counter-balance) the elected dimension of police governance with effective mechanisms of oversight, redress and public deliberation.

Notes

1   I wish to thank Jennifer Brown, Nicola Lacey and Elizabeth Turner for their constructive comments on the first draft of this chapter.
2   In London, the elected Mayor appoints a deputy who assumes responsibilities broadly analogous to those of Police and Crime Commissioners.
3   Much was made in the immediate aftermath of the elections of the impact that low voter turnout may have on the legitimacy of the elected candidates and their ability to work effectively as the 'voice of the people'. I rather suspect that these concerns will recede as Police and Crime Commissioners begin their work – though the 'you have no mandate' charge will linger in the background and can be activated during any future conflicts. I also think the Conservatives were relaxed about the turnout figures on the grounds that it takes time to generate public interest in a new political office and that the problem will not recur in subsequent elections (in 2016 Police and Crime Commissioners will be elected on the same day as local councils, in 2020 on the same day as the general election). From a Conservative standpoint the important thing is that Police and Crime Commissioners are now in place. Moreover, 16 of them are Conservatives and several of the Independents are either ex-police officers and/or supportive of a 'crime-fighting' agenda – most obviously the winner in Surrey, Kevin Hurley, who campaigned on a 'zero tolerance' ticket.
4   Not just in the Conservative Party, it must be said. Having briefly promoted the idea of elected police authorities while in office, the Labour Party very publicly aligned itself with police opinion in opposing elected Police and Crime Commissioners and seems to have become generally lukewarm about the idea of democratizing the police.
5   The outsourcing of police functions has largely taken in the absence of public debate about the impact this might have on integrated policing, about how – given commercial confidentiality – it is possible to judge whether the police are acquiring trustworthy, value-for-money services, or about whether the police have the capabilities to be effective procurers and regulators of the private sector (cf. Ayling *et al.* 2010). All this changed somewhat when G4S very publicly failed to deliver on part of its contract to provide security staff for the London Olympics – a scandal that is causing forces to pause (either for reflection or until the dust settles) before venturing any further down the path of outsourcing services.
6   Having abolished the National Police Improvement Agency, and expressed doubts about ACPO's fitness for purpose, the government has established a College of Policing to provide research-based guidance to forces and assist in the professional development of officers. It also commissioned a Review of Police Leadership and Training conducted by Peter Neyroud. Both these initiatives have been couched in terms of transforming the police service into a profession (see Sklansky, this volume). It remains to be seen, however, whether they will form an effective counterweight to the crime-fighting narrative that animates government policy.
7   Brodeur reviewed 51 studies based on various sources. Of these studies, 46 showed that the proportion of police work devoted to crime was 50 per cent or less, two-thirds of them concluded that the percentage was 33 per cent or less (Brodeur 2010: 158–159).

8   Though, as I have argued elsewhere with Rick Muir, one mark of a progressive Police and Crime Commissioner will be the extent to which he or she uses the office to put in place such deliberative arrangements (Loader and Muir 2011).

References

Ayling, J., P. Grabosky and C. Shearing (2010) *Lengthening the Arms of the Law*. Cambridge: Cambridge University Press.

Berman, G., C. Coleman and M. Taylor (2012) *Police and Crime Commissioner Elections, 2012*. Research Paper 12/73, House of Commons Library; available at: www.parliament.uk/briefing-papers/RP12–73.pdf.

Bittner, E. (1990) *Aspects of Police Work*. Boston: Northeastern University Press.

Blair, I. (2012) 'Police Independence is Under Threat', *New Statesman*, 6 June.

Brodeur, J.-P. (2010) *The Policing Web*. Oxford: Oxford University Press.

Chakrabarti, S. (2008) 'A Thinning Blue Line? Police Independence and the Rule of Law', *Policing*, 2/3: 367–374.

Flinders, M. (2012) *Defending Politics: Why Democracy Matters in the Twenty-first Century*. Oxford: Oxford University Press.

Forsyth, J. (2009) 'Elected Police Commissioners Are a Test of Whether the Tories Are Serious or Not About Their Agenda', *The Spectator*, 20 November.

Herbert, N. (2010) 'Who Runs the Police?' Speech to IPPR; available at: http://www.nickherbert.com/media_centre.php/438/Who%20runs%20the%20police.

Hough, M., J. Jackson, B. Bradford, A. Myhill and P. Quinton (2010) 'Procedural Justice, Trust, and Institutional Legitimacy', *Policing*, 4/3: 203–210.

Loader, I. (1997) 'Policing and the Social: Questions of Symbolic Power', *British Journal of Sociology*, 48/1: 1–18.

Loader, I. and A. Mulcahy (2003) *Policing and the Condition of England: Memory, Politics and Culture*. Oxford: Oxford University Press.

Loader, I. and R. Muir (2011) *Progressive Police and Crime Commissioners: An Opportunity for the Centre-Left*. London: IPPR; available at: http://ippr.org/articles/56/7957/progressive-police-and-crime-commissioners-an-opportunity-for-the-centre-left?megafilter=young+people.

Loader, I. and R. Sparks (2012) 'Beyond Lamentation: Towards a Democratic Egalitarian Politics of Crime and Justice', in T. Newburn and J. Peay (eds.) *Policing: Politics, Culture and Control*. Oxford: Hart.

Loader, I. and N. Walker (2007) *Civilizing Security*. Cambridge: Cambridge University Press.

Manning, P. (1977) *Police Work: The Social Organization of Policing*. Prospect Heights: Waveland Press.

Manning, P. (2010) *Democratic Policing in a Changing World*. Boulder, CO: Paradigm.

Manning, P. (2012) 'Drama, the Police and the Sacred', in T. Newburn and J. Peay (eds.) *Policing: Politics, Culture and Control*. Oxford: Hart.

May, T. (2011) 'Speech to ACPO Summer Conference'; available at: http://www.homeoffice.gov.uk/media-centre/speeches/acpo-summer.

Reiner, R. (1992) 'Policing a Postmodern Society', *Modern Law Review*, 55/6: 761–781.

Reiner, R. (2010) *The Politics of the Police (4th edn)*. Oxford: Oxford University Press.

Rosanvallon, P. (2011) *Democratic Legitimacy*. Princeton, NJ: Princeton University Press.

Samuel, R. and P. Thompson (eds.) (1990) *The Myths We Live By*. London: Routledge.

Smith, D. (2009) *Democratic Innovations: Designing Institutions for Citizen Participation*. Cambridge: Cambridge University Press.

Sunshine, J. and T. Tyler (2003) 'The Role of Procedural Justice and Legitimacy in Shaping Public Support for Policing', *Law & Society Review*, 37/3: 513–548.

Tyler, T. (2004) 'Enhancing Police Legitimacy', *Annals of the American Academy of Political and Social Science*, 593: 84–99.

Tyler, T. (2012) 'The Virtues of Self-Regulation', in A. Crawford and A. Hucklesby (eds.) *Legitimacy and Compliance in Criminal Justice*. London: Routledge.

Walker, N. (2000) *Policing in a Changing Constitutional Order*. London: Sweet and Maxwell.

4

WHAT ARE THE POLICE FOR?

Re-thinking policing post-austerity

Andrew Millie

Introduction

In the context of the global financial crisis and after inheriting a record budget deficit, the British Coalition Government decided in 2010 that the best way forward was a programme of austerity. What followed were major cuts to public expenditure, including a substantial reduction in police budgets. Whether this was the right decision is beyond the remit of this chapter. However, the effect on the police has been substantial. The police in Britain had enjoyed a sustained period of growth – both in terms of police numbers and increased responsibilities undertaken by police personnel – despite increases in competition and falls in recorded crime (Millie and Bullock, 2012; Millie, 2013). This was to change. In Scotland cuts came through the merging of all eight forces into a single Police Service of Scotland (Police and Fire Reform (Scotland) Act 2012).[1] With the 2010 Comprehensive Spending Review (HM Treasury, 2010) government funding of the police in England and Wales was reduced by 20 per cent through to 2015. The scale of these cuts was unprecedented and has required police services to reconsider their priorities. At the same time the police have had to deal with major change in governance structures with the introduction of elected Police and Crime Commissioners in November 2012 – albeit following an election where only 15 per cent of the electorate turned up to vote (Rogers and Burn-Murdoch, 2012). The new policing landscape of fewer resources and (assumed) greater democratic accountability has generated a lot of uncertainty among serving police officers and questions over what form policing will take post-austerity.

In this context the question of what the police are for becomes pertinent and is the focus for this chapter. According to the current Home Secretary, Theresa May (2011a), the police's remit is simple: 'We need them to be the tough, no-nonsense crime-fighters they signed up to become.' Yet 50 years of police research has painted a picture that is far more complicated. According to McLaughlin (2007: 52):

Despite the central position of this 'cops and robbers' model in both police culture and the popular imagination, ethnographic researchers confirmed that the exact nature and scope of police activity is in fact difficult to define and, for the most part, unrelated to law enforcement and criminal detection.

According to Jean-Paul Brodeur (1983, 2010) the policing task can be divided between 'high policing' and 'low policing'. High policing is associated with the work of the intelligence community, whereas low policing is the domain of everyday (often uniformed) officers. This chapter is concerned with the activities of low policing which are conceptualised as being on a continuum between 'wide policing' and 'narrow policing' (Millie, 2013). A focus on 'cops and robbers' – or Theresa May's notion of 'no-nonsense crime-fighters' – may be too narrow a definition of policing. At the other extreme, Egon Bittner (1990/2005: 150) noted the police's role as intervening in 'every kind of emergency'. Police officers clearly do not intervene in 'every kind of emergency'; however, their remit has grown to such an extent that what is regarded as legitimate police activity is perhaps too wide. Contemporary policing activities include crime fighting, crime reduction, dealing with anti-social behaviour, tackling terrorism, public reassurance, traffic duties, immigration control, schools work, offender management, event security, disaster management, making people feel safer and so on. A narrowing of focus could be beneficial and the current cuts might provide the opportunity for this to occur with the possibility that post-austerity policing will be both slimmer and fitter.

What are the police for?

As noted, there is more to policing than fighting crime – however, fighting crime is clearly a significant aspect to police work; but it is only one aspect. If policing were to be defined narrowly along the lines of Theresa May's 'no-nonsense crime-fighters' then a lot of valuable police activity would be called into question. Politically attractive 'bobbies on the beat' would be the first to go. While visible patrols can assist with gaining local intelligence, they rarely deal with actual crime (Kelling *et al.*, 1974; Clarke and Hough, 1984). On a micro level visible patrol might deter criminal activity (Ratcliffe *et al.*, 2011), yet these crimes can simply be displaced elsewhere. For Wakefield (2007: 343), the value of visible foot patrol is that it reflects 'the symbolic function of policing as a sign of social order'. For Innes (2004) the visible officer acts as a signal of control. The value of visible patrol is not in terms of crime-fighting potential, but in reassuring the public that the police are there, are on the side of the public and will intervene if required. Such reassurance policing (Innes and Fielding, 2002; Millie and Herrington, 2005) can be seen as part of the police's social service function (e.g. Morgan and Newburn, 1997; McLaughlin, 2007), or as Punch (1979) once termed it, a secret social service function. The aims of reassurance policing have included improving quality of life and feelings of safety, and addressing fears of crime (Tuffin *et al.*, 2006).

By targeting such 'softer' issues the hope is to improve public satisfaction and confidence in the police. Of course, this would only be possible if *all* officers – including response and investigative teams – took public reassurance seriously, rather than just those tasked with 'reassurance' (Millie and Herrington, 2005). Mistreatment by response teams or high-profile cases of misconduct or corruption can have greater influence on public confidence. From recent history the cases of Stephen Lawrence (Foster *et al.*, 2005) and Ian Tomlinson (Greer and McLaughlin, 2012), the Hillsborough Independent Panel (2012) and the Leveson inquiry into press standards (2012) will all have a negative influence on the public image of the police that attempts at reassurance would have to counter. Theresa May (2011b) has commented that: 'I haven't asked the police to be social workers . . . I've told them to cut crime.' Cutting crime is important, but a focus on crime without considering the police's wider social service function can result in very bad practice. It is Packer's classic (1968) distinction between a crime control and due process model of justice – between getting things done and getting things done properly. True policing requires both. Similarly, there have been historic debates concerning whether the police are a force or a service (e.g. Avery, 1981; Reiner, 2013). The answer is that the police are both force *and* service.

An order-maintenance role has also been recognised alongside the police's crime control and social service functions. In fact, according to Reiner (2013: 166): 'Most police work is neither social service nor law enforcement, but order maintenance – the settlement of conflicts, potentially crimes, by means other than formal law enforcement.'

According to Banton (1964) this is the function of being a 'peace officer'. For Ericson (1982) the police's function is the reproduction of order: 'Their sense of order and the order they seek to reproduce is that of the status quo' (Ericson, 1982: 7). In Britain this is reflected in the requirement to 'maintain the Queen's peace'. The order-maintenance function is, therefore, conservative, reproducing order acceptable to those with power. There is clearly negative potential with such an approach, with those who challenge the status quo being seen as opposed to a conservative order and then disproportionately policed. For Brogden and Ellison (2013: 9) 'state policing has always been committed to maintaining a divisive social order' and certain 'usual suspect' groups – young Black males in particular – are disproportionately targeted by police action. But preserving social order is not all bad and according to Reiner (2012: 5), 'the crucial work of policing is maintaining order, on both the grand social scale and micro-social levels.' For Reiner (2012) order maintenance is not inherently divisive but a function akin to what he calls 'fire brigade policing' or 'first aid order maintenance'.

In summary, the policing task is wider than Theresa May's 'no-nonsense crime-fighters' including a combination of crime control, social service and order-maintenance functions. However, if these functions are defined too widely, then the police start to adopt roles more suitable for other agencies, community groups or volunteers. Reiner has noted elsewhere that 'good policing may help preserve social order: it cannot produce it. Yet increasingly that is what is being demanded of the police' (2000: xi). An emphasis on order preservation rather than order production is helpful for understanding the role of the police. Order production is for others such as parents and schools who have roles in producing orderly citizens (although, of course, also citizens that challenge the status quo). The police's role is different, in preserving the existing order. Yet, as Reiner notes, the police have increasingly been required to produce order. Areas where the police roles have been stretched perhaps too widely – including in the production of order – are considered next.

How did the police become so wide?

A wide definition of policing is not new. According to Lee (1901, cited in Banton, 1973: 19) the nineteenth-century police officer was also responsible for 'the compulsory education of children, the reformation of criminals, the observance of sanitary and hygienic conditions, the control of liquor traffic, and the prevention of cruelty to children and animals'. Many of these tasks were passed onto other agencies; however, others were added to the police remit such that, by the 1990s the Conservative government attempted to lighten the load – albeit unsuccessfully (Wilson et al., 2001). Tasks that were suggested as superfluous included missing persons, schools work, noise nuisance, event stewarding, court summons, court security, immigration and certain traffic duties (Millie, 2013). Some activities have since moved to other agencies, for instance, with local authorities taking over noise nuisance, private security being used for court work and Highways Agency Traffic Officers taking on some traffic duties.

Despite such developments, over time many responsibilities have been added to the police task, either by government or through processes of empire building. The question is why this might be the case. In the late twentieth and early twenty-first centuries 'risk' became a prevailing approach to social policy (Beck, 1992; Giddens, 1999). Drawing on actuarial work in the insurance industry it was the idea that future hazards could be planned for and prevented. As Giddens pointed out (1999: 3), it was not that the world had become 'more hazardous'; rather, society was 'increasingly preoccupied with the future (and also with safety)'. In this context it made sense for the police to have greater involvement in wider aspects of social policy. For instance, if a young person's engagement with schooling reduced the risk of following a career into anti-social and criminal behaviour, then it was logical to view education in terms of crime prevention, and thereby an activity that may fall within the remit of police involvement. With the Safer School Partnerships – which evolved from the 2002 Street Crime Initiative – this is what occurred (Briers and Dickmann, 2011). Drawing on US practice (Simon, 2007), police officers were routinely stationed within school premises to deal with student behaviour and to provide a permanent link between the school and police. In effect, discipline issues that were traditionally dealt with by the school became the concern of the police, in a form of criminalisation of education policy (Millie and Moore, 2011). According to the Police Foundation

(2011: 08) the role of officers within schools also expanded, 'to encompass identification of risk factors pointing towards future bad behaviour or extremism'. The Police Foundation also noted that, 'This area should be approached with caution' (2011: 08).

A risk paradigm was similarly used for what has became known as offender management – work traditionally carried out by probation and social workers but now also by police officers in what Kemshall and Maguire (2001) have called the 'policification' of probation. It was thought that future offending could be risk-managed. Police officers have worked as 'offender managers' as part of the Prolific and other Priority Offender Strategy (PPO) (Millie and Erol, 2006) and through Multi-Agency Public Protection Arrangements (MAPPAs) (Kemshall *et al.*, 2005). Individual officers may have the skills to fulfil these roles; however, the involvement of the police changes fundamentally the relationship between supervisor and offender. Alongside support for the offender, the police's role is intelligence gathering, a function that may be at odds with building trust.

The examples of police officers working within schools and as 'offender managers' are reflective of Jonathan Simon's 'governing through crime' meta-narrative (2007) – with tackling or preventing crime regarded as justifications for a wide range of state policies. If crime prevention is an overriding consideration then schooling is important because educated children are less likely to be criminals (inasmuch as going to school improves their life chances). Similarly, effective offender supervision becomes important because it reduces crime (as well as assists with the rehabilitation process). Such change in emphasis has alternatively been seen as the criminalisation of social policy (Crawford, 1997). If police officers become *less* involved in such activities – leaving school discipline to educators and offender supervision to probation workers[2] – then there is the prospect for the decriminalisation of aspects of social policy.

Other areas characteristic of wide policing and the 'policification'/criminalisation of social policy include disaster management, immigration control and event security (Millie, 2013). In these areas, too, the risk paradigm has been influential. For instance, the police's role in disaster management is in coordination of response, crowd control, riot prevention, family liaison and investigation. It is arguable whether the police are best suited for coordination, and whether this is a task more suited to the fire and rescue service. Similarly, others may be better placed for family liaison work. This is a task where the police's social service and crime-fighting functions can come into conflict. With a focus on minimising future risks, all police tasks are an opportunity for intelligence gathering. According to Davis (2012: 12):

> Police regard survivors', relatives' or witnesses' disclosures to partner agencies as potential evidence and/or intelligence and argue that there can be 'no absolute guarantee of confidentiality' . . . The idea of 'covert' use of a family liaison 'cover' by anti-terrorism officers has raised debate among police themselves.

The result of such an approach is that those seen by the police as 'suspect communities' (cf. Hillyard, 1993) might not wish to help the police or will not seek the assistance of family liaison.

A focus on risk has led to an expansion of policing responsibilities in other areas, even where such expansion causes conflict between these roles and traditional intelligence gathering. The police are actively involved in immigration control (Weber and Bowling, 2004; Cooper, 2009), working alongside the UK Border Agency. With a focus on controlling future risks, those seeking immigration or asylum can be seen primarily as potential criminals or terrorists. Controlling crime and terrorism are clearly important, but should only be part of immigration/asylum policy and not necessarily the defining characteristic.

Event security is also an example of wide policing that might be better suited to other providers. Potential conflict between crime control, order maintenance and social service functions was made clear in the report of the Hillsborough Independent Panel (2012: 8) which noted that during the Hillsborough football disaster of 1989 the police prioritised 'crowd control over crowd safety'. However, more recently the failure of private security firm G4S to provide adequate security personnel for the London 2012 Olympics (BBC Online, 2012) shows that private provision might not be the answer either.

The core policing task

If policing has become too wide then what should constitute the core policing task? This chapter has demonstrated that the policing task comprises a mix of crime-control, social-service and order-maintenance functions. Yet how these functions have been defined has been stretched to include activities that might be better suited to other agencies. With a focus on risk, the police have become involved in activities such as schools work, probation, event security, immigration control and disaster management. There is scope for less police involvement in all these activities, leading to the decriminalisation of areas of social policy. This chapter argues for a narrower definition of crime control, social service and order maintenance. For instance, within crime control is the job of crime prevention. A narrow conception of crime prevention would include crime prevention advisers working with young people, schools, businesses and community groups. A wide definition of crime prevention would, for example, include being stationed within schools to reduce future crime risks, immigration control to prevent terrorism and work with offenders to prevent reoffending.

Writing in the 1960s Michael Banton observed: 'A cardinal principle for the understanding of police organization and activity is that the police are only one among many agencies of social control' (1964: 1). As I have stated elsewhere, 'In simple terms, the police do not have to be doing everything' (Millie, 2013: 155). As noted, the experience of G4S at the London Olympics shows that outsourcing to private companies might not be the best alternative. However, there are other agencies, community groups and volunteers that are capable of fulfilling such roles.

In talk of budget cuts, rather than narrowing definitions of crime control, social service and order maintenance, policing policy and practice has, instead, focused on protecting the 'front line' (HMIC, 2011, 2012; Travis, 2012). Her Majesty's Inspectorate of Policing attempted to define 'front-line' police work, although it found this more difficult than anticipated. According to HMIC (2011: 6), front-line policing includes 'those who are in everyday contact with the public and who directly intervene to keep people safe and enforce the law'. 'Everyday contact' is seen to include both visible and specialist roles, as well as middle-office roles such as custody and call handling – in other words, just about everything except for back-office functions such as finance and police training. Following the examples of criminalisation/'policification' outlined above, this definition of the front line becomes even wider.

Using the HMIC definition it was estimated that 68 per cent of police employees in England and Wales were 'front-line' (61 per cent in visible and specialist roles and 7 per cent in middle-office roles) (HMIC, 2011). According to Nick Herbert MP – who until the September 2012 Cabinet reshuffle was the Police and Criminal Justice Minister – front-line policing 'includes neighbourhood policing, response policing and criminal investigation' (Herbert, 2011). This is, perhaps, as unhelpful as the HMIC definition. Yet, a large proportion of 'front-line' policing is in the form of neighbourhood policing. The populist politics of the last 20 years have repeatedly led to calls for more 'bobbies on the beat' (Loader, 2006; Millie, 2008). As a result, by 2008 the Neighbourhood Policing Programme in England and Wales consisted of approximately 13,000 police officers and 16,000 Police Community Support Officers (PCSOs) working in dedicated neighbourhood policing teams (HMIC, 2008: 4).

Being such an all-inclusive definition, 'front line' is not helpful in identifying what constitutes the core policing task. Furthermore, it would be a mistake to suggest that back-office functions are less important, as without them the so-called front line will be less effective – be they neighbourhood, response or investigative officers. Yet in a time of austerity the temptation is to cut the back office first. According to HMIC (2012: 30), 'forces currently plan to reduce frontline workforce numbers by 6% (8,100) and non-frontline workforce numbers by 33% (20,300) between March 2010 and March 2015'. Such back-office cuts may be short-sighted.

Another area facing cuts has been the police estate (Millie, 2012) – representing both front-line and back-office policing. For instance, Essex police planned to close 21 stations and Lancashire Police were to close 14 stations during 2012 (BBC Online, 2011a, 2011b). According to Surrey Police, 13 stations were to close to 'ensure an extra 200 frontline police officers' (BBC Online, 2011c). While not all stations could be said to be a reassuring presence in the community (Millie, 2012), the closure of stations shows a lack of interest in particular neighbourhoods, thereby affecting public confidence. For instance, in the context of the Metropolitan Police's estate strategy, according to McLaughlin (2008: 273), 'the police seem to be incapable of understanding that local communities are reacting so angrily because the closures are symptomatic of a wider pattern of state withdrawal'.

Conclusions: the shape of policing post-austerity

As things stand, post-austerity policing will be characterised by – as much as possible – a preserved 'front line'. Elected Police and Crime Commissioners will not want to be seen to cut the front line. However, having front-line policing defined so widely there is the prospect that police resources will have been stretched almost to breaking point. Cuts in personnel are inevitable and, with recruitment freezes, police forces are already shrinking. Forces are currently promoting the use of volunteers across many aspects of their work in an attempt to fill gaps as they arise.

So-called back-room functions and the police estate are facing more substantial cuts. In the current economic climate, police buildings may also be sold too cheaply. A lot could be learned from Harold Macmillan's (1985) famous 'selling the family silver' speech in relation to the Conservative government's privatisation programme (see *Daily Telegraph*, 2008). By selling so many stations the police could be selling some of its more prized assets in an attempt to shore up short-term funding of the so-called 'front line'. Longer-term impacts may be more serious.

Instead, a narrowing of the front line and a narrowing of the police task in general are required for the creation of a post-austerity policing that is both slimmer and fitter. Tasks that could be passed onto other agencies, community groups and volunteers have been highlighted, although it is acknowledged that they will have similar economic pressures and might not be able to pick up the slack completely. Government leadership would be required for tasks to be passed elsewhere. The benefit of less police involvement in such 'wide policing' activities will be the decriminalisation of aspects of social policy and the lessening of conflict, for instance, between support and intelligence gathering at disaster scenes, between crowd control and crowd safety at sports events, and between identification of risk factors for potential crime and terrorism and working to improve the education chances of children in schools.

Further areas where police activity could be transferred elsewhere include traffic duties. As noted, some traffic duties have been taken on by Highways Agency Traffic Officers. Providing there is political, legislative and popular support, further enforcement responsibilities could be passed to the Highways Agency, leaving the police to focus on its new, narrower front line.

As for what should be left for the police, the answer is not a shrinking of responsibility to Theresa May's notion of no-nonsense crime-fighters. Instead there needs to be a return to the fundamental roles of the police – these being crime control *and* social service *and* order maintenance:

• If the police's crime control function is defined too widely, then it includes tasks that perhaps ought to be decriminalised and undertaken by others. For instance, in terms of crime prevention, a narrow focus would include work with young people, schools, businesses and community groups, but not necessarily having officers permanently stationed within schools, permanent police involvement in immigration control to prevent terrorism or full-time police taking on probation duties to prevent reoffending.

- A clear social service function for the police is public reassurance with the aim to improve public confidence and legitimacy for policing decisions. If the police's social service role is defined too widely, then it includes activities that might be better suited to others, such as work in disaster management or probation where priority should be social welfare rather than intelligence gathering.

- As for the police's order-maintenance function, an important test is Reiner's (2000) distinction between preserving social order and producing social order. If a task is focused on order production (such as education), then perhaps it could be passed onto others more suited to the task, leaving the police to focus on preserving order. The priority for work within schools, for example, then shifts to improving educational chances rather than identification of risk factors for future anti-social behaviour, crime or terrorist extremism.

It is a question of what should be the focus of police work. Despite the current uncertainty associated with austerity, there is now an opportunity to rethink the shape of policing and thus create a leaner and fitter post-austerity police. Unfortunately, the populist politics that are associated with policing dictate that, rather than having an intelligent debate concerning the nature of the policing task, we have a simplistic idea that 'front-line' policing should be protected at all costs – and that this front line is defined so widely that it is inclusive of all policing activity, bar some back-room functions. How the newly elected Police and Crime Commissioners are going to react to the current fiscal challenges is not yet certain; however, they might not be willing to negatively impact the strength of the front line – no matter how widely this front line is defined.

Notes

1   See, for instance, the contribution to this volume by Nick Fyfe.
2   To further complicate the picture, in January 2013 the Coalition's Justice Secretary, Chris Grayling, announced greater involvement of the private and voluntary sector in probation provision.

References

Avery, J.K. (1981) *Police, Force or Service?* Sydney: Butterworths.
Banton, M. (1973) *Police Community Relations*, London: William Collins Sons and Co. Ltd.
Banton, M. (1964) *The Policeman in the Community*, London: Tavistock.
BBC Online (2012) 'London 2012: G4S's Nick Buckles regrets taking contract', *BBC Online*, 17 July. Available at: www.bbc.co.uk/news/uk-18866153 [accessed 18 February 2013].
BBC Online (2011a) 'Fourteen Lancashire police stations to close to public', *BBC Online*, 14 November. Available at: www.bbc.co.uk/news/uk-england-lancashire-15713575 [accessed 15 January 2013].
BBC Online (2011b) 'Essex police stations close to public', *BBC Online*, 28 November. Available at: www.bbc.co.uk/news/uk-england-15920344 [accessed 15 January 2013].

BBC Online (2011c) 'Surrey police stations: Seven more could be sold to cut costs', *BBC Online*, 1 September. Available at: www.bbc.co.uk/news/uk-england-surrey-14750305 [accessed 15 January 2013].

Beck, U. (1992) *Risk Society: Towards a New Modernity*, London: Sage.

Bittner, E. (1990/2005) 'Florence Nightingale in pursuit of Willie Sutton: A theory of the police', in: Newburn, T. (ed.) *Policing: Key Readings*, Cullompton: Willan, pp. 150–172. (Original work published in 1990).

Briers, A. and Dickmann, E. (2011) 'Safer schools partnerships', in: Hayden, C. and Martin, D. (eds.) *Crime, Anti-Social Behaviour and Schools*, Basingstoke: Palgrave Macmillan.

Brodeur, J.-P. (2010) *The Policing Web*, Oxford: Oxford University Press.

Brodeur, J.-P. (1983) 'High and low policing: Remarks about the policing of political activities', *Social Problems*, 30(5): 507–521.

Brogden, M. and Ellison, G. (2013) *Policing in an Age of Austerity: A Postcolonial Perspective*, London: Routledge.

Clarke, R.V. and Hough, M. (1984) *Crime and Police Effectiveness*, Home Office Research Study 79, London: Home Office.

Cooper, C. (2009) 'Refugees, asylum seekers and criminal justice', in: Bhui, H. S. (ed.) *Race and Criminal Justice*, London: Sage, pp. 137–153.

Crawford, A. (1997) *The Local Governance of Crime: Appeals to Community and Partnerships*, Oxford: Oxford University Press.

Daily Telegraph (2008) 'It's Labour's turn to sell the family silver', *The Daily Telegraph*, 24 August. Available at: http://www.telegraph.co.uk/finance/economics/2795226/Its-Labours-turn-to-sell-the-family-silver.html [accessed 15 January 2013].

Davis, H. (2012) 'Contextual challenges for crisis support in the immediate aftermath of major incidents in the UK', *British Journal of Social Work*: 1–18.

Ericson, R.V. (1982) *Reproducing Order: A Study of Police Patrol Work*, Toronto: University of Toronto Press.

Foster, J., Newburn, T. and Souhami, A. (2005) *Assessing the Impact of the Stephen Lawrence Inquiry*. Home Office Research Study 294. London: Home Office.

Giddens, A. (1999) 'Risk and responsibility', *Modern Law Review*, 62(1): 1–10.

Greer, C. and McLaughlin, E. (2012) '"This is not justice": Ian Tomlinson, institutional failure and the press politics of outrage', *British Journal of Criminology*, 52(2): 274–293.

Herbert, N. (2011) Police Numbers (Greater Manchester), *Hansard*, 7 March 2011: Column 628.

Her Majesty's Inspectorate of Constabulary (HMIC) (2012) *Policing in Austerity: One Year On*, London: Her Majesty's Inspectorate of Constabulary.

Her Majesty's Inspectorate of Constabulary (HMIC) (2011) *Demanding Times: The Front Line and Police Visibility*, London: Her Majesty's Inspectorate of Policing.

Her Majesty's Inspectorate of Constabulary (HMIC) (2008) *Her Majesty's Inspectorate of Constabulary – Serving Neighbourhoods and Individuals: A Thematic Report on Neighbourhood Policing and Developing Citizen Focus Policing*, London: Her Majesty's Inspectorate of Constabulary.

Her Majesty's Treasury (2010) *Spending Review 2010*. Cm 7942. London: TSO.

Hillsborough Independent Panel (2012) *Hillsborough: The Report of the Hillsborough Independent Panel, HC 581*. London: The Stationery Office.

Hillyard, P. (1993) *Suspect Community: People's Experience of the Prevention of Terrorism Acts in Britain*, London: Pluto Books.

Innes, M. (2004) 'Signal crimes and signal disorders: notes on deviance as communicative action', *British Journal of Sociology*, 55(3): 335–355.

Innes, M. and Fielding, N. (2002) 'From community to communicative policing: "Signal crimes" and the problem of public reassurance', *Sociological Research Online*, 7(2). Available at: http://www.socresonline.org.uk/7/2/innes.html [accessed 15 January 2013].

Kelling, G.L., Pate, T., Dieckman, D. and Brown, C.E. (1974) *The Kansas City Preventive Patrol Experiment: A Summary Report*, Washington, DC: The Police Foundation.

Kemshall, H., Mackenzie, G., Wood, J., Bailey, R. and Yates, J. (2005) *Strengthening Multi-Agency Public Protection Arrangements (MAPPAs)*, Home Office Development and Practice Report 45. London: Home Office.

Kemshall, H. and Maguire, M. (2001) 'Public protection, partnership and risk penality: The multi-agency risk management of sexual and violent offenders', *Punishment and Society*, 3(2): 237–264.

Lee, W.M. (1901) *A History of Police in England*, London: Methuen.

Leveson, Lord Justice (2012) *An Inquiry into the Culture, Practices and Ethics of the Press: Report*, HC 780-I, London: The Stationery Office.

Loader, I. (2006) 'Policing, recognition, and belonging', *The Annals of the American Academy of Political and Social Science*, 605(1): 201–221.

May, T. (2011a) *Theresa May Speech in Full*, 4 October. Available at: www.politics.co.uk/comment-analysis/2011/10/04/theresa-may-speech-in-full [accessed 15 January 2013].

May, T. (2011b) *Conservative Values to Fight Crime and Cut Immigration*, 4 October. Available at: www.conservatives.com/News/Speeches/2011/10/May_Conservative_values_to_fight_crime_and_cut_immigration.aspx [accessed 15 January 2013].

McLaughlin, E. (2008) 'Last one out, turn off the "blue lamp": The geographical "placing" of police performance management', *Policing: A Journal of Policy and Practice*, 2(3): 266–275.

McLaughlin, E. (2007) *The New Policing*, London: Sage.

Millie, A. (2013) 'The policing task and the expansion (and contraction) of British policing', *Criminology and Criminal Justice*, 13(2): 143–160.

Millie, A. (2012) 'Police stations, architecture and public reassurance', *British Journal of Criminology*, 52(6): 1092–1112.

Millie, A. (2008) 'Crime as an issue during the 2005 UK General Election', *Crime, Media, Culture*, 4(1): 101–111.

Millie, A. and Bullock, K. (2012) 'Re-imagining policing post-austerity', *British Academy Review*, Issue 19: 16–18.

Millie, A. and Erol, R. (2006) 'Rehabilitation and resettlement: A study of prolific offender case management in Birmingham, United Kingdom', *International Journal of Offender Therapy and Comparative Criminology*, 50(6): 691–710.

Millie, A. and Herrington, V. (2005) 'Bridging the gap: Understanding reassurance policing', *Howard Journal of Criminal Justice*, 44(1): 41–56.

Millie, A. and Moore, S. (2011) 'Crime, anti-social behaviour and education: A critical review', in: Hayden, C. and Martin, D. (eds.) *Crime, Anti-Social Behaviour and Schools*, Basingstoke: Palgrave Macmillan.

Morgan, R. and Newburn, T. (1997) *The Future of Policing*, Oxford: Oxford University Press.

Packer, H.L. (1968) *The Limits of the Criminal Sanction*, Palo Alto, CA: Stanford University Press.

Police Foundation (2011) 'Safer school partnerships', *The Briefing*, 2(2), November 2011. London: The Police Foundation.

Punch, M. (1979) 'The secret social service', in: Holdaway, S. (ed.) *The British Police*, London: Edward Arnold, pp. 102–117.

Ratcliffe, J.H., Taniguchi, T., Groff, E. and Wood, J. (2011) 'The Philadelphia Foot Patrol Experiment: A randomized controlled trial of police patrol effectiveness in violent crime hotspots', *Criminology*, 49(3): 795–831.

Reiner, R. (2013) 'Who governs? Democracy, plutocracy, science and prophecy in shaping policing', *Criminology and Criminal Justice*, 13(2): 161–180.

Reiner, R. (2012) *In Praise of Fire Brigade Policing: Contra Common Sense Conceptions of the Police Role*, London: Howard League for Penal Reform.

Reiner, R. (2000) *The Politics of the Police*, 3rd edition. Oxford: Oxford University Press.

Rogers, S. and Burn-Murdoch, J. (2012) UK election historic turnouts since 1918, *The Guardian Online*, data blog, 16 November. Available at: www.guardian.co.uk/news/datablog/2012/nov/16/uk-election-turnouts-historic [accessed 15 January 2013].

Simon, J. (2007) *Governing Through Crime: How the War on Crime Transformed American Democracy and Created a Culture of Fear*, Oxford: Oxford University Press.

Travis, A. (2012) 'Police jobs: nearly 6,800 frontline posts have been cut since general election', *The Guardian*, 10 September. Available at: www.guardian.co.uk/uk/2012/sep/10/frontline-police-jobs-cut-election [accessed 21 December 2012].

Tuffin, R., Morris, J. and Poole, A. (2006) *An Evaluation of the Impact of the National Reassurance Policing Programme*, Home Office Research Study 296, London: Home Office.

Wakefield, A. (2007) 'Carry on constable: Revaluing foot patrol', *Policing: A Journal of Policy and Practice*, 1(3): 342–355.

Weber, L. and Bowling, B. (2004) 'Policing migration: A framework for investigating the regulation of global mobility', *Policing and Society*, 14(3): 195–212.

Wilson, D., Ashton, J. and Sharp, D. (2001) *What Everyone in Britain Should Know About the Police*, London: Blackstone.

5

REINVENTING THE OFFICE OF CONSTABLE

Progressive policing in an age of austerity

Martin Innes

Introduction

With the benefit of hindsight, it is now easier to see how key developments in British policing over the past two decades have been presaged by a model of material and moral investment. There was a basic willingness to spend more on the police. This was a disposition framed by a rather more subtle 'moral investment' in policing, contending that the police as a visible arm of the state can and should legitimately be used to manage an expanding spectrum of problems from anti-social behaviour through to counter-terrorism.

This investment model is now being challenged by the age of austerity. There is broad acceptance that the longer-term trajectory is one of disinvestment in policing as part of a wider drive to reduce spending on public services. It is also, though, in part, a product of declining crime rates across the Western world whereby the perceived need for policing services is being reduced. In the UK, this inclination to material disinvestment has been accelerated by a process of moral disinvestment in policing induced by a number of public scandals, including: the revelations about the practices of undercover officers involved in surveilling 'domestic extremists'; the arrests and convictions of police officers stemming from Operation Elvedon in respect of them channelling information to the Press; and the revelations about the Hillsborough disaster in 1989.

Varieties of this disinvestment narrative can be detected in a number of reforms that are, at the time of writing ongoing and that possess the potential to profoundly reconfigure the delivery of policing to the public. The introduction of Police and Crime Commissioners exemplifies this pattern in that they were charged to constrain the power of senior police officers. More subtly though, a review of their early Police and Crime Plans suggests many of the new Commissioners are seeking a move away from orthodox models of reactive policing to an increased accent upon crime-prevention work.

Potentially most significant though, is how disinvestment is inducing a reversal in the gearing of police reform and a shift to a 'de-specialisation' paradigm in respect of the social organisation of policing. As Roberts and Innes (2009) identified, over the past two decades the police reform agenda and the internal development of policing have been predicated upon a model of increased specialisation. Particular crime problems have increasingly been assigned to and 'owned' by a plethora of specialist police squads and units, working to their own doctrines and standard operating procedures. In most forces this included differentiating between neighbourhood and response policing, and between 'burglary squads', 'street robbery units' and 'drugs squads'. Challenged by the financial reductions that police agencies are having to make, this model is rapidly being reversed, with former specialisms and squads being reintegrated and absorbed into each other.

This shift from investment to disinvestment requires us to think in ways different from those to which we have become accustomed in the recent past. The danger is that, beset by combined economic and political pressures, change is simply allowed to happen, resulting in a drift back to a 'residualised' response policing. An alternative trajectory is to explicitly set out to design a vision of policing suited to the prevailing times. Accordingly, this chapter sketches some new ways of thinking about the office of constable and what the police and policing could look like over the next decade. Specifically, it seeks to accomplish three things:

1   To set out a proposition for thinking about the social organisation of policing and how it might be conceptualised in ways appropriate for the new economic and political landscape.
2   To provide a more detailed example of how this new framing of a network-enabled policing might be practically delivered and operationalised in a way that is highly responsive to community needs and priorities.
3   To establish how the two preceding elements might provide the basis for a coherent progressive position on the future of policing.

Mapping the policing disciplines

Discussions of the future of UK policing are typically ritually prefaced by returning to consider the so-called Peelian principles. Such an approach is undoubtedly useful in thinking about the institutional position of the police in society, and the vision and values that underpin the police function. However, my interests herein are more focused upon thinking about the practical delivery of policing services. As such, a more appropriate launching point is to understand how the police do what they do.

Conventional contemporary accounts of police activity tend to pivot around describing particular policing styles, among the most notable of which are 'community', 'problem-oriented' and 'intelligence-led' 'policings'. There are several problems with these accounts. For as Brodeur (2010) has recently noted, they tend to accent the role of uniformed policing, neglecting less-visible roles. Relatedly, they do not provide a comprehensive picture of the diverse range of activity that collectively comprises the work of the modern police force. Instead, they tend to generalise from a partial view. Even an agency that is keen on developing and using intelligence does not deliver all its services through this approach, and the same is true of the other policing styles. As such, in terms of trying to design a progressive form of policing, it is probably worth starting with some first principles.

Police are engaged in the delivery of formal social control services. They are not the only institution who do this, but they are among the most important given their capacity to range across a diversity of settings and situations, and for the way they can intervene using coercive force in both private and public troubles. It is important, however, to recognise that in so doing, they augment and supplement more organic informal social controls. This was captured by Egon Bittner (1974) in his formulation that the fundamental role of police is the 'emergency maintenance of social order' – with the stress being upon emergency provision. What this implicitly recognises is the extent to which most social problems are not solved through the interventions of police, but through the activities of individuals, social networks and communities. What police afford is a capacity and capability for coercive intervention when social order is threatened or at risk. Intriguingly, five decades of research on policing have demonstrated that even as agents of formal social control, police tend to resolve most problems through informal means, invoking criminal law as a last resort (see Reiner 2010).

Given that this is the case, it is perhaps surprising that more effort has not been directed towards understanding how the provision of different styles of policing interacts with the informal social control capacities residing in communities. For example, to what extent do different policing styles 'leverage' or constrain community crime control efforts? A quick thought experiment can help to map out the key considerations in this regard. The contours of this are depicted in Table 5.1 below.

By separating out who takes responsibility for defining the presence of a crime or disorder problem, and who leads the implementation of a response it is possible to identify four key positions. For example, where police define and solve a problem, this equates to their mainstream, orthodox role. This has been supplemented by the investment in Neighbourhood Policing which has increased their capacity to react to problems defined by communities. There are, however, situations where communities identify issues and independently mobilise to deal with these without any input from police. Perhaps the most neglected mode of social control is where police identify the presence of a problem, but mobilise community assets to resolve

TABLE 5.1 Interactions between police and community controls

	Police defined	*Community defined*
Police intervention	Response and proactive policing	Neighbourhood and response policing
Community intervention	Co-produced social control	Informal social control

these in a form of what we might term 'co-produced social control'. The unique property of co-produced social control is that it involves both the community and police in: co-defining the presence of a problem; co-designing a response to this; and co-delivering this response.

In terms of the broader task of thinking about the social organisation of the police, it is relevant that it is the two forms in the lower half of Figure 5.1 that are considered relatively infrequently. Future designs for the organisation of policing should think more seriously about what impacts particular styles and configurations of police intervention have in terms of shaping informal social control capacities within communities. For example, do highly assertive policing styles defray the overall legitimacy of police action and thus reduce community compliance with the law? Alternatively, in particular settings and situations, do 'softer' forms of policing fail to provide sufficient levels of community confidence to enable community-based governance processes to be sustained? Consideration of such matters moves us on to thinking about the police function.

As outlined in the introduction to this chapter, over the past two decades or so policing has been progressively reconfigured around an increasing number of specialisms. There has been a move away from notions of there being a generalist police constable, to a series of specialist disciplines focused upon particular issues such as burglary, drugs, homicide, child protection and so forth. Even seemingly generalist roles such as responding to calls from the public have been reconfigured by this framing. This particular aspect of police work is delineated in increasingly specific levels of detail about what is and is not within the scope of that role, so that response officers just respond to emergency calls before passing cases over to their colleagues in other departments for any further work that might be required.

Framing police work as a series of inter-dependent and inter-related specialisms has, though, tended to obscure the commonalities present across the vast majority of interventions that police make. For instance, there are fundamentally three basic points of intervention for police action through which they achieve outcomes:

1   *People* – it is well documented that significant amounts of police activity focus upon dealing with people in a variety of roles, including suspect, victim and witness. Of these categories of people, it is the 'known' suspects and trouble-makers that consume an awful lot of police attention.
2   *Places* – there is increasing focus within policing organisations upon locations that are crime attractors and crime generators. Through developments such as 'hotspots policing' this has come to play an increasingly significant role in the policing enterprise (Braga, 2001).
3   *Problems* – a third way that focus can be brought to the activity of policing is by orienting around particular problems. This might include, by way of example, e-crime, street robbery or domestic violence.

Of course, some of the more successful examples of police impact are where their interventions tackle the intersection between people, places and problems.

This notwithstanding, in terms of thinking about the social organisation of policing, identifying that these are the basic points of intervention is a useful starting point. We can develop this line of thinking further by similarly mapping out the key modes of cross-cutting police action that they use in respect of people, places and problems.

- *Patrol and response* – uniformed patrol constitutes the most visible manifestation of police activity. Patrol work encompasses both the tasks involved in responding to emergency calls from the public, engaging with citizens and the provision of community reassurance.
- *Prevention and protection* – across a number of domains (such as domestic violence, counter-terrorism, and property crime) police have been significantly developing their application of forms of situational and social crime prevention. Allied to this are the protective functions that deal with the management of presenting risks and established threats.
- *Investigation and intelligence* – this covers the skills and competencies involved in managing and working with information to develop intelligence products and cases to support prosecutions.
- *Specialist services* – all officers are endowed with the authority to enact coercive force, but there are occasions when police organisations are required to use corporate forms of action. There are a number of aspects of policing, such as public order and firearms, that require very specialist knowledge and skills not shared across other dimensions of policing.

Delineating police work along these lines starts to set out what amount to the core disciplines of policing. They can be considered as disciplines on the grounds that they possess a unique knowledge base, defined methodologies and particular skill sets. The value of such an approach is that it starts to bring a greater degree of clarity to thinking about what the police do, and could be used as the basis of simplifying the organisation of police agencies. That is, rather than having individual units specialising in child protection, burglary prevention and preventing violent extremism, it might be possible to establish a group of officers who are responsible for all preventative activity, cutting across specific crime types. Likewise, all investigations would be conducted by a pool of officers who are fully trained in the methods of intelligence development and investigation.

By bringing these four key disciplines together with the three intervention points, we can establish an overarching framework that provides a useful overview of the organisation of policing. Table 5.2 shows how specific policing interventions and tasks can be fitted into this framework. This is not intended to be comprehensive in its coverage but, rather, illustrative of how such an approach captures the fundamentals of policing. It would also help in determining what training and education requirements there are for new officers, as well as what information and communication technologies they need to enable more effective policing (discussed further below).

TABLE 5.2 Overview of policing interventions

	People	*Places*	*Problems*
Prevention and protection	Manage PPOs; vulnerable victims	Target hardening; situational crime prevention	Partnership working on drugs, DV, etc.
Patrol and response	Visibility and reassurance; stop and search	Neighbourhood policing; hotspots policing	Emergency calls from public
Investigation and intelligence	Offender management	Online crime; hotspots analysis	Cases for prosecution; problem profiles
Specialist services	CT policing	Mass public events	Firearms deployments

PPO = prolific priority offender; DV = domestic violence

Simplification in this manner and cutting through the complexity that has grown up around the delivery of policing would be coherent with the prevalent feeling that policing requires a paradigm shift if it is to adapt rationally to the confluence of social, political and economic forces that are challenging it. Police leaders have become fond of saying that, confronted by the challenges posed by austerity their organisations will have to 'do more with less'. The approach mapped out above, in fact, suggests the possibility of 'doing less with more' (Innes, 2011). That is, if there are to be fewer police officers, then they will need to be more skilled and flexible to respond to the demands upon them. Particularly if the prevention dimension is developed, then it might be possible that, actually, police intervene less often in social life, but do so with more impact, and that, in terms of how we think about police, there can be fewer specialist departments and more transferable skills and knowledge.

The practical delivery of this kind of policing can potentially be facilitated by some of the emergent capacities and capabilities afforded by new 'disruptive technologies' that are changing how police can diagnose community concerns. The development and proliferation of social media and web technologies have altered the quantity, quality and speed of key information flows for all public services. For policing, they are inducing a new information environment that is shifting how police come to know about the presence and distribution of a range of problems, as well as how publics come to know about and perceive the work of the police. The critical issue for the future design of policing is how these new socio-technical assemblages are configured and 'plugged in' to the policing system. For example, technologies that process and mine large volumes of data could be used to provide evidence-based decision tools for front-line officers to assist them in dealing with real-time incidents. This might include pushing intelligence out to the officer about the people or place that they are dealing with. So although that officer is not a specialist they can be supported in dealing with the specific requirements of the situation more effectively.

In a recent study, Innes and Roberts (2011) introduced notions of the 'information environment' and 'situational intelligence' as conceptual tools for helping to make sense of the ecology of different types of information that are potentially available to the police from a variety of sources, including both 'online' and 'offline' formats. As a concept, the information environment has direct parallels with the idea of the operating environment that is well established in police thinking. But whereas the operating environment shapes and moulds police actions and interventions, the information environment influences how police come to know about what is happening.

To illustrate the real-world nature of these changes we might think about how:

- online environments are creating new ways to commit financial and hate crimes;
- emerging sentiment mining technologies are providing new ways for police to gauge public concerns and to obtain feedback on the social impacts of their interventions;
- it is unlikely to be long before police start to use aerial drone technologies to provide an enhanced surveillance capacity in complex urban settings.

Changes in the information environment are altering how police identify and develop intelligence, knowledge and evidence. Simply put, the fundamental information problem for policing has changed. In the past it was a question of how to uncover information that people do not want the police to access. It is now a problem of how to rapidly search through vast information flows to identify the important material from the 'noise'. At the same time, these information sources are revealing new risks and threats that potentially require preventative or protective interventions. They are also changing the nature of police visibility and presence within communities.

What this points to is how, in delivering the four key policing disciplines outlined above, individual police constables are effectively participating in a variety of social and informational networks. These are processes and developments that are only likely to be accelerated by ongoing developments in the field of social informatics and, as such, any designs for future policing need to think about how they can be accommodated. For instance, it is entirely plausible to imagine that rather than front-line officers submitting intelligence reports, these being analysed, and then officers being briefed and tasked on the basis of the results, instead, the data might be centrally stored and front-line officers request 'on-demand' analyses of what they want to know there and then by using a series of 'apps'. In effect, basic intelligence analysis products are automated and based upon algorithms, rather than reliant upon a small cadre of analysts. Likewise, each individual officer might be able to use a mobile device to 'visualise' where all the other local policing assets are positioned; in effect, creating a much greater situational intelligence capacity.

The take-home point is that in terms of how they prevent, investigate or protect, police are likely, through a variety of technologies to have access to ever increasing volumes of data and information. Any meaningful attempt to design a vision of the future role and work of the police constable needs to factor in these technological innovations. This is constitutive of the shift from a command and control model of policing, to one where front-line officers are more empowered, agile and flexible in terms of how they work – in keeping with the de-specialisation trend highlighted earlier. Rather than being conceived simply as the 'limbs' and 'sensors' of the 'big brain' at the centre of the organisation, front-line officers enabled by informatics technologies could be re-shaped into more networked, self-organising forms of police activity that are potentially better suited to meet changing political and public expectations of their work. The change from previous formulations would be that rather than conceived as relatively autonomous individuals, in terms of conducting their work they would be enabled by the social and informational networks in which they are located.

The final question for this chapter, then, is how the various trajectories mapped out in the preceding sections could be accommodated and harnessed within a progressive position on policing. In terms of the politics of policing, there is a clear drive, crossing political affiliations, to render police organisations more transparent and accountable (Savage, 2007). The tenor of these shifts can be summarised as requiring that police: see like a citizen; engage in participative policing; and provide 'see through' services. The first of these involves an expectation that police should be responsive to the needs expressed by local communities, rather than the organisation defining their operational priorities, as has perhaps tended to happen in the past. Participative policing reflects an expectation that other agencies and the public should be enlisted in efforts to improve community safety. The provision of 'see through' services is a response to the political demand for increased transparency and that key decisions should be rendered publicly accountable. Command and control based models of policing that currently continue to predominate, seem to be in tension with these more 'localising' political currents. Aspects of the reinvention that is being proposed herein, might be more suited to meeting these political and public expectations.

To illuminate what this might look like, I want to briefly describe a blending of aspects of the Neighbourhood Policing approach, with a more disciplined approach to knowledge development and use, to craft a viable policing model. It is an approach pivoting around the development of a rich, deliberative picture of local problems and priorities based upon a process of systematic engagement to establish community intelligence. Reflecting its blending of the community policing and intelligence-led traditions, it has been dubbed 'community intelligence-led policing' (CILP) (Innes *et al.*, 2008; Lowe and Innes, 2012).

Community intelligence-led policing

Elements of the CILP approach were originally developed and tested as part of the National Reassurance Policing Programme (NRPP). The quasi-experimental forerunner of Neighbourhood Policing demonstrated that an appropriately configured policing designed to systematically identify and respond to public concerns at a very local level, can reduce crime, fear of crime and promote public confidence in the police (Tuffin *et al.*, 2006). Although much of the subsequent debate and commentary about Reassurance Policing has focused upon the public value attached to police visibility and presence, this neglects the significance of some of the other components that were integral to the delivery model – most saliently a process of systematic community engagement to identify the signal crimes and disorders that alter public perceptions of local security.

Neighbourhood Policing is important inasmuch as it started to rethink, in a number of important respects, what the police constable role might involve (Savage, 2007). For example, rather than just working on organisationally determined priority crimes, it was acknowledged that a neighbourhood officer ought to be diagnosing what their local community members priorities are and addressing these. In a break from the previous regimen, this could occur outside of the centralised police intelligence apparatus. Equally important, though, was how the neighbourhood officer was conceived as providing a degree of community leadership, building social networks and local social capital to resolve problems locally. Where Neighbourhood Policing failed to deliver its full potential was in respect of ensuring it always engaged with a wide range of groups to develop a full community intelligence picture of their issues, perceptions and concerns. Accordingly, subsequent to the original NRPP trial, a six-year programme of field trials has been ongoing that has sought to develop aspects of this approach into a fully fledged form of CILP.

Community intelligence is information that, when analysed, provides insight and foresight into the crimes and disorders that alter collective perceptions and experiences of safety. Its value to policing is that it provides a perspective on the local crime and anti-social behaviour problems that matter to the public. It is thus different from the crime and criminal intelligence that are more usually the focus of police knowledge-work.

Based upon a series of field trials conducted across the South Wales Police (SWP) area, it is possible to distinguish four main phases of activity in a CILP process. It starts with systematic and structured community engagement to establish community intelligence on the crime and disorder problems causing harm within and across neighbourhoods. The critical methodological innovation is in turning engagement into a proactive task of Neighbourhood Policing teams. So, rather than holding PACT (Police/Partners and Communities Together) meetings and waiting to see who turns up, or who responds to a postal survey, local police go and actively seek out the views of residents in a neighbourhood face-to-face, one-to-one. In so doing, they are provided with a sampling frame in terms of profiling who to engage with, to ensure a diversity of voices informs their community intelligence picture that is broadly representative of the demographic profile of the local population. The Neighbourhood Policing team (NPT) staff are also directed to ensure that they engage with community representatives in different geographic areas to ensure that coverage of the issues from all neighbourhoods in a target area is achieved. The police–public engagement interactions have been structured around an interview instrument designed to elicit the prevalence and distribution of different kinds of crime, physical disorder and social disorder in the local area, along with a measure of the relative harm these are causing. These data are captured on a qualitative GIS software package meaning that the location of all individual incidents and problems recalled by a respondent are geo-located on a map.

Having conducted multiple interviews with people residing in a neighbourhood, but who are typically unknown to each other, the next stage involves analysis of the data collected to identify those places and issues where there is a collective view that a problem exists. The analysis seeks to identify both those problems affecting a lot of people, as well as those that affect a relatively small number of individuals but in an acute way.

Next these data are played into community meetings employed as deliberative fora for prioritising interventions. Under the current approach to Neighbourhood Policing, 'beat meetings' or 'PACT meetings' are used as vehicles for generating community intelligence. It is proposed, however, that they are better suited to making choices about which problems should be treated as priorities for intervention, and to provide some indications as to the type of response that might be deemed locally effective. This reflects Loader and Sparks' (2012) assertion that a social democratic approach to criminal justice should incorporate processes that are democratically responsive.

Finally, targeted interventions to provide solutions to these public priorities are enacted. Having used public meetings to try to align police and partner interventions with those matters having most impact upon local communities, the next phase of the process involves the actual delivery of a response to the issues identified. This can involve: identifying vulnerable victims who require enhanced levels of protection; implementing social crime-prevention interventions to tackle emergent problems; and altering levels of visible police patrolling to target fear of crime hotspots.

When aspects of this approach were applied in the London Borough of Sutton over a four-year period, it was found that by targeting local priorities on the basis of community intelligence: the overall prevalence of community security problems identified by the public reduced by around one third; some problems were no longer being prioritised at all because they had been resolved; and there was a shift from people talking about problems 'in my neighbourhood' to the more generic public spaces in Sutton (Lowe and Innes, 2012). The importance of the South Wales field trials are that they demonstrate it is possible to implement this intensive approach to community engagement 'at scale', across very different communities and environments. Moreover, they evidence how a rich community intelligence picture can be used to drive a variety of policing interventions spanning prevention, protection, patrol and investigation.

Between 2008 and 2010, nearly 4,500 in-depth face-to-face community engagement interviews were conducted by researchers and NPTs right across Cardiff, Swansea and the South Wales Valleys. Limited space precludes detailed discussion of the very detailed community intelligence that resulted and how it was used.

However, a number of benefits were identified, including:

- When compared with the existing mechanisms for community engagement used by SWP, the new approach broadened the range and diversity of people whose perceptions and experiences of crime and disorder were gauged. Around 73 per cent of those engaged reported never having previously been consulted by police.
- The process also extended the geographic distribution of police contacts with communities. An empirical test of who the police were engaging with previously, demonstrated a clustering of contacts in the relatively affluent and low-crime neighbourhoods in Cardiff. This clustering was substantially reduced by the new methodology.
- An additional benefit was that it widened the 'police's radar' to allow them to understand the full range of issues that were negatively impacting upon conceptions of neighbourhood security, rather than police relying upon what they assumed was important.
- Police were using the public as sensors telling them about emerging problems. In effect earlier identification of issues afforded opportunity for police to engage more 'soft power' influence effects, preventing the emergence of more serious problems requiring more coercive interventions.
- Analysis of the community intelligence data measuring the impacts or 'effects' of crime and disorder suggests that at both individual and community levels vulnerability to being negatively impacted can arise from personal characteristics, the situation in which one is located and/or the nature of the incident to which you are exposed.
- Possession of a sophisticated community intelligence picture afforded a 'smarter', more agile and flexible response to community-defined problems. For example, rather than instigating a city-wide anti-public drinking campaign, the community intelligence showed where to target resources because citizens were saying this was a problem impacting upon their quality of life. So, rather than spreading resources 'thinly' across a whole city, they could be concentrated upon those locales where need was most acute.
- The intelligence was found to usefully inform tactical interventions in respect of particular issues in particular neighbourhoods, but it also afforded a strategic assessment.
- The community intelligence provided a shared intelligence picture for police and their partners. Because it allowed respondents to define any issues impacting upon their neighbourhood security, it ranged from acute crime issues to more chronic issues with damage to the built environment. In so doing, it provided the basis for co-productive working between agencies to resolve problem people, places and events.
- Arguably the key benefit for the police was the ability of the community intelligence to 'cut through'. What it provided was an evidence-informed perspective about which of all the crime and disorder problems that are known to police

should be prioritised because they are having the greatest impact upon how local citizens are thinking, feeling and acting in relation to their neighbourhood security.

An important aspect of the Welsh field trials is that they suggest a potential for CILP to be of benefit beyond purely local policing issues. In Cardiff, community intelligence was picked up about an open drug market in a particular area of the city. When this was cross-checked with the police intelligence databases it was found that this was not known to police. In order to check the veracity of the community intelligence, undercover officers were despatched to the area. Albeit initially sceptical they confirmed the community intelligence – there was indeed a large overt drugs market in operation. As a result Operation Michigan was subsequently launched leading to a large number of arrests and convictions, along with significant seizures of cash and Class A narcotics.

This example illustrates how community intelligence should be treated. The public in terms of the sorts of problems they report, are aware of the symptoms of an underlying pathology. They need the police to use their expertise to diagnose the cause of the symptoms and provide an effective treatment. It is also suggestive of the contribution that the implementation of a CILP strategy could make to a more responsive and socially impactive policing of serious and organised crime.

Delivered in this way, we can start to map out the potential benefits offered by a form of CILP. By actively listening to communities in a systematic way, and doing something about the priorities they define, it appears possible to improve community confidence and reduce the prevalence of incidents. The first generation of Neighbourhood Policing provided the foundations for such an approach, which have been significantly developed through the work in Sutton and South Wales. Importantly, though, some of the new technologies identified earlier (such as sentiment mining of publicly available social media data) will provide new channels for generating community intelligence.

Prospective design blueprints for future policing need to integrate such informatics technologies into their key processes and systems. Plugged into the CILP approach they offer a possibility of making community intelligence more flexible and agile than it is currently, in order that it can improve the situational awareness of police officers and their agency partners on the ground. There is no reason why, as the police constable moves around an area, the information network into which they are plugged should not be updating them with relevant situational intelligence about the area and those present within it. They might also be receiving dynamic feedback on community impacts of any local police interventions that have occurred.

There is one final point to be made about this approach. That is its role in 'problem-finding'. Discussions of community and Neighbourhood Policing frequently stress the importance of problem-solving and using research evidence to address problems effectively and efficiently. What has been happening in South Wales is the use of evidence-based ways of working to engage in 'problem-finding' work. That is, to work out what the public's priority problems are, and then direct police interventions towards these. This approach represents a rather different way of delivering evidence-based policing. It moves beyond just identifying 'what works' to engage with questions of 'what matters' most to the public.

Conclusion

Social democratic political philosophy has always had something of an ambivalent relationship with the criminal justice process in general and the police in particular (Loader and Sparks, 2012). This stems, in part, from an understanding that crime and disorder are products of macro-structural social and economic forces. As such, there has been a preference for focusing upon other public services to tackle problematic behaviours and their protagonists.

However, in the context of a prolonged and acute retraction in public services, it is vital to think about what role an appropriately configured policing could play in protecting social order. We know that insecurity triggered by crime and disorder corrodes the social and economic fabric of communities. As such, using policing to manage these problems seems to be important in creating a space where other forms of social intervention can gain traction and hopefully work to preserve and propagate neighbourhood security.

Informed by an ongoing empirical research programme, in this chapter I have sought to suggest some key elements of what a modern progressive vision of policing might involve. The CILP approach outlined above integrates several qualities that should provide a gravitational pull upon any social democratic position on policing. Namely:

- *Priorities* – it integrates a deliberative method for democratic influence in terms of deciding how the public's problems are defined as police priorities. Moreover, it facilitates a more agile and adaptive policing response.
- *Prevention* – by using community intelligence to spot emerging trends and the predicates of more serious crimes, police can operate more effectively through influence effects and thereby reduce their reliance upon coercive social control.
- *Protection* – the community intelligence identifies the most vulnerable people, places and events to ensure that they are supported first.
- *Partnering* – the community intelligence provides the basis for more effective co-productive partnership working by providing a common picture of what are the key people, places and problems that have to be managed by local agencies.

Blending, as it does, elements of the community policing and intelligence-led traditions, the CILP approach is significant in that it integrates capacities that should enable it to adapt to the demands of the new information environment, and changing political and public expectations about what policing is for. It imagines a police constable who is plugged into a variety of community intelligence 'feeds', using policing informatics to make sense of these data to steer their decisions about how and when to intervene. A critical point being that the informatics technologies de-centre the knowledge-work involved, moving it out from central units to locations far closer to the point of delivery.

In this regard, the development of such approaches needs to be set against a backdrop where there is a need to rearticulate and reimagine some of the key elements of contemporary policing. Currently, there are early indications that de-specialisation is starting in police organisations and, over the medium-term, any approach founded upon lots of specialist units and squads is unlikely to be sustain-able given the scale of the financial challenges that we face. Instead it has been proposed that we can identify several key disciplines that provide the basis for the vast majority of police interventions. The critical point is that police technological and social organisational structures need to be reformed to support this approach. The information and decision support needs of front-line officers will be different if they are less specialised. Likewise, the education and training requirement, and the basic skill sets of officers required to manage a diversity of crime and incident types will be different from where they are tasked to respond to just one type. In this respect it is important to start thinking seriously about how police can do less with more.

In the context of a likely decade-long era of constrained public sector funding, the provision of such deliberative fora seems to be an important instrument for securing a degree of public accountability and transparency in terms of the hard choices that will have to be made. Demand for police services from the public always outstrips the capacity to supply. A deliberative process, working on the basis of a robust local evidence base, seems to be a reasonable process for taking decisions about how scarce resource should be allocated.

References

Bittner, E. (1974) 'Florence Nightingale in pursuit of Willie Sutton: a theory of the police', in H. Jacobs (ed.) *The Potential for Reform of Criminal Justice*. Beverly Hills: Sage.

Braga, A. (2001) 'The effects of hot spots policing on crime', *Annals of the American Academy of Political and Social Science*, 578: 104–25.

Brodeur, J.-P. (2010) *The Policing Web*. New York: Oxford University Press.

Herbert, S. (2006) *Citizens, Cops and Power*. Chicago: University of Chicago Press.

Innes, M. (2011) 'Doing less with more: the new politics of policing', *Public Policy Research*, June–August: 73.

Innes, M., L. Abbott, T. Lowe and C. Roberts (2008) 'Seeing like a citizen: field experiments in community intelligence-led policing', *Police Practice and Research*, 10/2: 99–114.

Innes, M. and C. Roberts (2011) *Policing, Situational Intelligence and the Information Environment*. London: HMIC.

Loader, I. and R. Sparks (2012) 'Beyond lamentation: towards a democratic egalitarian politics of crime and justice', in T. Newburn and J. Peay (eds.) *Policing: Politics, Culture and Control*. Oxford: Hart.

Lowe, T. and M. Innes (2012) 'Can we speak in confidence? Community intelligence and neighbourhood policing v2.00', *Policing and Society*, 22/3: 295–316.

Reiner, R. (2010) *The Politics of the Police* (5th edn.). Oxford: Oxford University Press.

Roberts, C. and M. Innes (2009) 'The "Death" of Dixon? Policing gun crime and the end of the generalist police constable in England and Wales', *Criminology and Criminal Justice*, 9/3: 337–57.

Savage, S. (2007) *Police Reform*. Oxford: Oxford University Press.

Tuffin, R. *et al.* (2006) *The National Reassurance Policing Programme: A Six Site Evaluation*. London: Home Office.

6

POLICE FUTURES AND LEGITIMACY

Redefining 'good policing'

Ben Bradford, Jonathan Jackson and Mike Hough

Introduction

How can criminal justice institutions encourage law-abiding behaviour? What constitutes success in terms of police activity aimed at reducing crime? Answers to questions of this type often revolve around the idea that crime occurs when the criminal justice system provides insufficient likelihood of punishment, or when insufficiently tough sentences are imposed. Mechanisms of coercive social control and credible risks of sanction hope to persuade *Homo economicus* that – while other-wise desirable – a criminal act is not worth the risk (Tyler, 2008, 2011a; Schulhofer *et al.*, 2011), and police and other criminal justice agents should signal effective-ness, force, a high probability of detection and a swift recourse to justice in order to deter people from committing offences (Hough *et al.*, 2010; Schulhofer *et al.*, 2011; Jackson *et al.*, 2012a).

But there is another model of policing that speaks to a rather different set of motivations and behaviours. People (usually) obey the law and cooperate with the police and criminal courts because they think it is the right thing to do, or because they have simply acquired the habit of doing so. The fact that most people obey most laws, most of the time, suggests that criminal justice policy makers should profitably spend more time than is currently the case thinking about sources of voluntary compliance and cooperation, rather than triggers for offending and what should be done *after* an offence has occurred (important as these latter two aspects of policing continue to be).

That normative and moral considerations are an important influence on people's law-related behaviours poses a number of important but widely ignored questions for criminal justice policy. Can the central institutions of justice – and particu-larly the police – influence those processes of normative compliance (often taken for granted) upon which the criminal justice system in essence relies? Can police encourage people to 'do the right thing' and thus reinforce normative compliance, or is the role of the police simply to be a force for deterrence and coerced compliance? And if police activity can be calibrated to encourage normative compliance, what are the implications for our understanding of what 'good policing' looks like?

An emerging body of research – based initially on survey data but being strengthened by experimental and qualitative work from across the world (e.g. Reisig and Lloyd, 2009; Murphy et al., 2009; Van Dijke et al., 2010; Gau and Brunson, 2009; Elliott et al., 2011; Hasisi and Weisburd, 2011; Bradford et al., 2013; Mazerolle et al., 2013) – suggests that institutions of justice can indeed strengthen people's normative commitment to legal authority and the law by acting according to principles of procedural justice and by wielding their power in a fair manner (Tyler, 2006a, 2006b). Tyler's process-based model of policing (Sunshine and Tyler, 2003) states that when institutions act according to principles of procedural fairness, this sustains and strengthens the ability of legal authorities to encourage self-regulation among citizens (Tyler et al., in press). This is a normative model of crime-control based in part on the psychology of legitimacy and procedural justice. It posits that institutions can secure compliance and cooperation by developing policies that generate legitimacy as well as deterrent threat (Tyler and Huo, 2002; Huq et al., 2011). Appealing not only to self-interest but also to normative or ethical considerations, procedural justice and legitimacy motivates people to behave in line with their moral principles and to respect the rights of others.

At a time when many people are considering the future of policing in England and Wales, any consideration of policing policy and practice must encompass the legitimacy of the police in the eyes of the policed and, through this, the influence that police and other legal authorities can exert on the law-related behaviour of citizens. In this chapter we outline a model of policing based upon procedural justice. Considering the notion of 'good' policing in the light of this perspective, we summarise Tyler's argument that procedurally just institutions can help avoid the cost, danger and alienation that are associated with policies based on external rules underpinned by deterrent threat (Schulhofer et al., 2011). If the normative route to compliance with the law can be achieved, it is likely to be more durable and less costly than the coercive route that requires a credible deterrent threat (Tyler, 2006a, 2006b). A model of policing based primarily on procedural justice and policing by consent will also, if successful, free police and other criminal justice agents to concentrate on the 'hard-core' of offenders who might not be amenable to such interventions. And, while the focus of this chapter is on legitimacy of the police as perceived by the public, our analysis also raises issues about the legitimacy of the police organisation, as experienced by those within it.

What is legitimacy?

The notion of legitimacy is bound up not just with the right of an individual, organisation or institution to govern (to exist, to hold power, to have authority), but also with the recognition by the governed of that right. Individuals in society confer authority to institutions, believe they are morally and normatively justified to hold power, and judge that institutions respect the rule of law. Theorists from Weber onwards have viewed legitimacy as a vital component of social institutions, both in the long run for their very survival, and also on a day-to-day basis since people will defer to and assist institutions they feel to be legitimate.

But what constitutes legitimacy? Under what conditions can we say that an authority is viewed by citizens within a given system as legitimate? This is a question drawing considerable debate at the current time (e.g. Bottoms and Tankebe, 2012; Tyler and Jackson, 2013). Following Beetham (1991), we regard subjective legitimate authority as made up of three elements:

1   *Legality* (acting according to the law) – a legitimate authority follows its own rules and is seen to follow its own rules.
2   *Shared values* (values that are shared by those with authority and those subject to that authority) – a legitimate authority acts in ways that accord with the values and morals of the wider social group, and its power is justified in the lights of shared normative frameworks.
3   *Consent* (the sense among the policed of a moral obligation to obey the authority) – a legitimate authority garners obedience and support from citizens.

Viewed in this way, legitimacy is both an *orientation toward* and a *justification of* power (European Social Survey, 2011, 2012; Jackson *et al.*, 2012a, 2012b). The police are legitimate not only when and to the extent that people recognise the authority of officers and feel a corresponding duty of deference to them (consent). Police are also legitimate when and to the extent that people believe they have a proper moral purpose (shared values) and follow their own rules, as well as the rules that govern everyone in society (legality and lawfulness). Conversely, when people do not feel a duty of deference toward the police, do not feel that police share their values, and when they believe the police do not abide by the rules, legitimacy is fragile and may, in certain circumstances, be effectively absent.

What is procedural justice?

Procedural justice theories are – in essence – theories about the use of authority and power. They state that people place great importance on the justice or fairness of the behaviour of authority figures. People are less interested in the effectiveness of the authority, or in the *outcomes* it provides, than in the *processes* by which it makes decisions and in the motivations behind its actions. What looms most prominently in people's minds is the fairness of the processes by which power holders wield their power. Indeed, people appear ready to forgive or discount unfavourable or unsatisfactory outcomes if they believe that the processes that led to those outcomes were fair (Tyler 2006b), and the experience of procedural justice is linked to motive-based trust, a form of trust linked to assessments of motivation rather than performance (Tyler and Huo 2002).

Applied to the police, Tyler's procedural justice model predicts that when officers treat people with respect and dignity, utilise neutral and fair decision-making processes, and allow them a voice in the interaction, those officers communicate messages of status and worth to the individual concerned (that the individuals concerned are valued and respected members of the social group the police represent); they also demonstrate that their power is balanced by due process and that they are acting in accordance with values of legality and propriety. When officers act in a procedurally fair way the people they police are more likely to regard them as legitimate, to defer to their authority, and to feel that the power they wield is justified (Sunshine and Tyler, 2003; Tyler et al., in press; Jackson et al., 2011). Procedural justice promotes internalisation of the idea that one should obey the police and strengthens people's identification with the moral group that the police represent, and this translates into feeling that (a) one has a duty to allow the police to dictate appropriate behaviour, and (b) the police operate within appropriate ethical or normative frameworks (Jackson et al., 2012a).

Social identity thus energises procedural justice theory. The experience of procedurally just policing encourages a sense that both individual and police are 'on the same side'. People are motivated to feel valued members of social groups; they derive self-relevant information through the quality of their interactions with group representatives such as the police (Tyler et al., 1996). In positioning the police as a proto-typical group representative (Sunshine and Tyler, 2003), procedural justice models resonate with sociological accounts of policing that have pointed to its role as representative of, jointly and variously, nation, state and 'community' (Jackson and Bradford, 2009; Loader and Mulcahy, 2003; Reiner, 2010; Waddington, 1999). How police officers treat individuals shapes people's sense of identity, and police behaviour can strengthen their connection to society when it indicates they are valued.

The idea that police activity fosters or inhibits the formation and reproduction of social identities is of obvious relevance in the context of British policing (Bradford, 2012). Ever since the founding of the modern police, officers have been key agents in the social sifting and classification of individuals and groups (cf. Ericson and Haggerty, 1997). Until recently, such classificatory work was assumed to be largely negative in implication. Police activity does often place people in categories detrimental to themselves as well as the social groups of which they are members – from 'police property' and 'rubbish' (Reiner, 2010) to 'Black muggers' (Hall et al., 1978). Indeed, police activity may be instrumental in *creating* denigrated social categories (ibid.). It is of particular relevance, therefore, that studies have shown that procedural injustice can communicate stigmatisation by legal authorities (Tyler and Wakslak, 2004). If people perceive that their treatment by police officers is based not on what they are doing, but on their race, gender or age, the police behaviour carries significant negative identity implications. Unfairness casts doubt on the idea that they are members of the superordinate group(s) police represent, accorded the rights pertaining to group membership; at the same time, it may *label* that individual as a member of a marginalised, excluded or denigrated outgroup.

By contrast, procedural *fairness* can have positive effects on group identification. Police activity can promote positive, inclusive group identities and communicate to people they are valued members of society, and such inclusion has – in terms of the functioning of the criminal justice system – some important implications. People are more likely to cooperate with organisations when those organisations serve the social function of providing individuals with a favourable identity and a positive sense of self (Blader and Tyler, 2009). If people feel pride in the group, and if they believe that they are accorded respect, then their motives will be transferred from the personal to the group level. Defining themselves in terms of their group membership, they will be more willing to act cooperatively on its behalf, and in alignment with its representatives.

It is important to note that the notion of social identity used here is both expansive and non-exclusive (Moghaddam, 2008). It recognises that people have multiple group affiliations; it also allows that social identities in a complex society such as the United Kingdom do not overlap perfectly. Sets of individuals might feel they share group membership in one context while in another they might lack such a common identity (and might even have conflicting affiliations). It follows that is not necessarily important that police officers share all the identity characteristics of those they police, as long as they have some group affiliation in common – recognised membership of a particular nation-state, for example. Equally, police activity which strengthens identification with superordinate identities may encourage community cohesion, reminding individuals from diverse social groups that they also share things in common.

Is it only contact that counts?

Thus far we have primarily considered, implicitly and explicitly, the point of contact between police and citizen. Does procedural justice only matter to people's specific encounters with legal authorities; and can police only influence people's beliefs and actions via the specific encounters they have with officers? According to the available evidence, this does not seem to be the case. On the one hand, experience of the police is unlikely to be limited to direct personal contacts. People will often see officers interacting with others (perhaps their friends and family) in the areas in which they live. Such 'vicarious' experiences have been shown to be an important predictor of public opinions of the police (Miller *et al.*, 2004, Rosenbaum *et al.*, 2005). For example, a recent study showed people who had seen a police officer act in a violent manner were more likely to distrust the police compared to those people who had not seen a police officer act in such a manner. Indirect – vicarious – experience of the police shapes people's more general sense that the police can be trusted to treat people fairly and make fair decisions (Jackson *et al.*, 2012b). Wider vicarious – or mediated – contact with the police may also influence people's perceptions, possibly in highly complex and even contradictory ways. Press reports of police corruption may, for example, undermine people's sense that police act in a procedurally fair manner, while perceptions might simultaneously be buffered by the cultural repertoire of police dramas, which still tend to paint officers in a positive light (Reiner, 2010).[1]

On the other hand, whether or not they have experienced direct contact with police officers people retain a general sense of the procedural fairness of the police. When people believe that the police would treat them with respect and dignity (if they were to come into contact with officers) and when people believe that the police are 'out there' making decisions in a procedurally fair manner, these are expressions of *trust about procedural fairness*. Similarly, while most people will have little clear idea about how effective the police are in the tasks they undertake, they retain a level of trust in the effectiveness of the police – or they lack such trust. To trust the police (as officers and as institution) is to make a set of assumptions about both the way they (or it) will behave in the future and the way they (or it) generally behaves in the present. People have incomplete information about police activity and behaviour (and there is inherent risk and uncertainty involved; police officers might not be treating people fairly and they might not be effective at their job). But people can and do come to conclusions about the fairness and effectiveness of the police: thus conceived, trust is the belief that the police have the right intentions and are competent in the tasks assigned to them (Jackson and Bradford, 2010; Jackson *et al.*, 2011; European Social Survey, 2012; cf. Hardin, 2002).

Although to believe that the police are effective and fair is, in a sense, to take a leap into the dark (Mollering, 2006), public trust that it has the right intentions and is competent to do what is it tasked to do still undergirds legitimacy, and, crucially, the link between people's trust in the police and their beliefs about its legitimacy is robust even among those who have had no recent contact with officers. A number of studies have shown that encounters with officers can shape people's trust in the police, and people's trust in the police explains variation in legitimacy, cooperation and compliance (Sunshine and Tyler, 2003; Jackson *et al.*, 2012a; Mazerolle *et al.*, 2013). But people without direct personal experience also make judgements about the trustworthiness of the police, and these judgements seem to be important predictors of their beliefs about its legitimacy.

The importance of legitimacy in compliance with the law and cooperation with legal authorities

Based on the assumption that people's reasons for law-breaking are based on self-interested calculation, deterrence models of crime-control are designed to secure *instrumental compliance*. Deterrence models are based on the idea that offenders and would-be offenders are responsive primarily to the risk of punishment. They assume that, before committing a crime, people balance the benefits of doing so against the risk of being caught and punished. On this account, agents of criminal justice need to send out signals of strength, force, detection and justice. Social control mechanisms and credible risks of sanction hope to persuade rational-choice individuals that – while otherwise desirable – a criminal act is not worth the risk.

Compliance must be secured by the presence of formal or informal mechanisms of social control, as well as the existence of severe sanctions for wrong-doers.

But what if most people are not driven by this utilitarian reasoning? What if most people obey most laws, most of the time, because they think it is the right thing to do or they have acquired the simple habit of doing so? If variation in offending is explained primarily by variation in the value judgements individuals make in specific circumstance – and not in terms of utilitarian judgements concerning risk and reward – institutions will struggle to influence behaviour through traditional forms of force, censure and punishment.

Rather than concentrate solely on deterrence, those responsible for crime-control should recognise that the formal criminal justice system – via the threat it poses to law-breakers – is only one of many systems of social control, most of which have a significant normative dimension. Individuals comply with the law for reasons other than instrumental calculation of the benefits and risks of offending and, all else being equal, most people obey most laws, most of the time, because they think that to do so is the 'right thing'. Socialisation, psychological development, moral reasoning, community context, social norms and networks all sustain the routine compliance that is ingrained in everyday life.

It is here that the importance of the legitimacy of justice institutions and the legal system becomes evident. A legitimate police service has the right to exercise power: it commands consent (a sense of obligation to obey) grounded in legality and moral alignment, which, in turn, are evidenced to those interacting with or observing officers by the procedural fairness of their activities, above all, but also by the apparent effectiveness of policing and the equity with which the goods and impositions of policing is distributed across different population groups (Tankebe, 2013).

Importantly, legitimacy shapes law-related behaviour: when people believe that the police and legal system are legitimate, they *recognise* the power of these institutions to determine proper behaviour (and consequently feel a sense of obligation to obey the police and the law) and they *justify* this power by feeling that the ethical and normative standpoints inherent in the system are aligned with their own. People who see the police, courts and legal system as legitimate tend to obey the law *because it's the law*; they also tend to cooperate with authorities because they believe *it is the right thing to do* (European Social Survey, 2012).

Naturally, we do not claim that the procedural fairness and the legitimacy of justice institutions are the only non-instrumental reasons why people comply with the law and cooperate with legal authorities. What we do claim, however, is that among often competing theories of 'crime-related behaviour' procedural justice should take a privileged place because it suggests concrete possibilities for action to policy makers across the criminal justice system, and particularly in relation to policing. Criminologists might like to see the crime-preventive dividend of a fairer distribution of income and wealth, for example (Wilkinson and Pickett, 2010; Reiner, 2007; Cavadino and Dignan, 2006, 2013), but for ministers and senior justice officials such arguments are at best subsidiary to those pertaining to what they should do 'here and now'. Some of this activity will inevitably, and rightly, revolve around the harder-edged aims of policing. Yet, the apparent importance of procedural justice in terms of people's 'law-related' behaviours points to the *practical* – and increasingly well-evidenced (e.g. Mazerolle *et al.*, 2013; Papachristos *et al.*, 2012; Jackson *et al.*, 2013) – possibility of creating a form of social order which is based more on the willing consent and cooperation of citizens than on the threat of punishment. If such a vision is to be even partly achieved, we need to nudge political and public debate towards a greater appreciation of the normative dimensions of behaviour regulation, and we need to generate more understanding among officers of the consequences of police activity experienced as fair, or unfair, by citizens.

Lessons for the future of policing in England and Wales

Issues of the fairness, effectiveness and legitimacy – and continued debate over the importance and meaning of the idea of policing by consent – are especially pertinent in present times. Intense debate centres over the August 2011 riots, disproportionality in the use of stop and search powers, and the policing of demonstrations such as the 'Occupy' movement. The election of the first wave of Police and Crime Commissioners (PCCs) in November 2012 marked what appears to be a significant turning point in the governance of policing England and Wales. The effect of these developments on the legitimacy of the police, and its ability to foster normative compliance with the law, remains to be seen.[2] What is certain, however, is that a narrative of decline underpins these and many other accounts and developments. On this account, trust and legitimacy are on a downward sloping curve, and efforts need to be made to reverse this decline.

There are two ways to trace the historical trajectory and current distribution of police legitimacy in England and Wales. On the one hand there is the macro-level story of scandals concerning the treatment of ethnic minorities, the policing of riots and other public order events, corruption, and the extent of political interference in policing. These and related issues have a long pedigree – concerns about a loss of trust in, and respect for, the police, were raised by the 1929 Royal Commission on the Police (Weinberger, 1995), as well as by its counterpart in 1962 (Royal Commission on the Police, 1962) – as well as significant present-day salience. The legitimacy of the police is continuously at stake in the scandals and furore that erupt with alarming regularity. Equally, concern about the 'reassurance' gap (that public trust in the police did not increase substantively as crime fell over the period from the mid-1990s onwards) centred on the idea that public perception – and the reality – of crime is an important factor undermining trust and the legitimacy of the police.

While we have considerable sympathy with the first part of this account, if, perhaps, not the second (see below), it occludes an important empirical reality. Trust and confidence in the police have, on most accounts, been increasing since the early years of the new millennium (ONS, 2012), and in any case never fell, at the national level at least, to quite the low levels that accounts of the 'collapse' in legitimacy suggested (Loader and Mulcahy, 2003). Interwoven with the macro-level story is another account that is perhaps better able to explain this empirical reality: that of the everyday, mundane encounters between police and public that make up the vast bulk of the interaction between officers and citizens and which are a vital source of, and key threat to, trust and legitimacy (Bradford *et al.*, 2009; Jackson *et al.*, 2012b; Skogan, 2006). For every full-blown scandal involving police mistreatment of ethnic minority groups there are a thousand stop and search and other encounters. Many cause relatively little disturbance but all are 'teachable moments' (Tyler, 2011a), holding the potential to enhance or diminish police legitimacy, encourage or undermine positive social identities, and strengthen or weaken normative compliance with the law. Furthermore, citizen's quotidian experiences of policing exist alongside similar experiences of low-level crime, disorder and social cohesion in local communities and networks, and research has shown that it is these experiences, not concerns about the national crime picture, that hold implications for trust and legitimacy (Jackson and Bradford, 2009; Gau *et al.*, 2012). Indeed, *improvements* in people's perceptions of crime in their local area could be partly behind the increase in trust and confidence described above (Sindall *et al.*, 2012).

In order to outline some of the lessons notions of procedural justice and legitimacy hold for the practice of policing in England and Wales, we will concentrate on this second account and consider primarily aspects of the everyday practice of policing. This is not to claim that efforts to clamp down on corruption and other high-level malpractice should not continue, nor that these aspects of policing do not affect trust and legitimacy. However, we believe that officers' interactions with citizens, the way police treat victims of crime and deal with the kind of low-level issues that comprise the bulk of their workload, contain the clearest policy-relevant messages for how policing should be conducted and the clearest lessons in terms of what policy makers might do to enhance trust and legitimacy. Furthermore, consideration of the everyday practice of policing highlights what many police officers might find somewhat controversial – the idea that their legitimacy springs, at least in part, from public assessments of their actions, and that this legitimacy is contingent and subject to revision subsequent to citizens' experience of police activity. What, then, can police actually do – or perhaps, stop doing – that might enhance legitimacy and encourage normative compliance with the law?

Unsurprisingly, we suggest that developing styles of leadership, and accompanying structures and processes, that encourage officers to treat citizens in a procedurally fair manner should form a key component of any such attempt. Yet, arguably, this idea runs against some of the most fundamental aspects of police organisational culture. Indeed, the nature of the police organisation is itself often cited as a key barrier to attempts to improve the relationship between officer and citizen (Foster, 2003; Skogan, 2008; Stanko *et al.*, 2012). Suspicious, isolationist, conservative, cynical, and with a strong sense of internal solidarity (Loftus, 2009; Reiner, 2010), police culture is also often highly action-oriented and rather dismissive of 'soft skills' such as listening and explaining decisions (Myhill and Bradford, 2012, 2013).

Such viewpoints appear likely to inhibit officers' propensities to treat all – or at least as many as possible – citizens they encounter in a respectful and open manner. We outline below a few brief examples of the problems raised by current practices in terms of enhancing trust and legitimacy and suggest some ways these might be circumvented.

Victims of crime and police performance targets

While considerable strides have been made toward improving the experience of victims of crime within the criminal justice system, significant problems remain (Hoyle, 2012). Overall levels of 'victim satisfaction' are high, but many victims still do not feel they receive the care and attention from police they deserve. When it comes to judging their contacts with police subsequent to victimisation it seems most people place a significantly greater emphasis on the way they are treated by officers dealing with their case than on the outcome they receive (in terms, for example, of stolen goods returned or offenders arrested) (Myhill and Bradford, 2012). While victims certainly do care about these latter, more instrumental, factors, good interpersonal treatment and a tailored response to their case appears to matter considerably more (see also Bradford *et al.*, 2009; Creative Research, 2007, unpublished).

The policy implications are clear. Rather than concentrating solely on getting a 'result' officers should attend to the way in which they interact with victims. People value reassurance, and a sense of engagement and dialogue. However a focus on policing styles that might promote a sense of procedural justice and legitimacy among crime victims runs contrary to what is often the dominant performance culture within policing organisations. Performance targets in England and Wales were, until very recently, focused disproportionately on reducing volume crime (e.g. burglary and theft) and increasing detection rates (Flanagan, 2008; Hough, 2007), a focus that may have encouraged response and investigative officers to prioritise outcomes over process. After a brief shift during the third term of the New Labour administration, with its emphasis on public confidence as the overall measure of police performance (Stanko *et al.*, 2012), the Coalition Government appears to have returned to the idea that policing is, above all, about 'getting results' in relation to crime (Home Office, 2010). While the instrumental aim of dealing with crime will always be an important factor in assessing police performance, and notions of procedural justice and the more instrumentally oriented aims of policing are not inevitably in contradiction with each other (see below), it is not hard to imagine that emphasis on the latter – in terms of training, resource allocation or occupational 'canteen-culture' – may often come at the expense of attention to the former.

Conversely, when organisational priorities do shift away from 'fighting crime' as *the* end of policing, a space for improving officer/victim interactions may be opened up. The last Labour government's promotion of what became known as the 'confidence agenda' (Jackson and Bradford, 2010), suggests one way in which space might be created. On the one hand, the focus on a single item measure of public opinion as the paramount performance for police was deeply problematic (Myhill *et al.*, 2011). Yet, on the other hand, there is little doubt that this change focused senior officers' minds on victims' and indeed all citizens' opinions of the police and what police might profitably do to affect public trust in the service (Stanko *et al.*, 2012). Rather suddenly, police managers became very interested in how the actions of front-line officers affect and shape the opinions of those they interact with. High-level decisions made by governments may thus filter down to street level and change the context of encounters between officer and citizen. While the extent of genuine commitment among officers to process-based styles of policing is often unclear (Myhill and Bradford, 2012) the confidence agenda and other policies, such as 'reassurance policing', do appear to have moved the police some way toward policing styles more closely attuned to the ideas of procedural justice. Whether this movement continues in the current period of financial constraint and renewed emphasis on a narrow crime-fighting agenda is unclear; what *is* clear, however, is that police performance targets can be calibrated in ways that either reinforce or undermine the development and reproduction of trust and legitimacy. Naturally, we might note with some irony the idea that police practice directed too narrowly at fighting crime could, in the long run, undermine normative compliance with the law and promote offending.

Stop and search

Stop and search provides a key example of the potential tensions between existing policing practice and the possibility of police promoting normative compliance with the law. Stop and search and related behaviours have historically been blamed for low levels of trust in the police among ethnic minority groups, and although variation in levels of trust between different ethnic groups have grown markedly smaller this has largely been due to declining trust in the White population rather than increases elsewhere (Bradford, 2011). Viewed from one perspective, procedural justice theory might be said to provide a set of tools with which to address the problems thrown up by stop and search practice. If officers are respectful to the people they stop, explain what is going on and why, and involve them in some level of conversation about the events (allowing them a voice), the potentially negative effects of stop and search activity might be ameliorated or even reversed (Mazerolle *et al.*, 2013; Tyler and Wakslak, 2004). On this account effort is needed from police managers and street-level officers in relation to changing existing practice, which is often based on unfounded suspicion and prejudice (Quinton, 2011a) and can also be unnecessarily confrontational and aggressive (Hough, 2012; Sharp and Atherton, 2007). Greater emphasis is needed on gaining consent from citizens who, after all, have been stopped from going about their lawful business.

Desirable as a less confrontational method of conducting stop and searches might be, however, there is reason to suggest that this would not be enough to allay concerns among the communities most affected by this type of police activity. The sheer volume of stops experienced by members of some minority groups is, in itself, perceived as unfair (and indeed is almost certainly *actually* unfair). It could well be the case that procedural fairness at the level of interpersonal interaction cannot overcome the wider problems that surround stop and search practice as currently constituted. Embedding procedurally fair practice into this type of police work might involve a project more extensive than simply encouraging officers to treat those they do stop in fairer and more respectful ways. We might also note here that because contact experiences (of any type) have an 'asymmetric' effect on trust and legitimacy (Skogan, 2006), the net effect of any form of contact with police is negative (i.e. trust and legitimacy are, on average, lower among those who have had recent contact with the police). Police may garner a net 'uplift' in trust and legitimacy merely by decreasing the number of elective, confrontational contacts (such as stop and search) they have with members of the public.

However, efforts to modulate stop and search practice face many obstacles. This is one of the key tools of British policing; its use under various powers has grown substantially in recent years, although there has also been significant year on year variation (MoJ, 2012). Many police officers appear to have an almost mystical belief in the power and efficacy of stop and search (despite the low arrest rates it generates); not least as a way of 'taking control' and exerting a visible, powerful presence on the streets (Hough, 2013). Equally, government has often been very keen to grant police new powers to stop and search citizens (see Bowling and Philips, 2007). Yet, all current evidence suggests stop and search activity has a net negative effect on trust in the police, on legitimacy and, therefore, on compliance and public cooperation (Bradford *et al.*, 2009; Jackson *et al.*, 2012b; Myhill and Bradford, 2012; Skogan, 2006), pointing to a fundamental imbalance between the intention behind stop and search (to prevent and deter crime) and its actual effects (undermining normative compliance). Far from being a tool of crime prevention, stop and search could be both actively criminogenic and serve to undermine the cooperation on which police rely to solve crimes and deal with disorder.

Order maintenance and social cohesion

Thus far we have concentrated on sources of trust and legitimacy that relate primarily to direct contact between police officer and citizen. There is, of course, a much wider range of processes underpinning the extent to which people trust and legitimise the police, ranging from psychological needs for order and stability to macro-level social processes that affect trust in institutions and generate cynicism about existing political and legal structures. While many of these are clearly beyond the control of the police and criminal justice system there is a sub-set of important predictors of trust and legitimacy which might, at least initially, appear to be within the police's power to influence: namely, perceptions and experiences of low-level crime, disorder and social cohesion.

A number of recent studies have pointed to the importance of low-level disorder and social cohesion as correlates of trust and legitimacy (e.g. Jackson *et al.*, 2012b). In essence, these studies argue that the position of the police, representative of order, stability and cohesion, suffers when communities are experienced as disorderly, lacking in cohesion, and unable to regulate themselves. When order is seen to be failing the police are seen to be failing, trust declines, and legitimacy is withdrawn. What is particularly intriguing is that these concerns do not primarily revolve around crime per se so much as sub-criminal disorder and the wider condition of local communities as this relates to a sense of shared goals and shared understandings of how to achieve them (Sampson, 2012). It certainly seems that people do not 'blame' police for crime in some overall, or national, sense, nor do they withdraw trust when they are worried about crime; but they do hold police responsible if they find their neighbours disorderly or 'out of control', and their trust in the police is related to experiences of crime and (dis)order in their local areas (Jackson *et al.*, 2012b; Sindall *et al.*, 2012).

This set of concerns appears to exist in a separate category to the interpersonal interactions described above. In both cases citizens grant police legitimacy only contingently, and that legitimacy is both mutable and contestable. Yet, on the one hand, police legitimacy, and the normative compliance it may purchase, is formed and influenced via experiences and perceptions of the way police officers treat members of the public with whom they interact. On the other hand, however, legitimacy is influenced by a wider range of factors and processes that are concerned with low-level disorder (which could shade over into criminality), social cohesion, and collective efficacy. It might be tempting, therefore, to suggest that as well as attending to the quality of interpersonal interaction with citizens, attempts to strengthen police legitimacy should also attend to efforts toward order maintenance and deal with the types of minor annoyance that are linked with legitimacy in people's minds.

We think such efforts would be mistaken. Not only would they likely be largely ineffective in the long run (while police efforts can address localised problems of crime and disorder this usually takes the form of successful 'fire-fighting' rather than long-term structural change), but they could also be counter-productive if they were applied in ways such that those on the receiving end perceived the activity to be procedurally unfair. Take, for example, the classic 'problem' of teenagers 'hanging around' the streets that so often seems to concern certain people in local areas. Anxieties of this kind are consistently linked to lower police legitimacy in cross-sectional public attitude surveys, something that might prompt attempts at a police response. However, continuously moving groups of teenagers on, a process possibly ending in some more formal sanction, is likely to be found profoundly unfair by the young people involved. If the predictions of the procedural justice model are correct, this experience of unfairness would actually *increase* the likelihood of their offending in the future; it would seem almost certain to damage their relationship with local police, reduce cooperation, and increase tension. Clearly a sensible balance has to be struck. We are not suggesting a complete retreat from the policing of low-level disorder. However, it is essential that the resolution of conflicts of this sort should be done in a way that is both fair to both sides and fully accountable to the law.

Success in policing

The current emphasis on, and continuing expansion of, Tyler's work on procedural justice casts new light on our ideas of what constitutes success in policing and
about how this success should be obtained via policy. Commonly stated criteria for
success in policing can be loosely placed into one of three categories. For some,
policing is successful when it reduces crime. Policy should be oriented toward
developing practice that is effective in achieving this end, resulting in myriad policing programmes from POP to hot-spots to 'zero-tolerance' (see Telep and Weisburd (2012) for a review of 'what works'). Academic research in this area tends to
stress targeted, almost surgical, 'applications' of policing, and examines the efficacy
of such approaches in reducing specific crimes in specific contexts; more popular,
and political, accounts tend to stress a much wider – and very possibly mythical
– police ability to fight crime in all its guises.

For others, policing is successful when it builds strong links with communities,
and acts to reassure people and provide them with a sense of security (Loader and
Walker, 2007). On this account, we should accept the fact that there is relatively little police can do to influence the overall volume and nature of crime, and acknowledge that officers spend a large amount of time dealing with non-crime-related
issues. Instead of a constant recourse to 'fighting crime', police attention should be
directed toward mitigating the effects of crime on individuals and communities,
promoting a wider sense of order, and developing notions of policing that are true
to the actual practice of officers and not to the idealised accounts of media and politics (Brodeur, 2010). Developing alternative strategies of crime reduction that do
not rely on criminal justice responses should be a much wider policy concern, one
that addresses the social and economic 'root causes' of crime (Reiner, 2007).

On the third account, policing is successful when it is just. Before concentrating
on instrumental outcomes or providing a 'deep' sense of security, we should ensure
that the goods and impositions of policing are equitably distributed across individuals and social groups (Bowling and Philips, 2002). Accounts in this strand stress the
unfinished business of asserting fair, equitable policing, and that it is imperative to
address the unfair distribution and application of policing before moving on to its
outcomes.

These categories of success are, at least potentially, complementary and, of
course, police organisations should be effective, provide a sense of order and security *and* be fair to the maximal degree possible. While we have privileged notions of
fairness here, all three elements are likely sources of legitimacy, a characteristic that
almost all accounts of the nature and aims of the public police agree is a key feature
of policing in democratic states and a vital characteristic of police organisations if
they are to function effectively and in a sustainable manner. Yet, the idea that the
varying ends of policing might complement each other is often obscured. Policy
debates often revolve around implicit zero-sum equations. Attempts to enhance
effectiveness pay scant attention to fairness; indeed, 'human rights' are proposed as
an *impediment* to effectiveness and, as Loader (this volume) notes, something that

restrains the police's 'inner crime-fighter'. Similarly, providing a sense of security to citizens often appears an aim only in relation to certain sections of the population – those that need protection, perhaps, from the dangerous classes the police patrol who, in turn, are the targets of excessive amounts of police attention. Accounts that stress the importance of fairness pay, on the contrary, less attention than they perhaps should to the idea that police can, and should, be effective 'crime-fighters' in some minimal sense, or to the idea that police can and should provide a feeling of security to those they police. Alternatively, there are calls for 'good enough' policing and for modes that *balance* fairness and effectiveness (Bowling, 2008), once more implicitly setting these aspects of policing in counter-distinction with one another.

We have much sympathy with the approaches of Bowling and others. Certainly, policing is not 'good enough' when it is regularly conducted in an unfair manner (ibid.: 30). There is an element in police practice that is inherently confrontational, and a set of ends of policing that are inextricably linked to the application of coercive force (indeed, in some circumstances, confrontation and force are not only necessary but desirable, as when officers act to break up fights or to stop serious crimes in the act of commission). Yet we should strive to minimise this aspect of police behaviour by, among other things, constantly holding it up not against any instrumental gains it might achieve but against well-developed standards of justice and probity. Except in the most extreme cases heavy-handed, aggressive, procedurally unfair policing is not justified simply by being effective and, in many situations effectiveness *should* be contrasted with fairness. Equally, aggressive policing tactics might reassure certain sections of the population (the second criteria of success in policing outlined above) yet, at the same time, be instrumental in undermining the sense of security and inclusion of others.

Counter-posing fairness and effectiveness, however, this argument remains on the territory staked out by opponents of rights-based approaches to policing and exponents of 'law and order': more fairness, at least implicitly, means less effectiveness. By contrast, procedural justice theory offers the possibility of moving from a zero- to a positive-sum context. Put simply, policing that is experienced as fair by citizens, that builds trust and legitimacy, will in the long run be more effective. Legitimate policing encourages normative compliance with the law and garners public support in dealing with those crimes that do occur. Furthermore, citizens' sense of security and embeddedness in wider social structures can be enhanced by precisely the same process. A 'thick' sense of security (Loader and Walker, 2007) may be encouraged when people feel they are governed by authorities that accord them dignity, worth and respect, when they feel included in self-relevant social groups, and when they are reassured that the structures of the law correspond with their own sense of right and wrong and are enforced in an equitable manner.

Some final thoughts

This final section offers some thoughts on what may actually be involved in introducing into police practice some of the principles outlined above. No organisational change is cost-free, but achieving a different quality of relationship in encounters between police and public is not necessarily expensive. Changes in styles of policing are achieved more through positive leadership than through training (Myhill and Bradford, 2013) or the re-engineering of formal procedures. Police leaders need to communicate clearly that procedural fairness is a core aspect of police work. An important part of this communication process lies in ensuring that internal management actually commands legitimacy in the eyes of the workforce. Recent research has suggested that procedural justice could be just as important *within* policing organisations as it is in the *relationship* between police and public. Corresponding with the wider organisational justice literature (Colquitt *et al.*, 2001; Greenberg, 2011), this work has suggested that police officers' perceptions of procedural justice in their relationships with managers – particularly concerning the fairness of procedures, and the quality of interaction and communication – are strongly linked to their compliance with organisational goals and to 'organisational citizenship behaviours' that might enhance their willingness to engage with members of the public in positive and constructive ways (Myhill and Bradford, 2013; Quinton, 2011b; cf. Tyler, 2011b; Tyler and Blader, 2000). Just as procedural fairness indicates shared group membership to individuals when they are dealing with police officers, organisational justice provides for a sense of value and integration among officers, enhances internal legitimacy, and encourages positive orientations toward service-oriented policing. Unfair organisations, by contrast, are unlikely to encourage such positive attitudes among their staff. The five years from 2010 involve significant contractions in budgets (of around 20 per cent) and this will inevitably lead to organisational strain as the system is required to rise to the challenge of 'doing more with less' (or indeed 'less with less' – Innes (2010)). With threats to the *volume* of available services, securing some counterbalance in terms of improved *quality* might be a very wise investment.

As for the targeting of strategies designed to bolster the legitimacy of the police among the public, those sectors of the community that are best able to demand change are probably less significant in policing terms; it is those with less social capital who are over-represented in the (overlapping) populations of crime victims and offenders. Where trust and legitimacy are most needed is in the most socially and economically marginalised communities where crime is highest. What this means in practice is that strategies of procedural justice should be targeted at hard-to-police areas where everyday exigencies push policing in precisely the opposite direction (cf. Hough, 2012, 2013). Of course, the demands made on the police in such areas are often non-criminal – or lie on the margins of criminality – but the handling of each of these incidents remain 'teachable moments' (Tyler, 2011a) that concern the trustworthiness and legitimacy of the police.

There is a close correspondence between notions of what procedurally just policing might look like and neighbourhood policing strategies, which have been a feature of criminal justice policy in England and Wales since the turn of the century. In particular the emphasis on the geographical stability of neighbourhood policing teams seems likely to promote trust between officers and local residents, as do principles of responsiveness to public priorities. However, these principles of responsiveness can be strained in divided communities where different groups have different priorities. For example, as we noted above, inter-generational conflict is well illustrated by the frequent complaint that young people are being anti-social simply by 'hanging around' in public space. Principles of procedural justice remind us that the police need not only to be responsive wherever possible, but to retain some degree of *distance* from communities, resolving conflicts by reference to criteria of fair process and legality rather than majority preference.

These thoughts might suggest that there is a need to more clearly fix responsibility for issues of legitimacy within the police governance framework. If, as we have argued, procedural justice is a precondition for effective policing, then it should be a preoccupation of chief officers. But equally, HM Inspectorate of Constabulary and the Independent Police Complaints Authority both have some *locus* as guardians of legitimacy. To our minds, however, the new PCCs could and should play a central role here. Although they are not explicitly charged with this responsibility in the legislation, there is clearly scope for them to guide the policing style and philosophy of their force, while leaving enough space for their chief officers to exercise their 'operational independence'. A good PCC will be one who focuses attention on procedural fairness and system legitimacy and, to return to the issue of assessing performance, PCCs should arguably be less concerned with the crime rate in their area (over which the police have relatively little control) than with the strength of the relationship between police and local communities.

It is worth finishing on a note of caution. There is an inherent risk in policy based on principles of procedural justice. The legitimacy of the police is partly about perceptions, and partly about reality. In a complex world where ideas about institutions are shaped by a growing range of powerful media, there is a risk that strategies to improve the legitimacy of the police degrade into little more than public relations exercises – securing the right media messages, and ensuring that staff remain 'on message' in their contacts with the public. Such strategies of appearance management might yield some short-term results, but they are inherently dangerous, given that they are about trust-building. When any gaps between appearance and reality surface – as is likely, if not inevitable – the costs to legitimacy can be very high indeed. In other words, improvements in trust and legitimacy have to be earned, and not simply claimed.

Notes

1   Although we would note that evidence for a direct impact of media representations on people's opinions of the police is thin indeed – see Jackson *et al.* (2012b).
2   On the one hand, elections could encourage a sense of public 'ownership' of the police and foster a sense of value alignment, and thus legitimacy. On the other, those who back the losing candidate(s) for PCC might experience a distancing from the police, who become associated with the values of the winner. It is interesting to note in this light the unexpectedly large number of Independent candidates elected as PCCs. Many voters, it seems, voted against party political involvement and for candidates not so strongly associated with a particular set of political values.

References

Beetham, D. (1991) *The Legitimation of Power*. London: Macmillan.

Blader, S. and Tyler, T. R. (2009) Testing and expanding the group engagement model. *Journal of Applied Psychology*, 94: 445–464.

Bottoms, A., and Tankebe, J. (2012) Beyond procedural justice: A dialogic approach to legitimacy in criminal justice. *Journal of Criminal Law and Criminology*, 102: 119–170.

Bowling, B. (2008) Fair and effective policing methods: Towards 'good enough' policing. *Journal of Scandinavian Studies in Criminology and Crime Prevention*, 8(1): 17–32.

Bowling, B. and Philips, C. (2002) *Racism, Crime and Justice*. London: Longman.

Bowling, B. and Philips, C. (2007) Disproportionate and discriminatory: Reviewing the evidence on police stop and search. *The Modern Law Review*, 70: 936–961.

Bradford, B. (2011) Voice neutrality and respect: Use of victim support services procedural fairness and confidence in the criminal justice system. *Criminology and Criminal Justice*, 11(4): 345–366.

Bradford, B. (2012) Policing and social identity: Procedural justice, inclusion and cooperation between police and public. *Policing and Society*, iFirst (www.tandfonline.com/doi/full/10.1080/10439463.2012.72406).

Bradford, B., Jackson, J. and Stanko, E. (2009) Contact and confidence: Revisiting the impact of public encounters with the police. *Policing and Society*, 19: 20–46.

Bradford, B., Huq, A., Jackson, J. and Roberts, B. (2013) What price fairness when security is at stake? Police legitimacy in South Africa. *Regulation and Governance*, doi: 10.1111/rego.12012.

Brodeur, J.-P. (2010) *The Policing Web*. Oxford: Oxford University Press.

Cavadino, M. and Dignan, J. (2006) *Penal Systems. A Comparative Approach*. London: Thousand Oaks/New Delhi: Sage Publications.

Cavadino, M. and Dignan, J. (2013) Political economy and legal systems. In S. Body-Gendrot, R. Lévy, M. Hough, S. Snacken and K. Kerezsi (eds) *The Routledge Handbook of European Criminology*. London: Routledge.

Colquitt, J., Conlon, D., Wesson, M., Porter, C. and Ng, K. (2001) Justice at the millennium: A meta-analytic review of 25 years of organizational justice research. *Journal of Applied Psychology*, 86: 425–445.

Creative Research (2007, unpublished) *Exploring ethnic differences in victim's expectations of police service provision: The potential impact of expectation fulfilment on satisfaction*.

Elliott, I., Thomas, S. D., Ogloff, M. and James, R. P. (2011) Procedural justice in contacts with the police: Testing a relational model of authority in a mixed methods study. *Psychology, Public Policy, and Law*, 17(4): 592–610.

Ericson, R. and Haggerty, K. (1997) *Policing the Risk Society*. London: Clarendon.

European Social Survey (2011) Trust in justice: Topline findings from the European Social Survey, *ESS Topline Results Series Issue 1*. Authors: Jackson, J., Hough, M., Bradford, B., Pooler, T. M., Hohl, K. and Kuha, J.

European Social Survey (2012) Policing by consent: Understanding the dynamics of police power and legitimacy. *ESS Country Specific Topline Results Series Issue 1 (UK)*. Authors: Jackson, J., Hough, M., Bradford, B., Hohl, K. and Kuha, J.

Flanagan, R. (2008) *The Review of Policing: Final Report*. London: Home Office.

Foster, J. (2003) Cop cultures. In T. Newburn (ed.) *The Handbook of Policing*. Cullompton, Devon: Willan.

Gau, J. M. and Brunson, R. K. (2009) Procedural justice and order maintenance policing: A study of inner-city young men's perceptions of police legitimacy. *Justice Quarterly* 27(2): 255–279.

Gau, J. M., Corsaro, N., Stewart, E. A. and Brunson, R. K. (2012) Examining macro-level impacts on procedural justice and police legitimacy. *Journal of Criminal Justice*, 40(4): 333–343.

Greenberg, J. (2011) Organizational justice: The dynamics of fairness in the workplace. In Z. Sheldon (ed.) *APA Handbook of Industrial and Organizational Psychology, Vol. 3: Maintaining, expanding, and contracting the organization*. Washington, DC: American Psychological Association, pp. 271–327.

Hall, S., Crichter, C. and Jefferson, T. (1978) *Policing the Crisis: Mugging, the State and Law and Order*. London: Macmillan.

Hardin, R. (2002) *Trust and Trustworthiness*. New York: Russell Sage Foundation.

Hasisi, B. and Weisburd, D. (2011) Going beyond ascribed identities: The importance of procedural justice in airport security screening in Israel. *Law and Society Review*, 45(4): 867–892.

Home Office (2010) *A New Approach to Fighting Crime*. London: Home Office.

Hough, M. (2007) Policing, new public management and legitimacy. In T. R. Tyler (ed.) *Legitimacy and Criminal Justice*. New York: Russell Sage Foundation.

Hough, M. (2012) Researching trust in the police and trust in justice: A UK perspective. *Policing and Society*, 22(3): 332–345.

Hough, M. (2013) Procedural justice and professional policing in times of austerity. *Criminology and Criminal Justice*, 13(2): 181–197, doi: 10.1177/1748895812466399.

Hough, M., Jackson, J., Bradford, B., Myhill, A., and Quinton, P. (2010) Procedural justice, trust and institutional legitimacy. *Policing: A Journal of Policy and Practice*, 4(3): 203–210.

Hoyle, C. (2012) Victims, the criminal process and restorative justice. In M. Maguire, R. Morgan and R. Reiner (eds) *The Oxford Handbook of Criminology*. Oxford: Oxford University Press, pp. 398–425.

Huq, A. Z., Tyler, T. and Schulhofer, S. J. (2011) Mechanisms for eliciting cooperation in counterterrorism policing: A study of British Muslims. *Journal of Empirical Legal Studies*, 8: 728–761.

Innes, M. (2010) *Plenary address at the 2010 conference of the Scottish Institute of Police Research*, 14–15 September, West Park Centre, Dundee.

Jackson, J. and Bradford, B. (2009) Crime, policing and social order: On the expressive nature of public confidence in policing. *British Journal of Sociology*, 60(3): 493–521.

Jackson, J. and Bradford, B. (2010) What is trust and confidence in the police? *Policing: A Journal of Policy and Practice*, 4(3): 241–248.

Jackson, J., Bradford, B., Hough, M., Kuha, J., Stares, S. R., Widdop, S., et al. (2011) Developing European indicators of trust in justice. *European Journal of Criminology*, 8(4): 267–285.

Jackson, J., Bradford, B., Hough, M., Myhill, A., Quinton, P. and Tyler, T. R. (2012a) Why do people comply with the law? Legitimacy and the influence of legal institutions. *British Journal of Criminology*, 52(6): 1051–1071.

Jackson, J., Bradford, B., Stanko, E. A. and Hohl, K. (2012b) *Just Authority? Trust in the Police in England and Wales*. Oxon: Routledge.

Jackson, J., Huq, A., Bradford, B. and Tyler, T. R. (2013, forthcoming) Monopolizing force? Police legitimacy and public attitudes towards the acceptability of violence. *Psychology, Public Policy and Law*.

Loader, I. and Mulcahy, A. (2003) *Policing and the Condition of England: Memory, Politics and Culture*. Oxford: Oxford University Press.

Loader, I. and Walker, N. (2007) *Civilising Security*. Cambridge: Cambridge University Press.

Loftus, B. (2009) Police occupational culture: Classic themes, altered times. *Policing and Society*, 20(1): 594–604.

Mazerolle, L., Antrobus, E., Bennett, S. and Tyler, T. R. (2013) Shaping citizen perceptions of police legitimacy: A randomized field trial of procedural justice. *Criminology*, 51(1): 33–63.

Miller, J., Davies, R., Henderson, N., Markovic, J. and Ortiz, C. (2004) *Public Opinion of the Police: The Influence of Friends, Family and New Media*. New York: Vera Foundation.

Ministry of Justice (2012) *Statistics on Race and the Criminal Justice System 2010*. London: Ministry of Justice.

Moghaddam, F. M. (2008) *Multiculturalism and Intergroup Relations: Psychological Implications for Democracy in Global Context*. Washington, DC: American Psychological Association Press.

Möllering, G. (2006) *Trust: Reason, Routine and Reflexivity*. Oxford: Elsevier.

Murphy, K., Tyler, T. R. and Curtis, A. (2009) Nurturing regulatory compliance: Is procedural justice effective when people question the legitimacy of the law? *Regulation and Governance*, 3(1): 1–26.

Myhill, A. and Bradford, B. (2012) Can police enhance public confidence by improving quality of service? Results from two surveys in England and Wales. *Policing and Society*, 22(4): 397–425.

Myhill, A. and Bradford, B. (2013) Overcoming cop culture? Organizational justice and police officers' attitudes toward the public. *Policing: An International Journal of Police Strategies & Management*, 36(2): 338–356.

Myhill, A., Quinton, P., Bradford, B., Poole, A. and Sims, G. (2011) It depends what you mean by 'confident': Operationalizing measures of public confidence and the role of performance indicators. *Policing: A Journal of Policy and Practice*, 5(2): 114–124.

ONS (2012) Focus on Public Perceptions of Policing. Findings from the 2011/12 Crime Survey for England and Wales. London: Office for National Statistics.

Papachristos, A. V., Meares, T. L. and Fagan, J. (2012) Why do criminals obey the law? The influence of legitimacy and social networks on active gun offenders. *The Journal of Criminal Law and Criminology*, 102(2): 397–439.

Quinton, P. (2011a) *The impact of information about crime and policing on public perceptions: The results of a randomised controlled trial*. London: National Policing Improvement Agency.

Quinton, P. (2011b) The formation of suspicions: police stop and search practices in England and Wales. *Policing and Society*, 21(4): 357–368.

Reiner, R. (2007) *Law and Order: an Honest Citizen's Guide to Crime Control*. Cambridge: Polity Press.

Reiner, R. (2010) *The Politics of the Police* (4th edn). Oxford: Oxford University Press.

Reisig, M. D. and Lloyd, C. (2009) Procedural justice, police legitimacy, and helping the police fight crime: Results from a survey of Jamaican adolescents. *Police Quarterly*, 12(1): 42–62.

Rosenbaum, D., Schuck, A., Costebllo, S., Hawkins, D. and Ring, M. (2005) Attitudes toward the police: The effects of direct and vicarious experience. *Police Quarterly*, 83: 343–365.

Royal Commission on the Police (1962) *Final Report*. Commissioned 1728. London: HMSO.

Sampson, R. (2012) *Great American City*. Chicago: Chicago University Press.

Schulhofer, S. J., Tyler, T. R. and Huq, A. Z. (2011) American policing at a crossroads: Unsustainable policies and the procedural justice alternative. *Journal of Criminal Law and Criminology*, 101: 335–375.

Sharp, D. and Atherton, S. (2007) To serve and protect? The experiences of policing in the community of young people from black and other ethnic minority groups. *British Journal of Criminology*, 47: 746–763.

Sindall, K., Sturgis, P. and Jennings, W. (2012) Public confidence in the police: A time-series analysis. *British Journal of Criminology*, 52(4): 744–764.

Skogan, W. (2006) Asymmetry in the impact of encounters with the police. *Policing and Society*, 162: 99–126.

Skogan, W. (2008) Why reforms fail. *Policing and Society*, 18(1): 23–34.

Stanko, E. A., Jackson, J., Bradford, B. and Hohl, K. (2012) A golden thread, a presence amongst uniforms, and a good deal of data: Discourses of confidence in the London Metropolitan Police. *Policing and Society*, 22(3): 317–331.

Sunshine, J. and Tyler, T. (2003) The role of procedural justice and legitimacy in public support for policing. *Law and Society Review*, 37(3): 513–548.

Tankebe, J. (2013) Viewing things differently: Examining the dimensions of public perceptions of police legitimacy. *Criminology*, 51(1): 103–135.

Telep, C. W. and Weisburd, D. (2012) What is known about the effectivesness of police practices in reducing crime and disorder? *Police Quarterly*, advance access.

Tyler, T. R. (2006a) Psychological perspectives on legitimacy and legitimation. *Annual Review of Psychology*, 57: 375–400.

Tyler, T. R. (2006b) *Why People Obey the Law*. Princeton: Princeton University Press.

Tyler, T. R. (2008) Psychology and institutional design. *Review of Law and Economics*, 4(3): 801–887.

Tyler, T. R. (2011a) Trust and legitimacy: Policing in the USA and Europe. *European Journal of Criminology*, 8: 254–266.

Tyler, T. R. (2011b) *Why People Cooperate: The Role of Social Motivations*. Princeton: Princeton University Press.

Tyler, T. R., Degoey, P. and Smith, H. (1996) Understanding why the justice of group procedures matters: A test of the psychological dynamics of the group-value model. *Journal of Personality and Social Psychology*, 70(5): 913–930.

Tyler, T. R. and Blader, S. (2000) *Cooperation in Groups: Procedural Justice, Social Identity, and Behavioral Engagement*. Philadelphia, PA: Psychology Press.

Tyler, T. R. and Huo, Y. J. (2002) *Trust in the Law: Encouraging Public Cooperation with the Police and Courts*. New York: Russell Sage Foundation.

Tyler, T. R. and Wakslak, C. J. (2004) Profiling and police legitimacy: Procedural justice, attributions of motive, and acceptance of police authority. *Criminology*, 42(2): 253–281.

Tyler, T. R. and Jackson, J. (2013) Future challenges in the study of legitimacy and criminal justice. In J. Tankebe and A. Liebling (eds) *Legitimacy and Criminal Justice: An International Exploration*. Oxford: Oxford University Press.

Tyler, T. R., Jackson, J. and Bradford, B. (in press) Social connections and material interests: On the relational basis of voluntary cooperation with legal authorities. In N. Harris (ed.) *Encyclopedia of Criminology and Criminal Justice*. Springer-Verlag.

Van Dijke, M. H., De Cremer, D. and Mayer, D. (2010) The role of authority power in explaining procedural fairness effects. *Journal of Applied Psychology*, 95(3): 488–502.

Waddington, P. (1999) *Policing Citizens: Authority and Rights*. London: University College Press.

Weinberger, B. (1995) *The Best Police in the World: An Oral History of English Policing from the 1930s to the 1960s*. Aldershot: Scholar Press.

Wilkinson, R. and Pickett, K. (2010) *The Spirit Level: Why Equality is Better for Everyone*. London: Penguin.

PART II
Culture

7

POLICE CULTURE AND THE NEW POLICING CONTEXT

Matthew Bacon

Introduction

'Police culture' has been a lasting topic of interest and debate in the field of police studies for the past fifty or so years, a constant presence in policies, politics and public discussions about policing, and a 'convenient label for a range of negative values, attitudes, and practice norms among police officers' (Chan 1996, p. 110). When people think of 'the police' and 'policing' it is more than likely that images generated by ideas about police culture will spring to mind.

Research and reflection have consistently recognised the significant role that the 'occupational culture' of the police plays in shaping their decisions and actions. Police researchers have argued, for example, that the cultural elements of police organisations are the main reason why laws, policies and directives do not translate directly into practice, that they help officers determine how to exercise their discretionary powers, and that they mediate the demands of the job with the exigencies of everyday life. Police culture has been held accountable for a host of the deviant and discriminatory attitudes and behaviours that are occasionally exhibited by some police officers. It has also proven to be stubbornly resistant to changes in policing, and capable of under-mining efforts to reform the police. Perhaps the most important point to be taken from what is known is that if we do not understand the nature and influence of police culture we cannot hope to understand police practices or the realities of policing in society. The crucial matters under discussion in this chapter are the concept of police culture and the implications for the delivery and reform of policing and the police.

What is police culture?

Despite its explanatory power, extensive usage and influence, the concept of police culture remains somewhat complicated, contested and, at times, contradictory. It goes by different names and is conceptualised, employed and analysed in different ways. Some prefer the term 'police subculture' to 'police culture'; others opt for 'occupational culture', 'organisational culture', 'cop culture' or 'canteen culture'. Many writers and commentators use the terms interchangeably. Into the bargain, there has been a move away from looking at police *culture*, as scholars have developed the view that there are a number of distinctive police *cultures*. There is, therefore, a pressing need for some form of clarification. This section will attempt to make sense of various terminological issues and explain what is meant by police culture.

Definitions

Although it is unlikely that there will ever be a definition that encapsulates all of the themes and concepts identified in the extensive body of literature on the subject, the likenesses between existing definitions suggests that there exists a prevailing understanding of what is broadly meant by the term. What researchers have called police culture, by whichever name, is essentially the anthropological sense of the concept of 'culture' wedded to the police occupation. It provides officers with frames of reference, coping strategies, practical knowledge and 'commonsense' understandings about how to view their external environment and how and why policing should and can be done in any situation. The following box exemplars mostly point to sets of shared beliefs and values that influence the routine conduct of police officers.

BOX 7.1 EXAMPLE DEFINITIONS OF 'POLICE CULTURE'

- Holdaway (1983, p. 2) argues that 'a residual core of beliefs and values, of associated strategies and tactics relevant to policing, remains a principal guide for the day-to-day work of the rank-and-file officer'.
- Manning (1989, p. 360) considers it to be the 'accepted practices, rules, and principles of conduct that are situationally applied, and generalised rationales and beliefs'.
- Chan (1997, p. 43) proposes that the concept emerged from studies of police work that 'uncovered a layer of informal occupational norms and values operating under the apparently rigid hierarchical structure of police organisations'.
- Reiner (2010, p. 118) suggests that cop culture 'offers a patterned set of understandings that helps officers cope with the pressures and tensions confronting the police'.

Notwithstanding the tendency to lump cultural manifestations and fundamentals together under the same umbrella, if we are to understand the nature and influence of police culture it is necessary to distinguish between them. According to Schein (2004; cited in Cockcroft 2012, pp. 6–7), there are three levels of culture:

'artefacts'; 'espoused beliefs and values'; and 'underlying assumptions'. With regard to the police, artefacts are phenomena associated with members of police organisations and include ceremonies, language, stories and modes of address and behaviour. Espoused beliefs and values are conscious and explicitly articulated police philosophies that will lead to some observable expressions and could become underlying assumptions if they work in practice and provide meaning to the social experience of police officers. Such assumptions are internalised at an unconscious level and are embedded sufficiently to ensure their taken-for-granted validity. Reform initiatives may be deemed successful by virtue of them bringing about changes in expressed behaviour and explicit philosophy but unless they can alter the bedrock of police culture fundamental change will not occur.

Culture or subculture?

The term 'culture' is usually reserved for large, ordered social systems, a community, for instance, a city, a country, or an organisation, whereas 'subculture' is used to refer to the smaller micro-cultures that exist within the macro-culture (Geertz 1973; Goodenough 1976; Tylor 1871). Subcultures develop as modes of expression and rational means of resolving contradictions and solving problems that are created by the incompatible demands of existing cultural and structural circumstances. Given that the police can be viewed as both an organisation and a distinct social subgroup, it is perfectly fine to use either term to refer to their ethos and everyday practices.

That said, since criminologists have tended to use subcultural theories to understand forms of deviance, I would argue that, while the notion of police subculture is both terminologically and conceptually sound, the term itself will have negative connotations for certain audiences and so its usage should be avoided or at least carefully considered. Subcultural theories are, for example, particularly useful tools for examining tensions between formality and informality within organisational contexts. Using symbolic organisation theory as an approach to analysing the deep structures of organisations, Jermier *et al.* (1991) distinguish between the concepts of 'official organisational culture' and 'organisational subculture'. For them, official culture refers to the formal structures of police organisations that are established, in large part, by top management and oriented towards legitimating existing practices publicly. It is characterised by uniformed dress, an apparently rigid rank hierarchy of authority, mission statements and codes of conduct. The organisational subculture, on the other hand, refers to accepted practices that emerge in groups of officers and their shared understandings about the police mission and standards of conduct.

Before progressing any further with the discussion it should be noted that the police, like any other culture or subculture, are distinctive but not wholly distinct from the rest of society. Generally speaking, there has been a tendency to look at the police in isolation from the landscape and population that surrounds them. This blinkered approach has caused researchers and commentators to overstress the distinctiveness of police officers and overstate the explanatory power of the concept of police culture. The fact of the matter is the police are actually akin to their fellow citizens in many of their general attitudes. Waddington (1999a, p. 291), for example, proposes that the widespread sexism frequently found among police officers is probably influenced more by patriarchal beliefs embedded in society than the macho elements of their occupational culture. An understanding of police culture must situate it in the social context of policing and recognise whether the cultural expressions of the police are specific to their organisation/social subgroup or part of the wider culture.

The occupation of policing and the police organisation

Policing is an occupation practised by the police in formal organisational contexts, which goes a long way towards explaining why the terms 'occupational culture' and 'organisational culture' are used synonymously in much of the literature. Nevertheless, even though the occupation of policing and police constabularies have been intricately connected ever since the birth of the public police service in 1829, it is important to recognise that the occupation (a set of social control activities) and the organisation (a set of actors engaged in social control activities) are two different phenomena and can, therefore, influence police culture in both combined and separate ways.

By and large, the term organisational culture is used when referring to the observable expressions, explicit philosophies and underlying assumptions shared by members of an organisation (Sackmann 1997; Schein 2004; Weick 2001). Occupational culture, on the other hand, refers to filtered and often divergent versions of the organisational culture that are shaped by the particular roles and experiences of different occupational groups within an organisation. Paoline (2003) suggests that a fundamental difference between organisational and occupational cultures is that the former are top-down and driven by management whereas the latter are bottom-up and driven by the rank-and-file.

From a purely organisational perspective, the police are relatively similar to any other large, bureaucratically organised occupation. The range of business terminologies, principles and practices that have been introduced with the implementation of 'new public management' reforms over the last two decades has made these similarities all the more salient (Hood 1991; McLaughlin et al. 2001). Furthermore, it is widely recognised that most occupational groups 'develop understandings about how to interpret conduct, retain loyalties, express opinions, use or abuse authority' (Skolnick 2008, p. 35). As Loftus (2009, p. 199) stresses, however, 'the police remain in the unique position of enforcing the law in a liberal democratic society'. In the performance of their duties they are authorised to act in ways that would otherwise be 'exceptional, exceptionable and downright illegal' if undertaken by anyone else (Waddington 1999b, p. 156). Van Maanen (1978a, 1978b) suggests that few organisations experience the same degree of occupational identification as the police.

Being a 'police officer' is the occupation shared by most members of police organisations and, arguably, the defining occupation of the police service. Officers are, however, usually employed in a variety of roles during the course of their careers and thereby become members of different occupational groups. Accordingly, to quote and paraphrase Fielding (1988, p. 157), '"the" occupational culture is actually many subcultures', with myriad variations and nuances arising from idiosyncrasies and regional differences. There are well-documented distinctions between 'street cops' and 'management cops', for example, their cultures stemming from the distinct experiences and expectations associated with their organisational positions. Reuss-Ianni (1983, p. 6) argues that management cop culture finds 'its salience and meaning not in the traditions of the job, but rather in theories and practices of scientific management and public administration'. The detective literature gives prominence to the cultural transition that takes place when uniform officers join the Criminal Investigation Department (CID). According to Hobbs (1991, p. 599), the 'quicker new recruits to the CID can purge themselves of what is perceived as the plodding, mechanistic, reactive operational style of the uniform branch, the quicker total immersion in detective culture can be achieved'. Fielding (1995), to give another example, in his study of community policing, argues that at the lower echelons there are distinct subcultures among officers engaged in routine patrol, on the one hand, and 'community constables', on the other. Studies have also shown how police culture is shaped by the differing patterns and problems of the external environment. Cain's (1973) work, for example, explores how policing conditions and styles differ between rural and city areas, as does Young's (1993) research on cultural identity 'in the sticks'. Punch's (1979, p. 133) study of the Amsterdam police illustrates how their work is 'mediated by a complex unwritten code' that is 'rooted in the specific cultural norms of cosmopolitan inner-city life'. Likewise, Hobbs' (1988, p. 84) study of detectives in the East End of London suggests that the nature of CID work 'is influenced by its occupational environment to the extent of adopting crucial characteristics of the culture generated by that environment'. There is nothing intrinsically wrong with different occupational groups and geographical areas having different cultural traits and working practices, so long as they are ethical and appropriate to the situational demands of policing. It can, however, make problematic the implementation of national or force-wide policies.

On the whole, the research-based evidence indicates that the informal social systems of occupational groups have a greater impact upon cultural orientations than the wider organisation. Still, overemphasising the culturally determining influence of occupations can preclude deeper analyses of policing as an organisation and as a practice. A narrow focus on occupational culture, Manning (2007) argues, can neglect the political role the police play in the field of national and local policies, the internal nuances, dynamics and politics of the police organisation, the bureaucratic constraints such as authorisation procedures and paperwork, and the tensions between formal realities, individual commitments and the situated nature of police work.

'Cop culture' and 'canteen culture'

The relationship between thought, talk and action is complex and by no means easy to fathom, for what a person thinks they should do or says they have done or will do is not always what they actually do. Smith and Gray (1985), for example, found that police attitudes relating to race were not necessarily consistent with their behaviour towards black people. Similarly, Waddington (1994) found that, even though officers were generally homophobic, they went to great lengths to facilitate gay rights demonstrations and to protect the annual 'Gay Pride' march through central London.

Police scholars have developed the important conceptual distinction between 'cop culture' and 'canteen culture' as a means of understanding police practices and the discordance between their talk and action (Fielding 1994; Hoyle 1998; Waddington 1999a). The term cop culture is used when referring to the orientations implied and expressed by officers in the course of their work, whereas canteen culture refers to the way in which officers use cultural themes to communicate with their peers and establish a shared identity. For Hoyle (1998, p. 75), canteen culture 'allows officers to articulate their fears, and vent their frustrations and anger' about the role of the police and the demands of operational policing. She stresses that, while attitudes certainly have some impact on behaviour, they do not cause police officers to behave in a particular way or necessarily correspond to their practices. The stories and jokes told in the canteen should not be assumed to reveal the underlying assumptions of police culture or accurately reflect what really takes place. It is important, therefore, when formulating understandings of police culture, to take note of whether the evidence focuses on police work or relates solely to attitudes and accounts expressed in privacy, low-visibility situations or during off-duty socialising. The crucial matter is the relevance of cultural values and beliefs to actual behaviour and it is this that is regularly deemed to be in need of reform.

The relationship between culture and practice

The recognition that the rank-and-file exercise a considerable amount of discretion in the performance of their duties raises questions about some of the extra-legal factors influencing police decisions and actions. From the 1960s onwards attention focused on the occupational culture as one important set of factors. The relationship between culture and practice, however, is fraught with complexity and a source of much confusion and contention.

Research that has scrutinised the context within which decisions are made illustrates how culture is a determinant of action but does not determine how officers exercise their discretionary powers. Chatterton (1983), for example, describes the relevance of police culture to police practice in terms of a 'concept of style'. Manning (1989) suggests that police culture is 'sort of' rule guided by referring to the directions of the police culture as 'rules of thumb'. What can be discerned from the literature is that discretion provides the context in which police culture can influence the use, manipulation and circumvention of the laws, policies and directives that are flexible, indeterminate or deemed situationally inappropriate for the exigencies of police work (Dixon 1997; Holdaway 1989; McBarnet 1981).

The rules that routinely structure the exercise of police discretion are what Smith and Gray (1985) termed 'working rules', which are those that officers develop through operational experience and internalise as commonsense ways of dealing with specific incidents. This idea is developed by Hoyle (1998) in her study of the police response to domestic violence, in which she illustrates how working rules are applied on the basis of 'working assumptions'. The officers she observed arrived at working assumptions by interpreting information provided in advance or gathered at the scene about the suspect, the victim and the occurrence; a process that was informed by their knowledge of laws, policies and procedures and shaped by their norms, values and beliefs. This clearly demonstrates that a combination of factors impact upon how and why police officers decide to act in any situation. Moreover, it indicates that it is possible to define new ways of working and then inculcate a new set of assumptions to create new working models.

Acculturation

Police officers are not institutionalised clones. Trainees and new recruits do not automatically assimilate the ways and means of police culture upon joining the police, nor do they passively and predictably acculturate as time progresses. They are a heterogeneous group of people who carry with them a history of learning and socialisation, of values, beliefs and personal ideologies that affect their interpretation of the police role and their adjustment to the demands of police work. It is, therefore, necessary to recognise the agency of officers in making up their own minds and structuring their understandings of the organisation and its environment. While there are common elements to the acculturation process, learning how to interact with members of the public, for instance, or how to 'back up' colleagues in dangerous situations, others are shaped by the importance of factors unique to the individual. Variables such as age, gender, ethnicity, education and level of police experience have an effect on how officers interpret, adopt and adapt police culture. Some wilfully embrace it without question, or perhaps succumb to peer-pressure and play along, whereas others, as Chan (1997, p. 73) found in her study of racism and reform in an Australian police organisation, play a more active role in 'developing, reinforcing, resisting or transforming cultural knowledge'. Reform initiatives should utilise the capacity of individuals to develop police culture and bring about transformation.

The social networks officers find themselves in play a significant part in their acculturation, cultural passage and policing style. Culture is learnt, expressed and sustained in the context of social interaction, the everyday conversations between officers about the job and how to do it, the imparted words of wisdom, the narratives recounting past events and the glorified folklore. In an insightful take on the subject, Shearing and Ericson (1991) argue that the police use stories as a way of communicating the craft of policing to others. For them, such stories 'capture the sedimented residue of generations of police experience and convey it in a form that police officers can capture and use to construct their actions on an ongoing basis' (pp. 491–2). Socialisation and storytelling are central to the identification and dissemination of 'best practice'. These aspects of police culture can also inhibit change unless new stories are told to unlearn the past and inform officers about the present and future of policing.

A key stage in the development, reinforcement and transformation of values, beliefs and underlying assumptions is when new recruits are socialised into occupational groups and taught the 'informal code' (Cain 1973, p. 198). This tends to be undertaken by more experienced group members. Innes (2003, p. 17), for example, notes that trainee and novice detectives customarily undergo some form of 'apprenticeship', which 'continues to be important in relaying and transferring the tacit and informal knowledge of detective work, of how to get the job done in "the real world", and the recipe knowledge, working rules, and attitudes that will facilitate this'. Supervisors and managers are particularly influential figures and have the capacity to establish professional boundaries within a group, acknowledge and encourage positive contributions, and challenge negative behaviours and attitudes. Sergeants, in particular, play a key role in this respect, as they interpret the operational meaning of official policies, are directly involved in delivering policing on the ground, and supervise what the rank-and-file do on a day-to-day basis.

The dominant culture

When describing police culture, researchers and commentators have tended to concentrate on commonalities and make generalisations in order to identify characteristics that unite police officers across jurisdictions and over time. Taken collectively, the 'core characteristics' revealed in a longstanding tradition of police research – sense of mission, action orientation, cynicism and pessimism, suspicion, isolation and solidarity, conservatism, machismo, racial prejudice, and pragmatism (Reiner 2010, pp. 118–32) – can be viewed as encapsulating the 'dominant' occupational culture of the police. The adjective dominant is used here not only to capture the powerful influence of this cultural core over police officers and the occupation of policing, but also to imply that it predominates over perceptions of police culture. Sklansky (2007) goes so far as to argue that preoccupation with the dominant culture has resulted in a sort of 'cognitive burn-in' that obscures variations in police culture and policing styles.

Knowledge and understanding about the dominant occupational culture of the police has its origins in the wave of ethnographic studies of routine patrol work that started to emerge from the 1960s (e.g. Banton 1964; Bittner 1967; Cain 1973; Holdaway 1983; Manning 1977; Punch 1979; Reiner 1978; Skolnick 1966; van Maanen 1978c; Westley 1970). In these early studies of the uniformed rank-and-file and those that followed in their wake the characteristics of police culture are portrayed as being rooted in the recurrent experiences, problems and tensions inherently associated with being in the office of constable. Skolnick (1966), for example, argues that the constant risk of danger that officers face, their designated authority and capacity to use force against citizens, and the pressure to perform their duties effectively and efficiently, generates a 'working personality' characterised by suspiciousness, internal solidarity, social isolation and conservatism. Van Maanen (1978c), to refer to another classic study, observed that police officers tend to view their occupational world as comprised exhaustively of three types of citizens: 'suspicious persons', 'assholes' and 'know nothings'. To understand this typology, he suggests, it is necessary to understand the conditions of policing for patrol officers. He also suggests that such types serve a purpose in guiding police action, establishing social distance between the police and their segmented audiences, helping police officers make sense of seemingly meaningless behaviour, and providing an expressive outlet for them to let off steam.

Given the nature of their work, officers typically view their job as a vocation and develop a heightened sense of mission. This can be expressed in a positive manner through dedication, professionalism and a genuine concern for victims of crime. It can also lead to an inflated sense of authority, an exaggerated impression of the police role in society, and an overemphasis on enforcing the law and bringing criminals to justice. The crime-fighting mentality of the police has actually found support in the Coalition Government's political rhetoric and reform agenda. Empirical accounts of 'what the police do', in contrast, have repeatedly demonstrated that officers spend most of their time maintaining order and resolving minor social conflict (Brodeur 2010; Reiner 2010). It could be argued, therefore, that the police are oriented towards the action, danger and excitement of crime fighting not because police work itself is principally so, but rather because police culture feeds off such activities to provide stimulation and reinforce an image of what 'real' policing is all about. A negative upshot of this is that what the police perceive as 'not real' police work is often consigned to an inferior position or even considered irrelevant. An underlying assumption is that citizens' requests for police service are not sufficient to merit their recognition as a priority. Loftus (2009, p. 92), for example, found that domestic violence incidents and neighbour disputes are routinely relegated to the lower end of officers' 'sense of crime hierarchy'. Research has also highlighted the tendency of the police to view partnership work as 'soft' policing and a low priority (McCarthy 2012).

Scholars have shown how solidarity provides the cultural foundation for the social identity of the police as they perform their duties and interact with other social groups (Crank 1998). The value placed on trust, loyalty, cooperation, reciprocity and peer approval also has a significant impact upon how different occupational groups relate to each other within organisational contexts. Most significantly, studies of police solidarity have drawn attention to the existence of an 'us-and-them' mentality and the so-called 'blue code of silence' (Westmarland 2005). An unwanted corollary of these aspects of police culture is a mistrust of the community. When combined with the expectation of effectiveness and efficiency, they also put tremendous pressure on individual officers to conform and overlook or even cover up unethical or corrupt behaviour. Chan *et al.* (2003), for example, in her study of new recruits, found that they were very quickly being socialised into a culture of not telling and internal resolution. It is generally assumed that whistleblowers will be stigmatised by their colleagues. Furthermore, officers appear to lack confidence in management and believe that their information will have no effect on either the organisation or the individual in question. Creating an environment in which officers are willing to challenge inappropriate attitudes and behaviours and report instances of misconduct is a significant obstacle to police reform.

Police organisations are often portrayed as worlds of masculine values and exploits, where female and homosexual officers are discriminated against and find it difficult to gain acceptance and recognition (Brown and Heidensohn 2000; Burke 1993; Westmarland 2001). Racial prejudice and discrimination within the police workforce has been verified by the findings of industrial tribunals, research studies and analyses of officers' experiences (Foster *et al.* 2005; Holdaway 2009). Stereotypes are commonly used to classify members of the public on the basis of their sex, sexuality, race or ethnic origin. Black people, for example, are thought to be more prone to violent crime and drug abuse, to be incomprehensible, suspicious, hard to handle, naturally excitable, aggressive, lacking brainpower, troublesome and 'tooled up' (Bowling *et al.* 2008). There is also a plentiful supply of evidence of prejudice and discrimination in police practice. The Macpherson Report (1999) found the over-representation of racial minorities in the national stop and search figures to be a clear case of racist stereotyping. This apparent intolerance of 'otherness' can be conceived as both a symptom and a cause of police culture. Burke (1993), for example, explains the deviant status and marginalisation of gay and bisexual male officers by suggesting that stereotypes of homosexuality do not sit well with the conservativism of the dominant culture. He also suggests that the stereotypical association of homosexuality with effeminacy and weakness challenges the old-fashioned machismo images of police work. Reiner (2010) similarly argues that racial prejudice is an important aspect of police conservativism and insularity that is accentuated with work experience. More importantly, he comes to the conclusion that police racial prejudice is, in part, 'a reflection of general societal prejudice', since police recruits 'share the values of the social groups from which they are drawn' (p. 130). In consequence, unless such cultural attitudes alter as a result of more profound societal transformations, reforms in recruitment, training programmes and sanctions against individual officers will not bring about fundamental change.

The dominant culture is said to exist because the police are constantly reinventing and reproducing it in response to the common problems that arise from their role and the constraints of legality and bureaucracy (Loftus 2009; Reiner 2010). Whatever their later specialisms and ranks, it is important to remember that all officers have similar beginnings and shared experiences, which enable them to relate to each other on one or more cultural levels. As has been discussed above, however, the existence of a dominant culture among the uniformed rank-and-file does not mean police culture is monolithic, universal or unchanging. It should not be assumed that the core characteristics are cultural constants, or that officers and occupational groups adopt them in equal measure. Loftus and Goold (2012, p. 285), for example, in their study of covert policing, argue that 'the occupational commonsense inherent to surveillance work reveals a distinctly erudite working culture which operates in isolation from the clichéd cultural expressions of uniformed police that have been the focus of much scholarship'. It should also be acknowledged that much of the fieldwork-based literature from which understandings of police culture are largely derived is perhaps now lacking in contemporary relevance, as it relates to past policing contexts and portrays a police service that no longer exists in exactly the same form or functions in exactly the same way.

Cultural change and changing police culture

Far from being static, the field of policing is actually in a state of constant change, not least because of the need to react to the often conflicting and arguably insatiable demands and expectations that have come to be attached to the police service (Loader and Mulcahy 2003). Reiner (1992) describes the police as like 'litmuspaper' reflecting the unfolding dynamics of society. They are, in other words, pushed and pulled by the shifting social, economic and political tides with and against which we all swim. Police culture is, hence, constantly evolving as officers adapt to accommodate new structures, experiences and ideologies.

The police have been the subject of such a sustained programme of reform that they are said to exist in a state of 'permanent revolution' (McLaughlin *et al.* 2001). Community policing philosophies and practices have now been adopted by nearly all police forces throughout the Western world (Fielding 1995); for example, concerns about the lack of confidence in the police have led to a drive to reassure the public through initiatives such as neighbourhood policing and police community support officers (PCSOs) (Duffy *et al.* 2008; Johnston 2007), and the shift towards a more pluralised approach to policing means that the police now find themselves with a mandate to work in partnership with a wide spectrum of groups and organisations (Crawford 2008). Another pivotal development in the post-Macpherson era has been the emergence of respect for diversity and the recognition of cultural and gendered identities. Constabularies have come to be staffed by notably more minority ethnic, female and homosexual officers (Loftus 2009). There has also been an increase in the number of mature and educated officers (Punch 2007).

Reforms are implemented, in large part, by the officers to whom they are addressed. More often than not, therefore, unless police reformers enlist the support of the lower ranks their efforts will not succeed in changing policing on the frontline. Police studies have repeatedly shown that the rank-and-file dislike, dismiss and deride certain organisational rules and procedures and engage in informal work practices in order to circumvent or subvert them. They are also known to be critical and cynical about some of the laws and policies they are expected to enforce, affirm and act in accordance with. This is particularly true for programmes invented by civilians.

Police officers are traditionally adverse towards the involvement of politicians, academics and community activists in defining their work or evaluating their performance (Skogan 2008). Managerial reforms can also lead 'street cops' to believe that 'management cops' are out of touch with the realities of operational police work and to question and oppose their agendas (Cockcroft and Beattie 2009). Criticisms of police attitudes and behaviours and attempts to correct them are often perceived as a direct threat to their integrity and authority, which, according to Crank (1998), reinforces rather than diminishes the pervasive influence of the occupational culture. The key point to be taken from the available evidence is that reforms have habitually failed to override police culture when they conflict with established values, beliefs and assumptions. Change is resisted when it challenges existing worldviews, when it requires officers to break from their established routines, and when it does not accord with their intuitive commonsense.

There is, however, ample evidence to support the claim that the reform initiatives and changing social conditions of recent decades have affected police culture. O'Neill and McCarthy (2012), for example, show that, in the context of neighbourhood policing, police work has been reframed as a diverse range of community problem-solving tasks. Once officers had experienced the pragmatic and beneficial elements of partnership work they generally embraced it and valued their relationships with colleagues in partner agencies. The research findings suggest that, rather than acting as a barrier to change, police culture actually facilitated the development of multi-agency policing and adapted by developing new formations and expressions. Indeed, it is a classical sociological tenet that the more a social group extends its relationships outside its specific enclave the more it tends to lose its distinctive identity and culture.

Loftus (2009), in her recent ethnographic study of police culture, describes a reduction in openly expressed prejudice and discrimination and compliance with aspects of diversity and domestic violence policies. Be that as it may, she questions the extent to which the dominant occupational culture has actually changed and persuasively argues that while 'there have been important breaks with the past, the manifest continuities with older patterns should not be overlooked' (p. 188). What her research documents is a police organisation in which many of the core characteristics persist and coexist with new ways of thinking about and doing police work. The crime-fighter mentality, defensive solidarity and masculine ethos found expression within a resentful posture of white, heterosexual, male officers who considered themselves as challenged, beleaguered and unrecognised. The hostile comments put forward by some such officers clearly indicate that exclusion and 'othering' has extended into the post-Macpherson era. Furthermore, Loftus also found strong evidence of 'class contempt' and argues that the official emphasis on respect for diversity has had 'the unfortunate effect of delivering up powerless white males as uncontentiously legitimate terrain for the unchallenged exercise of police discretion and authority' (p. 184). This trend is likely to have been exacerbated by the riots of 2011 and the criminalisation of the so-called 'feral underclass'.

In my ethnographic study of detectives, drug law enforcement and proactive investigation (Bacon, forthcoming), I focus on the development of intelligence-led policing, the implementation of the National Intelligence Model (NIM), and the rules governing covert policing practices since the enactment of the Regulation of Investigatory Powers Act (2000). The reforms have altered practice by limiting decision-making autonomy through the establishment of rigid organisational rules, procedures and disciplinary mechanisms. However, while the detectives accepted the need to play by, or pay lip service to, the rules, they were above all viewed as how policing *must* be done rather than how it *should* be done. Consequently, when the rules were not enforced, were seen as unenforceable or allowed for the exercise of discretion, the detectives – especially the older generation – expressed themselves and acted in ways that resonated with the traditional themes of their occupational culture. They disliked bureaucracy, believed that strict adherence to the rules had a negative impact on operational efficiency, and resented the loss or lack of control over the informers, intelligence and cases that were perceived as their territory.

What police scholarship tells us, then, is that changing police culture is difficult but not impossible. Importantly, it suggests that cultural change cannot be forced but will happen when the police are ready, either because of an external crisis or internal forces towards change (Schein 2004). Police officers must believe that there is a need to change, be convinced that the proposed policies of reform are both necessary and appropriate, and be properly motivated and equipped to introduce and maintain support for the changes in their everyday activities. The question of how to do this begins with chief officers understanding the nature of the occupational cultures in their organisation and the ways in which they can inhibit or facilitate change. Then they need to use a variety of strategies and tactics to deal with the negative aspects of the organisational culture or particular occupational cultures. Given that culture is learnt through on-the-job socialisation, policymakers can define new working models that will gradually alter values, beliefs and basic assumptions if they are of practical benefit and provide meaning to the social experience of police officers. As a general rule, however, this will occur only if new ways of working are considered to work better than existing practices and make more sense than traditional understandings.

If reform initiatives are to fundamentally change police practice it is essential that cultural images of police work represent reality not myth. The diversity of the police role should be enshrined in their philosophies and take centre-stage in their performances until it becomes taken for granted that policing is about so much more than fighting crime through the use of force. Reward systems should be changed to reflect 'good policing' rather than promote a 'results' ethos that leads to unnecessary pressure upon police officers to tick boxes. Training programmes should be reconfigured so that they are delivered in partnership with universities to expose officers to a broader spectrum of experience and education and help broaden their knowledge base and thereby change their attitudes.

One of the most frequently advocated models of reform involves the development of 'professionalism' in police work (Neyroud 2011). Professionalism, which emphasises expertise, integrity, accountability and the application of an established body of knowledge, can be viewed as offering an alternative set of norms, values and beliefs to those of the occupational culture. Genuinely transformative organisational change also needs to be reinforced by each occupational group and supported by appropriate leadership strategies. The notion of 'transformational' leadership has been forwarded as one such strategy (Cockcroft 2012, pp. 131–44). This approach involves workforce consultation about what constitutes good policing and how it might be measured. It also involves effective role modelling and mentoring. We know that sergeants' supervision of constables is particularly important and that their management by inspectors upwards needs to be reformed. No matter how refined polices aimed at reforming police culture might be, however, they will struggle to bring about fundamental change unless there is 'a reshaping of the basic character of the police role through wider social transformation of the structures of economic inequality and power' (Reiner 2010, p. 138).

Conclusion

Police culture is an incredibly useful conceptual, analytical and rhetorical device for understanding how police officers approach and do their job. Yet, despite its explanatory power, extensive usage and influence, the concept remains somewhat complicated, contested and at times contradictory. Nevertheless, if we do not understand the nature and influence of police culture we cannot hope to understand police practices or the realities of policing in society.

Every occupational experience, every law, policy and training session, every social event with actual or potential implications for the police, is viewed through their cultural lens and woven into the social processes that reinvent and reproduce police culture. In effect, it helps mend the occupation of policing, holds the police organisation together, and supports officers in the performance of their duties. At the same time, however, it is partly responsible for a range of deviant and discriminatory attitudes and behaviours and is capable of undermining efforts to reform policing and the police. Some aspects of police culture should thus be praised, encouraged and preserved. Others should be challenged and are long overdue for a change.

Recent developments in the social context of policing have presented the police with significant challenges and seem to be challenging traditional ideas about their role and what is expected of them. Many aspects of their world are being shaken up and will continue to undergo trials, tribulations and transformations for the foreseeable future. In times of change, an understanding of police culture is even more vital than usual, for there is a need to know how things are perceived and play out on the frontline if we are to see the direction in which they are going or could potentially go. The million-dollar question is how the culture of the police will evolve as officers react to the changing experiences, problems and tensions of their work.

References

Bacon, M. (forthcoming) *Taking Care of Business: Police Detectives, Drug Law Enforcement and Proactive Investigation*, Oxford: Oxford University Press.

Banton, M. (1964) *The Policeman in the Community*, London: Tavistock.

Bittner, E. (1967) 'The Police on Skid Row: A Study in Peacekeeping', *American Sociology Review*, 32.

Bowling, B., Parmar, A. and Phillips, C. (2008) 'Policing Minority Ethnic Communities', in Newburn, T. (ed.) *Handbook of Policing* (2nd edn.), Cullompton: Willan.

Brodeur, J.-P. (2010) *The Policing Web*, Oxford: Oxford University Press.

Brown, J. and Heidensohn, F. (2000) *Gender and Policing*, Basingstoke: Macmillan.

Burke, M. (1993) *Coming Out of the Blue*, London: Cassell.

Cain, M. (1973) *Society and the Policeman's Role*, London: Routledge and Kegan Paul.

Chan, J. (1996) 'Changing Police Culture', *British Journal of Criminology*, 36(1): 109–34.

Chan, J. (1997) *Changing Police Culture: Policing in a Multicultural Society*, Cambridge: Cambridge University Press.

Chan, J., Devery, C. and Doran, S. (2003) *Fair Cop: Learning the Art of Policing*, Toronto: University of Toronto Press.

Chatterton, M. (1983) 'Police Work and Assault Charges', in Punch, M. (ed.) *Control in the Police Organization*, Cambridge, MA: MIT Press.

Cockcroft, T. (2012) *Police Culture: Themes and Concepts*, London: Routledge.

Cockcroft, T. and Beattie, I. (2009) 'Shifting Cultures: Managerialism and the Rise of "Performance"', *Policing: An International Journal of Police Strategies and Management*, 32(3): 526–40.

Crank, J. (1998) *Understanding Police Culture*, Cincinnati, OH: Anderson.

Crawford, A. (2008) 'Plural Policing in the UK: Policing Beyond the Police', in Newburn, T. (ed.) *Handbook of Policing* (2nd edn.), Cullompton: Willan.

Dixon, D. (1997) *Law in Policing: Legal Regulation and Police Practices*, Oxford: Oxford University Press.

Duffy, B., Wake, R., Burrows, T. and Bremner, P. (2008) *Closing the Gap: Crime and Public Perceptions*, London: Ipsos MORI.

Fielding, N. (1988) *Joining Forces: Police Training, Socialisation and Occupational Competence*, London: Routledge.

Fielding, N. (1994) 'Cop Canteen Culture', in Newburn, T. and Stanko, E. (eds.), *Just Boys Doing Business: Men, Masculinity and Crime*, London: Routledge.

Fielding, N. (1995) *Community Policing*, Oxford: Clarendon Press.

Foster, J., Newburn, T. and Souhami, A. (2005) *Assessing the Impact of the Stephen Lawrence Enquiry*, London: Home Office.

Geertz, C. (1973) *The Interpretation of Cultures*, New York, NY: Basic Books.

Goodenough, W. (1976) 'Multiculturalism as the Normal Human Experience', *Anthropology and Education Quarterly*, 7(4): 4–7.

Hobbs, D. (1988) *Doing the Business: Entrepreneurship, the Working Class and Detectives in the East End of London*, Oxford: Oxford University Press.

Hobbs, D. (1991) 'A Piece of Business: The Moral Economy of Detective Work in the East End of London', *British Journal of Sociology*, 41(4): 597–608.

Holdaway, S. (1983) *Inside the British Police*, Oxford: Basil Blackwell.

Holdaway, S. (1989) 'Discovering Structure: Studies of the British Police Occupational Culture', in Weatheritt, M. (ed.) *Police Research: Some Future Prospects*, Aldershot: Avebury.

Holdaway, S. (2009) *Black Police Associations: An Analysis of Race and Ethnicity within Constabularies*, Oxford: Oxford University Press.

Hood, C. (1991) 'A Public Management for All Seasons?', *Public Administration*, 69: 3–19.

Hoyle, C. (1998) *Negotiating Domestic Violence: Police, Criminal Justice and Victims*, Oxford: Oxford University Press.

Innes, M. (2003) *Investigating Murder: Detective Work and the Police Response to Criminal Homicide*, Oxford: Oxford University Press.

Jermier, J., Slocum, J., Fry, L. and Gaines, J. (1991) 'Organizational Subcultures in a Soft Bureaucracy: Resistance Behind the Myth and Façade of an Official Culture', *Organizational Science*, 2: 170–94.

Johnston, L. (2007) '"Keeping the Family Together": Police Community Support Officers and the "Police Extended Family" in London', *Policing and Society*, 17(2): 119–40.

Loader, I. and Mulcahy, A. (2003) *Policing and the Condition of England*, Oxford: Oxford University Press.

Loftus, B. (2009) *Policing Culture in a Changing World*, Oxford: Oxford University Press.

Loftus, B. and Goold, B. (2012) 'Covert Surveillance and the Invisibilities of Policing', *Criminology and Criminal Justice*, 12(3): 275–88.

Macpherson, W. (1999) *The Stephen Laurence Inquiry*, London: HMSO.

Manning, P. (1977) *Police Work: The Social Organization of Policing*, Cambridge, MA: MIT Press.

Manning, P. (1989) 'Occupational Culture', in Bailey, W. (ed.) *The Encyclopaedia of Police Science*, New York and London: Garland.

Manning, P. (2007) 'A Dialectic of Organisational and Occupational Culture', in O'Neill, M., Marks, M. and Singh, A. (eds.) *Police Occupational Culture: New Debates and Directions*, Amsterdam, the Netherlands: Elsevier.

McBarnet, D. (1981) *Conviction: Law, the State and the Construction of Justice*, London: Macmillan.

McCarthy, D. (2012) 'Gendering "Soft" Policing: Multi-Agency Working, Female Cops, and the Fluidities of Police Culture/s', *Policing and Society*, iFirst article: 1–18.

McLaughlin, E., Muncie, J. and Hughes, G. (2001) 'The Permanent Revolution: New Labour, New Public Management and the Modernisation of Criminal Justice', *Criminology and Criminal Justice*, 1(3): 301–18.

Neyroud, P. (2011) *Review of Police Leadership and Training*, London: Home Office.

O'Neill, M. and McCarthy, D. (2012) '(Re) Negotiating Police Culture through Partnership Working: Trust, Compromise and the "New" Pragmatism', *Criminology and Criminal Justice* (in press).

Paoline, E. (2003) 'Taking Stock: Towards a Richer Understanding of Police Culture', *Journal of Criminal Justice*, 31(3): 199–214.

Punch, M. (1979) *Policing the Inner City: A Study of Amsterdam's Warmoesstraat*, London: Macmillan.

Punch, M. (2007) 'Cops with Honours: University Education and Police Culture', in O'Neill, M., Marks, M. and Singh, A. (eds.) *Police Occupational Culture: New Debates and Directions*, Amsterdam, the Netherlands: Elsevier.

Reiner, R. (1978) *The Blue-Coated Worker*, Cambridge: Cambridge University Press.

Reiner, R. (1992) 'Policing a Postmodern Society', *Modern Law Review*, 55(6): 761–81.

Reiner, R. (2010) *The Politics of the Police* (4th edn.), Oxford: Oxford University Press.

Reuss-Ianni, E. (1983) *Two Cultures of Policing: Street Cops and Management Cops*, New Brunswick: Transaction Books.

Sackmann, S. (1997) *Cultural Complexity in Organizations: Inherent Contrasts and Contradictions*, Thousand Oaks, CA: Sage.

Schein, E. (2004) *Organizational Culture and Leadership* (3rd edn.), San Francisco, CA: Jossey-Bass.

Shearing, C. and Ericson, R. (1991) 'Culture as Figurative Action', *British Journal of Sociology*, 42(4): 481–506.

Sklansky, D. (2007) 'Seeing Blue: Police Reform, Occupational Culture, and Cognitive Burn-In', in O'Neill, M., Marks, M. and Singh, A. (eds.) *Police Occupational Culture: New Debates and Directions*, Amsterdam, the Netherlands: Elsevier.

Skogan, W. (2008) 'Why Reforms Fail', *Policing and Society*, 18(1): 23–34.

Skolnick, J. (1966) *Justice Without Trial: Law Enforcement in Democratic Society*, New York: Macmillan.

Skolnick, J. (2008) 'Enduring Issues of Police Culture and Demographics', *Policing and Society*, 18(1): 35–45.

Smith, D. and Gray, J. (1985) *Police and People in London: The PSI Report*, London: Policy Studies Institute.

Tylor, E. (1871) *Primitive Culture*, New York, NY.

van Maanen, J. (1978a) 'Observations of the Making of Policemen', in Manning, P. and van Maanen, J. (eds.) *Policing: A View from the Street*, Santa Monica, CA: Goodyear.

van Maanen, J. (1978b) 'Kinsmen in Repose: Occupational Perspectives of Patrolmen', in Manning, P. and van Maanen, J. (eds.) *Policing: A View from the Street*, Santa Monica, CA: Goodyear.

van Maanen, J. (1978c) 'The Asshole', in Manning, P. and van Maanen, J. (eds.) *Policing: A View from the Street*, Santa Monica, CA: Goodyear.

Waddington, P. (1994) *Liberty and Order: Public Order Policing in a Capital City*, London: UCL Press.

Waddington, P. (1999a) 'Police (Canteen) Sub-culture: An Appreciation', *British Journal of Criminology*, 39(2): 287–309.

Waddington, P. (1999b) *Policing Citizens: Authority and Rights*, London: UCL Press.

Weick, K. (2001) *Making Sense of the Organization*, Malden, MA: Blackwell.

Westley, W. (1970) *Violence and the Police: A Sociological Study of Law, Custom and Morality*, Cambridge, MA: MIT Press.

Westmarland, L. (2001) *Gender and Policing: Sex, Power and Police Culture*, Cullompton: Willan.

Westmarland, L. (2005) 'Police Ethics and Integrity: Breaking the Blue Code of Silence', *Policing and Society*, 15(2): 145–65.

Young, M. (1993) *In the Sticks: Cultural Identity in a Rural Police Force*, Oxford: Oxford University Press.

8

RACE AND POLICING

Michael Rowe

Introduction

Strained relations between various Black and Minority Ethnic (BME) communities and the police in England and Wales have formed an enduring and complex narrative for many decades. Although it is widely understood that poor relationships between sections of the black community and police have recurred since the mid-1970s, studies have suggested that elements of these problems were apparent even longer ago than that (see Whitfield, 2004). Across much of the twentieth century there is evidence that police officers have harassed BME communities and failed to provide a robust response to racist violence. It continues to be the case that BME communities are broadly under-represented among police staff and that this under-representation is more pronounced among higher than lower ranks.

Issues relating to race and racism have underpinned some of the most significant crises that contemporary police services have faced, including the failed investigation of the murder of Stephen Lawrence in 1993 and many instances of serious urban disorder. In his enquiry into the Brixton disorders of 1981, Lord Scarman (1981) described the history of police relations with minority ethnic communities as a 'tale of failure'. More than 30 years later, as is outlined further below, it is clear that additional unhappy chapters have been added and that significant concerns mean that police relations with BME communities continue to pose major questions for the future of policing in England and Wales.

Although there continue to be concerns about the impact of many aspects of policing on BME communities, it is also clear that over the last fifteen years or so there have been intensive efforts to address many of the problems that developed over preceding decades. Some of the initiatives that have been instigated in terms of stop and search, recruitment and retention, and responses to racist hate crime are outlined in the discussion that follows. It is apparent that the persistence of troubled police relations with BME communities does not reflect a lack of institutional innovation or indifference towards reform. As is also shown in the discussion below, while some problems endure, other aspects of police relations with some BME groups seem to have improved. The discussion below reviews current prospects for police relations with BME communities in regard to stop and search, workforce diversity, and responding to racist hate crime. In terms of each aspect, key challenges and opportunities that arise from current debates about police reform are considered. In conclusion it is argued that ethical and moral imperatives to address problems of racism offer important dividends in terms of police legitimacy and operational performance. Following Bowling's (2007) discussion, it is argued that the development of policing that is perceived to be 'fair' ought not to be regarded as being in tension with the pursuit of effectiveness. Rather, it is argued, the promotion of ethical policing that is 'racially just' is central to current discourses of police professionalism and underpins effectiveness in operational terms.

Stop and search

The over-representation of many BME communities in stop and search practices has been apparent in ethnic monitoring data that has been compiled since the early 1990s. The over-policing of black, and more recently Asian, communities – especially young males – in terms of their experience of stop and search is stark. In relation to searches conducted under the 1984 Police and Criminal Evidence Act (PACE), the largest category, Ministry of Justice data shows 17.9 in 1,000 white people were stopped and searched in England and Wales in 2009/10. For black people the rate was seven times higher (125.7 per 1000). The discrepancy between white and Asian people was less marked but the latter still experienced a rate more than double that of the former: 40.2 per 1,000 population. Interpreting this and similar data is made more difficult for a number of reasons – including concerns about the viability of ethnic classifications and the validity of using resident population statistics as a benchmark (Rowe, 2012). Despite these methodological concerns and the challenge of explaining disproportionality there can be little doubt that many BME communities are stopped and searched more frequently than other groups and that these disparities are widely cited as a major source of tension between BME (and other) groups and the police.

Stop and search was a key aspect of police discrimination and disrespect cited as a major cause of the 2011 riots (*Guardian*/LSE, 2011; Riots Communities and Victims Panel, 2012). In 2010 the Equalities and Human Rights Commission (EHRC) reported that disparities in the use of stop and search powers against different ethnic groups were rooted in police policies and practices that could not be justified in terms of offending rates or demographic trends. The Commission (EHRC, 2010) threatened to issue enforcement notices against police forces that continued to exhibit high levels of disproportionality against black and Asian people and, in 2011, agreed a programme of measures with two police services (Leicestershire and Thames Valley) designed to remedy identified problems.

Concerns about the over-representation of BME groups in stop and search have generally been expressed in terms of police powers under PACE but extend to more recent anti-terrorism and public order legislation. Section 44 of the 2002 Terrorism Act (TA) gave police power, in defined localities, to stop and search vehicles, people in vehicles and pedestrians for articles that could be used for terrorism 'whether or not there are grounds for suspecting that such articles are present'. In this way the Act moved beyond PACE provisions that require officers have 'reasonable grounds' relating to individuals who are stopped and searched. In the last quarter of 2010, 19.7 per cent of those stopped and searched under s44 powers were Asian (Home Office, 2010: 17). Similarly, the provisions of section 60 of the 1994 Criminal Justice and Public Order Act give officers the power to stop and search any individual in a designated area regardless of whether there is reasonable suspicion that they have committed or intend to commit an offence. Politicians, police and other commentators have sometimes maintained that Asian people, likely to be identified as synonymous with Muslims, can expect to be stopped and searched more frequently and that security demands prevail over civil rights concerns (as though the two are mutually exclusive). Controversies arising from analysis of the use of these powers include that they have little impact in terms of preventing or detecting terrorism, that they are used too broadly to stop and search people where there is no credible relation to terrorist action, and, coupled with these problems, that their disproportionate use against minorities might serve to undermine community relations and so prove counter-productive. The limitations and negative repercussions of the use of these powers have been identified by campaign groups, such as StopWatch, and by the Independent Reviewer of Terrorism Legislation (2012).

Concerns about the effectiveness of s44 TA powers and the prospect that the disproportionate impact on Asian people might fuel radicalisation, coupled with legal rulings about their incompatibility with Article 8 of the European Convention on Human Rights, led the Home Secretary to suspend these powers in July 2010. The 2012 Protection of Freedom Act removed the s44 powers and provided for more subscribed use of stop and search, although officers continue not to need 'reasonable suspicion' in relation to individual stops. The 2012 Act curtails stop and search powers by requiring authorisation from an ACPO-level officer, by requiring that the geographical remit of the powers be closely defined, and through specifying that the powers normally should only endure for 48 hours. For these reasons it might be expected that the new provisions will result in fewer such stop and searches, but the new requirements do not contain measures that will necessarily reduce disproportionality. Fewer people may be unnecessarily stopped and searched but a higher rate for some BME groups may persist.

Criticisms of police stop and search stem in part from the very small number of arrests that result from these practices. In the last quarter of 2010 the 17,926 s.44 stop and searches conducted yielded only 54 arrests, and many of those were for offences unrelated to terrorism. Similarly, less than 10 per cent of PACE stop and searches led to an arrest in 2008/09. Neither of these legal provisions to stop and search has been effective in terms of detecting crime. While other potential benefits, relating to deterrence or intelligence-gathering, might be identified these practices are beyond the legal basis of police stop and search powers that are clearly grounded in crime detection and investigation and not these other outcomes. Moreover, as Bowling and Weber (2011) have argued, there is no reliable evidence that stop and search has a deterrent effect, either in terms of individual or aggregate patterns of offending.

The small proportion of stop and searches that result in arrest suggest that these police powers offer little in terms of crime investigation and detection. In relation to BME communities more specifically these concerns are heightened in the light of evidence that suggests that higher levels of disproportionality are associated with lower levels of sanctioned detection and arrest. Bradford's (2012) analysis of stop and search data across police force areas in England and Wales between 2002/03 and 2009/10 found that those areas that had higher ratios of disproportionality between black and white and Asian and white populations tended to have lower levels of sanctioned detection and arrest. Figure 8.1 shows that police force areas (each dot on the graph represents the data for one police force area in one particular year) that had high levels of black/white disproportionality in stop and search had a lower success rate in terms of arrests resulting from stop and search.

A similar trend emerges in relation to Asian disproportionality and arrest rates from stop and search. In respect of the broader category of 'sanctioned detections' (i.e. resulting in a charge, a caution, a fixed penalty for disorder, a summons, or when an offence is taken into consideration at the sentencing stage), Bradford's (2012) analysis also suggests an inverse relationship with disproportionality. Figure 8.2 shows that the proportion of stop and searches resulting in a sanctioned detection fell as the disproportionality ratio between Asian and white people increased.

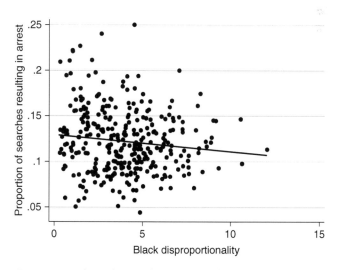

FIGURE 8.1   Proportion of searches resulting in arrest by black/white disproportionality, by police force area, 2002/3 to 2009/10

Source: Bradford (2012)

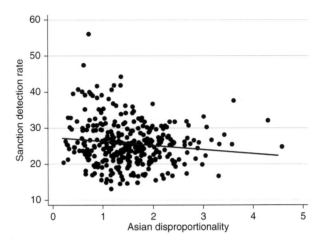

FIGURE 8.2   Proportion of searches resulting in sanctioned detection by Asian/white disproportionality, by police force area, 2002/3 to 2009/10

Source: Bradford (2012)

Again, the data relate to all police force areas for the stop and searches between 2002/3 and 2009/10.

Figures 8.1 and 8.2 suggest that higher levels of disproportionality are associated with a lower 'return' in terms of the crime detection impact of stop and search. Bradford's (2012) analysis suggests further cause for concern in relation to the negative consequences of disproportionate stop and search in respect of complaints made against the police. Figure 8.3 indicates that the number of allegations

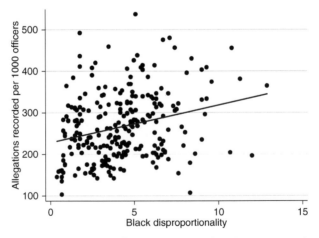

FIGURE 8.3   Allegations per 1,000 officers and black/white disproportionality, by police force area, 2002/3 to 2009/10

Source: Bradford (2012)

recorded per 1,000 officers was higher in police force areas that had higher levels of black/white disproportionality, a similar trend was found in relation to Asian/white disproportionality.

The disproportionate impact of police stop and search on BME communities is clearly evident in terms of practices undertaken in relation to the various legal provisions outlined in the discussion above. The consequences of this over-representation have been widely noted in terms of the legitimacy of the police and the deleterious effect on relations between police and the community. These data demonstrate that disproportionality is also related to ineffective police performance in terms of the core mandate of crime detection and investigation. It was perhaps for a combination of these reasons that the Home Secretary announced, in June 2013, a fundamental review of police stop and search powers. That issues relating to the policing of BME communities can be considered in relation to operational performance, as well as being matters of significant ethical and moral concern, is returned to in the discussion at the end of this chapter.

Challenges and opportunities

The contemporary context of police reform and restructuring suggests that reducing problems of disproportionality in police stop and search practices is likely to face considerable challenges. To some extent these stem from developments external to police services. The continuing economic recession will mean that many groups already at the social and economic periphery are likely to experience yet further marginalisation and this might meant that they are more likely to become 'available' to police stop and search practices. Unemployment, the withdrawal of Educational Maintenance Allowances, and the closure of public sector facilities will mean that young people (not just those from BME communities) living in poverty might be more likely to congregate in public spaces that are subject to higher levels of police stop and search. Consolidating these risks is the prospect that Police and Crime Commissioners might pursue 'tough' law and order approaches that combine with racialised media representation of crime problems in ways that also serve to further identify young BME people as a legitimate focus of police attention. National and local political efforts to centre policing around crime control – 'releasing the police's inner crime-fighter', as Loader argues in this volume – are likely to chime with those aspects of police policy and occupational culture that focus on controlling problematic populations on the street. For this related set of reasons there are grounds for concern that historical disproportionalities are set to continue.

Conversely other aspects of current attempts to reconfigure policing might provide grounds for optimism. As has been demonstrated, established policies, patterns and practices of stop and search provide a poor return in terms of criminal justice outcomes. Moreover, they have been widely identified as having significant negative repercussions in terms of allegations against police and reduced legitimacy. If ongoing financial pressures provide impetus to identify aspects of police work that could be relinquished, then stop and search practices seem likely to prove a fruitful focus of attention. Coupled with this is the demand to develop police professionalism. While professionalism remains a contested concept – as several contributions to this collection demonstrate – there is a broad agreement that it entails officers acting as reflexive practitioners who operate on the basis of evidence. Again, this ought to mean that the conduct of stop and search powers becomes subject to greater critical scrutiny such that disproportionalities are reduced.

Recruitment and retention

Perhaps to a greater extent than many other public bodies, the police service has experienced sustained pressure to recruit a workforce that reflects the profile of the general population. This might be due to the relatively high visibility of the police and their pivotal role as gatekeepers to the criminal justice system and that, individually and collectively, police exercise discretionary powers over fellow citizens that are particularly stark. A litany of enquiries, reports and policy statements has developed over recent decades to recommend that police services must increase the number of minority ethnic officers. The 1999 Macpherson Report, following the public enquiry into the racist murder of Stephen Lawrence in London in 1993, included three recommendations relating to the recruitment and retention of minority ethnic police officers (Macpherson, 1999). That report led to the establishment of detailed targets for each police service, based on the proportion of the local population in each service area that was of a minority ethnic background, and so established a specific framework of action not always stipulated by other analysts. However, the need to develop more effective recruitment had been iterated many times. In the mid-1990s two reports, one produced by the Commission for Racial Equality (CRE, 1996) and one by Her Majesty's Inspectorate of Constabulary (HMIC, 1996), urged that steps be taken to ensure that the ethnic diversity of British society was more closely reflected within the police service. Both of these studies noted that demands to improve equal opportunities had been made in earlier documents. The CRE report, for example, pointed out that a 1990 policy document issued by the Association of Chief Police Officers (ACPO) *Setting the Standards for Policing: Meeting Community Expectations* had argued 'forces should strive to improve equal opportunities within the organisation'. It also referred to a 1992 HMIC report, *Equal Opportunities in the Police Service*, and one from the late 1980s, *Employment in Police Forces: a Survey of Equal Opportunities*. Additionally the CRE report noted that the 1981 Scarman Inquiry had emphasised that (Scarman, 1981: 5.12):

> A police force which fails to reflect the ethnic diversity of our society will never succeed in securing the full support of all its sections.

Turning to the Scarman Report itself, it too noted that the under-representation of black and Asian people within the police had been a fairly long-standing matter of concern and that various attempts to rectify the problem had been made since the mid-1970s. Scarman (1981: 5.6) pointed out that while the service had made efforts to recruit minority officers, there was clearly some reluctance among the black community to seek careers within the police service. More recently a study by Stone and Tuffin (2000) found that a perception that police work is a low-status occupation deterred some BME communities from pursuing a police career. The apparent intractability of the issue is worth noting at this stage. Report-upon-report, and those mentioned above are but a few of the total, have apparently expressed concern and dismay at the situation, suggested broadly similar solutions, and then joined the litany of documents to be cited in subsequent investigations. It is not being suggested that the police service has done nothing to address the problems so frequently identified. However, despite decades of recruitment drives and associated activity, the number of minority ethnic police officers remains low, as Table 8.1 indicates. The 2011 figure of 4.9 per cent of officers being of a minority ethnic group represents a significant increase from a decade earlier – in 2001, 2.9 per cent of police officers were of a minority ethnic background. While this rise is welcome, progress has been at a slow pace. If that trajectory continues then it might take another decade for the proportion of police of a BME background to match that of the overall population aged 10 and over, of which 10.6 per cent was BME according to the Office of National Statistics data (MoJ, 2011: 8).

Moreover, as Table 8.1 also indicates, minorities are further under-represented amid the higher ranks of the police service.

It might be that future representation of minorities becomes more aligned to that of the general population as a higher proportion of new entrants to the police service are of a minority ethnic background compared to the overall profile of the 43 English and Welsh forces. Of 'joiners' to the service in 2010/11, 7.5 per cent were of a minority ethnic group, a higher rate than across the service as a whole (5.9 per cent) (Ministry of Justice, 2011). Only 3.1 per cent of leavers were of a minority background. The nature of police careers and the structure of the promotion system clearly mean that officer progress up the rank hierarchy develops over time, which might mean that relatively recent increases in recruitment have yet to lead to improved representation in middle and senior positions.

TABLE 8.1 Percentage ethnicity of police officer strength (full time equivalent), by rank, 31 March 2011

Grade	White	Mixed	Asian	Black	Chinese/Other	Not Stated	Total
ACPO	95.8	0.0	0.9	0.0	0.0	3.3	100
Chief Inspector	95.4	1.1	1.4	0.8	0.2	1.0	100
Chief Superintendent	96.7	0.7	1.7	0.7	0.0	0.2	100
Superintendent	96.2	1.4	1.1	0.8	0.2	0.3	100
Inspector	95.8	0.9	1.3	0.6	0.3	1.0	100
Sergeant	95.4	0.9	1.3	0.9	0.4	1.2	100
Constable	93.6	1.4	2.0	1.1	0.6	1.2	100
Total	94.1	1.3	1.9	1.0	0.5	1.2	100

Source: Ministry of Justice (2011)

As was argued in relation to patterns of stop and search practice, the position and representation of BME staff within the police service is significant in legal terms, for reasons of legitimacy, and in respect of police operational performance. Clearly, in 2000, the Race Relations (Amendment) Act added impetus since the police service is subject to the same legal requirement to promote 'racial equality' and tackle discrimination that extends to the public sector more widely. Unlike some previous pieces of equalities legislation, this Act did not exempt the police service. In terms of legitimacy, as the discussion above indicates, the establishment of an ethnically diverse police service has been regarded as a key priority. The extent to which such claims are supported by clear evidence is unclear, however. While it is axiomatic that public services that are seen to exclude minorities might be regarded as less legitimate than those that perform better in terms of diversity, it does not necessarily follow that an improved pattern of representation yields improvements in terms of public trust and confidence. There are a number of reasons for caution. First, the performance of police services might be regarded as more significant than the profile of the staff that deliver them. Second, the ethnic identity of police staff might be less important in terms of relations with the public than their professional identity as police officers. Related to this is a third concern that a focus on the ethnicity of officers ignores inter-sectionality such that other dimensions of multiple identities, including age, gender, class, status and religion, also shape police–public relations. For these and other reasons it might be that the operational benefits of recruiting a more ethnically diverse police force are limited, although still necessary for other reasons. Policies to improve the recruitment, retention and promotion of minority staff might be considered as necessary but insufficient conditions to bring about change.

Challenges and opportunities

The most significant challenge in relation to recruiting a more ethnically diverse police service relates to the reductions in expenditure and decline in officer numbers that will continue at least until 2015. An HMIC (2011) review of police force expenditure plans estimated a reduction in police officers, Police Community Support Officers and police staff of 34,100 over the period March 2010 to March 2015. This will mean that by 2014/15 police officer numbers will be back to the position of 2001/02 and the total workforce will return to the level of 2003/04. The impact of this reduction on the ethnic profile of the police workforce is difficult to predict but it seems unlikely that the overall number of BME officers and staff will increase against a wider background of a decline in police force strength.

However, wider proposals relating to leadership, training and professionalism suggest that some progress might be possible. Changes to recruitment and training proposed in the Neyroud Report (2011) are likely to prove significant. Proposals for a Police Initial Qualification to be delivered through greater involvement of the FE and HE sector, coupled with the broader promotion of professionalism, might address negative perceptions of the occupational status of policework that have been identified as barriers to recruitment among some BME communities (Stone and

Tuffin, 2000). While Winsor's (2012) recommendations relating to fast-track promotion and the direct entry of external staff into leadership roles are controversial, they do suggest one means for better BME representation among higher ranks.

Policing racist hate crime

In contrast to debates about stop and search, discussion of the policing of racist hate crime has focused on under- rather than over-policing. Much of the research evidence has shown that police services have tended not to provide a professional response to victims of racist hate crime (Bowling, 1998; Solomos, 1988; Hall, 2005). A combination of factors explains this failure. Key among these has been a tendency for officers not to recognise that the racist component of an incident can qualitatively alter the nature of victimisation such that an otherwise minor incident of criminal damage, for example, has a much more significant negative impact than a non-aggravated offence. As in other areas, the Macpherson Report (1999: 313) gave official endorsement to claims widely articulated by campaign groups and academic commentators for several decades when it noted:

> [Minority ethnic communities'] collective experience was of senior officers adopting fine policies and using fine words, but of indifference on the ground at junior officer level. The actions or inactions of officers in relation to racist incidents were clearly a most potent factor in damaging public confidence in the Police Service.

Crucially, the Macpherson Report provided, and police services quickly adopted, a definition of a racist incident that was based upon a prima facie model that has been applied more widely to crime recording. The Macpherson Report definition that any incident be treated as a 'racist incident' if the victim, a witness, the officer or any other party identifies it as such, has underpinned a range of complementary initiatives to improve the response to racist crime. Alongside extensive training programmes, for example, have been changes to recording practices such that racist incidents are 'flagged' so that patterns and potential 'hot spots' can be identified, and the progress of investigation more easily monitored (Rowe, 2004). Crucial to improving the police response to hate crime has been the identification of operational and managerial tasks that produce better outcomes. Embedding general imperatives to provide a more professional service to victims into routine activities of police investigation has proven a relatively effective approach. Along similar lines, Hall (2011) argued that measures to improve the policing of hate crimes in the London Metropolitan Police Service were successful relative to responses developed in the New York Police Department because they were aimed at 'administrative' tasks that officers were required to complete. This aspect of improving police relations with BME groups has been rooted in improvements to core police business of investigating offences and assisting victims. Ministry of Justice (2010) data show that the clear-up rate for all racially or religiously aggravated offences was higher than for non-aggravated offences (at 41 per cent compared to 28 per cent in 2008/09). However, for the largest category of racially or religiously aggravated offences – incidents of harassment – the clear-up rate was lower than that for non-aggravated offences, at 43 per cent compared to 63 per cent. Included in the clear-up rates for racially and religiously aggravated offences were the 11,228 persons cautioned or proceeded against in court in 2008, a slight decrease on the 2007 figure of 11,465 (Ministry of Justice, 2010).

The operational imperative to tackle racist hate crime offenders is given further impetus by research findings that demonstrate that perpetrators of such incidents tend to commit other violent crimes and engage in anti-social behaviour more generally (Sibbitt, 1997). Ray *et al.*'s (2004: 351) study of racist offenders in Greater Manchester found that they were 'very rarely specialists in racist violence' but had a wider repertoire of offending such that the effective investigation of racist incidents might offer positive externalities in terms of responding to crime more generally:

> Apart from a handful who claimed (we were not always able to check) that the offence in question was their first, all – including the small minority who offered some kind of political justification of racist violence – had convictions for other offences, usually theft, burglary, drug dealing and assault. It was clear that, for many, violence was a routine resource for solving problems and dealing with conflicts.

Challenges and opportunities

Although it remains unclear how reductions in police officer numbers will impact operationally, there might be a risk that training in the investigation of hate crimes and the specialist roles and support staff will be reduced in response to budget cuts. The negative impact of any depletion in police capacity will be compounded by cuts to third party and public sector agencies that have provided important means by which the reporting and recording of racist hate crime has been increased (Chakraborti and Garland, 2009).

Efforts to promote police professionalism might offer signficiant opportunities to improve effectiveness in terms of the response to racist hate crime. As noted, better detection and investigation of racist hate crime perpetrators will also yield operational benefits in terms of other forms of offending. An important aspect of racist hate crime is the broader impact such offences have in terms of victimisation. While providing a quality response to immediate victims is clearly a signficant aspect of professionalism in relation to any offence, in the context of hate crimes – intended to challenge the status of entire communities – this professional imperative becomes magnified.

Embedding diversity in professional policing

The police service has much to gain in operational terms from tackling over-representation of BME communities in stop and search, the under-representation of minorities from the police workforce, and from providing a more effective response to racist hate crime. Considerable police resources are expended on stop and search with very little return in terms of arrests or sanctioned detections. There is little evidence that other benefits – perhaps in terms of deterrence or intelligence-gathering – accrue, and it is widely perceived that stop and search has a deleterious effect on police–public relations (Bowling and Weber, 2011). The over-representation of minorities in stop and search is stark and has been sustained for many years, and the associated sense of injustice has been cited as a significant factor in relation to numerous incidents of public disorder and other crime problems. Research evidence suggests that perceptions that police fail to act in ways that are procedurally just are associated with distrust and lack of confidence in the police service and the rule of law more generally (Tyler, 2007; Hough *et al.*, 2010). The need to address disproportionality can and should be expressed in terms of legal, moral and ethical imperatives that public services deliver their roles fairly, impartially and without discrimination. Clearly these factors provide compelling reasons to address some of the problems outlined in this chapter. Developing the professional status of policing entails ensuring that activities such as stop and search are discharged ethically and with legitimacy. Moreover, though, an emphasis on evidence-based policing requires that officers operate as reflexive practitioners and discontinue aspects of police work predominantly based upon traditional custom and practice.

The promotion of professional policing also has implications for the development of workforce diversity. The need to recruit, retain and promote the most talented personnel makes it imperative that discrimination is tackled and provides a strong impetus to proactively target under-represented groups. Neyroud (2011) argued that demonstrating ethical behaviour and integrity are key elements of successful leadership and a commitment to tackling workplace discrimination is clearly important in terms of this aspect of police professionalism. Moreover, developing the professional status of policing, including a commitment to tertiary sector education and training, might also pay dividends in terms of recruiting from sections of the community that have not tended to regard policing as an attractive career.

Delivering a quality service to crime victims is clearly integral to professionalism and the aggravated impact of hate crime, including the broader victimisation of wider communities, means that responding to racist crime is particularly significant. In terms of delivering on a core police mandate of crime prevention and detection then research evidence pointing to the wider offending behaviour of perpetrators of racist hate crime suggests that there are solid operational reasons why improving the police response to such offenders ought to be prioritised.

For these reasons, addressing the 'tale of failure' of police relations with BME groups needs to be prioritised. In the past the case for doing so has often been couched in moral terms relating to police legitimacy and the principle of policing by consent. These continue to provide a valid rationale and demonstrate that many of the problems reviewed only briefly in this chapter are closely aligned to wider questions of police governance and accountability. The need to tackle disproportionality can also be expressed in terms of improving police performance, delivering services more effectively and efficiently, and enhancing the professional status of policing. Approached along these lines the promotion of equitable, just and non-discriminatory practice might be more effective if firmly embedded in the operational delivery of professional policing.

References

Bowling, B. (1998) *Violent Racism: Victimisation, Policing and Social Context*, Oxford: Oxford University Press.

Bowling, B. (2007) 'Fair and Effective Policing Methods: Towards "Good Enough" Policing', *Journal of Scandinavian Studies in Criminology and Crime Prevention*, 8(1): 17–32.

Bowling, B. and Weber, L. (2011) 'Stop and Search in Global Context: An Overview', *Policing and Society*, 21(4): 480–488.

Bradford, B. (2012) 'Effectiveness of Stop and Search', paper presented to *Effectiveness of Stop and Search and Alternative Policing Approaches* seminar, StopWatch/King's College: London, 3 September.

Chakraborti, N. and Garland, J. (2009) *Hate Crime: Impact, Causes, and Consequences*, London: Sage.

Commission for Racial Equality (1996) *Race and Equal Opportunities in the Police Service: A Programme for Action*, London: CRE.

Equalities and Human Rights Commission (2010) *Stop and Think: A Critical Review of the Use of Stop and Search Powers in England and Wales*, London: EHRC.

Guardian/LSE (2011) *Reading the Riots: Investigating England's Summer of Disorder*, London: Guardian.

Hall, N. (2005) *Hate Crime*, Cullompton: Willan Publishing.

Hall, N. (2011) 'Policing Hate Crime in London and New York City: Some Reflections on the Factors Influencing Effective Law Enforcement, Service Provision and Public Trust and Confidence', *International Review of Victimology*, 18(1): 73–87.

Her Majesty's Inspectorate of Constabulary (1996) *Developing Diversity in the Police Service*, London: Home Office.

Her Majesty's Inspectorate of Constabulary (2011) *Adapting to Austerity: A Review of Police Force and Authority Preparedness for the 2011/12–14/15 CSR Period*, London: HMIC.

Home Office (2010) *Operation of Police Powers under the Terrorism Act 2000 and Subsequent Legislation: Arrests, Outcomes and Stops & Searches, Quarterly Update to September 2009*, Statistical Bulletin 0410, London: Home Office.

Hough, M., Jackson, J., Bradford, B., Myhill, A. and Quinton, P. (2010) 'Procedural Justice, Trust, and Institutional Legitimacy', *Policing*, 4: 203–210.

Independent Reviewer of Terrorism Legislation (IRTL) (2012) *The Terrorism Acts in 2011: Report of the Independent Reviewer on the Operation of the Terrorism Act 2000 and Part 1 of the Terrorism Act 2006*, London: IRTL.

Macpherson, Sir W. (1999) *The Stephen Lawrence Inquiry: Report of an Inquiry by Sir William Macpherson of Cluny*, CM 4262-1, London: HMSO.

Ministry of Justice (2010) *Statistics on Race and the Criminal Justice System 2008/09*, London: Ministry of Justice.

Ministry of Justice (2011) *Statistics on Race and the Criminal Justice System 2011*, London: Ministry of Justice.

Neyroud, P. (2011) *Review of Police Leadership and Training*, London: Home Office.

Ray, L., Smith, D. and Wastell, L. (2004) 'Shame, Rage and Racist Violence', *British Journal of Criminology*, 44: 350–368.

Riots Communities and Victims Panel (RCVP) (2012) *After the Riots: The Final Report of the RCVP*, London: RCVP.

Rowe, M. (2004) *Policing, Race and Racism*, Cullompton: Willan Publishing.

Rowe, M. (2012) *Race and Crime: A Critical Engagement*, London: Sage.

Scarman, Lord (1981) *The Brixton Disorders: 10–12 April 1981 – Report of an Inquiry by the Rt Hon. Lord Scarman, OBE*, London: HMSO.

Sibbitt, R. (1997) *The Perpetrators of Racial Harassment and Racial Violence*, Research Study 176, London: Home Office.

Solomos, J. (1988) *Black Youth, Racism and the State: The Politics of Ideology and Policy*, Cambridge; Cambridge University Press.

Stone, V. and Tuffin, R. (2000) *Attitudes of People from Minority Ethnic Communities towards a Career in the Police Service*, Police Research Series Paper 136, London: Home Office.

Tyler, T. R. (2007) *Legitimacy and Criminal Justice*, New York: Russell Sage Foundation.

Whitfield, J. (2004) *Unhappy Dialogue: The Metropolitan Police and Black Londoners in Post-war Britain*, Cullompton: Willan Publishing.

Winsor, T. (2012) *Independent Review of Police Officer and Staff Remuneration and Conditions*, London: The Stationery Office.

9

WOMEN POLICE

Potential and possibilities for police reform

Penny Dick, Marisa Silvestri and Louise Westmarland

Introduction

As a highly politicised organisation, it is by no means straightforward for the police service in England and Wales to secure legitimacy from the public and other key stakeholders (Manning, 1997). Unfortunately, recent events, including the death of Ian Tomlinson during the G20-summit protests in London in 2009; the Leveson Inquiry (2011) into police–media relations and possible corruption in the Metropolitan Police Service (MPS); the report of the Hillsborough panel into the 1989 Hillsborough disaster (2012); and the ACPO report into the abuse of police powers to perpetrate sexual violence (2011) have greatly damaged police legitimacy. Add to these events, the results of a recent survey by Brown (2012) which shows a disaffected police uniformed workforce, with 56 per cent of officers expressing the desire to resign from the service, and it is probably no exaggeration to claim that the police are facing a serious and extremely worrying legitimacy crisis.

Research indicates that some of the problems that underpin these events and workplace disaffection are located deep in police culture and how this produces particular beliefs about what policing should be about (crime versus community) and how policing should be enacted (control versus collaboration) (Brown, 1981; Conti, 2010; Shapland and Vagg, 1988; Southgate and Crisp, 1993; Sykes and Brent, 1983; Waddington, 1999). Given some recent work which suggests that many police officers would welcome and, indeed, desire an occupational culture that emphasises collaboration and the chance to participate in steering and shaping the future of the police (Brown, 2012), it is clear that we are now facing a window of opportunity for police reform.

In this chapter, we want to argue that one important route to reform is increasing the numbers of policewomen. Our position is derived not from a feminisation thesis, i.e. the belief that more women means that a different and more feminised police culture will evolve (Dick and Nadin, 2006), but from a practice-based perspective, which sees women as having a fundamental impact on dominant, taken-for-granted work practices which, we will argue, are the chief carriers of some of the more problematic and troublesome aspects of contemporary policing and police organisations. To illustrate our position we will first provide a very brief outline of what a practice-based approach to understanding workplace transformation involves, before moving on to discuss what women bring to police practice that might offer transformational potential. We then move on to explore current barriers to such transformation as well as current transformational spaces. We conclude the chapter by outlining what our review implies for police reform, what this might look like and, more importantly, how a practice-based approach to transformation might help us identify specific targets for bringing this reform into being.

A practice-based approach to understanding police reform

Traditional theories of organisational transformation see this as proceeding from an external shock or jolt that causes the organisation to fundamentally re-think and change its existing activities and routines (Smets et al., 2012). Practice theory, in contrast, suggests that transformation may be a more endogenous process, proceeding from how small adjustments and improvisations to everyday activities and routines (practices) may cause a shift in how actors come to understand what these routines and activities mean (Giddens, 1984; Orlikowsi and Yates, 2002). A practice-based approach to understanding organisational transformation, therefore, focuses on the relationships between practices, actions and meanings (Zilber, 2002, 2009). All organisations function through everyday practices. While these can be habitual, and enacted without a great deal of thought or reflection, all practices have to be adjusted, adapted and modified to enable actors to respond to unforeseen exigencies, disruptions or changes that are brought about by external or internal circumstances (Smets et al., 2012). Thus practices, while to some extent regulated by historical norms and rules (meanings), are always open to improvisation and change as individuals make these everyday adjustments through their enactments of these practices. As these adjustments are made, the norms and rules that govern these practices may also be adjusted, reconfigured or even challenged and changed (Feldman and Pentland, 2003). In the following sections, we want to illustrate these relationships by reviewing some of the more recent literature on women police which suggests that they are having a fundamental impact on everyday practice through their external and internal interactions. Before we do so, we want to briefly examine a key external driver, public perceptions of procedural justice, which could provide momentum for the forms of endogenous changes we explore in the sections that follow.

Potential and possibilities: external drivers for reform

The benefits of recruiting a more diverse police workforce have gained increasing prominence in recent years and are neatly encapsulated in a recent joint report published by ACPO, APA and the Home Office, *Equality, Diversity and Human Rights Strategy for the Police Service* (2010). Drawing on both 'external' impacts with communities and 'internal' impacts with organisational members, the report outlines a number of benefits in relation to the recruitment of a more diverse police workforce. These include the potential to achieve: a broader range of information for decision making and a wider range of possible solutions; a willingness to challenge established ways of thinking and consider new options; improvements in the overall quality of the team; better staff management, leading to improvements in staff satisfaction; a reduction in the number of employees leaving the service, and fewer grievances and complaints; and better relationships with the community, resulting in a more effective service and better quality services, leading to increased public confidence.

The issue of improving public trust and confidence in policing is particularly salient to our discussion and the literature on procedural justice provides a useful framework within which to make sense of the potential impact of policewomen on everyday practices. There is a now growing body of research evidence in support of procedural justice theories (Bradford, 2011; Hough *et al.*, 2010; Jackson and Bradford, 2009, 2010; Jackson *et al.*, 2012; Myhill and Bradford, 2012; Tyler, 2003, 2007; Tyler and Huo, 2002; see also Bradford *et al.*, this volume). Drawing on various public surveys, Tyler (2003) emphasises that procedural justice – that is, fair and respectful *treatment* that 'follows the rules' – is more important to people than obtaining *outcomes* that they regard either as fair or favourable to themselves. Here, the fairness of police procedures and the quality of individuals' interactions with officers are identified as central to the project of bringing about improved police–public relations. Hence, Bradford (2011: 181) argues that 'public confidence can be enhanced if the way people as *individuals* are treated can be improved'. The importance of the personal encounter is emphasised further by Myhill and Bradford (2012: 399) as a 'powerful "lever" for affecting an improved relationship between police and public', something they note as having particular resonance in contemporary times of budgetary constraint – treating people with respect is not dependent on financial resources.

Thus, perceptions of procedural justice may play a vital role in improving and maintaining police legitimacy. What follows is an exploration of how policewomen's interactions with both 'external' communities and 'internal' organisational members might help foster such perceptions.

Interactions with communities

In an era where the emphasis on service in policing has become paramount, evidence suggests that women may have a positive impact on shifting policing philosophy away from a crime control- to a community and citizen-focused approach. Women officers demonstrate a strong 'service oriented' commitment to policing, emphasising communication, familiarity and the building of trust and rapport with communities (Brown and Woolfenden, 2011; Davies and Thomas, 2003; Fleming and McLaughlin, 2010; Heidensohn, 1992). Miller (1999) found that women police are perceived as 'friendly and service oriented' by members of their communities. Brown, Fielding and Woolfenden (2009) present evidence to demonstrate that the members of the community itself see the value of an increased representation of women and the importance of a more diverse police service, expressing preferences for women police to deal with victims and missing persons. The Patten Report (1999) has also emphasised the positive effect of having a much higher proportion of women officers on enhancing the effectiveness of policing within the community.

In relation to their enactment of everyday practices, specifically, interacting with and apprehending potential or actual perpetrators of crime, research shows that, when compared to men, women police appear to be less 'trigger happy' and much less likely to use deadly force (Brown and Langan, 2001; McElvain and Kposowa, 2008; Waugh *et al.*, 1998), utilise threats, physical restraint, force and arrest (Rabe-Hemp, 2008b; Shuck and Rabe-Hemp, 2005). Such findings echo and concur with earlier findings by Belknap and Shelley (1992); Bloch and Anderson (1973); Grennan (1987); Linden (1983); Lunnenborg (1989); Sherman (1975). In a study of conflict management, Braithwaite and Brewer (1998) found that male officers were twice as likely as female officers to engage in threatening behaviour and physical contact with members of the public, which in turn elicited greater resistance and aggression. Such findings appear to provide explanations for evidence which demonstrates that women are less likely to abuse their power and attract complaints and allegations of misconduct (Brereton, 1999; Corsianos, 2011; Lonsway *et al.*, 2002). Waugh *et al.* (1998) found that male police attracted two and a half times as many allegations of assault as female police. Moreover, successive inquiries into corruption and police misconduct in Australia have concluded that there is a direct association between increasing the number of women police officers and reducing levels of corruption (Fleming and Lafferty, 2003).

Positive outcomes in relation to policewomen's enactments of police practices can also be found in relation to their interactions with victims of crime, particularly those that have experienced sexual offences and domestic violence. Research by Brown and King (1998), Page (2007) and Schuller and Stewart (2000) found that women police officers are more likely to believe victims, attribute less blame to the victim and be less accepting of rape myths than their male counterparts. Research by Rabe-Hemp (2008b, 2009) also suggests that women officers bring a high level of empathy in serving the needs of women and children, especially those that have been subject to violent or sexual abuse. Using data collected by a large-scale observational project on the impact of officer gender on police response to domestic violence, Sun (2007) found that while there was no significant difference between female and male officers in their exercise of control actions towards citizens, there is some evidence to support the link between officer gender and non-coercive actions. Such findings are echoed in a recent review of global policing which has emphasised the positive effects of women for police conduct and police–community interactions, in the management and de-escalation of conflict situations and in the support for victims of crime (Brown, 2012). In line with the procedural justice model, findings from Myhill and Bradford (2012) suggest that victims of crime place a greater emphasis on process than outcome.

Jackson *et al.* (2012) emphasise that improving the quality of mundane officer–citizen encounters may reap significant rewards in terms of securing greater legitimacy and compliance with the law. We propose that the positive accounts of women's enactments of everyday practices that are related to police–public encounters outlined above, offer considerable opportunities for building greater trust, confidence and, ultimately, greater consent and legitimacy in policing (Brown *et al.*, 2006; Miller, 1999, Murphy *et al.*, 2008; Prenzler *et al.*, 2010).

Interactions 'within' policing

An exploration of women's enactments of practices 'within' policing offers further opportunities to observe how a practice-based approach might lead to broader transformations in the police service. Research has emphasised women's greater association with adopting a transformative leadership style, with some commentators theorising that the employment of more senior policewomen will lead to new forms of cooperative, transformative management and leadership (Brown, 2003; Heidensohn, 1992; Rabe-Hemp, 2008a; Silvestri, 2003, 2007). Embodying positive leadership traits emphasising participation, consultation and inclusion, a transformational style fits well with contemporary organisational change and management theory, which highlights the need for organisations to become less bureaucratic and hierarchical in favour of participation, team orientation and flexibility (Kark, 2004). The benefits of such a style have been emphasised by a number of police commentators, who argue that the use of participatory transformative leadership styles is more likely to bring about successful long-term change in policing and move the service in line with a greater 'ethical' and 'quality of service' culture (Adlam and Villiers, 2003; Casey and Mitchell, 2007; Densten, 1999; Dobby *et al.*, 2004; Hassell and Brandl, 2009; Marks and Fleming, 2004; Villiers, 2003; Wood *et al.*, 2008).

Evidence of senior policewomen 'doing' and 'championing' a transformational leadership style can be found in the work of Silvestri (2003) and Whittred (2008). Silvestri (2003), for instance, argues that senior policewomen adopt a more holistic style of leadership, not traditionally associated with the police organisation. She argues that through willingness to challenge established ways of thinking, such a style has immeasurable benefits for securing better relations within staff teams and between organisational members. Senior women in her study associated themselves strongly with a transformational approach, which included behaviours aimed at including staff in decision-making processes and supporting staff with family commitments. Such leadership styles were evidenced in the rigorous, thoughtful and consultative approach adopted in senior women's decision making when taking account of subordinate staff as individuals with obligations and lives that extend beyond their jobs. Senior women, here, were 'conscious and active' in providing support for officers with family commitments to work more flexibly wherever possible. The importance of such leadership practice takes on additional significance in light of the recent finding that four in 10 women police officers have considered leaving the force because of low morale, concerns regarding flexible working and child care considerations (Brown, 2012).

Policewomen, practice and police culture: barriers to transformation

Overall, therefore, the evidence suggests that policewomen enact policing in fundamentally different ways to men. However, a practice-based approach draws our attention to the fact that enactment is only one aspect of the relationship between individuals, practices and broader structural and institutional processes. In short, actions alone cannot bring about the transformation in policing that we have suggested is required. We have to understand actions as embedded within everyday practices and the meanings that such practices carry (Zilber, 2002). One fundamental issue here is that police culture, especially at grass roots level, is characterised by a form of hegemonic masculinity (Connell, 1995) that is pervasive in police forces (Smith and Gray, 1983; Westmarland, 2001a, 2001b). This hegemonic masculinity is reflected in dominant understandings of 'real' police work as involving crime fighting and the use of force (Reiner, 2000). These understandings, in turn, are embedded in everyday practices; practices which act as barriers to the potential transformation that women's enactments of policing might produce.

One such set of practices relates to the deployment of women officers and how they are often perceived as 'specialists', best suited to roles dealing with domestic violence, sexual offences and children (Wertsch, 1998; Westmarland, 2001a). Such deployment acts to not only reinforce and reproduce stereotypes regarding women, but also to reproduce the dominant understandings of 'real' police work we have outlined above. Such understandings act to marginalise women officers because they are perceived as unsuitable for these tasks (Westmarland, 2001a). Moreover, such understandings, it is claimed, undermine women's efforts to gain the range of experiences, particularly in departments such as CID, that are deemed important for promotion (Anderson *et al.*, 1993; Heidensohn 1992; HMIC 1996; Jones, 1986; Walklate, 2001). While there is scant evidence to support this claim (Westmarland, 2001a), there is evidence that women police believe that they lack the 'presence' of male officers in the eyes of the public, especially in relation to the maintenance of public order (Heidensohn, 1994). In sum, because police work is generally understood by both insiders and outsiders as primarily concerned with crime control, the different enactments of policing that women bring risk being marginalised and designated as lying outside the remit of 'real policing'.

Another set of practices that act as carriers of these dominant meanings of police work are those that are the products of how work is organised and designed in police forces, such that the ideal police officer is constructed as being 'ever-available' and without family commitments (Charlesworth and Whittenbury, 2007; Dick, 2009; Dick and Cassell, 2004; Silvestri, 2003). Examples include the five-week rotating shift system; the routine use of over-time to complete tasks that are unfinished at the end of a particular shift; and, related to the latter, the individualised nature of task allocation, which produces the necessity for high levels of individual continuity. All these activities are justified through the conceptions of policing and police work that we have discussed above, conceptions that are social constructions, not facts about policing (Dick and Cassell, 2004; Waddington, 1999). These activities act to exclude women by making it difficult for them to continue working full-time when they have children and by influencing how part-time police officers are perceived in police forces – often as less professional and less committed (Charlesworth and Whittenbury, 2007). This, in turn, affects the promotion aspirations and opportunities of policewomen, representing an 'irresolvable conflict' between balancing family commitments and a career in policing and a major barrier for women looking to progress to police leadership ranks (Dick and Cassell, 2004; Silvestri, 2003).

A further set of deterring practices are those related to police leadership. The leadership styles of women, outlined above, have much potential to effect change in the internal relationships between police officers. Through injecting a higher degree of emotion into *doing* leadership, police officers may become more emotionally aware of themselves and others. In turn, this can become the basis for a 'new emotional orientation that seeks creative solutions to issues confronting police' (Drodge and Murphy, 2002: 432). Indeed, the very presence of women officers at all ranks may generate broader transformations and organisational change. Nonetheless, Silvestri (2003) points to the practical and symbolic difficulties experienced by senior women in 'doing' transformational leadership. Women leaders, for instance, have reported disapproval by management peers and senior management over the length of time taken to reach decisions. Senior policewomen's leadership styles are also regularly challenged on the grounds of their effectiveness, and women are repeatedly made to feel 'too sensitive' and unable to withstand the rigours and demands required of police leaders. As a result women experience difficulty in exerting managerial authority with peers and are often perceived to be the weak and soft link in the managerial chain. The transformational style is deemed too 'feminine' in orientation and thus at odds with the more traditional command and control style of leadership found in the police organisation. These deterring practices are the products of the rigid, competitive, quantitative police performance culture which encourages a focus on ends rather than means, and which encourages police leaders to enact leadership so that work centrality is seen to be critical to effective leadership, demonstrated through working long hours (Provost, 2009).

All of this suggests that, in line with the extant literature on institutional maintenance and transformation (Lawrence and Suddaby, 2006; Lawrence *et al.*, 2011), change is likely to proceed from conscious attempts to change and challenge taken-for-granted practices that reproduce dominant conceptions of policing and the police identity. As we will now move on to discuss, it is the presence of women and their inevitable impact on the enactment of the everyday practices we have discussed in this section, that carry the potential for the kinds of endogenous change we believe to be critical to police reform.

Transformational spaces

Research indicates that women officers are not only more likely to be absent more frequently than men (Brown *et al.*, 2009), but that they are much more likely to ask to work reduced hours at some stage in their career (Brown, 2012). For instance, one in five of the women surveyed by Brown (2012) were working part-time and nearly 5 per cent were working restricted duties due to pregnancy. One of the probable underlying causes for the higher rate of female absenteeism is the attempt to meet family and domestic demands within current rigid temporal structures that are part and parcel of taken-for-granted working arrangements for police officers, specifically, the five-week rotating shift system (or other similar rotation). One very important locus of transformation, therefore, resides in thinking more creatively about these temporal structures and how and why they are enacted as they are.

Dick and Collings' (2012) work on the integration of part-time working into operational police units, sheds some light on transformational possibilities here. Their work illustrates that the vast majority of part-time arrangements are managed by attempting to align them within existing temporal structures. Thus, for example, an officer who chooses to drop 20 per cent of their hours on return from maternity leave will typically be expected to work in ways that align these hours with those of her existing workgroup. However, the fact that such officers either typically work fewer shifts than the rest of their workgroup, or are not able to work routine overtime to complete tasks at the end of a shift creates significant problems within workgroups. These include problems such as increased work-loads for colleagues and lack of continuity for tasks that require an external interface (Dick, 2006, 2009). Dick and Collings (2012) argue that, paradoxically, as the numbers of part-time workers within a particular workgroup increases, this appears to trigger responses from managers which are aimed at more creatively integrating the part-time officer with, potentially, beneficial outcomes for workgroups.

Cross-shift working, for example, which is one response to being unable to align a part-time officer's preferred pattern of hours with that of a single shift or relief, appears to be very welcomed by those workgroups involved. In such cases, the part-timer (who is typically very experienced and trained in some or other specialist skill) is seen as an additional and skilled resource. In one unit participating in Dick's (2005a) research project, part-time staff were placed in mentoring roles with probationer constables and were perceived by all parties as adding, not taking away from, the resources available within workgroups. In short, part-time working, while potentially a source of significant problems when squeezed into existing institutional arrangements, may, in fact, carry significant transformational potential.

The more novel attempts to integrate part-time workers by allowing them to work across shifts or by re-defining their roles within specific shifts, act to challenge some of the more dominant ideas that reproduce the temporal structures referred to above, including the notion that continuity of cover needs to be understood in terms of quantity not quality; the notion that officers need to be monitored by one supervisor; and the notion that individuals need to be members of a specific, permanent shift (Dick and Collings, 2012).

Thus, we recommend that the design of police work needs a fundamental re-think especially around the issue of individualised work-loads and handovers. The long hours culture in police services should be a key target for future reform because it is this which reproduces some of the dominant 'myths' about policing that are embedded in what people do and in their sense of identity as police officers (Dick, 2005b; Dick and Cassell, 2004; Waddington, 1999). Police officers often claim, for instance, that the long working hours are necessitated by the fact that policing is so unpredictable, that officers might need to attend incidents shortly before retiring from their particular tour of duty and that they need to remain on duty until the 'incident' has been dealt with. Not only does research suggest that the degree of unpredictability in policing is far less severe than officers perceive it to be (McLean and Hillier, 2011), but also the requirement to remain on duty is a product of individualised work-loads, exacerbated by a lack of protocols to enable effective handovers (see Briscoe (2007) for a discussion of this issue as it applies within hospital medical roles).

Alongside this, we propose that the police service continues to develop a culture of flexible working, in which undertaking part-time work is not read as a lack of commitment to the police career but, rather, is seen as evidence of an officer's ongoing commitment to the job, while balancing work and family. We anticipate that such reform and shift in perception will go some way towards enabling women to progress to police leadership ranks.

We also recommend that the different enactments of policing that women offer, especially with respect to conflict management and other public–police interactions are recognised and rewarded, first at line management level and then upwards from there. Such recognition need not necessarily mean being fast tracked or identified as potential for promotion but, following good practice from research we have conducted, could involve encouraging more skilled and experienced women to act as mentors for newly recruited police officers – this offers a potentially transformatory approach to police socialisation practices which too often breed the cynical lie-low and keep quiet approach to the job identified by Van Maanen and colleagues in the 1970s.

Finally, the importance of improving the 'personal encounter', either between police officers and citizens or between police officers themselves, should not be underestimated for its power to improve police legitimacy. The positive aspects of policewomen's impact on everyday practice reported in this chapter hold much transformational power in relation to contemporary debates about what we as citizens expect and want from our police service in the twenty-first century.

Turning transformational spaces into more widespread change: concluding thoughts

The emerging literature on practice-based change in organisations has revealed some important insights into how fundamental organisational transformation may occur. Changing everyday practices in organisations is a very difficult process, largely because most organisational practices are highly institutionalised, taken-for-granted as the way things are (Orlikowski and Yates, 2002). The literature on practice-based change suggests that some practices which are dominant carriers of organisational culture (or meanings, to use the language we have adopted in this chapter) are targeted for change often as the consequence of regulatory pressures (Briscoe, 2007; Currie *et al.*, 2012; Kellogg, 2009). Such practices, in short, are targeted for change because they are perceived as problematic in some way. Our review suggests that this is a potential sticking point for police reform because some of the dominant practices that we would see as potential targets for change are not currently perceived, by either outsiders or insiders, as problematic. Specifically, deployment practices, routine overtime and working long hours, and management by the measurement of quantitative, target-driven outputs are some of the dominant, yet highly legitimised carriers of several of the more problematic aspects of police culture. Nonetheless, we do see the increased presence of women as providing the impetus for problematising these practices simply because, as their numbers increase, they cannot maintain their careers within existing institutional constraints. This, coupled with equality legislation, might mean that more women will be prepared to mount legal challenges against forces if they feel their employment and career opportunities are being compromised by existing practices (Dick, 2009). Thus, one argument for increasing the presence of women is that they could bring about regulatory change (similar to that which led to the widespread introduction of reduced working hours) which will then enable some of these current practices to be targeted for reform.

Regulatory pressures alone, however, cannot bring about changes to existing everyday practices. For that to happen, there has to be support for such changes. Research indicates that two important issues need to be considered. First, when practices are targeted for change there is often widespread resistance from those actors whose interests might be compromised by such changes, be those interests material or symbolic (Kellogg, 2009, 2011). Thus, for instance, within the police service, the long hours culture that we would suggest needs to be a target for change provides symbolic and material incentives for actors. Materially, for example, the existing shift system and its reliance on the use of routine overtime, means that officers benefit economically, while symbolically, working shifts provides officers with a sense of mechanical solidarity which, while highly functional in some ways (Zerubavel, 1979), may be highly dysfunctional in others (Dick, 2005b). Thus, widespread support for such changes is, in current circumstances, difficult to envisage. Nonetheless, the literature does suggest that where actors stand to benefit from proposed changes to practices, and where those actors can both mobilise their collective interests and find spaces to discuss how to implement change so that it can work, transformation is a possibility (Kellogg, 2009). Again, we would argue that increasing the numbers of women police will act as the catalyst for garnering support for practice change, as it is they who are most likely to benefit from changes to the practices we have been discussing. Finally, we need to understand that practice-based change has to be sustained. Too frequently, old habits die hard and any number of highly persuasive justifications can be mobilised against change (Kellogg, 2011). The literature shows clearly that sustained change happens only when meanings as well as practices change. That is, there has to be a collective effort to think differently about what it is that the organisation is doing and why it is doing it, if practice-based change is to take root and diffuse. Reform, in short, has to be championed and supported, and reformers must be able to develop a sense that change can be brought about. We believe that of crucial importance here, is the need for women to extend and develop a collective and shared interest with men. This could be particularly pertinent given the number of police officers who either co-habit with, or are married to, other serving officers (Archbold and Hassell, 2009). As more men take on a greater share of caring responsibilities, male police officers also stand to benefit from a more progressive and flexible workplace culture. It is these groups that we see as those most likely to act as change champions.

References

Adlam, R. and Villiers, P. (2003) (eds) *Police Leadership in the Twenty-First Century: Philosophy, Doctrine and Developments*. Winchester: Waterside Press.

Anderson, R., Brown, J. and Campbell, E. (1993) *Aspects of Discrimination Within the Police Service in England and Wales*. London: Home Office.

Archbold, C.A. and Hassell, K.D. (2009) Paying a marriage tax: an examination of the barriers to the promotion of female police officers. *Policing: An International Journal of Police Strategies and Management*, 32(1): 56–74.

Belknap, J. and Shelley, J.K. (1992) The new Lone Ranger: policewomen on patrol. *American Journal of Police*, 12: 47–75.

Bloch, P. and Anderson, D. (1973) *Policewomen on Patrol: Major Findings: First Report*. Washington, DC: Police Foundation.

Bradford, B. (2011) Convergence, not divergence: trends and trajectories in public contact and confidence in police. *British Journal of Criminology*, 51: 179–200.

Braithwaite, H. and Brewer, N. (1998) Differences in conflict resolution of male and female police patrol officers. *International Journal of Police Science and Management*, 1(3): 276–287.

Brereton, D. (1999, July). *Do women police differently? Implications for police–community relations*. Paper presented to the Second Australasian Women and Policing Conference, Brisbane.

Briscoe, F. (2007) From iron cage to iron shield? How bureaucracy enables temporal flexibility for professional service workers. *Organization Science*, 18(2): 297–314.

Brown, J. (2003) 'Women leaders: a catalyst for change'. In R. Adlam and P. Villiers (eds) *Leadership in the Twenty-first Century: Philosophy, Doctrine and Developments*. Winchester: Waterside Press.

Brown, J. (2012) Facing the future. *Police Magazine*. Available at: http://www.policemag.co.uk/editions/709.aspx.

Brown, J. and King, J. (1998) Gender differences in police officers' attitudes towards rape: results of an exploratory study. *Psychology, Crime and Law*, 4(4): 265–279.

Brown, J. and Langan, P. (2001) Policing and homicide, 1976–98: justifiable homicide by police, police officers murdered by felons. Washington, DC: US Dept of Justice.

Brown, J. and Woolfenden, S. (2011) Implications of the changing gender ratio amongst warranted police officers. *Policing*, 5(4): 356–364.

Brown, J., Fielding, J. and Woolfenden, S. (2009) *Added Value? The implications of increasing the percentages of women in the police service by 2009*. A report commissioned by the British Association for Women Policing.

Brown, J., Hegarty, P. and O'Neill, D. (2006) *Playing with numbers: A discussion paper on positive discrimination as a means for achieving gender equality in the Police Service in England and Wales*. Department of Psychology, School of Human Science, University of Surrey.

Brown, M. (1981) *Working the Street: Police Discretion and the Dilemmas of Reform*. New York: Russell Sage Foundation.

Casey, J. and Mitchell, M. (2007) 'Police–community consultation in Australia: working with a conundrum'. In J. Ruiz and D. Hummer (eds) *Handbook of Police Administration*. CRC Press New York: Taylor and Francis.

Charlesworth, S. and Whittenbury, K. (2007) Part-time and part committed? The challenge of part-time work in policing. *Industrial Relations Journal*, 49(1): 31–47.

Connell, R.W. (1995) *Masculinities*. Cambridge, UK: Polity Press.

Conti, N. (2010) *Weak links and warrior hearts: A framework for judging self and others in police training*. International Police Executive Symposium, Geneva Center for the Democratic Control of Armed Forces, Working Paper no. 24.

Corsianos, M. (2011) Responding to officers' gendered experiences through community policing and improving accountability to citizens. *Contemporary Justice Review*, 14: 7–20.

Currie, G., Lockett, A., Finn, R., Martin, G. and Waring, J. (2012) Institutional work to maintain professional power: recreating the model of medical professionalism. *Organization Studies*, 33(7): 937–962.

Davies, A. and Thomas, R. (2003) Talking cop: discourses of change and policing identities. *Public Administration*, 81(4): 681–699.

Densten, I.L. (1999) Senior Australia law enforcement leadership under examination. *Policing: An International Journal of Police Strategies and Management*, 26(3): 400–418.

Dick, P. (2005a) *Developing flexible working practices in police work*. ESRC Project Final Report.

Dick, P. (2005b) Dirty work designations: how police officers account for their use of coercive authority. *Human Relations*, 58(11): 1363–1390.

Dick, P. (2006) The psychological contract and the transition from full to part-time police work. *Journal of Organizational Behavior*, 27(1): 37–58.

Dick, P. (2009) Bending over backwards? Using a pluralistic framework to explore the management of flexible working in the police service. *British Journal of Management*, 20(1): 182–193.

Dick, P. and Cassell, C. (2004) The position of police women: a discourse analytic study. *Work, Employment & Society*, 18(1): 51–72.

Dick, P. and Collings, D.G. (2012) Temporal asymmetry and the disruption of the socio-temporal order: institutional maintenance as an unintended consequence of practical-evaluative agency. Working paper, Sheffield University Management School.

Dick, P. and Nadin, S. (2006) Reproducing gender inequalities? A critique of realist assumptions underpinning personnel selection research and practice. *Journal of Occupational and Organizational Psychology*, 79: 481–498.

Dobby, J., Anscombe, J. and Tuffin, R. (2004) *Police leadership: expectations and impact.* Home Office online report 20/04, Research Development and Statistics Office, London.

Drodge, E. and Murphy, S. (2002) Interrogating emotions in police leadership. *Human Resource Development Review*, 1(4): 420–438.

Feldman, M. and Pentland, B.T. (2003) Reconceptualizing organizational routines as a source of flexibility and change. *Administrative Science Quarterly*, 48: 94–118.

Fleming, J. and McLaughlin, E. (2010) 'The public gets what the public wants?' Interrogating the 'public confidence' agenda. [In special issue: Public confidence in the police] *Policing: A Journal of Policy and Practice*, 4(3): 199–202.

Fleming, J. and Lafferty, G. (2003) Equity confounded: women in Australian police organisations. *Labour and Industry*, 13(3): 37–50.

Giddens, A. (1984) *The Constitution of Society: Outline of the Theory of Structuration.* Berkeley, CA: University of California Press.

Grennan, S.A. (1987) Findings on the role of officer gender in violent encounters with citizens. *Journal of Police Science and Administration*, 15: 78–85.

Hassell, K. and Brandl, S. (2009) An examination of the workplace experiences of police patrol officers: the role of race, sex, and sexual orientation. *Police Quarterly*, 12(4): 408–430.

Heidensohn, F. (1992) *Women in Control: The Role of Women in Law Enforcement.* Oxford: Oxford University Press.

Heidensohn, F. (1994) 'We can handle it out here'. Women in Britain and the USA and the Policing of Public Order. *Policing and Society*, 4: 293–303.

HMIC (1996) *Developing diversity in the police service: equal opportunities thematic inspection report.* London: Home Office.

Hough, M., Jackson, J., Bradford, B., Myhill, A. and Quinton, P. (2010) Procedural justice, trust and institutional legitimacy. *Policing: A Journal of Policy and Practice*, 4: 203–210.

Jackson, J. and Bradford, B. (2009) Crime, policing and the moral order. *British Journal of Sociology*, 60(3): 493–522.

Jackson, J. and Bradford, B. (2010) What is trust and confidence in the police? *Policing: A Journal of Policy and Practice*, 4(3): 241–248.

Jackson, J., Bradford, B., Hough, M., Myhill, A., Quinton, P. and Tyler, T. (2012) Why do people comply with the Law? Legitimacy and the influence of legal institutions. *British Journal of Criminology*, 52(6): 1051–1071.

Jones, S. (1986) *Policewomen and Inequality.* London: Macmillan.

Kark, R. (2004) The transformational leader: who is (s)he? A feminist perspective. *Journal of Organisational Change Management*, 17(2): 160–176.

Kellogg, K.C. (2009) Relational spaces and microinstitutional change in surgery. *American Journal of Sociology*, 115(3): 657–711.

Kellogg, K. (2011) Hot lights and cold steel: cultural and political toolkits for practice change in surgery. *Organization Science*, 22(2): 482–502.

Lawrence, T.B. and Suddaby, R. (2006) 'Institutions and institutional work'. In S. Clegg, C. Hardy, T.B. Lawrence and R.W. Nord (eds) *The Sage Handbook of Organization Studies.* London: Sage.

Lawrence, T.B., Suddaby, R. and Leca, B. (2011) Institutional work: refocusing institutional studies of organization. *Journal of Management Inquiry*, 20(1): 52–58.

Linden, R. (1983) Women in policing: a study of lower mainland Royal Canadian Mounted Police detachments. *Canadian Police College Journal*, 7: 212–229.

Lonsway, K., Wood, M. and Spillar, K. (2002) Officer gender and excessive force. *Law and Order*, 50: 60–66.

Lunnenborg, P.W. (1989) *Women Police Officers: Current Career Profiles.* Springfield, IL: Thomas.

Manning, P.K. (1997) *Police Work: The Social Organization of Policing*. Prospect Heights, IL: Waveland.

Marks, M. and Fleming, J. (2004) 'As Unremarkable as the air they breathe?' Reforming Police Management in South Africa. *Current Sociology*, 52(5): 784–808.

McElvain, J.P. and Kposowa, A.J. (2008) Police officer characteristics and the likelihood of using deadly force. *Criminal Justice and Behavior*, 35(4): 505–521.

McLean, F. and Hillier, J. (2011) *An Observational Study of Response and Neighbourhood Officers*. London: NPIA.

Miller, S.L. (1999) *Gender and Community Policing: Walking the Talk*. Boston, MA: Northeastern University Press.

Murphy, K., Hinds, L. and Fleming, J. (2008) Encouraging public cooperation and support for police. *Policing and Society: An International Journal of Research and Policy*, 18(2): 136–155.

Myhill, A. and Bradford, B. (2012) Can police enhance public confidence by improving quality of service? Results from two surveys in England and Wales. *Policing and Society*, 22(4): 397–425.

Orlikowski, W.J. and Yates, J. (2002) It's about time: temporal structuring in organizations. *Organization Science*, 13(6): 684–700.

Page, A.D. (2007) Behind the blue line: investigating police officers' attitudes toward rape. *Journal of Police and Criminal Psychology*, 22(1): 22–32.

Patten Report (1999) *A New Beginning: Policing in Northern Ireland*. The Independent Police Commission on Policing in Northern Ireland.

Prenzler, T., Fleming, J. and King, A. (2010) Gender equity in Australian and New Zealand Policing: a five year review. *International Journal of Police Science and Management*, 12: 584–595.

Provost, G. (2009) A profession in process: the atypical rise of women to the high rank of Police '*Commissaire*' in France. *Sociologie du Travail*, 51: 34–48.

Rabe-Hemp, C. (2008a) Survival in an 'all boys club': policewomen and their fight for acceptance. *Policing: An International Journal of Police Strategies and Management*, 31: 251–270.

Rabe-Hemp, C. (2008b) Female officers and the ethics of care: does officer gender impact police behaviours? *Journal of Criminal Justice*, 36: 426–434.

Rabe-Hemp, C. (2009) POLICEwomen or PoliceWOMEN? Doing gender and police work. *Feminist Criminology*, 4: 114–129.

Reiner, R. (2000) *The Politics of the Police (third edition)*. London: Harvester Wheatsheaf.

Schuck, A.M. and Rabe-Hemp, C.R. (2005) Women police: the use of force by and against female officers. *Women and Criminal Justice*, 14(4): 91–117.

Schuller, R.A. and Stewart, A. (2000) Police responses to sexual assault complaints: the role of perpetrator/complainant intoxication. *Law and Human Behavior*, 24: 535–551.

Shapland, J. and Vagg, J. (1988) *Policing by the Public*. London: Routledge.

Sherman, L. (1975) Evaluation of policewomen on patrol in a suburban police department. *Journal of Police Science and Administration*, 3: 434–438.

Silvestri, M. (2003) *Women in Charge: Policing, Gender and Leadership*. Cullompton, Devon: Willan Publishing.

Silvestri, M. (2006) 'Doing time': becoming a police leader. *International Journal of Police Science and Management*, 8(4): 266–281.

Silvestri, M. (2007) 'Doing' police leadership: enter the 'new smart macho'. *Policing and Society*, 17(1): 38–58.

Smets, M., Morris, T. and Greenwood, R. (2012) From practice to field: a practice driven model of institutional change. *Academy of Management Journal*, 55(4): 877–904.

Smith, D. and Gray, J. (1983) *The Police in Action. Police and People in London: Vol. 4.* London: Policy Studies Institute.

Southgate, P. and Crisp, D. (1993) *Public Satisfaction with Police Services.* Research and Planning Unit Papers No. 72, London: HMSO.

Sun, I.Y. (2007) Policing domestic violence: does officer gender matter? *Journal of Criminal Justice*, 35: 581–595.

Sykes, R.E. and Brent, E.E. (1983) *Policing: A Social Behaviourist Perspective.* New Brunswick, NJ: Rutgers University Press.

Tyler, T. (2003) 'Procedural justice, legitimacy and the effective rule of law'. In M. Tonry (ed.) *Crime and Justice: A Review of Research, Vol. 30*, pp. 431–505. Chicago: University of Chicago Press.

Tyler, T. (2007) *Legitimacy and Criminal Justice.* New York: Russell Sage Foundation.

Tyler, T. and Huo, Y. (2002) *Trust in the Law: Encouraging Public Cooperation with the Police and Courts.* New York: Russell Sage Foundation.

Van Maanen, J. (1975) Police socialization: a longitudinal examination of job attitudes in an urban police department. *Administrative Science Quarterly*, 20: 207–229.

Villiers, P. (2003) 'Philosophy, doctrine and leadership: some core beliefs'. In R. Adlam and P. Villiers (eds) *Police Leadership in the Twenty-first Century. Philosophy, Doctrine and Developments.* Winchester: Waterside Press.

Waddington, P.A.J. (1999) Police (canteen) sub-culture: an appreciation. *British Journal of Criminology*, 39(2): 287–309.

Walklate, S. (2001) *Gender, Crime and Criminal Justice.* Cullompton: Willan.

Waugh, L., Ede, A. and Alley, A. (1998) Police culture, women police and attitudes towards misconduct. *International Journal of Police Science and Management*, 1(3): 289–300.

Wertsch, T.L. (1998) Walking the thin blue line: policewomen and tokenism today. *Women and Criminal Justice*, 9(3): 59–68.

Westmarland, L. (2001a) *Gender and Policing: Sex, Power and Police Culture.* Cullompton: Willan.

Westmarland, L. (2001b) Blowing the whistle on police violence: gender, ethnography and ethics. *British Journal of Criminology*, 41(2): 523–535.

Whittred, J. (2008) *A qualitative exploration into the transformational leadership styles of senior policewomen.* Unpublished MSc in Police Leadership and Management, University of Leicester.

Wood, J., Fleming, J. and Marks, M. (2008) Building the capacity of police change agents: the nexus policing project. *Policing and Society*, 18(1): 72–87.

Zerubavel, E. (1979) *Patterns of Time in Hospital Life.* Chicago: Chicago University Press.

Zilber, T.B. (2002) Institutionalization as an interplay between actions, meanings and actors: the case of a rape crisis center in Israel. *Academy of Management Journal*, 45(1): 234–254.

Zilber, T.B. (2009) 'Institutional maintenance as narrative acts'. In T.B. Lawrence, R. Suddaby and B. Leca (eds) *Institutional Work: Actors and Agency in Institutional Studies of Organizations.* Cambridge: Cambridge University Press.

Websites

http://hillsborough.independent.gov.uk/repository/report/HIP_report.pdf
http://www.acpo.police.uk/documents/reports/2012/201209AbPPtPSV.pdf
http://www.levesoninquiry.org.uk/

10

A DIVERSITY STONE LEFT UNTURNED?

Exploring the occupational complexities surrounding lesbian, gay and bisexual police officers

Matthew Jones

Introduction

Within the reconfigured dynamics of post-Macpherson (1999) policing, diversity and difference have been embraced as a rationale through which police forces across England and Wales can build connections with their heterogeneous publics, enhance legitimacy and bring about meaningful internal cultural change. A central part of this new policing mind-set has been the active recruitment and integration of individuals from minority groups into the ranks – among which lesbian, gay and bisexual (LGB) individuals have been a target demographic despite relatively raw hostilities between the police and LGB communities. Yet, despite growing empirical coverage into how women and black and minority ethnic (BME) officers have fared within this new organisational rubric (Holdaway, 2009; O'Neill & Holdaway, 2007; Rabe-Hemp, 2008; Silvestri, 2007), the occupational experiences of LGB officers have, until recently, been – symbolically some claim – overlooked. Yet, it will be argued that the experiences of LGB officers reflect more broadly the health of police organisations at a given time and that as a subaltern group they hold considerable potential to contribute to meaningful internal cultural change. Accordingly, drawing on the recent findings of a national research project conducted by the author (Jones, 2013a), the aim of this chapter is to redress this empirical imbalance by highlighting some of the main occupational complexities experienced by this subaltern group today, before presenting some practical recommendations on how these experiences can be further improved and utilised within policing futures.

Empirical neglect: the story for LGB officers so far

In order to explore the contemporary complexities and appreciate the progress made by police organisations in regard to the employment of LGB personnel, it is first appropriate to reflect on a time, not that long ago, when difference and deviation from historically embedded sub-cultural policing standards were strongly resisted.

Now twenty years old, research by Burke (1993, 1994, 1995) had been, until recently, the only empirical project to exclusively examine the relationship between homosexuality and policing in England and Wales. His findings painted a rather bleak picture, describing the status and perception of LGB officers as deviant in the minds of their heterosexual colleagues and as representing the most serious kind of contamination and threat to the integrity of the British Police Service. LGB individuals who chose to be open about their sexual orientation at work, or who were merely suspected as being homosexual by colleagues reported turbulent career trajectories characterised by persistent prejudice and discrimination from across the police organisation. Examples of the former include being subjected to derogatory discourse, professional humiliation, physical violence and the refusal from some heterosexual officers to work in close proximity with LGB officers. In regard to the latter, respondents reported adverse treatment during the recruitment process, psychologically damaging experiences during training, unfair allocation of duties, and bars to promotion and development.

In an attempt to explain the antithetical relationship between homosexuality and policing, Burke (1994) offers three key explanations. First, the stereotypically grounded, non-conformist perceptions of homosexuality are deemed to directly oppose the conservative, conformist and role-appropriate behaviours that have become synonymous with the dominant yet unwritten sub-cultural constitution that underpinned police behaviours. Second, in a similar vein, the stereotypical association of homosexuality with effeminacy and weakness was seen to pose a direct threat to the supremacy of masculinity – a central and celebrated requirement of police work and a driving force behind police sub-cultural practices. As a result, those who deviated or threatened the integrity of the prescribed norm instantly forfeited their masculinity in the minds of their colleagues, along with the fraternal bonds and protection which it affords. Third, Burke offered a two-pronged criminality hypothesis as a justification to resistance. This encompasses the view that the fresh memory of homosexuality as illegal, coupled with a historically routed antagonistic relationship between the police and LGB communities as a result of policing public sex environments and drug consumption, created a natural association between homosexuality and criminality in the minds of heterosexual officers, who naturally see this community as a legitimate target for suspicion as a result.

Faced with the prospect of such hostility, a central tenet of Burke's research is identification of the double life strategy that the invisibility of sexuality affords. In summary, many LGB officers chose to camouflage their sexual orientation with a performance and illusion of conformist heterosexuality at work. Although being a common path and appearing to be an antidote to the aforementioned shackles of prejudice and discrimination, this path did bring with it considerable cautionary risks; most notably detriment to mental health, an inability to give maximum attention to police duties, difficulties in forming lasting professional relationships, and low levels of job satisfaction. Whatever the choice, either to be open and transparent about their sexual orientation, or opting for the illusion of professional heterosexuality, Burke identified that the plight of an LGB officer is desolate and challenging, with many failing to last for the full tenure of their police career due to either being pushed out by the heterosexual majority, or experiencing psychological breakdown rendering them unfit for the job.

Making a difference through difference: a reconfigured organisational core

The report of Sir William Macpherson (1999) condemned the insular and anti-quated cultural climate as encapsulated by Burke and brought about a contemporary reform agenda that transformed the way that the police approached their internal composition and relationships between themselves and their diverse publics (Hall *et al.*, 2009). Loftus (2009) asserts that as a consequence of Macpherson, diversity became a politicised priority within twenty-first-century policing.

A central component of this post-Macpherson reform agenda was to recruit and build up a diverse workforce with the aim of diluting the counterproductive subcultural dominance of masculinity, to establish and build relationships with diverse communities, explore new ways of thinking about the policing mission beyond 'crime fighting', and to restore the public faith in the competence of the police which had been dwindling for many years (HMIC, 2003; Home Office, 2005a). LGB officers were seen as key agents of change within this new organisational strategy, although the hostile relationship between the police and LGB communities as highlighted by Burke could not be overlooked. Consequently, police forces nationally set about introducing a wide portfolio of initiatives that aimed at breaking down negative attitudes towards homosexuality and promoting the benefits of increasing LGB representation within the ranks. Examples included: (i) the active recruitment of LGB officers through marketing campaigns and engagement initiatives within the LGB community; (ii) investment and expansion of the national Gay Police Association and Local Gay Staff Networks; (iii) symbolic commitment to LGB initiatives and the wider police diversity mission from senior officers (e.g. leading the police march at GayPride events); and (iv) establishment and investment in LGBT Liaison Officers[1] (see Godwin (2007) for a case study into the LGB initiatives introduced by a progressive English police force). These efforts were complemented externally by the introduction of The Employment Equality (Sexual Orientation) Regulations 2003 which legally barred, for the first time, discriminatory workplace practices and set a minimum standard throughout organisations, including the police.

As a consequence of this new workplace framework, LGB officers have reported significant improvement in their professional treatment and workplace environment – going as far as to acknowledge a recent upgrade from historically passive victims to empowered and protected members of the modern police family. This satisfaction was reflected within a recent survey of 836 LGB police officers across

England and Wales where 75.1 per cent reported that their force does enough for their LGB staff, 86.6 per cent reported a career in the police that has been free from organisational discrimination, and 79 per cent considered themselves to be 'out' at work (Jones, 2013b). This vast transformation has been afforded to a new organisational commitment to diversity, the protection of minority staff as a valued resource, widespread intolerance to bigoted and discriminatory behaviours and the establishment of formal procedures that impose professional penalties on those who fail to meet the requirement standard of conduct.

Within this contemporary environment, LGB officers report being able to make a unique contribution to policing through a unique skillset and alternative approach. Just as Brown & Heidensohn (2000) and Rabe-Hemp (2008) discuss how women police officers can offer a more empathetic and emotional response to operational policing, LGB officers believe that their unique contribution is their ability to: diffuse violent situations verbally rather than physically, identify and respond to the emotional needs of victims, encourage supportive and problem-orientated discourse among colleagues, and to offer a minority perspective – drawing on their own life experiences – when interacting with the vast array of police stakeholders.

Yet, despite the antithetical experiences of LGB officers today compared to those included in the work of Burke (1993), it should not be considered that the contemporary diversity agenda is complete. Currently, LGB officers do experience some resistance within their everyday working environments which, although less emotive, restrict their ability to maximise their contribution and bring about meaningful change. Accordingly the diversity agenda should be conceptualised as a long-term, embedded policing priority that requires considerable investment and continual evolvement. In the next section of this chapter some selected examples of resistances are discussed, as well as the reasons for their occurrence.

Contemporary hurdles faced by LGB police officers

As discussed at length in other chapters within this edited collection, *the police* as a focus of empirical investigation and understanding is quite schizophrenic, in that it is characterised by the good intentions of its formal organisational culture as well as informal sub-cultural codes of the rank and file. The latter has come to refer to the ways in which occupations 'develop understandings about how to interpret conduct, retain loyalties, express opinions [and] use or abuse authority' (Skolnick, 2008, p. 35), which, in relation to the police, refers to a historically embedded set of occupational rules and standards which are celebrated and direct the conduct of the rank and file. It is some of these dominant and, some argue, antiquated standards that have been the target of the post-Macpherson reform agenda. Breakwell (1986) argues that when dominant identities are threatened in this way, those who are threatened resort to fuelling ideals of their dominance and the ineffectiveness of those who pose the biggest threat to them. In this vein, some of the main resistances experienced by LGB police officers today relate to their integration into the dominant police sub-cultural mind-set – mainly that of police machismo – and associated attempts to discredit the contribution to be made by subaltern police officers to modern policing. Some of these main forms of resistance will now be addressed.

Developing a professional identity within a masculine occupation

The invisibility of sexuality affords LGB police officers considerable discretion as to when to disclose their sexual orientation at work. As Burke (1995) and Ward & Winstanley (2005) discuss, this process of disclosure is highly emotional, psychologically draining, subjectively laden and unique to every LGB individual. What makes it particularly challenging for LGB police officers is that the decision is often determined by the individual's interpretation of police sub-cultural standards – of which masculinity and the ability to fulfil the iconographic role of a 'crime fighter' are still paramount.

A large proportion of LGB officers make an active decision not to come out at work at least for the first twelve months of their service, with a large majority extending that initial period of non-disclosure until up to five years of service. This is rationalised as a period during which they can build up and establish a reputation as 'a good police officer' – a standard which they judge against their ability to conform, perform and be accepted within traditionally masculinist police structures. Many LGB officers fear that being open about their LGB status will forfeit their professional integrity; create risks to their personal safety due to a potential lack of support from colleagues in violent operational settings; cause them to become typecast into roles that are associated with the soft side of policing (e.g. domestic violence, sexual offences); and make them the target of ridicule and gossip within professional circles. By reaching this subjective standard and achieving the reputation as a 'good cop', LGB officers believe that the process of disclosing their sexual orientation to police colleagues will become less turbulent and is less likely to attract stereotypical associations or ridicule. In reality, those who chose to come out at work from the outset report positive experiences on the whole, and are often credited with respect from colleagues who appreciate the bravery required to be honest about their sexuality within a masculine fuelled occupation.

Reflecting McLaughlin's (2007) discussion of 'nostalgic policing' these anxieties underpinning reluctance to come out at work are often fuelled by historical myths and internal folk tales, rather than lived experience, which continue to be promoted by the threatened subscribers to traditional police sub-cultural ideals. These myths relate to the 'good old days' where force, violence and brawn were a prerequisite of the crime fighter role in which difference had no place (see e.g. Holdaway, 1979, 1983). However, these are highly influential and falsely inform the mind-set of new minority officers. This leads to many LGB officers experiencing the adverse effects of pursuing a dual persona for at least a short period of their police career, only to then find that the foundations of their anxieties are subsequently not met and regret not coming out sooner.

This is not to say that masculinity in policing is merely a historical myth. On the contrary, Brown (2007) and Rabe-Hemp (2008) both argue that the cult of masculinity and its overarching prominence within policing is still alive and well. This is evident in the attempts of LGB police officers to form professional bonds with police colleagues and integrate into the fraternal team working. Those whose behaviours and mannerisms conform to traditional standards of masculinist policing experience the least resistance and rejection. For example, those who are naturally effeminate or unable to 'hold their own' in violent police situations are instantly rejected and ridiculed by colleagues. Identity performance is, therefore, common-place for LGB officers who often, unconsciously, manage their external behaviours so as to avoid common LGB stereotypes which appear to be the kryptonite of police cultural ideals (Myers *et al.*, 2004). A consequence of this is that the major-ity of LGB officers choose not to engage with other LGB officers or with organi-sational initiatives aimed at LGB staff, due to fears of being labelled political or overtly resistant and challenging. Further, within this conformist mind-set a large proportion of LGB officers fail to utilise their sexuality as an operational resource, as per the rationale of their inclusion within the post-Macpherson reform agenda (HMIC, 2003). Thus, while the shackles of dominant masculinist ideals continue within policing, the propensity for LGB and other minority officers to bring about change and make a unique contribution is significantly diluted.

New forms of resistance

Reconfigured organisational and legislative intolerance towards prejudice and dis-crimination has forced once overt displays of resistance towards LGB to evolve. Extreme resistance is uncommon today, but where it does occur it now mani-fests itself strategically so as to avoid detection. Holdaway & O'Neill (2007) when exploring the occupational experiences of BME police officers found that although organisations can establish formal organisation cultures and policies which are built on moral grounds, employees are under no obligation to conform to both behav-ioural and moral expectations. In fact, in a professional environment, police offic-ers' behaviour can be exemplary but their core attitudes, which have been socially constructed within their personal lives prior to joining the police, can contradict the rationale for these required behaviours. Instead, compliance can be a form of insincere performance aimed at avoiding professional penalties, resorting to overt expressions of prejudice (e.g. racism, sexism and homophobia) in situations where the propensity for detection is at its lowest.

The dynamics of covert homophobia and prejudice are a reality faced by all LGB officers at some point during their careers today. It often occurs within infor-mal settings – e.g. after-work drinks, team nights out or while on patrol away from earshot of any other colleagues – and often encapsulates individual prejudices associated with the Burke era. However, the most common expression of cov-ert homophobia today is through humour. Kehily & Nayak (1997) explore the micro-political dynamics of homophobia expressed through humour in relation to teenage male friendships, but their thesis is very much applicable to professional male-dominated interactions such as policing. Humour allows the author to express and reinforce their non-desirable homophobic views within a public setting, leaving the target questioning the sincerity of the ridicule as actual humour or something more sinister, yet providing an insincere defence of 'only joking' for the author if anyone were to challenge his/her behaviour. This largely subjective test is extremely hard to prove and challenge and has been a dilemma for the majority of LGB officers today, who are often left personally grappling with determining the point at which a professional line has been crossed (Jones, 2013a).

Beyond – yet not unrelated to – personal expression of prejudice, instances of formal organisational discrimination targeted at LGB police officers still occurs today. Colvin (2008) in his American study of LGB police officers found that formal discrimination occurred in areas where supervisory discretion is at its highest. This is reflected within the experiences of LGB police officers in England and Wales, where perceived discrimination was reported most frequently in areas of deployment and training (Jones, 2013b).

Professional insecurities

The propensity for LGB officers to fully utilise their unique skillset within modern policing is being considerably restricted by chronic insecurities surrounding the longevity of organisational commitment to the diversity agenda. Extreme pessimism exists as a consequence of traditionally reactionary police reform agendas with fears that diversity, and the protection of minority officers, is only in vogue until the next disaster/organisational crisis diverts the dominant policing lens. Examples of reduced funding and withdrawn LGB initiatives continue to grow (Brown & Bear, 2012; Clemence, 2011), fuelling concern that the diversity reform agenda is grinding to a sudden halt in the face of its likely successor, austerity. LGB officers report widespread insecurity surrounding their future role within the police organisation and the wider commitment of police constabularies to invest in the on-going improvements to their workplace experiences and trajectories. As a consequence they feel that it is the safe option to conform, rather than experiment with how their unique skillset could bring about positive change. These insecurities are particularly prevalent among officers with more than ten years' service who experienced first-hand the speed of reform post-Macpherson, who have worked first-hand within the pre-Macpherson climate and are deeply fearful that a reduced impetus surrounding diversity at this point could easily allow police forces nationally to default into their pre-Macpherson mind-set.

Beyond the monolithic

The socially constructed nature of both sexuality and policing dictate that the experiences of LGB police officers, discussed above, cannot be seen as monolithic or universal – rather, the examples above have been selected as the most prominent difficulties faced by LGB police officers today for analytic convenience. Chan (1996) calls for a more holistic and heterogeneous understanding of modern policing cultures, and it is in this vein that some common variances in the experiences discussed above are now highlighted.

Gender/sexual orientation

It is common practice when talking about diversity to aggregate the experiences of lesbian, gay and bisexual individuals into one sexual orientation strand or variable – i.e. 'LGB'. However, in reality the experiences of these distinct categories vary enormously. Due to the continued dominance of masculinity within policing, male officers continue to experience the highest levels of resistance and adverse treatment. The claim that 'a "real" man is the one who is the least open to the charge of homosexuality' (Hoch, 1979) still resonates today, with the sexual threat that male gay officers pose towards heterosexual officers being a common justification for aversion, resistance and rejection. Male gay officers who are civil partnered and/or who have children are more readily accepted, due to a reduced propensity that they will make sexual advances towards their male colleagues. Alternatively, despite common objections as to their suitability for traditional police work (Brown & Heidensohn, 2000; Rabe-Hemp, 2008; Westmarland, 2001), women gay/lesbian officers report considerably less resistance due to their sexuality. Despite having to juggle the intersectional realities of being a double minority in policing – i.e. a woman and gay/lesbian – the majority ascribe any resistance as being due to their gender. In reality the sexual fantasy of lesbianism is strongly encouraged and explored with intrigue by the masculinist majority, encouraging little resistance beyond male chauvinism. Bisexuality is widely overlooked, both by society and within an occupational context. It is often deemed as a sexual rather than emotional construct, although recent empirical insights identify that this is not the case (Giles, 2006; Rodriguez Rust, 2009). Within the aforementioned survey of LGB officers, only 18.4 per cent of bisexual male officers and 40 per cent of bisexual women officers considered themselves to be out at work – a direct contrast to reported levels of disclosure by gay men and lesbian/gay women officers – giving rise to claims that further empirical attention is needed to explore the experiences of this overlooked niche group.

The central role of middle management

A dominant architect in the career experiences of LGB officers is his/her immediate supervisor/manager. It is this influential figure that has the capacity to establish professional boundaries and behaviours within a team, acknowledge and encourage unique contributions made by LGB staff, and challenge negative behaviours and attitudes. Alternatively, they hold the potential to ruin and marginalise LGB officers if they fail to establish the requisite professional standards and employ discriminatory attitudes themselves. Both Morris (2004) and Home Office (2005b) highlighted the failure of police organisation to fully embrace and integrate diversity. Specifically they highlighted the lack of true understanding of diversity issues, especially among middle management officers. Since then, improvements have been made, however a large proportion of LGB officers choose not to talk to their immediate line manager about personal issues relating to their sexual orientation and associated private lives, often choosing to compose alternative reasons to justify requests for personal and emotional leave. Those who are managers/supervisors themselves associate this aversion to the lack of LGB training currently provided for lower management officers, paving the way for awkward and uncomfortable scenarios in this context.

LGB police officers of rank

Van Ewijk (2011) aptly asserts that diversity per se within policing rank structures diminishes according to increased levels of seniority. Yet, senior LGB officers have reported that personal anxieties surrounding the management of their sexual orientation diminishes as their rank increases due to the growth of respect and associated power that comes with seniority. Despite this, many senior LGB officers are still reluctant to become role models and take the lead within their organisations on diversity issues, offering their support only on rare occasions and away from the limelight. In some instances, those who have aims to achieve ACPO rank choose not to disclose their LGB status at all in professional settings due to growing accusations surrounding promotion equity and positive discrimination on the grounds of diversity – an anxiety which is a cause for concern across all ranks. However, this lack of transparent leadership is a consistent form of disappointment for lower ranking officers who see the actions of their senior officers as a reflection of their force's commitment to translating policy and rhetoric into meaningful practice. Those LGB officers who are aware of the LGB status of their senior management but know that they choose not to come out at work are not encouraged to disclose themselves, again diminishing their potential contribution.

Variances in geography/force type

The current centralisation of police diversity policy and guidance aims to ensure a minimum standard across all 43 police forces. However, smaller, non-urban forces often fail to translate these policy directions into tangible initiatives, instead branding diversity as an urban problem (Morant & Edwards, 2011). In reality, the working lives of LGB officers in non-urban settings are extremely complex – often working and living within less progressive populations, with a smaller number of colleagues, within more isolated and concentrated settings (Holloway, 2005; Mawby & Yarwood, 2010). Thus, the margin for error for LGB officers in smaller/rural forces – in terms of managing the risks associated with potential adverse reactions from colleagues with these non-progressive settings – is significantly reduced, forcing many to camouflage their LGB status in order to conform. LGB officers outside urban settings, therefore, report feelings of organisational neglect and the existence of diversity envy relating to the substantive initiatives employed by neighbouring urban forces. These force variances are often overlooked, with policies and guidance often lacking the malleability to reflect differing requirements.

Policing futures for LGB police officers

The analysis above identifies considerable improvement in the workplace climate for LGB police officers today. However, despite this, the true potential of integrating subaltern officers into a new police force for the twenty-first century is not currently being maximised due to the strong resonance of historical sub-cultural masculinity that is being fed, rather falsely yet successfully, by the dominant mindset of the rank and file. Accordingly, the future of policing for LGB police officers rests on the ability to considerably dilute and eradicate this association of policing with masculinity and, instead, to celebrate the contribution that diversity and difference can make. The following recommendations are grounded in the views of LGB police officers on how these sizeable aims can be practically achieved:

- Insecurities currently held by LGB and other minority police officers regarding the longevity of the diversity agenda need to be addressed as a matter of urgency. Specifically in the face of financial austerity, anxiety is growing among LGB officers that recent efforts relating to their representation, integration, protection and improved work environment will grind to a halt and that forces will revert back to a pre-Macpherson mind-set. In such times of insecurity LGB officers are not inspired to utilise and explore the benefits of their unique skillset. To combat this, the establishment of a long-term proactive diversity strategy is needed, requiring long-term investment and reassurances from the Home Office and dominant police stakeholders. An example of this might include the establishment of a singular *Police Diversity Association* which would attract universal funding and encourage collaborative innovation among all diversity strands within policing.
- In order to dilute the prevalence of masculinity and negative behaviours, the mechanisms used to assess the calibre and core social values of potential new recruits need to be further reformed. The existing SEARCH and application form processes allow new recruits to create an illusion of diversity appreciation and adherence due to their short and formal nature. An alternative process based on a military model is encouraged, where the behaviours and social skills of applicants can be observed over a longer residential period. Similarly the expansion of a recent practice by some police forces to only recruit new police constables from their special constabulary stock is strongly encouraged. This allows the attitudes and behaviours of new recruits to be monitored and tested in a unique police environment prior to joining as a full-time remunerated police officer, with those who fail to demonstrate and meet the requisite standards being identified by the organisation and rejected before they can cause harm to future reform efforts.

- Reform of the initial two-year probation period for new recruits is also needed to expand the operational experiences of probation constables. Under the current system, new recruits are often placed in emergency response teams where masculinist expectations and behaviours are at their highest concentration. After two years in this climate new constables are often normalised into this policing mind-set, creating a benchmark against which all future professional experiences and expectations are judged. To combat this, lessons from professional legal training can be learned, specifically where trainee solicitors are required by the regulator to experience three different areas of law during their two-year workplace training (see SRA, 2012). Under a similar model for trainee police officers, after the initial 35-week IPLDP (Initial Police Learning and Development Programme), new recruits should be required to complete three placements in different areas of policing, where different skills, mind-sets and policing strategies are required. As a consequence, the need for and benefits of diversity and different policing styles beyond machismo can be practically experienced and explored from the outset of a new police officer's career.
- A comprehensive review of diversity training and pedagogic platforms used by the police is strongly encouraged. Currently, the effectiveness and impact of e-learning and generic training strategies to bring about meaningful attitudinal change and cultural understanding is called into question amongst minority officers. Instead, a training strategy based on experiential reflexive learning should be devised, as advocated in the chapter on police education within this edited collection. It is only when police officers understand *why* they are required to do something (through an understanding of diversity theory and histories) and are given the opportunity to moot *how* different actions can potentially impact police reputation, community interactions and workplace experiences of colleagues within a pseudo-intellectual space, that embedded and symbolic change of attitudes can be brought about.
- The traditional iconography of policing needs to be reviewed and updated to reflect modern policing roles and contributions. Brown (2007) discusses how police images and marketing material continue to only represent policemen in traditional police roles, despite the prominence of community, problem-orientated and multi-agency policy models today. These outdated images, she argues, reinforce masculine police associations, fuel the internal cult of masculinity and do little to promote the impact of diversity reform agendas. In future, contributions and representations of minority officers – including LGB officers who are often overlooked due to the invisibility of sexuality – should be included as part of a wider educational strategy to celebrate difference internally and to promote the effects of reform to the general public.
- Finally, the existing territorial set-up and geographical disparate nature of our 43 police forces across England and Wales present unique challenges to the execution of police diversity often leading to disparate experiences for LGB police officers. In future, inter-force collaboration and the establishment of a

platform through which police forces nationally can showcase and share best practice is strongly encouraged.

Note

1   These are formal positions that dedicate the remit of the officers – who are not necessarily LGB themselves – to LGBT (lesbian, gay, bisexual, transgender) community policing issues.

References

Breakwell, G. (1986). *Coping with Threatened Identities*. London: Methuen & Co. Ltd.

Brown, J. (2007). From Cult of Masculinity to Smart Macho: Gender Perspectives on Police Occupational Culture. In M. O'Neill, M. Marks & A.-M. Singh (Eds.), *Police Occupational Culture: New Debates and Directions*. Oxford: Elsevier.

Brown, J. & Heidensohn, F. (2000). *Gender & Policing: Comparative Perspectives*. Basingstoke: Palgrave Macmillan.

Brown, J. & Bear, D. (2012). Women police officers may lose equality gains with the current police reform programme | British Politics and Policy at LSE. *London School of Economics & Political Science Blog*. Retrieved November 1, 2012, from http://blogs.lse. ac.uk/politicsandpolicy/2012/07/02/police-reform-programme-bear-brown/

Burke, M. (1993). *Homosexuality in the British Police*. PhD Thesis. University of Essex.

Burke, M. (1995). Identities and disclosures: The case of lesbian and gay police officers. *The Psychologist*, *8*, 543–547.

Burke, M. (1994). Homosexuality as deviance: The case of the gay police officer. *British Journal of Criminology*, *34*(2), 192–203.

Chan, J. (1996). Changing police culture. *British Journal of Criminology*, *36*(1), 109.

Clemence, H. (2011). Diversity in policing: Putting money where the mouth is. *Jane's Police Review: Reporter's Reflections Blog*.

Colvin, R. (2008). Shared perceptions among lesbian and gay police officers: Barriers and opportunities in the law enforcement work environment. *Police Quarterly*, *12*(1), 86–101.

Giles, J. (2006). Social constructionism and sexual desire. *Journal for the Theory of Social Behaviour*, *36*(3), 225–238.

Godwin, K. (2007). Staffordshire Police: Working to a different beat. *Equal Opportunities Review*, 164.

Hall, N., Grieve, J. & Savage, S. (2009). Introduction: The Legacies of Lawrence. In N. Hall, J. Grieve & P. Savage (Eds.), *Policing and the Legacy of Lawrence* (pp. 1–21). Cullompton, Devon: Willan.

HMIC. (2003). *Diversity Matters*. London.

Hoch, P. (Ed.). (1979). Masculinity as the Avoidance of Homosexuality. *White Hero, Black Beast: Racism, Sexism and the Mask of Masculinity*. London: Pluto Press.

Holdaway, S (Ed.). (1979). *The British Police*. London: Edward Arnold Publishers.

Holdaway, S. (1983). *Inside the British Police*. Oxford: Basil Blackwell Publisher Ltd.

Holdaway, S. (2009). *Black Police Associations*. Oxford: Oxford University Press.

Holdaway, S. & O'Neill, M. (2007). Where has all the racism gone? Views of racism within constabularies after Macpherson. *Ethnic and Racial Studies*, *30*(3), 397–415.

Holloway, S. L. (2005). Articulating Otherness? White rural residents talk about Gypsy-Travellers. *Transactions of the Institute of British Geographers*, *30*(3), 351–367.

Home Office. (2005a). *It Works . . . The Operational Benefits of Diversity for the Police Service.* London.

Home Office. (2005b). *Assessing the Impact of the Stephen Lawrence Inquiry. Research Study 294.*

Jones, M. (2013a). *Cultures of Difference: Exploring the Occupational Complexities Faced by Lesbian, Gay and Bisexual Police Officers across England and Wales.* PhD Thesis. Cardiff University.

Jones, M. (2013b). Who forgot lesbian, gay & bisexual police officers? Findings from a national survey (forthcoming).

Kehily, M. J. & Nayak, A. (1997). 'Lads and laughter': Humour and the production of heterosexual hierarchies. *Gender and Education, 9*(1), 69–88.

Loftus, B. (2009). *Police Culture in a Changing World.* Oxford: Oxford University Press.

Macpherson, S. W. (1999). *Report of an Inquiry by Sir William Macpherson Of Cluny.* London.

Mawby, R. I. & Yarwood, R. (2010). *Rural Policing and Policing the Rural: A Constable Countryside?* (p. 261). Ashgate Publishing, Ltd.

McLaughlin, E. (2007). *The New Policing.* London: Sage.

Morant, N. & Edwards, E. (2011). Police responses to diversity: A social representational study of rural British policing in a changing representational context. *Journal of Community & Applied Social Psychology, 21*(4), 281–296.

Morris, S. (2004). *The case for change: People in the Metropolitan Police Service. The Report of the Morris Inquiry.* London: Metropolitan Police Authority.

Myers, K., Forest, K. & Miller, S. (2004). Officer friendly and the tough cop: Gays and lesbians navigate homophobia and policing. *Journal of Homosexuality, 47*(1), 17–37.

O'Neill, M. & Holdaway, S. (2007). Examining 'window dressing': The views of black police associations on recruitment and training. *Journal of Ethnic and Migration Studies, 33*(3), 483–500.

Rabe-Hemp, C. E. (2008). POLICE women or PoliceWOMEN? Doing gender and police work. *Feminist Criminology, 4*(2), 114–129.

Rodriguez Rust, P. (2009). No More Lip Service: How to Really Include Bisexuals in Research on Sexuality. In W. Meezan & J. Martin (Eds.), *Handbook of Research with Lesbian, Gay, Bisexual, and Transgender Populations.* Oxon: Routledge.

Silvestri, M. (2007). 'Doing' police leadership: Enter the 'new smart macho'. *Policing and Society, 17*(1), 38–58.

Skolnick, J. H. (2008). Enduring issues of police culture and demographics. *Policing and Society, 18*(1), 35–45.

SRA. (2012). Solicitors Regulation Authority: Training Contract Guidelines. Retrieved from http://www.sra.org.uk/training-contract/

Van Ewijk, A. R. (2011). Diversity within police forces in Europe: A case for the comprehensive view. *Policing, 6*(1), 76–92.

Ward, J. & Winstanley, D. (2005). Coming out at work: Performativity and the recognition and renegotiation of identity. *The Sociological Review, 53*(3), 447–475.

Westmarland, L. (2001). *Gender & Policing: Sex, Power and Police Culture.* Cullompton, Devon: Willan.

INTRODUCTION TO PARTS III AND IV

The practice of policing

Jennifer M. Brown

Introduction

Parts III and IV of the book address issues reflected in the Commission's terms of reference to do with relationships, delivery and resourcing. Chapters in Part IV take us into the territory of what has been termed 'high' and 'low' policing (Innes and Thiel, 2008). The latter is concerned with the everyday protection of the citizen and largely reacts to notification that a crime or some disorder is in progress or has taken place. The former is about matters that threaten the security of the state and is often proactive, involving infiltration, surveillance and intelligence gathering and analysis. What Innes and Thiel make apparent is that clear-cut boundaries between the two have changed over time and that having a national capability represents a departure from the local delivery and accountabilities of Peelian modes of policing said to characterise the British Model of Policing. The blurring of boundaries is reflected in the chapters in Part III with discussions of public–private provision.

The authors address a number of shibboleths: that the state or indeed the police have a monopoly over policing and, in particular, crime control; sanctity of the Peelian principles; the inexorable march of privatisation. The emergent themes that the chapters collectively bring out are, first, departures from the locally delivered tradition of the British Model of Policing; second, a blurring of the distinctiveness of the public and private sectors in respect to policing; third, the critical importance of community in operational policing; fourth, the emerging role of research to inform policing practices; and fifth, the requirement for the police to act within the law, especially in the arena of high policing.

The plurality of policing and the involvement of the private sector are the focus of the chapters by Adam Crawford and Mark Roycroft. Roycroft, in his chapter, describes early privately funded police that predated the establishment of the Metropolitan Police in 1829 which located responsibility for policing with the state. At the insistence of Sir Robert Peel, the primary aim of the 'new' police he founded for the metropolis was crime prevention. Adam Crawford (2008: 147) notes in modern times there has been 'a restructuring of the police and a proliferation of policing beyond the police as a result of which a more complex division of labour in the fields of policing and security has emerged'. As Sir Ronnie Flanagan observed, 'modern policing is carried out in partnership with a wide range of local agencies' (Flanagan, 2008: 7).

Adam Crawford, in his chapter, sets out some game changers: changes in land use, ideological shifts in favour of the private sector, introduction of locally elected Police and Crime Commissioners which, in conjunction with the pressures brought on by austerity, have opened up previously unthinkable arrangements for the delivery of policing. He shows how progressively legislation has interacted with these trends such that there has been an 'osmotic' diffusion which, in his view, blurs the distinction between the private and the public. On the one hand, the public police use their brand advantage to sell services and, on the other, the private sector are adopting public good sentiments. This means the previous, neater distinction between the 'public' police as agents of the state engaged in a public service for a communal good and 'private' agents being paid by the state to provide policing goods for profit has been lost. Tony Butler, a serving chief constable writing in the mid-1990s, predicted that the police will become 'just another service responding to the social market occupied almost entirely with pursuing a deterrence model of crime control' (Butler, 1996: 230). As discussed in several previous chapters in this volume there is a critical stance taken on the political emphasis on crime control models of policing. In this section there is a demonstration of how crucial it is to embed policing within the community, and the balancing act that must weigh protecting the public against reassuring the community, whether that be policing hate crime (Johnson), serious organised crime (Sproat), public order (Stott and Gorringe) or terrorism (Grieve). The community focus is developed in Megan O'Neill's chapter through her empirical research looking at delivery of neighbourhood policing and how success has shifted the value attached to this as a policing deployment. Alex Hirschfield and colleagues also provide a demonstration of this through the crime prevention arena.

Several authors, Grieve, Sproat, Stott and Gorringe, draw on academic research to demonstrate how this has informed developments in policing in areas of both high and low policing. Robin Engel and Samantha Henderson present an account of how academic police relationships have evolved and Karen Bullock provides a corridor through which systematic evidence-based approaches travel and meet operation policing in the form of the National Intelligence Model. Her chapter and the chapter by Engel and Henderson provide the platform for a discussion of police professionalism presented in Part V.

Crawford delineates dimensions differentiating traditional policing from private security: symbolic vs instrumental; reactive vs proactive; law enforcement vs loss prevention; detection vs risk reduction. Interestingly these overlap with, but in some respects are different from, the distinctions observed by Manning (e.g.

accountability, symbolic role in governance, use of violence and willingness to sacrifice life). Crawford's distinctions have become blurred through some pretty significant shifts in attitudes by police themselves and politically in the ideology of engaging the private sector in delivery of policing. The movement towards the private sector was discernible in Margaret Thatcher's introduction of New Public Management in the police which attempted to instil commercial efficiencies into management practices. Since then, enabling legislation has developed a more active participation of the private sector and, in the present fiscal climate, the emphasis has been on achieving economies by delivering aspects of policing services more cheaply. The implications of Crawford's argument is that there is a continuum rather than a dichotomy separating the public from the private. Mark Roycroft attempts to segment policing tasks in a way that takes account of the Manning distinctions and argues that, for those reasons, some duties should remain with the public police, whereas others can be outsourced and yet others delivered in com-bination. Manning tries to get at motive for involvement in policing by describing the contest between the vocabulary of economics (efficiency, effectiveness, value for money) and a moral vocabulary (equity, fairness, legitimacy). Part of the prob-lem in debating the relative merits of private versus public provision of policing, he says, is a lack of definitional precision and paucity of robust evidence to substantiate the outcome claims of both.

The 'appliance of science', as discussed by Brogden and Ellison (2013: 75) is another response to the depletion of police resources. Robin Engel and Samantha Henderson, in their chapter, note that early collaborations between the police and academia began in the 1900s. Whereas Stenson and Silverstone, in Chapter 27, discuss the role of research as an accountability mechanism, Engel and Henderson describe the increased effectiveness in policing which is made possible by evi-denced-based research interventions. Here then, potentially, is a version of Man-ning's competing vocabularies. As Stenson and Silverstone observe in their chapter, the academic community is not entirely disinterested in the research questions asked or the methods used, with quantitative methodologies tending towards the effective and efficiency objectives, and qualitative tending towards the moral.

Both Crawford and Roycroft discuss the symbolic role of the public police, identified previously by Manning who asserted that not only do the police send out messages about 'what is right, correct and trustworthy' but also that the virtue of their visible presence is a 'unifying and even comforting source of emotional and interpersonal support'. Manning argues, as does Roycroft, that allegiance to the shareholder could seriously undermine notions of 'democratic' policing. Roy-croft attempts to identify policing duties that require a publicly accountable police response, such as deployment of force, and those which do not, such as routine statement taking. This, he argues, can be provided by private contractors. Yet other activities may require a combination of police knowledge and commercial analytic skill, e.g. crime pattern analysis. As such, a 'blended' model of policing preserves degrees of separation between the public and private depending on requirements of skills, public expectations and accountability rather than the fluidity suggested by

Crawford's 'extended family' metaphor. Whichever plays out, these new arrangements represent, as Crawford declares, 'a fundamental departure in the organisation and delivery of British policing'. However, Crawford speculates that in the aftermath of G4S's failure to deliver its Olympic contract, together with the stance taken by many of the newly elected Police and Crime Commissioners as well as a measure of public disquiet, there has been a stuttering of momentum in private provision.

Other new ways of working are described by Megan O'Neill who employs the concept of occupational culture when reporting some of the results of her empirical studies in partnership working. This reveals that neighbourhood policing has become a space where boundaries of the crime control model have been stretched. In part, this has been achieved by an enhanced status accruing to neighbourhood policing which no longer carries a career limiting stigma. Here too, there is evidence of the duality described by Manning. On the one hand, some officers see neighbourhood interventions in the business sense by adding value through problem-solving solutions that save money, while others are committed to building partnership on the basis of shared values and changing the time horizon for outcomes. This marks a change in what Reiner portrays as a mentality in which 'police officers are concerned to get from here to tomorrow (or the next hour) safely and with the least fuss and paperwork which has made them reluctant to contemplate innovation, experimentation or research' (Reiner, 2010: 132).

Engels and Henderson also draw our attention to an analogous relationship to the one described by Megan O'Neill with respect to neighbourhood policing, in that the more likely productive partnerships to emerge between the police and researchers are those built on long-term commitment over many years, in which mutual trust develops through understanding each other's perspectives. These enduring relations are thought to deliver more fruitful results than collaborations built round a specific project. The consortium, such as the Scottish Institute of Policing Research (SIPR), is an example of the former and has pioneered a networked approach in which police and academics, together, set a research agenda over a longer time frame than any one project.

Alex Hirschfield, Rachel Armitage, Paul Ekblom and Jason Roach also pursue the building and boundaries of relationships, in this case relating to crime prevention. They distinguish between

> enforcement based judicial prevention in which the police service is heavily involved and the broader notion of civil crime prevention to which the police make valuable contribution through mobilising or working in partnership with local communities, statutory agencies, voluntary groups and the private sector.

Their chapter neatly segues between O'Neill's discussion and that of Engels and Henderson by examining evidence and theory considerations of crime prevention, which, like neighbourhood policing, was not considered a particularly high-profile policing activity. As they remind us, crime prevention takes us back to the early purposes of the 'new' police. Their new ways of thinking locates crime prevention in the moral domain because a preventative CJS 'helps to channel blame and revenge into a formal, controlled and relatively impersonal public arena'. The argument they present maps onto the duality discussed at the beginning; the oscillation between a welfarist approach and a security one.

This oscillation is also at the heart of chapters by John Grieve and Peter Sproat. Grieve, formerly a commander in the Metropolitan Police's anti terrorist branch and also famously involved in interventions post Lawrence, presents some of the dilemmas besetting the state in protecting citizens from the activities of terrorists. Drawing on his experiences in Northern Ireland, and also informed by the work he did with the Lawrence family after the murder of their son Stephen, he uncompromisingly affirms the criticality of engaging with communities because it is through them that the necessary intelligence can be gleaned. Over-emphasis on the operational tactics at the expense of community concerns can undermine confidence and exacerbate deep-seated resentments in order to achieve short-term objectives. Oppressive tactics that undermine the legitimacy of the policing might well interfere with the aim of the police in helping to bring communities back to normality. A version of this is discussed by Mike Rowe (Chapter 8) and the cycle of resentment that stop and search engenders in the ethnic minority communities. Understanding that intelligence is a given in countering terrorism, neverthless (a) dialogue and (b) informed research is pivotal in developing counter terrorist (CT) policing. Grieve argues that in the context of CT it is not simply a case of maintaining the peace, but of *winning* it (*my emphasis*). Thus, there is an important reservoir of knowledge to be drawn from people in constructing community-derived tactics to disrupt terrorist activity or facilitating arrests. Another source of knowledge is derived from research which helps understand the prejudices, extremism and processes involved in radicalisation that fuel the resentments and ideologies that contribute to acts of terrorism.

Clifford Stott and Hugo Gorringe also illustrate the importance of dialogue and research in their discussion of public order policing and the derivation of police liaison teams. Their chapter is another example of the disruption theme elucidated in Part I of the book. They assert that the police must seek and maintain public support by acting fairly and impartially. When they are policing a public protest, for example, they are caught between differing and conflicting interests: the right to protest, the potential disruption to business and transport, the counter interests of disagreeing parties. As in CT, the insensitive use of oppressive tactics in public order policing might bring about an immediate restoration of order but can undermine people's trust and confidence through perceived, or actual, partiality. Critically important, too, is the decision to use force only when persuasion has been tried and failed. Finally, it is necessary to understand the nature of crowds and the psychology of crowd behaviour to counter a belief that large groupings of people somehow act irrationally. They also advise on the importance of policing from *within* the community (*my emphasis*) and highlight the identification between the police and the policed. While they have not stated so in procedural justice terms, as discussed by Loader and Bradford and colleagues, ideas of fair treatment, and social and psychological identification are common ideas.

What they then describe is the evolving of a policing innovation – Police Liaison Teams' (PLTs). The logic which they draw out resonates with Dick and colleagues in formulating ways to change when they say the PLTs

> were deliberately re-branded to show a break from the past in terms of policing styles. These officers, trained in protest liaison skills and crowd psychology, were adept at communication and engagement. Indeed, they were chosen for their 'people skills' and several had no background in public order.

Thus, PLTs entailed 'root and branch' changes in the operational dynamics of the public order policing.

The changes Paul Johnson talks about in his chapter about hate crime derive from a 'cuture shift' following the Macpherson Report in 1999 which investigated the murder of Stephen Lawrence mentioned earlier. This had identified 'institutional racism' in the police service and called for the police to recognise different experiences, perceptions and needs of the diverse society they police. This critical event and its aftermath, development of guidance, creation of specialist units, buttressed by primary legislation led to a recognition of, and different response to, crimes motivated by bias and prejudice. But what Johnson discusses are some of the consequences of the plurality of policing and an ambiguity in Government policy as to whether the police are at the heart of, or peripheral in, dealing with hate crime. This, to some extent, represents the dilemma inherent in national policy and local delivery.

Peter Sproat and Karen Bullock identify similar problems when it comes to the policing of serious organised crime. Sproat argues that the Peelian mode of policing bequeathed a model of locally delivered, locally accountable services. The development of a national approach as in the National Crime Agency and its progenitors, is essentially a deviation from the Peelian conception. Bullock acknowledges the shortcomings of the random patrol, rapid response of local policing and shows how an intelligence-led approach and its embodiment in the National Intelligence Model offered standards and systematic use of intelligence both to understand problems and direct resources to better effect.

Some of the risks associated with a national approach are articulated by Sproat, not least of which is a coming together of the needs of the state and the investigative process which can undermine the independence of the police, illustrated by the uncoupling of 'agents' from the office of constable. Complementary risks are identified by Crawford when he talks about business regulatory models which are being brought in to govern the conduct of private security agents. Karen Bullock reminds us that, however good, analysts can only provide an indication, they cannot predict. Moreover, she draws our attention to a further example of the limits of private and public when she points out that civilian analysts might have no operational experience and her compromise is that the analyst can offer options but officers should decide where, when and how resources are deployed.

References

Brogden, M. and Ellison, G. (2013) *Policing in the Age of Austerity: A Post Colonial Perspective.* London: Routledge.

Butler, A.J.P. (1996) Managing the future: a chief constable's view, in F. Leishman, B. Loveday and S. Savage (eds) *Core Issues in Policing.* London: Longmans, pp. 218–230.

Crawford, A. (2008) Plural police in the UK: policing beyond the police, in T. Newburn (ed.) *Handbook of Policing.* Cullompton: Willan, pp. 147–181.

Flanagan, Sir Ronnie. (2008) *The Review of Policing: Final Report.* London: Home Office.

Innes, M. and Thiel, D. (2008) Policing terror, in T. Newburn (ed.) *Handbook of Policing.* Cullompton: Willan, pp. 553–579.

Reiner, R. (2010) *The Politics of the Police* (4th edn). Oxford: Oxford University Press.

PART III

Relationships

11

THE POLICE, POLICING AND THE FUTURE OF THE EXTENDED POLICING FAMILY

Adam Crawford

Introduction

'Policing' is too readily reduced to the activities of 'the police'. Subsequently, developments in the market, private and voluntary sectors and civil society are marginalised. Moreover, the implications of one of the most enduring lessons of decades of police scholarship from Banton (1964) to Brodeur (2010), namely the marginal place of the police in social control and crime prevention, are largely overlooked. Hence, much public debate and policy reform erroneously perpetuates the 'myth' of the sovereign state monopoly over crime control and policing; of the public monopoly over policing; and the police monopoly over crime.

The contentions of this chapter are fourfold. First, policing can no longer (if ever it could) be conceived as simply 'what the police do'. This necessitates an acknowledgement of, and political engagement with, the mixed economy of policing which is structured by a complex division of labour and multifaceted relations between plural providers, auspices and actors. Second, as a result of converging forces, changes in land-use and policy trends, we now stand on the brink of a new dawn for relations between private security and public police in Britain, with significant implications for policing and safety as a 'public good'. Third, the contemporary confluence of 'electoral answerability' in the form of the new governance structure of Police and Crime Commissioners (PCCs) and 'fiscal austerity' could prove to be a volatile mix; resulting simultaneously in pressures upon greater private sector involvement in the delivery of police services and provoking (insatiable) public expectations and demands for greater front-line public policing. Finally, in light of the above, any reform of policing and its governance must regulate and oversee the plurality of policing providers and seek to organise and coordinate relations between them in the furtherance of public safety.

The police in policing

In place of the dominant assumptions about the centrality of the police in policing and crime control, there is a prevailing need to appreciate policing as *the outcome of a constellation of actors, agencies and processes* both within and beyond the police organisation; as 'intentional action involving the conscious exercise of power or authority (by an individual or organisation) that is directed towards rule enforcement, the promotion of order or assurances of safety' (Crawford *et al.* 2005: 4). This challenges us to better understand: (i) the role and place of police within policing; (ii) the contribution and role of non-police (commercial, municipal, hybrid and citizen-based) agents to policing endeavours; and (iii) the relations within and between plural providers of policing – or what has become known as the 'extended policing family'. To do so requires us to think conceptually about the parameters of policing and the role of the police therein.

A key fault-line influencing the nature of plural policing has been the shifting relations between public police and private security; between the state and the market as providers of policing. The latter part of the twentieth century saw a significant growth in the private security industry and its role in the provision of policing. This contemporary pluralisation and expansion of private policing was, itself, a product of longer-term trends combined with more recent policy developments and market-based initiatives.

A significant finding of research into private security has been that the strategies of commercial security tend to differ significantly from those of the traditional police in that they are more instrumental than moral, offering a more proactive rather than reactive approach to problem-solving (Shearing and Stenning 1981). They tend to be concerned with loss prevention and risk reduction rather than with law enforcement or the detection and conviction of criminals. In 'mass private property' the regulatory force of 'membership' and 'access' are powerful modes of control. If the law is invoked it is often likely to be contract law, rather than the criminal law. The powers of removal, dismissal and exclusion – whether from a night-club or shopping mall – are potent administrative tools of policing (Stenning 2000). Private security managers and the shop owner have private, largely commercial, interests to secure that diverge from those of public prosecution. Security guards are more likely to prioritise the plugging of security breaches in the future, the exclusion of likely offenders and ensuring that security is not compromised. Symbolic and ritualistic punishments are not a commercial imperative. Rather, private security tends to inscribe incentives for conformity and orderly conduct. Shearing (2001) thus juxtaposes a past-regarding, reactive, morally toned and punitive mentality of 'justice' against a risk-based, instrumental and future-oriented mentality of 'security'. The former is associated with traditional aspects of police crime detection work (and the activities of state criminal justice agencies more generally). The latter is associated with commercial operatives and is exercised under plural auspices.

This juxtaposition provides a useful analytic framework. However, increasingly it is the osmotic relationships between state and commercial developments and the cross-fertilisation of techniques, practices and mentalities that dominate the field (Crawford 2011). As White and Gill (2013: 89) conclude, the growth of private policing has not simply resulted in a shift from a 'public good oriented system of policing to a market-oriented one as the ratio of private security to police actors has increased'. Commercially oriented strategies that combine dynamics of inclusion and exclusion now increasingly structure public ordering of city centres and street corners, while private security guards and managers appeal to the public good and have recourse to public powers. In the process, public values coalesce around, and collide with, private and parochial interests. Thus, it is less easy to differentiate between styles of policing dependent upon, or reducible to, the characteristics of those who provide or even authorise policing agents. The conceptual parameters for thinking about both the public goals and interests served by private forms of policing and the private or parochial nature of the public police have become more intimate and complex as there has been both a commercialisation of the public police and a publicisation of private security.

Policing policy developments

From within the field of policing there have been significant policy reforms that have also informed the mixed economy of plural policing. The steady marketisation of policing has seen the police involved more extensively both in buying and selling services (Ayling *et al.* 2009). While the Police Act 1964 allowed police forces to charge for 'special services', such as the policing of football matches, it was the Police and Magistrates Court Act 1994 that opened a wider space for the police to enter the market-place, including the contracting out of police officer time. The Police Reform Act 2002 not only gave the police a new commodity to 'contract out' through public–private partnerships, namely the Police Community Support Officer (PCSO), but also enabled chief officers to establish accreditation schemes that grant limited powers (fixed penalty notices) to non-police organisations to contribute towards community safety. The Act marked a watershed in fostering greater engagement with the private security sector.

The early 2000s also saw the further pluralisation of policing agents with the government-sponsored expansion of neighbourhood and street wardens (Crawford 2006). Nevertheless, the competition for local resources once central government funding ceased, resulted in a steady decline in the number of wardens as many councils subsequently diverted resources to part-fund the expansion of PCSOs. In an example of conflicting departmental priorities emanating from central government, councils were forced to choose to allocate scarce resources either to funding Home Office-sponsored PCSOs or Office of Deputy Prime Minister-promoted warden schemes. Little strategic thought was given to the relative benefits that adhere to the very different purposes, roles and rationalities of each of the differing policing actors.

Furthermore, community safety accreditation schemes have largely failed to take off to the extent initially envisaged; despite offering the police opportunities to influence the policing efforts of others and affording private security benefits from enhanced credibility. The business advantages to security providers were offset by the costs and the scheme foundered on the reluctance of many police forces to entertain the idea of granting additional powers to private operators. By the end of 2010, the number of accredited persons stood at only 2,219 across the 26 participating forces (ACPO 2011). The vast majority were local authority employed wardens or anti-social behaviour enforcement officers rather than staff employed by commercial security companies.

It was the Private Security Industry Act 2001 that possibly did more to lay the ground-work for current conditions. It established the Security Industry Authority (SIA), launched in 2003, to license and regulate all 'contract' private security providers. The SIA has two main responsibilities. The first is the compulsory licensing of individuals undertaking designated activities within the private security industry. The second is to manage the voluntary 'approved contractor' scheme, which measures private security suppliers against certain criteria. The Act was introduced, in part, to shift the industry into the mainstream of policing services by encouraging a higher degree of professionalism and to regulate unscrupulous operators. Regulation was a long-standing policy goal that powerful proponents within the industry had championed as the key to greater legitimacy and hence to open the gateway to wider policing markets. According to the SIA's Annual Report for 2011/12, membership of the approved contractor scheme stood at 736 companies (SIA 2012). Despite a number of 'false dawns' (White 2010), the SIA has helped move the private security industry into the mainstream. John Saunders, SIA Chief Executive between 2003 and 2006, reflected:

> the Act's most important contribution is that it provides sound foundations for introducing fundamental change, creating a private security industry that is healthier, more successful, dynamic and fit to pursue new market opportunities. Above all, an industry that is respected and proud of its reputation.
>
> *(Saunders 2004: 6)*

Following the Public Bodies Review in 2010, the Coalition Government concluded that the SIA's functions should be reformed and no longer conducted by a non-departmental public body accountable to the Home Secretary: 'The Review concluded that a new regulatory regime and new regulator should be established, reflecting the maturity of the private security industry and supporting the industry's willingness to take on further responsibility and be more accountable for its actions' (Home Office 2012: 7). In November 2012, the government published its preferred option for reforming how the private security industry is to be regulated, under which there would be a phased transition to a business regulation regime and a change to how individuals are licensed to work within the industry (Home Office 2012). The intention of the proposed changes is to achieve a reduction in the regulatory cost and burden on the private security industry as a whole. As a result the SIA is anticipated to be reconstituted as a new independent regulator outside of the public sector with increased representation from the security industry. The likely outcome will be that regulation will shift from licensing individuals to registering businesses, which will have to meet certain standards and conditions set by the new regulator.

Two phases: the rise and fall of police numbers

Figure 11.1 highlights two very distinct periods over the last 15 years. It illustrates the growth and subsequent decline of police numbers, which reflected and informed very different attitudes held by police managers towards the private sector. In the first phase (circa 2000–2010), against a background of expanding police numbers, senior police managers held a highly sceptical view of the private security sector. Relations were marked by hostility and a lack of trust by the police in the private security sector. Research at the time concluded:

> There persists a view within some police units that the police alone should provide patrols and that others merely get in their way rather than seeing others' policing efforts as a resource to be harnessed in the furtherance of public safety.
>
> *(Crawford and Lister 2004: x)*

This was combined with fears that the private sector might encroach onto, and stimulate, a market for policing services, including the sacred cow of neighbourhood patrols. The then Deputy Commissioner of the Metropolitan Police, Ian Blair (2002) somewhat apocalyptically captured this view in his warning of the possible 'Balkanisation of policing'. From this perspective, the growth of the private sector was something to be feared; as a result of which 'we may see hundreds of different law-enforcement agencies springing up across Britain' (Blair 2002: 23), thus, returning policing to the 'dark ages' before the rise of the professional police.

In the 2000s, police managers anticipated that they could expand and even capture markets from the private sector, given their brand advantage and their more competitively priced workforce, notably in the light of workforce modernisation and the introduction of PCSOs as compared to their constabulary colleagues. This view was captured again by Ian Blair in 2003 in his vision of a 'vertical model' of relations between the police and private sector; analogous to the monopolistic model outlined earlier:

> I have in mind two concentric circles. The inner, much smaller circle is coloured completely blue; this is the direct employees of the police service. The second circle is much larger and consists of all the personnel involved in community safety activity. I believe it is in the interest of social cohesion and public security for as much as possible of that circle also to be blue, in effect for the inner circle to widen.
>
> *(Blair 2003; cited in Crawford 2007a: 151)*

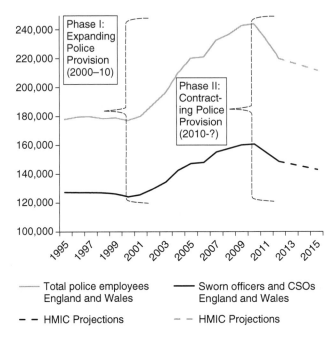

FIGURE 11.1 Number of police employees (at 31 March each year) with HMIC projections 1995–2015 for England and Wales (100,000 base-line)

Adapted from Dhani (2012) and HMIC (2012)

The private security industry at the time remained relatively immature in many traditional areas of police work. It was also preoccupied with addressing public legitimacy deficits and side-tracked with the burdens of regulation implied by the implementation of the 2001 Act.

By the time of the 2010 Comprehensive Spending Review, Britain had a more mature, self-confident and assertive private security industry. The implementation of the new, albeit relatively tame (within a European context) regulatory framework for the security industry coupled with innovative experiments in public–private partnerships has provided more fertile soil.

A major stimulus for transformation, however, was triggered by the banking crisis of 2008 which prompted dramatic austerity measures across the public sector. In this context, the ideological commitment to private sector involvement in the delivery of public services as the accepted response to conditions of austerity has quickly germinated. As the political taboo of decreasing police officer numbers was abandoned by the Coalition Government, so the transfer to the private sector of large aspects of policing has been placed firmly on the agenda. The subsequent scale of fiscal restraint on policing budgets has been unprecedented. Furthermore, the economic challenges go beyond the short-term spending period. HM Treasury (2012) has already indicated departmental expenditure limits until 2017. Moreover, the Winsor Review (2011) forecasts severe restraint in public service finances for decades to come. This new economic reality prompted the new Coalition Government to abandon the erstwhile political shibboleth of increased police officer numbers, allowing them to fall. By 2010, the size of the police workforce in England and Wales reached an all-time high, at just under 245,000, including just under 144,000 police constables and 17,000 PCSOs. According to the HMIC, total police employees are estimated to decline by 32,300 up to 2015; a 13 per cent fall from its 2010 peak. This includes reductions of 15,600 police staff, 15,000 police constables and 1,700 PCSOs (HMIC 2012: 20).

However, the police austerity programme was due not simply to economic pressures but also to ideological imperatives. The Coalition Government has made clear their political and ideological commitment to greater private sector involvement in the delivery of various public services as the 'rational response' to conditions of austerity. Oliver Letwin the minister responsible for coordinating government policy articulated the now prevailing ideological position. He declared that private companies working in hospitals, police and schools will 'no longer be a matter of political debate but straightforward and obvious as a way of conducting business in this country' (cited in Mason 2012). As such, austerity has become the justification for the headlong rush to private sector involvement as a means of making cost efficiencies in the face of considerable reductions in police budgets. Finally, the spectre of 'external' democratic control ushered by the advent of PCCs has – given their control of police budgets – added a further dynamic of political and policy uncertainty in relation to the police and their relations with non-police providers of policing.

Acknowledging this, the private sector has been adroit at responding to their changed fortunes. In November 2011, a roundtable meeting was held in Parliament, hosted by the British Security Industry Association (BSIA) to encourage greater private sector involvement in policing. A number of subsequent developments signalled a dramatic transition in the attitude of police managers towards private security in which the market came to be seen less as a threat to the public good and more as a possible saviour, providing opportunities for efficiency savings.

Pioneers of the new frontier?

The subsequent pace of events was nothing short of breath-taking. A landmark was set by Lincolnshire Police when they signed a £200 million contract with G4S in February 2012 to build and staff (for 10 years) a police station. The contract accounts for 18 per cent of the force budget, with estimated savings of £28 million. It incorporates a wide range of functions, such as: custody services ('street to suite'); town enquiry officers; force control room; and a crime management bureau. Under the initiative, half the civilian staff (some 575 employees) joined the private company. When the contract was put out to tender in March 2011, some 12 companies responded with submissions, highlighting the readiness of the private sector to respond to public sector outsourcing of policing.

West Midlands and Surrey Police forces followed this initiative by issuing a £1.5 billion procurement tender. This joint 'Business Partnering for Police' (BPP) initiative was supported financially, strategically and ideologically by the Home Office. Home Office backing provided what the West Midlands Police Authority (2011) subsequently described as 'significant protection from some of the reputational risks' associated with the programme. Crucially, the Home Office provided the essential momentum to initiate the procurement process, by funding the consultancy report (prepared by Impower Consulting) that generated the first stage of the work, indicating a willingness to provide additional finances to help support the procurement and pre-procurement stages, and creating a 'very positive dialogue with potential partners and providers' (ibid.). A procurement notice was published in January 2012 in the *Official Journal of the European Union* which led to approximately 300 'registrations of interest' from the supplier community.

The scale and breadth of the areas of policing covered in the procurement documents – including supporting victims and witnesses, managing high-risk individuals, patrolling neighbourhoods, managing engagement with the public, etc. – left few in doubt that it represented a fundamental departure in the organisation and delivery of British policing. A West Midlands Police Authority spokesperson explained: 'Combining with the business sector is aimed at totally transforming the way the force currently does business – improving the service provided to the public' (cited in Travis and Williams 2012). The Impower Consulting report provides crucial insights into the thinking and logic that lay behind the initiative, the goals of which were described as constituting:

> the rapid transformation of key functions and activities, in particular to strengthen the relationship with the customer and citizen and invest in new technologies; the provision of functions and services to the public that are higher performing and cost less to deliver than is currently the case; the building of expertise and capability to meet the significant challenges for policing in the medium term and build 'continuous transformation'.
>
> *(West Midlands Police Authority 2012: 4)*

The report sets out the dimensions of the business case as strategic, economic, commercial, financial and management (following HM Treasury's Green Book), the nub of which was 'financial austerity' (ibid.: 4–5). By June 2012, the BBP programme had produced a shortlist of six groups to be taken forward into a further stage of tendering and negotiations. The contract notice was something of a scoping exercise both in its breadth and the fact that it was undertaken for the benefit of all police forces in England and Wales, to avoid subsequent costly procurement exercises. Subsequently, Cambridgeshire, Bedfordshire and Hertfordshire police all announced in June 2012 that they were considering privatising some services in an attempt to tackle a £73 million funding shortfall created by government cuts. Police authority members in the three counties were asked to consider how services including HR, finance and IT could be outsourced in line with the G4S contract in Lincolnshire as part of a joint recommendation made by the three chief constables. Similarly, in July 2012, the London Mayor, Boris Johnson revealed that huge parts of the Metropolitan Police could be privatised to cut costs; claiming that private firms could run some Scotland Yard services 'without making the thin blue line any thinner' (cited in Crerar 2012).

However, publication by *The Guardian* newspaper in March 2012 of the Surrey/West Midlands plans prompted a public furore. In light of the ensuing public debate, both police authorities agreed to a short pause in the contracting process to build public confidence in the contracting programme and to seek to dispel the idea that it was about privatising core police services. By contrast, the BSIA (2012) responded on the front-foot by welcoming the opportunity to take over certain police functions.

Attempts to differentiate between 'back-office' staff and 'front-line' personnel have been central to proponents' arguments that contracting out the former will allow police forces to dedicate more resources to the latter, enhancing public-facing police interactions. Yet, such distinctions are complex and frequently constitute something of a semantic fig leaf. Many of the tasks identified for private contracting in recent tenders involve contact with the public in some form or other. The patrol function has already largely been civilianised and devolved from the constabulary to PCSOs, who themselves have been the subject of public–private financing initiatives. Just as the work of traffic wardens (previously police employees) was passed to local authorities and private contractors, so too the work of other police staff following the Lincolnshire experiment has been handed over to private companies like G4S. In the near future, PCSOs could be in line for similar private management.

In June 2012, David Taylor-Smith, the head of G4S for the UK and Africa, predicted that private companies would be running large parts of the British police service within five years, driven by a combination of 'budgetary pressure and political will' (Taylor and Travis 2012). Revealingly, he went on to add:

> We have been long-term optimistic about the police and short-to-medium-term pessimistic about the police for many years. Our view was, look, we would never try to take away core policing functions from the police but for a number of years it has been absolutely clear as day to us – and to others – that the configuration of the police in the UK is just simply not as effective and as efficient as it could be.
>
> *(cited in Taylor and Travis 2012)*

However, the brakes to the privatisation juggernaut were spectacularly applied when, later the same month, on the eve of the Olympics, G4S announced its inability to meet the terms of its £284 million contract with the government to provide 10,400 security staff for the Olympic Games in London, requiring some 3,500 members of the armed forces to stand in. The 'G4S fiasco' underlined that the public sector will be required to bail out private companies when they default on their contracts. That is where, and if, sufficient capacity to do so remains. Inevitably, the more that privatisation through outsourcing bites into the provision of public safety, the more it will erode the public sector's capability to fill the vacuum created when the market fails. The G4S saga caused some government ministers, notably the Defence Secretary Philip Hammond, to reconsider the appropriateness of the involvement of the private sector in the delivery of certain services (Wright 2012). In the light of the G4S Olympic failure, Surrey police announced their intention to withdraw from their contract negotiations in the face of active campaigns against the move by some of the declared candidates for the Surrey PCC job (Travis 2012). The West Midlands Police Authority reacted to the Surrey announcement by postponing its decision on who should get the contract until after the election of their PCC. This sudden change of events underscores both the contingent nature of developments and the volatile condition of public debate with regard to policing, given the deeply held attachment of the British public to the emblematic 'Bobby' as the symbol of collective identity and public order (Loader and Mulcahy 2003).

The additional dynamic of democratic governance

The election of PCCs in November 2012 has added an interesting but volatile dynamic to debates about the future of outsourcing and private sector involvement in the police, specifically, and the nature of relations within and between the 'extended policing family' more generally. PCCs have considerable powers to shape not only the police organisation by holding the Chief Constable to account and setting five-year plans, but also to influence the broader policing terrain. Most specifically, how PCCs use their responsibilities to decide the local council tax precept and set (as well as allocate) the annual force budget will be pivotal. This is especially so given their legal powers to commission services from anyone within their force area, including the voluntary and private sectors. The irony is not lost that PCCs have arrived on the policing scene at the very time when outsourcing has been placed firmly on the agenda, against a background of unprecedented cuts to central police funding, and introduced by a government that is politically and ideologically committed to greater private sector involvement in the delivery of public services. And yet, the choice of the 41 individual PCCs charged with carrying the burden of these new responsibilities was left to the small numbers of electors (14.7 per cent of those eligible to vote across the 41 force areas) who made it to the polling stations or cast their postal vote.

In what were otherwise rather uneventful elections, the main conclusion, beside the record low turnout, was the victory of 12 independent candidates (out of 41). It would seem that this underlined a rejection of the mix of party politics with policing, thus questioning the very *raison d'être* of the reforms, namely the idea of a single individual responsible for oversight and budgetary control of policing elected through a process dominated by party politics. Many of the independent candidates stressed their independence from the political process. The results suggest that independence was perceived by electors to be an electoral strength for the role.

One of the only other prominent issues on which very distinct positions were taken by some candidates (more evident in some areas) was in relation to anti-privatisation and outsourcing. My own analysis of the content of formal election statements made by all candidates (see Figure 11.2)[1] reveals that most candidates preferred not to mention the issue of 'outsourcing' or private sector involvement at all, despite the extensive national debate about the issue in the months leading up to the elections. Those who did tended to do so from a critical perspective. This was particularly evident among Labour candidates most of whom (some 32 out of 41 – i.e. 78 per cent) adopted an anti-privatisation stance.

Figure 11.3, by contrast, identifies the range of views on privatisation and out-sourcing expressed in official statements by the successful PCC candidates. Successful Labour candidates made prominent reference to their opposition to privatisation and outsourcing in their election publicity. For example, Tony Lloyd, the PCC for Greater Manchester declared: 'Keep police on the beat not hand policing over to private companies. Our police are not for sale.' In a similar vein, Ron Hogg, the Durham PCC stated: 'I will resist the drive for privatisation of your police service, ensuring that policing remains for people and not for profit.' Of the four independent candidates that unequivocally opposed privatisation, three were successfully elected. This might appear to suggest that anti-privatisation as an issue (especially where detached from party politics) might well have been a vote-winner with the electorate. One of those who came out in opposition to privatisation plans was Ann Barnes, the independent candidate who won the Kent election. She simply declared: 'No privatisation of core Police services.' Likewise, the successful independent candidate in North Wales, Winston Roddick, stated: 'We need to protect

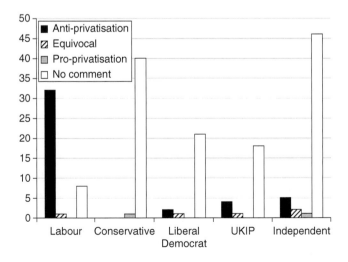

FIGURE 11.2   Views on privatisation in PCC candidates' election statements

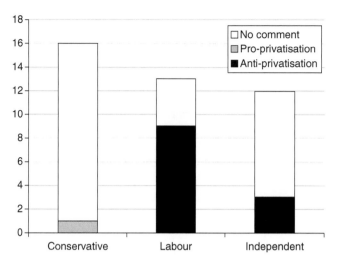

FIGURE 11.3 Elected PCCs' statements on privatisation

the service from devastating cuts and worrying proposals from Westminster for privatising police work.' In total, nearly a third of elected PCCs made it clear in their manifestos that they would oppose outsourcing to the private sector, leaving it unclear which way the other PCCs might lean in future debates. However, the four Labour PCCs who did not come out unequivocally against privatisation might be assumed to be more likely to be sceptical of outsourcing given the dominant view within the Labour Party generally.

Given the above analysis, one of the main legacies of the PCC elections might well be the extent to which outsourcing and private sector involvement moves ahead in some police force areas and not in others. Outside of Lincolnshire where it has already made significant inroads, this is most likely to occur in areas where successful Conservative (or possibly independent) candidates have been elected who failed to say anything explicit about outsourcing in their election statements, but who nevertheless subsequently decide to push ahead with such business-partnering initiatives. Consequently, over the coming years we might come to see an experimental policing patchwork quilt across the country in which some police forces embrace outsourcing, while others stridently resist it.

One of the first acts that the successful West Midlands PCC initiated on taking up the role on 22 November 2012 was to announce his intention to halt the privatisation of core police services. Bob Jones made sure that the symbolism of his first decision in the new role was not lost when he told a press conference that he had moved to scrap the 'Business Partnering for Police' programme just 10 hours after acquiring legal powers as Commissioner. He announced:

> It is also significant that what I am about to announce is my first decision since taking up office. This attests to the importance I attach to giving clarity

to the public and, equally as importantly, to the officers and staff of the Force on the future of the Programme. My decision is that the Business Partnering Programme will cease.[2]

As an alternative approach, Bob Jones asked his Chief Constable, Chris Sims, to convene a fast-track working party to devise a 'technology driven solution' to enable the force to deliver efficiencies and improvements.

It is also likely that the new PCCs will come under some considerable financial pressures, prompting from central government and lobbying from private sector firms, to consider and explore various outsourcing options in their attempts to cut millions of pounds from police budgets. It was therefore unsurprising that shortly after the elections, it was reported that private security firms had launched a major lobbying campaign targeting the newly elected commissioners in recognition of the evident. In an interview with the *Independent*, the Steria UK chief executive John Torrie, said of the approach taken by security, technology, and outsourcing companies: 'Some of the people in there at the present moment are new into this market and they see it as a potentially huge market. They've recruited big forces of people and they will be all over the police market like a rash' (cited in Peachey 2012).

All this suggests that as a result of converging forces and policy trends, we stand on the brink of a possible new dawn for relations between private security and public police in Britain (at least in some police force areas) with significant implications for policing and safety as a 'public good'. Nonetheless, the contemporary confluence of 'electoral answerability' and 'fiscal austerity' could prove to be an unpredictable mix given pressures towards greater private sector involvement in the delivery of police services and simultaneous citizens' (electoral) demands for greater front-line public policing.

Organising and regulating plural policing

Recognition that the provision of policing no longer resides solely with the public police but has become increasingly fragmented and multi-tiered, highlights acute coordination challenges and regulatory dilemmas. Regional policing boards might offer one possible solution to the trends towards geographically disjointed and pluralised provision of policing by affording a degree of holistic oversight, cross-force regulation and cooperation, promoting appropriate standards and effective joint-working, as well as safeguarding the public interest. How they might connect with the government's proposals for reform of private security regulation and the advent of PCCs is less evident.

Certainly, the introduction of PCCs offers the potential for a new form of democratic oversight of policing both in a narrow sense of what the police do and, to an extent, in a broader sense of relations between the police and non-police providers of policing. The latter will be facilitated not only by PCCs' legal responsibility to set annual force budgets, but also by the incorporation of community safety partnership funding, special grants (such as 'crime and drug grants') and new forms of income generation (such as the levy on night-time economy service users) into a single PCC funding pot by 2014/15. Much debate has focused on the responsibility that PCCs have over the police, but the function is a more extensive one than that – they are after all Police and Crime Commissioners, not simply Police Commissioners – and the role includes a duty to cooperate with community safety and criminal justice partners. Explicit in the role is the overarching statutory requirement to work in partnership across a range of agencies at local and national levels 'to ensure there is a unified approach to preventing and reducing crime' (Ss.10 & 88 and Schedule 11, Police Reform and Social Responsibility Act 2011). The role also encompasses a more generally responsibility to represent the public, the vulnerable and victims of crime. Consequently, there are evident possibilities (and some might suggest a distinct likelihood) that, over time, PCCs will become increasingly promiscuous in pushing the boundaries of their role more extensively into the domains of crime prevention and criminal justice.[3] As it becomes clearer to the incumbent PCCs that the police navigate and respond to the socio-economic and political 'tides and currents' that have their deeper origins far from the reach of the police organisation (Greene 2012), so too, they will be likely to be drawn into policy realms and social issues beyond the orbit of the police and policing narrowly defined.

There are, however, real dangers that the introduction of PCCs with a capacious role will reduce and subsume community safety and crime prevention to police-related policy concerns, rather than seeing policing as an element or sub-set of community safety. To do so, as I have sought to highlight, would be to retreat back to the myth of public monopoly over policing and police monopoly over crime. Just as Wiles and Pease (2000) argued that the Crime and Disorder Act of 1998 inappropriately subsumed community safety under a focus on crime reduction rather than a 'pan-hazard approach' to diverse harms, in the same vein, the Police Reform and Social Responsibility Act 2011 may come to· construct community safety through a narrow police (or at best policing) lens. Much of the recent history of community safety and the development of a partnership approach has been wrapped up with attempts to break free from the narrow constraints of a police focus endemic in much (notably situational) crime prevention work (Morgan 1991; Crawford 1997; 2007b). Furthermore, there are worrying signs that the current Coalition Government's narrowing of the police mandate to a focus on crime-fighting – as signalled in the 2010 White Paper declaration that the 'key priority for the police is to cut crime' (Home Office 2010: para. 1.22) – may see the police retract from wider community safety commitments and engagement with local partnerships.

Regardless, in discharging their functions in relation to the wider 'extended policing family', PCCs will be held back by the existing coordination deficits, segmented regulation and disjointed oversight mechanisms that cut across the plural providers of policing (Crawford et al. 2005). There is a strong case for a wider ranging and holistic review of policing in its broadest sense that breaks free of the police-centred approach adopted thus far. Hence, any future reform of policing and its governance must seek to regulate and oversee the plurality of policing providers and attempt to organise and coordinate relations between them more effectively in the furtherance of public safety. Despite recent reforms, and to some extent more so because of them, there remains a pressing need to consolidate and clarify relations between members of the 'extended policing family' and secure suitably robust forms of governance and regulation to ensure policing is delivered in accordance with democratic values of justice, equity, accountability and effectiveness.

Conclusion

This chapter has sought to contend that it is inappropriate and misleading to think about the future of policing solely, or even predominantly, in terms of the activities carried out by the state agency we refer to as 'the police'. Given the trends outlined above, the future of policing is likely to be increasingly pluralised and multifaceted. This process of pluralisation is to be found occurring both inside the police organisation – in terms of changes to the workforce, the fracturing of the notion of the omnicompetent police constable and the essential role played by civilians, not least PCSOs and 'designated officers' – and outside the police among the diverse providers of specialist policing functions, private security and novel kinds of formalised secondary social control. Most significantly, it has been argued that the role of the private sector will continue to enlarge both in size but also, more fundamentally, in terms of its pervasiveness and place within the policing division of labour. Changes in land-use and property relations will continue to provide private management companies with ample incentives and opportunities to deliver and/or direct their own policing and security services. They might look to the public sector to supply some of these services but will also wish to control or influence its performance.

The current drive for fiscal restraint is likely to loom large over future debates about the police workforce, its composition and relations with non-police partner agencies in the public, private and voluntary sectors. Undoubtedly, it will serve as a stimulus for experimentations that afford or offer possible economies. For some police managers, it will be the justification for hastening private sector involvement as a means of making cost efficiencies in the face of considerable cuts in police budgets. However, resultant business partnerships will be as much informed by conscious political decision-making and ideological commitments as economic imperatives. Furthermore, they are unlikely to be replicated in many, if any, European countries where there appears little appetite for such response to similar fiscal problems.

While David Taylor-Smith's predictions about private companies running large parts of the British police service within five years might seem somewhat far-fetched, the considerable momentum that developed behind the West Midlands/Surrey 'Business Partnering for Police' programme during 2012 is liable to resurface in some significant form or other. The G4S Olympic fiasco might have derailed the initiative in the short-term, but it also demonstrated the manner in which British society has accepted the pivotal reliance on the private sector in delivering security – for such a high-profile event as the Olympics – as well as the precarious nature of public opinion with regard to the spectre of privatising police functions. The 'Police for Public – Not for Profit' slogan to be found adorning Police Federation banners during the demonstrations in May 2012, which saw 30,000 police officers march against police reforms, budget reductions and pay cuts, and similar sentiments expressed in PCCs' election manifestos are testimony to the enduring 'sacred' place that the British 'Bobby' retains and the residual antipathy towards the idea of policing for profit. One possible future scenario could see the transfer of PCSOs to private sector management. However, given the vital role they play as the front-line 'face' of British policing, this might prove unpalatable to public sensibilities with significant implications for PCSOs' legitimacy and subsequent citizen compliance.

Much will depend on how PCCs use their extensive budgetary powers and how well experiments in outsourcing arrangements are received by local publics (and hence electors). The extent to which the complex plural policing landscape is harnessed to the benefits of public safety will be dependent on how well PCCs and central government come to terms with and seek to organise, regulate and coordinate the diverse efforts of and relations between policing providers. At the same time, they will need to do so without allowing the vagaries of unequal access and differentiated policing provision to segment populations further along lines structured by the inequitable distribution of security and demarcated by the capacity of citizens and organisations to purchase additional security or retreat from the public realm.

Notes

1   All candidates had their brief election statements published on the Home Office-sponsored website http://www.choosemypcc.org.uk/ from which this analysis was drawn. That there was much criticism of the limited publicity for the candidates, the lack of public funding for postal leaflets and the minimal coverage of the elections by the media, serves to underscore the importance of the information provided in these official statements.
2   See http://www.westmidlands-pcc.gov.uk/news/2012-news/statement-on-the-business-partnering-for-policing-programme/ [accessed 10 June 2013].
3   Interestingly, reflecting the promiscuous possibilities of the role, the Conservative PCC for Cheshire on his first day in office announced the setting up of a Sentencing Unit to campaign for 'tougher sentences'. See: http://www.cheshire-pcc.gov.uk/News-and-Events/News/2012/November/New-Commissioner-prepares-for-Work.aspx [accessed 10 June 2013].

References

Association of Chief Police Officers (2011) *A Survey of Employers Involved in the Community Safety Accreditation Scheme*, London: ACPO.

Ayling, J., Grabosky, P. and Shearing, C. (2009) *Lengthening the Arm of the Law: Enhancing Police Resources in the Twenty-First Century*, Cambridge: Cambridge University Press.

Banton, M. (1964) *The Policeman in the Community*, London: Tavistock.

Blair, I. (2002) 'The policing revolution: back to the beat', *New Statesman*, 23 September: 21–3.

Blair, I. (2003) 'Leading Towards the Future', The Future of Policing conference, LSE, 10 October. Available at: http://www.padpolice.com/futureofpolicing.php

British Security Industry Association (2012) 'MPs' talk of increased public/private sector partnerships is welcomed by private security firms', BSIA News. Available at: http://www.bsia.co.uk/home/bsia-police-public-private-sector-government-secur

Brodeur, J.-P. (2010) *The Policing Web*, Oxford: Oxford University Press.

Crawford, A. (1997) *The Local Governance of Crime*, Oxford: Clarendon Press.

Crawford, A. (2006) 'Fixing Broken Promises? Neighbourhood Wardens and Social Capital', *Urban Studies*, 43(5/6), 957–76.

Crawford, A. (2007a) 'Reassurance Policing: Feeling is Believing', in A. Henry and D.J. Smith (eds) *Transformations of Policing*, Aldershot: Ashgate, pp. 143–68.

Crawford, A. (2007b) 'Crime Prevention and Community Safety', in M. Maguire, R. Morgan and R. Reiner (eds) *The Oxford Handbook of Criminology* (4th edition), Oxford: Oxford University Press, pp. 866–909.

Crawford, A. (2011) 'From the Shopping Mall to the Street Corner: Dynamics of Exclusion in the Governance of Public Space', in A. Crawford (ed.) *International and Comparative Criminal Justice and Urban Governance*, Cambridge: Cambridge University Press, pp. 483–518.

Crawford, A. and Lister, S. (2004) *The Extended Policing Family*, York: JRF.

Crawford, A., Lister, S., Blackburn, S. and Burnett, J. (2005) *Plural Policing: The Mixed Economy of Visible Patrols in England and Wales*, Bristol: Policy Press.

Crerar, P. (2012) 'Thinner blue line? Boris reveals bid to privatise parts of Met', *London Evening Standard*, 11 July. Available at: http://www.standard.co.uk/news/mayor/thinner-blue-line-boris-reveals-bid-to-privatise-parts-of-met-7935900.html

Dhani, A. (2012) *Police Service Strength England and Wales, 31 March 2012*, HOSB 09/12, London: Home Office.

Greene, J.R. (2012) 'The Tides and Currents, Eddies and Whirlpools and Riptides of Modern Policing', *Journal of Police Studies*, 25, 29–54.

Her Majesty's Inspectorate of Constabulary (2012) *Policing in Austerity: One Year On*, London: HMIC.

HM Treasury (2012) *Budget 2012*, London: TSO.

Home Office (2010) *Policing in the 21st Century: Reconnecting the Police and the People*, London: TSO.

Home Office (2012) *Consultation on a Future Regulatory Regime for the Private Security Industry*, London: Home Office.

Loader, I. and Mulcahy, A. (2003) *Policing and the Condition of England*, Oxford: Oxford University Press.

Mason, R. (2012) 'Private companies in hospitals, police and schools are here to stay, says Oliver Letwin', *The Telegraph*, 1 March. Available at: http://www.telegraph.co.uk/news/9116667/Private-companies-in-hospitals-police-and-schools-are-here-to-stay-says-Oliver-Letwin.html

Morgan, J. (1991) *Safer Communities: The Local Delivery of Crime Prevention through the Partnership Approach*, London: Home Office.

Peachey, P. (2012) '"All over them like a rash": Lobbyists scramble to target newly elected police commissioners', *The Independent*, 8 December. Available at: http://www.independent.co.uk/news/uk/home-news/all-over-them-like-a-rash-lobbyists-scramble-to-target-newly-elected-police-commissioners-8393498.html

Saunders, J. (2004) 'Chief Executive's Review and Report', in Security Industry

Authority *Annual Report and Accounts 2003/4*, London: SIA. Available at: http://www.sia. homeoffice.gov.uk/Documents/annual-reports/sia_annual_report_03-04.pdf

Security Industry Authority (2012) *Annual Report and Accounts 2011/12*, London: TSO. Available at: http://www.sia.homeoffice.gov.uk/Documents/annual-reports/sia_annual_report_11-12.pdf

Shearing, C. and Stenning, P. (1981) 'Modern Private Security: Its Growth and Implications', *Crime and Justice*, 3, 193–245.

Shearing, C. (2001) 'Punishment and the Changing Face of Governance', *Punishment and Society*, 3(2), 203–20.

Stenning, P. (2000) 'Powers and Accountability of Private Police', *European Journal on Criminal Policy and Research*, 8(3), 325–52.

Taylor, M. and Travis, A. (2012) 'G4S chief predicts mass police privatisation', *The Guardian*, 20 June. Available at: http://www.theguardian.com/uk/2012/jun/20/g4s-chief-mass-police-privatisation

Travis, A. (2012) 'Surrey police shelve privatisation plan after G4S Olympic failure', *The Guardian*, 12 July. Available at: http://www.theguardian.com/uk/2012/jul/12/surrey-police-privatisation-g4s-olympic

Travis, A. and Williams, Z. (2012) 'Revealed: government plans for police privatisation', *The Guardian*, 2 March. Available at: http://www.theguardian.com/uk/2012/mar/02/police-privatisation-security-firms-crime

West Midlands Police Authority (2011) *Business Partnering for Police*: Report of the Chief Constable, 29 September.

West Midlands Police Authority (2012) *Business Partnering for Police*: Strategic Business Case, 5 July.

White, A. (2010) *The Politics of Private Security: Regulation, Reform and Re-Legitimation*, London: Palgrave Macmillan.

White, A. and Gill, M. (2013) 'The Transformation of Policing: From Ratios to Rationalities', *British Journal of Criminology*, 53(1), 74–93.

Wiles, P. and Pease, K. (2000) 'Crime Prevention and Community Safety: Tweedledum and Tweedledee?', in S. Ballintyne, K. Pease and V. McLaren (eds) *Secure Foundations: Key Issues in Crime Prevention, Crime Reduction and Community Safety*, London: IPPR, pp. 21–9.

Winsor, T.P. (2011) *Independent Review of Police Officer and Staff Remuneration and Conditions Part 1 Report*, London: HMSO.

Wright, O. (2012) 'G4S proves we can't always rely on private sector, says minister', *The Independent*, 14 August. Available at: http://www.independent.co.uk/news/uk/politics/exclusive-g4s-proves-we-cant-always-rely-on-private-sector-says-minister-8038760.html

12

A BLENDED MODEL FOR THE PUBLIC–PRIVATE PROVISION OF POLICING FOR ENGLAND AND WALES

Mark Roycroft

Introduction

The present economic problems besetting the United Kingdom have led to a renewed debate about the modernisation of policing and the possible private provision of services. The fiscal crisis has created an imperative to ask some fundamental questions about the role of the policing and who is responsible for carrying out tasks, and who governs and directs the police. There is a growing body of scholarship that suggests policing is in the midst of a new wave of reform. Indeed, McLaughlin and Murji (1999) have talked of the demise of public policing. The last decades have seen the increased pluralisation of policing with private security rising relative to the decline in the public police's numbers.

This chapter argues that lamenting the end of public policing is somewhat premature. What has progressively occurred over the last several decades has been an extension of policing activities by non-state agencies and the emergence of plural provision of police services (Bayley and Shearing, 1996). This gradual fracturing of the monopoly of the public police over the last 30 years is due to several factors. First, the demands placed on forces for an increased visible presence which led to the innovation of the non-warranted police community support officers (PCSOs) and rises in the number of volunteer special constables. Second, private security provision has risen as a consequence of liberalising powers granted in the 1994 Police Act. Third, the changing nature of public places has meant that private security within shopping malls and public stadiums have become the providers of public safety. Fourth, the private sector has been a response to cost cutting in order to make administrative functions cheaper as the particular nature of the current structure of 43 territorial forces of England and Wales (Schedule 1, Police Act, 1996) does not easily allow for economies of scale. Fifth, the liberalisation of the consumption of alcohol through changes to licensing laws has stimulated expansion in the private policing of pubs, clubs and other night-time outlets.

This chapter will examine the arguments about private sector involvement and how 'outsourcing' may be seen either as a crucial element in the modernisation agenda to free up trained officers to 'front line' duties, or as a creeping 'privatisation' with the state losing control of policing. Some commentators see private–public partnerships as a working together in order to transform policing in the twenty first century. Johnston (1991) for example states that

> fragmented, diverse, networked policing is to all intents and purposes here to stay indeed, current developments serve in many respects merely to accentu- ate and extend what has in fact long been a world of multiple provisions.

This chapter will argue for a model of 'blended policing' where it is recognised that some functions must remain the province of the public police, whereas other activities can be undertaken by the private sector and yet others may be a collabora- tion of the two.

The future of policing in England and Wales will depend in the main on how police forces are organised and led and in part on the performance of the private sector. The failure of the security company, G4S, to provide adequate security staff for the Olympics has drawn attention to the role of the public sector as agency of last resort. Ultimately the state should be responsible for security matters, but as Boutellier (2001: 27) suggests, police officers can adopt a 'liberal position' in which they support organisations and citizens with preventive practices as part of the con- tinuum of maintaining order and social control.

Evolution not revolution

Jones and Newburn (2002) state that the present state of plural provision of policing in England and Wales is not a break with the past but represents continuity with, and a formalisation of, a continuum of social control. Historical research shows that in the nineteenth century it was the thief takers in London and other commercial organisations that maintained order. For instance, the Harbours, Docks and Piers Clauses Act of 1847 allowed magistrates to swear in special constables within the limits of piers and docks, these constables have virtually been operating as a private police force for several decades. The Thames River Police was founded as a privately funded police force as a means to combat theft of cargo from the Pool of London.

Policing then is not an exclusive monopoly provided by the public administra- tion. In the words of Dutch sociologist Cachet (1990: 7), 'policing is not so unique as practitioners think. It belongs to a more general category of control mecha- nisms'. Geuss (2001: 6) states, 'there is no single clear-cut distinction between pub- lic and private but rather a series of overlapping contrasts, and [thus] the distinction between the public and the private should not be taken to have the significance often attributed to it'.

As Rawlings too pointed out (2002: 130) the vast bulk of policing has always been done by organisations and people other than the police. The substantial growth in most countries of the private security industry is not contested. A few examples illustrate this trend. In France, there was a growth of the industry from 100,000 personnel in 1982 to 160,000 in 2010; in Japan, from 70,000 guards in 1975 to 460,000 in 2003; in South Africa, from 115,000 in 1997 to 390,000 in 2010. In India there are 7 million security personnel, outnumbering police officers 4.98 to 1. In South Africa the figure is 2.57, in the United States of America 2.26, and in Australia 2.19 (UNODC, 2011).

Pressure on and managing of resources to fund the delivery of policing services has been on the political agenda since the 1980s. A Home Office Circular (114/83) placed limits on Chief Constables on the acquisition of additional resources and required them to consider greater cost efficiencies. Force strengths were reduced, forces re-structured and a 'civilianisation' programme accelerated whereby roles in research and development, personnel, finance and computing were reassigned to professional 'civilian' members of staff, ostensibly at lower cost, thereby encouraging the previous police officer incumbents to return to operational duties. In the 1990s, in England and Wales the Posen review distinguished between core and ancillary tasks with a reduction in police undertaking the latter and private security taking on the escorting of wide loads, custody services and prisoner escorts. Bayley and Shearing (1996: 585) argue that this, in the North American context, could be seen as 'when one system of policing finished and another took its place'.

The primary aim of the public police is to protect the citizen, by handling emergencies, resolving conflicts and, where necessary, utilising force. In addition there might be a requirement to arrest, thereby depriving the individual of their liberty. This involves direct public–police contact with differing levels of risk and their attendant consequences. Supporting functions, routine file preparation and administrative tasks, by and large, carry relatively low risk and little, if any, direct contact with the public. A third category of tasks might involve some public contact, require specialist knowledge or skills and could be accomplished by mixed teams of public police and private contractors. Table 12.1 illustrates possible differentiation of responsibility for delivering various policing functions (the list is not meant to be exhaustive).

The detection of both low-volume and high-volume crimes should remain part of the public police's core function. There is a public expectation that these are part of public sector responsibilities and that a warranted officer, with the underpinning governance deals with serious crimes such as murder and rape in a professional and sensitive way. It is unlikely that the multi-faceted aspects of such investigations, involving as they do covert surveillance, undercover operations, family liaison and forensic retrieval, could be appropriately carried out by private companies. Public order situations, such as the summer riots of 2011, require large reserves of uniformed officers who are garnered through mutual aid arrangements which it would be hard to envisage being an economic proposition for the private sector, given the unpredictability of such occurrences or their scale. Specialist activities such as missing person searches, firearms teams and anti-terrorist work should also remain within the public sector with their complex mix of demands and

TABLE 12.1 Functions to be performed by public police, private providers and combined capability

Task	Public police	Private provision	Combined
Minor crime investigation	Need for warranted powers for arrest	Routine statement taking Custody duties Scenes of crime	Interviewing Victim support Crime pattern analysis
Major crime investigations	Need for warranted powers for arrest/ detention/use of force Family liaison	Routine statement taking Custody duties Scenes of crime Asset recovery Transporting prisoners Forensic science analysis	Specialist investigations, e.g. e-crime and fraud Victim support Behavioural investigative advice
Public order	Political protest National prestige events	Football matches and smaller scale policing of events	Special events
Administration	Some file production	Back-office administration	Middle-office administration
Intelligence gathering	Covert surveillance Undercover work Electronic intercepts	Back office Routine intelligence gathering	Cyber crime
Emergency response	'Fire-brigade' policing	Managing police call centres	Disaster management
Counter terrorism	Covert surveillance Undercover work Electronic intercepts Local intelligence gathering Major operations	Routine statement taking Custody duties Scenes of crime Forensic science analysis	Combined arrest teams
Road traffic accidents	Fatal accidents, major traffic disruption	Routine patrolling traffic officers	Traffic investigation
Community engagement	Reassurance policing	Rostering duties	Community liaison Monitoring community tension MAPPA (multi-agency protection panels)

potential sensitivity of issues. The management of traffic flows, on the other hand, has already been partly privatised after the introduction of Highways Agency in 1994. As an Executive Agency of the Department for Transport (DfT), the Highways Agency is responsible for operating, maintaining and improving the strategic road network although the police still retain control over motorway incidents and fatal accidents.

Community engagement and the management of multi-agency protection panels (MAPPA) should remain within the public sector. This is because critical to the

British model of policing is the concept of policing by consent. Key to this is the notion of legitimacy. Weisel and Painter (1997) say, 'Without popular acceptance from the policed population, laws will not be respected and the policeman [sic] will not be obeyed'. The discernible presence of police and their relationship with the communities they serve is, in part, one of the means for developing trust, a key essential of legitimacy.

The public also have a right to expect that the exercising of force and the deprivation of a person's liberty are underpinned by accountability to law and appropriate levels of training and oversight. Article 4 of the Police Service of Northern Ireland's (PSNI) Code of Ethics is written from the UN principles on the use of force by law enforcement officials. Use of force by the police is critical to the 'relationship of the state to its citizens'. Weber (1972) argued that a monopoly over the legitimate use of force is a central defining feature of the modern state.

Private sector engagement in policing

Increased pressures upon the law enforcement community have resulted in the substitution of private contractors for some police functions. There has been load shedding, where the police withdraw from providing certain functions and private security fill the gap; contracting out, where services are still provided by the police but a contractor is used to supply that service; the embracement of private sector practices by the public police, such as charging for services and accepting sponsorship; buying in private sector know-how in order to train chief officer teams in business practices and process re-engineering.

The G4S security group has operations in more than 125 countries and 657,000 employees (it is the second largest private employer in the world). It specialises in outsourced business processes and facilities in sectors where security and safety risks are considered a strategic threat. Just over a quarter of G4S profit comes from the British Government (www.G4S.com). G4S has been contracted to design, build and run a police station in Lincolnshire, in the largest outsourcing deal seen so far in Britain. This means that almost half the force's 900 civilian workers will be transferred to G4S as a result of this arrangement and take responsibility for control rooms, custody services, ICT and Criminal Justice Services. The force hopes, thereby, to save £28 million over 10 years with G4S running custody suites, station offices, criminal justice units, and fleet management and finance units. There is emerging the concept of 'street to suite' teams where sworn officers arrest suspects and civilian personnel drive the suspects to the station and process them. Emergency calls in at least one police force, Cleveland, are being handled by a private company, Steria.

QUEST is a culture change programme run by the management consultants KPMG and is widely regarded as assisting the performance improvement programmes in UK policing. Fourteen forces have already benefited, reporting tangible and significant performance uplift and cashable benefits. The KPMG West Midlands Police QUEST collaboration is detailed here as an illustrative case history (KPMG and Home Office, 2010).

West Midlands Police is the second largest force in the UK. Following the government's comprehensive spending review in 2009/10, it had to cut its annual budget by £134 million within four years – a 20 per cent reduction. Performance and satisfaction levels had been deteriorating, crime levels rising and detection rates falling. KPMG were invited to look at five areas of the operations (covering 52 per cent of the force's budget): incident management; crime investigation; defendant management processes following an arrest; neighbourhood and proactive policing; intelligence. Through the QUEST approach, integrated teams of officers and consultants were formed whose main aim was transferring knowledge by means of formal training, coaching and continual support. The evidence from the QUEST approach showed West Midlands had large, inefficient response teams due to multiple roles of response, investigation, arrest and custody. Through the programme, roles were simplified and separate crime investigation was established to provide a better service for low-severity crimes. Dedicated prisoner handling teams were also set up, as were dedicated, proactive neighbourhood teams. This blending of private expertise with the public service ethos provides the basis for changing and improving performance. An evaluation showed that Greater Manchester Police (GMP) achieved significant productivity savings. For example, in the Salford division, the project enabled the force to free up the number of full-time employees by approximately 30 per cent, equating to savings of almost £2 million per year. For GMP as a whole, the £22 million that was projected to be the potential annual saving through improved productivity has been realised, representing a return on the project investment of more than 8 : 1 over its first three years.

The growing civilianisation of some police roles has been complemented in some forces by business partnerships with the private sector. In many respects such partnerships have enabled forces to realise significant savings, while redeploying warranted officers to duties more in keeping with their skills and capabilities. The use of private provision in custody suites has been shown to deliver significant savings, for example, a private custody suite at Cardiff Bay station in South Wales has enabled the force to deliver savings of £1.2 million a year, equivalent to around 30 per cent, while simultaneously improving the safety and quality of service. HMIC estimated this enabled 53 warranted officers to be released to the beat or other roles and represented savings of 57,855 police officer hours per annum. Thirty-six of the 43 forces continue to provide custody in-house, using over 5,000 police officers and support staff. The annual estimated cost of the police services' custody suites is £1.1 billion.

Potential benefits and concerns

Table 12.2 sets out some of the concerns about private sector involvement and the benefits to public policing of continued private provision of services. The concerns raised relate to accountability, transparency and governance of the 'new' service providers. One such concern is the perception that the private sector's engagement to deliver policing services is because the public police have failed, and this is potentially undermining of public confidence.

TABLE 12.2 Benefits, concerns and governance networks of private provision

Potential benefits	Concerns
Cost saving in times of austerity	Failures of private sector leave public sector as agency of last resort
Freeing up expertise, so allowing trained staff to undertake public police roles	Dispersed governance networks
	Use of force by non-licensed or regulated staff
Flexibility and innovation	Cherry picking to leave public police with the difficult confrontations
New skill sets acquired from mentoring in business practices and process engineering	Pluralisation of services, leading to unequal service distribution and exacerbating social division
Better quality of service in routine matters	Complaints procedure and transparency
Better running of middle- and back-room functions	Perceived failure of state policing
	Lack of training in private sector
Raises the profile of the public police officer	Private security accountable to paying clients/ shareholders rather than tax payer
	Possibility of strike action
	Increased surveillance culture with much surveillance in private hands

Deputy chair of the IPCC Deborah Glass comments

> We believe it is vital for public confidence that all those who perform police-like functions and powers are subject to independent oversight. It cannot be right for someone doing the same job as a police officer not to fall within the IPCC's remit simply because the police have contracted the job to a private company. But any change in this area requires a change in the IPCC's powers. We have told the Home Office that we believe these powers are necessary, indeed crucial.

There have been some examples of problems in the quality and provision of service by private companies and several cases of note are listed here. In 2011 G4S lost a major government contract after a record 773 complaints by immigration centre detainees, including 50 of assault. Recently, 160 staff and a range of 'back-office' services have been transferred back to the public sector in Avon and Somerset. These had been supplied by Southwest One in 2007 under a joint venture between IBM, Somerset council, the Avon and Somerset police and Taunton Deane borough council. The reversal followed losses of £31 million and failures to hit savings targets (see http://www.avonandsomerset.police.uk/operations_and_initiatives/collaboration.aspx).

The deaths of two prisoners while in G4S custody provoked concern from Lord Ramsbottom who has asked for a public enquiry into one of the cases. Mr Jimmy Mubenga died on 12 October 2010 after three G4S security guards used restraining techniques while he was on board a British Airways flight during his forcible deportation to Angola. There had been criticisms by the coroner in the case of Gareth Myatt; a 15-year-old who died in Rainsbrook secure training centre following the use of similar procedures for restraint by G4S guards. The Corporate Manslaughter and Homicide Act 2007 was extended to include police forces, prisons and immigration detention centres. This means prosecutions against public or private bodies following a death in police or private security custody are now possible but none, as yet, has been undertaken.

The limitations of the private sector have been shown by the G4S response to the 2012 Olympics in London where G4S could not supply its full quota of security staff to the Olympics. While it gave £2.5 million to the Armed Forces the shortfall in numbers presented a challenge to Locog, the Olympics organisers. This shortfall also demonstrates that private companies depend on 'short-term' employees with limited management structures, much more than public agencies. Public agencies such as the Police and the Army come from the opposite end of the spectrum where they have a permanent management and deployment capability for such 'emergencies'. It could also be argued that herein lies some built-in redundancy in that the public sector carries the risk of unpredictable outbreaks of disorder or civil emergencies in terms of scale and scope which the private sector is simply unwilling to bear.

Similarly if personnel are employed on a temporary basis there will be pressure on systems designed to deal with complaints about staff and retaining a level of investigation capacity of the Police Service's Professional Standards Units. Part of the future organising of policing provision must incorporate regulation and accountability mechanisms. The Independent Police Complaints Commission (IPCC) has a role to maintain public confidence in the handling of public complaints against the police and allegations of police misconduct matters. The IPCC also has oversight of instances when there has been a death or serious injury involving the police irrespective of whether there is a complaint or allegation of misconduct. The IPCC's guardianship function consists of four main elements:

- a duty to increase public confidence in the system as a whole;
- promoting accessibility of the complaints system;
- setting, monitoring, inspecting and reviewing standards for the operation of the whole system;
- promoting a learning culture so that lessons may be learnt from the system.

Yet the recent Home Affairs Select Committee report when reviewing the work of the IPCC concluded,

> the IPCC is woefully under equipped and hamstrung in achieving its original objectives. It has neither the powers nor the resources that it needs to get to the truth when the integrity of the police is in doubt. Smaller even than the Professional Standards Department of the Metropolitan Police,

the Commission is not even first among equals, yet it is meant to be the backstop of the system. It lacks the investigative resources necessary to get to the truth; police forces are too often left to investigate themselves; and the voice of the IPCC does not have binding authority.

The Committee was of the view that the IPCC is not capable of delivering the kind of powerful, objective scrutiny that is needed to inspire public confidence. It is hard then to envisage that it will be able to extend its remit to incorporate the privately contracted workforce within its oversight, especially if there is no increase in its resources.

Another matter of concern is the ethical milieu in which policing operates. The Police Service of Northern Ireland (PSNI) are the first police force in the UK to publish a Code of Ethics. Box 12.1 contains an abbreviated summary.

BOX 12.1 SUMMARY OF PSNI CODE OF ETHICS

- *Professional duty*: Uphold the law, protect human dignity and uphold human rights, with the cooperation of local community and shall not play an active part in politics
- *Police investigations*: Conducted promptly, thoroughly, impartially treating victims with sensitivity and respect for their dignity, gathering, retaining and using information with regard to respect for family and personal life.
- *Privacy and confidentiality*: Gather, secure and use information in accordance with the right to privacy and family life
- *Use of force*: Restraint in the use of force
- *Detained persons*: Treated in a humane and dignified way
- *Equality*: Act with fairness, self-control, tolerance and impartiality
- *Integrity*: Respect and obey the law
- *Property*: Ensure property, monies and equipment handled as required by law, and gratuities received, authorised
- *Fitness for duty*: Fit to carry out duties
- *Duty of supervisors*: Be the primary promoters and positive agents of good conduct

---

Arising from this is the potential tension between the commercial imperatives of the private sector and the public good mandate of the public police. This is not to say that the private sector is bereft of ethical practice or that the police service itself is always exemplary in its conduct, but returning to the principle of thief takers who arrest for profit would defeat the democratic process and limits put in place over the last almost 200 years of public policing in the UK. Commercial sensitivity and privileged financial information may place transparency of budgets, contract bidding and procurements in jeopardy. The public service ethos and holders of the office of constable may put their lives in danger for the public good, which sacrifice could be a limiting factor to those under stricter contractual obligations.

Conclusions

The police modernisation project does not necessarily mean provision by either private companies or the public police. Rather, what is being advocated is a 'blended' model where there is a clear separation of tasks to be undertaken by the public police, those that can be privately contracted and those where there could be a collaboration between public and private within a public accountability model.

The warranted officer should retain those tasks that require force, arrest and access to sensitive information. There is clearly a role of the public police to maintain public order and be responsible for the security of the state and the citizen. Some street patrolling, investigation of offences and the control of public disorder should also be retained by the public sector, but more mundane activities such as statement taking, dealing with vulnerable witnesses, missing person enquiries and support functions can be considered for provision by a private sector partner alone or by a mixture of private and public resources. This provision has to remain under the accountability of a Chief Constable and his or her Police and Crime Commissioner.

One potential future could be a continuum with progress towards streamlining service provision with both the specialised and back-room functions being improved. South (1988: 127) had previously suggested the usefulness of employing such a model in which both the public and private contributors exchange expertise, key personnel and, importantly, accommodate each other's shifting parameters of operation and priorities in action. The 'continuum mode' sees a shared project of social control, through informal neighbourhood watch and citizen engagement, and formal policing supported by private contracts. Bayley and Shearing (1996) suggest that the sworn or warranted police should concentrate on law enforcement, leaving crime prevention and community safety functions to municipal civil and commercial bodies. They state 'late modernity has altered the morphology of governance, there is a need to construct a model of optimum policing where security is neither excessive nor quantitatively invasive'.

There are, however, some limits to private sector involvement in policing. Legislation is needed to set out what private industry is prohibited from carrying out. The purpose of clearly defining the limits of private security powers is to prevent their abuse and ensure that the rights of other citizens are protected. To effectively regulate the conduct of private security personnel, the adoption of a code of conduct/ethics with accompanying sanctions for infractions, should be considered. Legislation regulating private security might need to include the requirement for a designated person responsible for the entity; a minimum level of insurance; appropriate equipment; a minimum level of resources. In many regulatory systems once a provider is authorised to provide private security there are additional requirements they must keep in order to have their authorisation regularly renewed, e.g. lists of employees, records of incidents, having to inform authorities of specific kinds of incidents, and having to wear identification. The Private Security Industry Act 2001 does set out licensing requirements for certain private security occupations and this is regulated by the Security Industry Authority. But as Button (2007) warns,

> the system to be introduced for security guards in England and Wales falls below European norms and needs to be more demanding if the performance and accountability of the industry are to be enhanced and the industry is to play the expanding role in policing that many increasingly expect.

An agenda to secure a blended model of policing provision might include:

- incorporation by the public police of private sector knowledge within their management remit;
- a robust complaints procedure and model based on the existing police professional standards should be introduced for privately contracted staff who engage in public duties and that this be managed independently;
- the IPCC remit should be extended to include serious complaints within the private sector and should be included in the IPCC guardianship model;
- the training of all privately contracted staff should be formalised and certificated (the new College of Policing might provide the means to achieve this) backed by sanctions in the event of misconduct and incompetence;
- a code of ethics to be published for the security industry and private providers that reflects the values of the public police;
- accountability in law for any misuse of force by private security staff;
- training should be provided for police leaders to accommodate the private sector within its management system.

References

Bayley, D. and C. Shearing (1996) 'The future of policing', *Law and Society Review*, 30(3): 585–606.

Boutellier, J.C.J. (2001) 'The convergence of social policy and criminal justice', *European Journal on Criminal Policy and Research*, 9(4): 361.

Button, M. (2007) 'Assessing the regulation of private security across Europe', *European Journal of Criminology*, 7(3): 214–234.

Cachet, A. (1990) *Police and Social Control*, Arnhem, Gouda Quint.

Geuss, R. (2001) *Public Goods, Private Goods*, Princeton, Princeton University Press.

Johnston, L. (1991) 'Privatisation and the police function: From "new police" to "new policing"', in R. Reiner and M. Cross (eds) *Beyond Law and Order: Criminal Justice Policy and Politics into the 1990s*, London, Macmillan, pp. 18–40.

Jones, T. and Newburn, T. (1998) *Private Security and Public Policing*, Oxford, Clarendon.

KPMG and Home Office (2010) Operation QUEST: Transforming policing. Available at: http://www.kpmg.com/UK/en/IssuesAndInsights/ArticlesPublications/Documents/

PDF/Market%20Sector/Public_Sector/Operation-QUEST-report.pdf (accessed 17 June 2013).

McLaughlin, E. and Murji, K. (1999) 'After the Stephen Lawrence Report', *Critical Social Policy*, 19(3): 371–385.

Rawlings, P. (2002) *Policing: A Short History*, Cullompton, Willan.

South, N. (1988) *Policing for Profit: The Private Security Sector*, London, Sage.

UNODC (24/8/11) Civilian private security services: their role, oversight and contribution to crime prevention and community safety. Available at: http://www.unodc.org/documents/justice-and-prison-reform/Expert-group-meeting-Bangkok/IEGMCivilianPrivateSecurity/UNODC_CCPCJ_EG.5_2011_1_English.pdf (accessed 20 January 2012).

Weber, M. (1972) *From Max Weber: Essays in Sociology* (ed. and trans. H. Gerth and C. Wright Mills), London.

Weisel, D.L. and Painter, E. (1997) *The Police Response to Gangs, Case Study of Five Cities*, Washington, Police Executive Research Forum.

13

PLAYING NICELY WITH OTHERS

Lessons from successes in partnership working

Megan O'Neill

Introduction

Like many public service organisations, the police do not operate in a vacuum. They collaborate with other public sector workers from a variety of agencies on a regular basis in the course of fulfilling their duties. These could be from education services, health, probation, social services, environmental services or other emergency services such as the fire service. This list is by no means exhaustive. The police also work with members of the private sector (such as social landlords), local government officers and representatives from the voluntary sector (such as the National Society for the Prevention of Cruelty to Children). Increasingly, policing is a complex task, performed in myriad ways with multiple service providers in many diverse locations. As Bittner said (nearly 50 years ago), policing 'appears to be a solution to an unknown problem arrived at by unknown means' (1967: 701). Policing is not quantifiable as a series of tasks (Wright 2002), and thus police officers and staff find themselves working far beyond a simplistic conception of 'crime control'. The police are often the first port of call for people in distress, and finding a suitable remedy for these situations might require the skills and resources of many agencies. Thus it is imperative that the police build and maintain good working relationships with their 'partner' agencies, to either hand over the case to the most appropriate agency or to help design and implement a long-term problem-solving strategy (and many options in between). This not only makes practical sense from a police point of view, but is in fact the reality for a modern policing organisation which is accountable to its citizens and works in a community policing context. However, this is of course more easily said than done.

Traditional writings on the police and its occupational culture regularly reported a suspicion of 'outsiders', among them, social services and other public sector groups (Reiner 2010). Far from being viewed as helpful to police work, these staff were seen as threatening and challenging (Holdaway 1983, 1986). The situation has changed a great deal from these early writings and, as this chapter will discuss, the police are much more open now to working in partnership, in addition to being legally mandated to do so by the Crime and Disorder Act 1998 (CDA 1998). However, not all sections of the police have embraced this method of working and not all partnerships work well. This chapter will explore why this is the case and what steps might be taken to help the police 'play nicely with others', especially in a context of fiscal constraint.

Historical look

Partnership can be defined as

> a way of enhancing performance in the delivery of a common goal, by the taking of joint responsibility and the pooling of resources by different agents, whether public or private, collective or individual. A partnership may serve crime prevention or another aim.
>
> *(Ekblom 2011: 231)*

Partnership working had been taking place in the public sector before the CDA 1998, but it is this piece of legislation which made it a statutory requirement for the police and local authority to do so and named them as responsible agencies (Bullock *et al.* 2006). This responsibility was later extended to police authorities, the fire service and the health service (Crawford 2006). Before the national roll-out of Neighbourhood Policing in 2008, partnership working tended to be located in Crime and Disorder Reduction Partnerships, which were tasked with undertaking crime audits of the local area and then designing and implementing crime-reduction projects which might call upon the skills and expertise of those outside the police. However, enshrining partnership in law did not guarantee that these arrangements would work well or that all parties would be fully engaged in the process. The fact that the legislation had to be modified to include other services as responsible agents suggests that they had not been embracing this arrangement (Crawford 2006). Many practical issues were encountered in partnerships, such as in data sharing, mixed agendas, lack of focus to projects, lack of project ownership and a lack of expertise in problem-orientated working (Bullock *et al.* 2006).

Besides the practical difficulties cited above, there have been many political and cultural issues with which partnerships contended. Gilling (2007) and Hughes and Rowe (2007) discuss how the various agencies had different internal pressures, plans and priorities to meet with often limited resources. If an agency did not normally see 'crime' as part of its core business, it was difficult for that agency to muster the kind of enthusiasm and commitment to the crime-reduction projects that appease the political powers-that-be for whom crime is an all-encompassing issue. As Hughes (2007) elaborates, some agencies, such as social services, probation and education, saw the exclusive, enforcement-driven, crime-reduction approach favoured by the police as anathema to their ways of working, which tend to be more inclusive, liberal and orientated around community safety. Police officers, for their part, commented on their frustration in working with agencies that seem to lack a clear chain of command and hierarchy as well as the ratio of talk to action not being to their liking. Despite this, they were often accused of dominating partnerships and using them for their own ends (Pearson *et al.* 1992; Edwards 2002).

Current situation

While partnership working did indeed experience many difficulties in the early days of its formalised existence, there is reason to believe that this is not quite the case anymore. Work conducted by this author[1] (O'Neill and McCarthy 2012) and others (see McCarthy (2011, 2012) for youth services and Mawby and Worrall (2011) for probation partnerships) presents a more optimistic picture. In these cases, police officers, staff (such as Police Community Support Officers (PCSOs)) and partner agents not only sang the praises of partnership working (for the most part) but often said that they would be incapable of doing their jobs without it. What made this change and why has it been so successful?

One reason for this success (from the police point of view) could be that partnership working is now an embedded part of Neighbourhood Policing (although it exists elsewhere, such as in road safety), and Neighbourhood Policing has been a nationwide project. In addition the CDA 1998 requires all local authorities and their various agencies to work in partnership, and addresses previous issues in the Data Protection Act to allow this to happen. This created a situation where, first, the police were legally mandated to work in partnership and then, in 2008, a more obvious and facilitating context was created in the national roll-out of Neighbourhood Policing. To work at a 'neighbourhood' level would be difficult for the police to do in isolation, as the ethos behind this method of local policing requires engagement with the local community, as well as with local services (see Innes 2005). Crime and Disorder Reduction Partnerships (CDRPs) were the initial focus for partnership working in local areas after the creation of the CDA 1998. While these have a 'crime' focus, they are meant to involve all relevant public sector groups (such as youth services, education, housing, health, local officials, etc.). However, these seemed to struggle in many places in that the non-police partners did not always see how their work could relate to 'crime' (Gilling 2007; Hughes 2007). Neighbourhood Policing, on the other hand, is less about 'crime' and more about the needs of a local community as expressed by that community, whatever that or whoever they might be. Concerns tend to focus on relatively low-level issues such as dog fouling, graffiti, litter and young people loitering. All of these kinds of issues, which are often not about 'crime', can only be effectively addressed if services, other than the police, are involved.

Just because Neighbourhood Policing provided an enabling context did not necessarily mean that partnership working would function well. However, in many areas researched by this author this did, indeed, prove to be the case. There were many reasons that emerged, which will be examined in more detail below. Overall, the police participants in the study seemed to value the *pragmatic* elements of partnership working. Pragmatism is one of the classic elements of police culture cited by several scholars, as it provides a useful way to deal with the 'police predicament' (Reiner 2010). While these established versions of police culture have been challenged over the years (such as by Waddington (1999) and Sklansky (2007), see Bacon and also Jones, this volume), more recent work on policing has revealed a consistency with past analyses, although altered for modern times (Loftus 2007, 2010). While not all police forces and police officers are the same, there remains a recurring pattern in the way police officers adapt to their 'predicament', and pragmatism is one of them.

Because police officers are often called to address problems, and do so quickly, they tend to rely on methods of working that 'make sense' or show a practical value. Partnership working has provided the kind of pragmatism that police officers tend to seek, but by establishing new ways of working. For example, police officers who work closely with partners embrace opportunities for medium- to long-term problem solving (such as working with at-risk children or getting a housing provider to address a long-standing issue in their estate). This is a departure from previous conceptualisations of police pragmatism in that the police in question are not just looking to 'get from here to tomorrow (or the next hour) safely and with the least fuss and paperwork, which has made them reluctant to contemplate innovation, experimentation or research' (Reiner 2010: 132) but now will put in the time and effort required to fix problems for good (as much as they can be). For example, this on occasion meant police applying with partners for funding for community projects or developing complex interventions with young people.

Despite this rosy picture there were, of course, areas where partnership working was not a great success. Police officers complained about partners not turning up to meetings or not completing the tasks they were given. Again, the police took a pragmatic approach to these issues in that they would come to rely on a smaller number of known and trusted contacts in select organisations, who would be approached directly for assistance or support. These smaller sub-groups proved to be more effective than the larger one and while this does undermine the principle of partnership working to an extent, the needs of the community in question were still being addressed. The fact that the police were willing to take these steps to ensure that the community work was done reflects their commitment to it. If they were not sold on the idea of partnership and community working, they would not have put in the effort to make these contacts and approach them individually, outside of meetings (see O'Neill and McCarthy (2012) for more on this).

We are now in a situation where the police in neighbourhood teams regularly work with those public sector groups who, not that long ago, would have been viewed as at best useless and at worst threatening to the police and their autonomy. How has this dramatic change happened to the occupational culture of these officers? Here I will refer to Wood (2004) who in turn draws on Chan (Chan 1997; Chan *et al.* 2003). Chan, using Bourdieu's conceptualisations of the field of policing as a social space for competition and struggle for control over certain types of power, proposes that this is constructed with elements such as the wider political context, government policy, approaches to the policing of ethnic minorities, systems for police accountability, etc. These elements shape police culture by forming the 'rules of the game' (Chan 1997; Chan *et al.* 2003). Actors in the field compete for different types of capital (cultural, social, symbolic – see Bourdieu and Wacquant (1992)). The other relevant Bourdieu concept is 'habitus' referring to a set of 'dispositions', based on past experiences, which help police officers get a 'feel for the game' (Chan 1997; Chan *et al.* 2003) and allow them to cope with unexpected situations. This integrates different forms of 'cultural knowledge' which convey how the police approach their work and the people they encounter. Chan argues that by altering the field of policing, cultural change can be possible. Actors in the field, through the course of their struggle for capital, modify the field itself and are modified by it. Thus to change the field can engender a complementary change in habitus, the 'feel for the game'.

Wood (2004), building on Chan's work, discusses how 'zero tolerance' policing found such a warm welcome in policing in North America. This is because it not only did not threaten the field and habitus of these officers, it chimed rather well with their existing conceptualisations of these. Police were keen to address 'quality of life' issues in communities and found zero tolerance policing a nice fit. This allowed them to position the disadvantaged and the underclass as the problem, and thus worthy of punishment rather than help. This type of enforcement approach to low-level disorder (begging, street sellers, squeegee kids) allowed the police to utilise their legitimate use of force to remove these undesirable figures from the streets, the idea being that to root out low-level disorder would prevent higher level crimes from happening (Wilson and Kelling 1982) as well as potentially revealing more serious crimes such as hidden weapons and drugs. The police were able to employ their existing habitus as the field had not changed a great deal. The underclass and the disadvantaged were already conceived in the same category as other 'disarmers' (Holdaway 1983) such as social workers, so the introduction of zero tolerance did not disrupt the existing police culture.

However, what has been developing in recent years with partnership policing in England and Wales *does* present a new configuration of the policing field and has required the police officers involved to alter their habitus as a consequence. In terms of the wider political context, the law was changed to make partnership work compulsory in the public sector (in the CDA 1998) and Neighbourhood Policing was adopted across England and Wales in 2008 which came with dedicated funding and ministerial expectations. Police forces were required to fundamentally alter their way of working, which was endorsed from the top of the organisation downwards. There was no way to avoid it, as well as a great deal of political and public pressure to adopt it (Innes 2005). As discussed above, partnership work found a natural home in Neighbourhood Policing and became an integral part of this method of policing. Thus, the field of policing has changed markedly across the ranks. The 'rules of the game' are different: community (neighbourhood) policing is no longer the side car to the policing motorcycle to which weaker, older or recuperating officers were condemned. It is now the main driver of police work with an enhanced status becoming the guiding force in how police work is operationalised (through their multiple Neighbourhood Policing teams, many of which are now coterminous with local authority ward areas). As a consequence, those officers involved in neighbourhood work with partner agencies had to alter their habitus; to get a new 'feel for the game'. This did not happen overnight, but once the benefits of partnership working were experienced and the practical elements made clear, and the changes made, this was welcomed by many. The new field of policing, where partnership working is now a core feature, tapped into the existing value placed on the pragmatic by many officers in their habitus. What was new was that this conception of pragmatism in the habitus could now take a longer-term view and could rely upon non-police actors to bring it about, a change to the previous 'cultural knowledge' (Chan 1997; Chan et al. 2003) of the police. Social workers, probation officers, etc. were no longer a threat, but actually fundamentally important in helping the police to address the needs of their communities. The police are now 'playing nicely with others' in the public sector.

What should be made clear here, however, is that while the broader field of policing did change, this change was not felt in the same way by all police officers. Those officers who remained in response-based roles or specialist teams (such as detectives or firearms) will have had little direct experience of the benefits of partnership work. They may accept the role that partnership can play *in principle*, but until it occupies a prominent position in their lived experience of the policing field, their existing construction of their policing habitus will not be directly challenged in any great way. Like the officers in Wood's (2004) analysis of zero tolerance policing, they have not been faced with too much competition in the new policing field and their capital remains largely intact. Likewise, police officers who have had poor relationships with partner agencies and staff will also not be challenged on their traditional cultural knowledge of working with outsiders to the organisation, nor on the benefits that partnership working can bring to their workloads and effectiveness. Partnership working can indeed bring about a dramatic change to the world view of some police officers and lead to working practices that are more open to regular engagement with other public sector services, perhaps even to seeing members of the public as 'partners'. However, this change has not been organisation-wide, and thus the 'old way' of doing things remains in certain pockets or in certain forces.

Good practice

Previous research studies have shown how a lack of internal support, both at middle-management level and at a higher strategic level, can severely undermine efforts at partnership working in the police. For example, Rogers (2004) noted that while the police officers assigned to a particular partnership group in England were very enthusiastic about the project, they had little to no support from their sergeants and inspectors for this work. It was seen as a distraction from 'real' policing, taking staff away from work in the evenings. Enthusiasm quickly faded. Fleming (2006) discusses the situation in Australia where there is no legal mandate for partnership working and no dedicated funding to support it. Policing in Australia (as elsewhere) is committed to managerial measurements of success, which do not sit well with policing through networks and community partnerships, as these do not tend to provide quantifiable results. In addition to which, police officers change roles frequently, which is problematic in terms of building successful relationships with community groups and partners. The policing organisations in Australia speak favourably about partnership work in public, but the internal systems, processes and reward mechanisms that would enable it to flourish are absent.

These situations, by and large, are no longer the case in England and Wales. Not only is there a national legal mandate to support partnership work, but it has found a welcoming home in Neighbourhood Policing (which had not yet been rolled-out nationally at the time of Rogers' research), supported by dedicated funding (at least until 2013). This works to the extent that in some areas, police officers are co-located with their public sector partners (as was envisioned by Bowling and Foster back in 2002). While these co-location arrangements can be complex to set up and bring with them a degree of cost, the police officers involved report that it is of huge benefit to their work to be in such close proximity to their partners. Conversations about ongoing work can be had on the spot, without the need for scheduled meetings or phone calls. Information sharing is greatly eased and relationships with partners made all the stronger. Thus at the strategic level, policing in England and Wales has gone a very long way to enable partnership working.

In terms of middle-management support, this was expressed throughout the research interviews. Sergeants and Inspectors all reported support for partnerships, for a variety of reasons. For some, it was about making more successful interventions in the community, with groups or with specific individuals. For others, it was valued largely for its business sense: non-police tasks are given to the appropriate groups saving police time; long-term problem solving saves money (eventually). Many acknowledged that partners did not always work the way the police expected and could let them down, but overall the method was valued. By having the support of middle-managers, police officers and staff were able to undertake the work they needed to do without having to justify it (as Fleming reported was the case in Australia). In addition, there was some evidence from the research interviews that systems for promotion within the police in England and Wales are changing so that officers who remained in Neighbourhood Policing for a long period of time (two years or more) were viewed favourably (or at the very least a long term of office in Neighbourhood Policing was not a negative mark on a career record). This also enhances partnership working in that the police officers who conduct partnership work in the context of Neighbourhood Policing have the time to build relationships with key partners and community members. Partnership working does often involve attendance at multiple meetings (less so for those officers who are co-located with partners) but this was seen as a price worth paying for the benefits to be had from greater familiarity with partners individually, better understanding of each other's roles and resources and better communication of data and progress reports.

Berry *et al.* (2011) analysed research findings from a number of partnership projects in the USA. While methodological issues prevent firm conclusions to be drawn, the analysis suggests the following elements to be important in the success of partnership work: strong leadership, data sharing and a clear problem focus, communication and co-location, flexible structures, clear accountability, and experienced team members. These findings support the discussion above in that police collaborating in non-traditional ways with the public sector is crucial to the success of partnership working. While the police have been criticised in the past for dominating partnership arrangements, this might not be as problematic as it seems. The police, by the nature of their organisation, are more able to respond quickly to events as they unfold (especially in the evenings or at weekends), as well as make decisions and follow up tasks in a timely manner, than their partner agencies might be. That the police might end up chairing or leading partnership groups in some areas can be a benefit for all as the police can provide the leadership that is needed to keep partnerships functioning well (O'Neill and McCarthy 2012). Thus they might be better at being facilitators, but (according to the research participants) do *not* wish to be the lead in all aspects of the partnership's activities. The Berry *et al.* research also lends support to the finding that co-location is good practice, to facilitate information sharing, flexibility and improving communication between the partners.

Problems

Although the research project discussed here demonstrates successes in partnership working and a general endorsement of the practice, there were of course problems and shortcomings. The discussion above alludes to some issues, such as partners not attending meetings or not fulfilling the tasks they were set. Police officers who were invested in these partnerships and wanted them to be successful would find ways to work around these problems such as by seeking out specific partners who could be relied upon outside of meetings or forming smaller working groups (O'Neill and McCarthy 2012). One police force in the study seemed to have rather entrenched problems with partnerships which stemmed from multiple and ineffective layers of management. This resulted in little accountability for those partners who did not uphold their role in the partnership and much apathy from the police officers concerned. Any practical benefits that might have arisen from partnerships were outweighed by the effort required to make them work. However, in the forces where partnership was embraced at all levels (strategic and operational) and supported well, there was a large degree of will to work through problems which arose.

Despite much commitment from all parties for partnership working, there did seem to be a degree of 'meeting overload' for some police officers. Being a traditionally task-focused organisation, it is not a surprise that some officers resented the number of meetings they had to attend and the length of time they were in these meetings. This also points to the importance of co-location wherever possible, as well as encouraging police officers and staff to make direct connections with specific individuals in the partner groups. This can reduce the reliance on meetings to get tasks completed or can make those meetings that do take place more productive. However, as mentioned earlier, co-location arrangements carry with them a degree of cost and can be complex to set up. Police databases would need to be accessible to the police officers in a co-location arrangement, but in such as way as to ensure that the information could be accessed in line with the Data Protection Act. These officers will also need to do more travelling between the various police stations and the shared location. The current budget constraints for the public sector presents perhaps the biggest problem for partnership working, in that all partnership groups, including the police, are facing many years of restricted budgets and shrinking teams. This means that there are fewer staff available for partnerships who have fewer resources on which to draw to do this work.

Data Protection presents a related problem for partnerships. Research interviews revealed that in the beginning of partnership working there was a great deal of uncertainty about what information could be shared between partners and this presented a great barrier to the successful implementation of the method. However, the Crime and Disorder Act 1998 did allow for amendments to the Data Protection Act to facilitate data sharing between partners to enable them to do their 'joined-up' working. Once these changes were better understood, partnership working became much easier. It was reported in the interviews that partnership group members will sign disclosure agreements to set in writing an understanding of what is and is not allowed. However, this does raise the concern at the ease at which various sections of the public sector can share detailed and rather personal information about specific individuals (Hughes and Rowe 2007). The police I interviewed often mentioned how partners were very helpful in filling in gaps in each other's information about a person or family, enabling more intervention from these services. While this did tend to have a benevolent tone to it, one wonders if the end result is that it is more difficult for these individuals (who tend to be from disadvantaged communities and backgrounds) to escape the security gaze of the state (O'Neill and Loftus 2013).

Finally, Hough (2006) has warned that the police (as well as the Home Office) tend to operate with rather simplistic notions of crime control. He warns that this could disenfranchise partners who perhaps are working with a more holistic view of social problems and would seek to avoid quick, uninformed decisions about how to address them (see also, Hughes 2007). Although Hough was writing in the context of CDRPs, the warning can apply to other types of partnerships in which the police are involved. While it can be a strength of the police that they are willing and able to work quickly to remedy a problem, this can also be a shortcoming. The post-2008 embeddedness of partnership working in a Neighbourhood Policing context may help to alleviate this problem to a degree in that the police are, ideally, working in one area for an extended period to help implement long-term solutions as one part of a larger team.

Suggestions for the future

Neighbourhood Policing should continue in all areas, even low-crime ones. While the police may see this as comforting the 'worried well', the residents in question will not and do not see their concerns as trivial. This is, of course, the very ethos on which Neighbourhood Policing was developed (Innes 2005; see also Innes, this volume), to address the priorities of the residents, not of the police, in a local area. What England and Wales has done well, which has not been replicated in other countries (Australia or the USA, for example) is to have a nationwide project with dedicated funding and support, which has fundamentally altered the core of the organisation. This is the only way to significantly alter the policing field to the extent that the policing habitus likewise changes to enable it to succeed. Piecemeal, local projects without organisation-wide structural support will not, in my view, lead to the type of highly respected and responsive profession that the police aim to be.

In terms of developing individual officers as effective partners in the public sector through Neighbourhood Policing, it is useful to draw upon some of the points made in other chapters in this volume. Innes discusses the future of the neighbourhood constable as one who is directly gathering, through door-to-door contact with residents, a more holistic view of the issues in a neighbourhood. These officers in Innes' vision will be supported by intelligence systems that allow them to see and process intelligence feeds for each area directly and quickly, rather than that intelligence being processed centrally. He calls this 'Community Intelligence-Led Policing (CILP)'. Laycock and Tilley (this volume) have examined ways in which Problem Orientated Policing (POP) can be better embedded in the police organisation and that the police actors involved can be better aware of and trained on this method, operating as it does on multiple levels (local, force, national and international). This method of policing seeks to view crimes and other events in an area collectively so that the root of a community problem can be addressed, rather than repeatedly addressing individual symptoms. Both Innes and Laycock and Tilley are describing the police as problem-solvers. For the former the police gather their information about problems directly from the public, for the latter it is a case of the police assembling information from formal crime reports which have come in (or arrests the police have made). While there may be a degree of overlap here, to a certain extent the source of the information about problems affecting a police force is different for each vision. What is common to both, is the role that other public sector (as well as private and third sector) partners can play in these processes. In order for community problems to be effectively addressed, at local, force, national or international levels, the police must seek the help of other agencies. They are unable to fully address all the problems that might arise in an area on their own.

In order for these partnerships to work well and to respond effectively to the needs of communities and police forces, various techniques can be used such as co-location, a clear goal, national and force-level support, clear leadership and clear accountability. Effective partnerships mean that the police and their partners are not only distributing work to the most appropriate agency, they are also accessing each other's resources (in terms of staff time, skills and budgets), which is important in terms of cost savings more generally. However, what leads to good partnerships in the first place (in addition to legal mandates) is well-developed social capital. Police actors develop a series of networks with the various agencies through regularly meeting with the same people over a long period of time. This social capital means that they know who to go to for quick, effective responses to problems, in addition to the formal channels which must also be pursued. The police do not necessarily receive formal training on this; it tends to be picked up along the way as its practical benefits become manifest (O'Neill and McCarthy 2012).

The question remains of how to better develop skills in acquiring social capital and the resulting networks with partners so that these processes are as efficient as possible. One answer lies with PCSOs.[2] Often overlooked by policy-makers and senior level officers, PCSOs can and do gather a wealth of local knowledge on people, places and events. Their local social capital and networks can be very detailed and for those who have been patrolling the same area for a number of years, have a long historical view. They are the members of the Neighbourhood Policing teams who have the time to speak to residents, to do door-to-door enquiries on the low-level incidents that tend to impact on daily life the most, and who are processing information about people and events as the reports come in to the station (sometimes acting immediately on this knowledge). Thus, they are already, to an extent, acting as the technologically supported community intelligence-led officers that Innes envisions, and know to whom to turn for local problem-solving tasks (which may also impact on the force, national and international levels as Laycock and Tilley describe). While it is tempting to turn to neighbourhood police officers for these tasks, the reality is (certainly at the moment anyway), that neighbourhood officers do not have the time to gather the level of local information and develop the networks that are needed for this method of working. They should, of course, be involved, and try to get out and speak to their community members whenever they can. However, the team members with the time to develop the most extensive and detailed knowledge of an area and its public sector partners are the PCSOs.

In keeping with the forward-facing focus of this section of the chapter, I suggest the following to ensure that police officers and staff are best prepared to work in partnership with other agencies in the future. First of all, the role of PCSO needs to be the first rung on the police ladder, i.e. all applicants to the police should spend at least two years as a PCSO in a Neighbourhood Policing team. This model is already in place in the Netherlands (although with full powers of arrest and a baton, which I would not suggest for the UK (see Hofstra and Shapland 1997, Hauber et al. 1996)) and would also help demarcate the work of the PCSO from that of the community warden (funded by the local council but often with overlapping responsibilities). By spending two years doing intensive community work as PCSOs first, police officers would have a more mature sense of interpersonal communication, of the role and impact of the police in the local community, of the interconnectedness of local social problems and issues, and will begin to get a sense of how the various public sector agencies work and interact. This would also ensure that PCSOs have a route to promotion should they wish it (something currently denied them). Second, in order to boost the skills and credentials of PCSOs in a professionalised policing organisation (see Sklansky, this volume), PCSO training needs to be accredited and lead to a recognised (and transferable) qualification. It is only fitting that if police officers are becoming policing professionals, especially with the formation of the College of Policing, that these professionals are supported by a team of recognised paraprofessionals, the PCSOs. Their training would need to be enhanced to allow them to gain a qualification from it, but this would also go a long way to addressing the lack of professional development in the role. Part of this training would include developing local networks and contacts, working with partner agencies, and a detailed understanding of the public sector system. Finally, the role of PCSO should be enhanced with optional specialisms. This is where the link with Innes' CILP and Laycock and Tilley's enhanced POP can be promoted. PCSOs who have demonstrated skill at developing local social capital and building community networks, including with local public sector partners, could apply to be POP PCSOs or CILP PCSOs. These staff members would have additional responsibilities for working with local partners to address community problems that come in via either police recording systems (POP) or from consultations with the local community (CILP – which the PCSOs will carry out, door-to-door). Working with the neighbourhood police officers and their local connections, these PCSOs could take the lead on creating and running projects and interventions to address low-level issues. This would ensure that police officers are being used for tasks that demand their additional powers and skills and that officers have the support they need to ensure that all community issues (no matter how trivial they might seem) are being addressed. These enhancements of the PCSO role will ensure that police partnership work and problem solving is more effective, that PCSOs gain the internal and external recognition that they deserve for the work that they already do, and that they can access promotion and professional development. In this way, the police organisation would become a truly professionalised community service.

Notes

1 This research was conducted in 2008/09 and was funded by the British Academy (BA), award number SG-46702. The support of the BA is gratefully acknowledged. The author conducted semi-structured interviews with a range of police officers, from the rank of constable to inspector (plus one superintendent). This covered four police force areas, two of which were largely urban and two of which were largely rural. Six officers from each force were interviewed, two from each rank, for a total of 25 interviews (six of which were women). Chief inspectors provided the names of potential participants, whom the researcher then invited to interview directly. The chief inspector selected the names based on criteria supplied by the researcher – some were to be involved in Neighbourhood Policing and partnership working and some were not, to get a balance of perspectives. Respondents were made aware before the interview date that their participation was voluntary and that all information would be kept in confidence and used in publications anonymously. Interviews were transcribed and analysed using MaxQDA software.

2   The following discussion is based on preliminary findings from my ongoing research on PCSOs, funded by a Leverhulme Trust Research Fellowship.

References

Berry, G., Briggs, P., Erol, R. and van Staden, L. (2011) 'The effectiveness of partnership working in a crime and disorder context: A rapid evidence assessment'. Research Report 52. London: The Home Office.

Bittner, E. (1967) 'The Police on Skid Row: A Study of Peacekeeping', *American Sociological Review*, 32(5): 699–715.

Bourdieu, P. and Wacquant, J.J.D. (1992) *An Invitation to Reflexive Sociology*. Chicago, IL: University of Chicago Press.

Bowling, B. and Foster, J. (2002) 'Policing and the Police', in M. Maguire, R. Morgan and R. Reiner (eds) *The Oxford Handbook of Criminology*. Oxford: Oxford University Press.

Bullock, K., Erol, R. and Tilley, N. (2006) *Problem-Oriented Policing and Partnerships*. Cullompton: Willan Publishing.

Chan, J. (1997) *Changing Police Culture: Policing in a Multicultural Society*. Cambridge: Cambridge University Press.

Chan, J., Devery, C. and Doran, S. (2003) *Fair Cop: Learning the Art of Policing*. Toronto: University of Toronto Press.

Crawford, A. (2006) 'Networked Governance and the Post-Regulatory State?', *Theoretical Criminology*, 10(4): 449–479.

Edwards, A. (2002) 'Learning from Diversity: The Strategic Dilemmas of Community-Based Crime Control', in G. Hughes and A. Edwards (eds) *Crime Control and Community: The New Politics of Public Safety*. Cullompton: Willan Publishing.

Ekblom, P. (2011) *Crime Prevention, Security and Community Safety Using the 5Is Framework*. Basingstoke: Palgrave Macmillan.

Fleming, J. (2006) 'Working through Networks: The Challenge of Partnership Policing', in J. Fleming and J. Wood (eds) *Fighting Crime Together: The Challenges of Policing and Security Networks*. Sydney: University of New South Wales Press.

Gilling, D. (2007) *Crime Reduction and Community Safety*. Cullompton: Willan.

Hauber, A., Hofstra, B., Toornvliet, L. and Zandbergen, A. (1996) 'Some New Forms of Functional Social Control in the Netherlands and their Effects', *British Journal of Criminology*, 36(2): 199–219.

Hofstra, B. and Shapland, J. (1997) 'Who is in Control?' *Policing & Society*, 6(4): 265–281.

Holdaway, S. (1983) *Inside the British Police*. Oxford: Basil Blackwell.

Holdaway, S. (1986) 'Police and Social Work Relations: Problems and Possibilities', *British Journal of Social Work*, 16: 137–160.

Hough, M. (2006) 'Hands On or Hands Off? Central Government's Role in Managing CDRPs', *Community Safety Journal*, 5(3): 14–19.

Hughes, G. (2007) *The Politics of Crime and Community*. Houndmills: Palgrave MacMillan.

Hughes, G. and Rowe, M. (2007) 'Neighbourhood Policing and Community Safety: Researching the Instabilities of the Local Governance of Crime, Disorder and Security in Contemporary UK', *Criminology and Criminal Justice*, 7(4): 317–346.

Innes, M. (2005) 'Why "Soft" Policing is Hard: On the Curious Development of Reassurance Policing, How It Became Neighbourhood Policing and What This Signifies About the Politics of Police Reform', *Journal of Community and Applied Social Psychology*, 15(3): 156–169.

Loftus, B. (2007) 'Policing the "Irrelevant": Class, Diversity and Contemporary Police

Culture', in M. O'Neill, M. Marks and A.-M. Singh (eds) *Police Occupational Culture: New Debates and Directions*. Oxford: Elsevier.

Loftus, B. (2010) 'Police Occupational Culture: Classic Themes, Altered Times', *Policing and Society*, 20(1): 1–20.

Mawby, R. and Worrall, A. (2011) '"They Were Very Threatening About Do-Gooding Bastards": Probation's Changing Relationships with the Police and Prison Services in England and Wales', *European Journal of Probation*, 3(3): 78–94.

McCarthy, D.J. (2011) 'Classing Early Intervention: Social Class, Occupational Moralities and Criminalization', *Critical Social Policy*, 31(4): 1–22.

McCarthy, D.J. (2012) 'Gendering "Soft" Policing: Female Cops, Multi-Agency Working, and the Fragilities of Police Culture/s', *Policing and Society*, first published as doi:10.1080/10439463.2012.703199.

Noaks, L. (2008) 'Private and Public Policing in the UK: A Citizen Perspective on Partnership', *Policing and Society*, 18(2): 156–168.

O'Neill, M. and McCarthy, D. (2012) '(Re)Negotiating Police Culture through Partnership Working: Trust, Compromise and the "New" Pragmatism', *Criminology and Criminal Justice*, first published as doi:10.1177/1748895812469381.

O'Neill, M. and Loftus, B. (2013) 'Policing of the Marginalised: The Everyday Contexts of Social Control', *Theoretical Criminology*, first published as doi: 10.1177/1362480613495084.

Pearson, G., Blagg, H., Smith, D., Sampson, A. and Stubbs, P. (1992) 'Crime, Community and Conflict: The Multi-Agency Approach', in D. Downes (ed.) *Unravelling Criminal Justice*. London: Macmillan.

Reiner, R. (2010) *The Politics of the Police* (4th edn). Oxford: Oxford University Press.

Rogers, C. (2004) 'Separated by a Common Goal: Some Problems of Interagency Working', *Community Safety Journal*, 3(2): 5–11.

Sklansky, D. (2007) 'Seeing Blue: Police Reform, Occupational Culture and Cognitive Burn-in', in M. O'Neill, M. Marks and A.-M. Singh (eds) *Police Occupational Culture: New Debates and Directions*. Oxford: Elsevier Science.

Waddington, P.A.J. (1999) 'Police (Canteen) Sub-Culture: An Appreciation', *British Journal of Criminology*, 39(2): 287–309.

Wilson, J.Q. and Kelling, G.L. (1982) 'Broken windows', *The Atlantic Monthly*, March, pp. 29–37.

Wood, J. (2004) 'Cultural Change in the Governance of Security', *Policing and Society*, 14(1): 31–48.

Wright, A. (2002) *Policing: An Introduction to Concepts and Practice*. Cullompton: Willan Publishing.

14

BEYOND RHETORIC

Establishing police–academic partnerships that work

Robin S. Engel and Samantha Henderson

Introduction

Partnerships between police agencies and academics have existed in one form or another for the past century. However, it was not until the last three decades that the two entities have partnered more regularly to form both short- and long-term working relationships. Most recently, partnerships have begun taking on the form of long-term collaborations, focusing on ongoing research and knowledge transfer rather than individual projects. Despite the increasing prevalence of this type of partnership, relationships between police and academics still vary widely in their length and composition. Regardless of their make-up, these relationships have undoubtedly benefited both the police and the academics involved in them. However, as we describe, there remains significant room for improvement if police–academic partnerships are to reach their full potential.

In this chapter, we present an overview of police–academic partnerships by first discussing the background and current prevalence of the phenomenon. Thereafter, we provide a brief overview of the benefits and obstacles to these partnerships. Borrowing from Bradley and Nixon (2009) we also describe the varying types of police–academic partnerships that have emerged (critical, policy, and fully collaborative), and document the available case studies that describe these types of partnerships. We focus more specifically on full collaborative partnerships by identifying the three distinct structural forms these collaborative partnerships have generally taken (i.e., individual researchers working directly with agencies; an academic unit within a single university working directly with agencies; and collaborations of researchers across academic institutions working directly with agencies). In conclusion, we provide our view on the future of police–academic partnerships and advocate for the advancement of fully collaborative research partnerships. In particular, we argue that structured collaborations that span multiple universities and police agencies will be most effective at advancing evidence-based practices in policing agencies.

History of police–academic partnerships

The first known police–academic partnership began in the early 1900s (Rojek *et al.*, 2012) when August Vollmer, the Chief of Police in Berkeley, California, paired with the University of California, Berkeley to offer instructional courses to officers (Vollmer & Schneider, 1917). Partnerships incorporating research did not occur until some 40 years later, when agencies began pairing with academics and allowing them access to their officers and data. For example, by the late 1960s, the United States government had developed a funding source for police research, available through the National Institute of Law Enforcement and Criminal Justice (now the National Institute of Justice) (Rojek *et al.*, 2012). More recently, these grants have been targeted at increasing police–academic partnerships, with the hopes of expanding evidence-based police practices through partnered research. Likewise, in the United Kingdom, funds are available to support partnered research via the Home Office (Hanak & Hofinger, 2005).

Despite this lengthy history, until recently little was known about the prevalence of police–academic partnerships. A recent national survey conducted in the United States, however, has shed light on the number of agencies engaging in such relationships. In the five years prior to 2010, less than one-third of American police agencies participated in some form of academic–policing research partnership. Of those, the vast majority were short-term partnerships, with only a handful reporting long-term collaborations (Rojek *et al.*, 2012). The authors found that there was a positive correlation between agency size and the prevalence of partnerships – a mere 7 per cent of agencies with nine officers or fewer engaged in any form of partnership, while 48 per cent of those with over 100 officers did so.[1] Additionally, larger agencies were more likely to engage in long-term partnerships, while smaller ones more often participated in short-term project-based collaborations.

The reason for the limited number of partnerships could be the lack of importance policing agencies place on research. A recent European study, for example, reported that police forces in almost half of the 26 countries studied placed a low value on policing research, while only 15 per cent considered it highly valuable (Hanak & Hofinger, 2005). Additionally, only half of the countries included in the study reported having a unit devoted to research within their agency. In these countries, empirical research does not often contribute to policing-policy decisions. In contrast, in those countries which place a high value on police research, policy decisions are largely driven by study findings. This study also reported that in the United Kingdom, police research is frequently conducted and has the support of the Home Office. Additionally, partnerships between police and universities are emphasized, and occur often.

Benefits and obstacles of police–academic partnerships

While the benefits and obstacles of police–academic partnerships have been described in detail elsewhere (e.g., Bradley & Nixon, 2009; Engel & Whalen, 2010), it is valuable to reiterate several of the most important for both practitioners and academics. There are a number of benefits for police agencies when they engage in partnerships with academics. The first, and most important, is the increased effectiveness that comes along with basing their work on empirical research (Engel & Whalen, 2010; Whalen, 2012). By basing their operational decisions on research findings, policing agencies simultaneously increase their effectiveness, and provide themselves with an externally valid source of support in the event that their decision-making is scrutinized. Collaborating with academics also enables agencies to receive feedback throughout the duration of a research project (Bradley & Nixon, 2009; Foster & Bailey, 2010; Guillaume et al., 2012). This is preferred to having to wait for final reports, which take a while to complete, and as such often arrive after they are no longer useful.

Academics also benefit from engaging in such partnerships. Importantly, engaging directly with the police will not lessen academic quality but, rather, enhance it. By listening to the needs of police practitioners, they can target their research toward in-demand topics, so their results have more impact (Engel & Whalen, 2010). Additionally, partnering with police agencies enables academics to maintain relationships with an entire police agency, rather than just individual officers (Boba, 2010), which affords them ongoing access to the data they require to engage in research (Beal & Kerlikowske, 2010; Engel & Whalen, 2010). Finally, continual collaboration on research can lead to the formulation of trusting relationships (Boba, 2010; Wuestewald & Steinheider, 2010), and to increases in police acceptance of the use of empirical based evidence (Innes, 2010).

Despite the advantages of police–academic partnerships discussed above, the prevalence rate of these relationships remains quite low (Rojek et al., 2012). This is largely due to a number of barriers that persist for both police and academics. For instance, practitioners and researchers often have conflicting perspectives and goals (Fleming, 2012; Wuestewald & Steinheider, 2010). This can lead to both police resistance to research (Foster & Bailey, 2010; Knutsson, 2010), and to communication issues between police and academics (Fleming, 2012).

Additionally, officer turnover can make it difficult to establish the trusting relationships required to engage in long-term partnerships (Engel & Whalen, 2010; Henry & Mackenzie, 2012), and agencies might be unwilling to implement research findings – either because they disagree with them (Knutsson, 2010), or because they arrive too late to be useful (Engel & Whalen, 2010). This latter obstacle is a particularly common complaint, as practitioners and researchers operate on differing timelines, with agencies expecting feedback more quickly than researchers provide it. Finally, obtaining consistent funding for research can prove difficult (Boba, 2010; Bradley & Nixon, 2009), as funding sources such as grants are often designed to support short-term projects, rather than long-term collaborations.

Types of police–academic partnerships

It is believed that at least some of the barriers noted above can be removed based on the type and structure of the police–academic partnership. Our review of the literature produced 16 published case studies available regarding specific types of police–academic partnerships in seven countries. Note that our review does not include descriptions of specific projects where an academic team evaluated a police intervention; rather, we focus specifically on descriptions of police–academic partnerships. As documented in Table 14.1, these police–academic partnerships varied widely in location, structure, duration, scope, activities, and funding. This reported variation across case studies clearly demonstrates that the form and structure of police–academic partnerships vary dramatically. Despite this wide variation, Bradley and Nixon (2009) have suggested that police–academic partnerships can be categorized within three distinct groups: critical, policy, and full collaborative. Using their work in Australia as an example of a successful police–academic partnership, they strongly advocate for the fully collaborative approach.

Bradley and Nixon (2009) draw on MacDonald's (1986) 'dialogue of the deaf' to describe the relationship between academics and police practitioners in critical partnerships. In his writing, MacDonald presents a fictitious conversation between an academic and a police officer. During the dialogue, both parties remain unsympathetic to the perspective of the other, while emphasizing their own expectations. Unconcerned with the needs of police agencies, researchers in critical partnerships keep their subjects at arm's length, and regularly find fault in the practices of the police (Bradley & Nixon, 2009). Researchers who adopt this approach typically do not seek to alter police practices directly. Rather, the goal is to contribute to the general knowledge base on the subject, while informing governmental decision-making and the development of legislation (Bradley & Nixon, 2009).

The critical approach to research dominated much of the work conducted in the 1960s–1980s and formed a lasting legacy that contributed greatly to police reform during its time. However, this approach now hampers the expansion and growth of police–academic partnerships. Policing research emerged from the 1960s as an enterprise seeking to better understand the role of police in society. A series of rich ethnographic works describing police behaviour and organizations demonstrated that an understanding of the law gave little insight into police in action (e.g., Black, 1980; Goldstein, 1960, 1963; LaFave, 1962; Muir, 1977; Reiss, 1971; Skolnick, 1966; Westley, 1970; Wilson, 1968). In the United States, this research challenged conventional wisdom and exposed the power of governmental agents. It described the use and abuse of discretion, along with the functions and dysfunctions of police organizations. These studies set the stage for inquiries over the next several decades (Walker, 1992). But it also led researchers to have a fundamental and deep-seated suspicion of the police. Researchers often saw their role as exposing poor police practices, and police naturally retreated from partnerships.

In contrast to the approach, the policy approach to police research is grounded in practical applications, and seeks to influence police practices directly (Bradley &

TABLE 14.1 Police–academic partnerships

Author(s)	Location and participating agencies	Type of partnership	Description	Funding source	Notable benefits/obstacles of partnership
Alemika, 2009	Africa	Non-existent	Prevalence of police–academic research partnerships is on the rise in Africa, but is predominantly limited to individuals who on their own personal resources to conduct research.	Funding for research is largely lacking in most African countries	**Obstacles**: political climates in most African nations are hostile to research, and police forces in African countries are either unaware of, or ignore, research findings
Beal & Kerlikowske, 2010	New York, USA: Buffalo Police Department and the University of Buffalo School of Management	Long-term collaboration between university and police department	Ongoing project-based relationship whereby individual projects are completed by researchers and by students in the management school.	No dedicated source of funding, many pro bono projects to give graduate students experience	**Benefits**: Provides easy access to data, and gives graduate students experience in the field
Boba, 2010	Florida, USA: Port St Lucie, Florida Police Department, and Florida Atlantic University	Long-term collaboration between a single academic and local police department	Ongoing relationship between a single academic and a local police department.	Various grants	**Benefits**: Development of trust through long-term partnership enabled researcher to maintain relationship over time
Bradley & Nixon, 2009	Australia: Victoria Police and various academics	Long-term pursuit of partnered research by police department	Police department actively seeks out academics who meet their research needs and apply for grants to support participatory action research projects with	Australian Research Council	**Obstacles**: Access to funding is contingent on receiving grants **Benefits**: Practitioners have a say in what is researched, and pairing with academics means that the police

TABLE 14.1 Continued

Author(s)	Location and participating agencies	Type of partnership	Description	Funding source	Notable benefits/obstacles of partnership
			them; have paired with more than 20 universities in Australia and elsewhere, and with more than 120 researchers and 25 doctoral research students.		department does not have to wait until the end of the study for a large final report
Davis, 2010	Texas, USA: Caruth Police Institute at Dallas	Research Institute	Ongoing partnership between the Dallas Police Department, the University of North Texas, and the University of Texas at Dallas, who have joined together to form a research institute. The institute is involved in both police-related research and the education of police officers.	Communities Foundation of Texas – startup funds from $10 million (USD) grant	**Benefits**: Development of institute with both practitioner and research partners ensures ongoing research collaborations
Engel & Whalen, 2010	Ohio, USA: University of Cincinnati Policing Institute and the Cincinnati Police Department	Long-term collaboration between university-based research institute and local police department	Ongoing relationship between university research institute and a local police department that promotes evidence-based practices and procedures. In addition to pairing for research purposes, Cincinnati Police officers are able to obtain Criminal Justice graduate degrees through the Chief Scholar's Program at the University of Cincinnati.	Various state grants, city contracts, and pro bono projects for graduate student experience	**Benefits**: Combining the interests of researchers and the police has led to enhanced police services being provided to the citizens of Cincinnati

Citation	Location/Participants	Type of partnership	Description	Funding source	Obstacles/Benefits
Fleming, 2012	Australia: Single Australian police organization and two researchers	Short-term partnership	Short-term partnership designed to aid a police organization in designing and evaluating a community policing strategy.	N/A	**Obstacles**: Communication issues, sense of 'us' vs. 'them'
Foster & Bailey, 2010	Norfolk, UK; Norfolk Constabulary and single academic	Long-term collaboration between single academic and local police department	Ongoing partnership between a single academic and a local police constabulary focusing on the development of evidence-based approaches to improving police services. Emphasis on action research.	N/A	**Obstacles**: Initial resistance to allowing academics into the organization **Benefits**: Partnership enabled department to receive feedback quickly
Fyfe & Wilson, 2012	Scotland; Scottish Institute for Policing Research and the Scottish Police	Long-term partnership across universities to provide long-term collaboration with CJ agencies	Ongoing strategic partnership between the Scottish police service and 12 Scottish universities forming the Scottish Institute for Policing Research (SIPR). SIPR is organized around three research networks: police—community relations, evidence and investigation, and police organization. Research activities are coordinated from the University of Dundee's administrative hub. Appropriate researchers are paired with practitioners to work on projects. A professional development programme is delivered at the police college by SIPR researchers and police practitioners.	Association of Chief of Police Officers in Scotland, the Scottish Funding Council, and from participating universities	**Benefits**: Regular interaction between officers and researchers has resulted in a culture of engagement whereby both parties are committed to producing research together

TABLE 14.1 Continued

Author(s)	Location and participating agencies	Type of partnership	Description	Funding source	Notable benefits/obstacles of partnership
Guillaume, Sidebottom, & Tilley, 2012	Warwickshire, UK: Jill Dando Institute of Security & Crime Science at Univ. College London, Warwickshire Police, Warwickshire County Council	Short-term project-based partnership	Practitioner-led Problem Oriented Policing project in which advising and evaluation was provided by university research institute.	UK Home Office	**Benefits**: Practitioners stated that working with academics was beneficial, as they were able to test their ideas and give advice throughout the project
Henry & Mackenzie, 2012	Scotland: Single Scottish police organization and two researchers	Long-term collaboration between a local police department and two researchers	Three-year Knowledge Transfer relationship designed to aid in the transfer of research and findings. Focus on the development of Community Oriented Policing practices.	UK Arts and Humanities Research Council	**Obstacles**: Officer assigned to integral position changed four times throughout the project; funding applications and cycles did not match up with police demands
Innes, 2010	Wales: South Wales University Police Science Institute	Research Institute	Ongoing partnership between Cardiff University, Glamorgan University, and the South Wales Police who have joined together to form a research institute. In addition to partnering with	N/A	**Benefits**: Approaching the police–academic relationship from multiple fronts has contributed to a cultural shift in the police department that is more accepting of the use of research-based evidence

outside agencies to conduct research and help implement findings, police recruits are trained at one of the partnering universities, and some senior officers pursue post-graduate studies at the partnering universities.

Knutsson, 2010	Sweden: Single researcher and the Swedish National Police Board	Short-term project-based partnership	Short-term partnership to evaluate the effects of a crime-prevention programme.	Swedish National Police Board	**Obstacles**: Police Board refused to accept the null finding result, and continued to implement the crime prevention measure
OCJS, 2013; Engel, Latessa, Corsaro, 2012	38 researchers from 11 Ohio, USA universities	Long-term partnership across universities to provide long-term collaboration with CJ agencies	Research consortium pairs criminal justice agencies seeking research assistance with academics that have relevant expertise.	Ohio Office of Criminal Justice Services	**Benefits**: Agencies are matched with local experts and provided research at low/no cost on topics that they deem relevant
Scott, 2010	Wisconsin, USA: University of Wisconsin Law School and various outside law agencies	Long-term pursuit of partnered research by academics	University faculty actively seek out and engage in policing research and are involved in the education of practitioners. Additionally, students at the law school are given internships with the Wisconsin police department and prosecutors office so that they can conduct action research.	Various	N/A

TABLE 14.1 Continued

Author(s)	Location and participating agencies	Type of partnership	Description	Funding source	Notable benefits/obstacles of partnership
Wuestewald & Steinheider, 2010	Oklahoma, USA: Broken Arrow, Oklahoma Police Department and University of Oklahoma, Tulsa Graduate College	Long-term collaboration between single academic and local police department	Ongoing partnership between an organizational psychologist (and a network of their graduate students) and a local police department. Relationship initially began as a single project to address low staff morale, but evolved into a long-term partnership with a focus on action research.	N/A	**Obstacles**: Differing perspectives initially led to conflicting goals **Benefits**: Action research approach ensured that all parties had their needs addressed, enabled them to develop trust

Nixon, 2009). The goal of this approach differs from that of the critical approach: rather than generating research which contributes to a broad knowledge base, policy researchers focus on establishing practically relevant research that affects police policies. Although promising, policy type partnerships have not been as successful as originally anticipated, and the 'dialogue of the deaf' still persists. This may be due, in part, because the same academics that conducted critical research then tried to engage in policy partnerships, yet never fully embraced their goals (Bradley & Nixon, 2009). Additionally, there have been barriers to implementing research findings based on this approach.

Despite these shifts in research and the continued discussion about police–academic partnerships, very few academic institutions and police agencies actually develop mutually beneficial relationships designed specifically to improve police practices (Engel & Whalen, 2010). The ability to get data from a police agency is not a sufficient condition for claiming to have a partnership. Partnerships are long-term commitments that require trust and consultation (Braga & Hinkle, 2010). They require a commitment to conducting rigorous research over many years that could result in the improvement of police practices. A collaboration built around a specific project or grant is unlikely to result in a partnership unless considerable effort is made before and after that grant is awarded. This will require change on the part of both academic researchers and the police (Beal & Kerlikowske, 2010; Bradley & Nixon, 2009; Engel & Whalen, 2010).

In order to rectify the issues present within critical and policy partnerships, Bradley and Nixon (2009) suggested a third type of partnership, emphasizing both collaboration and length. This type of partnership (which we refer to as fully collaborative), is conscious of both organizational culture and agency policies (Bradley & Nixon, 2009). This approach encourages long-term partnership between practitioners and researchers, where researchers remain involved from the inception of the study right through the implementation of the findings. However, it is unclear from Bradley and Nixon's description what organizational forms these fully collaborative partnership should take. Again, Table 14.1 demonstrates a wide variation in the approaches used both across and within countries. Our review demonstrates that fully collaborative partnerships generally take one of three forms: (1) individual researchers working directly with agencies; (2) an academic unit within a single university working directly with agencies; (3) collaborations of researchers across academic institutions working directly with agencies.

In the small number of jurisdictions where fully collaborative police–academic partnerships actually exist, they likely take the form of an individual researcher establishing a relationship with a single police agency. For example, Boba (2010) describes her relationship with the Port St Lucie Police Department in Florida as a long-term 'partnership between individuals' (p. 124) that has led to a 'meaningful and ongoing level of trust' (p. 127) between herself and the police department she works with. This, she argues, is required in order to maintain a research relationship, and is more difficult to establish at the organizational level.

While Boba (2010) indicates that this partnership is strengthened because of the continuity of the researcher over time, we suggest that this type of relationship is actually the most limited form of a collaborative relationship because it is based solely upon a single researcher. Therefore, the sustainability of this approach is questionable, and the likelihood of moving beyond assistance with specific projects is unlikely.

This approach could be strengthened if the individual researcher was actually embedded in the organizational structure of the agency. This approach was used in the Redlands, California, USA Police Department, where a criminologist was hired as a member of the executive staff and reports directly to the Chief (Taniguchi & Bueermann, 2012). There are strengths to this approach, including gaining wider access across a variety of topics, and the ability to have direct impact within the agency. Employing the individual as non-sworn personnel, however, necessarily reduces the independence and objectivity of the researcher. This approach however, provides police agencies with an opportunity to take ownership of police science as advocated by Weisburd & Neyroud (2011). Unfortunately, very little has been systematically documented about the strengths and weaknesses of this organizational approach.

A second type of collaborative partnership involves establishing a relationship between an academic unit within a single university and a police agency. This approach has been successfully implemented in Cincinnati, Ohio, USA in a fully collaborative partnership between the University of Cincinnati School of Criminal Justice and the Cincinnati Police Department. The goal of this relationship is to promote evidence-based practices within the police department. As described by Engel & Whalen (2010), in order to better understand the context in which the police work, academics regularly attend command staff and crime analysis meetings, and ride with patrol officers and specialized units. Additionally, researchers have been granted full, unfettered access to all agency data. As the police department defines their organizational priorities, their research partners provide valuable insight and guidance regarding best practices. The partnership has led to increases in police efficiency (in both enforcement and data collection), and provided the agency with an externally valid source of support for their decision-making (Whalen, 2012).

The strength of this approach is that it is not dependent upon a single researcher and therefore is more likely to have sustainability and continuity over time. In addition, the scope and breadth of the expertise provided across topics will naturally expand with additional researchers involved in the partnership. Finally, there is an opportunity for police officers to become more fully engaged in the research process through training at the university via the *Chief's Scholars Program*. This programme allows specially selected Cincinnati police officers to maintain their on-duty status while studying full-time for their master's degree in Criminal Justice at the University of Cincinnati (Engel & Whalen, 2010; Whalen, 2012).

The final model of fully collaborative police–academic partnerships (i.e., collaborations of researchers across academic institutions working directly with agencies) takes the previously described model to scale. This approach is best exemplified by the Scottish Institute for Policing Research (SIPR) (Scottish Institute for Policing Research, 2011), a research consortium made up of the Scottish police service and 12 Scottish universities. Structured around three distinct research networks (Police–Community Relations, Evidence and Investigation, and Police Organization), the SIPR coordinates collaborations between academics and practitioners on topics relevant to police practice in Scotland. Additionally, the institute has developed a network of graduate students, and funds post-doctoral and PhD studentships in policing research.

Likewise, the State of Ohio, USA is currently developing an academic consortium to provide technical assistance, training, and consulting services directly to criminal justice agencies across the state (Engel *et al.*, 2012). The development of the Ohio Consortium of Crime Science (OCCS), housed at the University of Cincinnati's Institute of Crime Science (ICS), includes 38 criminology and criminal justice academic experts from 11 different Ohio universities and colleges (OCJS, 2013). The purpose of the OCCS is to link jurisdictions that have crime and criminal justice problems to local academics with expertise in crime prevention, policing, courts, juvenile justice, corrections, etc. Experts associated with the OCCS provide technical assistance, consultation, training, and evaluation services to state and local jurisdictions in Ohio based on requests for assistance vetted and funded through the Ohio Office of Criminal Justice Services (OCJS). To our knowledge, this is the first such statewide consortium in the United States designed to create and sustain local collaborative practitioner–academic partnerships.

The future of partnerships

The small number of long-term and productive police–academic partnerships in existence is undoubtedly due to many of the obstacles noted previously. Several scholars have argued that even the few productive partnerships that exist cannot save the policing practice, which is fundamentally flawed based, in part, on its organizational disconnect from social science research, and from unrealistic expectations and understandings of the police profession by academics (Hoover, 2010; Kennedy, 2010). For example, Kennedy described the movement toward collaborative police–academic partnerships in Australia, the USA, and elsewhere as:

> too little, too weak, and will not make much difference at all. The core orientations and activities of both police and the academy will be little altered. Relatively little research will be done, and it will have little impact on practice. Outcomes with respect to crime and public safety – what matters the most, in the end – will be minimal.
>
> *(Kennedy, 2010: 166)*

But we believe that the successful partnerships established in some American cities and in jurisdictions across the United Kingdom give us some reason for optimism. The academic field of policing research is changing, as is policing itself. These changes lend themselves to the establishment of collaborative partnerships for the mutual benefit of both entities.

As an academic field of study, policing lags behind many other areas in social science. However, over the past 50 years, there has been incredible growth in policing research, with expansion in several critical areas that has provided a solid base upon which to build. Policing research has also helped change policing practices. There are obvious gaps in our knowledge, however, that suggest police researchers might want to creatively reexamine the contributions of our field. In particular, a reexamination of the purposes of police research appears necessary. Is our research intended to foster discussion within academia? Is it to stimulate wider public debate on the role of policing? Is it to help police decision-makers improve their operations? Or, is it to drive change in policing practices? And if it serves all of these purposes, what is the priority we should attach to each? These are key considerations that have not been adequately addressed in our field of study.

There are many academics that remain leery of working directly with police practitioners. Indeed, there is some legitimate concern that researchers aspiring to provide utility to practitioners are potentially problematic for an academic discipline that strives to be scientific and unbiased. For example, some have described the problem as one of 'sleeping with the enemy', where naive researchers accept the fundamental mission and activities of police as benign. We believe that while this concern might have some merit, it is not supported by the limited evidence available. Consider that James Fyfe (1982, 1988), while conducting his research that arguably resulted in changes to use of force policies across the United States that saved the lives of hundreds of citizens, was a lieutenant within the New York City Police Department. Also consider that Herman Goldstein (1977, 1990), largely responsible for promoting a new model of problem-oriented policing, worked for the Chicago Police Department before developing his new approach. We believe the problem is not too much intimacy. Rather, the problem is that many researchers continue to view the police in an adversarial context – organizations to expose, rather than organizations to aid – and, as a result, remain aloof to the real difficulties of policing. Is it possible to establish research agendas that are beneficial to practitioners and to create effective practitioner–researcher partnerships, without sacrificing autonomy and objectivity? We believe it is not only possible, but likely necessary for producing research and insight that improves policing.

To be clear, we do not believe that focusing on research questions that have practical utility means that researchers should not examine these issues with a critical eye; our work must be independent, and often we must deliver unwelcome news to police administrators. The most meaningful policing research to date has been critical of police practices, but importantly, has also offered solutions. Police today are far more effective at dealing with crime and disorder than they were 20 years ago. Much of this is due to a few police–researcher collaborations that established sound research regarding the effectiveness of police strategies and tactics, and the police paying attention to this research. It is important to note that initially the policing community did not call for this research or frame the research questions, and was often deeply sceptical of the results. Relevancy was created by closely observing the police and developing insights that few inside policing had. It was developed neither by chummy pandering, nor by distant disparagement; behind every relevant insight that has changed policing is a deep criticism of some police practice.

Simultaneously, the field of policing is significantly changing. Due in part to the global economic downturn in recent years, coupled with the technology revolution, police agencies are being asked by the public they serve to do more with fewer resources. In short, they are expected to work smarter, and are being held accountable for their effectiveness, efficiency, and equity in dealing with crime and public safety (Eck & Rosenbaum, 1994; Bradley & Nixon, 2009). This will require that the police become more analytical in their approaches, and evaluate the outcomes of these approaches (Knutsson, 2010). Thus, the opportunity for expanding collaborative partnerships with academics is ripe.

Focus on knowledge exchange and the collaboration process

In an effort to refocus on the importance of partnerships and promotion of their strengths, Fyfe and Wilson (2012) have recently called on the policing field to 'reframe the debate about police–researcher collaborations' to focus more directly on knowledge use and exchange. These sentiments have been echoed by Henry and Mackenzie (2012) in their description of the development of community policing. Both sets of researchers argue that successful partnerships should focus on knowledge use, transfer, and exchange rather than individual projects, topics, or activities. The implication is that partnerships focused more directly on the *collaboration process* will increase the likelihood of sustainability over time. Describing this evolution in partnerships occurring in Scotland, Henry and Mackenzie noted that

> collaboration between academics and police is therefore a growing phenomenon, having moved from a position typified by one-shot or ad hoc work between single academics or teams and specific police departments, to a situation where we have overarching, reasonably stable, and sometimes national collaboration agreements between groups of researchers from multiple universities and the police institutions generally.
>
> *(2012: 316)*

While knowledge transfer and exchange is a commendable goal for police–academic partnerships, it is not without concerns. Even the terms themselves – knowledge transfer, knowledge exchange, knowledge interaction, knowledge mediation, knowledge integration, etc. – seem to be a matter of debate (Graham *et al.*, 2006; Davies *et al.*, 2008; Fyfe & Wilson, 2012). For example, there is some concern that the term knowledge transfer suggests a one-way direction of information from research to practitioner, while knowledge exchange demonstrates the value of two-way flows of information (Henry & Mackenzie, 2012). These debates are fuelled by the importance of better understanding the social processing of how information is most effectively generated and shared.

Yet perhaps one of the most important limitations in the transfer and exchange of knowledge in policing is the actual availability of the evidence-based information to be exchanged. As noted by Fyfe & Wilson (2012) much of the available evidence in policing research has been focused on demonstrating 'what works' to reduce crime (e.g., Braga & Weisburd, 2012; Braga *et al.*, 2012; Lum *et al.*, 2011; Sherman, 1998). While this is certainly an important area for knowledge transfer and exchange, most facets of policing do not have a robust body of evidence-based literature available for consideration. Further, academics quite routinely focus on outcome evaluations and not process evaluations – as a result, guidance about how to implement best practices is nearly non-existent. This is why partnerships that focus more on the collaboration itself are believed to be more successful. Yet this proposition itself is untested. Further, it remains unclear what form should these collaborations should take and how should they be funded.

We have travelled a long distance in the last decade. The central debate now among police effectiveness researchers is not *whether* to be relevant, but *how* to be relevant. Scholars debate the relative contributions of using experiments to demonstrate what works and what does not (Weisburd & Neyroud, 2011) versus developing the analytical craft in support of police operations and problem solving (Sparrow, 2011). Despite this debate, the police effectiveness literature provides quality research that has also shown great value to practitioners. Examining research questions that have utility to practitioners and the public does not mean that researchers cannot offer important critiques and objective criticism. It does mean, however, that criticism should be accompanied by actionable policy recommendations to reduce the problematic behaviour, strategies, or policies identified.

Who should own police research?

In a controversial piece, Weisburd and Neyroud (2011) suggested further room for improvement in police–academic partnerships, arguing that for policing to become an evidence-based profession, partnerships between academics and police must change from their current state. They argued that a paradigm shift must occur whereby police agencies place a higher value on empiricism, and academics become more cognisant of the needs of police agencies by integrating themselves into daily police practice. For this to happen, the authors argued that research must move from its current location at the periphery of organizations where its scope and depth is often determined by the interests of academic scholars. Instead, police agencies must take ownership over the research, so that they may guide the topics investigated and undertake research that best suits them. Writing about his experiences in Norway, Sweden, and Demark, Knutsson (2010: 134) concurs, suggesting that the future of policing is analytical and that there is only one route to achieve that – police must improve their ability to analyze data, and be more knowledgeable of what works with the effects and what does not work, and above all – to be able to make reasonable strict evaluations . . . this cannot happen without the police having a research capability of their own.

Likewise, Rojek *et al.* (2012) noted that there are currently not enough specially trained police researchers to partner with all the agencies that require them. The collective implication is that current partnerships will only serve temporary needs and, further, that the police must take ownership of research. This will require a paradigm shift in how policing is conceived and delivered, and researchers should not assume the lead role in this process.

While we believe there is some merit to this position, we argue that based on the evidence available, the most productive way forward is to continue to forge collaborative police–academic partnerships. Much discussion has been generated that compares policing to the medical profession, describing the need for the police to generate their own research as in the medical profession (Kennedy, 2010; Sherman & Berk, 1984; Sherman, 1998). These overly simplistic comparisons across two very different fields, however, fail to consider the obvious differences that clearly impact the ability to educate and fund personnel to engage in research. In addition, they often fail to recognize the important impact that agencies outside of medical practitioners (e.g., insurance companies, drug companies, governmental oversight, etc.) have over medical research. Further, they typically paint a somewhat romanticized version of the medical profession, glossing over the now well-recognized problems with the medical model (Thacher, 2001). Therefore, we remain unconvinced that advancing the medical model (with teaching hospitals and internal ownership of research), is a realistic future for policing.

Rather, we agree with Fyfe and Wilson (2012), among others, that the future of policing will be tied directly to the establishment of effective collaborative partnerships that span across multiple universities and police agencies. The SIPR in Scotland and OCCS in Ohio, USA, among others, are promising models that will facilitate incremental changes in police practices based on research. As reminded by Hoover (2010: 164), 'incrementalism is not a dirty word within organizational theory; indeed it is the recommended change model for healthy organizations'. Public and private investments in collaborative police–academic partnerships should be increased because the incremental change they have been shown to produce currently represents our best opportunity to advance evidence-based practices in policing.

Further, to facilitate partnerships, academics should be involved in programme implementation, as well as evaluation (Braga & Hinkle, 2010). At the same time, academics should recognize that much of modern police work now involves research. The patrol officer or detective trying to understand the nature of crime problems, the seemingly conflicting demands of citizens, or repeat victimization, are engaged in forms of research that are just as valuable as the work published in peer-reviewed journals. Partners need to treat each other as equals, not as enemies

– and they need to be collaborative in their exchange of information. Again, this does not suggest academics cannot be critical of police but, rather, a healthy dose of criticism coated in practical alternatives and solutions would go a long way. These types of successful partnerships have led Klofas, Hipple, and McGarrell (2010) to describe what they view as the 'new criminal justice', where actors across the criminal justice system (police, prosecutors, probation, parole) cooperate and collaborate with researchers to reduce crime. We agree – it is time to advance police–academic partnerships that work.

Note

1   Note that in contrast to the United Kingdom, there are over 18,000 different police agencies in the United States, close to half (49.5 per cent) have fewer than 10 officers, 5 per cent have 100 officers or more (Reaves, 2010).

References

Alemika, E.E.O. (2009). Police practice and police research in Africa. *Police Practice and Research: An International Journal*, 10(5/6): 483–502.

Beal, P. and Kerlikowske, R.G. (2010). Action research in Buffalo and Seattle. *Police Practice and Research*, 11(2): 117–121.

Black, D. (1980). *The Manners and Customs of Police*. New York: Academic Press.

Boba, R. (2010). A practice-based evidence approach in Florida. *Police Practice and Research*, 11(2): 122–128.

Bradley, D. and Nixon, C. (2009). Ending the 'dialogue of the deaf': Evidence and policing policies and practices. An Australian case study. *Police Practice and Research: An International Journal*, 10(5/6): 423–435.

Braga, A.A. and Hinkle, M. (2010). The participation of academics in the criminal justice working group process. In J.M. Klofas, N.K. Hipple, and E.F. McGarrell (eds) *The New Criminal Justice: American Communities and the Changing World of Crime Control*. London: Routledge Press.

Braga, A., Papachristos, A. and Hureau, D. (2012). Hot spots policing effects on crime. *Campbell Systematic Reviews*, 8. DOI: 10.4073/csr.2012.8.

Braga, A. and Weisburd, D. (2012). The effects of 'pulling levers' focused deterrence strategies on crime. *Campbell Systematic Reviews*, 6. DOI: 10.4073/csr.2012.6

Davies, H., Nutley, S. and Walter, I. (2008). Why 'knowledge transfer' is misconceived for applied social research. *Journal of Health Services Research & Policy*, 13: 188–190.

Davis, R.C. (2010). A new approach in Dallas. *Police Practice and Research*, 11(2): 129–131.

Eck, J.E. and Rosenbaum, D.P. (1994). The new police order: Effectiveness, equality, and efficiency in community policing. In D.P. Rosenbaum (ed.) *Community Policing: Testing the Promises*. Newbury Park, CA: Sage.

Engel, R.S., Latessa, E. and Corsaro, N. (2012). *Ohio Consortium of Crime Science*. Proposal prepared for the Ohio Office of Criminal Justice Services.

Engel, R.S. and Whalen, J.L. (2010). Police–academic partnerships: Ending the dialogue of the deaf, the Cincinnati experience. *Police Practice and Research: An International Journal*, 11(2): 105–116.

Fleming, J. (2012). Changing the way we do business: Reflecting on collaborative practice. *Police Practice and Research: An International Journal*, 13(4): 375–388.

Foster, J. and Bailey, S. (2010). Joining forces: Maximizing ways of making a difference in policing. *Policing: A Journal of Policy and Practice*, 4(2): 95–103.

Fyfe, J.J. (1982). Blind justice: Police shootings in Memphis. *Journal of Criminal Law and Criminology*, 73: 707–722.

Fyfe, J. J. (1988). Police use of deadly force: Research and reform. *Justice Quarterly*, 5(2): 165–205.

Fyfe, N.R. and Wilson, P. (2012). Knowledge exchange and police practice: Broadening and deepening the debate around researcher-practitioner collaborations. *Police Practice and Research: An International Journal*, 13(4): 306–314.

Goldstein, J. (1960). Police discretion not to invoke the criminal process: Low-visibility decisions in the administration of justice. *The Yale Law Journal*, 69(4): 543–594.

Goldstein, J. (1963). Police discretion: The ideal v the real. *Public Administration Review*, 23: 140–148.

Goldstein, J. (1977). *Policing a Free Society*. Cambridge, MA: Ballinger.

Goldstein, H. (1990). *Problem-Oriented Policing*. New York: McGraw-Hill.

Graham, I., Logan, J., Harrison, B., Straus, S., Tetroe, J., Caswell, W. and Robinson, N. (2006). Lost in knowledge translation: Time for a map? *Journal of Continuing Education in Health Professions*, 6(1): 13–24.

Guillaume, P., Sidebottom, A. and Tilley, N. (2012). On police and university collabora-tions: A problem-oriented policing case study. *Police Practice and Research: An International Journal*, 13(4): 389–401.

Hanak, G. and Hofinger, V. (2005). *Police Science and Research in the European Union*. Vienna: CEPOL.

Henry, A. and Mackenzie, S. (2012). Brokering communities of practice: A model of knowledge exchange and academic-practitioner collaboration developed in the con-text of community policing. *Police Practice and Research: An International Journal*, 13(4): 315–328.

Hoover, L.T. (2010). Rethinking our expectations. *Police Practice and Research*, 11(2): 160–165.

Innes, M. (2010). A 'mirror' and a 'motor': Researching and reforming policing in an age of austerity. *Policing: A Journal of Policy and Practice*, 4(2): 127–134.

Kennedy, D. (2010). Hope and despair. *Police Practice and Research*, 11(2): 166–170.

Klofas, J.M., Hipple, N.K. and McGarrell, E.F. (2010). The new criminal justice. In J.M. Klofas, N.K. Hipple and E.F. McGarrell (eds) *The New Criminal Justice: American Com-munities and the Changing World of Crime Control* (pp. 3–16). New York: Routledge.

Knutsson, J. (2010). Nordic reflections on the dialogue of the deaf. *Police Practice and Research: An International Journal*, 11(2): 132–134.

LaFave, W. (1962). The police and nonenforcement of the law – Part I. *Wisconsin Law Review*, 240: 104–137.

Lum, C., Koper, C. and Telep, C.W. (2011). The evidence-based policing matrix. *Journal of Experimental Criminology*, 7(1): 3–26.

MacDonald, B. (1986). Research and action in the context of policing: an analysis of the problem and a programme proposal. Unpublished document of the Police Foundation of England and Wales.

Muir Jr., W.K. (1977). *Police: Streetcorner Politicians*. Chicago: University of Chicago Press.

OCJS. (2013). OCJS partners with local universities to create the Ohio Consortium of Crime Science. *OCJS research brief*, 2(1): 4.

Reaves, B.A. (2010). Local police departments, 2007 (Report No. NCJ231174). Retrieved from Bureau of Justice Statistics: http://bjs.ojp.usdoj.gov/index.cfm?ty=pbdetail&iid=1750.

Reiss Jr., A.J. (1971). *The Police and the Public*. New Haven, CT: Yale University Press.

Rojek, J., Alpert, G. and Smith, H. (2012). The utilization of research by the police. *Police Practice and Research*, 13(4): 329–341.

Scott, M.S. (2010). Policing and police research: Learning to list, with a Wisconsin case study. *Police Practice and Research: An International Journal*, 11(2): 95–104.

Scottish Institute for Policing Research (2011). *Annual Report*. Scotland: SIPR.

Sherman, L.W. (1998). *Evidence-Based Policing: Ideas in American Policing*. Washington, DC: Police Foundation.

Sherman, L.W. and Berk, R.A. (1984). The specific deterrent effects of arrest for domestic assault. *American Sociological Review*, 49: 261–272.

Skolnick, J.H. (1966). *Justice Without Trial: Law Enforcement in Democratic Society*. New York: Wiley.

Sparrow, M.K. (2011). *Governing Science: New Perspectives in Policing*. Washington, DC: Department of Justice, National Institute of Justice.

Taniguchi, T. and Bueerman, J. (2012). The embedded criminologist: Leveraging the community's investment in the police. Presentation given at the Police Foundation Board Meeting in Washington, DC, on 8 November 2012.

Thacher, D. (2001). Policing is not a treatment: Alternatives to the medical model of policing research. *Journal of Research in Crime and Delinquency*, 38(4): 387–415.

Walker, S. (1992). Origins of the contemporary criminal justice paradigm: The American Bar Foundation Survey, 1953–1969. *Justice Quarterly*, 9: 47–76.

Weisburd, D. and Neyroud, P. (2011). *Police Science: Toward a New Paradigm*. Cambridge, MA: Harvard Kennedy School Program in Criminal Justice Policy and Management.

Westley, W.A. (1970). *Violence and the Police: A Sociological Study of Law, Custom, and Morality*. Cambridge, MA: MIT Press.

Whalen, J.L. (2012). Cincinnati police team up with academics. *The Gazette*, 74(4). Retrieved from http://www.rcmp-grc.gc.ca/gazette/vol74n4/coverstory-reportage-eng.htm#unity.

Wilson, J.Q. (1968). *Varieties of Police Behavior: The Management of Law and Order in Eight Communities*. Cambridge, MA: Harvard University Press.

Wuestewald, T. and Steinheider, B. (2010). Practitioner-researcher collaboration in policing: A case of close encounters? *Policing: A Journal of Policy and Practice*, 4(2): 104–111.

Vollmer, A. and Schneider, A. (1917). The school for police as planned at Berkeley. *Journal of the American Institute of Criminal Law and Criminology*, 3: 881–889.

PART IV
Delivery

15

FROM SIR ROBERT PEEL TO PLTs

Adapting to liaison-based public order policing in England and Wales

Clifford Stott and Hugo Gorringe

Introduction

The death of Mr Ian Tomlinson during the protests surrounding the 2009 G20 International Summit in London began a series of public statements, news articles and revelations which culminated ultimately in what is arguably one of the most serious critical incidents in British policing. The loss of public confidence in the police is central to the definition of a critical incident which, when serious and widespread, stimulates political crisis and forces high-level reaction. In this case, Her Majesty's Inspectorate of the Constabulary (HMIC, 2009a, 2009b), the UK's main policing oversight authority, conducted a systematic and comprehensive analysis, resulting in the 'Adapting to Protest' (ATP) reports. The first report offered an analysis of the policing of the 'G20 protests' by the Metropolitan Police Service (MPS); the second, a more comprehensive overview of public order policing in England and Wales.

The headline finding of ATP – emphasising the need to 'nurture' the consensus basis of British policing – has been widely discussed, but there has been less systematic consideration of what this means in terms of how it is to be nurtured. This chapter, therefore, overviews the key areas of the policy framework put in place by HMIC and some of the evidence bearing upon subsequent reform to police policy, guidance and practice. It will be argued that the policy guidance emerging for these reviews was reasonably clear-cut about the future direction of reform, but the means through which these recommendations can, and indeed are, being achieved operationally is less transparent. Indeed, we assert that if police organisations within England and Wales are not willing or able to embrace the full implications of what is required, these recommendations might not be obtainable. First, though, we offer an overview of the main themes of ATP: the philosophical underpinnings of British policing; the legal framework within which the police operate; the legality of police recourse to force; and the scientific evidence supporting the HMIC recommendations.

Philosophical framework: The British Policing Model

The second of the two HMIC reports subtitled '*Nurturing the British Model of Policing*', makes two issues immediately salient. First, that policing in England and Wales is fundamentally about an approach to policing that focuses upon 'the preservation of peace within a tolerant, plural society', free from political interference, and prioritises the protection of the rights of the people through the commitment to a policing style that is 'approachable, impartial, accountable' and 'based on minimal force' (p. 5). Second, that the 'British model is easily eroded' by 'premature displays of formidable public order protective uniform and equipment' (p. 5). In other words, the policing of public order in England and Wales is as much about maintaining a democratic policing style as it is about protecting a democratic society from crime and 'disorder'.

The British Policing Model (BPM) revolves around the development of nine principles attributed to the then Home Secretary Sir Robert Peel which provided a philosophy for ethical policing. These principles were formalised in the Metropolitan Police Act of 1829 which laid the foundation of the nation's approach to policing (Inwood, 1990).[1] Reith (1956) suggests that while the principles define the primary duty of the police to be the prevention of crime and disorder, it is important to recognise that this objective was framed from the outset as an *alternative* to repression by military force and legal punishment. Moreover, it was recognised that the power of the police to fulfil this function was dependent not upon their capacity to generate fear and deterrence but upon public approval and cooperation – primarily among those communities who were themselves involved in the very 'disorder' the police service was designed to 'control'.

What is perhaps most interesting about these founding 'Peelian' principles is the centrality of police legitimacy and dialogue. First, the principles assert that the police must seek and maintain public support – or legitimacy – by acting impartially. Second, that the police should use force (i.e. coercion) only when persuasion had been *tried and failed*. Finally, the principles also point toward the centrality of policing from within the community and, as such, highlight the importance of the psychological identification between the police and those that are policed; 'the police are the public and the public are the police' (HMIC, 2009b, p. 12).

In effect, the BPM is founded upon the idea that the police are 'ordinary citizens' who are warranted to focus on the duties that every citizen is assumed to hold in preventing crime and disorder. Therefore, the role of the police was not to replace but to promote the communities' ability to 'self-regulate' through maintaining – as far as was possible – the perceived legitimacy of police authority among those communities.

Legal framework: The Human Rights Act

Another central focus of ATP was on clarifying the law for policing protest in England and Wales and on ensuring that its application is compliant with the European Convention of Human Rights (ECHR). Since it became enshrined in domestic law, the Human Rights Act (1998; HRA) makes it unlawful for any public body in England and Wales – and therefore the police – to act in a way that is incompatible with the rights protected under the ECHR. Consequently, while the police have statutory powers and duties in relation to the policing of protest[2] under existing domestic law in England and Wales, these must be interpreted and applied in a manner that is compatible with the Convention.

Although the HRA was fully enacted on 2 October 2000, no systematic analysis of how it applied to policing protest had previously been conducted. In this sense alone the HMIC analysis was long overdue, but the legal framework created by the HRA is complex and it is far from straightforward to understand the nuanced interactions between the ECHR, domestic law and the policing of crowd events. For example, while there is not a specific right protecting protest within the ECHR, Article 9 protects freedom of thought, conscience and religion along with the right to manifest that religion or belief. Article 10 protects the freedom of expression and Article 11 the freedom of association or assembly. It is the interaction between these three articles that constitutes the right to protest peacefully. At the same time, however, protesters cannot simply demonstrate where and when they choose. For example, these rights only apply in public places and any attempt to hold a peaceful assembly on private land can be considered trespass in line with Article 1 of Protocol No. 1 to the ECHR, which provides that every person is entitled to the peaceful enjoyment of their possessions including their property.

Articles 9, 10 and 11 are 'qualified' rights and therefore the police are entitled – indeed often obliged – to impose restrictions on these freedoms where necessary. While any conditions must be imposed proportionately, in pursuit of legitimate aims and in accordance with the law, the ECHR is applied universally. Consequently, it is not just the right of those who wish to protest that are protected but also others such as counter-protesters, residents, property owners, workers, spectators, and indeed police officers. For example, Article 2 of Protocol 4 protects the freedom of movement (although this has not been ratified by the UK). Thus, while the right to peaceful assembly is protected, where this occurs on the public highway it can infringe others' rights to the freedom of movement. The police must then make decisions based upon balancing one set of rights (right to protest) against another (impact upon another's freedom of movement) bearing in mind that (a) peaceful protest is protected under the ECHR and is considered to be reasonable use of the highway; and (b) the rights protected under the ECHR cannot be used to infringe the rights of others. To add to the complexity for police decision-making, the ECHR creates both negative and positive obligations on the police. For example, with respect to Article 11, the police not only have the negative duty *not* to act in a manner that restricts peaceful assembly,[3] they also have a positive duty to take reasonable and appropriate steps to *facilitate and protect* those who want to peacefully exercise their rights.

In effect, ATP sets out a different understanding of the legal context surrounding public order policing in England and Wales. The consequence was that fundamental change was required to shift the policing approach from merely managing the potential for disorder posed by crowd events to managing this potentiality within a legal framework of sometimes competing and contradictory rights; a framework that requires the police to actively facilitate peaceful assembly, the freedom of expression and the right to freedom of beliefs, privacy and so on.

Dialogue and police use of force

A third central strand of analysis within ATP begins to address the question of how the police might meet their legal requirements. It relates directly to an 'absence of clear standards on the use of force for individual officers' as one of the core factors undermining the BPM in the public order environment (p. 5). As such, ATP provides an analysis of how the law as it currently stands in England and Wales applies. The first, and perhaps most important, issue is that police officers and commanders are individually accountable and responsible for any use of force and must be able to justify their actions in law.[4] The second is that the use of force must be proportionate (i.e. the minimum necessary). The third – reflecting Peel's principles – is that in carrying out their duties police officers should, as far as possible, apply non-violent methods (i.e. persuasion) *before* resorting to force. While police officers have the right to use lethal or potentially lethal force, they can only do so when judged to be absolutely necessary to protect life because of their obligations under Article 2.

The ATP highlights that any lawful recourse to the use of force requires that less restrictive alternatives have been already explored, from the planning stages of an operation through to its conclusion. In other words, the prior failure of persuasion is the legal justification for use of minimum force. This is, of course, entirely in line with the foundation principles of the BPM. The central problem is that in the context of public order the capacity for tactical intervention capable of engaging crowd participants in negotiated solutions to emergent problems is currently, arguably, rather limited, particularly with those 'hard to reach or resistant communities' (p. 73) who are deeply antagonistic toward the police (Hoggett & Stott, 2010; Stott, 2009).

The need to engage in dialogue with protesters, combined with the benefits this brings in terms of achieving proportionality, has been recognised by the police in England and Wales for many years. ATP makes reference to units of officers called Forward Intelligence Teams (FIT) that were a direct product of this early realisation. These units were developed to establish dialogue with individuals and groups 'to gather information and intelligence'.

However, ATP points out that 'while the original intention was that FIT officers would act as a link between protesters and the police . . . the role has shifted significantly' to concentrate on gathering criminal intelligence on protesters. Furthermore, a lack of clarity with respect to surrounding policy has created 'the potential' for FIT officers to 'act outside their lawful powers' (p. 128). This has helped create a situation in which some protest groups have justifiably argued that their rights under ECHR Article 8[5] have been infringed by FITs which, in turn, has created a hostility toward them that has contributed to an irretrievable breakdown in their – and therefore police – capacity to engage in genuine dialogue with those protesters.

Crowd psychology and dynamics

It can be argued that FITs' focus on the collation of intelligence and removal of protesters' anonymity derived, in large part, from an outmoded understanding of how crowds work. A fourth area of policy analysis introduced by ATP, therefore, was an unequivocal call to reform the theoretical basis for understanding the psychology and behaviour of crowds in public order policing. In particular, ATP acknowledged that command level public order training relied on what is referred to as 'classic theory' as its foundation for understanding crowds. This was a serious problem not just because the theory that was being utilised in police command training was outdated and unsustainable scientifically, but also because police understandings of crowds based upon classic theory negatively influences police strategy and tactics (Hoggett & Stott, 2010; Reicher *et al.*, 2004, 2007; Stott & Drury, 2000).

By decontextualizing and reifying them, classic theory conveys the idea that physical crowds are single psychological entities posing inherent and unavoidable dangers to public order (Reicher, 1982, 1987). From this perspective, crowds are understood as irrational, inherently unpredictable, volatile and dangerous. It, therefore, becomes almost self-evident that crowds – particularly those containing groups with a history of 'disorder' – need to be controlled. The assumption of irrationality implies that this control must be exerted primarily through the threat or use of force (e.g. containment, arrest or dispersal), often against crowds as a whole (Drury *et al.*, 2003; Hoggett & Stott, 2010; Stott & Reicher, 1998). The available science, however, suggests that the indiscriminate use of force can and does negatively impact upon crowd psychology in such a way as to increase the likelihood that conflict will develop and become widespread. Tactics premised on classic crowd theory can, thus, become a self-fulfilling prophesy (Reicher *et al.*, 2004; Stott *et al.*, 2008b; Stott & Drury, 2000; Stott & Reicher, 1998).

Recognising these issues, ATP rejected classic theory in favour of the Elaborated Social Identity Model of crowd behaviour (ESIM) as the future theoretical rationale for police understanding of collective action during crowd events. The ESIM is a theory that articulates the group-level processes of crowd events and recognises that collective action is meaningful to those involved. These psychological processes revolve around crowd participants' shared, socially and historically determined, identity. This social 'identity' is a shared cognitive self-representation among crowd participants that is defined in terms of the nature, legitimacy and power of the relationships they share within the surrounding social context.[6] When shared and salient, social identity is therefore the psychological basis for collective action in crowds. Moreover, this psychology of 'us' and 'them', affects the social influence processes within the crowd (e.g. who individuals within 'crowds' are prepared to listen to or follow) and sets in motion group-level dynamics that need to be managed.

Since ESIM is able to define and test these processes, it has been extensively validated via studies of a wide range of different 'riots' (see Stott (2011) for a summary). The model attracts extensive support within the academic community, despite the assertion of some that there are fuller, more powerful explanations available (Waddington, 2012). But ESIM's utility resides primarily in its ability to predict both the negative (i.e. conflict increasing) and the positive (i.e. conflict reducing) impacts that police tactics can have upon crowd psychology, dynamics and behaviour. Most importantly, the theory helps us to understand why it is that where intergroup relationships – particularly with the police – are perceived as legitimate there is a marked reduction in 'disorder' (e.g. Stott & Reicher, 1998; Stott *et al.*, 2007, 2008a, 2012a, 2012b). ESIM[7] suggests that this occurs primarily through an emergent identification between crowd participants and the police and a 'self-regulation' culture within the crowd that flows from this (Stott *et al.*, 2012a, 2012b).

As a consequence, the theory has been able to derive a series of principles for good police practice that have been implemented by police forces, producing outcomes that were effective at reducing 'disorder' (see Reicher *et al.* (2004, 2007) for a fuller explanation). Drawing directly upon these ESIM principles and combining them both with the principles of the BPM and ECHR, ATP asserts that police strategy and tactics should be oriented both strategically and tactically toward proactively enhancing and actively creating perceptions of police legitimacy among crowd participants through (a) a strategic orientation toward the facilitation of peaceful behaviour within a crowd; (b) a graded and information-led tactical profile which has a dynamic capacity for achieving dialogue and communication before, during and after the event; and (c) the avoidance of the undifferentiated threat or use of force wherever possible and reasonable (HMIC, 2009b; Association of Chief Police Officers (ACPO), 2010).

A framework for the future

Taking these issues together, it is our assertion that ATP sets out a clear and coherent analytical framework for the future policing of public order in England and Wales. First, and perhaps most importantly, the emphasis is upon democratic policing, independent of political interference and a policing style based upon dialogue rather than coercion; a model aimed at producing police legitimacy and public consent, designed primarily to enhance the ability of communities to 'self-regulate'.

Second, that police officers must act lawfully and therefore understand their obligations under the ECHR and HRA. For all the concerns expressed about

European law imposing itself on the British context, a close analysis reveals that the ECHR is entirely consistent with the BPM's stress upon the protection of the rights of 'ordinary' people. The HRA merely creates a positive duty for police to actively protect and facilitate these rights among those who peacefully assemble, while balancing this against the rights of others. Third, the protection and balancing of these rights has to sit within a clear, transparent and consensually accepted framework for police use of force. On the one hand, because police use of force can inadvertently create the very disorder the police are trying to avoid. On the other, the police have a legal obligation to demonstrate that everything reasonable has been done – from the planning stages onward – to avoid the use of force and that – if it was necessary – it was applied proportionately.

In other words, as with the BPM, the police have to adopt an approach where the primary tactical intervention should be focused upon negotiated solutions rather than the use of force. Moreover, everything possible should be done to maintain the primacy of this approach even where 'risks' to public order have emerged. Finally, through its promotion of crowd psychology, ATP effectively asserts that public order policing should be evidence-based. Indeed, it is our assertion that the science actually supports the British model because it makes clear that police intervention based upon dialogue, and designed to generate perceptions of legitimacy among those being policed, is an effective tool for reducing conflict. It also suggests that this relationship exists because such interventions create a social and psychological context that empowers those communities to 'self-regulate'. In other words, where the people are the police they will police themselves. The issue is then; how can and are these recommendations being translated into practice?

Post HMIC reforms

ATP was published in late 2009. Subsequently, ACPO had to consider the ATP recommendations within its revision of the manual of guidance 'Keeping the Peace' which did not see publication until early 2010. Following this, the main body responsible for setting the training curriculum, then the National Police Improvement Agency (NPIA),[8] had to incorporate these recommendations into the redesign of its training courses.[9] Thus, despite the initially rapid response of the HMIC it was not until 2011 – almost two years after Mr Tomlinson's death – that the new national police guidance and training environment was in place.

What then began was the slow, and perhaps even more challenging, process of cascading this policy down through the regional training centres and from there into operational practice. While there have been early, piecemeal attempts to pick up on these policy reforms, there have also been major setbacks. In particular, the 'outing' of Mark Kennedy and Bob Lambert as police 'spies', along with the on-going activity of FIT officers, has further undermined police legitimacy and trust among large sections of the protest community. Also, the invasion of Millbank tower by angry student protesters in November 2010, the subsequent 'rioting' in Parliament Square in December of that year, the occupation of Fortnum and Mason's by 'UKUncut' and subsequent 'mass arrest' in March 2011 all led prominent figures and protest organisations to assert publicly that the HMIC reforms were either fundamentally flawed or simply not taking place (Stott et al., 2010).

The summer 'riots' of 2011 then posed further challenges. Not only was the high-profile political analysis of their underlying cause at complete odds with the science of crowd psychology; the Government during the disturbances, the mass media and subsequent high-profile formal inquiries attributed blame to a somewhat 'soft' policing response (Reicher & Stott, 2011; Home Affairs Select Committee, 2011). Subsequently, there has been a £427,000 investment by the Home Office in AEP's munitions[10] and the MPS has openly undertaken consideration of the use of water cannon. While the MPS inquiry report into the riots does acknowledge failures of dialogue and community engagement (MPS, 2012), the focus nationally has been primarily on improving the speed and regionalisation of PSU mobilisation along with training and policy development in the use of firearms in public order situations. The HMIC has recognised that the public, on occasion, actually support (indeed, actively call for) more forceful intervention and reinforced its call for transparent criteria for police use of force, including lethal force, in the context of riots and public disorder (HMIC, 2011). The Home Office has also undertaken a formal consultation on creating police powers to impose curfews (Home Office, 2011; cf. Stott et al., 2012a). Tie all of this in with the new PCCs, Winsor reforms and cutbacks and one would be entirely forgiven for thinking the 'Adapting to Protest' reforms were essentially redundant.

But, as we have asserted, ATP has actually set out some core fundamentals that frame the future for public order policing in England and Wales in terms of philosophy, legality and evidence that, we would argue, have not been superseded by subsequent events. Moreover, the ATP reforms have as yet to fully materialise in terms of operational practice, so they can hardly be a causal factor in any of the above circumstances. Moreover, there is a realistic consensus that there is a meaningful distinction to be drawn between the 'day-to-day' business of policing crowds and that of responding to serious urban disorder. As such in the world of protest-related public order policing – despite the potential for setback – the bureaucratic, but therefore steady, progress of reform has now begun to materialise in the form of systematic developments in operational policing. Perhaps the first major implementation of these policy reforms actually occurred some four months before the 2011 riots. Operation 'Obelisk' was the South Yorkshire Police operation surrounding the 2011 Liberal Party Spring Conference in Sheffield. Given the earlier rioting of students in Parliament Square, the 50,000 student population of Sheffield, and the fact that the city is Nick Clegg's constituency, there were solid reasons for assuming that the two days of protests planned around the conference posed significant threats to public order.

While Obelisk mobilised a large number of PSUs, a primary strategic objective of this operation was to facilitate and work with protest groups rather than simply 'manage' protest. 'Police Liaison Teams' (PLTs) created to achieve this objective, were deliberately re-branded to show a break from the past in terms of policing styles. These officers, trained in protest liaison skills and crowd psychology, were adept at communication and engagement. Indeed, they were chosen for their 'people skills' and several had no background in public order. Their primary role was to enhance police communications at street level, facilitate peaceful protest and to build trust confidence by enhancing perceptions of police legitimacy among protesters.

But the potential effectiveness of the PLTs actually began at the planning stages. From the outset the facilitation strategy was combined with a command protocol that made police commanders aware of different ways that tactical primacy for the PLTs could be maintained even in situations of increased threat. Thus, PLTs were not just about 'talking to protesters' they entailed root and branch changes in the operational dynamics of the operation. With the right strategy and command protocols in place the PLTs were able to work with protesters both before and throughout the event, even when situations developed that were seen by commanders as posing threats to public order. By developing and then maintaining positive relationships, the PLTs were better positioned than any other resources to understand what was actually happening and to provide real-time dynamic risk assessments. Moreover, by being in place at the right time and having established relationships within the crowd, the PLTs were able to negotiate solutions to low-level difficulties that prevented unnecessary escalations in the policing response.

The PLT officers were not just about communication. Here, as in Scandinavia, they were 'problem solvers' who tactically resolved issues and reduced tension through dialogue, and enabled the police to retain proportionality. The outcome was a highly successful event without any incidents of disorder. Associated academic research suggests that this success was primarily because the PLTs were not so much 'policing the crowd' as working with the crowd to facilitate their protest by promoting 'self-regulation' among protesters and 'policing the police' (Gorringe et al., 2012; cf. McSeveny & Waddington, 2011; Waddington, 2012). Indeed, it should be noted that despite being one of England's major cities Sheffield did not experience any major rioting during August 2011. Senior Commanders have acknowledged that, at least in part, this was linked to the tactical capacity for dialogue that was developed during Obelisk being set to work preventatively on the streets of Sheffield in the days following the initial rioting in London (HASC, 2011). The success of the PLTs within Obelisk has subsequently seen the model adopted and cascaded out nationally. Subsequently, the first author has been involved as a consultant in projects stimulating the creation and development of PLTs in other forces; the first with the MPS and the second with Sussex Police. As part of this work, observations of PLT deployment across a number of protest events have provided some powerful and significant learning points that begin to confirm initial findings from Obelisk but also set out some of the key challenges of the liaison-based approach to public order policing (Stott et al., 2013).

Conclusions

In sum, it is our contention that the HMIC reforms remain the necessary founda-tion for the future of public order policing in England and Wales and are gradually filtering into genuine reforms of police practice. Workshops undertaken by the authors on behalf of sponsoring forces have demonstrated that there is a willingness among a new generation of commanders to move public order policing toward a more facilitative, ethical and evidence-based platform. This trajectory has not been undermined by the events that have taken place since the publication of ATP in 2009. Commanders are also beginning to understand the relationship between police tactics and crowd dynamics in terms of raising and reducing tension, and we are now witnessing the creation of PLTs across the UK.

Positive change is clearly upon us but to be successful it needs to be grasped with both hands before this hard-won opportunity is lost. On the one hand, the vulnerability is because many protest groups have a profound and deeply histori-cally rooted mistrust of the police. Some are already promoting the view that PLTs are an attack on the right to protest through an insidious form of deceptive control (Gorringe *et al.*, 2011). Unless these perceptions are tackled carefully through the appropriate use of PLTs, alongside a coherent standard operating procedure that is transparent to the public – particularly concerning PLT compliance with ECHR Article 8 issues surrounding information gathering and its retention – we may subsequently see the opportunity for conflict management that PLTs offer being irreparably damaged. For an example of how this can occur one need look no fur-ther than the case of FITs (see HMIC, 2009b, p. 128).

On the other hand, the tensions and barriers are not only among the protest community. Police themselves have to confront the cultural tensions that the use of PLTs can and do create within their own organisations (see Holgersson & Knuts-son, 2011; Stott *et al.*, 2013). It is our assertion that such 'organisational' barriers can, and perhaps will, undermine police capacity to realise the BMP set out in ATP. In the context of public order, a failure to manage the reforms internally could also mean that policing will remain reliant on the heavy and expensive use of resources – and possibly even distance weaponry such as AEP and water cannon – simply because police tactics lack the capability to reduce community tensions over the longer term through genuine dialogue. Moreover, it is our contention that the use of force – especially in the form of distance weaponry – is an approach that will actually erode police legitimacy over the longer term (Sharp & Atherton, 2007; Stott *et al.*, 2012a, 2012b).

Our argument is that to avoid this black hole of resourcing – and the 'open day' for critical incident development that flows from the use of AEPs – there is an urgent requirement for forces across England and Wales: (1) to draw accurately upon the lessons of the earlier deployments of PLTs (Gorringe *et al.*, 2012; Stott *et al.*, 2013); (2) to further embrace an evidence-based approach to the policing of public order (Hoggett & Stott, 2012); and (3) to recognise that the effective use of PLTs goes hand in hand with training for public order commanders on how to work with them. Crucially, we would concur with ATP in stressing that this 'liaison-based approach' should not be seen as an unwarranted or imported model of policing; rather, it is the historical essence of the British approach. To this extent the question for the future is still exactly that which it was in 2009, but now with a slight caveat. We should not just ask to what extent can the BMP be maintained in the policing of public order; we should also ask why is it that the obvious requirement for liaison-based public order policing has been so hard to achieve and may yet not actually survive?

Notes

1 These principles must be understood in context. First, the principles, and the police forces emerging to apply them, were created at a time of industrialisation in which mass society and its associated problems of controlling 'disorder' among the 'working classes' were becoming a salient social and political issue. Attempts to deal with such issues, however, were flawed if the working classes themselves did not at some level accept the legitimacy and authority of the newly formed police.
2 Including those set out in the Public Order Act (1986), the Criminal Justice and Public Order Act (1994), the Criminal Law Act (1967), the Police and Criminal Evidence Act (1984) and in common law including powers to prevent breaches of the peace.
3 Except to the extent allowed by Article 11(2).
4 This is particularly challenging because police support units are often ordered into highly charged situations but then individually left fully accountable for use of force in a situation they had not chosen to place themselves in.
5 ECHR Article 8 protects individual's right to privacy and family life. This Article is also qualified and police are entitled to collect and store data on protesters only on the understanding that certain strict criteria are met.
6 In any given context people can form group-level psychological bonds of similarity and solidarity with those who are understood to *share* their values and outlook. This collective sense of self is defined in terms of *differentiation* to others along those very same identity-defining dimensions.
7 This theoretical interpretation is also in line with Procedural Justice Theory which argues that people are as concerned about *processes* as outcomes. See Stott *et al.* (2012b) for an analysis of the similarity between the two approaches.
8 Currently this function is served in England and Wales by the College of Policing.
9 These included the NCALT basic training along with new training courses for Bronze, Silver and Gold Commanders (formerly IPOC (Initial Public Order Trained Commanders) and APOC (Advanced Public Order Trained Commanders).
10 Although according to press reports these munitions did not adhere to UK safety standards and could therefore only be used for training purposes.

References

ACPOS. (2010) *Manual of Guidance on Keeping the Peace*. Specialist Operations Centre, Wyboston: On behalf of the Association of Chief Police Officers and ACPO in Scotland by the National Policing Improvement Agency.

Drury, J., Stott, C. & Farsides, T. (2003) 'The role of police perceptions and practices in the development of public disorder', *Journal of Applied Social Psychology* 33(7): 1480–1500.

Gorringe, H., Rosie, M., Waddington, D. & Kominou, M. (2011) 'Facilitating ineffective protest? The policing of the 2009 Edinburgh NATO protests', *Policing and Society:* DOI:10.1080/10439463.2011.605260.

Gorringe, H., Stott, C. & Rosie, M. (2012) 'Dialogue police, decision making, and the management of public order during protest crowd events', *Journal of Investigative Psychology and Offender Profiling* 9(2): 111–125.

Her Majesty's Inspector of Constabulary (2009a) *Adapting to Protest*. London: HMIC.

Her Majesty's Inspector of Constabulary (2009b) *Adapting to Protest: Nurturing the British Model of Policing*. London: HMIC.

Her Majesty's Inspector of Constabulary (2011) *The Rules of Engagement: A Review of the 2001 Riots*. London: HMIC.

Hoggett, J. & Stott, C. (2010) 'Crowd psychology, public order police training and the policing of football crowds', *Policing: An International Journal of Police Strategies & Management* 33(2): 218–235.

Hoggett, J. & Stott, C. (2012) 'Post G20: The challenge of change, implementing evidence based public order policing', *Journal of Investigative Psychology and Offender Profiling* 9(2): 174–183.

Holgersson, S. & Knutsson, J. (2011) 'Dialogue policing: A means for less collective violence?' in T. Madensen & J. Knutsson (Eds), *Crime Prevention Studies: Preventing Collective Violence*. Boulder, CO: Lynne Rienner Publishers, pp. 191–216.

Home Affairs Select Committee (2011) *Policing large scale disorder: Lessons from the disturbances of August 2011*. London: House of Commons.

Home Office (2011) *Consultation on police powers to promote and maintain public order*. London: Home Office, October.

Inwood, S. (1990) 'Policing London's morals: The Metropolitan Police and popular culture, 1829–50', *London Journal* 15(2): 129–167.

McSeveny, K. & Waddington, D. (2011) 'Up close and personal: the interplay between information technology and human agency in the policing of the 2011 Sheffield anti-Lib Dem protest', in B. Akhgar & S. Yates (Eds), *Intelligence Management: Knowledge Driven Frameworks for Combating Terrorism and Organised Crime*, Part 3. London: Springer-Verlag, pp. 199–212.

Metropolitan Police Service (2012) *4 Days in August: Strategic Review into the Disorder of August 2011*. London: MPS.

Reicher, S. D. (1982) 'The determination of collective behaviour', in H. Tajfel (Ed.), *Social Identity and Intergroup Relations*. Cambridge, UK: Cambridge University Press.

Reicher, S. D. (1987) 'Crowd behaviour as social action', in J. Turner (Ed.), *Rediscovering the Social Group: A Self-categorization Theory*. Oxford: Blackwell.

Reicher, S. & Stott, C. (2011) *Mad Mobs and Englishmen*. London: Constable and Robinson.

Reicher, S., Stott, C., Cronin, P. & Adang, O. (2004) 'An integrated approach to crowd psychology and public order policing', *Policing* 27(4): 558–572.

Reicher, S., Stott, C., Drury, J., Adang, O., Cronin, P. & Livingstone, A. (2007) 'Knowledge-based public order policing: principles and practice', *Policing* 1(4): 403–415.

Reith, C. (1956) *A New Study of Police History*. London: Oliver & Boyd.

Sharp, D. & Atherton, S. (2007) 'To serve and protect? The experiences of policing in the community of young people from Black and other ethnic minority groups', *British Journal of Criminology* 47(5): 746–763.

Stott, C. (2009) 'Crowd psychology and public order policing: an overview of scientific theory and evidence'. *Submission to the HMIC of Public Protest Review Team*. Liverpool: University of Liverpool.

Stott, C. (2011) 'Crowd dynamics and public order policing', in T. Madensen & J. Knutsson (Eds), *Preventing Crowd Violence*. London: Lynne Reinner Publishers Inc.

Stott, C., Adang, O., Livingstone, A. & Schrieber, M. (2007) 'Variability in the collective behaviour of England fans at Euro 2004: hooliganism, public order policing and social change', *European Journal of Social Psychology* 37: 75–100.

Stott, C., Adang, O., Livingstone, A. & Schreiber, M. (2008a) 'Tackling football hooliganism: a quantitative study of public order, policing and crowd psychology', *Psychology, Public Policy, and Law* 14(2): 115–141.

Stott, C., Bradford, B., Pearson, G. & Jackson, J. (2012a) *Response to the Home Office Consultation: Police Powers to Promote and Maintain Public Order.* CCM Ltd: Wirral Merseyside.

Stott, C. & Drury, J. (2000) 'Crowds, context and identity: dynamic categorisation processes in the poll tax riot', *Human Relations* 53: 247–273.

Stott, C., Gorringe, H. & Rosie, M. (2010) 'HMIC goes to Millbank: public order policing following student disorder', *Police Professional* 232, November 25.

Stott, C., Hoggett, J. & Pearson, G. (2012b) '"Keeping the peace": social identity, procedural justice and the policing of football crowds', *British Journal of Criminology* 52(2): 381–399.

Stott, C., Livingstone, A. & Hoggett, J. (2008b) 'Policing football crowds in England and Wales: a model of "good practice"?' *Policing and Society* 18(3): 258–281.

Stott, C. & Reicher, S. (1998) 'Crowd action as intergroup process: introducing the police perspective', *European Journal of Social Psychology* 28(4): 509–529.

Stott, C., Scothern, M. & Gorringe, H. (2013) 'Advances in liaison based public order policing in England: human rights and negotiating the management of protest?' *Policing: A Journal of Policy and Practice* 7(2): 212–226.

Waddington, D. (2012) 'A "kinder blue": analysing the police management of the Sheffield anti-"Lib Dem" protest of March 2011', *Policing and Society* 23(1): 46–64 (Online First).

16

LANDSCAPING THE POLICING OF ORGANISED CRIME

Some designs and reflections

Peter Sproat

Introduction

The overarching objective of the Independent Policing Commission (IPC) is to examine the roles and responsibilities of the police service in England and Wales in the twenty-first century while giving consideration to the relevance of the nine 'Peelian principles'. In contrast, the focus of this chapter is the policing of organised crime, and one of my first thoughts was to wonder whether the Peelian principles are relevant to the policing of organised crime today. Presently the latter is conducted by a national state agency rather than local 'Bobbies' with whom Sir Robert Peel is associated after helping establish the first of England's many constabularies.[1] It is this issue of distinctiveness that constitutes the starting point for these reflections on the policing of organised crime and it is to facilitate the reading of points made later, that this chapter starts with a brief explanation of how we arrived at the situation we find ourselves in today.

A brief history of the policing of organised crime

When writing about the policing of organised crime as distinct from the policing of 'ordinary' crime, commentators often start with the creation of the first centralised or 'national' institution to conduct policing operations against organised crime in England and Wales – i.e. the National Crime Squad (NCS) in 1998. According to Harfield, prior to this, any organised criminality that crossed constabulary boundaries in England and Wales was investigated by nine, and later six, regional crime squads. These were run as collaborative ventures between police forces supplemented by a non-executive national coordinator based in London since the mid-1960s. In contrast, the NCS constituted a significant departure from the British tradition of policing locally delivered and locally accountable, because it was a national entity. As such it was able to conduct its own national investigations and support locally based intervention against organised crime in accordance with an agreement negotiated with the Association of Chief Police Officers. Commanded by an executive director-general – the rank equivalence of Chief Constable – it seconded its officers from local police forces and levied its finances from them too (Harfield, 2008). A few years later, the NCS was made a non-departmental public body with the Home Office responsible for its work (Segell, 2007).

The NCS was supported in its investigations and operations by the National Criminal Intelligence Service (NCIS). The latter was created out of the Home Office's National Drugs Intelligence Unit in 1992. In addition to producing a national threat assessment, the NCIS collected information and produced profiles on major criminals and criminal organisations for partners including the NCS and the regional crime squads before it. During this period other agencies such as HM Customs and Excise and the Home Office were responsible for policing serious drug-trafficking at the borders and organised immigration crime and the seizure of their assets (Bowling and Ross, 2006; Segell, 2007). In 2002 the government attempted to increase the latter by introducing the Proceeds of Crime Act. It enabled the state to take up to six years of assets from 'lifestyle criminals', authorised the forfeiture of 'criminal' assets by civil courts and taxation and created the Assets Recovery Agency to proceed such cases.

Four years later, and only eight years after the creation of the NCS, the government re-designed the landscape by creating the Serious Organised Crime Agency (SOCA). It brought together staff from the NCS and the NCIS along with those from the UK Immigration Service and HM Revenue and Customs who had dealt with organised immigration crime and drugs trafficking and associated criminal finance, respectively. The new organisation was designed to address problems of duplication and coordination and it was suggested its greater consistency of approach would create a critical mass of competence that would focus efforts on front-line intelligence and investigation. It was envisaged that the SOCA would benefit from the opportunities for economies of scale and reduced bureaucracy resulting in an organisation that would be 'more than the sum of its parts' according to the Home Secretary (Home Office, 2004: iii). Two years after its creation, the SOCA absorbed the Assets Recovery Agency (bar its training section).

In contrast to the NCS, the SOCA was not staffed by police officers aided by colleagues from customs or immigration. Instead, its operational staff were authorised to: 'use the powers of a constable, the powers of a customs officer, and the powers of an immigration officer' as the task demanded. This provided a 'very powerful mix of authorities' according to its first Chair, Sir Stephen Lander – whose background was in the intelligence, rather than police, service. The legislation also enabled the SOCA to share and receive information from anybody – a power that overrode duties of confidence (Lander, 2007) and made a 'no comment' interview to a SOCA agent an imprisonable offence. It was because of such 'unprecedented law enforcement powers' coupled with 'secrecy and centralised control' and a move away from 'independence and account-ability' that Bowling and Ross described the SOCA as a 'transformative leap in British policing'. Never before had central government 'commanded such a high degree of control over police agents, who have traditionally been independent, swearing allegiance to the Crown' (Bowling and Ross, 2006: 1033). In terms of political accountability, they pointed out that while its director-general had a degree of operational independence not dissimilar to that of a Chief Constable – in that s/he decided which particular operations were to be mounted and how such operations were to be conducted – the Home Secretary could 'command considerable degree of control over both the day-to-day running and general management' of the non-departmental public body by use of several mechanisms. These included an ability to: determine the timing and amount of funds available to the Agency and its strategic priorities; appoint all 11 members of the SOCA's governing board; hire and fire the director-general; and issue codes of practice for its agents who – unlike police constables – had not sworn allegiance to the Crown (Bowling and Ross, 2006: 1026–28).

The existence of a national operational and intelligence-gathering agency pos-sessing unprecedented policing powers is one of the reasons for suggesting the contemporary policing of organised crime was distinctive. Another is the novel strategic *approach* it has used to police organised crime. This is not a reference to the suggestion that the SOCA has acted like an intelligence agency with an enforce-ment arm[2] but, rather, to the 'harm-reduction strategy' used by the SOCA. As a Parliamentary Under-Secretary once put it, the SOCA was to 'adopt a wholly new approach by having as its core objective the reduction of harm caused by organised crime'. She explained this would involve 'traditional investigations and prosecutions' and 'all other methods at its disposal to disrupt, dissipate and destroy organised criminal gangs'.[3] Moreover, the variety of disruption techniques placed at the SOCA's disposal was increased over the next few years so that three years later another Government Minister could declare:

> SOCA's remit is to reduce the harm caused to the UK by serious organised crime. To achieve this SOCA deploys a range of tools. These include: crimi-nal justice interventions (arrests and prosecutions); action to deny criminals access to assets through the use of proceeds of crime legislation and other measures; the disruption of criminal markets and organisations; and the use of ancillary orders such as Serious Crime Prevention Orders. The use of these tools is mainstreamed into the operational activity of the agency. Most opera-tions deploy a number of these tools.[4]

Finally, after describing how we arrived at the distinct structure, powers, accountability mechanisms and strategic approach of the agency that now polices organised crime in England and Wales, it is worth noting where we might be in the very near future. This is because four years after the creation of the SOCA a parliamentary election produced a new government which announced it would replace the SOCA with the National Crime Agency (NCA) by the end of 2013. The plans envisage the NCA having the power to 'task and coordinate' the policing of organised crime by local police and other law enforcement agencies (the Bill going through Parliament declares the director-general 'may direct' the 'chief officer of an England and Wales police force' and 'the Chief Constable of the British Transport Police', 'Commissioners for Her Majesty's Revenue and Customs'; the 'Director of the Serious Fraud Office'; and 'the Director of Border Revenue').[5] Despite the appointment of a former Chief Constable to head the new body and an increased emphasis in the use of the term 'law enforcement' in the official rhetoric on organised crime, the latter continues to refer to 'harm reduction' and 'disruption' in positive ways.[6] The other step-change, if not step back, is the reduction in the funding going to the national policing organisation. For while the SOCA had a 'net expenditure of £476.0m' in 2009–10, it is envisaged the funding for the NCA in the first full financial year it will be operational (2014–15) will be in the region of £407m.[7] In comparing the two figures one should not only factor in five years of cumulative inflation but also the fact that by then the NCA will also include parts of the National Policing Improvement Agency.

The options

So how does all of this description help answer the immediate question of whether the Peelian principles have anything to do with the policing of organised crime today? It reveals four issues need to be considered when landscaping the policing of organised crime. The main one is the structural arrangements – i.e. the nature of the bodies used to police organised crime and the relationship between them. From this flow questions concerning the powers, strategic approach and accountability mechanisms of any *distinct* national entity authorised to carry out operations against organised crime. Here is an apt place to note the chapter distinguishes between two key policing tasks, namely: gathering, analysis, prioritisation and production of intelligence packages (intelligence task); and investigating, disrupting and enforcing (operational task).

The chapter provides a framework for understanding the range of designs that are possible. To facilitate the description of the framework it is useful to reveal each of the potential landscapes resulting from the two possible answers (i.e. yes or no) to four questions that derive from the issues of structure and powers. These are:

1   Should the design include a national intelligence entity?
2   Should the design include a national operational entity?
3   Should the design include a national entity that combines these two functions?
4   Should the operational entity hold solely police powers or a SOCA-like multitude of powers?

These alternate answers enable the production of Table 16.1.

TABLE 16.1 Designs for the landscape of policing organised crime

Name of (akin to)	Nature of OCGs (Levels)[8]	National intelligence entity?	National operational entity?	Combined intelligence & operational entity?	Access to multiple powers?
Peelian	1, 2	**No**	**No**	n/a	n/a
Reversed NCA	1, 2	**No**	**Yes** (not autonomous)	n/a	n/a
NCIS 1992–98 *Reform's model*	1, 2, 3	**Yes** *(yes MPS)*	**No**	n/a	n/a
NCIS & NCS 1998–2006	1, 2, 3	**Yes**	**Yes**	**No**	**No**
NCIS & Agency	1, 2, 3	**Yes**	**Yes**	**No**	**Yes**
SCDEA *Police Scotland*	1, 2, 3	**Yes**	**Yes**	**Yes**	**No**
SOCA *NCA*	1, 2, 3	**Yes**	**Yes**	**Yes**	**Yes**

The table contains ten designs (found in seven distinct sets). Moreover, this helps explain how the total number of potential designs doubles if we consider the third issue – that of strategy (i.e. whether to use 'harm reduction'). That said, the total number of possibilities is actually far greater because there are so many different ways of making any operational body accountable. The chapter then uses the same framework to lay out the advantages and disadvantages of the designs.

As already noted, permutations arise by considering whether the policing of organised crime should be distinct from a pure Peelian arrangement involving numerous local constabularies. The fact that a national entity to police organised crime exists presently, does not per se justify its existence, for if such reasoning was valid the original de-centralised structure would not have been questioned or changed! Instead one is left to consider why we would want to create a distinct institution or institutions to police organised crime. One way of addressing this is to ask a further question: is there something qualitatively different about organised crime that suggests it should be policed by a distinct entity? One credible answer to this is that some organised crime is distinct in scope, i.e. some organised crime groups (OCGs) are organised on a national basis. If this hypothesis is correct, such a distinction would be very important to those designing the landscape of public policing for it would mean that a policing response based solely upon local constabularies would leave some members of nationally organised OCGs beyond reach because there would be no one gathering, collating and analysing intelligence on the 'clean skins' within each national group – be they living outside of the local force (or regional) boundaries and/or operating behind the scenes.

If organised crime is distinct in scope because it includes criminal groupings organised on a national basis then it would be logical to include an institution to gather, process and distribute intelligence on everyone involved in national or Level 3 OCGs. Indeed, not including an entity to produce intelligence at a national level only makes sense if one believes Level 3 OCGs do not exist or they exist on such a small scale it is not worth funding a national intelligence body. Rationally, those holding either of these latter views would want to re-design the existing structural arrangements for policing organised crime, for there would be no obvious reason to maintain a national intelligence-gathering capability. There are, of course, a number of structural arrangements the adherents of such a belief could logically accept, and one way of identifying them is to ask the second key question: should the design include a national operational entity? A negative answer to this question, – in the context of a 'no' answer to the first one – leads to a design in which there is neither a national intelligence nor operational entity. Instead local constabularies (or their regional arrangements) would be left to gather intelligence and conduct operations against Level 1 and 2 OCGs (for in this scenario Level 3 groups do not exist). Such a 'constabularies only' arrangement can be described as a pure Peelian one and is akin to that which existed prior to the creation of the NCIS in 1992.

In contrast, a positive answer to this second question – following a negative answer to the first question – leads to a design in which there is no central intelligence-gathering entity but there *is* a national operational entity. In this rather awkward design, the latter would not be an autonomous operational entity (be it a police one or an agency) carrying out its own work, for it would have no intelligence to base it on. Instead it would constitute a central resource the local constabularies (and any regional arrangements) could call upon when they required an additional capacity or even specialist capability to deal with Level 1 and 2 OCGs. Such an arrangement could be seen as something akin to a reversal of the proposed plans for the NCA which envisages 'tasking and coordinating' the work of local constabularies *by* the central operational entity – albeit for use against Level 1 and 2 OCGs (hence it is entitled a Reversed NCA in the table).[9] These two designs constitute the only ones that flow from the belief that national OCGs do *not* exist. They do not lead to any other designs in our table because one cannot ask any of the follow-on questions about whether to combine or separate the national intelligence and operational entities because the two do not exist at the same time. Nor can the fourth key question concerning the powers of the *distinct* operational entity in the second design be asked – never mind questions about its approach and accountability mechanism – simply because it does not exist as an *autonomous* operational entity (instead the local constabularies holding only police powers would lead the operations against organised crime in both these designs).

All of the other options considered here flow from the belief that national OCGs exist – a view held by almost all in officialdom and academia. Moreover, this belief lends itself to many designs, all of which logically include a national entity that scans for intelligence on national (if not international) OCGs. Once again the various possible designs flowing from such a view can be distinguished from each another by simply asking the remaining follow-on questions. In this context, the answer 'no' to the question of whether to have a national operational entity to deal with organised crime, immediately leads to a set of designs in which a national intelligence entity exists but a distinct national *operational* entity does not. The first of the landscapes in this set is one akin to that which existed between 1992 and 1998 when the NCIS processed intelligence but the operational activity was carried out by the local constabularies, including their regional arrangements. Unsurprisingly this is labelled NCIS 1992–98 in Table 16.1. The second design, or perhaps more accurately, a variation of this, is the structural arrangement akin to those suggested by the think-tank Reform which involves 'sub-contracting' the central intelligence-gathering task to the largest existing constabulary – the Metropolitan Police Service – while the local forces (and any regional arrangements) carry out policing operations. Hence it is referred to as *Reform's model*.[10] Once again this set of designs can go no further because one cannot ask the follow-on questions concerning the nature of powers of the *distinct* national operational entity simply because no such entity is envisaged, as the operational capability lies with the local constabularies.

There are six more designs noted in the table, situated within four distinct sets, all of which flow from a positive answer to both the first and second key questions. The four sets can then be distinguished from each other according to the answers to the third and fourth key questions, namely, whether the intelligence function and operational functions should be combined *and* whether the operational entity should possess a SOCA-like multitude of powers, respectively. That is, the first two sets envisage a landscape which separates the national intelligence entity from the central operational entity. In turn these two designs can be differentiated because one involves a national operational entity staffed by police and the other an agency whose operational staff possess a multitude of powers. The other two sets of designs involve the intelligence and operational functions being combined in one entity, be it one run by the police or as an agency.

In terms of the table, the first of these four sets of designs is similar to that which existed between 1998 and 2006 in which the national intelligence entity – the NCIS – was kept separate from the national operational entity – NCS. The latter was staffed by police officers and therefore did not possess multiple powers. It is for this reason this is referred to as NCIS/NCS 1998–2006 in the accompanying table. The second consists of a design that allows the operational entity to be an Agency with a multitude of powers rather than a police squad. Entitled NCIS & Agency in the accompanying table such a design has yet to be tried in the UK.

The two remaining sets of designs both involve a national intelligence *combined* with an operational entity. The difference is that in one the operational entity would be purely a police entity, although there are two variations within this set. The first is a national anti-organised crime police unit. This is probably best envisaged as an NCS-like entity that has been combined with a police-run intelligence capability – very much like the Scottish Crime and Drug Enforcement Agency which existed until recently (hence it is described as akin to the SCDEA in the table). The second design in this set can be viewed as an anti-organised crime *squad* within a single national police force – a model recently introduced into Scotland, although neither of these variations in this set has been tried in England and Wales (hence it is described as akin to *Police Scotland* in the table).

The final set of designs in the table consist of an agency in which the intelligence and operation functions are combined and whose operational staff have access to a variety of powers. Unsurprisingly, because the arrangement is akin to that which exists presently this is referred to as SOCA in the table. The proposed *NCA* can be seen as a variation of this in that it is a distinct national entity that has combined the intelligence and operational functions in an agency. The most important difference is, at the time of writing, the Bill for the NCA allows the central combined agency to 'direct' the work of local constabularies (and others) creating a central operational entity holding more powers than even a national police force and with the ability to direct more than just the police.

As already noted the number of possible designs is greater than the ten highlighted here, and the total would be even greater if a further variable was added, i.e. a distinct 'harm-reduction strategy'. This total could also be multiplied by the number of different accountability mechanisms. It is for this reason the chapter examines only a limited number, but hopefully the table and accompanying explanation has provided a framework for identifying the range of designs that are possible.

Reflections

There are, of course, advantages, disadvantages and issues surrounding each of the limited number of designs examined here. However, rather than repeat them frequently while describing each of the ten designs, the following section aims to describe the strengths and weaknesses of the alternate answers to the four key questions found in each of the four main columns of the table (marked in **bold**), before considering some that relate to the use of a 'harm-reduction' strategy. It also provides a few suggestions to reduce some of the potential problems.

The implications of the alternate answers found in the first of the table's four main columns are few. As noted earlier, the decision to include a distinct *intelligence-gathering* body simply depends upon whether it is believed that OCGs are organised on a national basis. If so it is logical to have one. In contrast, any design involving numerous decentralised entities collecting intelligence will have difficulty identifying anyone working for an OCG beyond a force or region. There is also likely to be a little duplication of effort on gathering intelligence on members of Level 2 OCGs, although given local constabularies already gather intelligence at a local level this financial inefficiency is not likely to be great. In sum, only the 'no' answer produces a major potential problem – namely, the inability to look at national OCGs should they exist.

In terms of the second column the choice of whether to have a single national operational entity or a number of decentralised policing entities can be viewed as a 'trade off' between a potential risk to liberty and a possibility of financial savings. Theoretically, any design that incorporates staff with specialist skills in a single entity *should* be more cost-effective than any decentralised design that envisages each force holding specialist operational capacity that is used less often. The question for politicians is whether these potential savings are worth the risk that a central operational force could become too powerful in its own right, or as the operational force of the executive. This risk could be reduced by introducing checks, if not balances. This is where consideration of accountability mechanisms comes in. The accountability arrangements for the SOCA – especially the Home Secretary's ability to fund it, determined its strategic priorities and the hire and fire of the director-general (Bowling and Ross, 2006) – concentrate too much power in the hands of the England and Wales' equivalent of a minister of the interior and the executive generally. This position is made worse by the fact its operational staff hold so many powers – including illiberal ones – and are not holders of the Office of the Constable who have sworn allegiance elsewhere. The latter could constitute some sort of check, just as the actual existence of many independent police forces outside of the Metropolis could make any grab for a monopoly of police power more difficult. The accountability mechanisms of NCA are no less frightening.

This analysis gives an indication of the political (dis)advantages of the various designs. It is posited here that the landscapes can be ranked according to the risk each poses to political liberty and it is to this that the chapter briefly diverts. In detail, the pure Peelian decentralised arrangement constitutes the antithesis of the centralised structures favoured by history's 'police states'. This is closely followed by the Reverse NCA design because neither envisages a central operational entity and police power is fractured. These are ranked slightly ahead of the two designs that allow local constabularies to exist independently alongside a national intelligence-gathering entity be it on its own, i.e. NCIS 1992–98 or *Reform's model*. These are viewed as posing a slightly greater risk to political liberty because they allow a central authority to gather intelligence on potential targets. In contrast, all of the remaining designs envisage the latter *and* the existence of a national operational entity. Of these, the designs that *separate* the operational activity from the intelligence-gathering function pose a smaller risk to political liberty than those which combine the two (simply because the latter needs the former to operate). This means the NCIS & NCS 1998–2006 design is next in this ranking ahead of the NCIS & Agency design because staff in the latter's operational entity have access to a greater range of powers and have not sworn an oath to the Crown.

As for the designs that combine the two functions, it is posited that the arrangement referred to here as SCDEA (a national anti-OC police unit) would be slightly more favourable than the SOCA design if strictly adhered to, but that the latter is more preferable to a national police force akin to *Police Scotland* from a liberty perspective (depending of course on the nature of the powers held). This might seem counter-intuitive given the SOCA's operational staff possess a multiplicity of powers, but it is based upon the fact that in the latter arrangement, 43 operationally independent police forces exist and the SOCA has no authority over them. Using the same logic, it is suggested the SOCA arrangement is preferable to a design that allows a SOCA-like body to 'task and coordinate' local constabularies. Such an arrangement – referred to here as the *NCA* – constitutes the greater risk to liberty, greater even than that posed by a national police force, for while both arrangements allow a combined national entity to instruct local police officers via their Chief Constables, the director-general of the *NCA* could instruct other agencies too, and its operational staff would hold more powers but no allegiance to the Crown, and its funding and governance would be accountable to the equivalent of the interior minister.

As for the alternate answers found in the third column, those designs that combine the intelligence and operational functions in a single national entity *should* – at least in theory – produce savings in terms of backroom staff, such as senior management, administration and human resources, and central resources, for example, buildings and IT. However, combining the two functions produces an obvious conflict of interest and a potential source of different, and possibly much larger, financial costs. This is because combining the intelligence and operational functions produces a situation in which the organisation supplying the operational policing of OCGs is the same one that supplies the threat assessment upon which the demand for such services is based. Obviously, this potential conflict of interest does not arise with separation, but another potential disadvantage of separating the two functions – in addition to potentially greater overheads – is that those who use the intelligence packages as the basis of action lose the ability to instantly, and easily, clarify any issues arising out of them. Here it is suggested that should the politicians choose separation, they could also attempt to reduce the impact of both by situating the two different organisations in the same building as happens within some multi-agency arrangements. Alternatively, if a combined entity were favoured then it would seem a good idea to have the funding or staff devoted to intelligence gathering and processing limited by ring-fencing or monitoring by the body to which the operational entity is accountable. Such oversight might help prevent a drift away from operational 'actions' towards deskwork – a point to which we will return.[11]

The answers in the final column concern the question of whether those working for a national operational entity should have a multitude of enforcement powers. Presently, this is the case with the SOCA but there are no *inherent* reasons why this must be so. Indeed, police officers *could* work, and indeed have worked, alongside customs or immigration staff from the HMRC and Borders Agency, respectively, in a multi-agency response to the policing of organised crime. As already noted, this was the practice in England before the creation of the SOCA, and until recently this occurred in Scotland. Instead, the main argument in favour of providing a 'SOCA–style' multiplicity of powers to operational staff within a national entity boils down to a belief that any cooperation in multi-agency approaches *will* suffer from the tensions inherent in the different, if not competing, procedures, practices, priorities and budgets held by the various operational entities. Put another way, the most credible non-political reason for creating a design in which the investigators can access this variety of enforcement powers is a belief that their operational efficiency would be greater than one in which police investigators were involved in a multi-agency approach.

Allowing investigators of a national operational entity to hold three types of powers – as in the SOCA – presents a measure of unease. It is the nature, not the number, of powers that constitutes the more important problem for those who desire a liberal criminal justice system. Thus the primary objection is not to the fact that members of the operational entity can choose from a variety of powers, but to the illiberal nature of some of them, such as the power that makes it a criminal offence to be silent when questioned by the SOCA.[12] However, should politicians choose to continue to provide such authoritarian powers they might like to consider introducing some sort of check, if not balance. For example, they could provide all of those charged by staff holding such extraordinary powers the right to trial by jury so the public could find the persecuted 'not guilty' if they felt the prosecution had become a political persecution as happened in the Ponting case.[13]

As noted earlier, the number of designs in the table could be almost doubled by including consideration of our third issue, which could have been phrased as a fifth key question, namely: should any distinct operational entity use a 'harm-reduction' strategy? This approach proudly emphasises 'disruption' as well as 'prevention' and the use of traditional law enforcement methods. In terms of whether a distinct entity tasked with policing organised crime should use a SOCA-like 'harm-reduction strategy' the answer depends upon how the nature and extent of organised crime is viewed, as well as political considerations. At present, the official discourse describes organised crime as a threat to national security and suggests 38,000 people are involved in it in the UK – which works out at approximately 31,931 once one excludes those in Scotland and Northern Ireland.[14] Unfortunately, less than 1 per cent of those who are said to constitute a threat to national security are convicted each year by the SOCA. If one truly believes many of the remaining 99 per cent constitute an actual, rather than theoretical, threat to national security then the use of a harm-reduction strategy which leaves so many of them at liberty is appeasement. However, while the publicly available official literature proclaims the threat to national security from organised crime it provides little evidence to support it. If no more than a few OCGs constitute a threat to national security then harm reduction does look like a logical way of setting priorities for pro-actively policing organised crime, and there is little doubt that disruption – a key element in the harm-reduction strategy – is, as Innes and Sheptycki (2004: 13) put it: 'a way of overcoming some of the problems' encountered by policing organisations 'in coping with heavy workloads' which is undoubtedly the scenario they face. The use of prevention is also in accord with the other Peelian principles and can constitute a more effective use of public funds in the long term.

However, there are other, more practical, potential problems with harm reduction which are worth considering. Here it is hypothesised that if not properly managed, a strategy of 'harm reduction' can produce a drift from 'blue-collar' to 'white-collar' policing, a movement from operational activity, be it law enforcement *or* disruption, towards desk work such as collating and analysing data, producing intelligence packages and pondering the meaning of harm.[15] Furthermore, this effect is likely to be worse in landscapes that combine the intelligence and operational functions in one central entity.[16] There are a number of factors behind this hypothesis. The first is the apparent lack of 'blue-collar' activity by the SOCA relative to the dramatic increase in its funding. For example, the average number of convictions achieved each year by the more powerful and far better resourced SOCA (279.5) is far smaller than the number (345.75) obtained by its main predecessor – the NCS – in the last four years of its existence.[17] Similarly, the number of policing 'operations' it carried out does not seem to suggest the SOCA became much more than the sum of its parts – although it is accepted it is very difficult to make an exact comparison on the limited publicly available data. The second is that even when limited to illegal activities, the concepts of 'harm' and 'harm reduction' are open to many competing interpretations and different ways of measurement as David Bolt the Director of Intelligence in the SOCA once noted. More importantly he went on: 'You can tie yourself in knots with such arguments and, as a result, become risk averse to the point of inaction' (Bolt, 2009: 26). In truth, the phrase 'harm reduction' combines two vague words in the way 'community policing' does and, like the latter, this enables a range of credible but very different definitions to be produced. Without clarity as to the meaning of the phrase, any organisation set up to implement 'harm reduction' is left with a credible excuse for procrastination rather than action. If politicians authorise a harm-reduction strategy the meaning of the ambiguous phrase needs to be clearly identified in advance. In detail the latter should occur only after a joint commission of practitioners and academics have produced a report pointing out the implications of the range of competing operational definitions to the politicians.

Finally, in reference to harm reduction, it is necessary to highlight that *some* disruption – including that which Innes and Sheptycki describe as extra legal – is contrary to the principles that underlie a liberal criminal justice system. In detail, the Common Law system of England and Wales is based upon the assumption of innocence. Thus the system requires the (state) prosecution to persuade an independent jury, lay magistrate or judge there is no reasonable doubt that those it accuses were responsible for criminal acts or omissions. This 'due process' constitutes one method by which the individual is provided with some protection against a(n authoritarian) state simply imprisoning those *it* labels as criminal. In *some* uses of disruption there is a danger that policing entities act as 'judge and jury', or more accurately accuser and judge, on the basis of their intelligence packages. Put another way, intelligence packages are not proof of guilt, but one danger of intelligence-led disruption is that the operational entity assumes the intelligence packages show the individual 'deserves' or 'needs' to have their activities (or indeed liberty) curtailed by the use of disruption. In such situations disruption is not used with the correct intention. Outside of situations where the agents of the state threaten or use violence to prevent immediate harm to a person or their property, its threat or use of violence against an individual is legitimate only because its use is intended to produce a specific goal – namely, to take an individual through the court system.

It is this due process which establishes the legitimacy of the use of force in a criminal justice system and it is for that reason liberal societies insist that the individuals carrying out an arrest *genuinely* possess a 'reasonable suspicion' that the suspect has broken the law. Therefore outwith self-defence or necessity (both of which are immediate), the application of the police power to particular individuals without a genuinely held intent to process the latter through the court system is illegitimate. Those who doubt this, should imagine what would happen if private individuals decided to use the same techniques – such as following people about and having a 'word in their ear' – against other fellow citizens in situations where we held no intention of preventing immediate damage to property or people or arresting the victim of our actions. This would likely result in an arrest for offences such as harassment, breach of the peace, if not actual assault. Peelian principles *demand* the same rules apply to organised 'citizens in uniform'.

Conclusion

This chapter has highlighted that there are many different ways of landscaping the policing of organised crime in England and Wales and each has its strengths and weaknesses. As for which is the most appropriate, this depends upon how one views the nature and extent of the problem as well as one's political priorities and values. My conclusion is that the issue of political liberty takes priority, and the preferred design reflects this. It is for the latter reason I reject the purest Peelian structural arrangement noted here but propose a 'Peelian'-friendly design akin to NCIS & NCS 1998–2006 – albeit with the national operational entity staffed by police clearly following a 'harm reduction strategy'. In detail it seems unrealistic not to have a structural arrangement in which a central entity collects intelligence on OCGs that operate across the UK. At the same time this should be separate from a central unit of police officers specialising in conducting operations against serious organised crime in England and Wales. Here an arrangement is envisaged that requires the national operational entity to obtain the consent of the local Chief Constable in order to conduct operations. The separation of the two national units from one another (and the other 43 local constabularies) not only favours liberty, it arguably favours financial efficiency in that it should reduce the ability of those currently policing organised crime to create the demand for such a service in the immediate future. Moreover, it also helps ring-fence the resources dedicated to 'white-collar' policing. Indeed, any landscape that envisages the separation of a single central intelligence-gathering entity for the whole of the UK and a separate police operational entity for England and Wales produces a much more equitable fit with the *de facto* arrangements that exist in the rest of the UK. That is, it would produce a situation in which one truly national (as in UK-wide) entity gathered information on nationally organised OCGs for three 'regional' entities that carried out operations against organised crime – even if the detail of the arrangements within some of the regions were different.

The preferred design reflects an ideological belief in a liberal criminal justice system and a fear that a central police force could become the political arm of an overbearing executive or too powerful in its own right. The concentration of police power in the hands of a few individuals would make it much easier to focus unbearable state power on particular individuals or groups. In this context, the exact nature of the arrangements for the NCA eventually passed by Parliament will be incredibly informative. If it is allowed to 'task and coordinate' and *direct* the activities of the local police in England and Wales the Conservative–Liberal Democrat coalition government will have created a centralisation of police power – albeit by use of a particularly powerful agency accountable to the Home Secretary – that surely would have outraged the Tory and Whig politicians of the early 1900s who rejected the idea of a single national police force for fear of an authoritarian state. That said, the chances of a centralised policing force or agency suddenly metamorphosing into a nationwide police state across the whole of the UK (as opposed to one that can make the lives of individuals and groups in society particularly unbearable) can easily be overstated in an era of financial austerity. Moreover, even the plans for the NCA recognised the devolution of some operational activity, thus creating another obstacle to implementation of a nightmare scenario outside of England and Wales. If, in the end, the proposed constitutionally important changes are rejected and the NCA is merely able to propose tasks, coordinate and encourage, then the NCA will pose no more risk to political liberty than the SOCA. In sum, despite implications to the contrary, Peelian ideas *can* and *should* constitute major aspects of a contemporary landscape for the policing of organised crime, but for this to happen politicians need to remember to fracture police power and maintain prevention as the key aim of policing.

Notes

1 Despite the fact Peel proposed a single national force for Ireland, Peel is associated with the decentralised arrangement of policing as a result of his involvement in the creation of the Metropolitan Police in 1829.

2 In part, this has been suggested because many board members – including its first Chair, Sir Stephen Lander – had career backgrounds in the intelligence agencies. The other reason is Harfield's suggestion that the methodology of the intelligence arm of SOCA would combine the roles of intelligence officer and analyst, which is the approach adopted by MI5, whereas, historically, the police service has separated the roles (Harfield, 2006: 746).

3 Caroline Flint, then Parliamentary Under-Secretary for reducing organised and international crime, anti-drugs coordination and international and European issues, *Hansard*, House of Commons Debate, 7 February 2005, c1309. The White Paper which proposed the new agency mentioned the words 'harm' and 'disruption/disrupt' 50 and 22 times, respectively. Unsurprisingly, the SOCA has adopted this rhetoric and approach with its website declaring that the agency: 'uses whatever lawful methods have the maximum impact against organised criminals. We investigate wherever possible, and we also go much further. By using non-criminal justice tools and proceedings, we ensure that all organised criminals are within our reach and that once they are in our sights we keep them there' (http://www.soca.gov.uk/about-soca/how-we-work/new-approaches (accessed 23 January 2013)).

4 Alan Campbell, then the Parliamentary Under-Secretary of State for the Home Department *Hansard*, House of Commons Debate, 20 July 2009, c100WS. For more details of each, see Sproat (2012).

5 See, for example, Schedule 3 11(1) of the Crime and Courts Bill before the House of Lords (as amended in Public Bill Committee) 14 February 2013.

6 The document Home Office (2011) uses the words 'harm' and 'disrupt or disruption' 14 and 16 times, respectively. The phrase 'harm reduction' is even mentioned in the Bill, see for example, Part 1 Section 1 (4) which states: 'The NCA is to have the function (the "crime-reduction function") of securing that efficient and effective activities to combat organised crime and serious crime are carried out (whether by the NCA, other law enforcement agencies, or other persons).' Crime and Courts Bill before the House of Lords (as amended in Public Bill Committee) 14 February 2013.

7 Serious Organised Crime Agency (2010: 39). The figure for the NCA is the most recent the author could find. In detail Jeremy Browne, Minister of State, Home Department, stated: 'for the first full financial year of operation – 2014–15 . . . the NCA's indicative budget for planning purposes will be around £407 million'. *Hansard*. Public Bill Committee, Tuesday 22 January 2013.

8 Here, the term 'Level 3' refers to OCGs operating at the national level (and international) level. Level 2 or regional crime crosses force boundaries, while Level 1 crime is that capable of being managed by local constabularies. This is broadly in line with the use of these terms in the police's National Intelligence Model, although strictly speaking, Level 1 involves crimes affecting a Basic command unit (BCU) or small force area, while Level 2 consists of 'cross-border' issues affecting more than one BCU *within* a force as well as that affecting another force or regional crime activity and usually requiring additional resources. Level 3 is therefore: 'Serious and organised crime usually operating on a national and international scale, requiring identification by proactive means and a response primarily through targeted operations by dedicated units. It is also likely to require a preventative response on a national basis' (National Centre for Policing Excellence 2005: 12).

9 Regardless of whether the central resource was an agency or a police service such an arrangement would be rather difficult to organise because there would be no accounting for when each force decided to approach the centre.

10 The author over-simplifies the proposals from Reform but suggests his simplification is not far from the essence of what it proposes, given that Reform envisages 'local forces' retaining a 'responsibility for information gathering, intelligence sharing and operations in their area' and no central operational entity, this presumably leaves the MPS to analyse and prioritise the intelligence (Basset *et al.*, 2009: 36). Another problem with the author's central resource design would be the temptation for the intelligence unit in the MPS to prioritise the demands coming from the operational unit inside the same force, not only because they would share the same bosses but because of their proximity. This could become an issue with the other forces.

11 In a similar vein, the former Home Secretary Jack Straw suggested 'Police officers prefer warmth of police station to catching criminals' (www.telegraph.co.uk/news/politics/6916946/Police-officers-prefer-warmth-of-police-station-to-catching-criminals.html (accessed 30 January 2012)).

12 This power is also objectionable when held by the Serious Fraud Office – an organisation with a smaller range of powers.

13 Clive Ponting was a civil servant who was tried under the Official Secrets Act for leaking information about the sinking of the Belgrano in 1984 to an MP. He was acquitted by a jury.

14 According to the latest organised crime strategy, 'Organised crime poses a threat to the UK's national security . . . there are around 38,000 organised criminals impacting on the UK' (HM Government, 2011: 5). To identify those in England and Wales the author removed an estimated 6,069 for the number of individuals in Scotland and Northern Ireland. The latter consisted of the 3,663 reported by the *Daily Record* (2012); plus an esti-

mate of 2,406 for Northern Ireland. The latter was produced by multiplying the average number of people in an OCG in Scotland 13.36861 (= 3,663/274 gangs reported in the said media story) by 180 – the number of crime gangs said to be operating in Northern Ireland according to the BBC (2012).

15 For Innes and Sheptycki one potential problem with the use of intelligence-led policing (ILP) is the increased use of intelligence results in a 'drift' in the objectives of law enforcement interventions towards the use of disruption, as advocates of ILP exhibit a marked preference for disruption, often seeing such operations as easier, less time consuming and therefore more cost-effective. Innes and Sheptycki cite Johnston (2000: 61) who suggests, 'the rationale' of disruption 'is to circumvent the formal justice system in order, more easily, to effect the speedy closure of a given problem'. In this sense 'disruption is a way of overcoming some of the problems encountered by police organizations in coping with heavy workloads' (Innes and Sheptycki, 2004: 13).

16 It might even be worse still when the entity is a brand new agency (staffed by 'civilians') rather than a police force with a culture of enforcing the law (among other tasks).

17 The comparison is with figures from the final four years of the NCS only (the author has yet to find figures for the years 1998–2002 inclusive). The annual number of convictions achieved by the NCS were: 2002–03, 358; 2003–04, 335; 2004–05, 286; 2005–06, 404, an average of 345.7 (1,383/4). In contrast the annual number of convictions achieved by the SOCA was 2006–07, 271; 2007–08, 276; 2008–09, 266; 2009–10, 315; 2010–11, 240; 2011–12, 309, an average of 279.5 (1,677/6). See Sproat (2012).

References

Bassett, D., Haldenby, A., Thrives, L. and Truss, E. (2009) *A New Force*. London: Reform.

BBC (4 July 2012) *Police waging war on 180 crime gangs* (http://www.bbc.co.uk/news/uk-northern-ireland-18709892 (accessed 14 March 2013)).

Bolt, D. (2009) 'Tackling serious organised crime drug harms', *Safer Communities*, 8(1): 24–28.

Bowling, B. and Ross, J. (2006) 'The Serious Organised Crime Agency – should we be afraid?' *Criminal Law Review*, (Dec.): 1019–1034.

Daily Record (22 September 2012) 'Revealed: the shocking scale of organised crime in Scotland' (http://www.dailyrecord.co.uk/news/crime/revealed-the-shocking-scale-of-organised-crime-1337429 (accessed 14 March 2013)).

Harfield, C. (2006) 'SOCA: a paradigm shift in British policing', *British Journal of Criminology* (July), 46(4): 743–761.

Harfield, C. (2008) 'The organization of "organized crime policing" and its international context', *Criminology & Criminal Justice*, 8(4): 483–507.

HM Government (July 2011) *Local to Global: Reducing the Risk from Organised Crime*. London: Home Office.

Home Office (2004) *One Step Ahead: A 21st Century Strategy to Defeat Organised Crime*. London: The Stationery Office.

Home Office (June 2011) *The National Crime Agency: A Plan for the Creation of a National Crime-Fighting Capability*. London: The Stationery Office.

Innes, M. and Sheptycki, J. W. E. (2004) 'From detection to disruption: intelligence and the changing logic of police crime control in the United Kingdom', *International Criminal Justice Review*, 14: 1–24.

Johnston, L. (2000) *Policing Britain: Risk, Security, and Governance*. Harlow, UK: Longman.

Lander, Sir Stephen (2007) 'Soca: One Year On'. Speech delivered on 13 February 2007 (http://www.crimeandjustice.org.uk/news_1s18x19x20o10.html (accessed 23 January 2013)).

National Centre for Policing Excellence (2005) *Guidance on The National Intelligence Model 2005*. ACPO Centrex.

Segell, G. M. (2007) 'Reform and transformation: The UK's Serious Organized Crime Agency', *International Journal of Intelligence and Counter Intelligence*, 20(2): 217–239.

Serious Organised Crime Agency (July 2010) *Annual Report and Accounts 2009–10*. London: The Stationery Office.

Serious Organised Crime Agency 'How we work: new approaches' (http://www.soca.gov. uk/about-soca/how-we-work/new-approaches (accessed 23 January 2013)).

Sproat, P. A. (2012) 'Phoney war or appeasement? The policing of organised crime in the UK'. *Trends in Organized Crime*, 15(4): 313–330.

The Telegraph (2009) 'Police officers "prefer warmth of police station to catching criminals"' (www.telegraph.co.uk/news/politics/6916946/Police-officers-prefer-warmth-of-police-station-to-catching-criminals.html (accessed 30 January 2012)).

17

THE ROLE OF THE POLICE IN COUNTER TERRORISM

John G. D. Grieve

Introduction

This chapter explores some similarities and differences in current and earlier policing counter terrorism (CT) policies and practices. It argues that there are more
similarities with the past than are sometimes identified by proponents of the 'new
terrorism' thesis. Here I will focus on policing and not the wider aspects of what
unfortunately has been called 'the war on terror'. So I assume a criminal justice
rather than military model of CT.

It has always been difficult to write something useful for public consumption
about CT as there are issues of the Official Secrets Act, ongoing cases and contempt
of court, disclosure and other demands under the Freedom of Information Act.
The situation is not helped by the recent Boston College case in USA involving
UK material apparently retained for academic purposes.[1]

I have not used any secret or sensitive material. The debrief material was either
made in my presence, desensitised, anonymised, and noted in my mind maps,
abstracted by others from material that has been generalised and made anonymous
and desensitised, or obtained from desensitised published material (e.g. Alison and
Crego, 2008; HMIC/Audit Commission 2009a and b). I have not got nor have I
used direct quotations from any such material. The quotations I have used are from
material specifically collected by me for this chapter (see also the section on methodology below). It is not my intention to write anything either unhelpful or potentially compromising. Although two of my predecessors as CT leaders have fallen
foul of the issues I have described, a growing number of CT leaders and politicians
have successfully published accounts (e.g. Rimmington, 2001 (but see also Norton-
Taylor (2013) for reservations about this publication); Manningham-Buller, 2012;
Mowlem, 2002; Powell, 2008; Hayman and Gilmour, 2009 (although there were
initial problems with this publication); Stevens, 2005; Blair, 2009; Quick, 2012)
offering me precedents.

The chapter will develop an alternative thesis to that proposed by many commentators that the post-9/11 world is 'new terrorism' (see Quick, 2012). I will argue that current terrorism is a continuation of much earlier patterns of political or extremist violence and although there are considerable differences, there are important similarities. I come to very different conclusions about the consequences of this thinking for policing policy to those reached by Mythen and Walklate (2012). They conclude that the state should be examined for its own terrorist activities. The conclusions reached here are about *the dialogue* between, engagement of, and empathy with, the diverse communities I have served. These have practical consequences for policing, e.g. in the publicity attendant upon successful prosecutions, the support for investigations, information available to police interviewers post arrest and the involvement of families of potential terrorists in preventing radicalisation (see examples of all of these in Laville and Dodd (2013) and discussed below). Other implications might be how police communicate with communities, not least post Leveson (2013) and Filkin (2012).

I focus on what might be learned from the past CT 'hypothesis' 'not to over react', and consider 'not doing anything stupid' and 'winning the peace'. The chapter examines several theories and then explores what some police officer 'practitioners' think is important, their values, and compares them with what a range of 'experts' think. It follows similar thinking in other studies in this volume by O'Neill and by Stott.

While I am not talking about 'new terrorism' I do identify some new dimensions. I would be surprised if any of what I write is new to the current heads of a highly successful policing CT strategy and tactics and the equally successful Security Service intelligence lead. What I will suggest has implications for CT and presents a useful structure to the argument about the importance of policing which is wider than the public police or state agencies as it involves the role of diverse communities. This is significant in my view because it can be related to a wider policing philosophy dating back to Robert Peel and the first Commissioners. Finally, as noted above, it is written by someone who has performed some versions of the tasks that society now faces.

Setting the scene

Since 9/11 in the UK over 300 people have been arrested and prosecuted to conviction by the courts on terrorist related charges, over 70 people have been murdered by terrorists including two police officers, a number of terrorist suicide bombers have lost their lives as has an innocent member of the public shot during a CT operation (Brain, 2010; Manningham-Buller, 2012). Therefore, the context against which to consider CT is of sustained intensity in an age of generally reduced policing resources (if not in CT policing) and a confluence of turbulence deriving from a combination of austerity and political demands for changes in police leadership, governance and practice, not least the demand of localism.

Since 9/11, three out of the five most senior police leaders of UK counter terrorist response have left as a consequence of criticism after intense public scrutiny of matters not always directly related to their CT activities. There are versions of this in the Northern Irish experience of post peace process reviews, coroners' inquests and public inquiries (which includes international dimensions) and can be seen as attempts to 'win the peace process'. While this is part of some wider learning about the nature of CT operations in the twenty-first century, it does not suggest to me that this is a new dimension to our thinking. It can, however, be described as different in scale and its expansion to a deeper UK-wide public scrutiny of policing. For example, there is a major ongoing review as a result of continuing public outrage over the alleged covert, long-term infiltration tactics used by undercover police officers in cases where criminal damage and civil disobedience of 'green issues' appears to have been equated with other aspects of 'domestic' terrorism. There has been major criticism and investigation of the robust (at best) and insensitive (at worst) tactics of stop and search and early intervention search warrants. The pervasive reality for those involved in CT policing is not only the complex and difficult environment, but also the potentially career threatening risks of those strategically involved at senior level and operationally engaged on the ground. In my view this is because of government concerns with police governance and leadership, fascinating international links and a sceptical media's deep scrutiny of the issues involved and the previous public persona of the senior officers concerned. Again this is not per se new. It is, however, different in scale and can be related to an argument I develop below in that the state has overreacted, done 'something stupid', which can be as debilitating to the CT efforts as an exploding terrorist device. All this has an effect on public confidence and leads to new challenges about police leadership not least in CT policies and practice.

Some guiding principles

While not a fashionable claim, the UK police learned much during the NI terrorist campaigns of the 1970s, 1980s and 1990s.[2] I present a number of exhortations for all involved in policing, police, those concerned with the Criminal Justice System, but also including politicians, local and national, community leaders and intelligence officers, derived from that learning. Each, however, is accompanied by a corollary and poses a dilemma for policing. Policing is never simple and never easy and CT policing is at the extreme.

My first exhortation to the police in counter terrorist operations and policy is '*do not over react, that is what the terrorists want you to do*' (see historical examples such as the attempts by Michael Collins in the fight for an Irish Free State, Mao Zedong, during the modernisation of China, Che Guevara and Regis Debray in Bolivia). Famously, T.E. Lawrence engaged in provocation in his efforts against the Turks to inspire an Arab rebellion (Gearty, 1987; Laqueur, 1987; Cronin and Ludes, 2004; Cronin, 2009). The corollary is *never give in to terrorists*.

My second exhortation is '*do not leave a festering mess for your successors*'. This is closely related to the first. The police should obey, to the letter, the rule of law, and use the Criminal Justice System rigorously and without exceeding lawful powers. But, it is as much neglect of duty to fail to use audacious endeavour within the law as it is to act unlawfully, in any fashion. The aim during conflict is to prepare for peace and return to normality. The police will never achieve this if they over-react, indeed if they incite politicians to overreact. As Eliza Manningham-Buller has recently pointed out, the erosion of democratic rights and freedoms for the attacked citizens are the very sort of overreaction the terrorists seek; 'rushing to legislate is . . . often a mistake' (Manningham-Buller, 2012: 44–48, 61, 76; Norton-Taylor, 2012). The corollary is *overreaction is downright stupid.*

My third exhortation is '*try not to do anything stupid*'. On one occasion I incited a Home Secretary to improve our CT stop and search powers for small size impro-vised explosive devices (IEDs). Widespread personal search counter terrorist legis-lation had a severely detrimental effect on wider community confidence in policing and legitimacy of the Criminal Justice System (CJS) and, in turn, CT policing. Even where the intention is good, i.e. to improve police capability to detect small audio cassette size incendiary devices, the outcome can be disastrous for minority community relations, with allegations of racial stereotyping for CT stop and search. The intention was not to overreact, but the outcome was that the sheer scale of police activity was interpreted in that way. The corollary is *intelligence-led policing must be intelligent.* This brings me to my fourth exhortation: '*contribute to finding a balance between protecting a community and keeping its confidence*'.

Prevention has been a core police task since Peel, Rowan and Mayne. Stopping a terrorist attack is better than catching the terrorists afterwards. Of course, the cor-ollary is that *you may not find the evidence you need for a prosecution or you may leave legal defences open to the terrorists.* In the case of CT policing, prevention is achieved by the intelligence services, communities and police providing intelligence that is used in pre-empting attacks. But at the same time the police have the task of winning hearts and minds (an expression derived from the military as Kevin Stenson has recently pointed out), also known as the more general police task of community confi-dence maintenance. Community confidence is a direct result of engagement and individual police interactions with citizens. Community intelligence which derives from this engagement is predicated on engagement informing harm and impact assessments. Where to strike a balance in that engagement without compromising secret intelligence operations? Where that balance is struck is the subject of intense debate, not to say vicious disagreement, as the former police officer Bob Lambert (Lambert, 2011: 254) has pointed out. Innes and Levi (2012: 676), in their useful analysis of some CT policies, generally consider not only police-derived tactics involving communities but also community-derived ones. In the following matrix they help identify where such a balance might lie. This seems to fit the exhortations and the other theories of English and Cronin that follow.

Laville and Dodd (2013) reporting the cases of Ashik Ali, Irfan Khalid and Irfan Naseer, who plotted murder on a horrendous scale inspired by Al-Qaeda, illustrate several aspects of these four modes of prevention. The case involved conspiracy to cause more deadly explosions than 7/7. Some of the investigation was covert surveillance to obtain evidence for a CJS intervention – an example of protective mode of multiple communities (consider the diverse nature of the victims of 7/7).

TABLE 17.1 Police- and community-derived CT tactics

	Police-defined	*Community-defined*
	Protective	*Type 1 Co-production*
Police-delivered	The police own the intervention, determine what tactics to use and might or might not involve community.	Police work directly with an informed community who have brought the problem to their attention.
	Type 2 Co-production	*Mobilisation*
Community-delivered	Police encourage community responses to a problem they have identified.	Here the community takes action and might or might not involve the police. The decision making about intervention is outside the police.

Based on Innes and Levi (2012: 676; Table 22.1)

On the other hand, potential recruits to the conspiracy were dissuaded by family and community intervention (including bringing them home from alleged terrorism training camps). Finally, in the closing stages, local officers were deployed in both type 1 and type 2 co-productions to encourage dialogue and avoid misunderstandings in both arrest and prosecution phases (Laville and Dodd, 2013).

None of what I have written here is new, or unique to CT policing. What I am describing goes on, on a daily basis, not just in the CT arena. The founders of policing concluded something along the lines of 'Police are the Public; Public are the Police' (Peel, as arranged by Reith).[3] Much has been said and written about the vulnerability of communities to terrorism, including the importance to the terrorists of economic and iconic targets, the particular vulnerability of twenty-first-century communities through interconnectivities, open sources of information about people and infrastructure (e.g. electricity and transportation systems). The example of extreme weather shows the narrow margin between comfort and social chaos and illustrates how thin the veneer of civilisation can be. It is this fragility that the twenty-first-century terrorist seeks to use. The need for electricity, the transportation of supplies of food, the need to get to work, are but examples. Of course, the IRA knew this in 1939 as did the Provisional IRA in the 1990s. The speed at which the terrorist can broadcast messages of fear is virtually immediate. But the very interconnectedness of communities that makes them vulnerable also makes the terrorist vulnerable. They need recruits, bomb making equipment, transportation, safe houses, and that opens them up to the eyes of others and potentially the kinds of interventions described by Innes and Levi (2012). The speed of communication that benefits the terrorist's message is also available to the police and the state. So, on a note of optimism, it can be argued that terrorists are as vulnerable as the communities they use because of the same open sources and interconnectivity; what we might call mirrored vulnerability in an optimistic mood. Terrorists potentially have more threats from the state and communities because they are a tiny minority.

They are 'fish in the sea of the community' (Mao Zedong). And that community sea can be made a hostile environment for the terrorists using media and the speed of communication, as the UK police are learning.

This is not the grounds for claiming there is a completely new terrorism – unique aspects there may be, as many contributors to Cronin (2004) point out – this can be argued to be a fourth wave as Rapoport (2004) identifies in the same volume. This fourth wave we are facing is sometimes said to be religious. The previous waves of modern terrorism are anarchist, anti colonial, new left in this model (Rapoport, 2004). 'Kill 3 frighten 3000 or kill 3000 frighten 300 million' is age-old strategy. Proponents of the new terrorism thesis might argue that the global links of IT communications make this fourth wave so different as to be new. Yet despite the power in that thesis there are nine lessons from NI that suggest a continuity and that it would be foolish to forget these hard-earned experiences.

Practice-learning the lessons

Nine lessons and experiences from Northern Ireland?

This is my formulation of the opportunities offered by the Independent Monitoring Commission's (IMC) experiences and debriefing. Though bound by our anonymity, security and confidentiality rules, the theories below played a part in our processes.

- 'Communities defeat Terrorism': this mantra is derived from the core philosophy of policing in the UK that the 'Police are the Public; Public are the Police' (Peel, arranged by Reith (1938)).
- The development of the strategic architecture includes international, coordination and planning, currently manifested in CONTEST, the cross-party agreed framework of prepare, prevent, protect, pursue (Home Office, 2006/2011) but also local policing arrangements.
- The development of a tactical doctrine that includes everything from threat levels to training for CT investigators and prosecutors. Specialist Officers, Scene/Investigation Management and Prosecutors, International Liaison, and Regional CT Units and local borough activities.
- The use and research of modern technologies to counter a variety of terrorist techniques.
- Everything was intelligence led. The intelligence lead given to the Security Service but with vital roles for the police at every level. Intelligence structures were developed for information flow, for example protocols for Covert Human Intelligence Sources (CHISs) and the CT Hotline.
- The need to understand hatred, bias, prejudice, extreme violence and the violent radicalisation process.
- The roles, positive and negative, that could be played by prisons, schools, colleges, universities, and the complex role of religion was also examined in the Northern Irish context.

- Resilience and recovery to normality after CT incidents were explored, best practice developed and debriefed.
- Winning the Peace – the importance of the role of any of those in public offices not to have done anything stupid, for example undermining CJS legitimacy (Bowcott, 2013) during their tenure, nor to have left a festering mess for their successors (Sanderson (2012) is an interesting recent example about the long shadows of the past) (see also, for example, Home Office, 1996). This can be identified through investigations into miscarriages of justice, Public Inquiries. For example, those seven initiated as a result of the reviews by Judge Cory or the Bloody Sunday Inquiry, cases being investigated by the Coroner, some involving the so-called shoot to kill (40+ cases) allegations, the post peace agreement alliances – politicians, journalists, lawyers that have led to the collusion investigations by the Police Ombudsman for NI. Winning the peace also includes the requirement of anyone in the process not to undermine the central role of the criminal justice process.[4]

These nine lessons were learned with much pain and courage in the NI experiences of the police and communities. The last, 'winning the peace', which is ongoing, is a summation of all that has gone before.

Some theory

I have been influenced by Manningham-Buller (2012), Lambert (2011), Omand (2010), English (2009), Cronin (2009), Cronin and Ludes (2004), Butler (2004), Matassa and Newburn (2003), and all the police officers, intelligence officers, experts and academics I met as a Commissioner on the IMC between 2004 and 2011 (see, for example, IMC 26th Report (2011). I have also for a number of years been pursuing an agenda of community-friendly police intelligence (see Grieve, 2003/2008; Harfield *et al.*, 2008).

Professor Richard English (2009) considers the following menu which maps onto some aspects of the nine lessons listed above. This is perhaps unsurprising as he was drawing these from his research in Northern Ireland.

- Learn to live with some aspects and incidents of terrorism.
- Address the underlying causes where possible.
- Avoiding over militarisation, in particular emphasise the role of police in the Criminal Justice System.
- Primacy of rule of democratic law and the role of the Criminal Justice System.
- Central, vital role of intelligence and the role of the Security Service.
- Coordinate all measures, e.g. finance, technology.
- Strong public arguments need to be made against the terrorists and their megaphones, to undermine their credibility.

Audrey Kurth Cronin, a Professor at the War College in Washington, in her book *How Terrorism Ends* (2009) gives an optimistic account of the history of over 70 terrorist organisations which suggests there are possibly successful outcomes.

BOX 17.1 CT OUTCOMES (AFTER CRONIN, 2009)

1   Decapitation – kill or capture the leadership.
2   Negotiation – politics resolves the situation.
3   Success – the terrorists achieve their intent.
4   Failure – they implode, there is a backlash, and they are marginalised.
5   Repression – they are crushed by force.
6   Reorientation – they are recategorised as criminals, or as Organised Crime.

Some empirical research

I wanted to discover if my emerging thinking was mirrored by other CT practitioners. I explored various data, some collected in my presence by Jonathan Crego using 10kv debriefing (see methodology note below) analysed at the time by me, and some collected by him using the same methodology but not in my presence, of decision-making, computer-generated simulations. I then reviewed the answers from the 300 or so CT Police Officers ('practitioners') who had been asked to answer the question 'What matters in CT?' Broadly the non-secret, non-sensitive answers fell into the five following themes:

1   Police and communities.
2   Intelligence, knowledge and intelligent policing.
3   Training.
4   Investigation and prosecutions.
5   Financing terrorism.

Although the first two seemed consistent with what I had previously identified from my own CT and IMC experiences, I interpreted the communities and intelligence themes more widely. This emphasises not only that the community aspects were covered because of the scale of unprompted responses from some highly specialised officers, but also that this is a clear arena of other police work. It also touches directly on the exhortation not to do anything to undermine policing legitimacy. The categories were not clear-cut and I have included some answers from all the other categories which appear to relate to the policing of communities. I then set about matching this material with that which I had received from a group of CT knowledgeable individuals ('experts') (see note on methodology below). Here are some illustrative analyses (the non-sensitive non-secret from some 200 answers) from a variety of respondents about answers related to the community category. I have anonymised these responses.

TABLE 17.2 CT professionals' responses to the question 'What matters in CT policing?'

'*Know the enemy*'
- 'Develop as complete an understanding as possible of what it is that motivates the terrorists, their objectives, methodology, etc., how serious a threat they pose, what level and degree of support they have in the wider community, any developments in their thinking and strategy and any changes in their thinking and direction. I have the XY model in mind here'.
- 'What is it that keeps groups together? How do they construct their enemy? (Remember: needing an enemy is a key factor in maintaining unity).'

NB The XY model is anonymised here and refers to a particular community response. This response is relevant to English's (2009) account of the need to address the underlying causes; to do that you have to understand them.

'*Real-time analysis*'
- 'Use of multiple intelligence sources – open and closed, but also incorporating CCTV, target tracking. There are now software systems which are fearfully expensive, but they bring together, and analyse many information sources simultaneously'.

NB It is the open aspects and the need for community support for such endeavours I am identifying from these respondents.

'*Enhanced relations with the intelligence community*'
'This is a necessity in order to connect the minutiae – more use of internet and open source information as the intelligence value is astounding.'

NB this respondent is emphasising the open source and its relationship to community support and confidence which is relevant by avoiding the allegation of over-surveillance.

'*Internet scrutiny*'
- 'The police (+ Security Service) cannot surf the entire internet, but must develop the capacity to closely follow the sites that radicalise, and continuously search for existing and new posters of messages. The Clean IT Project, a European initiative led by the Dutch National Coordinator for Counterterrorism and Security, but also involving other regional units, is suggesting very close and continuous surveillance of the internet, with automated detection systems, flagging systems, etc.'

'*Greater fusion of public data*'
- 'Particularly biometrics. Greater use of multi-modal biometrics in public data – e.g. driving licences, social security, entry to the UK. More effective sharing/corralling of UK public biometric data to support identification of threats. More effective sharing of International biometric data related to CT threats – currently poor with few bilaterals in place'.

NB These two highly effective yet expensive preventive/pre-emptive measures have the capability to undermine community confidence if not properly explained and democratically accountable.

'*Creation of an international/European CT intelligence hub*'
- 'Which provide a fusion capability to identify and defeat trans-national CT threats . . . currently pretty ineffective in terms of Interpol/Europol.'

'*Comprehensive strategies*'
- 'Examining [the threat] in the round and identifying all areas where a concerted effort on the part of state agencies can contain or set back the terrorists' efforts, carefully cultivate and work on multi-agency cooperation to ensure full effect. Prioritise soundly based and effective gathering, analysis and deployment of intelligence'.

NB These are the ideals of any community-friendly policing intelligence system (Grieve, 2003/2008).

There were a variety of views about the effectiveness of European cooperation expressed. The relevance of this to the arguments presented here is also pertinent to the global interconnectedness and the speed of communication and the potential to undermine positive messages about policing.

There was a considerable commentary on the improved, supportive attitudes of many communities and much is already being done to develop community relationships, as one respondent pointed out:

> The relationship is crucial . . . if the relationships are there, it is a case of bonded in crisis we can articulate what a successful police/community partnership looks like and this will be further evidence to prove that the way to deal with this threat is to invest in stopping people becoming terrorists as much as or even more than catching them planning what they intend to do.

This respondent went on:

> [R]obust partnerships with the community contributed most to the sense of success; in psychological terms, it is likely that these were underpinned by a common super ordinate social identity and, therefore, a sense that everyone was on the same team working towards a common goal.

However the same respondent also noted:

> We have a national strategy for combating terrorism. Local communities and law enforcement agencies have the biggest role in this. Muslims and non-Muslims alike have said that community building is the solution. The stronger your ties with the community, the less likely you are to seek out a terrorist group to be part of. It is incumbent upon community leaders to denounce acts of violence. . . . We go to the community meetings with our agenda and forget about what the community really wants to talk about. You have to separate what you want and what the community wants.

But other respondents described what more could be done. The direct relevance to CT policing is that in the desire to prevent terrorist activities and pre-empt conspiracies in a robust fashion the need to work with communities can become secondary – the baby can be thrown out with the bath water.

Two other ideas drew on elements of professional ethic and can be given the shorthand, 'moral moments' and 'public spirit'. This latter is a practical application of the moral dimension and together these offer an opportunity to fuse the current political localism agenda with a central direction needed when dealing with a national threat.

> Police should look for 'moral moments', that is, when there is a moment of reconsideration and moral reflection about violence by those who perpe-

trated it or who are involved in it. Police should look beyond the stereotype which avoids nuance and difference. It is this nuance and difference which police should constantly search for.

Harness the can do wave of Olympics in terms of the volunteer programme – Reflecting the public spirit across counter terrorist support and maintain the 'worth' of individuals who raised their game to support the public good.

Establishing clearly identified community CT representatives and public safety community structure.

Primary and Secondary education introduced around 'life skills' focused upon threats of crime and terrorist events which provides a platform for a 'good citizen' approach in collaborative behaviour/public spirit.

This emphasis on good citizenship is interesting as it offers a way to link policing countering violent extremists with continuation of the traditional Peelian values.

Good community policing – by which I mean old fashioned 'deep knowledge' of the area being policed, in order to develop community intelligence. Almost certainly beat officers are the heart of the system.

Police need to be culturally sensitive (and knowledgeable) when dealing with/interviewing, etc. members of differing cultures with respect to terrorist entities. Law Enforcement needs to build bridges within our multicultural communities, work with pro-active community based organisations. Police need to be versed on the religious holy days and days of cultural significance to various cultures. Police need to be aware of events of significance on a global scale, especially when dealing with International entities, for what occurs today, may be representative of an historic event, etc. Law Enforcement needs to be politically aware.

Police should attempt to understand the metaphors that groups refer to and seek to undermine those metaphors where possible by offering other ways to imagine problems and identity. Police should seek to build contacts with figures seeking to find a way out of violence and help to create positive developments which can be sold to volunteers. This should be done slowly and deliberately in order to show the gains of moving away from violence. When there is no sign of figures seeking to end violence police should talk up the benefits of doing so and use other civil groups, charities, etc. to reinforce the credibility of the argument.

Developing better understanding of the radicalisation processes, and the ideologies (Islamist, extreme right, anarchist, etc.) that drive them. A very valid criticism of Britain's CT effort, in the past (and possibly still) has been that we don't understand ideology, and are therefore ill-prepared to counter the consequences of radicalisation.

These latter points look to the training, indeed education of the police themselves as preparation for a dialogue with communities.

Political violence often occurs because groups perceive being in a position of weakness. Police need to respect this but also challenge it in order to make it harder for groups to pedal clichés about isolation, etc. Frames of justification must be constantly challenged and the disadvantages of violence reiterated at all times (alongside articulation about clear advantages which may emerge when and if violence stops).

Associated with the question of ideology is that of keeping a closer eye on those who make violent pronouncements, in private or public. We frequently get the impression that the police discount the violent sayings of some Middle East focused groups, unless there is an absolute breach of the POA. Groups now know the parameters within which they are free to incite hatred, without making themselves liable to prosecution. But you see the consequence when volunteers go off to Somalia, Yemen, Syria, etc.

These two points look to extremely sophisticated roles for policing and perhaps the requirement for some additional skills and the training and education previously identified.

Lone operators – a growing issue but there has to be a better way to spot the drop outs and those who pass rapidly through extremist groups, being radicalised in the process, but not ascending the hierarchies, without compromising democratic norms and processes.

It could be argued that although the lone operator might be difficult to spot, the community might be more ready to give up such potentially isolated individuals. But the issue is highlighted here because the community and police tasks might be very much more difficult to prevent or even pursue.

Establishing an annual public event focused upon CT from an awareness/prevention perspective. . . . National No Smoking day . . . National CT Day . . . and running this in conjunction with a community intelligence effort.

I have juxtaposed these two points as the latter might be an answer to the former.

Try to avoid 'own goals', i.e. policing actions that generate sympathy or support for the terrorist cause (especially important if there is a body of hitherto non-involved sympathisers in the community).

This goes to the heart of 'not to do anything stupid' and 'not to leave a festering mess'.

> Have a well considered communications policy that puts across the police perspective on the terrorist campaign, and the response to it, in the media in an effective and rounded way on an ongoing basis. Also, engage publicly and with key actors on what the police are doing and are trying to achieve in the fight against terrorism.

> Influence politicians and policy-makers to make any changes in legislation or in policy that police experience suggests will enhance the fight against terrorism. But avoid coming up with knee-jerk suggestions in the immediate aftermath of atrocities or in order to pass the buck for lack of progress in the fight against terrorism to politicians.

These two latter go to the heart of policing in an interconnected, communication-rich world. These and many other answers from my respondents appear to envision a more sophisticated community CT role for policing with major implications in the political and social context outlined at the start. An issue might be the dilemmas, misinterpretations and misunderstandings that might occur through the dual purpose of collecting intelligence and protecting the community. There is, it seems to me, a world of difference in the active moral autonomy philosophy of 'communities defeat terrorism', something they do for themselves, and the state acting to 'prevent' terrorism, something that is done to communities. It is here that policing is at the nexus of where the political localism agenda meets the central focus of dealing with a threat to the state.

Another issue that emerges most strongly is the tension between the kind of role envisioned here and the more robust, sometimes highly covert, police tactics, difficult sometimes to explain openly, that might be used in such critical incidents as preventive arrests, widespread stop and search and CCTV installation. This can be referred to as the balance between need to know and need to protect. Another issue, highly pertinent to the age of austerity might be the amount of resources not least people, training and time required to engage long-term in such subtle analytic or explanatory communication activities in a time of austerity.

Synthesis and conclusions

This chapter has considered similarities with earlier CT policing, in particular the learning deriving from NI both for practice and policy there but also elsewhere in the UK and more widely geographically. In particular, it has emphasised the role of communities in policing and the wider police family of agencies and institutions that follows some of the thinking elsewhere in this volume. This all seems very basic and not new, Peelian probably, certainly reminiscent of Chief Constable John Alderson (Alderson 1979, 1984, 1998) if detailed to a particular aspect of contemporary policing. As one respondent in my empirical analyses wrote:

It is unfortunately common to be dismissive of research unless it uncovers startlingly new findings (the 'Didn't tell me anything I didn't already know' grumble). Even if nothing surprisingly new were to emerge . . . they are nonetheless valuable. It is worth reminding the more cynical of the most elementary rule for new detectives: there is a difference between 'what we know' and 'what we think we know'.

The chapter has also been exploring a philosophy I have been fascinated with for some years: how to use basic policing skills and techniques to avoid losing the peace. To quote a philosopher of conflict, '[G]rand strategy looks beyond the war to the subsequent peace. It should not only combine the various instruments, but so regulate their use as to avoid damage to the future state of peace – for its security and prosperity' (Liddell Hart, 1954: 336). Liddell Hart and others since classical times have considered the juxtaposition: 'In peace prepare for war' and 'In war prepare for peace!' This implies not only intelligence activity in both periods, but also community policing in dialogues with the enemy (the title of Scott Atran's 2010 book *Talking to the Enemy*) and their supporters or defenders with all the difficulties that Lambert (2011) has described. This can be seen to be preparation for 'winning the peace' but also the avoidance of 'a festering mess' left for one's successors (Sanderson (2012) is a useful recent case study). There are also implications about not unnecessarily undermining the legitimacy of the CJS during disputes amongst CT leaders and other public figures about CJS uses (Bowcott, 2013; Blair, 2009).

The core of my conclusions are about the dialogue between, engagement of, and empathy with the diverse communities I and my respondents have served. These have practical consequences for policing, e.g. in the publicity attendant (perhaps even the much maligned background briefings criticised by Leveson (2012) upon successful prosecutions, the support for investigations, information available to police interviewers post arrest and the involvement of families of potential terrorists in preventing radicalisation (for examples of all of these, see Laville and Dodd (2013)).

Another set of implications are the relationship of the foregoing with all the media and putting matters into the public domain post Leveson (2012). For example, the apparent limitations placed on dialogue with communities via those most obvious wide ranging of broadcasters (in their original scattering information sense), journalists.

Thinking the issues through and building local relationships and structures can help us analyse the community police aspects of the problems from their apparent difficulties and generate solutions. Open source intelligence, explained to help build community confidence in the CT structures and operations, can be used to prevent violent radicalisation. In turn it can be used to build confidence in more covert intelligence tactics where less information can be made available. In this way we might avoid the 'festering mess' and not 'doing anything stupid' lessons so painfully learned from the last few decades. In that way the police can continue to contribute to 'winning the peace' in an age of austerity and localism.

A note on methodology

I admit that the qualitative semi-structured hybrid methodology adopted here can be challenged, or even rejected, but the chapter opens some new material for others to think about into the public domain. I have used some innovative rigorous debriefs, non-sensitive, non-secret, anonymous (Alison and Crego, 2008) answers to the introductory 'what matters in CT?' question (n = 300+). I have then assessed this against a convenience sample of experts in the field of CT policing, as well as police officers, both former and serving. I have been assisted by diplomats, intelligence officers, and academics with expertise in CT work. They were all asked to answer the question 'what 10 things do you think the police should do or not do in CT?' (n = 20+) (see Eyre et al. (2008) for a description and assessment of these hugely useful debriefs and methodology from which I and many others learned much).

Notes

1 Following the peace process in Northern Ireland in the 1990s/2000s, a decision was made that a record should be maintained of the activities of some of the combatants. This was based on the precedent of a military history archive about, for example, Michael Collins and his followers in an earlier phase of the conflict (see Hart, 2005). It was decided that to assist anonymity during the life time of the participants it would be held in the USA at Boston College. The anonymity and lack of access has been challenged in the US courts (a good starting pont is the *Time* newspaper 09.07.12).

2 Clutterbuck (2004: 159) identifies 3,601 casualties related to Northern Ireland terrorism between 1969 and 1999. Between 1972 and 1999 there were 582 bomb attacks and 33 shootings of which 365 and 17, respectively, occurred in London. I had the privilege to investigate several of these. This gives some idea of the scale of the pain across NI and of the available learning. The Royal Ulster Constabulary GC lost over 300 officers, murdered between 1969 and 1999; a measure of their pain and courage.

3 Peel, never a democrat in modern terms, never actually wrote this or specified his so-called Peelian principles. They have to be derived from his speeches and letters. However, he did write that he 'did not want gentlemen'. Reith (1938) concluded from the material he analysed on Peel that drawing the police from those he wanted policed and drawing the public into policing was a good way forward. I and many others agree. (See Emsley (this volume); Alderson (1979, 1984, 1998); and many others).

4 This latter responsibility was recently eloquently but forcibly pointed out to me by Mike Hough (2012) in a discussion about the summer 2011 London public disorders. The exhortations themselves as a methodology are not far from the format of Alderson 1979.

Bibliography

Alderson, J. (1979). *Policing Freedom*. Plymouth UK. Macdonald and Evans.
Alderson, J. (1984). *Law and Disorder*. London UK. Hamish Hamilton.
Alderson, J. (1998). *Principled Policing. Protecting the Public with Integrity*. Winchester UK. Waterside Press.
Alison, L. and Crego, J. Eds. (2008). *Policing Critical Incidents*. Devon. Willan.
Atran, S. (2010). *Talking to the Enemy. Violent Extremism, Sacred Values and What It Means to be Human*. London UK. Allen Lane.

Blair, I. (2009). *Policing Controversy*. London UK. Profile Books.

Brain, T. (2010). *A History of Policing in England and Wales from 1974. A Turbulent Journey.* Oxford UK. Oxford University Press.

Butler, R. (2004). *Espionage and the Iraq War*. HC 898. London UK. The Stationery Office.

Clutterbuck, L. (2004). *Law Enforcement.* Chapter 6 in Cronin, A.K. and Ludes, J.M. (Eds) *Attacking Terorism. Elements of a Grand Strategy.* Washington DC USA. Georgetown University Press.

Cronin, A.K. (2009). *How Terrorism Ends. Understanding the Decline and Demise of Terrorist Campaigns.* Princeton USA. Princeton University.

Cronin, A.K. and Ludes, J.M. Eds. (2004). *Attacking Terrorism. Elements of a Grand Strategy.* Washington DC USA. Georgetown University Press.

English, R. (2009). *Terrorism. How to Respond.* Oxford UK. Oxford University Press.

Eyre, M., Crego, J. and Alison, L. (2008). *Electronic Debriefs and Simulations as Descriptive Methods for Defining the Critical Incident Landscape.* In Alison, L. and Crego, J. (Eds) *Policing Critical Incidents.* Devon. Willan.

Gearty, C. (1987). *The Future of Terrorism.* London UK. Phoenix.

Grieve, J. (2003/2008). *Developments in UK Criminal Intelligence.* Chapter in Ratcliffe, J. (Ed.) *Strategic Developments in Criminal Intelligence.* Devon UK. Willan and Federation Press.

Hart, P. (2005). *Mick. The Real Michael Collins.* London UK. Macmillan.

Hayman, A. and Gilmore, M. (2009). *The Terrorist Hunters.* London. Bantam Press.

HMIC (2009a). *Prevent: Progress and Prospects.* London UK. Her Majesty's Inspectorate of Constabulary.

HMIC (2009b). *Stockwell – MPS Progress.* London UK. Her Majesty's Inspectorate of Constabulary.

Home Office (1996). *Prof. Brian Caddy. Assessment and Implications of Centrifuge Contamination.* TSO. Cmnd 3491 presented to Parlt. December 1996.

Home Office (2006/2011). *Countering International Terrorism* (London: Command Paper 6888, as updated by Command Paper 7547 (2009), Command Paper 7833 (2010), Command Paper 8123 (2011). London UK. HMSO.

IMC (2004–2011). *Reports Numbers 1–26 of the Independent Monitoring Commission.* London. The Stationery Office. (Can also be found at www.independentmonitoringcommission. org).

Innes, M. and Levi, M. (2012). *Terrorism and Counter-Terrorism.* Chapter in Maguire, M., Morgan, R. and Reiner, R. (Eds) *The Oxford Handbook of Criminology.* 5th Edition. Oxford UK.

Lambert, R. (2011). *Countering Al-Qaeda in London. Police and Muslims in Partnership.* London UK. C. Hurst and Co.

Laqueur, W. (1987). *The Age of Terrorism.* London UK. Weidenfeld and Nicolson.

Laville, S. and Dodd, V. (2013). *Guilty: gang who thought 7/7 wasn't deadly enough.* London UK. Guardian newspaper 22.02.13.

Leveson, L.J. (2012). *The Leveson Inquiry into the Culture, Practice and Ethics of the Press.* London UK. TSO.

Liddell Hart, B. (1954). *Strategy: The Indirect Approach.* London UK. Faber and Faber.

Manningham-Buller, E. (2012). *Securing Freedom. BBC Reith Lectures 2011.* London. Profile Books by arrangement with BBC.

Matassa, M. and Newburn, T. (2003). *Policing and Terrorism.* Chapter in Newburn, T. (Ed.) *Handbook of Policing.* Cullompton, Devon UK. Willan Publishing.

Mowlem, M. (2002). *Momentum.* London UK. Hodder and Stoughton.

Mythen, G. and Walklate, S. (2012). *Global Terrorism, Risk and the State.* Chapter in Hall, S. and Winlow, S. (Eds) *New Directions in Criminological Theory.* London UK. Routledge.

National Commission on Terrorist Attacks on the USA (2004). *The 9/11 Commission Report.* Washington USA. US Government.

Norton-Taylor, R. (2012). *Mr Grayling take note.* London UK. Guardian newspaper 05.09.2012.

Norton-Taylor, R. (2013). *Spies chilled about spooks but military heated over memoirs.* London UK. Guardian newspaper 05.09.13.

Omand, D. (2010). *Securing the State.* London UK. C. Hurst.

Powell, J. (2008). *Great Hatred, Little Room. Making Peace in Northern Ireland.* London UK. Bodley Head.

Quick, R. (2012). *Counter Terrorism: The Next Decade.* In Neyroud, P. (Ed.) *Policing UK 2013. Priorities and Pressures: A Year of Transformation.* London. Witan Media, pp. 88–91.

Rapoport, D. (2004). *The Four Waves of Modern Terrorism.* Chapter 2 in Cronin, A.K. and Ludes, J.M. (Eds) *Attacking Terorism. Elements of a Grand Strategy.* Washington DC USA. Georgetown University Press.

Reith, C. (1938). *The Police Idea: Its History and Evolution in England in the Eighteenth Century and After.* London UK. Oxford University Press.

Rimmington, S. (2001). *Open Secret. The Autobiography of the Former Director-General of M15.* London UK. Hutchinson.

Sanderson, D. (2012). *Lawyer murder collusion is shocking, admits PM.* London Times newspaper 13.12.12, page 24 and Leader page 2.

Stevens, J. (2005). *Not for the Faint Hearted. My Life Fighting Crime.* London UK. Weidenfeld and Nicolson.

Other works consulted and useful further reading

Alexander, Y. (2006). *Counter Terrorist Strategies. Successes and Failures of Six Nations.* Dulles VA USA. Potomac Books.

Aaronovitch, D. (2009). *Voodoo Histories. The Role of Conspiracy Theory in Shaping Modern History.* London UK. Jonathan Cape.

Bowcott, O. (2013). *Judge defends court role over terror suspects.* London UK. Guardian newspaper 05.03.2013, pages 1, 20 and Editorial page 34.

Dwyer, T. Ryle (2005). *The Squad and the Intelligence Operations of Michael Collins.* Cork Ireland. Mercier Press.

Elagab, E.O. (1995). *International Law Documents Relating to Terrorism.* London UK. Cavendish.

Foy, M.T. (2006). *Michael Collins's Intelligence War. The Struggle between the British and the IRA 1919–1921.* Stroud UK. Sutton Publishing.

Grieve, J. (2011). *Monitoring the Loyalist Paramilitaries in Northern Ireland.* Chapter in McAulay, J.W. and Spencer, G. (Eds) *Ulster Loyalism after the Good Friday Agreement.* London UK. Palgrave Macmillan.

Grieve, J. (2013 Forthcoming). *Thinking about Peace in Conflict.* In Pearse, J. (Ed.) *Counter Terrorism* (in preparation).

Grieve, J., Crego, J. and Griffiths, B. (2007). *Critical Incidents: Investigation, Management and Training.* Chapter in Newburn T., Williamson, T. and Wright, A. (Eds) *Handbook of Criminal Investigation.* Devon UK. Willan.

Grieve, J., Harfield, C. and MacVean, A. (2006). *Policing.* London UK. Sage Publications.

Grieve, J. and Howard, J. (Eds) (2004). *Communities, Social Exclusion and Crime.* UK. Smith Institute.

Guardian Obituary (14.02.1997). *Major Geoffrey Biddle G.M. 'Defusing Terror'.* London.

Hall, S. and Winlow, S. (Eds) (2012). *New Directions in Criminological Theory*. London UK. Routledge.

Harfield, C., Grieve, J., MacVean, A. and Phillips, D. (2008). *Handbook of Intelligent Policing*. Oxford UK. Oxford University Press.

Harnden, T. (1999). *'Bandit County' The IRA and South Armagh*. London UK. Hodder & Stoughton.

HMIC/Audit Commission (2008). *Preventing Violent Extremism*. London UK. Her Majesty's Inspectorate of Constabulary and the Audit Commission.

HMIC (2011). *Adapting to Austerity*. London UK. Her Majesty's Inspectorate of Constabulary.

HMIC (2012). *Policing in Austerity: One Year On*. London UK. Her Majesty's Inspectorate of Constabulary.

Hart, P. (2005). *Mick. The Real Michael Collins*. Macmillan. London.

Huntley, B. (1977). *Bomb Squad*. London UK. W.H. Allen. (See also *Daily Telegraph* Obituary 30.03.2001).

Laqueur, W. (1977). *Terrorism*. London UK. Weidenfeld and Nicolson.

Maguire, M., Morgan, R. and Reiner, R. (2012). *The Oxford Handbook of Criminology*. 5th Edition. Oxford UK.

Ryder, C. (2000). *The RUC: A Force Under Fire*. London UK. Arrow Books.

Savage, S. (2007). *Police Reform*. Oxford UK. Oxford University Press.

Spalek, B. and Lambert, R. (2008). 'Muslim communities, counter-terrorism and counter-radicalisation: A critically reflective approach to engagement', *International Journal of Law, Crime and Justice*, 36: 257–270.

Taylor, P. (2001). *Brits: The War Against the IRA*. London UK. Bloomsbury.

US Government. (2003). *The 9/11 Commission Report. Final Report of the National Commission on Terrorist Attacks upon the United States*. Authorised Edition. Washington USA.

Walker, C. (1992). *The Prevention of Terrorism in British Law*. 2nd Edition. Manchester University Press.

Wright, A. (2002). *Policing. An Introduction to Concepts and Practice*. Devon UK. Willan.

Wright, L. (2006). *The Looming Tower: Al-Qaeda's Road to 9/11*. London UK. Allen Lane.

18

INTELLIGENCE-LED POLICING AND THE NATIONAL INTELLIGENCE MODEL

Karen Bullock

Introduction

Intelligence-led Policing (ILP) is a relatively recent addition to the vocabulary of policing and one that has been seen as the most positive contribution that the police service can make to crime prevention (Ratcliffe, 2002). However, while the police service might have embraced the terminology of ILP in principle, its practice is rather less straightforward (Ratcliffe, 2002). This chapter considers the application of ILP in the UK. It covers key definitions; the rationale and impetus for the development of ILP; its operation in the UK; and potential challenges for the implementation of the approach in the future.

ILP and the National Intelligence Model (NIM)

The aim of ILP is to disrupt offending, where it is likely to yield the highest dividends, by bringing together and analysing information about criminals and their activities (Tilley, 2008). Ratcliffe (2003) notes that the objectives of ILP can be seen in the priorities of the UK National Intelligence Model (NIM), more on which shortly, which include: targeting offenders (especially active criminals through overt and covert means); the management of crime and disorder hotspots; the investigation of linked series of crimes and incidents; and the application of preventative measures, including working with local partnerships to reduce crime and disorder.

While ILP and the NIM have much in common, they are not one and the same thing. The term 'NIM' refers to the *specific* mechanisms through which ILP is implemented in England and Wales. The NIM has been described as a 'model for policing' (Kirby and McPherson, 2004: 36) and as a 'business model' (John and Maguire, 2003: 38). It incorporates a process for setting priorities and a framework through which the police service can seek to resolve problems (Kirby and

McPherson, 2004). John and Maguire (2003: 41) describe the Model as 'essentially the design for a comprehensive "business process" to rationalise and systematise the ways in which the police service handles information and makes key decisions about the deployment of resources'. In principle, the Model should drive all police business from neighbourhood policing to the investigation of serious and organised crime and terrorism (ACPO/NCPE, 2007b).

Rationale and impetus

The contemporary notion of ILP entered the UK police lexicon in the early 1990s (Ratcliffe, 2003) and has spread around the globe. The origins of ILP can be found in a range of factors that have shaped the contemporary policing landscape – social, technological and political – and cannot be easily located in one event. Ratcliffe (2008a) describes a number of drivers for change. These include greater complexity in the policing task (including the need to think differently about organised and transnational crime), the demands of formal risk management practice and recognition of the 'gap' between the numbers of police officers and the level of recorded crime. In addition, the limitations of the 'standard model' of policing (random patrol, rapid response and post-crime investigation) have been acknowledged (Ratcliffe, 2008a). All of these will be touched upon in this chapter. However, perhaps most significantly, the contemporary calls for an intelligence-led approach emerged in a political context where the police service was being asked to make more efficient use of resources and to better account for the resources it did use.

During the 1980s and 1990s, the police service, like all public sector organisations, came under pressure to demonstrate 'value for money' (Maguire, 2000). Early, and influential, UK government reports (Audit Commission, 1993; HMIC, 1997) made a case for greater proactivity and targeting of resources in the fight against crime. Reflecting the early Audit Commission report, more recent discourse makes very similar points about the need to find ways to reduce the demand on police services:

> [The NIM] is based on proactive policing which involves identifying, understanding and addressing underlying problems and trends. This broader perspective allows for prioritisation of police activity which makes it easier to respond to the increasing demands placed on the Police Service.
> *(ACPO/NCPE, 2007b: 6)*

ILP appears to offer a way of managing demand for police services through prioritising issues and resources in a targeted manner via the development of information and intelligence (ACPO/NCPE, 2007a). While the need to find more efficient uses of police resources was central to the development of ILP, the NIM also sought to bring clarity, structure and standards to police decision making, embedding greater 'rigour into the management decision-making processes for both strategic and tactical purposes' (NCIS, 2000: 7).

The operation of ILP in England and Wales

The origins of the NIM can be found in work led by the National Criminal Intelligence Service on behalf of the Association of Chief Police Officers (ACPO) (NCIS, 2000). The overall structure of the Model has been characterised as relatively simple, although this has become obscured by jargon and by the detail of its individual components (John and Maguire, 2003). This section summarises how the NIM should operate in principle throughout England and Wales, before returning to our knowledge of the operation of the Model in practice in later sections.

Analysis of information about crime and disorder is central to the operation of the NIM. In the context of contemporary ILP, intelligence refers to 'processed, actionable information derived from *any* number of sources' (Rogers *et al.*, 2011: 180; emphasis added), the nature of which will be returned to. The key is that 'these sources are analysed so that law enforcement managers can determine objective policing tactics in regard to enforcement targets, prevention activities and further intelligence operations' (Ratcliffe, 2009: 177). As guidance makes clear, to operate effectively the NIM is reliant on a clear framework to analyse information to facilitate a problem-solving approach to law enforcement and crime prevention (NCPE, 2004). Accordingly, the NIM is driven by a series of strategic and tactical assessments of crime problems. The NIM draws on four standardised 'intelligence products' each of which can use up to nine analytical techniques. The products are: the *Strategic Assessment* which comprises the 'big picture' within a police service area over a six-month period; the *Tactical Assessments* which consider trends over a much shorter time period; the *Problem Profile* which identifies potential crime and disorder problems; and the *Target Profile* which profiles suspects/offenders, identifies weaknesses in their criminal activities.

All of these assessments should go beyond description of the nature of crime and criminality within a locality to make recommendations for action. Accordingly, the analytical products feed into two sets of meetings which coordinate the allocation of police resources: Strategic Tasking and Co-ordinating Groups and Tactical Tasking and Co-ordinating Groups. The purpose of a Strategic Tasking and Co-ordinating Group, which should meet each six months, is to set the overall agenda for intelligence, prevention and enforcement priorities. The purpose of the Tactical Tasking and Co-ordinating Group is to implement the agenda set at the strategic level through a menu of tactical options and to manage any subsequent priorities that might arise (NCPE, 2004). This group should meet as frequently as is necessary in accordance with force policy, though this is much more regularly than the Strategic Tasking and Co-ordinating Group.

The process of generating analytical products and the structure of tasking is replicated at three levels of operational policing: Level 1 (the basic command unit or below) which focuses on local crime problems and anti-social behaviour; Level 2 (force, inter-force and regional criminal activity) which might require additional resources and coordination; and Level 3 (international level) which focuses on the most serious and organised crime (NCPE, 2004).

The idea is that intelligence, generated from the aforementioned assessments, can flow both within and between each of the levels of the NIM. Reflecting the point that the NIM should be an overall driver of policing, 'effective application of the National Intelligence Model should enable police forces to trace the continuum between anti-social behaviour and the most serious crime and then to identify those local issues in most urgent need of attention' (NCPE, 2004: 6).

Implementation in practice

Implementing the NIM represents a change to police practice and, as Kirby and McPherson (2004: 46) put it, whether these changes are implemented effectively 'depends on its leaders to make sure the infrastructure and direction is in place, and depends on practitioners to willingly exploit those new methods in the operational setting'. In fact, there has not been a great deal of academic research on the operation of the NIM. Extant studies are generally focused on the early days of its operation (Tilley, 2008). Accordingly, it is certainly too early to state whether the approach is effective or not in controlling crime (Ratcliffe, 2009). The following sections bring together what is known about the operation of ILP generally, drawing on evidence from around the world, and the NIM more specifically.

Leadership

Much early documentation on the development and operation of the Model stressed the importance of enthusiastic and energetic leadership (HMIC, 1997). Indeed, research on the implementation of ILP in the early to mid-1990s drew attention to how 'major organisational reforms can be successfully implemented *only* if there is wholehearted commitment to them from the most senior officers in the force' (Maguire and John, 1995: 54; emphasis added). Strong personal interest and endorsement from senior officers is important because it brings resources and gives authority to reforms. However, research on the implementation of the NIM has revealed that strong leadership was not evident in all police services. Simply, some senior officers were convinced by the need to implement an intelligence-led approach, others less so (Christopher and Cope, 2009).

Developing the infrastructure

The development of ILP typically involves reorganisation of the police structure, placing much greater emphasis on intelligence units and freeing resources to facilitate proactive working (Rogers *et al.*, 2011). Developing the structure to facilitate and support the development of ILP is a challenge. Early research demonstrated that while many police services were convinced of the need for proactivity within criminal investigations, not all were investing in organisational reforms to support this kind of work (Maguire and John, 1995). Guidance on the NIM certainly acknowledges the need for the development of infrastructure and draws attention to a wide range of operational, structural and human resource issues that need attending to (ACPO/NCPE, 2005, 2007a). Indeed, guidance on the nature of the infrastructure of the Model has become progressively more detailed over time, presumably reflecting acknowledgement of the complexity of this task, considered in detail in the following sections.

Generating intelligence

NIM guidelines draw attention to how data should be drawn from wide and varied sources. A primary source of data for analysing and interpreting the criminal environment are those routinely generated from administrative data sets, such as calls for service, police recorded crime and more specialist data sets, such as custody records. There is no need to rehearse here the myriad problems associated with police administrative data (see for example, Maguire, 2012). However, there are issues regarding the use of administrative data sets which are worth nothing in this context.

First is the role played by data generated from agencies other than the police service. While much has been made of the benefits of generating information from non-police agencies, such as the health and social services, police data sets tend to dominate. Data sharing problems have been explained in terms of cultural differences between agencies – often expressed as concerns about the confidentiality of certain data – as well as technical difficulties in data sharing (Bullock *et al.*, 2002; Phillips *et al.*, 2002). The problem is that a police view of local problems comes to dominate (John and Maguire, 2003; Bullock, 2013), a point that will be returned to in later sections.

Second is the role played by police 'intelligence systems'. Information contained on police intelligence systems – which allows the police service and other agencies to record, evaluate and disseminate wide ranging information about people and places (ACPO/NCPE, 2007b) – comprise a primary data source for ILP. The rule of thumb is that the systems could record *any* information that is not recorded elsewhere (ACPO/NCPE, 2007b). These data are wide and varied and may incorporate, but are not limited to, information given to the police by a member of the public; information from anonymous sources (e.g. Crimestoppers); information from non-police agencies; sanitised information derived from informants or by covert means; information obtained by police officers and staff in the course of their duties (e.g.patrol officers, front desk staff); and from interviewing offenders (ACPO/NCPE, 2007b). Research has drawn attention to a number of problems with the use of these data for analytical purposes. Some relate to the nature of the information submitted to the system. Cope (2004) identified the problem of 'policing-led intelligence' where the information that officers value, generate and so record coalesces around 'the usual suspects' and does not consider the nature of crime and criminals more broadly. There are also a number of issues about the storage and management of these data (see Sheptycki, 2004).

Collating and analysing information

The effectiveness of the NIM is heavily dependent on the generation of good quality analytical products. As John and Maguire (2003) note, substantial investment in analytical resources is necessary if products of a requisite standard are to be produced. However, the police service has been somewhat slow to invest in the development of systems to capture and analyse data. Read and Tilley (2000) reported that five out of the eight police services they visited had inadequate data recording systems and/or analytic software. John and Maguire (2003: 63) confirmed that 'this was an area in which considerable improvement is still needed'. More recently, Ratcliffe (2008b) drew attention to the significant technological barriers to the generation of analytical products. He points to the incompatibility of the diverse forms of information generated by the police service and the problems of marrying together information stored on different systems using different software. In short, 'there is no doubt that in most forces an "intelligence lacuna" existed, and in a few, still does' (Christopher and Cope, 2009: 240).

A related set of issues focus on the personnel required to develop analytic products. Traditionally, police intelligence analysts had quite varying career paths but many were police officers coming to the end of their careers with no specialist knowledge of data and analytic software (John and Maguire, 2003; Read and Tilley, 2000). The increased role of computerisation in the management of police information has resulted in changes in the role of the intelligence officer. Intelligence analysts need to be experts in data manipulation and data analysis packages and today the role is usually conducted by civilian staff, often social science graduates. While increasing computer power has improved the capacity to analyse information about crime, it has led to changes in the role of the intelligence officer and created challenges for police management (Maguire and John, 1995). The police service has struggled to introduce training and a career structure for its new breed of civilian intelligence officer. Training has certainly been variable but typically focused on standard analytical packages which are insufficient for crime reduction purposes (Read and Tilley, 2000: 28). A point confirmed by John and Maguire (2003) and Ratcliffe (2008b). Retention of staff has been a problem as analysts look to find career routes unavailable in the police service (John and Maguire, 2003; Read and Tilley, 2000).

Standardisation of analytical products

As we have seen, a primary aim of the NIM was to standardise the intelligence function within and between police services in order that information can flow between them. In fact, studies have demonstrated that the early aspiration of achieving standardisation was missed and that police services have developed their own processes and products (John and Maguire, 2003). On the one hand, as John and Maguire note, variation in the structure and content of intelligence products render effective collation and analysis throughout the level structure difficult to achieve.

On the other hand, the Model was criticised for attempting to impose a national standard with little appreciation for the diversity of policing at force, and particularly BCU, level (John and Maguire, 2003). It might then be that police services have developed structures which are more meaningful for their local contexts.

Influencing decision-makers

Being able to develop comprehensive assessments of crime and disorder problems is one thing but it is yet another to influence those who make decisions about resource allocation. In many police services, analytical products appear to have only a limited influence on decision making (HMIC, 2005). While police officers may state that the work of analysts is essential, in practice they may be 'silent partners' (Cope, 2004: 192), for a number of reasons.

First, the results of analysis 'compete' with a range of factors – from performance targets, to community concerns, to newspaper reports, to pressures from politicians, to the routine habits and preferences of officers –for police resources (Ratcliffe, 2003). Meeting performance indicators is pervasive (Ratcliffe, 2003; John and Maguire, 2003). Police managers have felt pressure to concentrate resources on crime problems which comprise the target of centrally determined performance indicators rather than ones that emerge from the findings of analysis. Second, officers might not have always found analytical products to be that useful. One has to caution against unrealistic expectations of what analytical products can provide – analysts cannot predict the future. Yet their products are sometimes categorised by officers as descriptive documents which add little to what they already know (Bullock, 2013). There is a risk of something of a 'vicious circle' developing: if products are perceived to be weak, their usefulness or 'added value' will remain questionable to the officers, who will struggle to see the value of investing further in analytical resources, which is a prerequisite of good quality analytical products (John and Maguire, 2003). Third, there is a question mark surrounding the nature of communication between analysts and officers and, pertinently, the nature of the recommendations analysts make.There are on-going debates regarding whether analysts, as civilian staff with little or no operational experience, should give operational instructions to police officers (see Evans, 2009). Some officers (and analysts) clearly believe that the role of analysts is to lay out the findings of research but that tactical and strategic decision making should be left to the officers (Bullock, 2013). It might be that there is room for compromise. In short, analysts might draw attention to options for where, when and how police resources could be deployed recognising that ultimately resource allocation will be made by police officers (Evans, 2009).

The nature of interventions and the role of partners

Although designed and developed as a model for policing, the discourse of the NIM has stressed the role of partnership from its inception (HMIC, 1997; NCIS,

2000). As early guidance notes: 'acceptance of the basic precepts of the model by other agencies will greatly aid the effort to "join up" law enforcement activity' (NCIS, 2000: 7). However, research suggests that this has not been realised in practice. We have already seen that there is a risk that analytical products become dominated by police-generated data. Evidence has also suggested that non-police agencies play a limited role in shaping responses to problems. John and Maguire (2003: 55) drew attention to how, outside of isolated examples of good practice, partnership involvement was regarded as an 'area for future development'. Maguire and John (2006) note that partnership working within the NIM framework, where it did exist, tended to be based on strong personal contacts rather than formalised institutional arrangements. They note that 'the absence of partners and their resources is a significant one' which limits the potential to encourage ownership of responses or effectively monitor progress against priorities (p. 82). The lack of partnership involvement could also mean that responses become limited to rather conventional police responses – such as patrol, arrest and incapacitation (Bullock, 2013). This issue is returned to in later sections.

Impact

The rationale for introducing ILP was to improve efficiency in the allocation of police resources. Ultimately, doing so was assumed to impact on crime rates and so on the demand for police services. Although, as Tilley (2008) notes, the approach seems *plausible* at the time of writing we do not know what impact ILP, or the NIM, has on crime rates and demand for police services.

As always, the devil is in the detail. Much depends on implementation and, as we have seen, there are question marks regarding whether ILP is operating as it should be. Much also depends on the nature of the tactics implemented. Ratcliffe (2002) notes that while there are limits to the ability of the police to affect crime rates, some tactics – such as directed patrols in hot spots of crime and the proactive arrest of serious repeat offenders – have been shown to be effective. However, there is a tendency for what really 'works' to be overshadowed by schemes that have significant public appeal, but for which the crime reduction evidence is disputed, such as establishing Neighbourhood Watch (Ratcliffe, 2002). More broadly, it is common for the police to revert to what they are used to (Bullock, 2013). Come what may, the impact of tactics at the local level is not always known. Research has suggested that evaluation, which officially should be part of the process, has not been fully integrated into the Model (John and Maguire, 2003). This is not much of a surprise since there is now a significant body of evidence which draws attention to the limitations of evaluation within policing and crime reduction practice (Bullock *et al.*, 2006).

Future challenges

The following sections consider challenges for the future of ILP.

A first challenge relates to the development of the infrastructure to support ILP. Achieving an intelligence-led police service is not resource free. Direct expenditure is involved in purchasing software and the development of the analytical role, and there are opportunity costs of investing in an intelligence system. Quite simply the officers (and others) operating the system could be doing something else.

A second challenge relates to the balance between law enforcement and wider crime reduction outcomes. As stressed, ILP seeks more efficient use of police resources and, ultimately, to reduce crime and public demand. At the time of writing, it is not clear that the Model is able to efficiently orient resources, not least because of the lack of systematic evidence on the issue. However, the focus would certainly seem to be on efficient use of police resources. There are obvious benefits of orienting police resources to where they are most needed, but these will be limited to short-term law enforcement goals unless the approach is viewed more widely. Achieving longer term crime reduction outcomes will be challenging without pooling wider resources and thinking about crime reduction as more than the enforcement of the criminal law.

A third set of challenges relate to priority setting within the NIM structure. While decisions about priorities are an inevitable feature of all police work, they are particularly important in proactive approaches to crime control which, due to its resource intensive nature, allows only a small number of initiatives to be conducted at any one time (Maguire, 2000). Questions regarding what – or who – is targeted, why and how, become pertinent. While much depends on how ILP is conceived and implemented (Ratcliffe, 2009), the approach is potentially intrusive and so there are implications for civil liberties and accountability (Maguire, 2000; Maguire and John, 2006; Ratcliffe, 2009). The intelligence systems contain highly sensitive information about individuals, their associates and their day-to-day routines. Questions must be asked about the nature of information collated; how widely it is shared (and with what purpose); and how long it is retained. Individual targets of proactive police work become subject to powerful tools – including surveillance devices and ever-growing powers under both civil and criminal procedures – which are intrusive and could have a major impact on a person's life (Maguire, 2000). The proportionality of the approach also becomes relevant. The NIM incorporates wide ranging behaviours from low-level disorder to terrorist activity, and pretty much anything in between. It could be that these techniques are applied to relatively low-level offenders (Ratcliffe, 2002). Questions about the potential for discrimination on racial or social class grounds are highly pertinent (Maguire, 2000).

A final challenge relates to measurement of effectiveness. Despite a clearly stated commitment to the evaluation of ILP – the then Chairman of the Association of Chief Police Officers Crime Committee, David Phillips, noted that 'the evaluation of this programme is one of the main planks to the ACPO Crime strategy' (NCIS, 2000: 4) – there has been no systematic independent evaluations of this approach. Given the nature of claims made about ILP, the amount of resources expended, observed implementation problems and concerns about civil liberties and accountability, this needs addressing. There are complexities in evaluating the impact of ILP. A distinction would certainly need to be made between the measurement of the overall impact of the approach on crime reduction at the macro level – a daunting task – or the micro level issue of whether tactics introduced as part of ILP are effective at the local level. The independence of evaluations is also important. A number of commentators have drawn attention to the validity of evaluations that are conducted internally by the police service. Leaving aside issues of whether the police service has the necessary skills to conduct evaluations (see Bullock *et al.*, 2006) there is pressure on officers to demonstrate success in reducing crime when documenting the impact of innovations in practice. As Ratcliffe (2002: 62) put it, 'it would be a brave [officer] indeed who could admit the failure of a crime reduction initiative, and under the critical gaze of the Commissioner it would be understandable if they succumbed to the allure of a less rigorous, more flattering and potentially erroneous evaluation'.

Conclusions

The NIM is a dominant model through which the police service in England and Wales has sought to allocate resources and shape business since the turn of the century. This chapter has examined the rationale for ILP and its operation in practice. In so doing, necessary conditions for the successful implementation and operation of the NIM and ILP have been identified. These include the prerequisite of committed leadership, the importance of investment, the need to reorient aspects of the police organisation towards greater proactivity and the requirement for coordination, standardisation and prioritisation in the policy process at the different levels of police governance. Although the principles of ILP have been widely endorsed, implementing the associated processes has not been without problems.

However, it should be stressed that implementing the NIM does not appear to have run into some of the difficulties that have befallen other contemporary reform movements. It could be that officers are broadly convinced of the benefits of a proactive, intelligence-led approach to policing (Maguire, 2000). Despite early problems, the police service might accommodate ILP more comfortably than other attempts at reform (Tilley, 2008). ILP resonates with the traditional model of policing. It has focused primarily on enforcement of the criminal law through disruption of offending and incarceration of offenders and it 'continues to be hard on the criminal' (Tilley, 2008: 396). In short, the NIM has not challenged the dominant model of policing in a discernible way (Tilley, 2008).

However, many commentators, inside and outside of the police service, have expressed reservations about the 'speed and wholesale commitment' with which intelligence-led approaches have been embraced by policy-makers and senior officers as well as the more controversial aspects of the model (Maguire, 2000: 320). This takes on a new meaning in the context of fiscal constraint. Much rhetoric has been focused on protecting 'the front line' of policing. Although their role is to *direct* the front line, 'invisible' civilian analysts are no doubt vulnerable to cost cutting exercises. There is a risk that the infrastructure on which ILP relies starts to be dismantled. Given that ILP developed as a response to the challenge of making policing more effective and efficient in the face of cost cutting within the public services, this is somewhat ironic.

References

ACPO/NCPE (2005) *Guidance on the National Intelligence Model*. Wyboston: NCPE.

ACPO/NCPE (2007a) *Practice Advice on Resources and the People Assets of the National Intelligence Model*. Wyboston: NCPE.

ACPO/NCPE (2007b) *Introduction to the National Intelligence Model*. Wyboston: NCPE.

Audit Commission (1993) *Helping With Enquiries: Tackling Crime Effectively*. London: Audit Commission.

Bullock, K. (2013) 'Community, intelligence-led policing and crime control'. *Policing and Society*, 23(2): 125–144.

Bullock, K., Farrell, G. and Tilley, N. (2002) 'Funding and Implementing Crime Reduction Initiatives'. Online report 10/02. London: Home Office. Available at: https://dspace.lboro.ac.uk/dspace-jspui/handle/2134/788 [accessed 5 July 2012].

Bullock, K., Erol, R. and Tilley, N. (2006) *Problem-oriented Policing and Partnership: Implementation of an Evidence Based Approach to Crime Reduction*. Cullompton: Willan.

Christopher, S. and Cope, N. (2009) 'A Practitioner's Perspective of UK Strategic Intelligence', in J. Ratcliffe (ed.) *Strategic Thinking in Criminal Intelligence*. Sydney: The Federation Press.

Cope, N. (2004) 'Intelligence-led policing or policing led intelligence? Integrating volume crime analysis into policing'. *British Journal of Criminology* 44(2): 188–203.

Evans, R. (2009) 'Influencing Decision-Makers with Intelligence and Analytical Products', in J. Ratcliffe (ed.) *Strategic Thinking in Criminal Intelligence*. Sydney: The Federation Press.

HMIC (1997) 'Policing with intelligence'. London: Her Majesty's Inspectorate of Constabulary. Available at: http://www.nationalarchives.gov.uk/erorecords/ho/421/2/hmic/pintell.htm [accessed 5 July 2012].

HMIC (2005) 'Closing the gap: a review of the fitness for purpose of the current structure of policing in England and Wales'. London: HMIC.

John, T. and Maguire, M. (2003) 'Rolling Out the National Intelligence Model: Key Challenges', in K. Bullock and N. Tilley (eds) *Crime Reduction and Problem-oriented Policing*. Cullompton: Willan.

Kirby, S. and McPherson, I. (2004) 'Integrating the National Intelligence Model with a "problem solving" approach'. *Community Safety Journal* 3(2): 36–46.

Maguire, M. (2000) 'Policing by risks and targets: some dimensions and implications of intelligence-led crime control'. *Policing and Society: An International Journal of Research and Policy* 9(4): 315–336.

Maguire, M. (2012) 'Criminal Statistics and the Construction of Crime', in M. Maguire, R. Morgan and R. Reiner (eds) *The Oxford Handbook of Criminology*. Fourth edition. Oxford: Oxford University Press.

Maguire, M. and John, T. (1995) 'Intelligence, Surveillance and Informants: Integrated Approaches, Crime Detection and Prevention Series Paper 64'. London: Home Office.

Maguire, M. and John, T. (2006) 'Intelligence-led policing, managerialism and community engagement: competing priorities and the role of the National Intelligence Model in the UK'. *Policing and Society* 16(1): 67–85.

NCIS (2000) *The National Intelligence Model*. London: NCIS. Available at: http://www. intelligenceanalysis.net/National%20Intelligence%20Model.pdf [accessed 5 July 2012].

NCPE (2004) *National Intelligence Model Code of Practice*. Wyboston: Centrex.

Phillips, C., Jacobson, J., Prime, R., Carter, M. and Considine, M. (2002) 'Crime and disorder reduction partnerships: round one progress'. *Police Research Series*, 151. Home Office, Policing and Reducing Crime Unit, London, UK.

Ratcliffe, J. (2002) 'Intelligence-led policing and the problems of turning rhetoric into practice'. *Policing and Society* 12(1): 53–66.

Ratcliffe, J. (2003) 'Intelligence-led policing'. *Trends and Issues in Crime and Criminal Justice* 248: 241–260. Canberra: Australian Institute of Criminology. Available at: http://www. aic.gov.au/publications/current%20series/tandi/241-260/tandi248.aspx [accessed 30 August 2012].

Ratcliffe, J. (2008a) *Intelligence-led Policing*. Cullompton: Willan.

Ratcliffe, J. (2008b) 'Knowledge Management Challenges in the Development of Intelligence-led Policing', in T. Williamson (ed.) *The Handbook of Knowledge-based Policing: Current Conceptions and Future Directions*. Chichester: Wiley.

Ratcliffe, J. (2009) 'Intelligence-Led Policing', in A. Wakefield and J. Fleming (eds) *The Sage Dictionary of Policing*. London: Sage.

Read, T. and Tilley, N. (2000) 'Not rocket science? Problem-solving and crime reduction'. *Crime Reduction Research Series*. Paper No. 6. London: Home Office. Available at: http:// www.popcenter.org/library/reading/pdfs/Rocket_Science.pdf [accessed 5 July 2012].

Rogers, C., Lewis, R., John, T. and Read, T. (2011) *Police Work: Principles and Practice*. Abingdon: Routledge.

Sheptycki, J. (2004) 'Organisational pathologies in police intelligence systems: some contributions to the lexicon of intelligence-led policing'. *European Journal of Criminology* 1(3): 307–332.

Tilley, N. (2008) 'Modern Approaches to Policing: Community, Problem-Oriented and Intelligence Led', in T. Newburn (ed.) *Handbook of Policing*, Second Edition. Cullompton: Willan.

19

HOLDING THE LINE

The sustainability of police involvement in crime prevention

Alex Hirschfield, Paul Ekblom, Rachel Armitage and Jason Roach

Introduction

In this chapter, we examine the role of the police in crime prevention in the UK, how it has developed over the years, the position that it has reached currently and where it should be heading in the future. We begin by defining what is meant by crime prevention, its relationship to similar functions, such as 'crime reduction', 'crime control' and 'community safety', and its dependence on law enforcement processes and the Criminal Justice System (CJS) which provides the very foundation underpinning the preventive process. We distinguish between enforcement-based 'judicial' prevention in which the police service is heavily involved and the broader notion of 'civil' crime prevention to which the police make a valuable contribution through mobilising, or working in partnership with, local communities, statutory agencies, voluntary groups and the private sector.

The roles of police Architectural Liaison Officers (ALOs) and Crime Prevention Design Advisers (CPDAs) are good examples of direct police involvement in offering advice – based on evidence, experience and theory – on designing out crime in new build and enhancing the security of existing properties. The delivery of Crime Prevention through Environmental Design (CPTED) has developed into a specialised service over the past two decades, supported by local planning policy and practice. The police role involves 'case work' such as reviewing major developments from a crime prevention perspective (scrutiny of Development Plans, analysis of crime data, site visits) and training others (e.g. town planners) in the principles and application of CPTED. Recent changes in both policy and practice run the risk of severely jeopardising both the delivery and quality of crime prevention advice. As a non-frontline service, posts in this area have been particularly vulnerable in the current economic climate: the number of ALOs/CPDAs fell by 32 per cent from 347 in January 2009 to 236 by August 2011, and as of June 2012 there were 196 ALOs, 44 per cent fewer than in January 2009. Furthermore, the Localism Act of 2011, in deregulating the planning system, has abolished Policy Planning Statements which stated the need to consider designing out crime in new developments and has placed the onus on local communities to develop their own neighbourhood plans. Planning deregulation, together with the downsizing of the ALO service, will restrict the community's ability to make evidence-based decisions regarding the crime risks of proposed developments in their areas. Drawing on both local and international experience, we discuss how communities in the future are likely to receive advice on what works in designing out crime and suggest alternative ways in which the dissemination of high-quality practice might be maintained.

The last 20 years have seen the development of various frameworks and analytical models such as Problem-Oriented Policing (Goldstein, 1990) the National Intelligence Model (National Criminal Intelligence Service, 2000) and the Crime Reduction Toolkits (http://webarchive.nationalarchives.gov. uk/20100413151426/crimereduction.homeoffice.gov.uk/toolkits/index.htm). A more recent model, discussed further below, is the 5Is Framework (Ekblom, 2011) which is a detailed process model for guiding prevention and capturing knowledge of practice. All of these have sought to equip the police with both the knowledge and skills to facilitate problem-solving and to make evidence- and theory-aware decisions on the targeting of crime prevention resources and interventions. Much has also been learned on the threats to effectiveness in crime prevention posed by implementation failure and how best to avoid or mitigate its impact. We expand on this later.

Access to and use of the results from good-quality crime prevention research and evaluation studies are necessary preconditions to effective problem-solving and the recognition and adoption of best practice in crime prevention. The capture, consolidation and dissemination of knowledge on what works in crime prevention are crucial to this process. We discuss attempts to manage practice knowledge over the past decade, the current situation and what needs to be done to ensure that lessons from past successes and failures in the design and implementation of crime prevention measures are not lost.

Crime prevention within the police service is not a particularly high-profile activity compared with other police functions and this is reflected in fluctuations over time in the prioritisation of crime prevention training for police officers whether provided in-house or outsourced. The Home Office Crime Reduction Centre (HOCRC), established in 1995, offered formal training to police officers and community safety practitioners and hosted the Crime Reduction Toolkits Website. The HOCRC closed in 2005 and the Crime Reduction Toolkits were archived in 2010. Police budget cuts in 2010 have been accompanied by a de-prioritisation of crime prevention training. Drawing upon personal accounts from police officers and trainers in a Northern Constabulary, we present views from the grassroots on recent changes in crime prevention training and where it might be heading in the future. We pay particular attention to the need for crime prevention training, the demand for it within the police service and by whom, where and how it should be provided.

Crime prevention: definition and police role

Many definitions of crime and its prevention exist. We define *crime prevention* as 'ethically acceptable advance action intended to reduce the risk of criminal events' (this and following definitions adapted from Ekblom (2011)). Risk reduction can be achieved through:

- eliminating the possibility of the criminal events, often by design;
- reducing the probability by intervening in the causes or, alternatively stated, by frustrating criminal goals by disrupting activities and organisations directed towards them; and
- reducing the harm by advance preparation to eliminate, reduce or mitigate it.

In all cases, the causes or risk and protective factors intervened in range from the immediate to the remote, and from the offender to the crime situation.

Crime reduction is a broader and simpler concept than prevention: any intervention made before, during or after criminal events to reduce their frequency or harm. Crime control involves holding the frequency of criminal events, or their harm, below a tolerable level, or halting their rapid growth. Much reduction and control is delivered via prevention. Community safety focuses less on individual criminal events and more on harm reduction and the positive quality of individual and collective life, e.g. delivered through reassurance (e.g. Ekblom, 2011).

It is rarely appreciated in crime prevention circles that the very existence of the CJS, in dispensing fair and satisfying justice, sets the conditions for all other forms of prevention to be possible. In this sense, the CJS is inherently preventive because it helps to channel blame and revenge into a formal, controlled and relatively impersonal public arena, and to avoid the slide into extremes of vigilantism, personal retaliation, feuding and 'terrorist justice'. Effective and pervasive law enforcement – both supported by, and contributing to, the wider climate of policing by consent – plays an enormous part in establishing these conditions and more prosaically in making society safe enough for 'civil prevention' to be workable. By this term we mean interventions in everyday life, ranging from youth shelters to parenting classes, and from secure car designs to better-managed bars, intended to reduce the risk of crime.

The police not only undertake the majority of prevention-through-enforcement (or more broadly 'judicial prevention' – Ekblom (2011)); they also contribute significantly to civil crime prevention, whether via preventive patrolling, resolving neighbour disputes, advising on building security or supporting interventions with young people at risk of offending. Other contributions that the police make to civil crime prevention, whether acting alone or with other agencies and individuals are through:

- the capture, maintenance and supply of crime data;
- their knowledge and expertise about local crime patterns;
- their awareness of local crime attractors, generators and risky facilities;
- their intelligence on local offenders;
- their expertise in crime and its prevention;
- acting as a channel of referral to third parties;
- their presence and authority to influence third parties (inherent legitimacy).

All of these qualities and skills underpin the success of repeat victimisation, one of the most successful crime prevention targeting strategies. For example, the particular variant of repeat victimisation known as 'Once Bitten' (Farrell and Pease, 1993) developed an explicit strategy of moving from *universal* situational prevention for all potential burglary victims, to *selective* additional situational prevention for those already victimised once, to *enforcement* by catching offenders by setting up surveillance and installing alarms for the few multiply-victimised homes. One might wish to consider whether interventions targeting repeat victims would have been feasible without *any* of the above-mentioned contributions by the police.

A more critical review of the preventive role of policing and that of other agencies and institutions comes from Hallsworth and Lea (2011). They take a perspective which sees a marked shift from the welfare state to the 'security state', controlling not just terrorism but risks of all kinds including from sub-populations marginalised by economic pressures and the global movement of business investment. From this viewpoint the coercive powers of criminal justice agencies are progressively being extended, in the service of boosting a flagging degree of community cohesion, to cover pre-crime and post-punishment phases – respectively, for example, the institution of ASBOs and the prolonged incapacitation of sex offenders on release from prison. Such 'pre-emptive criminalisation' (Fitzgibbon, 2004) can be classed as judicial crime prevention in the schema proposed above. However, from the critical perspective taken here we might debate the extent to which the interventions are 'ethically acceptable' as per the definition of prevention given above. The central (albeit not exclusive) role of the police in such coercive forcing of cohesion is certainly a topic for discussion. But one presumes the issue is the extent and nature of their involvement rather than the principle of pre-emption – it would be hard to envisage a society that got by without our long-standing anti-conspiracy laws, or 'going equipped' offences, for example.

Crime prevention design advice

Advice on CPTED in England and Wales is delivered on the ground by specialist police officers and civilians who have, until recently, worked within a broad regulatory and policy framework. Although some are called Architectural Liaison Officers (ALOs) and others Crime Prevention Design Advisers (CPDAs) their role is essentially the same. It involves liaising with planning officers, architects and developers to embed CPTED principles in design and developments, training activities and promoting the Secured by Design (SBD) award scheme. Historically, there has been at least one individual in each of the 43 police forces responsible for reviewing planning applications and offering CPTED advice.

Recognition of the role that planning and design can have in the reduction of crime has grown following the 1998 Crime and Disorder Act and this has been reflected in planning policy and guidance within England and Wales. Prior to 1998, the only policy which referred to crime prevention within the planning system was the 11-page circular 5/94 – Planning out Crime. This offered little in the way of guidance, other than highlighting the importance of consultation with police ALOs.

The publication of the Urban Policy White Paper – *Our Towns and Cities: The Future* (ODPM, 2000) emphasised the importance of crime, disorder and the fear of crime within urban renewal, development and the planning system. This communicated a clear message, namely, that 'good design of buildings and the way buildings and public spaces are laid out can help prevent crime' (ODPM, 2000), and that 'properly designed developments can also discourage crime' (ODPM, 2000). Crucially, the White Paper also included the recommendation to review and update circular 5/94, and in 2004 the joint ODPM/Home Office guidance *Safer Places – The Planning System and Crime Prevention* (ODPM/Home Office, 2004) was published.

Other guidance and legislation followed. The 2004 Planning and Compulsory Purchase Act required local authorities to produce Development Plans. Many local authorities declared, in their general statements contained within their Development Plans, that planning decisions should take crime prevention into account and reinforced these statements of intent with Supplementary Planning Guidance focusing solely on crime prevention. Additionally, Design and Access Statements, also brought in under the 2004 Act and submitted as part of the planning application process, had to demonstrate how crime prevention would be addressed in proposed developments.

Two further policy instruments, Planning Policy Statement (PPS) 1 on Sustainable Development and PPS3 on Housing were published in 2005 and 2006, respectively. PPS1, although not specific to crime prevention, emphasised the importance of crime prevention in good and sustainable design. It highlighted how 'poor planning can result in a legacy for current and future generations of run-down town centres, unsafe and dilapidated housing, crime and disorder, and the loss of our finest countryside to development' (DCLG, 2005, p. 2). It also stated that 'planning authorities should prepare robust policies on design and access . . . Key objectives should include ensuring that developments create safe and accessible environments where crime and disorder or fear of crime does not undermine quality of life or community cohesion' (DCLG, 2005, p. 15). PPS3, which was specific to housing, also emphasised that safety should be considered when assessing the design quality of property developments (DCLG, 2011).

In 2007, building codes and design standards were introduced that offered incentives to developers to embed security into their designs. The 2007 Code for Sustainable Homes awarded credits to developments that met certain sustainability criteria. Security was one of these (cf. Armitage and Monchuk, 2009) and credits were awarded for consulting with ALOs and for complying with the physical security element of the SBD Scheme. In the same year, the then Housing Corporation introduced various Design and Quality Standards one of which was the requirement for housing to be secure (Armitage et al., 2012).

By the end of the 2000s, there was a raft of guidance and legislation in place to facilitate the incorporation of CPTED principles into urban design and development. At around this time, a review of the ALO/CPDA service across England and Wales (Wootton et al., 2009) counted 347 ALO/CPDAs in post in England and Wales in January 2009 and showed that by August 2009, only 21 per cent of all police forces in England and Wales had two or fewer ALO/CPDAs in post – every force had at least one ALO. However, an update of this review in August 2011 revealed that the number of ALOs had fallen to 236, and although each police force still had at least one ALO, 31 per cent of forces (as opposed to 21 per cent) had two or fewer ALOs in post.

While it is clear that the period of 1998–2011 saw some major improvements in the consideration for crime prevention within planning policy, reforms introduced in 2011 have brought substantive changes. The Localism Act (2011) has introduced major alterations to the planning system within England. It has abolished regional planning in favour of neighbourhood planning and introduced Neighbourhood Development Plans and Neighbourhood Development Orders. The former allow communities to come together through a local parish council or neighbourhood forum to produce a plan which sets out policies in relation to the development and use of land within their neighbourhood. Although there could be many benefits to allowing those who live within a community (and know the local issues and concerns) to make decisions regarding planning and development, there are also risks, particularly where a lack of resources (ALO/CPDA cuts) and lack of guidance/policy (removal of Planning Policy Statements) restrict that community's ability to make evidence-based decisions.

In addition to the introduction of Neighbourhood Development Plans and Orders, the move from regional towards neighbourhood planning, and the associated emphasis upon deregulation, has also seen the replacement of 44 documents including PPS1 *Delivering Sustainable Development* and PPS3, *Housing*, by a solitary 59-page National Planning Policy Framework (DCLG, 2012). Besides replacing key Planning Policy Statements, the National Planning Policy Framework discourages the production of Supplementary Planning Documents, such as those that had a specific focus on crime prevention. Hence:

> Any additional development plan documents should only be used where clearly justified. Supplementary planning documents should be used where they can help applicants make successful applications or aid infrastructure delivery, and should not be used to add unnecessarily to the financial burdens on development.
>
> (DCLG, 2012, p. 37)

Importantly, the National Planning Policy Framework has retained some key references to the importance of considering crime prevention within planning and development and, crucially, these references refer to the consideration of crime prevention within the production of Local and Neighbourhood Plans: 'Planning policies and decisions should aim to ensure that developments . . . create safe and accessible environments where crime and disorder, and the fear of crime, do not undermine quality of life or community cohesion' (DCLG, 2012, p. 15).

There are two main problems with the current system – a lack of ALO/CPDAs to deliver an effective service on the ground, and also deregulation within the planning system. On the former, we have fallen back from a position where each police force had a senior Force ALO/CPDA and several ALO/CPDAs, each working closely with their respective local authority to offer CPTED advice (a reactive service) but also to influence local planning policy to enhance the consideration for security within design and development (a proactive service). Many police forces/local authorities had Supplementary Planning Guidance specific to crime prevention, and for those which did not, crime prevention was largely referred to as a recommended consideration within Development Plans. The cuts to police budgets have resulted in vast reductions in ALO/CPDA numbers meaning that many forces no longer have a Force ALO/CPDA to lead on strategic/policy issues, and there have been several police forces where ACPO CPI have had to intervene to avoid the loss of the one remaining ALO/CPDA. Not only does this mean that, for many forces, no major planning applications can be assessed, more crucially in the long term, it also means that ALO/CPDAs are reluctant to push for consideration for security within local planning policy because, should this occur, they would be unable to deliver the service. Historically, one of the main policy aims of ALO/CPDAs was to become statutory consultees. Yet, should this take place, the current cuts in services would mean that this would be impossible to deliver.

The second concern relates to the deregulation within the planning system, whereby neighbourhood planning has placed decision making in the hands of communities to decide where and what development should take place. Given the removal of national Planning Policy Statements and local Supplementary Planning Guidance, as well as the cuts in ALO/CPDA numbers, what resources will be available to these communities/neighbourhood forums to assist in making evidence-based decisions regarding the risks or benefits of proposed development within their area?

Throughout the budget cuts, one police force in England has managed not only to avoid cuts to ALO numbers, but also to develop and grow as a crime prevention service. Greater Manchester Police's (GMP) approach to delivering the ALO/CPDA role involves a team of consultants and one dedicated crime analyst under the title of *Greater Manchester Design for Security Consultancy* (GMP DfSC). Although the team is based within GMP Police Headquarters, has access to police recorded crime data, Neighbourhood Policing Teams (NPTs) and other relevant police intelligence, the DfSC consultants are civilian staff with a background in a built environment profession such as design, architecture or planning. While the (entirely) civilian background is unique to GMP, it is by no means the only difference in their approach. The second major variation is the emphasis placed upon pre-planning consultation between the developer and DfSC. Greater Manchester includes ten local planning authorities. Where a client wishes to apply for planning permission, the application which is made to the local planning authority must adhere to national planning policy, but also to the requirements of each local authority's Validation Checklist. The latter requires that the submission of a major planning application be accompanied by a Crime Impact Statement (CIS). The CIS contains an analysis of local crime figures, offender *modi operandi*, observations from site visits and specific recommendations by the consultant. While the local planning authorities inform clients that the CIS can be compiled by DfSC, there is no stipulation that it is they who *must* produce the report. However, given the content of a CIS, which relies upon police recorded crime data, knowledge of common offender *modi operandi* and local police intelligence, it is difficult to see how this could be delivered (to the required standard) by any other agency.

The final, unique, element to the delivery of the ALO role within GMP, and one that has proved able to protect the provision of this service within the current economic climate is that, although a not-for-profit organisation, DfSC does charge a fee for the production of a CIS. The fee is based upon the number of dwellings within the proposed development, and although this is a small proportion of the developer's costs, it provides DfSC with an income stream to support the retention of staff, a dedicated crime analyst, the provision of equipment and software besides Continuing Professional Development (CPD) and training opportunities.

Crime prevention knowledge management and dissemination

The need for managing knowledge of crime prevention and using this knowledge to design interventions and feed into training and on-the-job guidance is recognised internationally. This recognition accords a central role to evidence-based practice and policy (Sherman *et al.*, 2002; Pawson, 2006). That approach privileges knowledge obtained through rigorous research and evaluation of impact or cost-effectiveness, where possible assembled through the equally rigorous process of systematic reviews such as are conducted through the Campbell Collaboration[1] (Farrington and Petrosino, 2001). However, the knowledge required to help practitioners, delivery managers and policymakers *select* appropriate practices, programmes and policies from the record of prior art, *replicate* it intelligently customised to new contexts; and where evaluated knowledge does not exist (a commonplace occurrence), *innovate* based on first principles based on tested theory, is far wider than impact and cost-effectiveness alone (Ekblom, 2011: 265–6). The United Nations' (United Nations, 2006: 298–9) compendium of standards and norms in crime prevention and criminal justice, recommends that governments and/or civil society facilitate knowledge-based crime prevention by, among other things:

- supporting the generation of useful and practically applicable knowledge that is scientifically reliable and valid;
- supporting the organisation and synthesis of knowledge and identifying and addressing gaps in the knowledge base;
- sharing that knowledge, as appropriate, among researchers, policymakers, educators, practitioners from other relevant sectors and the wider community; and
- applying this knowledge in replicating successful interventions, developing new initiatives and anticipating new crime problems and prevention opportunities.

Various Home Office research and/or administrator-led efforts to capture, organise and disseminate practice knowledge have come and gone sporadically over the last decade or so. A good example is the development, around 2000, of the Crime Reduction Toolkits for guiding the on-the-job work of the (then) Crime and Disorder Reduction Partnerships. Although these were produced with some haste and lack of consistency, many were quite rich in content and drew on a combination of evidence and experience. Unfortunately, the maintenance of these only outlasted the 2005 demise of the HOCRC by a couple of years, and now they are embalmed in the National Archive following an across-the-board decision, by the Coalition Government, to freeze all prior government websites.

During the National Crime Reduction Programme (1998–2002) ad-hoc *practice guides* were also produced based on commissioned process and impact evaluations of interventions and covered not only what works and what does not, but also factors shown to be critical to successful implementation. Unfortunately, the Home Office Research and Statistics Directorate, manifesting what can only be described as vacillation between dedicating effort to supporting knowledge needs of policymakers and of the practitioners who delivered that policy, was unable to foster any continuity of these on closure of the programme and the 'Development and Practice Reports' series petered out in 2007 after some 40 volumes.

Maguire (2004) documents the failure to capitalise on what was originally planned to be a major opportunity to apply, create and assemble knowledge of what works in favour of a rush to get crime numbers down, and argues for the slow and steady accumulation of evidence rather than this failed 'big bang' approach. The long-running Police Research Series finished at number 155 in 2002.[2] The 2005 IPAK Initiative ('Improving Performance through Acquired Knowledge') appeared with ambitious aims of assembling examples of effective practice; knowledge about crime and crime types; and tacit knowledge/'know-how' of practice. A pilot evidence base on burglary was published but the initiative lapsed in 2007.[3] The street crime 'crisis' of 2003–4 engendered an ad-hoc assembly of preventive initiatives whose practice knowledge was systematically captured (Tilley *et al.*, 2004) while, ironically, draining resources from other preventive knowledge capture and application initiatives such as that on design of products against crime (Ekblom, 2012).

Much of the above remains available; while the original sources are now quite difficult to locate in the National Archive, the National Police Library[4] maintains a good collection for the police service.

Other sources of preventive knowledge have been more steadily developed and maintained, principally the peer- and academic-reviewed US POP (Problem-Oriented Policing) Center guides,[5] covering problems (e.g. theft of scrap metal), responses (e.g. sting operations) and problem-solving tools (e.g. using offender interviews), built up over some 11 years and, despite funding concerns, still going strong. While funded for and primarily oriented towards a US police practitioner audience, the guides draw on international experience including UK research and evaluation; indeed in some cases the authors have been British (e.g. Johnson *et al.*, 2008); and they are a useful resource for UK practitioners in all cases. Systematic Reviews under the international Campbell Collaboration[6] have also covered, for example, CCTV (Welsh and Farrington, 2008) and 'hot spot' policing (Braga *et al.*, 2012).

There is much evidence of implementation failure, whether of local civil crime prevention schemes (Hough, 2006) or within major national programmes, such as the US Community Crime Prevention Program of the 1980s (Rosenbaum, 1986), the UK Safer Cities Programme 1988–93 (Tilley, 1993; Sutton, 1996) or the UK National Crime Reduction Programme (Ekblom, 2002; Hirschfield, 2004; Bowers and Johnson, 2006; Homel, 2006). It is vital to document, explain and address such failure, not least in order to maximise the chances that the advice on police-related crime prevention emerging from the Stevens Commission successfully and durably influences practice and programme delivery rather than falling into the same traps. Implementation failure has variously been attributed to prosaic factors such as poor project management or centralised funding constraints, or organisational ones such as a police subculture and career/reward structure hostile to civil prevention, and deficient training. These might well be important but it has been argued (Ekblom, 2011: chapters 2–4) that underlying much poor performance and limitation of scope of civil crime prevention practice has been inadequacy in the management (including transfer) of knowledge. In particular, failure to know what works through evidence-based approaches drawing, in particular, on systematic reviews, and failure to share that knowledge nationally and internationally; failure to implement what we know to work, by matching 'what-works principles' to specific local problems and contexts (Pawson and Tilley, 1997; Ekblom, 2011); and failure to anticipate, innovate and adapt to emerging challenges from adaptive offenders exploiting social and technological changes. The latter may involve new forms of antisocial behaviour, new ways of stealing cars, new forms of criminal organisation or new techniques of terrorism (e.g. Ekblom, 1997; Pease, 2003; Ekblom and Pease, in press).

The police subculture and organisational ethos have rarely encouraged positive learning from mistakes and failures and such salutary lessons are rarely sought out, disseminated or acted on. More generally, the detailed study by Bullock *et al.* (2006) of UK entries to the Tilley Award for POP projects showed no trend of improvement in quality of entries over the period 1999–2005, a time of both intensive and extensive effort in communicating, implementing and funding POP principles. This shows, fairly conclusively, that knowledge is necessary but not sufficient in improving performance.

One approach that could be used in conjunction with hard 'what-works' reviews, is the 5Is framework[7] (Ekblom, 2011). This strives to capture and organise detailed information to enable intelligent, problem- and context-based replication and innovation rather than superficial 'cookbook-type' copying. However, it so far lacks institutional adoption (Sidebottom and Tilley, 2011), arguably because of an absence of 'official' support enabling investment in key practical infrastructure, e.g. in terms of an interactive tutorial, toolkit and knowledge bank. It should, though, be noted that despite decades of effort the more conventional model for POP, SARA (Scanning, Analysis, Response, Assessment) continues to face difficulties of adoption (Bullock *et al.*, 2006; Scott, 2006; Goldstein, 2003).

In early 2011, the National Policing Improvement Agency published a highly ambitious and wide-ranging Police Knowledge Action Plan based on wide consultation and sophisticated thinking which sought to integrate previous efforts (e.g. the POLKA knowledge bank) and establish a complete system for creating, sharing and using knowledge across the police service, addressing issues ranging from the cultural and organisational to the technical. However, uncertainties exist given the current winding up of the National Police Improvement Agency (NPIA) and replacement by the College of Policing, a 'professional body to increase professionalism in policing'. Whether the ambition remains, and whether it is adequately executed, resourced and maintained, or whether yet another initiative falls by the wayside, is a question whose answer should be of interest to all in the crime prevention world. Certainly the requirement for the knowledge function to be fully supported officially in one or other form is beyond all dispute; and the College of Policing, almost by definition, seems the right place to locate it.[8] However, that leaves unresolved the extent to which crime prevention knowledge is as valid for, and valuable to, a wider range of institutions than the police alone. On the one hand, we should ask how far the policing institution should keep the most developed knowledge of policing activity to itself, given that this activity is undertaken by many other institutions and informal interventions in society; and on the other, whether civil crime prevention knowledge in particular should be organised and supported in its own terms rather than tied to one, albeit dominant, institution.

Whatever the case, how crime prevention knowledge is managed has to adapt to wider changes than government-instigated 'institutional churn'. Relevant considerations include:

- Increased professionalism in a context of frequent staff moves which requires rapid and efficient transfer of expert knowledge (of the 'get smart quick' kind) rather than reliance on individuals building up that knowledge over a long-term career; and then that knowledge being placed in jeopardy when, as now, those experts are required to retire in cost-cutting exercises (as appears to have happened with police ALOs).

- The drive towards 'localism' which requires that professionalism is capable of adapting to local problems, contexts and priorities – in fact, this resonates with the message from research on the kind of approach to prevention that is most effective. How the knowledge of crime prevention will intersect with the heightened political dimension of local policing introduced by the advent of Police and Crime Commissioners (PCCs) is unknown territory – but these individuals, recently in post following the November 2012 elections, will require a good-quality and accessible knowledge bank for their own purposes. The Local Government Association has begun to develop such a bank at the time of writing.[9] It is a moot point whether a more specific and officially sanctioned knowledge bank (of the sort that, say, the Ministry of Justice prepares for Judges and Magistrates) is feasible or appropriate in this more political context; and whether policy/political issues surrounding prevention (such as fairness in distributing resources, or how to navigate the tricky waters between a criminal responsibility perspective and one of dispassionate causal analysis in support of 'rational' prevention) can be drawn out in a non-partisan way. The significant number of independent PCCs now in post (some 30 per cent) lacking a party briefing may indicate that some such support would be beneficial.

Although the crime prevention knowledge bank built up in the UK up to around 2007 remains available, albeit not always easily retrievable, what we have is essentially a 'wasting asset' as the material becomes rapidly out of date due to changes in police practice, organisation and operating environment (including in the law and in police powers); societal and technological change; and adaptations and innovations by offenders (Ekblom, 2005). This is not the best position to be in when there are growing expectations to deliver good practice in local settings (e.g. Neighbourhood Plans) against a background of diminishing back-office support and reductions in the number of police officers in the crime prevention arena.

Crime prevention training: past, present and future?

Crime prevention training in England and Wales has been subject to continual change, usually as a response to fluctuating perceptions held by politicians, police and public alike, of its level of priority in relation to other aspects of police work and training needs. It is not our intention to discuss these changes in depth here but, rather, to focus on the views and perceptions of a diverse group of police officers and police trainers from a police service in the North of England who were interviewed specifically for this chapter.

Crime prevention training for police has been a journey that started with the creation of the Home Office Crime Prevention College in 1964, through the centralised provision to police officers and members of the Crime and Disorder Reduction Partnerships (CDRPs) of the 1990s and early 2000s, to the idiosyncratic and eclectic mix of individual service level provision that we see today.

By the mid-1990s, the Home Office Crime Prevention College was providing a range of residential courses for police Crime Prevention Officers (CPOs), including the intensive two-week 'Standard Crime Prevention Course' and 'Architectural Liaison Officer' (ALO) courses. Demand remained high and waiting lists long, due primarily to the reputation of the courses and the fact that they were financed by the Home Office, so provided to police without charge.[10]

Following the 1998 Crime and Disorder Act, courses were provided not just for police, but also for their local CDRPs. Alongside formal training, the re-named Home Office Crime Reduction Centre (HOCRC) organised regular crime reduction conferences for practitioners and housed and maintained the Crime Reduction Website with its range of 'toolkits'.

By July 2004, the decision was made to stop providing the free Standard Crime Prevention Course and ALO courses and a year later, in an effort to save money, the HOCRC was closed. Responsibility for training police CPOs was shifted to *Centrex*, the National Police Training School. In 2007, Centrex itself was absorbed into the NPIA which took responsibility for most police training including crime prevention. Training provision is now subject to further change with the demise of the NPIA as part of the Coalition Government's reforms and reduced budgets announced in the 2010 Comprehensive Spending Review (CSR).

A recurrent theme from our interviews with police officers and police trainers was that the police budget cuts, announced in the 2010 CSR, had been a *major* factor in the general deprioritisation of crime prevention training, in favour of what were perceived to be more pressing 'frontline priorities' (i.e. detecting criminals rather than preventing crime). This shift was compounded by the fact that no targets for crime prevention were set in the 2010 CSR, which understandably led police service leaders to conclude that crime prevention was simply not a priority for them.

This deprioritisation of crime prevention has had an obvious 'knock-on effect' on those on the ground. Those trainers we interviewed said that the demand for crime prevention training at present was 'pretty non-existent' mainly because police managers (e.g. operational sergeants) did not see it as a priority. Consequently, they were less likely to sanction requests for training in this area, even if it was identified by their officers. Although we only interviewed trainers from a single force in the North of England, they were of the opinion that this situation applied more generally.

Outside of police service provision, crime prevention training is offered by some higher education establishments, and at a number of different academic levels, ranging from one-day courses focusing on CPD to Masters degrees (e.g. the Masters in Crime Science offered by the Jill Dando Institute of Crime Science at University College London).[11] Other universities offering criminology and crime science degrees with a strong practitioner emphasis include: Universities of the

West of England, Glasgow, Leicester De Montfort, Huddersfield, Northumbria, and the Open University. Although none of the officers and trainers we interviewed doubted the calibre of university-run crime prevention-focused courses, they did highlight practical considerations which often made them inaccessible to police officers: namely, their cost and the time an officer would need to be abstracted from frontline duties in order to attend and complete such courses.

In a recap of where crime prevention police training is now, we must not blame its apparent deprioritisation simply on the CSR of 2010. Crime prevention training began to decline after it ceased to be provided free of charge by central agencies such as the HOCRC and is best summed-up now as being both eclectic and idiosyncratic according to individual police service priorities and ethos. For example, the police trainers and officers we interviewed believed that the problem-solving element of crime prevention training was probably ingrained in their force because it was championed by the Deputy Chief Constable.

We arrive at two fundamental questions. Is there still a need for police crime prevention training? And if so, where and how should it be provided? One recurrent suggestion raised by the police trainers and officers we interviewed was that the term crime prevention was antiquated and pejorative in the sense that most officers considered it to be simply about locks, bolts and other techniques for 'target hardening'. Historically, the role of CPO was seen by many police officers to be the last role before retirement forever associated with giving crime prevention advice to home owners or organising Neighbourhood Watch areas. It appears that, for some, the term crime prevention is still inextricably linked with this perception. When asked if crime prevention training is needed, most officers will, therefore, answer 'no'. Many have changed their position to Crime Reduction Officers (a post itself now quite scarce in most police services) in an attempt to distance themselves from the past. One CRO we talked with suggested that the demise of the original crime prevention certificate meant that the role no longer had currency as there was no tangible evidence that they had been trained to do the role.

The point being made is that by framing questions about training need in terms of crime prevention, one is not likely to get a true reflection of levels of training need due to a pejorative interpretation of the term. We suggest that if trying to determine knowledge and training needs from police, the term 'crime reduction' be used instead, or the activity framed within a broader problem-solving context. Even though all our interviewees considered crime prevention knowledge to be vital in modern policing, only one stated that a central training agency (such as the HOCRC) should exist once again. All, however, considered the loss of the Crime Reduction Website, with its facility for sharing prevention ideas and practice, to be a far greater blow and all called for a similar facility to be available to all police and practitioners as soon as possible.[12] All of our interviewees emphasised the importance of the problem-solving element of crime prevention training (e.g. SARA) They considered this to be a vital aspect of all police training, and at all levels, not just for new recruits.

Conclusion

We strongly believe that the police should continue to play a key role in crime prevention but the sustainability of this is dependent on the core activities of preserving, building upon, disseminating and utilising the evidence base on effective practice in crime prevention. The three areas we have highlighted (designing out crime, knowledge management/transfer and crime prevention training) are all examples of where the continuity of these core activities may be seriously at risk. To address these concerns, we believe that careful consideration be given to the following.

Crime prevention design advice

- The role of providing crime prevention design advice (both anticipatory and remedial) is beneficial and must be maintained.
- Each police force should have at least one senior Force ALO to provide strategic input into local authorities and to ensure that crime prevention advice has a sufficiently high profile locally and nationally.
- There needs to be a sufficient number of crime prevention advisers on the ground to support local communities in knowing how to design out crime to comply with the spirit of the Localism Act 2011 that crime prevention be regarded as an 'important consideration' in Neighbourhood Plans. Therefore, priority should be given to a sustainable funding model for the crime prevention design advice service (ground staff).

In 2009, Armitage and Monchuk conducted a piece of research for ACPO, DCLG and the Home Office to investigate the feasibility of setting up a National Police Crime Prevention Service. This included an online survey of all ALOs and focus-groups with every police force in England and Wales. The results revealed large discrepancies in provision, management, training and delivery, and the report concluded that a National Police Crime Prevention Service would promote consistency and improve delivery. Unfortunately, this report coincided with the CSR and the recommendations have never been acted upon. Whether or not this can be revisited in the fiscal climate remains to be seen.

Crime prevention knowledge management and transfer

- High-performance policing in crime prevention needs a knowledge management plan that is thorough and adhered to consistently in the long term. However, evidence of past initiatives has shown failure to maintain any continuity and consistency of effort in the knowledge management area (e.g. toolkits).
- The Police Knowledge Action Plan of 2011[13] has the potential to offer this but there are serious questions about what will happen in the light of both history and the current context of financial cuts, abolition of the NPIA and transfer of responsibilities to the College of Policing.

Police crime prevention training

- The new College of Policing should recognise the importance of crime prevention training and give it a sufficiently high priority. The emphasis here is on assigning a high profile to crime prevention. Such training need not necessarily be provided at a central facility or at zero cost to the end user.
- The College needs to provide a repository of knowledge about effective crime prevention, and lessons learned from what does not work.

We have set out what we see as future priorities in the three areas that we have examined. In an age of austerity, where resources for policing are under severe pressure, reducing the demands on the police by preventing crime happening in the first place is more important than ever. To do so successfully, decisions about policy interventions and the targeting of scarce resources need to be informed by sound evidence, not only of what measures are most likely to be effective under different conditions, but also on how best to implement them.

Notes

1 www.campbellcollaboration.org
2 http://webarchive.nationalarchives.gov.uk/20110218135832/rds.homeoffice.gov.uk/rds/prgpdfs/prs155bn.pdf
3 http://webarchive.nationalarchives.gov.uk/20100413151441/http:/www.crimereduction.homeoffice.gov.uk/ipak/ipak01.htm
4 http://library.college.police.uk
5 www.popcenter.org
6 http://www.campbellcollaboration.org/crime_and_justice/index.php
7 http://5isframework.wordpress.com
8 Since this was written the College has become host to the What Works Centre for Crime Reduction, under a Cabinet Office initiative.
9 www.local.gov.uk/pcc/
10 We should acknowledge at this point that one of us worked as a trainer at the HOCRC from 2003 to its closure in 2005.
11 http://www.ucl.ac.uk/jdi/
12 The NPIA has recently developed a knowledge database (POLKA) for police personnel to access and exchange crime knowledge and practice, but this is exclusive to police, so does not permit any exchange with other non-police crime reduction practitioners.
13 http://www.college.police.uk/en/17092.htm

References

Armitage, R. and Monchuk, L. (2009) 'Reconciling security with sustainability: the challenge for eco-homes', *Built Environment*, 35(3): 308–327.
Armitage, R., Rogerson, M. and Pease, K. (2012) 'What is good about good design? Exploring the link between housing quality and crime', *Built Environment*, 39(1): 140–161.
Bowers, K. and Johnson, S. (2006) 'Implementation Failure and Success: Some Lessons from England', in J. Knutsson and R. Clarke (eds) *Putting Theory to Work: Implementing Situational Prevention and Problem-Oriented Policing*. Crime Prevention Studies, 20. Monsey, NY: Criminal Justice Press.

Braga, A., Papachristos, A. and Hureau, D. (2012) 'Hot spots policing effects on crime'. *Campbell Systematic Reviews* 2012: 8. Oslo: Campbell Collaboration.

Bullock, K., Erol, R. and Tilley, N. (2006) *Problem-Oriented Policing and Partnerships: Implementing an Evidence-Based Approach to Crime Reduction.* Cullompton: Willan.

Department for Communities and Local Government (2005) *Planning Policy Statement 1: Delivering Sustainable Development.* Available at: http://www.communities.gov.uk/publications/planningandbuilding/planningpolicystatement1. Accessed 21 March 2012.

Department for Communities and Local Government (2011) *Planning Policy Statement 3: Housing.* Available at: http://www.communities.gov.uk/publications/planningandbuilding/pps3housing. Accessed 21 March 2012.

Department for Communities and Local Government (2012) *National Planning Policy Framework.* Available at: http://www.communities.gov.uk/documents/planningandbuilding/pdf/2116950.pdf. Accessed 29 March 2012.

Ekblom, P. (1997) 'Gearing up against crime: a dynamic framework to help designers keep up with the adaptive criminal in a changing world', *International Journal of Risk, Security and Crime Prevention*, 2(4): 249–265.

Ekblom, P. (2002) 'From the Source to the Mainstream is Uphill: The Challenge of Transferring Knowledge of Crime Prevention through Replication, Innovation and Anticipation', in N. Tilley (ed.) *Analysis for Crime Prevention.* Crime Prevention Studies, 13. Monsey, NY: Criminal Justice Press.

Ekblom, P. (2005) 'How to Police the Future: Scanning for Scientific and Technological Innovations which Generate Potential Threats and Opportunities in Crime, Policing and Crime Reduction', in M. Smith and N. Tilley (eds) *Crime Science: New Approaches to Preventing and Detecting Crime.* Cullompton: Willan.

Ekblom, P. (2011) *Crime Prevention, Security and Community Safety Using the 5Is Framework.* Basingstoke: Palgrave Macmillan.

Ekblom, P. (2012) 'Introduction', in P. Ekblom (ed.) *Design Against Crime: Crime Proofing Everyday Objects.* Crime Prevention Studies, 27. Boulder, CO: Lynne Rienner.

Ekblom, P. and Pease, K. (in press). *Innovation and Crime Prevention. Encyclopedia of Criminology and Criminal Justice.* New York: Springer.

Farrell, G. and Pease, K. (1993) *Once Bitten, Twice Bitten: Repeat Victimisation and its Implications for Crime Prevention.* Police Research Group Crime Prevention Unit Series Paper 46. London: Home Office.

Farrington, D. and Petrosino, A. (2001) 'Systematic reviews and cost benefit analyses of correctional interventions', *The Prison Journal*, 81(3): 339–359.

Fitzgibbon, D. (2004) *Pre-emptive Criminalisation: Risk Control and Alternative Futures.* London: NAPO.

Goldstein, H. (1990) *Problem-Oriented Policing.* New York, NY: McGraw-Hill.

Goldstein, H. (2003) 'On Further Developing Problem-Oriented Policing: The Most Critical Need, the Major Impediments, and a Proposal', in J. Knutsson (ed.) *Mainstreaming Problem-Oriented Policing.* Crime Prevention Studies, 15. Monsey, NY: Criminal Justice Press.

Hallsworth, S. and Lea, J. (2011) 'Reconstructing Leviathan: emerging contours of the security state', *Theoretical Criminology*, 15: 141–157.

Hirschfield, A. (2004) *The Impact of the Reducing Burglary Initiative in the North of England.* Home Office Online Report 40/04, London: Home Office.

Homel, P. (2006) 'Joining Up the Pieces: What Central Agencies Need to Do to Support Effective Local Crime Prevention', in J. Knutsson and R. Clarke (eds) *Putting Theory to Work: Implementing Situational Prevention and Problem-Oriented Policing.* Crime Prevention Studies, 20. Monsey, NY: Criminal Justice Press.

Hough, M. (2006) 'Not Seeing the Wood for the Trees: Mistaking Tactics for Strategy in Crime Reduction Initiatives', in J. Knutsson and R. Clarke (eds) *Putting Theory to Work: Implementing Situational Prevention and Problem-Oriented Policing.* Crime Prevention Studies, 20. Monsey, NY: Criminal Justice Press.

Johnson, S., Sidebottom, A. and Thorpe, A. (2008) *Bicycle Theft.* Problem-Oriented Guides for Police. Problem-Specific Guides Series, No. 52. Washington: US Department of Justice.

Maguire, M. (2004) 'The Crime Reduction Programme in England and Wales. Reflections on the vision and the reality', *Criminology and Criminal Justice*, 4(3): 213–237.

National Criminal Intelligence Service (2000) *The National Intelligence Model.* London: National Criminal Intelligence Service.

Office of the Deputy Prime Minister (2000) *Our Towns and Cities: The Future – Delivering an Urban Renaissance.* London: ODPM.

Office of the Deputy Prime Minister and Home Office (2004) *Safer Places – The Planning System and Crime Prevention*, London: HMSO.

Pawson, R. (2006) *Evidence-Based Policy. A Realist Perspective.* London: Sage.

Pawson, R. and Tilley, N. (1997) *Realistic Evaluation.* London: Sage.

Pease, K. (2003) *Cracking Crime through Design.* London: Design Council.

Rosenbaum, D. (ed.) (1986) *Community Crime Prevention: Does It Work?* London: Sage.

Scott, M. (2006) 'Implementing Crime Prevention: Lessons Learned from Problem-Oriented Policing Projects', in J. Knutsson and R. Clarke (eds) *Putting Theory to Work: Implementing Situational Prevention and Problem-Oriented Policing.* Crime Prevention Studies, 20. Monsey, NY: Criminal Justice Press.

Sherman, L., Farrington, D., Welsh, B. and MacKenzie, D. (eds) (2002) *Evidence-based Crime Prevention.* London: Routledge.

Sidebottom, A. and Tilley, N. (2011) 'Improving Problem-Oriented Policing: The need for a new model?' *Crime Prevention and Community Safety*, 13: 79–101.

Sutton, M. (1996) *Implementing Crime Prevention Schemes in a Multi-Agency Setting: Aspects of Process in the Safer Cities Programme.* Home Office Research Study 160. London: Home Office.

Tilley, N. (1993) *After Kirkholt: Theory, Methods and Results of Replication Evaluations.* Crime Prevention Unit Paper No. 47. London: Home Office.

Tilley, N., Smith, J., Finer, S., Erol, R., Charles, C. and Dobby, J. (2004) *Problem-solving street crime: practical lessons from the Street Crime Initiative.* RDS Practitioners Guides. London: Home Office. Available at: http://webarchive.nationalarchives.gov.uk/20110218135832/rds.homeoffice.gov.uk/rds/pdfs04/pssc.pdf.

United Nations (2006) *Compendium of United Nations Standards and Norms in Crime Prevention and Criminal Justice.* New York: United Nations. www.unodc.org/pdf/compendium/compendium_2006.pdf.

Welsh, B. and Farrington, D. (2008) 'Effects of closed circuit television surveillance on crime'. *Campbell Systematic Reviews*, 2008: 17. Oslo: Campbell Collaboration.

Wootton, A., Marselle, M., Davey, C., Armitage, R. and Monchuk, L. (2009) *NPCPS: Implementation Planning Research Project.* Salford: Design Against Crime Solution Centre, Salford University.

20

HATE CRIME

Paul Johnson

Introduction

The concept of 'hate crime' has gained widespread acceptance in the criminal justice systems of the United Kingdom. Hate crime is an umbrella term that is used to capture a range of 'bias-motivated' crimes directed at individuals or groups because of their actual, or perceived, characteristics. Although hate crime is a recently conceived concept (Newburn and Matassa, 2002), it has rapidly become a significant aspect of both criminal justice vocabulary and practice. This is because, as Jenness and Grattet argue, the 'seemingly simple pairing of words – "hate" and "crime" – creates a signifier that conveys an enormous sense of threat and an attendant demand for response' (2004: 2). The growth in perception of the threat of hate crime in the UK and the demand to address it has resulted in a number of Government initiatives, the most ambitious of which is the *Challenge it, Report it, Stop it* plan announced in March 2012 (H.M. Government, 2012). This coordinated strategy, involving a wide range of criminal justice practitioners, outlines an ambitious scheme to tackle this 'particularly corrosive' form of crime (H.M. Government, 2012: 3).

Policing is often argued to be a vital element in the broader criminal justice response to hate crime in many jurisdictions around the world. For instance, the International Association of Chiefs of Police (2012) has stated that:

> Police officers and investigators have important roles to play in responding to hate incidents and crimes. By doing the job efficiently and carefully, police can reinforce the message that hate crimes will be investigated aggressively, thus enhancing the likelihood of a successful prosecution.

The claim that effective policing will 'reinforce the message' about a society's intolerance of hate crime is also bound up with the notion that the public police are implicated in achieving greater social cohesion between majority and minority groups. For example, the Community Relations Council of Northern Ireland (2012) has argued that the police should take a 'zero-tolerance' approach to hate crime and be 'active participants in ensuring that no foothold is given to the public expression of violent sentiment against any one or group'. If policing is to successfully fill this role – that is, to protect the safety of all sections of a community through the robust and vigorous investigation and prosecution of offenders – then it arguably depends upon a type of police practice that conforms to the Peelian principle of preventing crime and disorder through public approval for, and willing cooperation with, the police. In other words, the effective policing of hate crime requires the consent of minority and vulnerable individuals and groups who are engaged with policing in the broadest sense.

In this chapter I consider some of the key issues facing the Police Service of England and Wales in respect of hate crime. I examine the role of the Police Service in dealing with bias-motivated crime and consider how a concern with hate crime in police work relates to both the core Peelian principles of policing as well as the policy (and ideological) commitments of the current Government. Throughout the chapter I make a number of recommendations that are aimed at strengthening the role of the Police Service in reducing hate crime and increasing operational effectiveness in responding to it. These recommendations relate to the need for the Police Service to: clearly define its role in addressing hate crime; establish a common definition of hate crime across forces; improve recording and reporting mechanisms; ensure adequate officer awareness of hate-motivated behaviour; increase officer understanding of law; establish effective communication with victims; and ensure that the response to hate crime is incorporated into the 'bigger picture' of law enforcement activity.

The role of the Police Service in responding to hate crime

The term 'hate crime', which originated in the mid-1980s in the United States of America (Jacobs and Potter, 1998), began to be used widely in the UK from the late 1990s. The growing use and acceptance of the concept among legislators and criminal justice practitioners in the UK was closely bound up with criticisms of policing. The Macpherson Report (1999), which identified institutional racism in the Police Service and called for policing that recognized the different experiences, perceptions and needs of a diverse society, underpinned what many now recognize as a 'cultural shift' in policing (House of Commons Home Affairs Committee, 2009). The Macpherson Report was instrumental in generating a broad range of critiques about police occupational culture and behaviours in relation to minority groups. For example, as Matthew Jones (this volume) shows, Macpherson underpinned a 'climate of reform' in policing in respect of homophobia among police officers and, although the extent and success of that reform remains debated, it is clear that widespread changes in police culture have taken place.

At the heart of this cultural shift has been an embracement of the concept of hate crime by the Police Service and the development of operational strategies designed to respond to it. This began immediately following Macpherson and resulted in, for example, the establishment of the Metropolitan Police's Diversity Directorate which stated that '[i]mproving public confidence in the prevention and detection of hate crime is a policing priority' (Metropolitan Police Service, 2002: 40). A wide range of changes in the Police Service have been achieved through, for example, the creation of specialist units, the training of dedicated staff, and the development of intelligence-led responses to hate crime (Hall, 2005). Underpinning this have been two ACPO guidance documents (2000, 2005) designed to promote good practice and increase effectiveness in preventing and detecting hate crimes. These changes in policing have been driven by the enactment of a raft of primary legislation designed to make the Police Service more responsive to the needs of minority and vulnerable groups (Sibbitt, 1997; Virdee, 1997). In short, the development of the Police Service's commitment to addressing hate crime has been intimately bound up with police reform in light of past failures to adequately deal with bias-motivated crimes.

However, while the Police Service has been required to implement significant reforms in respect of their strategic and operational response to hate crime, the Government's vision of the role of policing in addressing hate crime often appears confusing. While the Police Service is sometimes imagined to be at the heart of dealing with hate crime, at other times policing is rendered marginal. For example, the Government's *Challenge it, Report it, Stop it* action plan states:

> The Government has set out a new approach to cutting crime, based on freeing professionals from top-down micro-management and performance targets, and making the police democratically accountable to the communities they serve. Elected Police and Crime Commissioners, street-level crime maps and regular beat meetings will all focus police forces on the issues that matter to local people. This means local areas will be free to develop hate crime strategies that reflect local needs, rather than the concerns of those across Whitehall.
>
> *(H.M. Government, 2012: 8)*

While this appears to put local policing at the centre of the Government's response to hate crime, an examination of the detailed action plan in *Challenge it, Report it, Stop it* – which is divided into the three areas of 'Preventing hate crime', 'Increasing reporting and access to support', and 'Improving the operational response to hate crimes' – reveals a more limited role for the Police Service. For instance, in terms of preventing hate crime, which the Government argues requires 'challenging the attitudes that underpin it, and early intervention to prevent it escalating' (H.M. Government, 2012: 9), the plan sets out a very limited role for the Police Service. Although ACPO are required to 'work through voluntary sector partners to make available to schools resources to help them tackle all forms of bullying, particularly bullying motivated by prejudice' (H.M. Government, 2012: 11), the plan outlines a limited role for policing in providing a 'long-term . . . solution [which] lies in stopping hate crimes happening in the first place – by challenging and changing the attitudes and behaviours that lead to hatred, and intervening early to stop tensions or incidents escalating' (H.M. Government, 2012: 10). In short, the plan does not imagine the Police Service to have a significant 'social welfare' role in intervening directly in the social relations that underpin hate crime. Similarly, in respect of increasing the reporting of hate crime, which the Government argues requires 'building victim confidence and supporting local partnerships' (H.M. Government, 2012: 15), the only requirement for the Police Service is that ACPO continues to develop True Vision (a police-funded national website for reporting hate crime). It is only in respect of improving the operational response to hate crime that the plan identifies a more significant role for the police, requiring ACPO to publish a new Hate Crime Manual, update training for all police roles involved in tackling hate crime, and host a national ACPO Hate Crime Conference. This 'manualized' approach to shaping policing (which is now a characteristic of many aspects of operational police work) is also limited because it omits, for instance, any necessity for the Police Service to consider how cultural and organizational change may be required to meet the aim of effectively policing hate crime. While all of the activities outlined for the Police Service in the plan are important, within the overall scope of the action plan the role of the Police Service in addressing hate crime can be interpreted as marginal.

Challenge it, Report it, Stop it reflects a trend in criminal justice responses to hate crime in the UK whereby the state simultaneously promotes increased safety and security for vulnerable groups but 'defines down' the role of policing in delivering this (Moran, 2012). Drawing on Garland's (2001) idea that the state is increasingly withdrawing from delivering crime control and placing responsibility for this on individual citizens, Moran notes an 'ironic effect' of contemporary criminal justice policy: 'Just as it becomes legitimate to turn to the state for safety and security, many current crime control institutions and strategies emphasize the subject's own role in ensuring safety' (Moran, 2012: 20).

This can be seen in ACPO's first statement on hate crime in 2000 that placed significant emphasis on communities and individual citizens: 'Hate Crime is a most repugnant form of crime. The police service alone cannot be effective in combating it. The active support of partner agencies, group leaders, communities, witnesses and victims is essential to effective prevention and investigation' (ACPO, 2000). While partnerships between the Police Service and other criminal justice agencies and the wider community are appropriate and necessary, commentators such as Moran argue that there is a tendency in policing to abdicate responsibility *to them* rather than work *with them*. This may be exacerbated by what Newburn and Matassa describe as 'massive problems in connection with inter-agency working in criminal justice – many of them related to organisational culture' (2002: 43). Yet it is also driven by the Government's lack of a clear vision about the role of the Police Service in respect of hate crime. Recent research shows that there is significant disagreement among legislators about how the Police Service should respond to and deal with complaints about hate crime (Johnson and Vanderbeck, 2011; Vanderbeck and Johnson, 2011). The current Government's approach to hate crime presents a significant challenge to the Police Service in clearly defining and articulating its distinctive role in combating hate crime. On the one hand, in the post-Macpherson climate the Police Service is expected to provide a robust form of social control that addresses and eliminates sectarian crime within society. On the other hand, the Government continues to define down the 'social welfarist' role of the police. *The Police Service, through ACPO, should produce a publically available national policy document that clearly defines and articulates its social, community and crime control roles and responsibilities in respect of hate crime.*

Definitional problems

One way in which the Police Service could more clearly articulate its distinctive mission in responding to hate crime is to ensure the implementation of a national standard for defining hate crime. There is significant inconsistency among police forces in England and Wales in how they define hate crime when communicating with the public. In 2007, the ACPO Cabinet agreed, with the Crown Prosecution Service, National Offender Management Service and other agencies, common definitions of 'hate motivation', 'hate incident' and 'hate crime' to ensure consistent working definitions that would allow accurate recording and monitoring. The definition of hate crime, which covers the five strands of race, religion, sexual orientation, disability, and gender identity, was agreed as:

> any criminal offence which is perceived, by the victim or any other person, to be motivated by a hostility or prejudice based on a person's race or perceived race [or: religion or perceived religion; sexual orientation or perceived sexual orientation; disability or perceived disability; transgender or perceived to be transgender].

This differs from the definition established by ACPO in 2005:

> A Hate Crime is defined as: Any hate incident, which constitutes a criminal offence, perceived by the victim or any other person, as being motivated by prejudice or hate.
>
> *(ACPO, 2005)*

Although these two definitions are similar, the 2007 definition usefully removes the word 'hate' and replaces it with the word 'hostility' to better clarify the motivations that underpin hate crime. Yet the ACPO 2005 definition continues to be used by many local forces in their published materials. In Lincolnshire Police's (2010) *Hate Crime Strategy 2010–2012* an even older and different ACPO definition of hate crime is used from 2000. More confusingly, some forces use neither the

ACPO nor a nationally agreed definition. For instance, Derbyshire Constabulary (2012) state on their website that:

> Hate crime is subjecting people to harassment, victimisation, intimidation or abuse because of their race, faith, religion, disability or because they are lesbian, gay, bisexual or transgendered.

> Please note that this kind of crime against lesbian, gay, bisexual or transgendered people is known as homophobic/transphobic crime.

> The police use the following definition when recording a hate crime: 'A crime where the perpetrator's prejudice against any identifiable group of people is a factor in determining who is victimised.'

West Yorkshire Police (2012a), in the *Hate Incidents Booklet* that they provide to all victims of hate crime, use a definition of hate crime that includes reference to race and sexual orientation but omits disability, gender identity and religion: 'A Hate Incident is defined as any incident, which is perceived to be racist or homophobic by the victim or any other person.'

However, at the same time, in collaboration with British Transport Police, West Yorkshire Police launched a poster campaign across the West Yorkshire travel network in 2012 in which any reference to sexual orientation was omitted: 'HATE CRIME REPORT IT. If you're hostile, prejudiced or show hatred because of: disability, race, religion, transgender, then you're committing a hate crime.'

While there are those who are critical of a standard vocabulary around hate crime because of its potential to gloss over the complexities of a wide range of behaviours (Garland, 2012; Garland and Chakraborti, 2012), there are advantages to harmonizing terminology: not least because it promotes uniform understanding of hate crime among both officers and the public. *The Police Service should ensure that all local forces adopt and use the single criminal justice system definition of hate crime established in 2007.* This should be mandated nationally by the Home Office (using mechanisms such as the Home Office circular), ACPO, and in all training provided by the College of Policing.

Reporting and recording hate crime

Harmonizing the definition of hate crime within and across local forces is essential to increasing the reporting of incidents by victims and improving the recording of crime by the Police Service. Both the reporting of hate crime and the recording of it require a stable national frame of reference that aids mutual communication, interpretation and understanding about incidents between victims and the Police Service. Since April 2008, all police forces in England and Wales have recorded hate crime in respect of the five monitored victim strands (prior to this data were limited to racially and religiously aggravated offences). Since

2011, ACPO have made national data on recorded crime publically available. In 2012, ACPO data showed that local forces had recorded 44,519 hate crimes in 2011 (these data are broken down into force area and by victim strand but not by crime type). The ACPO data show significant variations in levels of hate crime across forces that suggest either a reluctance of victims to report crime or a failure of officers to record it. For instance, in 2011 in Suffolk 165 hate crimes were recorded against disabled people in comparison to six crimes against disabled people in South Yorkshire. The amount of crime recorded by these forces for racially motivated hate crime is roughly equal. It is highly unlikely that these data accurately reflect real differences in levels of crime against disabled people in Suffolk and South Yorkshire but, rather, suggests variations in reporting and recording practices.

All available research suggests that hate crime is significantly underreported (e.g., Dick, 2008). Encouraging victims to report hate crimes should be a key task of the Police Service, regardless of whether policing is imagined to be playing either a social welfare or crime control role, or both. If policing is to be effective in reducing and detecting hate crime it must encourage the engagement of victims. However, encouraging victims to report hate crime must go hand-in-hand with the accurate recording of it. There continues to be a perception among victims that the Police Service routinely fails to recognize or acknowledge hate crime (e.g., Trailblazers, 2012) and, as a result, fails to accurately record it. More robust recording could be encouraged by requiring officers to collect more detailed information about hate crime and installing an oversight mechanism to ensure that this is routinely done. Requiring officers to provide a wider range of standardized information about incidents would both foster better practice in recording and produce a more nuanced picture of crime. For instance, as a result of criticisms about a failure to record anti-Semitic crime (see, e.g., Iganski, 2007) the Police Service now collects specific data on this aspect of hate crime.

The Police Service should consider introducing mechanisms for reporting and collecting national data in respect of more subtle dimensions of hate crime. These data might include wider information about the victim than is currently collected, such as the religious affiliations of victims, the disabilities of victims, and the sexual identities of victims. Such data collection could be achieved through the introduction of a nationally agreed hate crime reporting form to be used by operational police officers (it could be modelled on and extend the self-reporting form used on True Vision). Requiring officers to routinely and actively investigate the existence of a bias-motivation in all crime rather than in those cases identified by victims (a point I address below) and collect more thorough information would produce a wider and richer set of data that would help improve understandings of vulnerability and victimization and allow a more coordinated operational response to protect those most in need. At the very least, *all forces should record and collect hate crime data by crime type to facilitate a coordinated response to particular types of crime.* Currently only a minority of forces (17) collect hate crime data by crime type and submit it to the Home Office (Home Office, 2012).

Officer training in respect of recording hate crime

There is a persistent concern that police officers fail to acknowledge and record hate crime when it is reported by victims (Equalities and Human Rights Commission, 2011). There are a number of reasons why this might be the case but a central problem could be how officers and victims communicate with each other about their respective perceptions of an incident. The perception of the victim is the defining factor in determining whether a crime is categorized as a hate crime and this inevitably makes recording problematic. Victims might not perceive incidents as hate crimes and, in such cases, the Police Service needs to ensure that officers adequately clarify the nature of an incident with the victim prior to recording it as a non-hate crime. When police officers suspect that hate is a motivating factor they can record a hate incident without the corroborating perception of the victim but, again, adequate clarification should precede this. An absence of clarification of incidents by officers can result in both the over and under recording of hate crime. When victims do clearly state that they perceive incidents to be motivated by hate, robust systems should be in place for guaranteeing that hate incidents and hate crimes are recorded. In all circumstances, accurate recording of hate crime depends upon the knowledge and skills of officers. The ACPO 2005 guidance on hate crime notes that ensuring officers are knowledgeable about and sensitive to a wide range of crime types and behaviours (from hate mail, internet abuse, and problems in sport) is vital in guaranteeing the accurate recording of hate crime. Yet research shows that most police forces admit that their officers could be better at identifying and recording hate crime (Sheikh *et al.*, 2010). Both local force strategy documents and ACPO documents suggest a willingness to address this deficit. Training is a key means to achieve this.

Training is important in respect of hate crime because, as in other areas of policing, operational officers are required to be 'policy makers' (Bell, 2004). Hate crime is a moral category (Mason, 2007) and police officers are agents who not only respond to crime but also actively conceive and construct it in moral terms (Cohen, 2002; Hall *et al.*, 1978; Young, 1971). It is therefore important to ensure that officers' interpretative discretion in respect of offence categorization is shaped by a capacity to fully comprehend hate-motivated crimes. The death of David Askew in 2010 – a victim of 31 crimes over a three-year period which, although motivated by his disability, were never recorded as hate crimes – revealed a significant problem in officers' understanding of bias-motivated crime (Equalities and Human Rights Commission, 2011). Equipping officers with the analytic tools and skills to appropriately and accurately identify and classify incidents is vital. But this cannot be achieved simply by requiring officers to read a manual or attend a short course. Rather, it depends upon creating an organizational environment in which officers become the 'problem solvers' that Tilley and Laycock (this volume) call for, who routinely 'test the hypothesis' that hate might underpin any incident they are called to investigate.

Ensuring that operational officers continually 'hypothesis test' in respect of hate crime requires officers to have not only knowledge of policing strategies but also an awareness of the sociological factors that underpin hate crime. In other words, police officers need to understand the broader social contexts from which hate crime arises and to which it gives expression. The current ACPO (2005) perspective on hate crime limits a critical social perspective on hate crime by stating that:

> Hate crime is largely based on ignorance and motivated by prejudice and hostility rather than personal gain. It is important in the first instance that all police personnel, when dealing with hate crime victims, have an awareness of their unique needs and vulnerability.

The ACPO definition of hate crime depicts offenders as pathological individuals who deviate from the behaviour of 'normal' citizens; offenders who are 'ignorant' or have 'prejudice or hostility'. Yet while hate crimes are committed by individuals or discrete groups, the roots of such crime do not lie within them but in socially, culturally, and institutionally normative ideas often held by the majority of society. Racist hate crime, for example, does not result from the prejudice of a minority of deviant individuals but is underpinned by widespread conceptions embedded throughout society (something the Police Service have themselves been forced to confront, post-Macpherson, both in terms of their investigative practices and operational behaviour). Hate crimes are mundane 'everyday' events rather than rare or extreme incidents (Iganski, 2008). Therefore, any training designed to increase understanding among police officers about hate crime needs to pay careful attention to developing a reflexive awareness of how 'normal' attitudes (perhaps held by officers themselves) underpin and produce hate-motivated incidents. Such awareness is needed if, for example, anti-Muslim hate crime is to be recognized as often resulting from widespread and entrenched Islamophobia (Githens-Mazer and Lambert, 2010). Officers need a critical awareness of how hate crimes emerge from, and give expression to, the broader power relations of society (Kaplan, 2008). Being able to assess whether hate crimes are motivated by socio-economic conditions, social constructions of difference, or lack of offender self control – or an interaction of all three (Walters, 2011) – would enhance officers' ability to deal with crime in the context of the 'real world' that victims inhabit. Improvements in officer understandings will also allay fears that labelling crimes as hate crimes dramatizes problems rather than solving them (Ray and Smith, 2001). In short, *the Police Service needs to ensure that adequate training results in knowledgeable officers able to identify hate crime and record it.* This could be achieved through a number of mechanisms: for example, the educational requirement of an adequate sociological understanding of hate crime could be made part of the national policing curriculum mandated by the College of Policing and, furthermore, hate crime training could be strengthened during the probationary training period. All training should be based on an 'evidence-based policing' approach in order to encourage an appreciation of the social factors underpinning hate crime and the impact on these by police interventions.

Officer awareness of law

A key determinant of how police officers respond to hate crime is their knowledge of the comprehensive legislation that empowers them to deal with a wide range of bias-motivated crimes. There has been significant concern among legislators that operational police officers do not understand the scope of the law relating to hate incidents and fail to apply it correctly (Johnson and Vanderbeck, 2011). Current legislation requires police officers to make front-line decisions based on careful and subtle interpretations of particular types of behaviour. In other words, the legislation necessitates a 'problem-solving' approach as imagined by Tilley and Laycock (this volume). For example, in respect of words spoken in public that a victim has perceived to constitute speech motivated by hatred based on sexual orientation, police officers are able to utilize three sections of the Public Order Act (POA) 1986. Section 4 of the POA criminalizes 'threatening, abusive or insulting words or behaviour' if it is done with intent and causes a 'person to believe that immediate unlawful violence will be used against him'; sections 4a and 5 of the POA criminalize 'threatening, abusive or insulting words or behaviour, or disorderly behaviour' that intentionally or unintentionally causes 'harassment, alarm or distress'; and section 29B(1) of Part 3A of the POA criminalizes 'threatening words or behaviour' or the display of 'any written material which is threatening' if a person intends 'to stir up hatred on the grounds of sexual orientation'. The POA therefore requires police officers to be able to interpret particular forms of speech – for example, a sign displayed in public which states 'God Hates Gays' – to determine whether it is threatening, abusive or insulting and, if so, whether it is likely to cause violence against a person, cause a person harassment alarm or distress, or stir up hatred against a group of people on the grounds of their sexual orientation.

There are no available research data on operational officers' understanding and interpretation of the law on hate crime. Yet ensuring an accurate understanding of law is crucial if officers are to meet the Peelian principle of seeking and preserving public favour not by catering to public opinion but by constantly demonstrating absolute impartial service to the law. *The Police Service should ensure that effective training and on-going monitoring results in knowledgeable officers who are able to effectively interpret and apply the law.* This is vital because a comprehensive understanding of how particular forms of behaviour can be dealt with under existing legislation helps prevent arbitrary or inappropriate use of the existing law. Demonstrating that officers are adequately trained in respect of the legal landscape of hate crime would allay the concerns of those who argue that '[l]icensing the police to determine what does or does not constitute "hate crime" creates the potential for arbitrariness [and] for miscarriages of justice' (McLaughlin, 2002: 39). One way that the Police Service might meet the Peelian principle of impartiality within this highly contested terrain of decision making is to encourage police officers to understand how their use of legislation relates to the Human Rights Act 1998 (Bullock and Johnson, 2012). The Human Rights Act 1998 arguably provides a mechanism for ensuring proportionate policing that balances the (often competing) interests of a wide range of social groups and individuals.

Responding to victims' complaints

The Police Service faces significant challenges in effectively responding to the needs of victims of hate crime. These are recognized by ACPO (2005) who have provided specific guidance on the treatment of victims throughout the life of a case. Dyfed Powys Police (2012) summarize the role of the Police Service as providing 'reassurance and immediate support to the victim, as well as investigating the incident'. It is important to emphasize that victim support must not be at the expense of criminal investigation. In other words, attention must be given to caring for victims as well as providing an effective investigative response (Brown, 2011). In respect of homophobic hate crime, for instance, it has been found that victims are equally frustrated by a lack of support from officers as well as a failure to take investigations forward (Dick, 2008). Against a history of mistrust of the Police Service by particular minority groups, the commitment of local forces to routinely dispatch officers to visit all victims of hate crime in order to provide support and reassurance is a welcome development. It is certainly vital in meeting the Peelian principle of building trust in the Police Service among all sections of the community in order to ensure the legitimacy of policing. However, a key aspect of victim reassurance is the knowledge that crimes against them are properly investigated, and a belief that police officers will robustly investigate hate crime will encourage a culture of reporting it.

ACPO stated clearly in its 2005 guidance that officers must 'actively seek the suspect' after interviewing victims, and local force strategies often give a commitment to 'vigorously investigate all hate incidents' (West Yorkshire Police, 2012b). Recent data from the Crown Prosecution Service (2011) show that the Police Service has made significant improvements in referring cases for prosecution which, in turn, suggests improvements in investigative practice. Yet victims of hate crime often report a lack of confidence in the Police Service to actively pursue investigations (Dick, 2008; Sheikh *et al.*, 2010). What might be lacking is adequate communication between the Police Service and the public about the willingness to investigate hate crime. Greater Manchester Police (2012) have attempted to address this in their Hate Crime Policy by stating:

> We will follow a 'positive intervention' approach, by which we will take firm action against offenders whenever we have sufficient evidence . . . In the event of an offence being identified, a positive arrest and prosecution are the primary ingredients for a successful resolution of hate crime. That said, it is recognized in some circumstances that this may not be the best course of action for the victim or offender. In order to capitalize on all methods of a victim focused resolution, if there is clear evidence to suggest prosecution is an available option and it is concluded that proceedings are not to be pursued through the criminal justice process, the advice of a supervisor or person/s nominated by the Divisional Commander must be taken.

This policy communicates to victims of hate crime a clear presumption to investigate and prosecute offenders. *The Police Service should, in line with ACPO guidance, communicate effectively with victims to assure them that investigation of hate crime will be undertaken with a presumption to prosecute where possible.*

Officer awareness of the 'bigger picture' of hate crime

Foster *et al.* (2005: 91) found that there is a tendency among police officers to disparage the policing of hate crime as 'pink and fluffy' in contrast to the 'glamorous and sexy' work of other departments. This is because many police officers believe that dealing with hate crime is not 'real' police work but a form of 'social work' that should be undertaken by specialist staff. It is incumbent upon the Police Service to ensure that all operational officers understand that an effective response to hate crime is at the heart of the police mission. The Peelian principle that police officers are only members of the public who are paid to give full-time attention to duties related to community welfare which are the responsibility of every citizen should underpin a strong belief that policing hate crime is essential to maintain lawful communities. In this sense, the 'social welfare' role of the Police Service, regardless of how it is defined out by current political ideology or government, is fundamentally linked to its crime control role. As the Community Relations Council of Northern Ireland (2012) argues:

> [H]ate crime has to be stopped because of its potential to take root, spreading from individual acts to shaping the experience of whole groups. On the one hand, unless hate crime is identified specifically, its roots in wider social attitudes and behaviour are never exposed, and the requirement to address issues of exclusion and social rivalry is lost in the focus on the individual act. On the other, hate crime creates enormous anxiety among others who feel that they too could be the next targets of random violence. Acts which create polarising sense of group solidarity are the biggest longest term threat to ideas of social cohesion, potentially generating antagonistic communities with radically different experiences of social life and identification.

The policing of individual incidents of hate crime should therefore be understood within the 'bigger picture' of crime control. Operational police responses to individual victims of hate crime should be approached in terms of their potential positive and negative impact on wider communities. An effective police response to one hate incident could potentially reduce larger community tensions and prevent the escalation of more widespread crime. Alternatively, a failure to deal with individual incidents could result in repeat and proliferating victimization. The success or failure of operational police responses to hate crime therefore has wide ranging implications that include the economic cost of hate crime to both communities and the Police Service. It is therefore vital that hate crime is given significant priority in the 'hierarchy of police relevance' (Grimshaw and Jefferson, 1987).

Hall (2005) details changes within the Metropolitan Police Service that have been successful in incorporating a concern with hate-motivated behaviour into the mainstream business of police work, at the centre of which have been a number of intelligence initiatives aimed at increasing both the prevention and detection of (particularly racist) hate crime. ACPO (2005) provide specific guidance on the use of intelligence designed to increase the effectiveness of operational policing within communities and state that in 'essence hate crime should be treated no differently to other areas of core business and effective analysis should be at the heart of any response'. There is a clear commitment to applying the standards of the National Intelligence Model when dealing with hate crime to maximize the efficiency of any police response. *The Police Service, in line with ACPO guidance, should ensure that all operational officers understand and apply the standards of the National Intelligence Model when responding to hate incidents.* More generally, hate crime should not be seen as the business of specialist officers but as a core aspect of all police work. In thinking about how to encourage greater awareness of the implications of hate crime for crime and its control, key lessons can be learned from the history of changing police organizational responses to crimes such as rape and domestic violence. Both an awareness of, and response to, the wider crime dimensions of hate crime will fail unless the Police Service ensures – through the training and organizational mechanisms I have outlined above – that a concern with hate crime is incorporated into the root and branch of policing.

Conclusion

In this chapter I have discussed some of the key issues facing the Police Service of England and Wales in respect of hate crime. There is no doubt that the landscape of policing hate-motivated crime has significantly altered in the last decade. Police forces across England and Wales have embraced the concept of hate crime and implemented strategies and tactical operational plans designed to address it. There is no standard model for policing hate crime and local forces vary in terms of the existence of dedicated officers and specialist units (Sheikh *et al.*, 2010). A 'one size fits all' approach will not necessarily increase the effectiveness of policing hate crime but, as I have suggested, harmonization across the Police Service in respect of particular policies and practices is desirable. Effective training that results in officer awareness of hate-motivated crime is essential in ensuring the identification of hate crime, the accurate application of law in response to it, and the appropriate recording of incidents. One significant challenge facing the Police Service, in light of the current Government's approach to hate crime, is the need to more coherently conceptualize and communicate its distinctive role in responding to this form of criminal offending. Imagining how policing could be fully implicated in facilitating the social changes that are necessary to reduce hate crime is vital if the Police Service is to meet the Peelian principle that the test of police efficiency is the absence of crime and disorder, not the visible evidence of police action in dealing with it.

References

ACPO (2000) *ACPO Guide to Identifying and Combating Hate Crime.*

ACPO (2005) *Hate Crime: Delivering a Quality Service. Good Practice and Tactical Guidance.*

Bell, J. (2004) *Policing Hatred: Law Enforcement, Civil Rights, and Hate Crime.* New York: NYU Press.

Brown, J. (2011) 'We mind and we care but have things changed? Assessment of progress in the reporting, investigating and prosecution of allegations of rape'. *Journal of Sexual Aggression.* 17: 1–10.

Bullock, K. and Johnson, P. (2012) 'The impact of the Human Rights Act 1998 on policing in England and Wales'. *British Journal of Criminology.* 52(3): 630–650.

Cohen, S. (2002) *Folk Devils and Moral Panics: The Creation of the Mods and Rockers (3rd edition).* London: Routledge.

Community Relations Council of Northern Ireland (2012) 'Hate crime, policing and human rights in a violently divided society'. http://www.community-relations.org.uk/about-the-council/background-info/hate-crime-speech (last accessed 19/09/2012).

Crown Prosecution Service (2011) *Hate Crime and Crime Against Older People Report 2010–2011.* London: CPS.

Derbyshire Constabulary (2012) 'What is hate crime?' http://www.derbyshire.police.uk/Contact-Us/Hate-Crime/What-is-Hate-Crime.aspx (last accessed 19/09/2012).

Dick, S. (2008) *Homophobic Hate Crime: The Gay British Crime Survey 2008.* London: Stonewall.

Dyfed Powys Police (2012) *Hate Crime: Force Policy Document.* http://www.dyfed-powys.police.uk/sites/default/files/documents/PoliciesProcedures/HateCrime.pdf (last accessed 19/09/2012).

Equalities and Human Rights Commission (2011) *Hidden in Plain Sight: Inquiry into Disability-Related Harassment.* Manchester: Equalities and Human Rights Commission.

Foster, J., Newburn, T. and Souhami, A. (2005) *Assessing the Impact of the Stephen Lawrence Inquiry (Home Office Research Study 294).* London: Home Office Research, Development and Statistics Directorate.

Garland, D. (2001) *The Culture of Control: Crime and Social Order in Contemporary Society.* Oxford: Oxford University Press.

Garland, J. (2012) 'Difficulties in defining hate crime victimization'. *International Review of Victimology.* 18(1): 25–37.

Garland, J. and Chakraborti, N. (2012) 'Divided by a common concept? Assessing the implications of different conceptualizations of hate crime in the European Union'. *European Journal of Criminology.* 9: 38–51.

Githens-Mazer, J. and Lambert, R. (2010) *Islamophobia and Anti-Muslim Hate Crime: a London Case Study.* Exeter: European Muslim Research Centre.

Greater Manchester Police (2012) 'Hate Crime Policy: Delivering a Quality Service'. http://www.gmp.police.uk/live/Nhoodv3.nsf/WebAttachments/6FEEFDD73A5CD2C280257A640049A1F0/$File/Hate%20Crime%20Policy.pdf (last accessed 24/06/2013).

Grimshaw, R. and Jefferson, T. (1987) *Interpreting Policework.* London: Allen and Unwin.

Hall, N. (2005) *Hate Crime.* Cullompton, Devon: Willan.

Hall, S., Critcher, C., Jefferson, T., and Clarke, J.N. (1978) *Policing the Crisis: Mugging, the State and Law and Order.* London: Palgrave MacMillan.

H.M. Government (2012) *Challenge it, Report it, Stop it: The Government's Plan to Tackle Hate Crime.*

Home Office (2012) *Hate Crimes, England and Wales 2011 to 2012.* http://www.homeoffice.gov.uk/publications/science-research-statistics/research-statistics/crime-research/hate-crimes-1112/hate-crimes-1112 (last accessed 19/09/2012).

House of Commons Home Affairs Committee (2009) *The Macpherson Report: Ten Years On (Twelfth Report of Session 2008–09, HC 427)*. London: The Stationery Office Ltd.

Iganski, P. (2007) 'Too Few Jews to Count? Police monitoring of hate crime against Jews in the United Kingdom'. *American Behavioral Scientist*. 51(2): 232–245.

Iganski, P. (2008) 'Criminal law and the routine activity of "hate crime"'. *Liverpool Law Review*. 29: 1–17.

International Association of Chiefs of Police (2012) *Responding to Hate Crimes: A Police Officer's Guide To Investigation and Prevention*. http://www.theiacp.org/publicationsguides/lawenforcementissues/hatecrimes/respondingtohatecrimespoliceofficersguide/tabid/221/default.aspx (last accessed 29/10/2012).

Jacobs, J. and Potter, K. (1998) *Hate Crimes: Criminal Law and Identity Politics*. New York: Oxford University Press.

Jenness, V. and Grattet, R. (2004) *Making Hate a Crime?: From Social Movement to Law Enforcement?*. New York: Russell Sage Foundation.

Johnson, P. & Vanderbeck, R.M. (2011) '"Hit them on the nose": representations of policing in Parliamentary debates about incitement to hatred on the grounds of sexual orientation'. *Policing: A Journal of Policy and Practice*. 5(1): 65–74.

Kaplan, M.B. (2008) 'Hate crime and the privatization of political responsibility: protecting queer citizens in the United States?' *Liverpool Law Review*. 29: 37–50.

Lincolnshire Police (2010) *Hate Crime Strategy 2010–2012*. http://www.lincs.police.uk/About/Equality-and-Diversity/Engagement-and-Partnerships/Hate-Crime-Strategy.pdf (last accessed 19/09/2012).

McLaughlin, E. (2002) 'Cause for concern: the policing of hate crime'. *Criminal Justice Matters*. 48(1): 38–39.

Macpherson, W. (1999) *The Stephen Lawewnce Inquiry: Report of an Inquiry by Sir William Macpherson of Cluny*. London: TSO.

Mason, G. (2007) 'Hate crime as moral category: Lessons from the Snowtown case'. *Australian and New Zealand Journal of Criminology*. 40(3): 249–271.

Moran, L.J. (2012) 'The Changing Landscape of Policing Male Sexualities: A Minor Revolution?', in P. Johnson and D. Dalton (eds) *Policing Sex*. Abingdon: Routledge.

Metropolitan Police Service (2002) 'Structuring a police response: the diversity directorate'. *Criminal Justice Matters*. 48(1): 40–40.

Newburn, T. and Matassa, M. (2002) 'Policing hate crime'. *Criminal Justice Matters*. 48(1): 42–43.

Ray, L. and Smith, D. (2001) 'Racist offenders and the politics of "hate crime"'. *Law and Critique*. 12(3): 203–221.

Sheikh, S., Pralat, R., Reed, C. and Hoong Sin, C. (2010) *Don't Stand By: Hate Crime Research Report*. London: Mencap.

Sibbitt, R. (1997) *The Perpetrators of Racial Harassment and Racial Violence (Home Office Research Study 176)*. London: Home Office, Research and Statistics Directorate.

Trailblazers (2012) *Under Investigation: The Trailblazers' Hate Crime Report*. London: Muscular Dystrophy Campaign.

Vanderbeck, R.M. and Johnson, P. (2011) '"If a charge was brought against a saintly religious leader whose intention was to save souls . . .": an analysis of UK Parliamentary debates over incitement to hatred on the grounds of sexual orientation'. *Parliamentary Affairs*. 64(4): 652–673.

Virdee, S. (1997) 'Racial Harassment', in T. Modood, R. Berthoud, J. Lakey, J. Nazroo, P. Smith, S. Virdee and S. Beishon (eds) *Ethnic Minorities in Britain: Diversity and Disadvantage*. London: Policy Studies.

Walters, M.A. (2011) 'A general theories of hate crime? Strain, doing difference and self control'. *Critical Criminology*. 19(4): 313–330.

West Yorkshire Police (2012a) *Hate Incidents Booklet*.

West Yorkshire Police (2012b) 'Hate Incidents'. http://www.westyorkshire.police.uk/ about-us/policy-statements/hate-incidents (last accessed 19/09/2012).

Young, J. (1971) *The Drugtakers*. London: Paladin.

INTRODUCTION TO PARTS V AND VI

Supporting policing

Jennifer M. Brown

Introduction

Governance and accountabilities and the professionalising of the police are very much within the remit of the Commission's terms of reference. Standards of conduct and of competency matter not least, as Sir Christopher Kelly states in the opening statement to the 2013 annual report on standards in public life:

> They are particularly important where public money is being spent on public services or public functions. Citizens have a right to expect that holders of public office who take decisions which affect their lives should do so with impartiality, should be truthful about what they are doing and should use public money wisely. Society can expect better outcomes when decisions are made fairly and on merit and not influenced by personal or private interests. Organisations in every sector benefit from greater legitimacy when the public has confidence in their integrity.

The two parts of this last section of the book are about changing and how to enhance policing. The first set of chapters examines professionalism and the second governance. The former is about educating in what it is to be a good officer in the competency sense and the latter is about being a good officer in the conduct sense. The link between the two is knowledge. The questions addressed by the chapters are: What does a good police officer need to know? How does the officer acquire the relevant knowledge? How do we know the officer has the knowledge and applies this appropriately? Several authors debate the meaning of the terms profession, professional and the process of professionalisation. In Fleming's review the notion of a professional police officer is taken to mean: being college educated, having a career devoted to public service, a counter to unacceptable behaviours and is accompanied by a code of ethics, special knowledge, educational standards, autonomy and self-regulation. Sklansky shows how calls for democratic reforms in policing have been conflated with drives towards professionalising the police. He muses that professionalism, rather like democracy, is an elusive term but both convey an aspiration worth achieving.

Dingwall (2008) proposes the idea that being a professional in the realm of law and crime requires the acquiring of 'guilty' knowledge. In other words the law enforcer has to know and understand the how, what and why of law breaking. Engels and Peterson, Sklansky, and Bryant and colleagues contend that this knowledge may be acquired: through coaching and mentoring by front-line supervisors; 'on the job' through doing community policing; and/or through an accredited process of learning and systematised knowledge. Dingwall's point is that being the repository of guilty knowledge carries with it not only a privileged status but also the means for exploiting this knowledge for self-interested or nefarious purposes. Accountabilities protect both the public and the officer. The ensuing discussion in the chapters debates whether self-regulation is sufficient in preserving a sufficiently high standard of both conduct and expertise or whether higher degrees of internal or external regulation are required.

Central to the discussion about professionalisation is the notion of police culture and the need to change from its adverse features into behaviours, attitudes and ways of working that promote the public good. Laycock and Tilley, in their chapter, suggest what needs to be done is to integrate a problem-solving approach firmly into routine policing and for it to be seen as 'part of the job'. They, as do Fleming, Sklansky and Byrant and colleagues, recognise this is a non-trivial task and requires not only a fundamental change in the ways policing services are conceived and delivered but also in how police officers think. Such a transformation will take time.

Robin Engels and Samuel Petersen suggest in some cases front-line supervisors have actually frustrated the inculcation of problem-solving approaches because 'by changing a patrol officer's role to that of a problem-solver (where they are afforded more freedom, creativity, and autonomy), supervisors would not be able to rely on their ability to control subordinates with departmental restrictions and/or their formal authority as supervisors'. Supervisors, in their view must be taught to emphasise their role as a facilitator and coach.

Sklansky illustrates how efforts in America to professionalise the police in the period from the 1950s to 1970s foundered because they were focused on crime suppression and were overly reliant on technocratic approaches. Fleming shows that almost 30 years of effort to professionalise the Australian police foundered because of the bureaucratic approach taken and failure to obtain buy-in from officers themselves, as well as failure to overcome the disabling effects of vested local interests. This is not to say that nothing has been achieved. In the case of Australia and New Zealand there are some tangible successes: a code of ethics, partnership arrangements with universities and an information portal to communicate the results of research and practice. The successes achieved in the United States, as described by Sklansky, were attributed to the adoption of the community policing model in which the aspirations of professionalism were enacted through practice. Community policing contributed to a rebuilding of trust, increased legitimacy and making police more attentive to the totality of community needs not just crime control.

Interestingly, the essay by Aogán Mulcahy on the transformation of the Royal Ulster Constabulary (RUC) into the Police Service of Northern Ireland (PSNI) was built around the notion of community policing. The PSNI emerged in the aftermath of the cessation of sectarian violence in Northern Ireland, as a consequence of a major Commission of Enquiry led by Lord Patten. Mulcahy explains that the community was seen as central to the policing purpose and required a shift from an organisation that secured the state into one that protected the citizen. Impartiality and accountability were crucial if the new policing model was to be accepted by both the Catholic and Protestant communities. Community is also central to the new national police service for Scotland. Nicholas Fyfe outlines, in his chapter, that the purpose of the new policing organisation is to 'improve the safety and well-being of persons, location and communities', to be achieved in ways that are accessible and promote measures to prevent, crime, harm and disorder (again a tri-partite definition of function). He says (Fyfe, 2013: 17) that the approach in Scotland privileges bureaucratic and technocratic forms of accountability over electoral and democratic approaches. Thus within the United Kingdom we see a virtual experiment being conducted in the delivery and oversight of policing. Fyfe explains the emergent Scottish model of policing was one in which the majority party adopted an agenda that amalgamated the eight regional forces to create a national police organisation. The arguments for this were economies of scale achieved by reducing infrastructure costs of running separate forces, and the better access to specialist expertise for high-impact, low-frequency crime. Moreover, Fife points out that the inspiration to develop policing in Scotland came from Europe where many countries are rationalising their organisational structures. There is no political appetite for amalgamation in England and Wales. Westminster looked in the other direction, to America for its ideas, namely the introduction of elected Police and Crime Commissioners (PCCs) which consolidates the localism agenda. The Northern Ireland model owes much to the concept of reconciliation inspired to repair community relationships in South Africa. Engels and Petersen, interestingly, note that there are few lessons to be learnt from the United States about what makes a 'good' front-line supervisor (sergeant), noting a paucity of research examining this issue. This is despite the importance of their translating role between street and management cops, and their potential for directing resources and monitoring behaviour.

Robin Bryant, Tom Cockcroft, Stephen Tong and Dominic Wood also talk about what makes a 'good' officer. They draw on their extensive experiences as providers of police education. They briefly provide an account of developments from police training which has more to do with achieving professionalism through proficiency to a more intellectual approach. As previously discussed in Part II, this idea is about a shift away from *de facto* authority, towards *epistemic* authority; in other words, the ways in which an officer (or police staff member) obtains their knowledge. Interestingly they also passionately state the case for an immersive approach washing right through the organisation such that professionalisation becomes a more universal model of knowledge dissemination. This would be accompanied by a move towards a lessening of centralised controls. They offer a tangible ten-year programme through the newly established College of Policing by which this can be achieved. In such a transition they find a site of 'ressentiment' discussed earlier in reference to the police culture. Bryant and colleagues note the concerns and anxieties from some in the police service that something may be lost through an intellectualising of what they do.

The themes embedded in the Part VI chapters set out what the public have a right to expect and their degree of engagement in governance arrangements; models for managing and controlling police conduct; and identification of some inherent paradoxes. There is a continuation of a discussion of symbolism. Nicholas Fyfe suggests that the amalgamation of the police services in Scotland was a powerful statement about nationhood and the nationalism agenda of the present Scottish Government. Aogán Mulcahy spends some time explaining the importance of symbols in the reinvention of policing in Northern Ireland. The change of uniform and insignia as well as the name had powerful resonance with both communities. The idea of sovereignty is introduced whereby the police have a role in defining the nation, not as a nostalgic harking back to the past but more as a form of prophecy. Critically, the notion that the police might actually be a morally nourishing force can be found in ideas of procedural justice which is at the heart of the discussion about legitimacy.

A central question posed by these contributors is who guards the guards? The recent House of Commons Home Affairs Select Committee, when investigating the role of the Independent Police Complaints Commission, stated in the report's conclusion that: 'Police officers are warranted with powers that can strip people of their liberty, their money and even their lives and it is vital that the public have confidence that those powers are not abused.'

Thus public confidence and trust are crucial to the model with which we police in the United Kingdom, i.e. by consent. Adrian Barton and Nick Johns, in their chapter, and Kevin Stenson and Dan Silverstone in theirs, forensically dissect the proposition that not all citizens are treated fairly or have their expectations met. Social class, ethnicity, gender as well as the matter that may bring an individual into contact with the police are shown to result in differential experiences. Barton and Johns trace some of the historical origins of this, Stenson and Silverstone draw attention to the changing contours of groups (emergence of new alliances of interest such as environmentalists and feminists as well as newly constituting diverse communities). Bradford and colleagues, in Chapter 6, discussed the importance of alignment to a common set of values between the police and the policed.

These discussions lead into analysis of how the public can be incorporated into the oversight machinery. Stenson and Silverstone helpfully describe the current architecture of bodies having governance responsibilities and, in particular, draw our attention to PCCs. As an innovation of the present Coalition Government, PCCs are the elected authority providing local oversight of policing. Stenson and Silverstone, and Barton and Johns, concur with Ian Loader's assessment that while it is early days in the life of this instrument of accountability, PCCs are a flawed means of engaging the public in the process. This is because they, in common with the police themselves, are not representative of the communities served and the infinite regress problem, who guards the PCCs?

The chapters by Anja Johansen and by Louise Westmarland take us into other mechanisms of accountability. Johansen compares and contrasts European models of independent complaints authorities and Westmarland discusses the concept of ethical codes of conduct. Implicit in these, and the other chapters in this section, are the different approaches taken to hold police to account. Use of rule book methods derives from military models in the form of discipline codes. Here there is little room for interpretation and coercive pressures are used to enforce compliance, which as Westmarland demonstrates, can induce an informal blue code of loyalty to the group or immediate colleagues to frustrate the bringing to book of infractors. Politically mandated priorities and reforms are associated with performance indicators and risk assessments. Here the emphasis is on doing what is required to be measured. A useful precedent is in the analysis undertaken by Professor Eileen Munro who reviewed child protection procedure. She, (Munro, 2011) concluded that:

> Reforms have been implemented through top-down direction and regulation, which has contributed to problems and led to an over-standardised response to the varied needs of children. Managerial attention has been excessively focused on the process rather than the practice of work. In social work, targets and performance indicators have become drivers of practice to a degree that was never intended by those who introduced them. In turn, this has created an image of the inspection process that perplexes those Ofsted inspectors who seek to take a wider and more qualitative assessment of practice. This top-down approach has also limited the system's ability to hear feedback . . . [resulting in] poor ability to learn.

Similarly Robert Francis QC (2013), when reviewing the failures of Stafford hospital, concluded that patients were routinely neglected by an organisation that was preoccupied with cost cutting, targets and processes and which, in so doing, lost sight of its responsibility to provide safe care. Moreover, outside organisations who had responsibility to provide external oversight such as the Primary Care Trust (PCT) and the Healthcare Commission, or any of the local oversight and scrutiny committees, detected nothing wrong with the hospital's performance. Such criticisms are detectable within the police service. There is a cottage industry associated with measuring performance such that these performance measures become ends in themselves rather than a means to an end. This is evidenced in the conclusions of several Independent Police Complaints Commission (IPCC) reports into operational failures, especially in rape investigations. In the foreword of a recent investigation into the Southwark Sapphire Sexual Offences Unit (IPCC, 2013) it was stated that:

> The review found that Southwark Sapphire unit was under-performing and over-stretched and officers of all ranks, often unfamiliar with sexual offence work, felt under pressure to improve performance and meet targets. Its sanction-detection rate (the proportion of recorded crimes that proceed to prosecution) was poor, and management focused on hitting this target as a measure of success, rather than on the Metropolitan Police Service's standard operating procedure, which identified a much broader range of performance measures. We found that Southwark Sapphire had implemented its own standard operating procedure over this period to meet these targets. Essentially, this took the form of encouraging officers and victims to retract allegations (so that no crime was recorded) in cases where it was thought that they might later withdraw or not reach the standard for prosecution (which would have been recorded as an unsolved crime).

Thus there has been a recognition of the problems and shortcomings of bureaucratic modes of regulation. What Westmarland and others point out is that policing tasks and duties involve a great deal of ambiguity and conflict, and require interpretation, which are uneasily accommodated within rule books or political mandates. When infringements occur or targets are not met, simply ratchetting up to tighten the rules or demanding more measurement will not work and, if anything, allow a flourishing of the informal blue code. In the police arena such models are giving way to democratic oversight as exemplified by the PCCs, which as preceding comment observes, is said to be a flawed method.

What several chapters suggest is that a professional judgement model underpinned by ethical standards disrupts the comfort blanket afforded by the 'canteen' culture by inculcating a moral and evidence base in judgements employed when exercising discretion. Sklansky also discusses the idea of internal norms being the driver of moral conduct and competency and self-regulation in the manner of the professions. The case for movement of the police service towards the creation of a profession in which its legitimacy is founded on principles of procedural justice is detailed in the Bradford, Jackson and Hough chapter. The principle is straightforward: the process of treating people fairly both inside the organisation as well as outside, is more likely to result in acknowledgement of the entitlement (legitimacy) granted to those in authority and compliance of the subordinate. The model and its ramifications are more complicated. The procedural justice thesis holds that the achievement of a moral alignment between the police and the public, and within the internal community of those working for the police, should result in doing the right thing because individuals believe it is the right thing to do and becomes 'ingrained in everyday life'. Stenson and Silverstone, however, suggest that the degree to which the police can protect the public and win the respect and support of the population *just* (their emphasis) with procedural fairness, friendly engagement with local citizens and liberal criminal justice measures, is limited. They say that procedural justice must be intertwined with professionalism.

There are, however, some paradoxes associated with successes in oversight. Anja Johanson's critique of independent complaints bodies includes the problem of police, or former police officers becoming the guards who guard the guards. There is a potential danger that in this role, the potency of the police culture might limit their independence on the one hand, but, on the other, knowledge of the informal culture allows them to scrutinise places hidden to the naive investigator. Another of Johanson's criticisms is the opaqueness of the means for the public to complain. Making the process more open, for example, through online reporting, might increase the volume of complaints and inadvertently decrease the public's confidence in the integrity of staff because of the increasing number of complaints.

Stenson and Silverstone allude to the heterogeneity of the police service but point out new ethical risks posed by incorporating a wider and more diverse set of people (from the private sector) into the delivery of policing. Ideologically designed to save money and improve efficiency, this policy could have the unintended consequence of undermining the symbolic role of the police in demonstrating fairness of state machinery in dealing with people. They further argue that if the police are a core nation-building institution, symbolically representing basic national values, then their work cannot be outsourced 'like rubbish collection to commercial providers'. And as yet the private contracted staff are not incorporated within the accountability structures, such as the IPCC.

Finally there is an intriguing discussion to be had about other accountability mechanisms. Clearly formal complaints procedures, as Johanson points out, are but one arrangement. Stenson and Silverstone point to other formal means such as Parliamentary Committees and Her Majesty's Inspectorate of Constabulary. These authors also ask us to think about the ways in which evidence provides a means to justify action. The production of evidence is not an uncontested field and it is important to have a sophisticated debate about the biases, proclivities and, indeed, the potential self-interest of differing academics when persuading policy makers to adopt a particular approach. A mode of accountability inculcated by alignment of values is implicit in the procedural justice approaches. In order to achieve this, significant work will be required on the informal culture of the police (which is the subject of Part II). It is difficult to see how such an alignment can be achieved when there is a differential experience of policing by virtue of demographics, geography or motivation for a police contact.

References

Dingwall, R. (2008) *Essays on Professions*. Aldershot: Ashgate.

Francis, R. (2013) *Independent inquiry into care provided by Mid Staffordshire NHS Foundation Trust January 2005–March 2009*. London: HMSO.

Fyfe, N. (2013) A different trajectory? In Neyroud, P. (ed.) *Policing UK 2013; Priorities and Pressures; A Year of Transformation.* Oxford: Witan Media.

Independent Police Complaint Commission (2013) *Southwark Sapphire Unit's local practices for the reporting and investigation of sexual offences, July 2008–September 2009.* London: The Commission.

Kelly, Sir S. (2013) *Standards matter: A review of best practice in promoting good behaviour in public life.* London: Committee on Standards in Public Life. Cm 8519.

Munro, E. (2011) *The Munro review of child protection: Final report: A child-centred system.* London: Department of Education Cm 8062.

PART V

Professionalising

21

THE PROMISE AND THE PERILS OF POLICE PROFESSIONALISM

David Alan Sklansky

Introduction

In the ongoing story of police reform – which in the Anglo-American world has largely been the story of efforts to make policing both more effective and more 'democratic' – the ideal of professionalism plays an ambiguous role. On the one hand, there is a long tradition of calls for the police to be more 'professional'. In the United States, in particular, there was a period in the mid-twentieth century when virtually every effort at police reform marched under the banner of police professionalism (President's Commission, 1967: 20–21; Carte and Carte, 1975: 114–115; Sklansky, 2008: 35–37; Segal, 2001) and echoes of that period can be heard today in arguments for a 'new professionalism' in law enforcement (Stone and Travis, 2011). In the United Kingdom, where police reformers often hearken back to Sir Robert Peel, the term 'professional' is sometimes used to sum up what was distinctive about the style of law enforcement that Peel pioneered, and – to take a particularly important present-day example – Peter Neyroud's recent review of police leadership and training places heavy emphasis on the importance of developing 'a new and vibrant professionalism in policing' (Neyroud, 2011: 14). Nor are Britain and the United States unique in this regard. The ideal of police professionalism has long attracted reformers throughout the English-speaking world, and it continues to do so (Clarke, 2005: 642; Canadian Association of Chiefs of Police, 2012). For example, calls for police professionalism are heard loudly today in South Africa, where it is seen as a critical component of efforts to reduce corruption among law enforcement officers and to tame the use of deadly force by the police (Bruce, 2011: 6–8; Newham and Faull, 2011: 46–47, 51, 53).

On the other hand, professionalism has a bad reputation among many police reformers, particularly in the United States. For much of the past three decades, in fact, the 'professional model' has been taken by many American police reformers to encapsulate what they are *against*. Community policing, the enormously influential, if often frustratingly vague, reform agenda that took root in the United States in the 1980s and became something of an orthodoxy in the 1990s, was to a great extent conceived and defined as a rejection of police professionalism (Sklansky, (2011; Stone and Travis, 2011: 8–12). In Britain, meanwhile, the identification of Peel's Metropolitan Police as 'professional' has always been in some tension with the notion, attributed to Peel, that the police are merely citizens in uniform – that 'the police are the public and the public are the police'.[1]

The ambiguous role played by professionalism in the story of police reform – sometimes hero, sometimes villain – owes something to the elusive nature of the concept. Police professionalism means different things to different people, and sorting out those various meanings is a necessary part of thinking sensibly about how, if at all, the ideal of professionalism can usefully be employed in current efforts at police reform. But it is not all a question of semantics. The rhetoric of professionalism is not infinitely elastic. It comes with a certain set of connotations. It has certain inherent advantages as a loadstar of police reform – and certain inherent disadvantages, as well.

Four meanings of police professionalism

When Peter Neyroud calls for moving British policing from 'a service that acts professionally' to 'a professional service' (Neyroud, 2011: 11), his phrasing should make clear, if it was not clear already, that there is something protean about the concept of police professionalism. And indeed the language of police professionalism has been applied to at least four different ideas, alone or, more typically, in combination.

Sometimes professionalism simply means *high expectations*. Professional police are police who are held to demanding standards of conduct, whatever those standards might be. Professionalizing a police service, on this understanding of the term, means laying down the law: serving notice that slack performance, unkempt appearance, rude manners, and loose ethics will no longer be tolerated. This is the sense in which Peel's Metropolitan Police are often said to be the first 'professional' law enforcement service. It is a large part of what American reformers in the mid-twentieth century meant when they called for police professionalization. And it is part of what South African reformers have in mind today when they promote the ideal of professional policing.

Sometimes police professionalism means, instead, that the police should be *self-regulating*, in the manner of the legal profession or the medical profession or the accounting profession. Greater operational independence for the police is not, in the main, what reformers in South Africa today have in mind, but institutional autonomy – and, more specifically, freedom from political interference – was very much part of the agenda of mid-twentieth-century police reformers in the United States (Sklansky, 2008: 34–38) and it is part of what police professionalism has come to mean in Britain, as well. Thus, for example, Lawrence Sherman argues that the

Cold Bath Fields riot of 1833 'helped establish for the police one of the hallmark characteristics of a profession: the right to operational independence' (Sherman, 2011). Neyroud's 'professionalism' similarly has more to do with institutional autonomy than with high expectations: that is what he means when he contrasts a 'professional service' with a service that merely 'acts professionally'.

Neyroud's version of operational independence, though, is a good deal different from the kind promoted by mid-twentieth-century American reformers. It has less to do with freedom from political second-guessing[2] and more to do with standards of competence and achievement administered by a self-regulating professional society, together with a body of accumulated expertise – knowledge and best practices – over which the society and its members take collective responsibility. It draws in part, therefore, on a third meaning of professionalism: the sense in which professionals are distinguished from amateurs. Professional policing, in this sense, means policing that is reflective and knowledge-based, a matter of *expertise* rather than common sense, intuition, or innate talent.[3] One way this can be achieved is through greater reliance on, and perhaps greater input into and responsibility for, the work of academics who study policing and crime control (Neyroud, 2011: 14; Weisburd and Neyroud, 2011). Even among academics, though, there is disagreement about how much of policing can realistically be governed by social science (Sparrow, 2011).

Fourth and finally, police are sometimes said to be 'professional' when their actions are guided by *internalized norms* rather than by rules enforced through a bureaucratic command structure or a formalized system of external oversight. This was never a central theme of the police professionalism movement in the United States (Bittner, 1990: 357; Stone and Travis, 2011: 7), nor is it stressed by Neyroud. But it has always been latent in the rhetoric of police professionalism (Segal, 2001) and it has sometimes been seized upon by reformers as an alternative to rigid, top-down, command-and-control approaches to policing – an alternative that might fit better with the realities of the police work and the large amount of discretion inevitably entrusted to front-line police officers (Clark, 2005; Regoli *et al.*, 1981). It is a discernible thread, for example, in current discussions of police professionalism in South Africa. (Bruce, 2011: 8–9).

It should go without saying that these four meanings of police professionalism – standards, self-regulation, expertise, and norms – are not mutually exclusive. On the contrary, they can reinforce each other, and often have done so. Still, they do not necessarily travel together. The mid-twentieth-century American version of police professionalism, as already suggested, heavily emphasized high standards, organizational autonomy, and, to a lesser extent, accumulated expertise, but gave short shrift to the notion that the actual 'professionals' – individual police officers – should exercise broad discretion guided by internalized, occupational norms. It claimed autonomy 'primarily for the institution of policing, and only secondarily, and then only in a severely limited sense, for its functionaries' (Bittner, 1990: 426; Segal, 2001). In contrast, the police professionalism being advocated today in South Africa pretty plainly is not meant to include greater institutional autonomy for law enforcement, nor does it put much emphasis on expertise; it is mostly about high standards and internalized norms. Neyroud's version of police professionalism is closer to the United States' model in these regards, but it places a good deal more emphasis on expertise and somewhat less emphasis on organizational autonomy.

A debate about police professionalism can easily turn into a debate about semantics. If professionalism means arrogance and a lack of accountability, no one favors it; if it means thoughtful, reflective, ethical policing, no one is against it. Part of thinking sensibly about police professionalism is being clear about what we want the term to denote.

Given the varying and sometimes conflicting ways in which the concept of professionalism has been employed in discussions of police reform, there is a case for abandoning the term altogether and substituting less ambiguous language, simply in the interest of clarity. That case has never proven fully persuasive, however. The reason is that the rhetoric of police professionalism has certain inherent, enduring attractions.[4]

The promise of police professionalism

The ideal of professionalism retains its allure in policing for some of the same reasons it retains its allure in other fields: it conjures up a body of practitioners who bring meaning and dignity to their work through dedication, collective self-improvement, and ethical commitment, aligning their own interests with the interests of those they serve. If anything, that ideal has even greater appeal in law enforcement than in medicine or law, probably the two most paradigmatic professions, because aligning the interests of police officers – the personification of state violence – with the interests of the public has, for decades, been thought a particularly pressing and particularly vexing problem throughout the Anglo-American world.

For police reformers, professionalism offers an antidote to corruption and underperformance, and a way of emphasizing that the police have, or should have, special skills and knowledge that can be written down, taught, and continually improved. It offers, too, an avenue of reform that promises to enlist the police themselves in the cause of reform, by offering them pride, respect, and status (Sklansky, 2011: 7). Notwithstanding the considerable ambiguity of the term 'professional', the language of professionalism allows reformers to appeal to a shared, off-the-shelf image of a 'true' profession, a profession characterized by 'continuous training, ethical standards and professional pride' (Stone and Travis 2011: 2–3, 7–8, 12, 18, 20–21).

The attractions of police professionalism for the police themselves are considerable. Some of the skepticism that community policing has always elicited, and continues to elicit, has to do with the sense that the police will never embrace it enthusiastically, because it does not seem like 'real police work' (Ratcliffe, 2008: 263, 269). Police, it is said, want to be part of an elite crime-fighting force; they did not sign up to be social workers. This is plainly an oversimplification: it takes too little account of the challenges and rewards of community policing, the diversity and sophistication of today's police officers, and the ways in which even veteran officers can be won over to the philosophy of community policing (Miller, 1999).[5] But it probably is true, at least for many officers, that the kind of law enforcement called to mind by the rhetoric of police professionalism remains glamorous and exciting in ways that community policing often is not. That means that it might be easier to enlist the allegiance of the police themselves, or at least some segments of the police, in a reform program when it is couched in the language of professionalism.

Nor should the past achievements of police professionalism be minimized. In the United States, for example, the police professionalism movement of the mid-twentieth century did succeed in reducing corruption, tightening standards, and raising the bar for what counted as success in law enforcement.

It should be said, too, that in important respects police professionalism is more appealing today than in the past. For one thing, claims of expertise are more credible now, because law enforcement as a field knows more than it used to about how to fight crime. The police might not know as much as they think they know, but the state of knowledge about effective crime control is undeniably better today than it was in the mid-to-late twentieth century. And one thing that is now apparent is that the police can, in fact, improve their effectiveness by careful, objective analysis of crime data – often an important part of what people mean now when they speak of police professionalism. Calls for police professionalism today often include calls to embrace one or more of several other trends in modern policing – 'evidence-based policing', 'intelligence-led policing', and 'predictive policing' – each of which relies heavily on quantitative analysis of crime rates and patterns of offending.[6]

Yet another attraction of police professionalism in some quarters today is fiscal. As police departments face tighter budgets, the kinds of programs associated with community policing can seem like luxuries, and professionalism can appear to hold the promise of greater efficiency: doing more with less. From one perspective, the ideal of professionalism actually sits in considerable tension with the ideal of efficiency: in other fields, historically, professionalism has arisen partly in explicit opposition to a purely business-oriented approach. Being a professional lawyer or a professional physician is supposed to mean paying less, not more, attention to money. But public managerialism fits reasonably well with the emphasis on quantitative analysis shared by evidence-based policing, intelligence-led policing, and predictive policing, so advocates of versions of police professionalism incorporating one or more of those data-driven approaches can make claims of efficiency that deserve to be taken seriously – even if, for reasons to be discussed below, those claims should also receive a certain amount of skepticism.

The perils of police professionalism

Professionalism in law enforcement can mean so many good things – integrity, rigorous standards, esprit de corps, expertise, continuous self-improvement, efficiency

– that someone new to the subject of police reform might wonder how anyone could be against professional policing. The most important reason, perhaps, is the unhappy history of the police professionalism movement in the United States.

From roughly the 1950s through the 1970s, police professionalism was more or less synonymous with police reform in the United States. Part of this was just a matter of terminology: particularly in the 1960s and early 1970s, virtually every effort to improve American policing was called 'professionalization' (President's Commission, 1967: Carte and Carte, 1975; Sklansky, 2008; Segal, 2001). But the labeling reflected something substantive. Despite the ambiguities that have always surrounded the concept of police professionalism, the reforms that marched under that banner in mid-twentieth-century America tended to share three central features: they focused law enforcement agencies on crime suppression, pushing to the side other traditional functions of the police; they sought to have police departments operate objectively and scientifically, free from political influence; and they worked to centralize, rationalize, and bureaucratize lines of authority within law enforcement agencies (Fogelson, 1977; Manning, 1997; Sklansky, 2011: 1).

As already noted, this movement can credibly claim some significant successes. Nonetheless by the early 1980s it was widely discredited. It was blamed for making police departments throughout the United States insular, arrogant, resistant to outside criticism, and – perhaps most disastrous of all – feckless in responding to the social ferment of the 1960s and 1970s. Community policing, the reform movement that coalesced in the 1980s and that became, in the 1990s, the new orthodoxy of police reform, was very consciously a reaction against police professionalism. It emphasized the plurality of police functions rather than a single-minded focus on crime control; it prioritized community input and involvement over expertise and technical analysis; and it favored decentralization over centralized authority, and locally tailored rather than globally rationalized solutions (Sklansky, 2008: 74–105).

Community policing has its own weaknesses, beginning with a set of ambiguities that are, if anything, even deeper than the ones plaguing professional policing. (Who or what is the community? In what ways should the police 'partner' with the community, whatever or whoever it is?) Still, community policing is widely seen as a spectacular success, at least by observers outside law enforcement. It rebuilt trust between the police and the public, it bolstered the perceived legitimacy of the police, it refocused the police on issues of concern to their constituents, it leveraged police resources, and it made law enforcement more attentive and accountable to community interests. Scholars across the ideological spectrum now take community policing as a model for how other governmental services might usefully be reformed (Dorf and Sobel, 1998: 328–332). And even advocates of a renewed emphasis on professionalism in law enforcement tend to agree that '[c]ommunity policing was an important improvement on the style of policing it challenged' (Stone and Travis, 2011: 5.)

It is true that some police leaders have been saying for close to a decade now that it is time to move beyond community policing, and it is true that some more recent movements in American policing – including intelligence-led policing and predictive policing – represent a return, in key respects, to what community policing rejected: a heavy focus on crime suppression, an emphasis on expertise and objective analysis, and a reliance on centralized control (Sklansky, 2011). But most thoughtful police executives and most thoughtful students of American policing want to build on community policing, not to discard it. That is true notwithstanding budget pressures, in part because the trust and perceived legitimacy that community policing helps to build are so critical to success of the police mission (Tyler, 1990; Tyler and Fagan, 2008; Meares, 2002), and in part because one of the strengths of community policing is precisely that it can allow the police to leverage their assets by tapping into the knowledge, the resources, and the abilities of organizations and individuals outside of law enforcement.

Most advocates of a renewed emphasis on police professionalism seek to incorporate the core lessons of community policing, creating a 'new police professionalism' that avoids what gave the professional model such a bad name in the 1960s and 1970s. They reject, for example, the pervasive, unquestioning faith in random patrol and central dispatch as tactics for maximizing the effectiveness of police personnel – a characteristic feature of professional policing a half-century ago, at least in the United States. And most advocates of 'professional policing' today, in the United States and elsewhere, argue that professionalism means, in part, accountability, outreach, and an attentiveness to community concerns.

There is reason to fear, though, that any philosophy of policing built around the ideal of professionalism will tend to emphasize technology, objectivity, and expertise at the expense of imperatives that are at least as important for the police in advanced democratic societies, but harder to pursue – such as trust, legitimacy, fairness, accountability, and racial equality. It was precisely the downplaying of these values that led many advocates of community policing to frame their movement as a rejection of professional policing. The architects of police professionalism in the 1950s, 1960s, and 1970s were, at times, as explicit as anyone could want about the importance of fairness, accountability, and community partnerships (see e.g. Wilson, 1950, 1963). The problem was that these values got lost in the shuffle, and the worry is that a revival of police professionalism, no matter how it is packaged, could have the same consequence. And there is evidence that some newer versions of police professionalism – intelligence-led policing and predictive policing, in particular – are, in fact, having a similar consequence in some quarters, leading police again to over-hype technology, overpromise expertise, and under-emphasize trust, cooperation, consultation, and accountability (Manning, 2008; Sklansky, 2011).

Police professionalism in perspective

Police professionalism is an ambiguous term that carries good connotations but that can be blamed for some unfortunate developments. In these regards it is like many other things: medicine, for example, or democracy. Few people suggest that we should give up on drugs or elections. What should we make of the ambiguous role that the goal of professionalism has played in police reform?

One possibility is that police professionalism is like medicine: a good thing when done right. This is probably the position of most people who argue in the United States or the United Kingdom today for a renewed emphasis on professionalism in policing. That is the point of talking about a 'true' professionalism.

Another possibility is that police professionalism is like democracy – an example of what philosophers call an 'essentially contested concept' (Gallie, 1955/56). There is no hope of getting broad agreement on a definition of 'democracy', but democracy still seems worth pursuing, in part because the arguments about the definition of democracy are themselves important and valuable. Those arguments help focus our attention on the best way to be true to a set of historic exemplars: the 'demands, aspirations, revolts and reforms' through which our societies have gradually rid themselves of practices and institutions now widely condemned in retrospect as inegalitarian and illegitimately hierarchical (Gallie, 1955/56: 186). Arguing about the meaning of democracy is a way of arguing about how to be true to the spirit of Magna Carta, the American Revolution, the abolition of slavery, and so on.

But there is reason to doubt that police professionalism is either like medicine or like democracy. There is reason to believe that the problem with police professionalism in mid-twentieth-century America was not simply that it was implemented poorly, but that professionalism was the wrong lodestar to begin with. The point of any explicit model of philosophy of policing is to emphasize particular aspects of the police mission that, for one reason or another, need emphasizing. Mark Moore, a particularly thoughtful and influential advocate of community policing in the 1980s, argued for that framework partly on the basis that it 'challenge[d] the police in the areas in which they are least likely to make investments in repositioning themselves' – namely, 'forging a relationship with the community' that would allow the police to 'enlist their aid, focus on the problems that turn out to be important, and figure out a way to be accountable'. Moore did not doubt the importance of developing 'more thoughtful, more information-guided, more active attacks on particular crime problems'. But he suggested that this agenda – which was fundamentally an elaboration of key strands of police professionalism – would 'take care of itself', because it was 'much more of a natural development in policing' (Harmann, 1998: 5).

Relations between the police and the public were never as bad in Britain as they were in America in the 1960s and 1970s. And relations between the police and the public in the United States are better now than they were then. But it remains true in the United States and likely in Britain that working with communities to build trust, legitimacy, and accountability, rather than strengthening expertise, is the hardest task facing large law enforcement agencies, and the one that most needs emphasis, encouragement, and assistance. A society like South Africa, where police corruption remains a much larger problem, might well be different in this regard: there, the ideal of professionalism could well focus the police on precisely the issues – such as integrity and self-regulation – that deserve their greatest attention. But in a society such as the United States or Britain, where corruption is a less pressing problem for the police than engaging openly and productively with the public, a focus on professionalism in any guise might focus the police on the wrong priorities.

For similar reasons, it is likely a mistake, at least in a society such as the United States or Britain, to think of police professionalism as an 'essentially contested concept' – that is to say, as a goal that eludes definition but that is, nonetheless, and partly for that very reason, worth pursuing. Outside of policing, professionalism is sometimes said to be an 'essentially contested concept', but the people applying that term usually mean only that it is hard, maybe impossible, to reach agreement about what constitutes a profession (Green, 2011; Hoyle and John, 1995)[7] At least in the context of policing, and probably more generally, professionalism is not an 'essentially contested concept' in the philosophers' sense, because arguing about the meaning of professionalism is not a helpful way to structure discussions about how best to emulate an agreed-upon set of role models. For good reason, there is no widespread agreement that police officers should be more like doctors, or like lawyers, or like any other specific example of professionalism. There might be aspects of how lawyers and doctors operate that seem worth emulating in policing, and arguing about the 'true' nature of professionalism *is* a way to argue about which aspects those are. But that seems a far less pressing question than the questions to which other organizing principles of police reform – community policing, say, or even the Peelian principles – direct our attention.

Conclusion

The rhetoric of police professionalism is neither well defined nor infinitely elastic. The term has at least four different meanings: high standards, self-regulation, expertise, and internalized norms. These meanings overlap, and advocates of police professionalism rarely intend only one of them. But they usually do not intend all four. It helps to be clear, when discussing police professionalism, precisely what combination of these four meanings of the term are contemplated.

Ambiguity is not the reason, though, that professionalism has a bad name among some police reformers, especially in the United States. The bad reputation stems from the directions that police reform took in the United States from roughly the 1950s through the 1970s, when law enforcement was suffused with the rhetoric of professionalism and dominated by an institutional ideal that was technocratic, hierarchical, bureaucratic, and – far too often – aloof and arrogant. The community policing movement was, to a very great extent, a reaction against this version of police professionalism.

The debate about police professionalism today, especially in the United States but to a lesser extent elsewhere in the Anglo-American world, is in part a debate about rhetoric and in part a debate about substance. To the extent that the debate is about rhetoric, the question is whether community policing really was a rejection of 'professionalism', or simply a rejection of a particular kind of policing that called itself professional, and whether the language of professionalism is helpful in steering present-day police in the right direction. To the extent that the debate is about substance, it is about whether aspects of the professional ideal pursued in the 1950s through the 1970s are worth reviving and extending, albeit more thoughtfully and in some sense more 'professionally' than was done the last time around.

The answers to both these questions likely depend on the specifics of the society at issue and the particular challenges for policing in that society. In a society like South Africa, where the most pressing tasks for police leaders and police reformers are to rein in corruption and the use of deadly force, the ideal of professionalism, with its connotations of high standards and internalized norms, might be an effective way to use occupational pride to advance an agenda of integrity and restraint. It is less clear, though, whether professionalism is a useful frame for thinking about police reform in the United States or the United Kingdom, where police corruption is not as pressing a concern, and where a case can be made that the major challenges for policing remain centered around building and sustaining the right kind of relationship with local communities. What is needed in that kind of society might not be a more ambitious form of police professionalism but, instead, renewed commitment to the agenda of community policing.[8]

Notes

1 A point noted, for example, by Neyroud, who acknowledges the 'challenge in developing the professionalism of the occupation of policing in a way that avoids insularity and distancing of police officers from the public' (Neyroud, 2011: 44–45).
2 It will be interesting to see whether this becomes a more prominent theme in British discussions of police professionalism after the arrival last year of elected Police and Crime Commissioners.
3 Gloria Laycock and Nick Tilley mean much the same thing when they call for 'professional policing' in their thoughtful contribution to this volume. The 'professionalism' that Megan O'Neill endorses in her own very helpful chapter also is largely a matter of expertise and accumulated experience, albeit expertise and experience with regard to collaboration, partnership, and the other values at the heart of Neighbourhood Policing.
4 Some of the discussion that follows is drawn from Sklansky (2011).
5 See also Megan O'Neill's contribution to this volume.
6 On 'evidence-based policing,' compare Sherman (2011) and Weisburd and Neyroud (2011) with Sparrow (2011). On 'intelligence-led policing' and 'predictive policing' and their connections with police professionalism, see Sklansky (2011: 3–5) and Stone and Travis (2011: 17).
7 Waldron (2002) notes more generally that the term 'essentially contested concept' is often used loosely 'to mean something like "very hotly contested, with no resolution in sight"'.
8 For preliminary thoughts about the shapes that might take, see Sklansky (2011: 12–13) and Megan O'Neill's helpful contribution to this volume.

References

Bittner, E. (1990) The Rise and Fall of the Thin Blue Line, reprinted in Egon Bittner, *Aspects of Police Work*. Boston: Northeastern University Press.

Bruce, D. (2011) Beyond Section 49: Control of the Use of Lethal Force. *SA Crime Quarterly* 36 (June): 3–12.

Canadian Association of Chiefs of Police (2012) *Professionalism in Policing Research Project*: Recommendations.

Carte, G.E. and Carte, E.H. (1975) *Police Reform in the United States: The Era of August Vollmer 1905–1932*. Berkeley: University of California Press.

Clark, M. (2005) The Importance of a New Philosophy to the Post Modern Police Environment. *Policing*, 28: 642–653.

Dorf, M.C. and Sobel, C.F. (1998) A Constitution of Democratic Experimentalism. *Columbia Law Review*, 98: 270–473.

Fogelson, R.M. (1977) *Big City Police*. Harvard: Harvard University Press.

Gallie, W.B. (1955/56) Essentially Contested Concepts. *Proceedings of the Aristotelian Society*, 56: 167–198.

Green, J. (2011) *Education, Professionalism and the Quest for Accountability: Hitting the Target but Missing the Point*. Oxford: Routledge.

Harmann, F.S., ed. (1988) Debating the Evolution of American Policing. *Perspectives in Policing* (November). National Institute of Justice.

Hoyle, E. and John, P.D. (1995) *Professional Knowledge and Professional Practice*. London: Cassell.

Manning, P. (1997) *Police Work: The Social Organization of Policing*. 2nd ed. Long Grove, IL: Waveland Press.

Manning, P. (2008) *The Technology of Policing: Crime Mapping, Information Technology and the Rationality of Crime Control*. New York: New York University Press.

Meares, T.L. (2002) Praying for Community Policing. *California Law Review*, 90: 1593–1634.

Miller, S. (1999) *Gender and Community Policing: Walking the Talk*. Boston: Northeastern University Press.

Newham, G. and Faull, A. (2011) *Protector or Predator? Tackling Police Corruption in South Africa*, Institute of Security Studies. Monograph No. 182.

Neyroud, P. (2011) *Review of Police Training and Leadership*. London: Home Office.

President's Commission on Law Enforcement & the Administration of Justice (1967) *Task Force Report: The Police*, pp. 20–21.

Ratcliffe, J. (2008) Intelligence-Led Policing, in Wortley, R., and Mazerolle, L. (eds.) *Environmental Criminology and Crime Analysis*. Cullompton: Willan.

Regoli, R.M., Poole, E.D., and Hou, C. (1981) The Effects of Professionalism on Cynicism among Taiwanese Police. *Police Studies*, 4: 67–72.

Segal, J. (2001) 'All of the Mysticism of Police Expertise': Legalizing Stop-and-Frisk in New York, 1961–1968. *Harvard Civil Right-Civil Liberties Review*, 47(2): 573–616.

Sherman, L. (2011) *Professional Policing and Liberal Democracy*. Benjamin Franklin Medal Lecture, London: Royal Society for the Encouragement of Arts, Manufactures and Commerce, November 1.

Sklansky, D.A. (2008) *Police and Democracy*. Stanford, CA: Stanford University Press.

Sklansky, D.A. (2011) The Persistent Pull of Police Professionalism. *New Perspectives in Policing* (March). Harvard Kennedy School/National Institute of Justice.

Sparrow, M.K. (2011) Governing Science. *New Perspectives in Policing* (January). Harvard Kennedy School/National Institute of Justice.

Stone, C. and Travis, J. (2011) Toward a New Professionalism in Policing. *New Perspectives in Policing* (March). Harvard Kennedy School/National Institute of Justice.

Tyler, T.R. (1990) *Why People Obey the Law*. Yale University Press.

Tyler, T.R. and Fagan, J. (2008) Legitimacy and Cooperation: Why Do People Help the Police Fight Crime in their Communities? *Ohio State Journal of Criminal Law*, 6: 231–275.

Waldron, J. (2002) Is the Rule of Law an Essentially Contested Concept (in Florida)? *Law & Philosophy*, 21: 137–164.

Weisburd, D. and Neyroud, P. (2011) Police Science: Toward a New Paradigm. *New Perspectives in Policing* (January). Harvard Kennedy School/National Institute of Justice.

Wilson, O.Q. (1950) *Police Administration*. New York: McGraw-Hill.

Wilson, O.Q. (1963) *Police Administration*. 2nd ed. New York: McGraw-Hill.

22

THE PURSUIT OF PROFESSIONALISM

Lessons from Australasia

Jenny Fleming

Introduction

The professionalisation of policing has been the goal of various countries and significant progress has been made. In the United Kingdom policing is poised once again at the proverbial threshold, attracted by the positive attributes associated with professionalism – ethical codes, professional authority, community sanction, uniform standards, expertise and a systematic body of knowledge, yet it is unsure how to proceed. The new College of Policing, 'a new professional body for the police service' has been established to advance many ideals commensurate with the move to professionalisation, emphasising improved training, education and standards. The College has been formally designated as one of five 'what works' centres of excellence which commits the public sector in England and Wales to creating a systematic knowledge base and developing a platform for an 'evidence-based profession'. A professional development framework will provide the context to raise standards in training, leadership development, skills and qualifications. It is envisaged that eventually the new College will be replaced with a statutory professional body, a body that will potentially 'raise the professional status of police officers and police staff, allowing them to gain greater recognition and reward for accredited levels of expertise' (Home Office 2012). Such aspirations are impressive. Yet the task of pursuing professionalism in policing is a long and somewhat arduous process. White (2012) has noted the convergence of police professionalisation initiatives in Australia/New Zealand and the UK. As the new College of Policing gears itself to addressing ideals of police professionalism emphasising education, training and standards, and evidence-based knowledge, it might be of some value to consider the move towards police professionalism in Australia and the lessons learnt.

This chapter follows the pursuit of professionalism in Australasia[1] from the 1980s through to the present day.[2] It provides a guide to the various groups and institutions that have sought to progress the national professional agenda and future direction of Australasian policing. The narrative is not exhaustive but provides the landmark decisions since the late 1980s. It suggests that while significant progress has been made, the challenges associated with effecting such reform across states and territories have resulted in progress that has been incremental and is far from complete. While comparing the UK with Australasia might be akin to comparing apples and oranges in terms of political and organisational structures, the narrative provides some understanding around the challenges associated with persuading others that police professionalisation is a goal to strive for. Before addressing the history, a short discussion around definitional issues is in order.

Definitional issues

The thorny issue of definition has always been problematic for any discussion of police professionalisation. Scholars have found it difficult to specify the criteria by which 'professionalism' can be defined, particularly as it relates to policing. Sturma (1987) sees police professionalism being about a career commitment 'devoted to public service'. August Vollmer was an early advocate of a police college education many years ago in America (Carte 1973). Reiner (1986) and others have supported higher education recruitment and training standards (see also Bradley and Ciocca-relli 1992). Another emphasis is the role of professionalisation to counter unacceptable police behaviours and cultures (Chan 1999).

Most definitions encompass a core set of criteria outlining the characteristics of a profession: the provision of a public service; a code of ethics; the possession of special knowledge and/or expertise; education and training standards, autonomy and self-regulation (Dale 1994; Mecum 1979; Price 1979). Police themselves are often confused by the concept. Police at ground level often have a different view of what professionalisation means. For many it equates with more money, more prestige and better conditions, for some it means the emphatic demarcation of the police role. Few see it as changing the way they do business and even fewer link the notion of professionalism to better service delivery (Burgess *et al.* 2006).

Clearly professionalism means 'different things to different people at different times and serves various purposes' (Chan 1999: 5). This is true not just between organisations but within organisations. A commitment to professionalism (however it is perceived) within police organisations invariably varies between ranks (Manning 1977) and there remains ambiguity about whether professionalism is best understood in terms of its 'body of knowledge', the ethical qualities of individual police officers or whether it needs to be assessed in the context of officer performance (Rowe 2009: 4).

As Sklansky notes (this volume) such definitional difficulties can turn a debate about police professionalism into a debate about semantics. This is a valid observation but does not get us far. Lanyon (2009: 248) reminds us that literally, a *professional* is one who has 'attained the status of a profession' and *professionalism* is 'an ideology subscribed to by individuals aspiring to professional status within either an occupation or a recognised profession'. For Lanyon, the term police profession-alisation can be used to 'describe the process by which policing moves to become a profession'. Price concurs (1979: 95), arguing that 'a mature profession pays as much attention to the processes by which ends are achieved, as it does to the ends themselves'. This chapter considers police professionalisation in the context of the process by which police organisations *move* towards professionalism.

Australia

In 2013, Australia comprises six states, Queensland, Tasmania, New South Wales (NSW), Victoria, South Australia and Western Australia and, for the purposes of policing, two territories, Australian Capital Territory (ACT) and the Northern Territory. The Australian Federal Police is Australia's federal law enforcement agency; a total of nine police jurisdictions police 7,740,000 square kilometres of land; (compared to the 244,000 square kilometres of land in Great Britain).

There is no national legislation concerning policing standards, recruitment, training, practice or policy, nor is there any federal control of state police, although there are a number of national forums in which Police Commissioners, Police Min-isters and others come together to discuss issues of mutual interest. Each jurisdiction has its own Police Academy (Queensland has two). Each state and territory has its own Police Act and associated policy/legislation, its own Police Commissioner,[3] its own Minister responsible for Police and its own Premier. Funding for policing is the responsibility of individual states and territories (Fleming and O'Reilly 2008). There are approximately 65,000 sworn police officers across the country. Each state and territory also has its own Police Association/Union and nationally, the Police Federation of Australia (PFA) oversees what it considers 'national issues for police' as it strives towards uniform standards and police mobility across jurisdic-tions. It does not interfere with individual state and territory workplace concerns or the potential impact of professionalisation initiatives on jurisdictional structures. This is considered the domain of the state and territory police unions/associations. Such diversity has traditionally been problematic across a number of areas not least in cross-jurisdictional initiatives (Fleming 2012: 163–164). It has proved a signifi-cant challenge for those seeking to implement national standards and a common approach to professionalism.

Moves towards professionalism

As in the UK, efforts to promote police professionalism in Australia have long been associated with police education schemes (see Bryant *et al.*, this volume) and police reform generally. While the PFA might have emphasised the importance of national registration, inter-jurisdictional mobility and a connected body of knowledge (Burgess 2009), in Australia and New Zealand, education, training and standards have, as in most countries, come to be associated with the move towards police professionalisation. This was particularly true in Australia in the early discourse around 'professional standards, competencies and skills'. While some states and territories were more receptive to the discourse of professionalisation, by the 1980s, most jurisdictions were at least prepared to discuss the issue of further education and improved standards for the nation's police officers (Lanyon 2007).

Early observations about police professionalism in Australia were noted by Barlow and Proctor (1980) in the context of education and ethics. In 1986, the Rawson Survey documented the need for higher training and standards particularly for those officers 'preparing for higher office' (Rohl and Barnsley 1995: 243). Others reflected that Australian Police either 'embrace professionalisation with vigour, or as a vocation we continue to stagnate and ultimately regress (Eaton 1990, cited in Rohl and Barnsley 1995: 241). The Australian Police Ministers' Council[4] (APMC) moved quickly following the Rawson Survey to develop and approve a national police education statement that emphasised the importance of 'the attainment of full professional status'. The statement, considered at an APMC meeting in March 1990, was clear that the notion of 'full professional status' would be about the need for qualifications, a more coordinated approach to tertiary courses offered to police and uniform national standards. Essentially professional status would 'entail national educational standards, formal higher education qualifications, improved police practice, and the establishment of uniform anti-corruption strategies' (Lanyon 2007: 111). The resolution of the APMC had 'placed education as a focus of professionalization of policing' (Lanyon 2006: 13).

At the same meeting, the APMC established the National Police Professionalism Implementation Advisory Committee (NPPIAC) with a view to implementing a national strategy for police higher education. Within a year the NPPIAC had consulted with all Police Commissioners and all jurisdictions had signed up to a Statement of Strategic Direction (SSD), 'noting the commitment to the pursuit of police professionalism, and the recognition of policing as a true profession' (Lanyon 2007: 112). Again the ten-point statement had focused primarily on core standards, code of ethics, tertiary education, national rating systems, nationally accredited in-service courses and a national police education standards council that would monitor such initiatives. Notions of a formal learned body, an active research agenda and registration were, as yet, not on the agenda.

In developing the SSD, the Board of Control at the Australian Police Staff College (APSC) acknowledged that the educational initiatives would take time to develop and would only be progressed over several years. It was hoped that such an approach to the professionalisation of policing would, over time, facilitate professional mobility across jurisdictions (Rohl and Barnsley 1995: 245), a goal that had long been the aspiration of the police unions and associations both at the state/territory level as well as nationally. The SSD was well received by the various police unions whose own 'professionalisation agenda' was focused on common police qualifications that would allow for accreditation and transfer across Australasia, a National Core Training Curriculum and a Professional Police Registration Board (Burgess 2009).

Within six months, a National Police Education Standards Council (NPESC) was established by the Police Commissioners as the formal Competency Standards Body for the police industry. At the same time, the APSC became the Australasian Institute of Police Management (AIPM). The AIPM would become the formal vehicle whereby the aims and objectives of the SSD would be realised. However within two years it was NPESC that was formally and legally established as the primary vehicle through which the principles of the SSD would be implemented. By 1998, NPESC had become the Australasian Police Education Standards Council (APESC), a consequence of New Zealand becoming a full member of the Council.

By 2000 a Public Safety Industry Training Package was endorsed by the Australian National Training Authority. The package included several police-specific qualifications, such as, for example, the Diploma of Public Safety. The endorsement of the training package 'effectively brought to a close the competency project commenced in 1991' (Lanyon 2007: 114).

A Platform for Professionalisation

In May 2001, Richard McCreadie, long-standing Tasmanian Police Commissioner and Chair of APESC, proposed a review that would consider a more focused strategy to progress full professionalisation and a police profession that would seek the principles that traditionally underpinned established professions such as nursing and accountancy. The review established four principles that would embrace professionalism. These included, as well as formal education and a code of ethics, a 'distinct body of knowledge and practice' and a formal registration system. In the same year, APESC became the Australasian Police Professional Standards Council (APPSC) comprising Police Commissioners and the heads of the PFA and the New Zealand Police Association (Lanyon 2007), the name change once again seeming to reflect a new direction. Without access to original documentation it is difficult to accurately assess whether these name changes effectively changed the remit of these 'councils' to any significant degree. As Lanyon has suggested, some of the name changes were required for legal reasons (Lanyon 2006). The overall impression of the period under discussion suggests that the name changes heralded a new phase in the overall professionalisation project and possibly new leadership or ownership of a particular initiative. It is true that specific individuals would come to be associated with specific initiatives and be influential in changing the direction of the professionalisation agenda over time.

For those who had been optimistically pursuing the concept of professionalism for Australia's disparate police forces, the following years were probably disappointing. Despite the emphasis on a body of knowledge and registration during the Review, the *Platform for a Professionalization Strategy 2002–2005* was essentially another series of objectives that emphasised university-based education, a statement of ethics, on-going development of competencies, minimum educational requirements and a project to facilitate inter-jurisdictional mobility (see Lanyon 2007: 114–116).

At this time many jurisdictions both in Australia and the national police agency in New Zealand had established relationships with various universities and some, like the New South Wales Police were already delivering their foundational training through the university sector.[5] Individual officers were beginning to undertake tertiary education of their own. It was clear that a credentialist definition of police professionalism that had so dominated the early steering committees, reviews and council work was still primarily the dominant feature of 'police professionalism'.

From an occupation to a profession

In 2005, the Police Commissioners' Conference established another review that would further 'consider the scope and functions of APPSC with a view to further develop a professionalization strategy in order to progress policing from an occupation to a profession' (Lanyon 2007: 116). A steering committee comprising four Police Commissioners and a representative from the Federal Government's Attorney-General's department formally agreed that a higher education degree would be a 'desirable professional qualification for Australasian practitioners', as would an evidence-based body of knowledge, continuing professional development, a process for professional registration, and the establishment of a professional body for policing (Lanyon 2007: 116–121). This would be the first time that a commitment to a professional body with an evidence-based body of knowledge had been formally integral to an understanding of full professional status. Concurrently, the same group conducted a review of the numerous national 'common policing services' established over time (so for example, the Australasian Centre of Police Research) to ascertain how those bodies might serve the new 'professionalisation' agenda. In 2006, a report was generated entitled, 'Blueprint for future cross-jurisdictional arrangements'. The report proposed 'a revised collaborative delivery of services' – 'working to a different model, in a different way and through more effective relationships' (Proud 2013).

In 2007, 17 common police services were subsumed into a new body, the Australasian and New Zealand Police Advisory Agency (ANZPAA).[6] The APPSC was retained. ANZPAA would seek to simplify the national policing landscape; streamline management processes and deliver a range of services including the 'development and promotion of professional development and standards'. At the same time the new body was being created, the National Police Improvement Agency in the UK was being set up to 'bring together the national support to the police service in one place' through the 'merging of at least five different groups of staff [and] the streamlining of 500+ programmes and projects' (NPIA 2008: 9).

ANZPAA's Strategic and Business Plans are aligned with the Standing Council on Police and Emergency Management's (SCPEM) *Directions in Australia New Zealand Policing* which is a set of three-year strategic principles to guide policing activities in Australasia. SCPEM comprises all Australian and New Zealand Ministers who have responsibility for police and emergency services. Its stated role is to: 'Promote a co-ordinated national response to law enforcement and emergency management issues. SCPEM looks to develop a shared framework for co-operation and a basis for strategic directions for the policing and emergency services of Australia and New Zealand' (*Directions in Australasian Policing* 2012–2015).

Through its 'directions' SCPEM promotes professionalism through leadership development and training and education; the building of respectful cultures; the promotion of individual integrity and ethical behaviour and the 'implementation of strategies which enhance professionalism' (*Directions in Australasian Policing* 2012–2015).

ANZPAA is responsible for progressing work on behalf of APPSC. Since 2009, the key streams of work led by APPSC that have informed professionalisation activities have been an 'international benchmarking study' (2009); a Training and Education Stocktake (2009); an ANZ Police Training and Education Strategy; and, in 2012, the ANZ Leadership Strategy, implemented through the Australian Institute of Police Management as a cross-jurisdictional endeavour aimed at developing leadership in policing (White 2012).

In 2011, a Police Practice Standards Model (PPSM) was adopted and funded by all ANZ police jurisdictions, and the unions (the PFA and the NZPA). The PPSM aligns key professionalisation activities under one strategy and seeks to establish consistent training and education, professional standards and best practice guidelines for policing across jurisdictions. In July 2012, the first phase of this strategy was implemented (White 2012). As Proud (2013) notes, ANZPAA has acknowledged that 'policing is best served by practitioners developing through skills training as well as underpinning knowledge and education' and it is this emphasis on education and training and police knowledge that drives ANZPAA's professionalisation strategy.

This brief outline might imply that Australasia's move to professionalism within its police organisations is part of an inexorable march towards success – an upward slanting trajectory that has as its inevitable destination the full professionalisation of Australian and New Zealand police. Indeed, significant progress has been made, but it would be misleading to suggest the journey has been without its challenges. Over the past 25 years moves towards professionalisation in Australia have been fraught with inter-jurisdictional dilemmas, a lack of buy in from police officers and organisational considerations. Such challenges have considerably hindered progress of the many aspirations held by those who pursue police professionalism.

Inter-jurisdictional dilemmas

It is difficult for those who do not know Australia to appreciate how distinctive the various jurisdictions are. A single jurisdiction might police the diverse needs of cities, urban areas, rural towns and remote bush communities. Others have indigenous communities and vast geographical areas to police. To illustrate this last point, the force in Western Australian police a geographical area of 2.5 million square kilometres, the world's largest non-federated area of police jurisdiction. As a result, each jurisdiction has different cultures, different populations and different ways of doing business (Fleming and O'Reilly 2008). In terms of education and training, Western Australia, Queensland, New South Wales and, to a lesser extent, Tasmania all have, or have had links to their state university/ies. Since 1998, police recruit training in NSW has been a collaborative effort between Charles Sturt University and the NSW Police Force. It is still, at the time of writing, the only state that has recruits who undertake university studies and pay for their own pre-entry education (Mahony and Prenzler 1996).

The Australian Federal Police used to require a university degree as an entry requirement but has since abolished that condition. In Queensland, early ideals sought to ensure that individuals looking for promotion to Inspector should be in possession of a university degree. That too, was phased out. Other jurisdictional arrangements include encouraging officers to take university courses as a matter of personal choice; officers completing specific courses as an element or totality of their probationer training; fast-track promotion schemes that include tertiary study and the organisational sponsorship of individual officers to undergo post-graduate study (Rowe 2009: 2). Such initiatives are not always a priority. In states such as Tasmania, where austerity measures have involved recruit freezes, university teaching agreements have been cancelled or put on hold indefinitely.

Much of the early educational activity was motivated by ideals of professionalising police, although as others have noted, broader structural reforms both in policing and education (Rowe 2009; Chan 2003) and recommendations in the context of Royal Commissions into Police Misconduct (Fleming and Lafferty 2000) have all provided strong motivation for such reforms. Yet despite some of these common concerns, the diversity across the jurisdictions in terms of culture, leadership, organisational objectives and recruitment practices mean that despite the best efforts of APPSC and ANZPAA, there is 'no cohesive training and education strategy for policing'. As well, there is significant difficulty in developing common police qualifications in the context of tertiary education (White 2012).

Attitudes to police education and professionalisation

There is a wealth of evidence to suggest that police education has a positive impact on policing practice (Trofymowych 2007/8), yet there remains a significant band of officers who are ambivalent about the value of education as opposed to police academy training (Mahony and Prenzler 1996). Additionally, there are many officers who struggle with the notion of attaining professionalism – either because 'they already are professional' or because they believe that 'trying to obtain professional status for police is doomed to failure' (see Trofymowych 2007/8: 428–430). Others cite the perceived lack of organisational support for external learning, a lack of certainty around professional 'reward' for undergoing further education and a stated lack of ambition to warrant such commitment as reasons for not engaging with tertiary educational study (Fleming 2008). While both Australian and New Zealand federal police associations support the professionalisation thrust, their central concern is one of national mobility for police officers, a national registration scheme and core national standards. The PFA is unwilling to enter into individual state and territory concerns about recruitment, education and training out of respect for the individual state and territory police union/association agendas.

There is little research into police attitudes towards ideals of police professionalism and how education and training fits into that vision. Christine Nixon recalls the introduction of compulsory tertiary study for NSW Police recruits: 'When it was announced . . . there was uproar – we'd never get the recruits we needed, the system would collapse, the thin blue line would lose its muscle, and so on, and so forth' (Nixon with Chandler 2011: 101).

Fleming's unpublished study in Tasmania (2008) confirms such anxiety among some officers and suggests that commitment to further study and the ideals of the professionalism agenda increase as an individual moves up the ranks but more work needs to be done. Trofymowych's (2007/8) work suggests that not all police officers working in police education 'accept that police can obtain full professional status' (p. 430). Trofymowych's view (2007/8: 430) is that 'there is still a long way to go':

> If police are ever to attain professional status in Australia there needs to be a common vision and implementation plan which originates from the top of each organisation and is then championed and embraced by those working in key management and education roles.

A 'common vision and implementation plan' however would need the cooperation of individual organisations.

Organisational considerations

At the organisational level, the 'doing of' professionalism has implications for public administrations of efficiency, technological expertise, performance measurement and standards of excellence in recruitment and training. Codes of conduct, recruitment issues and potential 'mobility' plans have policy consequences at both the organisational and at the state/territory governance level. Scholars argue that to change the way a police organisation does business requires significant cultural change. Police cultural knowledge is a product of the structural conditions of work. A professional model, 'will not replace existing cultural knowledge unless such a change is reinforced by existing structural conditions' (Chan 1999: 137). Imposing change through external bodies or from 'the top' imposes a number of problems. Such changes do not always deliver the intended consequences and can be costly both in financial and administrative terms. In Australia, local concerns and state politics drives police organisational reform on a number of levels. This is true across all jurisdictions. As a result external bodies seeking to impose national guidelines on any issue that will impact on organisational imperatives often find themselves challenged by local issues and there is often a reluctance to accept 'common approaches'. In the context of ANZPAA and other bodies committed to the pursuit of police professionalism, this often means an inability to penetrate jurisdictional reform agendas, difficulty in standardising police practice and, perhaps more broadly, a limited ability to impose a common approach to police professionalism (see White 2012).

Where are we now?

Twenty years ago, the ASPC rightly predicted that initiatives relating to education, training, accreditations and standards would take time to develop and would only be progressed over several years (Rohl and Barnsley 1995: 245). Policing in Australia and New Zealand and in the context of professionalisation has yet to 'develop a professional culture underpinned by superior management practices and a commitment to corporate excellence' across all jurisdictions. The professionalisation of policing has not as yet facilitated professional mobility across jurisdictions; there is no National Core Training Curriculum and no Professional Police Registration Board. There is no formal body of knowledge made up of evidence-based research (although ANZPAA maintains the Australia New Zealand Policing Information Resource Exchange knowledge management portal – ANZPire). There is not yet a professional body to which all members would be ultimately accountable and 'responsible for self-regulation of the profession' (Rohl and Barnsley 1995: 241).

ANZPAA's self-perceived lack of influence over police reform agendas across jurisdictions, its difficulty in formalising police practice across state and territory boundaries, its limited control over what happens in police academies in terms of police qualifications, and its perceived failure to impose a common approach to police professionalism have already been noted. There is not yet an 'agreed definition' or a widespread professional culture. There is no collective research agenda (although individual forces such as Queensland and NSW, for example, actively pursue research partnerships with universities in their respective states) or an acknowledged consensually agreed corpus which aspirants have to learn and be accredited before they can profess the knowledge as a member of that profession.

Yet as we document these 'limitations' and note the ways in which aspirations have not yet been reached, we must also acknowledge the substantial, if incremental progress that has been made. This is true across the states and territories individually. Each jurisdiction has in its own specific way sought to advance the professionalisation agenda. Some have been more successful than others. In five years, ANZPAA and APPSC have between them provided the context in which police professionalisation is gathering momentum. White (2012) advises that there is an increased willingness across Australia and New Zealand jurisdictions to advance police professionalisation. International connections, particularly with the UK, have been 'mutually beneficial'. The commitment to police professionalisation at senior level has included the Australia New Zealand Police Leadership Strategy (a cross-jurisdictional endeavour aimed at developing leadership in policing); education and training guidelines have been developed, approved and disseminated in such areas as family and domestic violence and mental health. Further Education and Training Guidelines have been approved by the APPSC in areas such as emergency management and community engagement. Other guidelines such as the Practice Level of a Police Supervisor are under way.

In conjunction with APPSC, ANZPAA is currently conducting further research on elements of the PPSM (Practice Certificates and Continuous Professional Development). This will take into consideration Police Registration when responding to SCPEM regarding National Police Registration. The PFA and NZPA working within APPSC continue to pursue registration over the 'easier' option of certification. In 1998, the PFA applied successfully for a federal grant of A$110,000 to develop and market a Professional Registration Board for police to 'ensure the professional independence and integrity of the police profession' (Burgess 2009). In 2013, an election year, the PFA will once again turn to Australia's respective political parties to push its case for Professional Registration (Burgess 2013).

ANZPAA is currently in the process of developing a formal Australia and New Zealand Police Professionalisation Strategy for 2013–2018. The strategy will draw together all police professionalisation activities that are currently taking place across Australia and New Zealand policing, and provide a framework for future police professionalisation activities. The strategy is still currently in draft form and will be presented to APPSC later this year for approval.

Lessons learned

In many ways, the pursuit of police professionalism in Australia can be likened to an exercise in organisational change. There is little scholarship that examines the successful elements of change management and the process of institutionalising change in police organisations (e.g. Hart 1996; Ikerd 2010). What there is, however, tells us that there must be effective planning and preparation around any new agenda (Ikerd 2010), the local context needs to be factored into extensive consultation processes at all levels (Bayley 2005; Brodeur 2005) and middle-level management should be very much part of the agenda in the change process (Hart 1996; Ikerd 2010).

The Australian professionalisation agenda began slowly – there was a broad understanding of what needed to be done but despite small working groups and general ideals, the long-term preparation and planning were missing. The 'agenda' and direction changed constantly, sometimes because of external events (New Zealand becoming part of the broader picture in 1998), sometimes because of new personalities taking over various phases of the programme. The changing agenda was negotiated by Police Commissioners, ministerial staff and national police union representatives – there was little, if any recourse to middle management or the rank and file, especially at the local level. In a country like Australia with nine different police organisations (and Commissioners), all with different governance structures, different politics, funding regimes, legislation, policy and academies, attention to planning, consultation and local circumstances was crucial. It remains so.

In a country with so many political jurisdictions, politics and personalities are always going to be a factor. This is not the forum within which such issues need to be aired and discussed. But a reminder that both politics (little 'p' and big 'P') and personalities can move mountains but can also stop progress in its tracks. Being mindful of both is a lesson learned.

Conclusion

The move towards police professionalism in Australia and New Zealand has gained momentum over the past five years and significant progress has been made. It is true that many things have not been achieved and several initiatives remain to be activated, accepted or approved. It is true that working across jurisdictions, dealing with disparate politics and individuals may have reduced that progress. However, a professional conversation has begun – a conversation that has some clarity and purpose. There are tangible codes of ethics and statements of professional values and an acknowledgement of the value of education and training. There are collaborative partnerships among national policing bodies (such as, for example, the National Institute of Forensic Science) that have, in conjunction with ANZPAA created national standards in their field. ANZPAA and its various partners are in the business of knowledge creation, dissemination and persuasion. There is a commitment to police professionalism from ANZPAA, its partners and others who see the value of higher education, those who do not want to be passive recipients of research but who seek to be part of an active research agenda and who have aspirations to full professional status. However long it takes, it is the move towards professionalisation that matters. As one Western Australia officer has noted, 'occupations that fail to lead the agenda in advancing their own professionalization may well forfeit that role to other more influential agencies' (cited in Lanyon 2006: 18).

Notes

1 In 1998, New Zealand joined the National Police Education Standards Council. For the purposes of this chapter I have used Australasia throughout.
2 This chapter confines itself to the national approach to police professionalisation. The chapter does not allow for any serious discussion about state/territory initiatives in Australia or local initiatives in New Zealand.
3 In Victoria the Chief of Police is referred to as Chief Commissioner, and in the ACT the Chief Officer is called the Chief Police Officer.
4 The APMC was established to promote a coordinated national response to law enforcement issues and to maximise the efficient use of police resources. Its objectives in carrying out this national role included the further advancement of the professionalism of policing. It is now known as the Ministerial Council for Police and Emergency Management – Police.
5 The Australian Graduate School of Police Management was established between Charles Sturt University and the Commonwealth in 1992 which allowed senior police officers to be enrolled in part-time postgraduate courses by 1995. Prior to this, as Chan has noted, NSW under Commissioner John Avery had acknowledged the value of education for police officers since the mid-1980s. By 1992, many educational and leadership programmes were available to police officers in NSW (Chan 2003: 80–84).

6 It is important to note that the following discussion about ANZPAA in this chapter
reflects its activities in the context of education and training and the move towards
professionalisation generally. ANZPAA's work is broader than this discourse allows and
those who are interested in finding out more information about this organisation can
visit: http://www.anzpaa.org.au/about-us.

References

Barlow, V. and Proctor, B (1980) 'Professionalization and Ethics', *Australian Police Journal*,
34(2): 116–129.

Bayley, D.H. (2005) 'Police Reform as Foreign Policy', *The Australian and New Zealand
Journal of Criminology*, 38(2): 206–215.

Bradley, D. and Cioccarelli, P. (1992) 'National police education issues – the role of the
Australian Police Staff College: A discussion paper'. Volume one, Annexures, Sydney:
NSW Police, 1–70.

Brodeur, J.P. (2005) 'Trotsky in Blue: Permanent Policing Reform', *The Australian and New
Zealand Journal of Criminology*, 38(2): 254–267.

Burgess, M. (2009) 'Professional Registration of Australia's Police', Police Federation of Australia. Available at: http://www.pfa.org.au/files/uploads/Police_National_Registration_
Scheme.pdf (accessed 13 March 2013).

Burgess, M. (2013) Personal conversation with author, 5 March 2013.

Burgess, M., Fleming, J. and Marks, M. (2006) 'Thinking Critically about Police Unions in
Australia: Internal Democracy and External Responsiveness', *Police Practice and Research:
An International Journal*, 7(5): 391–409.

Carte, G. (1973) 'August Vollmer and the Origins of Police Professionalism', *Journal of Police
Science and Administration*, 1(3): 274–281.

Chan, J. (1999) 'Police Culture', in D. Dixon (ed.) *A Culture of Corruption: Changing an
Australian Police Service*, Hawkins Press, 98–137.

Chan, J. (2003) *Fair Cop: Learning the Art of Policing*, Toronto, University of Toronto
Press.

Dale, A. (1994) 'Professionalism and the Police', *The Police Journal*, 67(3): 209–218.

Directions in Australasian Policing 2012–2015, Standing Council on Police and Emergency
Management (SCPEM). Available at: http://www.anzpaa.org.au/corporate-news-and-
publications/news/7137 (accessed 13 March 2013).

Fleming, J. (2008) *Tertiary Education Assistance Scheme Policy*, Tasmania Police Focus Groups
Final Report, August.

Fleming, J. (2012) 'Policing Indigenous People in the NPY Lands', in S. Bronitt, C. Harfield
and S. Hufnagel (eds) *Cross-Border Law Enforcement: Regional Law Enforcement Cooperation – European, Australian and Asia-Pacific Perspectives*, Chapter 9, Routledge-Cavendish,
Oxford, 163–176.

Fleming, J. and Lafferty, G. (2000) 'New Management Techniques and Restructuring in
Police Organisations', *Policing: An International Journal of Police Strategy and Management*,
23(2): 154–168.

Fleming, J. and O'Reilly, J. (2008) 'In Search of a Process: Community Policing in Australia', in T. Williamson (ed.) *The Handbook of Knowledge Based Policing: Current Conceptions
and Future Directions*, John Wiley, Chichester, Sussex, Chapter 6, 139–156.

Hart, J.M. (1996) 'The Management of Change in Police Organizations', in M. Pagon
(ed.) *Policing in Central and Eastern Europe: Comparing Firsthand Knowledge with Experience
from the West (Part IV – Policing and Change)*, Ljubljana, Slovenia: College of Police and
Security Studies.

Home Office (2012) College of Policing, Home Office, London. Available at: http://www.
homeoffice.gov.uk/police/college-of-policing/ (accessed 13 March 2013).

Ikerd, T.E. (2010) 'Beyond "Flavor of the Month" – Institutionalizing Problem-oriented
Policing (POP) in the CMPD', *Policing: An International Journal of Police Strategies and
Management*, 33(1): 179–202.

Lanyon, I. (2006) 'Achieving Professionalization of Australasian Policing: The story thus
far . . . .'. Unpublished paper.

Lanyon, I. (2007) 'Professionalization of Policing in Australia: The Implications for Police
Managers', in M. Mitchell and J. Casey (eds) *Police Leadership and Management*, Federation
Press, Leichhardt, 107–123.

Lanyon, I. (2009) 'Professionalization', in A. Wakefield and J. Fleming (eds) *Sage Dictionary
of Policing*, Sage Publications, London, 248–250.

Mahoney, D. and Prenzler, T. (1996) 'Police Studies, the University and the Police Service:
An Australian Study', *Journal of Criminal Justice Education*, 7(2): 283–304.

Manning, P. (1977) *Police Work: The Social Organisation of Working*, MIT Press, Cambridge.

Mecum, R. (1979) 'Police Professionalism: A New Look at an Old Topic', *Police Chief*,
46(8): 46–49.

Nixon, C. with Chandler, J. (2011) *Fair Cop*, Victory Books, Carlton, Victoria.

NPIA (2008) Annual Report and Accounts 2007/2008. Available at: http://www.npia.
police.uk/en/docs/Annual_Report_2007–08.pdf (accessed 13 March 2013).

Price, B. (1979) 'Integrated Professionalism: A Model for Controlling Police Practices',
Journal of Police Science and Administration, 7(1): 93–97.

Proud, L. (2013) 'Police Professionalization and ANZPAA', *Australasian Policing: A Journal of
Professional Practice and Research*, 5(1): 19.

Reiner, R. (1986) 'The Modern Bobby: The Development of the British Police', *Policing*,
2(4): 258–275.

Rohl, T.F. and Barnsley, R.H. (1995) 'The Strategic Transformation of Policing from
Occupational to Professional Status', in B. Etter and M. Palmer (eds) *Police Leadership in
Australia*, The Federation Press, Leichhardt, 234–255.

Rowe, M. (2009) 'Police Education, Professionalism and Diversity', *Briefing Paper 9*, Tasmanian Institute of Law Enforcement Studies, University of Tasmania, 1–6, March.

Sturma, M. (1987) 'Policing the Criminal Frontier in Mid-Nineteenth Century Australia, Britain and America', in M. Finnane (ed.) *Policing in Australia: Historical Perspectives*,
UNSW Press, Kensington, 15–34.

Trofymowych, D. (2007/8) 'Police Education Past and Present: Perceptions of Australian
Police Managers and Academics', *Flinders Journal of Law Reform*, 10419–433.

White, J. (2012) 'ANZPAA', Paper presented at The Third Annual Conference of the
Higher Education Forum for Learning and Development in Policing (POLCON 3),
4–5 September.

23

THE POLICE AS PROFESSIONAL PROBLEM SOLVERS

Nick Tilley and Gloria Laycock

Introduction

This chapter returns to the raison d'être of policing. What is policing intended to do? We assume that it is still primarily about meeting its original mission: to prevent crime and to maintain the Queen's peace, using enforcement where necessary including, in particular, the detection of offenders. Despite various efforts to reduce the range of additional problems dealt with by the police they remain the 'agency of last resort'. Whether they should or should not be dealing with such a range of problems is not an issue for this chapter. The present reality is that in addition to crime there is a host of other issues the police are expected to deal with, such as neighbour disputes, missing children, rowdy youth, false alarms, public demonstrations, stray dogs, suicides, truancy, traffic accidents and medical emergencies. As Herman Goldstein (1990: 1), the doyen of police problem solving, put it:

> Our society requires that the police deal with an incredibly broad range of troublesome situations. Handling these situations within the limitations that we place on the police is the essence of policing. It follows that efforts to improve policing should extend to and focus on the end products of policing – on the effectiveness and fairness of the police in dealing with the substantive problems that the public looks to the police to handle.

Following Goldstein our argument is that policing needs to put this diverse business centre-stage, rather than management systems, leadership skills, performance monitoring and the organisational infrastructure which have preoccupied much of policing over recent decades. Good management and leadership skills are necessary to the delivery of 'professional policing' in the sense in which we mean it in this chapter, but the first priority is agreement on how the core business should be delivered and developed. We argue here that 'solving problems' fairly and effectively within the broad remit of the police is what they should be doing in order to deliver safer and more secure communities.

In the remainder of this chapter we discuss what we mean by this in more detail and consider the implications for police activity at tactical and strategic levels. In the next section we consider the notion of professionalism, and following that we return to the ideas inherent in police problem solving. We then discuss specifically why the police need to be professional problem solvers and the necessary conditions for doing this, before finally drawing some conclusions on what we feel needs to be done in the future.

Professionalism

Professionalism and professionalisation can have their downsides. At its worst professionalism can be associated with pretentious status-enhancement and self-aggrandisement; efforts to improve market position by excluding others; the introduction and institutionalisation of untested standard practices; reluctance to undertake work that is not commensurate with claimed professional standing; and a mix of conservatism and defensiveness as practitioners play safe by falling back on unchallenged orthodoxies.

In the United States the police were professionalised in the middle decades of the twentieth century in an effort to remove the abuses of discretion that allowed for 'corruption, physical and other forms of abuse, callousness, discourtesy, and inefficiency' (Goldstein 1990: 6). Controls were established on what officers did to ensure that they acted 'professionally', by which, at the time, was meant fairly, lawfully, consistently, and proportionately as law-enforcement officers. But the standard operating procedures that were introduced as part of this development were untested or found to be ineffective. Moreover, departures from them in practice were widespread. The focus of policing shifted to the management rather than the substance of policing. Instead of working out whether the problems the public expected the police to address were being dealt with effectively and fairly, police services and the 'professional' staff within them came to focus on operational efficiency through the introduction of new technologies.

When we talk about 'professional policing' here, we mean it to refer, as in medicine, to the application of an established body of knowledge and the completion of high-quality work with a considerable amount of delegated authority for staff following high standards of professional ethics which stress personal integrity and public service. A professional organisation supports this process in valuing equity, non-discrimination and in monitoring the work of members to ensure that standards are maintained. A professional organisation is also concerned with continuous improvement and continuing professional development of its members. While the police may argue that they are already operating professionally; under this definition and in relation to problem solving they are failing to do so to the extent that they do not routinely follow the standard problem solving practices to any significant extent, are not systematically trained in them, do not draw on the established knowledge base, do not have in place ethical or other governance procedures related to problem solving and have not integrated the processes into standard policing practice.

The 'professionalisation' of policing would require the establishment of a professional body to police the police: one that was responsible for ensuring that education and training were appropriate, that standards were maintained, that serving police officers were drawing on a body of established knowledge which was scientifically and ethically defensible and which had the confidence and support of the communities the police are intended to serve. Such a professional body would be able to strike members off if they failed to meet minimum standards of service and would also protect members from undue pressure from an employer if they were asked to behave in ways that did not accord with the profession's code of ethics. Many of these tasks form part of the agenda of the proposed new Police College and it would be a relatively short step to move from the current proposals for the Police College to something closer to the colleges familiar to other professionals with, specifically, the right to strike off individuals from the profession should they fail to meet the expected professional standards in any respect.

Problem solving in policing

We all solve problems every day – where to eat, what to buy, which route to take to work. Many actions follow 'standing decisions'. They require very little thought: we behave routinely. The authors have a standing decision not to rob a bank despite the fact that we think we might be able to plan it so well as to get away with it. Other decisions, such as which car to buy, whether to move house or where to move to are potentially life changing and would require much more thought. We would, for example, carry out some 'research' and perhaps a bit of analysis – what is available? What are its characteristics? What can we afford? How can we best balance our preferences? And so on.

Similar processes apply in any job, including policing. The police solve problems every day with issues ranging from 'I have lost my cat' to 'my child has disappeared'. For detectives there are particular problems in determining who committed a crime, finding the offenders and the evidence associated with the offence, taking it to court and so on. So there can be no doubt that the police address problems as part of their job. So what does it mean to talk about the police as professional problem solvers? Are they not that already?

Goldstein observed in the 1970s that the police tend to approach police business as a series of single incidents calling for a response (Goldstein, 1979). They might solve a crime, resolve a dispute, find a cat, and so on but they, or more likely a colleague on a different shift, might also be called back to the same place a short time later and go through the process again. Goldstein argued that by grouping similar incidents together and dealing with them collectively, problems could be reduced, removed or ameliorated in their harmful effects. He called this approach 'problem-oriented policing' (POP) and it is in his sense that we discuss problem solving here.

Subsequently Eck and Spelman (1987), working in Newport News in the USA, developed the acronym 'SARA', standing for scanning, analysis, response and assessment, as a means of assisting the police in the problem-solving process. There are now several acronyms associated with police problem solving, although SARA remains the most commonly used (Sidebottom and Tilley, 2011) including in the UK.

The process of problem solving associated with POP is akin to scientific method. Scientists use scientific method as a way of testing hypotheses, refining theory and improving knowledge. This is what the police should be doing under the heading of POP, but in practice its application is geographically patchy and generally lacks depth. In specifying problems on which to focus and in working out what they might do more effectively to address them, police need to test prevailing working theories as well as new conjectures on the conditions giving rise to those problems to find improved responses. Novel responses then comprise hypotheses that need to be tested on the ground by assessing their effectiveness, and, done well, this theory testing contributes new professional understanding on the basis of which further improvements in effectiveness are made possible. The notion of testing hypotheses as a process running routinely through professional police problem solving has received relatively little attention in discussions of POP, although we take it to be implicit in the process. SARA is intended to assist the movement from the identification and articulation of a problem through the development and implementation of a response to an assessment of whether or not the problem was thereby reduced. A brief example will show what we mean:

1   The police have a problem of personal theft.
2   Rates of personal theft against women increase with their age once they reach their 30s and the highest level at any age group is among the over 70s.
3   The police have been unable effectively to deal with the problem of theft from older women by their conventional enforcement/detection methods.
4   Older women often place their bags in trolleys as they shop in supermarkets.
5   Much personal theft against older women occurs in supermarkets.
6   When distracted while shopping, women placing their bags in supermarket trolleys are at heightened risk of having their bags and purses stolen.
7   One way of reducing the vulnerability of older women to theft in supermarkets is to provide a convenient safer place to store their bags while shopping, making theft more difficult for prospective offenders.
8   Supermarkets might provide redesigned trolleys to provide for a safe place within them to store their bags when shopping.
9   Responsible supermarkets, when alerted to the risk faced by elderly female customers, will be willing to experiment with redesigned trolleys.
10 The implementation of redesigned trolleys can be undertaken in a controlled way that will enable their effectiveness in reducing theft against older women customers to be tested.

This sequence of ten hypotheses was tested as part of a local, grass-roots problem-solving exercise in the West Midlands (a copy of the report can be found at http://www.popcenter.org/library/awards/goldstein/2009/09–16(F).pdf).

Every stage in the problem-solving process, therefore, involves the testing of hypotheses: Have we specified the problem correctly? Are our assumptions about it warranted? How successful are current ways of dealing with it? What might plausibly improve the effectiveness of our treatment of it? How do we implement that solution (which often involves working with partners)? And finally, did the solution achieve the desired result? If the problem is not clearly understood then other alternative accounts of its development, and particularly the opportunities that facilitated it, will have to be articulated and tested. Similarly in identifying a response, the mechanism through which it might achieve its desired effect would need to be identified. It is this mechanism that is being tested when the efficacy of the response is considered. The whole of this process can draw on and contribute to a body of research evidence with which the police need to be familiar. So the process of problem solving is not necessarily straightforward, and requires supporting infrastructure at the organisational level to ensure that it is implemented and maintained: More on this below.

Why the police need to be professional problem solvers

The police are unable to deal with the volume of calls received on a case-by-case basis. Moreover, although responding to incidents individually might make sense in terms of enforcement and reassurance, if calls are patterned or clustered (as they usually are) then devising strategies that prevent or reduce their recurrence is more efficient in terms of police resource use, is more effective in addressing issues falling within the police remit, and more fully answers community concerns.

Five major forms of crime concentration have been widely found, which can form the basis for aggregate problem solving. These forms of concentration relate to offenders, targets, locations, victims and times. In all, the so-called '80/20 rule' (or, more formally, the 'Pareto principle') operates. According to this, a high proportion of the phenomenon of interest (say, 80 per cent) is found in only a small proportion (say, 20 per cent) of potential cases. We know, for example, that:

- A small proportion of offenders account for a large proportion of all crime. In England and Wales up to age 32, seven per cent of males with six or more convictions have been found to account for 65 per cent of all male convictions (Home Office Statistical Bulletin, 1989).
- The acronym CRAVED has been devised to try to capture the attributes of objects that tend to be stolen most often: it refers to Concealable, Removable, Available, Valuable, Enjoyable and Disposable (Clarke, 1999). Cash, cars, purses, jewellery, cell phones, cameras and laptop computers are all typical examples.

- Just 3.3 per cent of addresses and intersections in Minneapolis were found to account for 50 per cent of all dispatched calls for service (Sherman *et al.*, 1989). Such concentrations are common in many cities.
- Across a sample of 17 countries the International Crime Victimisation Survey found that an average of 40 per cent of crimes against individuals and households were against targets already victimised that year (Farrell *et al.*, 2005: 143).
- Most crimes have distinct temporal patterns. Most obviously, city centre crime and disorder tends to be concentrated during weekend evenings; antisocial behaviour tends to peak around Halloween; lawn mowers are stolen most often in spring; and so on.

The problems dealt with by the police are found consistently across time and jurisdiction to be highly concentrated. These are the 'squeaks' on which problem-solving grease can best be targeted.

The evidence for the effectiveness of systematic, professional problem solving in dealing with these problems is plentiful. A large number of individual case studies, many submitted as entries for the International Goldstein Award or the British Tilley Awards, have been able to provide persuasive evidence on this point. Experiments have found that places where systematic problem solving is put in place outperform those where it is not (Weisburd *et al.*, 2010), and a review of general approaches to policing found problem solving to be most effective (Weisburd and Eck, 2004). Problem solving has also been found effective across a wide range of problem-types, including violence, missing persons, youth homicide, burglary, car theft, vandalism, theft of outboard motors, road traffic accidents, shop theft, antisocial behaviour, nuisance callers and so on.

Unfortunately, there is also ample evidence that the implementation of systematic problem solving is patchy, tends to be short-lived, involves only parts of police services, generally concentrates only on local, low-level problems, and is subject to poor internal assessment, if any. Although it is found that weak problem solving is better than no problem solving at all in its outcome effectiveness, the professionalisation of problem solving, as conceived in this chapter, promises much more. But its delivery turns on the creation of conditions in which it can flourish throughout the police service, and not as a residual activity carried out by individual enthusiasts.

Conditions for the police to be professional problem solvers

We have argued that the police should address the diverse range of problems falling within their remit, this being the core business of policing. But much more is required if this is to be achieved in practice. In this section we look at what must be done to embed professional problem solving within policing.

Problem solving can and should be carried out at all levels within policing. Some problems are easily and more appropriately solved on the streets, at a local level, while others are more efficiently dealt with at force, national or even international level. In addition to working on problem solving at force level, constabularies have a responsibility for formulating and implementing a strategy to support and develop problem solving throughout their organisations and thereby to provide the context and infrastructure within which the local-level work can be completed. Table 23.1 sets out some ideas on what might be done at local, force and national levels, for strategic ('Enabling and encouraging professional problem solving') and for tactical ('Doing and delivering professional problem solving'). As can be seen from the table, strategic and tactical activities operate at all levels and it is not the case, as is often assumed, that strategic activities take place exclusively at a high organisational level while all the action is reserved for the 'troops'.

By local level in Table 23.1 we include the basic command, operational policing and neighbourhood contexts at which the police deal with the bulk of 'regular' crime and disorder and where they come into contact with communities on a daily basis. In the sense in which we are talking about professional problem solving, it is most common at this level, although there are still shortcomings in terms of patchy or inconsistent training and supervision of the locally based staff, accessibility of data, time available for consideration of the nature of problems and their solutions, accessibility to the kinds of partners that might be involved in the solutions to crime

TABLE 23.1 Strategic and tactical problem solving at local, force and national levels

	Strategic (Enabling and encouraging professional problem solving)	Tactical (Doing and delivering professional problem solving)
Local	Sergeant/Inspector supervision and coaching	Local SARA-type professional problem solving
	↑	↓
Force	Development and implementation of force problem-solving strategy Education and training CPD delivery Data and intelligence provision Analytic services Performance management	Cross-boundary/major crime SARA-type professional problem solving Provision of leverage for local problem solving
	↑	↓
National	Education and accreditation including CPD course identification Research and Development for specific problems Support of good practice database Awards scheme to recognise and encourage problem solving	National and international SARA-type professional problem solving

and disorder problems, and the support necessary for later evaluation. There is also limited access to prior good practice or the structure necessary to contribute to a database of good practice following a successful problem-solving venture.

'Force level' relates to the major administrative unit for the majority of UK policing and it is here that the crucial task of developing the force strategy supporting local, and delivering force-wide, problem solving rests. That strategy, in turn, depends to some extent on activities at national level, which in the UK may mean ACPO and its associated committees, the National Crime Agency (in due course) or within central government, which would normally mean the Home Office. The Home Office, for example, financially supports the UK Tilley Award for Problem Solving Partnerships.

At whatever level it is being applied, SARA-type professional problem solving begins with scanning and analysis, which involve access to comprehensive data and intelligence systems. The combined aim of these activities is a thorough understanding of the problem of concern and, in particular, an appreciation of the opportunities that facilitated the behaviours at issue. It is the reduction of these opportunities that most often leads to the reduction of the problem. This means that officers need free access to data and force intelligence systems and need the skills to manipulate and understand that information – or access to staff (such as professional crime analysts) who do.

At national and force levels, as at local levels, hypothesis testing is crucial. Here is an example where the hypotheses were often quite difficult to test but where the outcome was ultimately that a persistent problem was very substantially reduced:

1   There is a national problem of theft of cars.
2   Theft of cars is a function of the desirability of the car for the prospective thief and the ease with which it can be stolen.
3   Car theft can be reduced by improvements in vehicle security, making them more difficult to steal, especially for the opportunist joy-rider.
4   Car manufacturers are reluctant to devote resources to improving the security of their products.
5   Car manufacturers producing cars stolen at a relatively high rate are open to shaming if the vulnerability of their products to theft is exposed.
6   The Home Office production of a Car Theft Index, systematically showing the broad bands of vulnerability to theft of differing makes and models of car, will enjoy broad credibility.
7   Car manufacturers will prefer to improve the security of their vehicles, reducing their vulnerability to theft, than to face exposure through later iterations of the Car Theft Index.
8   Improvements to the security of cars brought about by shaming manufacturers will produce a sustained and significant drop in car theft.

The development of response options requires some understanding of the mechanisms through which they might achieve the desired reductions (Tilley and

Laycock, 2002) and in most cases requires action by third parties. It is often difficult for junior officers to persuade partners to work on crime reduction projects and some 'leverage' might need to be applied to deliver the required responses (Scott, 2005). In the car theft example, although tactics are available at local level and force levels relating, for example, to alerting drivers to places where their cars are at high risk, to advising drivers on the use of security measures when they leave their cars, to persuading car park operators or local authorities to install CCTV, to the design of new housing developments which are not conducive to car crime, and to promoting secured car park schemes etc., as might be suggested by the analysis of the local problem, the broader issue of vehicle vulnerability was beyond their competence and called for national efforts.

Creating a context within which professional problem-solving activities might become embedded within the police service to the point at which they are seen as a necessary element of policing is perhaps one of the greatest challenges. As Goldstein (2003) reminds us, the police are rightly required to respond to calls for service as expected by communities and as, indeed, they like to do. This requirement provides a constant pressure against other activities, particularly those which do not play to the police strength as an action-oriented, rather gung-ho organisation. The slower pace of analysis and contemplation is not immediately attractive.

The first step might be the creation of a force-level strategy for the implementation and development of problem solving at the various levels described in Table 23.1. Some forces have done this and have been extremely effective at implementation, to the extent that they are acknowledged as world leading (Bullock *et al.*, 2006). But this has been done on the basis of the strong, determined leadership of a particular chief constable or ACC who, once they are transferred, leave the organisation at risk of movement in a different direction. It is the exception to find consistency over time, and we aspire to a more stable and uniform picture.

One of the key decisions to be made in developing a force strategy is the extent to which scanning and analysis is a specialist function to be completed by the analyst or whether it can and should be carried out by the front-line officers. Although there are examples where specialist crime analysis is required (for example, where complex mapping or programming is called for) there are many examples where a professionally educated and trained basic grade officer will be able to complete a problem-solving project on the basis of a basic understanding of data and the ability to ask sensible questions and hypothesise about what might be causing what. Sophisticated statistics are not required but a real affinity with data is. As more graduates join the basic policing ranks it becomes more plausible to expect a minimum level of numeracy at all levels within the police service, alongside an ability to complete a basic POP project and to manage (and ask the right questions) of an analyst completing a more complex task.

The kinds of problems we have in mind, which might be dealt with at the different organisational levels discussed, are shown in Table 23.2. There is an obvious sense in which all crimes are manifest locally. Although international drug dealing, for example, is a high-level problem, it manifests itself on the streets in communities where drug sales and associated addictions cause considerable local damage. There is, therefore, often a decision to be made about the locus or loci of a solution or set of solutions for a problem that is visible locally, as in the car theft example referred to earlier. In Table 23.2 we have shown some of the kinds of problems that might be dealt with at the levels discussed. We have added in an international row for illustrative purposes while acknowledging that the UK police can do little to influence the activities of EUROPOL or INTERPOL.

The offences shown are simply examples and the easiest way to differentiate between them is to ask the question 'can a solution be implemented at this level and/or do we have to pass it higher?' So for example, if we find antisocial behaviour on Friday and Saturday nights to be endemic and consistently linked to alcohol abuse (as we do) then there is a case for passing this problem up to national level and expecting central government to address the alcohol legislation, which is currently, perhaps, unhelpful.

The level at which solutions might be developed for the problems shown in Table 23.2 will vary with the exact characteristics of the problem. So, for example, the situation just described in which antisocial behaviour is linked to alcohol abuse and which calls for a national response is different from antisocial behaviour by a group of school children in a local school on buses at home time. This latter problem can probably be more appropriately and adequately dealt with through an active partnership with the school and local bus company.

TABLE 23.2 Different levels of problem and solution

		PROBLEMS			
SOLUTIONS	*Level*	*Local*	*Force*	*National*	*International*
	Local	Antisocial behaviour Neighbour disputes	House burglary	Drink driving	Animal poaching
	Force	False alarms Missing from children's homes	Organised crime families Travelling criminals	Metal theft	Counterfeit goods
	National (ACPO/ central govt)	Fuel drive-offs Shop theft at supermarkets	Car park car crime	Theft of insecure high-value cars	Drug production
	International	Trafficked prostitutes Theft of cars for export	Drug-trafficking	Over fishing	Industrial pollution

Conclusions

In this final section we suggest what needs to be done if problem solving is firmly to be integrated into routine policing and seen as 'part of the job'. We should first point out that this is a non-trivial task and requires a fundamental change in the way policing is conceived and delivered. In the space available here we cannot go into the detail required and have settled for making some general points. There has certainly been progress, but it has been rather slow, inconsistent and hesitant (Knutsson and Clarke, 2006). Indeed in 2003 Goldstein opined that,

> [M]any projects under the problem-oriented policing label are superficial, and examples of full implementation of the concept . . . are rare. . . . a much larger investment must be made within police agencies in conducting more in-depth, rigorous studies of police business, in implementing the results of these studies, and in the evaluation of implementation efforts.
>
> *(Goldstein 2003: 13)*

Elsewhere, in a review of what has been achieved over the past three decades we have laid out a general agenda for improvement in the delivery of problem-oriented policing (Tilley and Scott, 2012). Here we ask just what is the nature of this larger investment in the UK? Does it, for example, require major financial commitments, which in the present climate must be judged unlikely? Our feeling is that with relatively little investment, much of which would be in training and development, a real change might be achieved.

We have listed below what we feel is needed on the basis of discussion so far:

1 Change must come from the top where senior officers need a deep understanding of the potential of problem solving and do not perceive it as some pseudo-academic exercise that can be taken or left as fancy dictates. Senior police leadership needs, therefore, to be engaged in this process, and this means all at ACPO rank. A stronger problem-solving dimension needs to be built into the Senior Command Course where the advantages of problem solving might be spelled out together with the consequences for policing and police organisation of adopting this approach.
2 Guidance would be useful on the implications for the collection, sharing and analysis of data and intelligence. For example, police data systems are not best designed for problem-solving analysis. And there is an assumption against sharing data for fairly obvious data protection reasons. But it is frequently impossible to investigate problems (repeat victimisation is a good example), without access to personal data on who exactly was victimised and there are many other instances where the net gain from sharing outweighs the potential costs. Any guidance, therefore, needs to address the risk-averse nature of police agencies, in particular their data protection officers, who sometimes see their role as the protection of data rather than the protection of potential victims through the prevention, disruption or detection of crime.

3   Although in some areas there has been impressive progress, problem-solving capabilities at force level still need to be strengthened, and at national level would specifically need to be built in both SOCA/NCA and at all levels of government where such expertise is currently lacking. This applies to both the police themselves and the analysts working for them. There is little point, for example, in training analysts and sending them back to their home agency to be managed by police officers who do not appreciate the potential of the work that they are now better trained to do. Similarly the analysts themselves need to keep up to date with new ideas, techniques, research and development so that they are better placed to support problem solving. Doing so would offer great potential in dealing with organised crime for example.

4   All of these developments would require a national training and development strategy with agreement between central and local government, ACPO and the College of Policing. It is not the place to go into the detail of this strategy here, but we have in mind, for example, much greater integration of problem solving and crime prevention into basic police training and thereafter throughout the police career. At BCU Commander level, we suggest a level of knowledge commensurate with that of a hospital consultant in the medical field. At ACPO level, knowledge of more strategic issues might be a requirement. The College of Policing seems to be the appropriate context within which to develop these ideas and the appropriate place to locate the responsibility for their implementation.

5   An organisation akin to a national crime prevention council might oversee this process and subsequently take over responsibility for the development of national-level problem solving as described earlier in relation to car theft and as indicated in Table 23.1.

6   The College of Policing might take responsibility for the collection and dissemination of a repository of knowledge on problem solving. Some good websites already exist, particularly the US-based COPS site (www.popcenter.org), which *inter alia* provides information on all former Goldstein and Tilley Award winners, but there is a need for a widely available UK good practice database building on existing ACPO and Home Office resources. The College might also take responsibility for encouraging the proper evaluation of problem-solving projects thus increasing the knowledge base further.

7   There are also two obvious links with academe that might be encouraged in this area. First is training at higher and basic levels including the provision of CPD courses for the police and, second, support for the knowledge base through the development of new ideas and further theoretical development on which proper professionalisation depends.

The agenda we have set out is difficult at any time but in the present financial climate it is particularly challenging. But we are not starting from a zero base. Much of the work around the National Intelligence Model (NIM) and Crime and

Disorder Reduction Partnerships (CDRPs) has put the UK ahead of most other countries for the development and delivery of professional problem solving. Neither has been without difficulty (see the chapter by Bullock, in this volume, on intelligence-led policing and, in particular, the NIM), but both have been mandated nationally and both embrace problem solving, the collaboration of the police with other agencies, priority setting on the basis of evidence-based needs, analysis of problems as a basis for determining enforcement and other responses, and the routine assessment of the results of measures put in place. And although further change is time consuming and potentially costly, there is an opportunity to radically improve the way in which UK policing is delivered and to consolidate the changes that have already begun. Rather than see the present shortage of funding as a crisis, we prefer to see it as an opportunity to rethink the delivery of the service and, in that respect, the present review of policing is particularly welcome.

References

Bullock, K., Erol, R. and Tilley, N. (2006) *Problem-Oriented Policing and Partnerships: Implementing an Evidence Based Approach to Crime Reduction.* Cullompton, Devon: Willan.

Clarke, R. V. (1999) Hot Products: understanding, anticipating and reducing demand for stolen goods. Police Research Series Paper 112, Home Office, UK.

Eck, J. and Spelman, W. (1987) *Solving Problems: Problem-Oriented Policing in Newport News.* Washington: Police Executive Research Forum.

Farrell, G., Tseloni, A. and Pease, K. (2005) Repeat victimization in the ICVS and the NCVS. *Crime Prevention and Community Safety: An International Journal*, 7(3): 7–18.

Goldstein, H. (1979) Improving policing: a problem-oriented approach. *Crime & Delinquency*, 25: 236–258.

Goldstein, H. (1990) *Problem Oriented Policing.* New York: McGraw-Hill; Philadelphia: Temple University Press.

Goldstein, H. (2003) 'On Further Developing Problem-Oriented Policing: The Most Critical Need, the Major Impediments, and a Proposal'. In J. Knutsson (ed.) *Problem-Oriented Policing: From Innovation to Mainstream.* Crime Prevention Studies, Volume 15. Monsey, NY: Criminal Justice Press; Cullompton, Devon: Willan.

Home Office Statistical Bulletin (1989) *Criminal and custodial careers of those born in 1953, 1958 and 1963.* Home Office Statistical Bulletin 32/89. London: Home Office.

Knutsson, J. and Clarke, R. V. (2006) *Putting Theory to Work: Implementing Situational Crime Prevention and Problem-Oriented Policing.* Crime Prevention Studies, Volume 20, Monsey, NY: Criminal Justice Press.

Scott, M. (2005) 'Shifting and Sharing Responsibility to Address Public Safety Problems'. In N. Tilley (ed.) *Handbook of Crime Prevention and Community Safety.* Cullompton, Devon: Willan.

Sherman, L. W., Gartin, P. R. and Buerger, M. E. (1989) Hot spots of predatory crime: routine activities and the criminology of place. *Criminology*, 27: 27–55.

Sidebottom, A. and Tilley, N. (2011) Improving problem-oriented policing: the need for a new model? *Crime Prevention and Community Safety*, 13: 79–101.

Tilley, N. and Laycock, G. (2002) *Working out what to do: evidence-based crime reduction.* Crime Reduction Research Series Paper 11. London: Home Office.

Tilley, N. and Scott, M. (2012) The past, present and future of POP. *Policing*, 6(2): 122–132.

Weisburd, D. and Eck, J. E. (2004) What can the police do to reduce crime, disorder, and fear? *The Annals of the American Academy of Political and Social Science*, 593: 42–65.

Weisburd, D., Telep, C. W., Hinkle, J. C. and Eck, J. (2010) Is problem-oriented policing effective in reducing crime and disorder? Findings from a Campbell systematic review. *Criminology & Public Policy*, 9: 139–172.

24

POLICE TRAINING AND EDUCATION

Past, present and future

Robin Bryant, Tom Cockcroft, Steve Tong and Dominic Wood

Introduction

This chapter argues that higher education (HE) can, and does play a key role in enhancing the professionalism and professional status of policing in England and Wales. The chapter first provides the context of the relationships between universities and police services over the past 20 years and the current state of play of such associations. The chapter then focuses on future developments, for which we make a number of suggestions. In particular, we argue that the future engagement between universities and police services should engage with a full range of policing activities in England and Wales. There has been, in our experience, a focus on initial police training at one end of a continuum and an emphasis on the learning requirements of senior officers at the other end of the continuum. However, the vast majority of what the police do, and the vast majority of police officers, have received little or no consideration within university/police engagements. We argue that this 'excluded middle' needs to be given much more attention if the professionalism and professional status of policing are to be realised.

This is a particularly apt and appropriate time at which to reflect on the collaboration between HE and policing. The College of Policing was established in 2012 and officially launched in February 2013. The emergence of the College, underpinned as it is by the aspirations and ambitions articulated within Neyroud's (2011) recommendations, is indicative of the progress that has been made between universities and the police service in developing shared ideas about how to enhance the professionalism, and professional status, of policing.

Of course it would be misleading to suggest that the relationships between universities and police services have been entirely unproblematic (see Heslop 2010, 2011; Macvean & Cox 2012; Wood & Tong 2009). Likewise, it would be false to claim that further involvement of the HE sector has been universally welcomed across either the police service or the HE sector. The Police Federation (2011) has been particularly vocal in raising concerns about the Neyroud (2011) recommendations and the Home Office's (2012) arguments supporting the introduction of the College as the first step towards establishing a professional body for policing. As Sklansky notes (this volume) the very issue of police professionalism is fraught with problems and controversies.

There need to be opportunities for the voices of discontent among the policing ranks to be heard, listened to and addressed. Nonetheless, it is our aim to show that the College of Policing offers a momentous opportunity to raise the professional standing of policing in England and Wales, which will have long-lasting benefits to police officers, the communities that they serve, and the standing of British policing in the rest of the world (see Sherman 2011). A starting point for us at Canterbury Christ Church University (CCCU) has long been the recognition of existing good practice. Rather than beginning with a preconceived idea of what police professionalism is, we recognise where there is existing good practice, with the objective of helping to develop continuous improvement. Professionalism in this sense will be achieved through a process of continual development rather than established in the abstract.

While stating that the College of Policing is a fundamentally positive development, it is important that in order for the College to realise its ambitions, it must be much more aspirational than its predecessor organisation, the National Police Improvement Agency (NPIA). We will argue that HE has an important role to play in helping the College be successful but in order for this assistance to be meaningful, the engagement with police services in developing the professionalism and professional status of policing cannot be partial, selective and limited to specific roles or ranks within the police service. The engagement needs to be all encompassing. It cannot be treated as optional or as additional to requirements. Too often in the past those responsible for raising the professional standing of policing in the UK have been severely limited by the need to compromise on quality and appease all voices within police services, which has in turn established the lowest common denominator as the norm and the threshold to be met.

A final point by way of introduction is to state quite clearly that we recognise the importance of what is at stake here and what needs to be achieved. In looking forward to where we believe policing needs to be, we borrow from Patten (1999) in proposing a 10-year model of development. It is imperative the College of Policing (and subsequently the emergent professional policing body, whatever form that takes), be at the centre of this developmental plan. However, if it is to be successful we argue that further and higher education, alongside police services and the various police associations, will also need to be involved in a full and meaningful way. The College's independence from Government (see May 2012) is thus a welcome development as a bulwark against party political influence over these developments.

The developing relationship between universities and police services: the past and present situation

This first part of our chapter provides information on the different types of engagements and collaborations between universities and police services over recent years.

Understandably, at the time of writing (March 2013), the College has yet to give a clear indication of its future direction. There are, however, significant changes in the leadership of the College and its Board in particular, chaired by Professor Shirley Pearce, provides a different kind of pressure in determining the direction taken by the College.

Key developments between universities and police services over the past 20 years

There have been significant developments in the relationships between universities and police services over the past 20 years but these have taken different forms (Bryant *et al.* 2012). The intention here is not to provide a comprehensive list of all the programmes that have been developed, and we apologise to colleagues from universities not mentioned below. Our purpose is much more to provide an illustration of the various innovations that have emerged between universities and police services. These include 'in-service' programmes of study for serving police officers, 'initial service' study programmes organised around the training of new recruits into the police service, and 'pre-service' programmes that aim to meet the same learning requirements of an initial programme that can be completed prior to joining the police. These latter programmes normally require students to become Special Constables or PCSOs in order for them to be able to demonstrate practical competences alongside knowledge acquisition. There have been significant developments at a senior officer level and support from senior leaders within the police in establishing dedicated research centres focusing on policing matters. A selection of these various initiatives is listed below.

1   *In-service* – both Portsmouth University and CCCU have been offering part-time policing degrees for serving police officers for over 15 years. There have also been similarly long-standing programmes for serving police officers at postgraduate level, most notably through what was the Scarman Centre for the Study of Public Order at Leicester University (now the Department of Criminology). In-service programmes have attracted limited attention but offer opportunities to increase the engagement with officers at all ranks in different policing roles. As such, they provide a means of engaging with the 'excluded middle', the officers that are beyond initial training but unlikely to be promoted to senior ranks.

2   *Initial service* – following the Police Reform Act 2002 opportunities arose for universities to play an integral role in the delivery of the initial learning of new recruits into the police service, which has given rise to a number of Foundation and full honours Degrees linked to the Initial Police Learning and Development Programme (IPLDP). Such programmes have been offered by CCCU and the universities of Teesside, Glamorgan, Ulster, Huddersfield, De Montfort, Northampton and UCLAN. These programmes have suffered somewhat from the lack of recruitment into the police over recent years because of cutbacks in police budgets and many have been adapted into pre-service programmes.

3 *Pre-service* – the emergence of pre-employment policing programmes undertaken by individuals wishing to join the police has been boosted by the budgetary constraints placed upon the police. However, such programmes have been around for some time. We have offered a pre-service policing degree at CCCU since 2002 but it has gone through various guises over the years in response to the requirements of the police service. Other universities that offer pre-service programmes include Chester, Liverpool John Moores, Liverpool Hope, Wolverhampton, Plymouth and New Bucks. Such programmes have become increasingly attractive to the police against a backdrop of austerity because of the potential savings accruing from getting people to train before they are employed. This has led to the NPIA and Skills for Justice engineered Certificate of Knowledge of Policing (CKP) award that offers a partial pre-employment route into the police (see below). The CKP is not a mandatory qualification for joining the police but is becoming an increasingly attractive option for police services around the country because it shifts the burden of the cost of training on to the individual wishing to join the police, something that was suggested by Flanagan (2008) to bring policing into line with other areas of work. There is concern that pre-service programmes become attractive exclusively because they offer short-term financial savings. Private providers are successfully bidding to win contracts to deliver significantly shortened pre-service training packages for police services that could, in the long run, undermine efforts to raise the professional status of policing.

4 *Leadership programmes* – there have been meaningful engagements between the police and universities in developing potential leaders of the police service through the NPIA's High Performance Development Scheme (HPDS) in conjunction with the University of Warwick Business School. Similarly, there have been opportunities for the existing senior leaders of the police service to undertake the MSt in Applied Criminology and Police Management at the University of Cambridge. The recommendation within Winsor (2012) regarding direct entry to senior rank within the police provides further support for the development of such leadership programmes, that could remain the preserve for senior officers and those striving for promotion to such positions, but there is also scope for suitably qualified individuals seeking to enter directly into a senior police role to perhaps undertake a police leadership programme prior to recruitment into post.

5 *Research* – there have been significant developments in the openness of the police services to allow academic access to data for research purposes, and a much more committed approach to supporting evidence from academic research in considering police strategy and operational practice. The Universities' Police Science Institute (UPSI) was established in 2007 with the support of South Wales Police. It involves academics from Cardiff University and the University of Glamorgan. In London, the Jill Dando Institute was formed within University College London (UCL) in 2001 and has been at the heart of much of the crime science research undertaken by faculty within the Department of Security and Crime at UCL. Professor Lawrence Sherman,

Director of the Institute of Criminology at Cambridge University, has been at the forefront of promoting the idea of evidence-based policing for a number of years. He has been involved heavily in promoting the Society of Evidence-Based Policing. Recently, the Commissioner of the Metropolitan Police Service, Sir Bernard Hogan Howe (speaking at the Home Affairs Committee on Leadership and Standards in the Police Service in January 2013), has indicated his support in establishing and partly funding policing professorships within a number of UK universities. The value of research into policing is clearly seen as being important and a number of universities in the UK are well placed to support policing in developing such ventures further.

Beyond these different programmes and projects, there have been more general collaborations concerning police/university relationships emerging across the UK.[1] In early 2009 the Higher Education Forum for Learning and Development in Policing was formed, comprising representatives primarily from those universities engaged in initial service and pre-service policing programmes. The Forum has members representing over 20 universities from England, Wales and Northern Ireland, illustrating the extent to which police training has become an interest to the university sector. The Forum has organised an annual conference since 2010 and these have attracted high-profile speakers and a healthy audience from both the academic and professional worlds. Its focus has been, primarily, on getting more recognition from police leaders and Government on the need to take more seriously the learning requirements attached to all policing roles, including, as a core, the professional qualities associated with the office of constable.

Policing-related academic literature has increased dramatically over the past 10 years and there are now a number of well-established academic policing journals, e.g. *Policing and Society* and *Policing: A Journal of Policy and Practice*. The number of policing-related papers presented at the British Society of Criminology's (BSC) annual conference has increased to the point that the BSC Executive Committee established a Policing Network in 2011 in recognition of the extent to which policing had become a focus for many of the society's members. The UK also has many internationally renowned professors with expertise in policing, such as Robert Reiner, P.A.J. Waddington, Tim Newburn, and is well on its way to establishing second, third and fourth generations of policing academics across a wide selection of universities.

The current status of initial police learning: the professional status of the office of constable

We now turn our attention to the current situation regarding initial police training, as this is the aspect of police learning that attracts most attention. Here we provide details in terms of level, duration and related issues that we argue need attention if we are to take the professional status of policing seriously. It is our contention that the current approach being fostered falls short of what is required, particularly viewed from the perspective of the office of constable. Although there is debate and difference concerning the status of policing as either an occupation, craft or profession (Tong & Bowling 2006; Tong, Bryant & Horvath 2009) there has long been general agreement that policing is not simply another example of a 'job' but has a distinctive vocational dimension. The vocational claim for policing normally gravitates around the themes of consensual legitimacy, personal authority, the exercise of discretion; themes that support the notion of the office of constable (Police Federation 2008).

However the professional status of policing is defined, the issue of qualifications is unavoidable. The notion of a profession in the UK is intimately linked with that of qualification. For example, the definition of a 'regulated profession' is one 'where access to or practice of a profession is restricted by national law to those holding specific qualifications' (ECCTIS 2012). Policing is not currently a regulated profession in the UK, although the new College of Policing has been established by the Government as a stage towards formal professional status for policing. Fundamentally, a coherent, robust and demanding set of qualifications underpins a claim to professionalism. This is why a discussion concerning the qualifications structure of the police service is far from arcane but, rather, an important voice in the debate.

The Qualifications and Credit Framework (QCF) for England, Wales and Ireland and the Scottish Credit and Qualifications Framework (SCQF) are the official accrediting bodies for qualifications from 'entry' level to Level 8. For example, Level 3 qualifications on the QCF include 'A' Levels and NVQ Level 3. The QCF accredits three sizes of qualification: an 'Award' (1–12 credits), a 'Certificate' (13–36 credits) and a 'Diploma' (at least 37 credits). Awarding bodies (such as City & Guilds and Skills for Justice (SfJ) Awards) are accredited by QCF and, in turn, authorise organisations to deliver QCF-approved qualifications.

In HE there is the Framework for Higher Education Qualifications (FHEQ) covering Level 4 (Certificate of Higher Education), Level 5 (Foundation Degree), Level 6 (Bachelor's degree with honours), Level 7 (Master's degree) and Level 8 (Doctoral degree). Higher education institutions and some further education colleges have the right to award their own qualifications within the FHEQ. There is thus some overlap in levels between the two frameworks, at least in terms of notional level.

Each police force is responsible for devising and operating its own recruitment process, although the procedures must be in accordance with a national framework and comply with Regulation 10 of the Police Regulations 2003. At the time of writing, an applicant seeking to join the police service must first satisfy general eligibility conditions (age, nationality, security (criminal convictions), fitness and eyesight). The application is then processed in a 'paper sift'. In the final selection stage applicants attend an 'assessment centre'. The assessment centre process follows a nationally agreed format, often referred to as SEARCH.

In July 2012 the Police Advisory Board for England and Wales (PABEW) considered Winsor's (2012) recommendations and agreed that from April 2013, an additional qualification should be added to Regulation 10: candidates eligible for appointment to a police force should have either a Level 3 qualification, or a police qualification (such as the CKP) which is recognised by the sector skills council (SfJ), or service as a special constable or as a PCSO (or equivalent). The PABEW also decided that a chief officer could exercise discretion in terms of which of these requirements should apply to applicants for initial training in his or her force. In January 2013 the Home Secretary endorsed the recommendations of the PABEW.

In 2012, the College of Policing introduced a CKP as a pre-entry qualification at Level 3 on the QCF. It has been developed from the Initial Policing Curriculum and has 10 knowledge-based assessment modules. Universities offering pre-service policing programmes are required to incorporate the CKP, or articulate its learning requirement with their programmes in order to give them currency as a pre-service entry programme into a police service. There is thus a further requirement to obtain a licence from the College of Policing in order to gain access to the materials underpinning the CKP. The CKP is accredited by awarding bodies such as City and Guilds, OCR and SfJ Awards. A number of universities are in the process of applying for the College of Policing Licence alongside further education (FE) colleges and private providers.

The 2011 Neyroud Review proposed a new Police Initial Qualification (PIQ) at Level 4 (Neyroud, 2011: 85). Neyroud argued that the new qualification would align more closely to the principles of a professional body for policing and drew an analogy with the training of doctors, nurses and teachers. However, the primary qualification which underpins initial police training is the Diploma in Policing, consisting of 10 QCF units, all at Level 3 (see above).

There are a number of important issues that arise from the current status of initial police learning that require attention.

1   First, there are a number of key formal stages within initial police training that we feel need to be associated more formally with qualifications and professional status, e.g. attestation, independent patrol, confirmation. The timing of attestation varies across forces but is normally very soon after joining and, in most cases, it occurs before an officer could possibly understand fully what it means to be a sworn officer in any meaningful sense. More thought needs to be given to how individuals can be given the opportunity to perform certain policing tasks prior to being given the full powers of a warranted officer. The legal basis for attestation is set out in s. 29 of and Sch. 4 to the Police Act 1996, as amended by s. 83 of the Police Reform Act 2002. The timing has been the subject of some debate: for example, in 1999 the Select Committee on Home Affairs recommended that attestation in the Metropolitan Police Service (MPS) take place after six months of training (rather than at the onset) to make it easier to dismiss unsuitable trainees. However, in many forces the timing of attestation has remained unchanged for the past 150 years. If we are to take the office of constable seriously then attestation needs to be something that is achieved at the end of a process, rather than at the point of employment. A related issue at stake here is that the cost of paying

trainees a full salary from the outset means that police forces naturally look to balance 'input' with 'output' in the most cost-effective manner. The obvious and common solution is to recruit the number of new police officers needed to meet loss through retirement and resignation together with a small margin for 'wastage'. The implicit assumption is that the vast majority of new recruits will successfully complete their initial training. While this makes financial sense within the current set up, it does little to enhance or progress the professional standing of police training.

2   The current selection process is entirely independent of any partnerships a police force might have (including potential recruitment) with external education or training partners, including joint pre-entry schemes with further and higher education. Many of these pre-service programmes require students to sign up as special constables. However, when it comes to being selected, each candidate is judged independently of any current position held within a police organisation, and so a special constable could fail the assessment centre (and hence be deemed unsuitable for appointment as a police officer) but still retain the office and powers of a special constable. Importantly, special constables are sworn officers with the same powers as a serving police officer. It is, therefore, possible to have a situation in which someone is deemed qualified to have police powers if unpaid, but does not meet the requirements of becoming a paid warranted officer. The use of special constables as a route into the police is thus somewhat problematic and needs to be given more thought.

3   A further concern relating to initial police training is the growing recognition that professionalism in policing is also now being articulated through reference to a unique policing corpus of knowledge (Home Office 2012) and the need for police officers to demonstrate the acquisition of a set of professional reasoning and cognitive skills. The task of 'policing' is no longer an example of a general purpose job, if it ever was (Canter 2012) but initial training is still very much geared towards the 'generalist'. All police officers, irrespective of what role they will go on to perform, share the same initial police learning experience. More thought needs to be given to how specialist roles can be articulated and recognised as specific areas of police knowledge and skills.

It is too early to say whether the College of Policing will continue along the lines established by NPIA and SfJ or whether it will begin to adopt a different approach. We hope it will be the latter. We now turn to the future developments and present a number of recommendations that we believe will enhance learning within policing contexts.

The future of police training: taking the office of constable seriously

In assessing the role that HE should play in policing, it is imperative that we keep in mind what kind of police officers we want. Our assumption in this chapter is that society needs police officers that are equipped to make sound professional decisions in situations that are emotionally charged and of fundamental importance to the liberties and securities that affect the well-being of individuals and communities. However, we acknowledge that not only do police officers need to 'know things', they also need to be able to think and respond to situations appropriately (expressed as 'professional problem solvers' by Tilley and Laycock elsewhere in this collection).

In relation to what police constables need to know, there have been continued calls for improvements in police training over the past 30 years (Scarman 1981; Byford 1981; Foster 1999; Macpherson 1999; BBC 2003; HMIC 2002). Some of these calls have been sparked by examples of bad policing, such as Scarman (1981), Macpherson (1999) and BBC (2003) while other drivers have been more concerned with the reform and modernisation of policing (Audit Commission 1993; Sheehy 1993; Police Reform Act 2002; HMIC 2002).

A key question that needs to be addressed concerns the unique role discretion plays within policing and the extent to which it can or should be controlled (Van Maanen 1978). As Winsor (2012) notes, the degree to which new employees are granted original authority to make professional decisions is unique to policing. Discretion in policing is enshrined within the concept of the office of constable (Police Federation 2008). As Davis (1991) argues, top-down control has little impact on police use of powers. Moreover, it removes officers from decision-making and inhibits discussions around professional ethics. Rather than focusing 'professional knowledge' in the middle management ranks and above, the professionalisation thesis suggests a more universal model of knowledge dissemination that would be accompanied by a move towards a lessening of centralised controls.

Research increasingly points to a pronounced cultural divide between police officers and their managers (see, for example, Cockcroft and Beattie 2009). Fundamental to this tension is the apparent contradiction between the largely unsupervised discretion enjoyed by the police officer at street level in their dealings with members of the public and the highly regulated and structured management model under which they perform. The undermining of discretion is also seen as a contributing factor in the increasingly risk-averse culture within policing (Flanagan 2008; Heaton 2010) that restricts the extent to which police officers can fulfil their role as public servants in the ways expected by the public they serve. As indicated within this collection and elsewhere (Bradford et al. 2009; Myhill and Bradford 2011; Jackson et al. 2013), it is becoming increasingly apparent through research into procedural justice and its link to police legitimacy that the police are judged by the general public as much in terms of how the police conduct themselves as the results they achieve. While there might be limitations to understanding the learning requirements of policing exclusively through the conceptual lens of procedural justice, the degree to which police officers become increasingly risk aversive could well have long-term implications for the confidence and trust that the public have in police officers.

Indeed, the link between the legitimacy and effectiveness of the police, on the one hand, and the degree to which police officers enjoy discretion, on the other hand, has been well made by Bottoms and Tankebe (2012) in a critical reflection on the limitations of the procedural justice literature. They argue that the question of police legitimacy cannot be established exclusively in relation to the views of those who are policed, what Simmons (2001) refers to as attitudinal accounts of legitimacy. Police legitimacy also needs to pay attention to the power holders, the police themselves, in order to establish whether policing is legitimate or not. Importantly, Bottoms and Tankebe (2012) also note that a unique aspect of policing that is not anticipated within the political science literature on the legitimacy of power holders is the extent to which it is every police officer that holds such power, not just those at the top of the organisation. Again, it is the degree to which each and every warranted officer carries with them such authority and power that necessitates a full engagement with all police officers. There are simply too many opportunities for the 'excluded middle' to influence matters in ways other than those desired by reformers and police leaders. This has been demonstrated in relation to the re-schooling that occurs to initial recruits once they are released from the training centre and undertaking patrol (Chan 2003).

Discretion is integral to the police world and while this has been widely acknowledged, contemporary debates and commentary do little to highlight its importance to good police practice. Recognition of the importance of discretion to good police work is overdue.

Establishing Level 4 and above as the norm in police learning within a 10-year timeframe

It seems to us that establishing Level 4 learning and above as the norm within policing needs little justification if we start by establishing the various attributes required of a police officer, in terms of knowledge, skills, attitudes and behaviours. It is unhelpful to suggest that 'anyone' can do policing and yet the police appear to be one of the few employers willing to employ someone without any formal qualifications and pay them close to a full wage while they undertake basic training. We can put aside the question of an academic qualification at this point as a secondary matter. The primary concern is ensuring that our police officers know what they need to know and that they have the attributes that make for good policing.

The focus on recognition is crucial here. It inverts the relationship between having the appropriate attributes to be a good police officer and the necessity of having an academic qualification in order to be a good police officer. Importantly, academic qualities are required for a person to be able to demonstrate that they have the appropriate knowledge and attributes to be a police officer. The question of a qualification follows as a matter of justice and fairness; if people are demonstrating academic qualities then they should be rewarded appropriately.

There is concern that the requirement of an academic qualification could create an unnecessary barrier for those wishing to join the police. This argument is often developed in a particular way that emphasises the potential impact upon the diversity of officers recruited into the police. We are not convinced by this perspective.

First, the police have been far less successful than the HE sector in attracting people from diverse ethnic backgrounds and problems have been identified regarding the cultural biases of the psychometric tests used by police as part of the police application process.

There is also a suggestion that parents from some ethnic backgrounds discourage their children from joining the police because it is seen to lack professional credentials (when compared to, say, law or medicine). A reasonable assumption is that moving to a norm in which academic qualifications are required would enhance the professional status of policing and make it more likely for parents from these ethnic backgrounds to welcome their children's choice to pursue a career in policing.

Beyond ethnicity, it is also argued that the diversity of the police would suffer in other ways, especially regarding age and class.[2] Such arguments are premised upon misconceptions of the university as a place beyond the reach of ordinary people. This view of the university as an ivory tower is outdated. The HE sector has been transformed and the percentage of school leavers entering tertiary education has risen dramatically over the past 30 years. Higher education is becoming increasingly flexible in how programmes are delivered and, through the use of blended learning, are much more able to facilitate part-time students. This allows those with families and/or an existing career to attend university with a view to a career change over time.

Experience from a number of initial police training programmes delivered in universities has shown that those wishing to join the police are capable of demonstrating the appropriate level of academic ability to achieve a Level 4 qualification. At CCCU we had over 600 officers successfully complete a Level 4 Certificate of Higher Education in Policing over a four-year period. Many of those completing this programme had no idea that they would be required to do so until the point of actually joining the police. Concerns about good police officers failing to meet the academic requirements were unfounded. The same story is told by colleagues from other universities. Of the small number of officers who seriously struggle on the academic side of the programme, they are invariably also struggling to perform police duties effectively.

Policing is undoubtedly a highly practical and applied occupation that requires skills that are not exclusively academic. These practical components that inform what makes someone a good police officer are of equal importance, and recognising the academic qualities of serving police officers is not the same as suggesting police officers need to become more academic. Policing programmes should primarily enhance policing, not produce policing academics.

Academia has a unique role to play within developing policing and that is in providing the police service a degree of intellectual space. It is precisely because we recognise the extent to which policing is an applied and practical occupation that there need to be opportunities for policing issues to be considered, researched, questioned, challenged and critiqued outside of the normal environments in which policing occurs. Academia is the place reserved within liberal democratic societies for reflection and critical thought. Academia offers police services and police officers the intellectual space to consider policing matters away from the pressures of having to apply solutions to people's problems with little time for reflection. Academic policing programmes can become, in this respect, laboratories in which police practices can be subjected to academic scrutiny. It is in this respect that the real value of Level 4 and beyond learning within policing becomes most apparent.

We recognise that it will take time to realise this recommendation and it is for this reason that we suggest a 10-year timeframe for it to be achieved. But much can be done now. For example, there is a buoyant market for pre-service policing programmes in universities. There is not a shortage of those wanting to be police officers who are willing to commit their own time and money to studying on an academic programme at a university prior to joining the police. There has been a substantial increase in the number of pre-service policing programmes despite the recent hiatus in police recruitment, and despite the fact that these qualifications are not formally recognised within police services or the police recruitment procedures.

Those already employed within police services also recognise increasingly that the attainment of policing knowledge at an academic level is a normal and reasonable expectation for a police officer. We have witnessed a dramatic increase in the number of serving police officers applying to undertake the in-service Policing degree that we offer at CCCU. The numbers of serving officers choosing to study on a Policing degree at the university is growing significantly despite the fact that the fees have risen by over 40 per cent in 2012 and officers are expected to pay the fees themselves, as police services have cut back on the funding available for such staff development.

Distinguishing between good and bad policing

A residual problem in policing is that the absence of professional standards means that bad policing can coexist alongside good policing. Where this happens, it is the bad policing that attracts the media attention and informs public perceptions of the police. There have been welcome moves within the police service towards developing appropriate professional standards and this process is on-going. It will undoubtedly be a core aspect of the College of Policing's functions.

The process of establishing appropriate professional standards for all police roles leads to a transformation in policing, away from a preoccupation on rank, towards a much more explicit focus on the roles performed by officers. This represents a shift away from *de facto* authority, towards *epistemic* authority, and the more this happens, the more there is a role to be played by universities in helping the police to develop appropriate levels of knowledge required at various levels of policing and within a variety of policing specialisms. This also reinforces the idea that an individual can attain the required knowledge for a particular policing role, or for generic policing functions, prior to being employed by the police. There are opportunities here on pre-registration programmes for students to begin developing a specialist area of policing from the outset.

Importantly, linking to HE allows the police to develop its own professional voice. This has to be a central component of the College of Policing. As Sherman (2012) has argued, the introduction of the Police and Crime Commissioners demands a counterbalancing and constraining influence, to ensure the liberal democratic context within which policing occurs in the UK is not undermined.

Concluding remarks

To summarise the main points underpinning the argument within this chapter, we believe that:

- All police roles can be enhanced through the development of an empirical research base and the fostering of a normative appreciation of the purpose of police activities.
- The development of an empirical and normative knowledge base for policing allows for, and indeed demands, the requirement for all police officers, including the excluded middle, to be inducted into this body of knowledge, for professional progression of all officers to be linked to an increasing mastering of this knowledge, and for all officers to be regularly updated on advancements in policing knowledge.
- The development of this body of knowledge also allows for individuals to begin engaging with what a police officer needs to know before joining the police.

The College of Policing offers an opportunity for these points to be acted upon. There is an opportunity for the status of policing, and police officers, to be raised and for police work to be enhanced through an engagement with HE. There needs to be a creative engagement between police and HE to ensure programmes for all policing roles address both the underpinning knowledge for each area of police work, but also ways in which the practical application of policing skills can be assessed and captured in meaningful ways. Neither the police, nor HE can achieve this on their own.

The College of Policing has to be aspirational but we also recognise the need to be realistic. In order to really transform the way knowledge is perceived within policing there needs to be a thorough engagement with the vast majority of police officers and we recognise this might take time. Police services and serving police officers, alike, need to be given time to respond to the dramatic changes occurring within policing. We believe working to a 10-year plan would allow this to happen in a fair and appropriate fashion. Most importantly, though, we need to ensure that the opportunities emerging from the introduction of the College of Policing have led to real, tangible changes in the status and quality of police training by 1 January 2023.

Notes

1 We do not consider the Scottish Police College (SPC) within this chapter as it has developed quite independently of what has happened elsewhere in the UK. There is a need to consider the lessons that can be taken from the experiences of the SPC but, given the extent to which policing in Scotland is somewhat differentiated from policing within the rest of the UK (Walker 2000), such considerations are beyond the scope of this chapter.
2 The issue of gender does not appear to feature as a concern in this respect.

References

Audit Commission (1993) *Helping with Enquiries: Tackling Crime Effectively*, London: Home Office.
BBC (2003) *The Secret Policeman*, Panorama BBC.
Bottoms, A. & Tankebe, Justice (2012) 'Beyond procedural justice: a dialogic approach to legitimacy in criminal justice', *Criminology*, 102(1): 119–170.
Bradford, B., Jackson, J. & Stanko, E. (2009) 'Contact and confidence: revisiting the impact of public encounters with the police', *Policing and Society*, 19(1): 20–46.
Bryant. R., Bryant. S., Tong, S. & Wood, D. (2012) *ASC 547 Higher Education and Policing*, Report submitted to the Higher Education Academy Social Sciences Cluster.
Byford, L. (1981) 'The Yorkshire Ripper Case: review of the police investigation of the case', unpublished report for Her Majesty's Inspector of Constabulary.
Canter, D. (2012) *Do we need the Police?* [Online] Available at: http://eprints.hud.ac.uk/13088/1/Do_we_need_The_Police_.pdf.
Chan, J. (2003) *Fair Cop: Learning the Art of Policing*, Toronto: University of Toronto Press.
Cockcroft, T. & Beattie, I. (2009) 'Shifting cultures: managerialism and the rise of "performance"', *Policing: An International Journal of Police Strategies and Management*, 32(3): 526–540.
Davis, M. (1991) 'Do cops really need a code of ethics?', *Criminal Justice Ethics*, 10(2): 14–28.
ECCTIS (2012) *Regulated Professions* [Online] Available at: http://www.ecctis.co.uk/uk%20ncp/individuals/Coming%20to%20the%20UK/Regulated%20Professions.aspx.
Flanagan, Sir R. (2008) *Review of Policing: Final Report*, London: HMSO.
Foster, J. (1999) 'Appendix 22: Memorandum by Dr Janet Foster, Institute of Criminology, University of Cambridge', in *Home Affairs Committee, Police Training and Recruitment*: Volume Two, London: The Stationery Office, pp. 382–391.
Heaton, R. (2010) 'We could be criticized! Policing and risk aversion', *Policing: A Journal of Policy and Practice*, 5(1): 75–86. First published online: 11 May 2010.
Heslop, R. (2010) They didn't treat us like professionals: a case study of police recruits trained at a university. *Fourth Critical Perspectives on Professional Learning Conference*.
Heslop, R. (2011) 'Reproducing police culture in a British university: findings from an exploratory case study of police foundation degrees', *Police Practice & Research: An International Journal*, 12(4): 298–312.
HMIC (2002) *Training Matters* London: HMIC.
Home Affairs Committee (2012) *Written evidence: Leadership and standards in the police service* [Online]. Available at: http://www.parliament.uk/documents/commons-committees/home-affairs/121016%20Leadership%20evidence.pdf.
Home Office (2012) *Crime and Courts Bill Fact Sheet: Abolition of the National Policing Improvement Agency* (NPIA) [Online]. Available at: http://www.homeoffice.gov.uk/publications/about-us/legislation/crime-courts-part1/fs-nca-npia?view=Binary.

Jackson, J., Bradford, B., Hohl, K. & Farrall, S. (2009) 'Does the fear of crime erode public confidence in policing?' *Policing*, 3(1): 100–111.

Jackson, J., Bradford, B., Stanko, B. & Hohl, K. (2013) *Just Authority? Trust in the Police in England and Wales*, London: Routledge.

Macpherson, Sir William (1999) *The Stephen Lawrence Inquiry*, London: TSO.

Macvean, A. & Cox, C. (2012) 'Police education in a university setting: emerging cultures and attitudes', *Policing: A Journal of Policy and Practice*, 6(1): 16–25.

May, T. (2012) *Police Professional Body*. Written Ministerial Statement. Home Office [Online]. Available at: http://www.homeoffice.gov.uk/publications/about-us/parliamentary-business/written-ministerial-statement/college-of-policing/?view=Standard&pubID=1054677.

Myhill, A. & Bradford, B. (2011) 'Can police enhance public confidence by improving quality of service? Results from two surveys in England and Wales', *Policing and Society*, 22(4): 397–425.

Neyroud, P. (2011) *Review of Police Leadership and Training*: Volume One [Online]. Available at: http://www.homeoffice.gov.uk/publications/consultations/rev-police-leadership-training/report?view=Binary.

Patten Report (1999) *A New Beginning: Policing in Northern Ireland*, the Report of the Independent Commission on Policing in Northern Ireland. Belfast.

Police Federation (2008) *The Office of Constable. The Bedrock of Modern Day British Policing*, Surrey: Police Federation.

Police Federation (2011) *Review of Police Leadership and Training. Consultation response on behalf of the Police Federation of England and Wales*. [Online] Available at: http://www.polfed.org/documents/Neyroud_response_final.pdf.

Scarman, Lord (1981) *The British Disorders 10–12 April 1981: Report of an Inquiry*, Cmnd 8427, London: HMSO, November 1981.

Sheehy, P. (1993) *Inquiry into Police Responsibilities & Rewards*, Volume 1, CM2280 I, London: HMSO.

Sherman, L. (2011) *Professional Policing and Liberal Democracy*. Benjamin Franklin Lecture. Royal Society for the Encouragement of Arts, Manufactures and Commerce, London, 1 November 2011.

Sherman, L. (2012) 'A people's revolution is under way in the fight against crime', *Daily Telegraph*, 22 August, p. 15.

Simmons, A. J. (2001) *Justification and Legitimacy. Essays on Rights and Obligations*, Cambridge: Cambridge University Press.

Tong, S. & Bowling, B. (2006) 'Art, craft and science of detective work', *Police Journal*, 79(4): 323–329.

Tong, S., Bryant, R. & Hovarth, M. (2009) *Understanding Criminal Investigation*, Chichester: Wiley & Sons Publication.

Van Maanen, J. (1978) 'The asshole', in P. K. Manning and J. Van Maanen (eds) *Policing: A View from the Street*, Santa Monica, CA: Goodyear.

Walker, N. (2000) *Policing in a Changing Constitutional Order*, London: Sweet & Maxwell.

Winsor, T. P. (2012) *Independent Review of Police Officer and Staff Remuneration and Conditions*, Final Report Volume 1, Cm 8325-I, London: HM Stationery Office.

Wood, D. & Tong, S. (2009) 'The future of initial police training: a university perspective', *International Journal of Police Science and Management*, 11(3): 294–305.

25

LEADING BY EXAMPLE

The untapped resource of front-line police supervisors

Robin S. Engel and Samuel Peterson

Introduction

By the nature of their work, front-line police officers are afforded a large amount of discretion (Goldstein, 1963). To ensure officers are acting in accordance with the police organization's objectives, their decisions require a certain amount of direction and oversight. This responsibility falls primarily on front-line supervisors. Indeed, front-line officers often act as 'policy makers' in the sense that their decisions to invoke or not invoke the law and departmental policy affect the final form both laws and policies take on. For instance, supervision plays a part in the extent to which front-line officers engage in behaviour that reflects the current strategy of the organization (DeJong *et al.*, 2001; Engel & Worden, 2003).

Field supervisors perform a variety of important functions. First, they are tasked with directing and monitoring the day-to-day activities of their front-line officers. Relatedly, they are expected to relay organizational goals and strategies. This might include formal or informal training sessions, directives, incentives, or other forms of instruction. More recently, an emphasis on officer accountability has also required supervisors to focus more on tracking officer performance and identifying problem behaviours through early intervention systems (Walker *et al.*, 2005). Additionally, supervisors play important roles with their ability to synthesise information they receive from front-line officers to develop a 'snap shot' of what might be occurring on the street (Witte *et al.*, 1990). This collection of duties is rife with potential conflict balancing the priorities of front-line officers with the expectations of upper-level managers.

Whether or not supervisors have an empirically demonstrated impact on their subordinates, the reality remains that people in higher positions of authority (e.g., chiefs, political officials) expect supervisors to be effective leaders. Supervisors are increasingly responsible for responding to and providing direction during critical incidents. This often makes them the public face of the police department and accountable for any mistakes (HMIC, 2008). Indeed, examinations into police corruption and ineffectiveness in both the United States and the United Kingdom find that ineffective training, poor selection/promotion processes, and low levels of organizational support are quite common in police agencies around the world (Rowe, 2006).

In this chapter, we present an overview of the current state of knowledge on front-line police supervision. More specifically, we summarize the current literature on front-line supervision, highlight some important gaps in the current knowledge base, and provide some recommendations for improving our empirical understanding of front-line supervision. We begin with a review of the early research which, while somewhat mixed, recognized the complexity and importance of the supervisory role. Then we discuss the potential impact of supervisors. We emphasize that this is somewhat speculative, given how little is currently known in this area. This is followed by a discussion of the current research focusing on the varied ways in which supervisors influence subordinate behaviour. Finally, we contend that the way forward requires the development of a structured research agenda that emphasizes developing evidence-based practices in order to provide agencies and supervisors with some consensus and confidence regarding the supervisory role.

Early police supervision research

Early ethnographic research portrayed the role of field supervisors as a multifaceted combination of responsibility *to* superior officers, responsibility *for* subordinate officers, and self-interest. This research also highlighted the difficulty in successfully performing this role while also controlling subordinate behaviour, given that supervisory power is often limited to departmental rules, regulations, and organizational resources (Van Maanen, 1983, 1984). Despite this position of authority, field supervisors are evaluated primarily according to their subordinates' behaviours and whether organizational expectations are met. To manage their situation effectively, field supervisors engage subordinates in a process of informal, and often subtle, 'exchanges' (Manning, 1977; Van Maanen, 1983; Brown, 1988). These exchanges provide supervisors with power to influence subordinate behaviour – albeit in a more abstract form than the manipulation of organizational resources – through obligation, respect, or fear (Reuss-Ianni & Ianni, 1983; Van Maanen, 1983). Supervisors seem to develop effective mechanisms of control over the work environment and subordinate behaviour through their existing duties of personnel brokering (e.g., tasks and work schedules) or institutional documentation and display (e.g., proof of accountability and performance monitoring). Additionally, front-line supervisors are in a unique position to control the flow of information throughout the organization. For example, messages from the command staff often take the form of listless office memos that must be 'translated' into a message the officers will not completely disregard. In this sense, first-line supervisors are translators, making information from the top of the organization relevant to line-level officers (Van Maanen, 1983). Equally important, supervisors control bottom-up information from the front line by either protecting their subordinates from investigation or by disciplining officers who take information outside the chain of command (Van Maanen, 1983).

There is understandably variation across officers in terms of how they adapt and define their role. Generally, ethnographers lumped supervisors into two styles that reflected their prior experience and cultural influences that are an outgrowth of the supervisors' unique position: 'street cops' or 'street sergeants' and 'management cops' or 'station house sergeants' (Reuss-Ianni & Ianni, 1983; Van Maanen, 1983, 1984). Additionally, these styles were associated with different emphases and effects on subordinate behaviour. Based on these ethnographic findings, researchers have sought to examine which supervisor characteristics seem to be important, and attempted to quantify the mechanisms by which supervisors influence subordinate behaviours.

Despite these early examinations of police supervision, however, a comprehensive quantitative research agenda did not follow, as was the case with other types of police behaviour. Despite an incredible growth in police research, with great consideration devoted to understanding patrol officer behaviour and police effectiveness, advances in research methods and statistical techniques, and the establishment of effective police–academic partnerships, the exploration of police supervision remains in its infancy. Given the importance of first-line supervision within police agencies, the lack of available research dedicated to better understanding their role, effectiveness, selection, training, and influence over subordinate behaviour is shocking. Many policing experts note the need to enhance line-level supervision, but it is still unclear how to accomplish this. What makes a good field supervisor? How can these qualities be systematically identified? What type of training is the most beneficial for enhancing quality field supervision? How can police managers reward and inspire good field supervisors? As noted by Dobby, Anscombe, and Tuffin (2004: v), 'to date, no research evidence has been provided to show a clear link between particular styles of police leadership and police effectiveness'.

Recent large-scale reviews from Great Britain demonstrate the renewed recognition that front-line supervisors are critical for the development and attainment of a more effective police force. For example, Dobby et al. (2004) conducted a study examining expectations and the impact of police leadership. Likewise, the thematic review, Leading from the frontline, conducted by Her Majesty's Inspectorate of Constabulary (HMIC, 2008) looked in depth at the current role of the front-line police sergeant. Most recently, Neyroud (2011) wrote a report for the Home Office, entitled Review of police leadership and training, that focused on the police service overall while highlighting the importance of adequate selection, training, and professional development of front-line management.

While slightly different in scope, these three reports produced some key themes with regard to front-line police supervision and management. First, there are no conclusive 'evidence-based' recommendations for improving front-line supervision (e.g., selection, training); second, evidence regarding the evaluation of leadership development programmes is lacking; third, weaknesses of directly applying findings from the private sector to policing were noted; fourth, there is wide variation in the way police organizations prepare their front-line supervisors, (a startlingly high number of officers feel unprepared for the demands of the job and organizational support (e.g., training) is often non-existent or ineffective); finally, although the role is often undefined and has become increasingly complex it appears there is some consistency in the characteristics of good supervisors, despite variation in the strategic goals across agencies. Supervisors must have strong leadership skills and have enough experience and training to manage the supervisory role effectively (HMIC, 2008). These reports suggested the broad areas surrounding the role of the front-line supervision that should be targeted for improvement include: (1) confidence (to lead); (2) capability (to act); (3) standards (for uniformity); and (4) status (to enhance leadership) within the position.

Unfortunately, research efforts in the United States continue to lag behind efforts in the United Kingdom regarding research on police leadership, supervision, and management. Notably, reports similar to those described above from the UK are nonexistent in the United States. While leadership training is provided by a variety of organizations including the International Association of Chiefs of Police (IACP), evaluation studies are nonexistent. Other agencies, including the Police Executive Research Forum (PERF), have published reports regarding the application of business management principles to policing (Wexler, Wycoff, & Fischer, 2007), but these ideas have not translated into systematic implementation and evaluation. Other interest in the role of front-line supervisors examines how the supervisory role is impacted by the implementation of new strategies such as Compstat, but neglects the more basic elements of their job (Willis, 2011). Additionally, the existing research regarding supervisory influence on subordinate behaviour is not well suited to recommendations for how to better utilize the supervisory role. A quantitative association between supervisors' attitudes or behaviours and subordinates' attitudes or behaviours is enlightening, but often provides little detail and questionable methodological rigour (e.g., few longitudinal studies). Thus, the evidence from the United States has tended to research the importance of the supervisor without a clear definition or understanding of their exact role.

This critical lack of research on police supervision, however, is exemplified by its absence in findings reported in the United States by the National Research Council (NRC) in 2004. In the early 2000s, the NRC convened the *Committee to Review Research on Police Policy and Practices* to review the volumes of research that had amassed regarding policing in the United States (Skogan & Frydl, 2004). Yet, the NRC's policing committee did not raise the topic of police field supervision in their review. As police agencies in democratic countries around the world begin to embrace and promote evidence-based practices, the scarcity of available evidence on 'what works' for police supervision is incredibly problematic. Nevertheless, there are a handful of studies that have considered the impact of police supervision over subordinate behaviour, and may be used as a foundation for future research, policy, and practice. These studies are reviewed in greater detail below, followed by recommendations of where we should go from here.

The potential impact of police supervisors

Initially, researchers were sceptical about the ability of field supervisors to have a significant impact over subordinate behaviour. As poignantly described by researcher Richard Lundman 'to a large extent, the work of the patrol officer is unsupervised and, to a lesser extent, it is unsupervisable' (1979: 160). Indeed, police work falls under the umbrella of 'low visibility' decision making whereby officers often encounter any number of situations in a given day that require them to use their discretion in deciding on the appropriate course of action (Goldstein, 1988). Research on a variety of police decisions (e.g., arrest) and behaviours (e.g., coercion) has reported that situational variables are key determinants of officer decision-making (Worden, 1989; Riksheim & Chermak, 1993). Thus, due to the nature of police work, much of officers' time is unstructured, involves a great deal of discretion, is ultimately unsupervised, and as previously noted, is arguably unsupervisable (Van Maanen, 1984; Lundman, 1979). Further, regardless of the current emphasis on focused policing, problem-oriented policing, community policing, intelligence-led policing, evidence-based policing, or any of the other numerous reform efforts, a large portion of police work remains reactive, unsupervised, and defies regulation (Klinger, 2004).

Researchers first raised the question of the quantity of supervisor–subordinate contact during police–citizen encounters in the 1970s. It was reasoned that the mere presence of field supervisors was the most direct way to manage and control subordinate behaviour. Early quantitative research using data collected in 1977 from systematic observation of 24 police departments in three metropolitan areas in the United States (Police Services Study data) operationalized supervision as the number of times supervisors had face-to-face or radio contact with a subordinate (Allen, 1980, 1982). This research found that field supervisors were present at only 7 per cent of all the police–citizen encounters observed; yet supervisors ranged dramatically in their amount of subordinate contact. Using systematic observation data collected two decades later, Famega, Frank, and Mazerolle (2005) reported that an average of 75 per cent of officers' working time is unassigned, and further that only 6 per cent of this unassigned time involved any direction by supervisors, dispatchers, other officers, or citizens. In addition, this research found that supervisor directives were often vague, general in form, and did not adhere to departmental strategies (e.g., problem-oriented policing). Out of 2,339 observed activities, a mere 19 (0.8%) were in response to a specific directive from a supervisor. This might explain other researchers' conclusions that the effect of supervisors on behaviour is ultimately marginal (Brown, 1988).

One possible reason for the marginal findings regarding supervisor influence on officer behaviour is that some supervisors often fail to engage in influential behaviours (Schafer, 2010). Without appropriate direction, officers are free to use their discretion to choose which activities to engage or not engage in. Additionally, Riksheim and Chermak (1993) explain that other sources of variation in officer behaviour, such as individual characteristics (e.g., education), situational factors (e.g., suspect demeanour), and organizational factors (e.g., enforcement strategy), all play a role in determining how officers behave. Thus, a supervisor's ability to influence their subordinates' behaviour is often limited by extraneous factors beyond their control.

Despite this, supervisor performance is commonly judged by their subordinates' behaviour. This makes understanding the mechanism through which supervisors affect, as well as the extent to which they are able to influence, subordinate behaviour, all the more important. Ethnographers initially described field supervisors as primarily engaging in transactional leadership – i.e., leadership based on an exchange or transaction between leaders and followers (Downton, 1973; Burns, 1978). Based on these accounts, the potential of field supervisors to significantly impact subordinate behaviour was called into question. Further, some researchers emphasized the negative impact that field supervisors could play in subverting reform efforts, such as problem solving and community-oriented policing. For example, when describing problem-oriented policing, Goldstein (1990) noted the hesitancy of field supervisors to embrace a new role for patrol officers and, consequently, a new role for themselves. Goldstein suggested this reluctance was because traditional policing greatly simplified the work of a supervisor. By changing a patrol officer's role to that of a problem-solver (where they are afforded more freedom, creativity, and autonomy), supervisors would not be able to rely on their ability to control subordinates with departmental restrictions and/or their formal authority as supervisors.

Goldstein, and other researchers, argued that field supervisors must be taught to rely less on their formal authority and, instead, to emphasize to subordinates their role as a facilitator and coach (Sparrow *et al.*, 1990; Weisburd *et al.*, 1988; Wycoff & Skogan, 1994). In short, researchers interested in police reform were early advocates for transformational leadership styles. As described by Bass and Avolio (1994: 2), leaders with a transformational style

> stimulate interest among colleagues and followers to view their work from new perspectives, generate awareness of the mission or vision of the team and organization, develop colleagues and followers to higher levels of ability and potential, and motivate colleagues and followers to look beyond their own interests toward those that will benefit the group.

Transformational leaders are believed to do more than establish exchanges between themselves and their subordinates. While transactional leadership is based on contingent rewards, transformational leadership is based on idealized influence (leader as a role model), inspirational motivation, intellectual stimulation, and individualized consideration (Bass & Avolio, 1994). Yet later research indicated that supervisors embracing more 'innovative' approaches actually had less influence over their subordinates than those who led by example in the field (Engel, 2001, 2002, 2003).

The most recent and thorough inquiries into police leadership and organizational considerations related to front-line supervision have been conducted by the

British Home Office and HMIC. These reviews suggest, not surprisingly, that there is considerable variation in police organizations regarding selection, training, and other organizational factors (e.g., administrative workload) that affect front-line supervisors. However, as Klinger notes (2004), there is a dearth of systematic research into the extent to which organizational (e.g., department size) and environmental (e.g., neighbourhood crime rate) factors influence police behaviour in general. There is even less attention to the role that police supervision plays in this interaction (e.g., developing workgroup norms). Therefore, a key organizational issue for improving the potential influence of police supervisors is to both find the right people for the job and provide them with the adequate training and technical skills. In this sense, the initial selection and training of first-line supervisors is critical to realize their potential within police organizations. The limited descriptive evidence in this area has focused on leadership ability as an important criterion for successful first-line police supervisors. Yet, some research has suggested leadership ability is an inherent personal characteristic, rather than something that can be trained or taught (HMIC, 2008). In this regard, the selection of police supervisors becomes of primary import.

How supervisors influence subordinate behaviour: the importance of style

While researchers and practitioners alike now generally agree that the role of the supervisor is unquestionably important in influencing front-line officer behaviour, serious inquiry into the *how* is rare. The evidence base for improving police supervision is limited in the sense that most of the research is descriptive rather than comparative. This limits the ability to provide clear directions for the most efficacious and appropriate (i.e., evidence-based) model for the key areas of police supervision. Such a model should include recommendations about supervisor selection, training, and retention, as well as organizational recommendations that promote particular supervisory styles over others. The limited research available is reviewed below; note, however, that this body of research is characterized more by what we do not know than what we do know. As Klinger (2004) observed, most police departments are deeply connected with external entities and environmental forces, which precludes a thorough understanding of organizational accounts of police operations. This external interdependency creates doubt about the generalizability of police organizational research, despite the importance in understanding these mechanisms. Fortunately, some research evidence does exist concerning which supervisor characteristics make 'good supervisors'. Most of this research focuses on officers' perceptions regarding effective supervisors, as well as the potential mechanisms through which supervisors demonstrate influence over subordinate behaviour.

As noted previously, early research on the influence of front-line supervisors focused on very basic information, such as supervisor presence at a crime scene. Here, the evidence suggests the presence of a supervisor and variables related to supervisor presence (e.g., the number of contacts and interaction time) increases the amount of officer work output (e.g., time spent at citizen encounters; Allen, 1982). Additionally, supervisory presence at an encounter increased the likelihood of arrest (Smith & Klein, 1983; Smith, 1984). Nevertheless, the overall effect of mere supervisor presence seems to be somewhat limited. This is not surprising considering this construct does not account for what supervisors actually do when they are present, and ignores other potentially influential factors that do not require supervisory presence.

One way to identify the effective supervisory characteristics is to ask subordinate officers for their opinions regarding what constitutes a high-quality supervisor. This research approach, however, has a number of limitations. First, this research has often neglected to examine whether supervisor characteristics influence actual subordinate behaviour, as opposed to morale, perceptions, or attitudes. While officer morale is an important consideration, whether it should be the primary factor regarding supervisor selection and performance evaluation depends on the agency's priorities. Clearly, agencies would like to have supervisors who are capable of achieving the desired outputs along with high morale. However, front-line officers surveyed about leadership qualities might be less concerned or informed about managerial and agency goals, and therefore place more value on their daily interactions and experiences with their supervisors. Additionally, even supervisors with good leadership qualities might not produce the expected results, while poor leaders can get the job done (Schafer, 2010). It is also not clear whether perceptions of what makes a good patrol officer should be extrapolated to the supervisory level. Indeed, the necessary skills for effective supervision might diverge dramatically from the necessary skills for effective front-line police work (Schafer, 2010). Despite these considerations, there are a few pervasive themes in the reporting of officers' perceptions of effective supervisors and leaders. Not surprisingly, officers seem to emphasize operational credibility and experience as vital characteristics of good supervisors (Hogan et al., 2011; Rowe, 2006; Schafer, 2010). This emphasis on experience and credibility is likely related to other key supervisory behaviours, such as deployment, mentoring, and generally understanding the work environment and needs of front-line officers. In contrast, poor supervisors seem to be more self-interested or out of touch, and tend to act in ways that reflect this, such as being closed-minded, micromanaging, 'playing politics', and failing to support subordinates (Dobby et al., 2004; Rowe, 2006; Schafer, 2010).

Another way supervisors might influence officer behaviour is through the specific directives or instructions they give to their officers. This communication should provide officers with an understanding of what types of behaviours are expected. However, observational research suggests that, in at least one city, supervisors rarely provided directives to front-line officers. When they did provide directives, they were typically not very specific (Famega et al., 2005). This finding might reflect a variety of other issues (e.g., poor communication or excessive workloads for supervisors), but it potentially explains why the research findings regarding the effects of supervisors on officer behaviour are typically marginal or null. It is possible that there is a necessary level of supervisor directives required in order for their influence to be recognized.

Directives play a partial role in expectancy motivation theory. In order for employees to understand which behaviours are most worthy of their effort, they must perceive that certain behaviours are desired by their superiors, that the behaviours are associated with (organizational) rewards, and that those rewards are of value (Mastrofski *et al.*, 1994). Applications of expectancy theory on police behaviour have found that supervisor or management expectations for certain activities (e.g., problem-solving time or drug arrests) are significantly and positively related to officers engaging in the corresponding behaviour (DeJong *et al.*, 2001; Johnson, 2009).

Supervisor styles

As is true with most human characteristics, there is variation in supervisory and leadership styles. Supervisory styles include a variety of attitudinal dimensions, expectations, and behaviours of supervisors that influence the way they supervise and direct subordinate behaviour. One of the most comprehensive studies examining supervisory styles was conducted using officer and supervisor survey data, along with systematic observation of those officers and supervisors in the field. Data for the study came from the Project on Policing Neighborhoods (POPN data) collected in 1996–1997 in Indianapolis, Indiana and St Petersburg, Florida (Engel, 2000, 2001, 2002, 2003; Engel & Worden, 2003). Engel analysed surveys and observations of 97 sergeants and lieutenants observed across 155 work shifts, and 322 patrol officers across 696 work shifts. She identified and measured nine leadership constructs and, using factor analysis, classified supervisors into four different supervisory styles based on their individual factor loadings. Observations and surveys of officers were then matched with their supervisors across shifts, and both supervisor and officer behaviours were compared across supervisory styles.

Engel (2001) identified four supervisory styles: traditional, innovative, supportive, and active. Supervisors identified as 'traditional' expected subordinate officers to produce measurable outcomes – particularly arrests and citations – along with an emphasis on paperwork and documentation. These supervisors expected officers to patrol aggressively, but not be bothered with order maintenance or quality of life issues. When in the field, these supervisors tend to take over incidents or tell officers how to handle them, and thus were more likely to make decisions. These supervisors were less likely to interact with citizens or develop relationships with subordinates, and their emphasis was on task completion, with a strict adherence to the rules and regulations of the organization.

In contrast, supervisors identified as 'innovative' scored the highest on power, relations-orientation (i.e., they perceive more officers as their friends), and community relations. These supervisors were more confident that officers could solve problems on their own, embrace new policing strategies, and spend more time interacting with citizens. The third identified style – labelled 'supportive' – emphasized protecting subordinates (e.g., from criticism or discipline from upper management). Supportive supervisors were low on task orientation (e.g., giving directives), and more likely to engage in inspirational motivation (e.g., team building, developing common goals). These officers are also more likely to reward or praise subordinates.

Finally, 'active' supervisors exhibited both the highest levels of activity and the most positive evaluations of their subordinates. They self-reported relatively high levels of power and decision-making as well. Active supervisors were defined by their emphasis on leading by example in the field. Although active supervisors felt they had considerable influence over decisions, lower scores on the inspirational motivation scale showed they were less likely to directly help subordinates. As described by one active supervisor, they maintained a fine line between being active and micro-managing.

Mechanisms of influence

The importance of identifying different types of supervisory styles is based on the premise that these styles have differential impacts over subordinates' attitudes and behaviours. As suggested by Sir Ronnie Flanagan, 'the key role of the frontline sergeant is in translating vision and strategic intent into day-to-day policing reality. The quality of the leadership provided by frontline sergeants to their teams is the one key factor that makes the difference' (HMIC, 2008: 1). Yet, there is limited research regarding the actual relationship between subordinate officers' behaviours and supervisory styles or other key aspects of leadership.

Some initial findings suggest that leading by example is likely the most fruitful opportunity to influence police subordinates' behaviour. Engel's (2000, 2001, 2002, 2003) examination of the relationship between supervisory styles and subordinate behaviour remain the only known empirical studies connecting identified supervisory styles with directly observed officer behaviour in the field. These analyses demonstrated that supervisors identified as having an 'active' style had significantly more influence over subordinate behaviours (Engel, 2000, 2002, 2003). This finding extends across a variety of officer behaviours including arrest, use of force, administrative activities, and engagement in proactive or self-initiated problem solving and community policing activities. Specifically, patrol officers with active supervisors were more likely to engage in proactive policing and problem solving/community policing (Engel, 2002), more likely to use force (Engel, 2000), and less likely to engage in administrative activities (Engel, 2002). Notably these supervisory effects were found after controlling for officer, situational, legal, and organizational characteristics (Engel, 2000, 2002). Further, additional analyses demonstrated that supervisors identified as 'active' were involved in more use of force incidents compared to their non-active supervisor counterparts, as were their subordinates (Engel, 2001). As such, Engel concluded that promoting active supervisory styles and leading by example could be a double-edged sword, as supervisors may set either positive or negative examples for their subordinates.

Other studies have also reported support for the hypothesis that police subordinates model their field supervisors' behaviour. For example, while Johnson (2006, 2011) found that officer and supervisor preference for traffic enforcement were not related to actual traffic enforcement, supervisor modelling was positively related to officer behaviour. Thus, it appears supervisor behaviour is an important consideration when evaluating the relevance of actual and perceived supervisor expectations. Other research focused on the amount of time officers spend on personal business, and demonstrated that face-to-face contacts with their supervisor were negatively associated with work shirking (suggesting a deterrent effect). In contrast, the amount of time their supervisor spent on personal business was positively associated with work shirking (Johnson, 2008). Note, however, that studies examining modelling have not included measures to identify whether subordinates actually witnessed their supervisor engaging in these particular behaviours.

Huberts, Kaptein, and Lasthuizen (2007) found that, in a sample of Dutch police officers, supervisor modelling of integrity violations was positively related to the amount of all types of integrity violations by their subordinates. In other words, the more often a supervisor engaged in violations, the more often their supervisees would. The violations most strongly associated with supervisor modelling included interpersonal ethical issues. Survey responses from police officers support the notion that modelling plays a part in this process, with teaching, role-playing, and feedback serving as important elements as well (Schafer, 2009).

Another behavioural principle that has been found to influence front-line officer behaviour is reward, or the expectation of rewards, for particular behaviours. It is not particularly difficult to see how. When there is discretion in decision making, people will choose to make decisions and engage in behaviours that are associated with a tangible reward. Accordingly, officers must perceive that the reward has value to them and, not surprisingly, there is individual variation in preference for particular rewards as well as the perceived severity of particular punishments (e.g., more experience was negatively associated with the perception that verbal or written reprimands were severe punishments; Johnson, 2009). This suggests that it is important for supervisors and agencies in general to have a variety of rewards and punishments available. Johnson's (2006, 2011) research on expectancy theory has consistently found that the expectation of agency rewards for certain behaviours is positively related to officers engaging in such behaviour. As managers, supervisors have the ability to apply direct rewards to officers for approved behaviour including verbal praise, priority in shift assignments, performance evaluations, etc. Likewise, supervisory behaviour can be influenced by contingency rewards as well (Correia & Jenks, 2011; Schafer, 2009).

The work that remains: toward evidence-based supervisory practices

While the identified link between supervisory styles and officer behaviour is illuminating, supervisory styles do not necessarily provide a causal explanation for how supervisors influence officer behaviour. Additionally, styles include a combination of officer characteristics, attitudes, and behaviours – some of which might not be easily identifiable or flexible enough to inform promotion or training purposes. Further, supervisory styles are likely not constant, as supervisors evolve over the course of their career. And finally, the approach that supervisors adopt likely varies across the particular subordinates they are supervising. This potentially leaves a gap between the knowledge base and practice regarding how to improve supervisory influence on subordinate behaviour.

Better understanding the link between officer attitudes and behaviour is also critical for supervision research. In his study of patrol officer behaviour, Worden (1989) concluded that the influence of attitudes on police behaviour in general is limited. However, in situations where attitudes and expectations for behaviour are congruent, there is a higher likelihood that behaviours will correspond with attitudes. The corresponding prediction is that supervisors who impart particular attitudes upon their subordinates might also create environments that foster such attitudes to manifest in behaviour. However, there has been no direct empirical inquiry into this prediction. In general, the influence of supervisor attitudes on officer attitudes and subsequent behaviour appears to be fairly weak.

This discrepancy is evidenced elsewhere, as Johnson (2011) found that front-line officer traffic citations were positively related to their own attitudes and negatively related to their supervisor's actual preference. Correia and Jenks (2011) found that attitudes associated with policing strategies (e.g., community policing) actually change in response to the level of engagement that officers have with the strategy. That is, changes in behaviour might lead to changes in attitude rather than the converse. This highlights the importance of using longitudinal data to measure the impact of supervisors on their subordinates, especially when examining the attitude–behaviour link.

Further, a systematic study examining the impact of supervisors' preferences over subordinates' behaviour demonstrated that large discrepancies exist between supervisors' reported preferences and subordinates' reported perceptions of their supervisors' preferences. Engel and Worden (2003) found that officers with supervisors who preferred aggressive law enforcement spent less time engaging in problem solving. However, front-line officers' perceptions of their supervisors' priorities are often inaccurate, but did influence the amount of time spent engaging in problem solving (Engel & Worden, 2003). In short, supervisors' preferences are not well communicated to subordinates. Engel & Worden's (2003) work demonstrated that patrol officers often engage in behaviour that they believe is related to their supervisors' preferences, but they often misinterpret their supervisors' preferences. This finding is critical for enhancing first-line supervision because it demonstrates the problem is not that subordinate officers' behaviour cannot be impacted through supervision, but rather that supervisors fail to effectively communicate their preferences and therefore their potential to impact behaviour often goes untapped.

To improve first-line police supervision, the development of an empirically based set of best practices is desperately needed. To move in this direction, there needs to be some consensus and clear description in the field about what good supervision looks like, and how it should be measured. This starting point is reminiscent of a similar problem within the larger body of police research. For years, researchers and practitioners struggled with defining and measuring 'good policing' (Fyfe, 1993). In the 1990s, researchers shifted their focus and began to use scientific principles to help the police identify effective crime fighting practices rather than to simply look for failures in policing (Sherman, 1998). Over the next two decades, a body of literature developed that emphasizes 'what works' in policing, and has ushered in a trend toward evidence-based, data driven strategies in policing (Weisburd & Eck, 2004). This literature was able to develop based on the core understanding that 'good policing' included concepts such as effectiveness, efficiency, and equity (Eck & Rosenbaum, 1994), and that these concepts could be readily measured. Accompanying this trend toward evidence-based practices is now an increased interest in police legitimacy, and a renewed focus on citizens' perceptions about the policing they receive (Brunson, 2007; Engel, 2005; Skogan, 2006; Tyler, 2003; Tyler & Wakslak, 2004). Agencies are now recognizing the need to measure 'good policing' not just through measures of effectiveness and efficiency, but also perceptions of legitimacy and equity (Mazerolle *et al.*, 2013).

However, police agencies' self-inspection has been somewhat limited to measuring and evaluating individual patrol officers' behaviour, along with aggregate measures of outcomes (e.g., use of force, arrests, citations, crime rates, etc.), but not through examination of supervisory practices. For example, police agencies now routinely use early warning systems (and other data-based managerial oversight mechanisms) to identify potentially problematic officers based on a pre-determined set of criteria. While these efforts have become an additional resource for monitoring officers' behaviour, less has been discussed about how first-line supervisors should best use these mechanisms, or how supervisors can use this information to redirect and retrain officers initially flagged as problematic. Likewise, the movement toward Compstat in the United States left a void in the discussion about *how* to hold officers accountable for their assigned areas and reduce reported crime in those areas, and further what the role of field supervisors in the Compstat process should be.

We believe researchers and practitioners need to take a step back to understand the larger scope of supervisory influence. Unfortunately, when asked *how* first-line supervisors can enhance effectiveness, efficiency, and equity in policing, the silence from the literature is deafening. It still remains unclear how to best select, train, and retain good supervisors – or even what a 'good' supervisor is. Our limited understanding of the mechanisms related to field supervision indicates that subordinate officers often model their behaviours based on their perceptions of their supervisors' priorities and expectations. This suggests that there is a tremendous untapped potential of first-line police supervision. We also know that priorities and expectations are often miscommunicated between supervisors and subordinates, and as a result, better understanding of effective communication is imperative for enhancing the potential impact of field supervision. Great consideration should be given to the reports regarding field supervision already conducted in the United Kingdom (e.g., Dobby *et al.*, 2004; HMIC, 2008; Neyroud, 2011), and future research should be based on their foundation. We agree that confidence, capability, standards, and status are important considerations for strong leadership skills and enhancing supervisory efficacy. But to get there, we must first embrace a renewed recognition of the importance of field supervision, and forge a commitment to better understand its potential.

References

Allen, D. (1980). Street-level police supervision: The effect of supervision on police officer activities, agency outputs, and neighborhood outcomes. PhD dissertation, Indiana University. Ann Arbor, MI: University Microfilms International.

Allen, D. N. (1982). Police supervision on the street: An analysis of supervisor/officer interaction during the shift. *Journal of Criminal Justice*, *10*, 91–109.

Bass, B. M., and Avolio, B. J. (1994). *Improving organizational effectiveness through transformational leadership*. Thousand Oaks, CA: Sage Publication.

Brown, M. K. (1988). *Working the street: Police discretion and the dilemma of reform*. New York: Russell Sage Foundation.

Brunson, R. K. (2007). 'Police don't like black people': African American young men's accumulated police experiences. *Criminology & Public Policy*, *6*, 71–101.

Burns, J. M. (1978). *Leadership*. New York: Harper and Row.

Correia, M. E., and Jenks, D. A. (2011). Expectations of change: The congruency between Beat Officers and Supervisors and its impact on programmatic change. *Police Practice & Research*, *12*(1), 16–34.

Dejong, C., Mastrofski, S. D., and Parks, R. B. (2001). Patrol officers and problem solving: An application of expectancy theory. *Justice Quarterly*, *18*, 31–61.

Dobby, J., Anscombe, J., and Tuffin, R. (2004). *Police leadership: Expectations and impact*. London: Home Office.

Downton, J. V. (1973). *Rebel leadership: Commitment and charisma in the revolutionary process*. New York: Free Press.

Eck, J. E., and Rosenbaum, D. P. (1994). The new police order: Effectiveness, equality, and efficiency in community policing. In D. P. Rosenbaum (ed.), *The challenge of community policing: Testing the promises* (pp. 3–23). Thousand Oaks, CA: Sage.

Engel, R. S. (2000). The effects of supervisory styles on patrol officer behaviour. *Police Quarterly*, *5*, 262–293.

Engel, R. S. (2001). Supervisory styles of patrol sergeants and lieutenants. *Journal of Criminal Justice*, *29*, 341–355.

Engel, R. S. (2002). Police supervision in the community policing era. *Journal of Criminal Justice*, *30*, 51–64.

Engel, R. S. (2003). How police supervisory styles influence patrol officer behaviour. *Research for Practice*, National Institute of Justice. Washington DC: U.S. Department of Justice.

Engel, R. S. (2005). Citizens' perceptions of distributive and procedural injustice during traffic stops with police. *Journal of Research in Crime and Delinquency*, *42*, 445–481.

Engel, R. S., and Worden, R. E. (2003). Police officers' attitudes, behaviour, and supervisory influences: An analysis of problem solving. *Criminology*, *41*, 131–166.

Famega, C. N., Frank, J., and Mazerolle, L. (2005). Managing police patrol time: The role of supervisor directives. *Justice Quarterly*, *22*(4), 540–559.

Fridell, L., Maskaly, J., Cordner, G., Mastrofski, S., Rosenbaum, D., Banfield, G., Lanterman, J., and Donner, C. (2011). *The longitudinal study of first line supervisors*. Washington, DC: National Institute of Justice.

Fyfe, James J. (1993). Good policing. In Brian Forst (ed.), *The socioeconomics of crime and justice* (pp. 269–289). Armonk, NY: M.E. Sharpe.

Goldstein, H. (1990). *Problem-oriented policing*. New York: McGraw-Hill.

Goldstein, J. (1963). Police discretion: The ideal v the real. *Public Administration Review, 23,* 140–148.

Goldstein, J. (1988). Police discretion not to invoke the criminal process: Low visibility decisions in the administration of justice. In George C. Cole (ed.), *Criminal justice law and politics, 5th Edition* (pp. 83–102). Pacific Grove, CA: Brooks/Cole Publishing Co.

Her Majesty's Inspectorate of Constabulary. (2008). *Leading from the frontline*. London: Home Office.

Hogan, J., Bennell, C., and Taylor, A. (2011). The challenges of moving into middle management: Responses from police officers. *Journal of Police and Criminal Psychology, 26,* 100–111.

Huberts, L. W. J. C., Kaptein, M., and Lasthuizen, K. (2007). A study of the impact of three leadership styles on integrity violations committed by police officers. *Policing: An International Journal of Police Strategies and Management, 30,* 587–607.

Johnson, R. R. (2006). Management influences on officer traffic enforcement productivity. *International Journal of Police Science and Management, 8*(3), 205–217.

Johnson, R. R. (2008). Field supervisor behaviour and officer on duty personal business. *International Journal of Police Science and Management, 10*(3), 339–348.

Johnson, R. R. (2009). Patrol officer perceptions of agency rewards and punishments: A research note. *Journal of Police and Criminal Psychology, 24*(2), 126–133.

Johnson, R. R. (2011). Officer attitudes and management influences on police work productivity. *American Journal of Criminal Justice, 36*(4), 293–306.

Klinger, D. A. (2004). Environment and organization: Reviving a perspective on the police. *AAPSS, 593,* 119–136.

Lundman, R. J. (1979). Police misconduct as organizational deviance. *Law and Policy Quarterly, 1,* 81–100.

Manning, P. K. (1977). *Police work*. Cambridge, MA: MIT Press.

Mastrofski, S. M., Ritti, R. R., and Snipes, J. B. (1994). Expectancy theory and police productivity in DUI enforcement. *Law & Society Review, 28,* 113–148.

Mazerolle, L., Bennett, S., Davis, J., Sargeant, E., and Manning, M. (2013). Legitimacy in policing. *Campbell Systematic Reviews 2013, 9*(1).

Muir, W., Jr. (1977). *Police: Street corner politicians*. Chicago: The University of Chicago Press.

Neyroud, P. (2011). *Review of police leadership and training*. London: Home Office.

Reuss-Ianni, E., and Ianni, F. (1983). Street cops and management cops: The two cultures of policing. In M. Punch (ed.), *Control in the police organization* (pp. 251–274). Cambridge, MA: MIT Press.

Riksheim, E. C., and Chermak, S. M. (1993). Causes of police behaviour revisited. *Journal of Criminal Justice, 21,* 353–382.

Rowe, M. (2006). Following the leader: Front-line narratives on police leadership. *Policing: An International Journal of Police Strategies & Management, 29,* 757–767.

Schafer, J. A. (2009). Developing effective leadership in policing: Perils, pitfalls, and paths forward. *Policing: An International Journal of Police Strategies & Management, 32*(2), 238–260.

Schafer, J. A. (2010). The ineffective police leader: Acts of commission and omission. *Journal of Criminal Justice, 38*(4), 737–746.

Sherman, L. W. (1998). *Evidence-based policing: Ideas in American policing.* Washington, DC: Police Foundation.

Skogan, W. (2006). *Police and community in Chicago: A tale of three cities.* New York: Oxford University Press, Inc.

Skogan, W., and Frydl, K. (eds). (2004). *Fairness and effectiveness in policing: The evidence.* Committee on Law and Justice, Division of Behavioral and Social Sciences and Education. Washington, DC: The National Academies Press.

Smith, D. (1984). The organizational context of legal control. *Criminology, 22,* 19–38.

Smith, D. A., and Klein, J. R. (1983). Police agency characteristics and arrest decisions. In G. P. Whitaker and C. D. Phillips (eds), *Evaluating performance of criminal justice agencies.* Beverly Hills, CA: Sage.

Sparrow, M. K., Moore, M. H., and Kennedy, D. M. (1990). *Beyond 911: A new era for policing.* New York: Basic Books.

Tyler, T. R. (2003). Procedural justice, legitimacy, and the effective rule of law. In M. Tonry (ed.), *Crime and justice: A review of research Vol. 30* (pp. 283–358). Chicago: University of Chicago Press.

Tyler, T. R., and Wakslak, C. J. (2004). Profiling and police legitimacy: Procedural justice, attributions of motive, and acceptance of police authority. *Criminology, 42,* 253–281.

Van Maanen, J. (1983). The boss: First-line supervision in an American police agency. In M. Punch (ed.), *Control in the police organization* (pp. 227–250). Cambridge, MA: MIT Press.

Van Maanen, J. (1984). Making rank: Becoming an American police sergeant. *Urban Life, 13,* 155–176.

Walker, S., Milligan, S.O., and Berke, A. (2005). *Supervision and intervention within early intervention systems: A guide for law enforcement Chief Executives.* Washington, DC: Police Executive Research Forum and the Office of Community Oriented Policing Services.

Weisburd, D., and Eck, J. E. (2004). What can the police do to reduce crime, disorder, and fear? *The Annals of the American Academy of Political and Social Science, 593,* 42–65.

Weisburd, D., McElroy, J., and Hardymann, P. (1988). Challenges to supervision in community policing: Observations on a pilot project. *American Journal of Police, 7,* 29–50.

Wexler, C., Wycoff, M. A., and Fischer, C. (2007). *'Good to great' policing: Application of business management principles in the public sector.* Washington, DC: Police Executive Research Forum.

Willis, J. J. (2011). First-line supervision and strategic decision making under Compstat and Community Policing. *Criminal Justice Policy Review,* 1–22.

Wilson, J. Q. (1968). *Varieties of police behaviour: The management of law and order in eight communities.* Cambridge, MA: Harvard University Press.

Witte, J. H., Travis III, L. F., and Langworthy, R. H. (1990). Participatory management in law enforcement: Police officer, supervisor, and administrator perceptions. *American Journal of Police, 9,* 1–23.

Worden, R. (1989). Situational and attitudinal explanations of police behaviour: A theoretical reappraisal and empirical assessment. *Law and Society Review, 23*(4), 667–711.

Wycoff. M. A., and Skogan, W. G. (1994). The effect of a community policing management style on officers' attitudes. *Crime and Delinquency, 40,* 371–383.

PART VI

Governance

26

ENGAGING THE CITIZEN

Adrian Barton and Nick Johns

Introduction

Quis custodiet ipsos custodies?

While the above quote from Juvenal, the Roman poet writing around two thousand years ago, may seem clichéd it is still worth reminding ourselves that how we control the police in a democratic society is not a contemporary question. Indeed in the United Kingdom (UK) the sentiment has created debates around both the principle and the practice of control and accountability which have reoccurred with the regularity of cause célèbre since the inception of modern policing in the nineteenth century. Why is this the case and are we any closer to finding a solution that suits all interested parties and allows for more democratic control over the police than we were at the time of Robert Peel? This chapter seeks to provide an answer to the first part of that question by locating the police within the broader philosophical and political context of the state and state power. The second part of the question is more difficult to fully resolve but we will try to provide an answer by offering a review of the UK's latest attempt to create a truly democratic control mechanism for the police. In sum, the chapter will begin by locating the police and policing within the state, looking particularly at state power and control, the manner in which police manifest such control and the problems that can emerge should state power, as delivered by the police, become too partisan or self-serving. Nothing could be more topical for, as we write, a report has been produced into the South Yorkshire Police Service's handling of the Hillsborough stadium football disaster in 1989 in which 96 spectators died.

Recently, too, the former New Labour Home Secretary, Jack Straw, has accused the Conservative administrations led by Mrs Thatcher of 'politicising' the police during the conflict with organised labour in the 1980s. This led, in his view, to a feeling that the police were above the law: 'The Thatcher government, because they needed the police to be a partisan force, particularly for the miners' strike and other industrial troubles, created a culture of impunity in the police service' (BBC News, 2012a). In response, Norman Tebbit, a senior Conservative figure and former Cabinet Minister in the Thatcher Government, dismissed the claims as 'silly' student politics. However, such claims are not the preserve of youthful rebelliousness (itself not to be dismissed) but they constitute part of a very serious question about how we are policed and in whose interests (Benyon and Solomos, 1988; Sullivan, 1998; Loveday, 1999). In recognition of this, the chapter provides a brief historical overview of the evolution of the police and the methods used to ensure some form of democratic accountability over their work. It is important, therefore, to include the latest development in this on-going democratic struggle – the creation of Police and Crime Commissioners (PCC). We will conclude the chapter with some final thoughts on the efficacy or otherwise of PCCs in engaging and representing citizens.

The state and the police

The starting point for any discussion around why we continue to seek to find a way in which to make the police accountable, and some would argue, controllable, is to remind ourselves of the role of the state in democracies. Ling (1998) suggests that the modern state rests on three inter-related characteristics: institutional capacity; legitimacy; and coercion. Institutional capacities reflect the manner in which the state developed organisations staffed by specialist workers designed to serve, administer, manage and deliver its three areas of influence on, and power over, its citizens, namely executive, legislative and judicial. Legitimacy refers to a legal claim to sovereignty and a democratic claim to represent all its citizens. As such, the state and its agencies need to remain within the law and to operate in a manner that does not favour one group over another. Coercion relates to the ability of the state to enforce its will on its citizens and to control the actions of its population. It is true to say that modern democracies tend to veer toward what Foucault termed 'discipline' (Foucault, 1972/1969), which we can define as soft control mechanisms through various forms of surveillance and low-level interventions by 'experts' such as medical professionals, social workers and, of course, the police. However, it is equally true that modern states are also not slow to invoke a more obvious and violent form of coercion should the situation arise. There are daily examples of agents of the state using physical violence to invoke its will (see, for example, http://police-brutality-uk.co.uk/) and leading human rights lawyers' identification of riot squad tactics aimed at a student demonstration in 2011 as a means of suppressing political protest per se (McVeigh and Townsend, 2011). Put simply, in democracies, the state is a jealous guardian of its ultimate form of coercion: the legitimate use of force and even the most benign and liberal states can and do resort to state sanctioned violence.

While the police display aspects of all the above characteristics of state agencies – they are an established institution with a legitimate democratic mandate –

arguably one of their primary roles as far as the average citizen is concerned is that of an agency of coercion and control (a review of British Crime Survey data and polls conducted by Bradford *et al.* (2009) appears to offer some support for this interpretation, although empirical work by Jackson and Sunshine (2007) paints a slightly different picture). What is clear is that research around public attitudes about the role and performance of policing need to be extended (Jackson and Sunshine, 2007). In the main, most citizens encounter the police in what might be termed a benign disciplinary role. That is, coercion and control are conducted through 'soft' measures and often citizens encounter this control in an unreflexive and frequently unnoticed manner mainly because they permeate their everyday lives. Soft measures can be as little as a physical presence such as patrol – what Reiner (1992) calls the 'scarecrow function' – which, for example, might make a motorist slow down; through to police-led technological surveillance approaches of control (speed cameras; number plate recognition technology, CCTV and so forth). Beyond the everyday encounters with 'soft' police control, some sections of the population will occasionally encounter 'harder' control tactics such as low-level physical restraint and containment in public order situations (political demonstrations, for example, but more regularly crowd control at sporting events such as football matches). However, from time to time individuals and sections of the population are at the receiving end of more violent or partial forms of state coercion and control, where the state invokes its right to use the legitimate use of violence and force to impose its will on its citizens. This is evident in the case of stop and search as it impacts upon black and minority young people in particular, whereby Bowling and Phillips (2007) have argued that it is so disproportionate and discriminatory in its operation that it should be abandoned as a legitimate policing strategy (see also Rowe, this volume).

On occasion, state-approved violence can and does lead to the death of a citizen at the hands of the police, working on behalf of the state. As such, this puts the police at the heart of any debates about state legitimacy as it is vital that citizens are assured that questions surrounding the how and for what state-sanctioned, police-led force is used. For example, we might need to be assured that violence is undertaken as a last resort and is not undertaken for any political, partisan or self-serving reasons. While the general population do not often openly engage in such debates, the state's ability to be able to defend and support its use of violence (or partiality) is at the heart of any functioning democracy.

Even a cursory thought about the mechanics of ensuring accountability and control in those situations will lead to the conclusion that the control and management of the police is a matter of great concern, not just to the institution in terms of ensuring internal policy and best practice is adhered to, but also to the state and its citizens in terms of ensuring democratic legitimacy – making sure that state institutions operate within the law; and ensuring democratic representation – making sure that the police did not act in a self-serving, partisan or overtly political manner. Thus it is clear that in democratic societies the police, be that an individual officer, a force or the institution itself, needs to be accountable. It is centrally important that we also reflect on the questions of to whom do the police need to be accountable AND what are the best mechanisms to guarantee such accountability?

Police development and accountability – a brief historical tour

Why have the police?

Like much contemporary policy, we find the roots of policing in the urbanisation and industrialisation that occurred around the beginnings of the nineteenth century. According to Reiner (2000: ch. 1) orthodox history would locate the rationale for the creation of the police as the need to create a force able to deal with the social, economic and political dislocation capitalist development carried in its wake. The previous ad hoc system was not fit for purpose given the growth of the urban environment. However, we can also adopt a more critical view of why the 'new' police force was created in 1829: put simply, capitalism places great stress on individual rather than collective ownership and the police were needed to ensure that private property was protected. Given that the rich owned most of the property (then as now), the police were created to protect the rich from the 'dangerous classes' and politically marginalised or the residiuum, so much feared by respectable Victorian society (Lea, 2000).

But we can also see the creation of the police in terms of the development of the democratic state and the accompanying need to have robust institutions and rational frameworks within which it could operate and enforce its will. It is, however, possible to argue that as the state machinery developed it needed structured, controllable and accountable institutions to ensure that the newly bureaucratised and codified state powers were delivered by equally bureaucratised and codified institutions. As a result of this need, a formalised and homogeneous form of policing emerged able to fit the needs of a rationalised and bureaucratised state, as well as providing the basis for commerce which paved the way for a growth in enterprise and business (a need recognised at the birth of capitalism by its earliest 'worldly philosopher' Adam Smith (2012, see also Heilbroner, 2000).

Which social groups do they primarily serve?

Theoretically, in a democratic state, the police are impartial and for everyone. This would certainly represent the Tebbit view outlined earlier. However, is this the case? Certainly in historical terms there was a fair degree of opposition to the police from all sides of society. However, orthodox history sees this as merely a passing phase and once the value (and alleged impartiality) of the police became universally recognised, opposition dwindled, not least because all citizens felt protected and served by the police force. Moreover, orthodox history suggests that the working-class poor are the greatest supporters of the police simply because the police protect the very weakest members of society. Thus from this perspective the police are for all citizens and all citizens are treated equally by the law enforcement arm of the state.

The more radical view of history challenges this. It notes that the rich were initially against the police, based in the main on having to fund a service they did not believe they needed, but subsequently the opposition to the police from the wealthy came in the form of concerns about the form and control of the police. However, radical historians note that the main opposition toward the police actually came from the working class. Initially, this focused around the disenfranchised who had little or no democratic control over the police. While this form of opposition began to dwindle and we moved to a full democratic system, working-class opposition remained in the form of resentment toward the police for disturbing and controlling forms of street life and being seen as a tool of the 'bosses' in strikes, legitimate protests and industrial disputes. From this perspective, the police were for the property owning and wealthy sections of society and not an even-handed enforcer of equal rights as argued by Brogden and Ellison (2012: 20) 'state policing is primarily a practice of enforcing unequal laws within an unequal social order mandate against unequal peoples'.

We point to an early codification of offences by Redgrave, who in 1834 created a typology of offences, mostly with reference to property. Redgrave's work took place a mere five years after the creation of the Metropolitan Police Force in the midst of the spread of the establishment of police forces across the country. Once Redgrave codified the law, the state agency charged with enforcing the law would have little choice but to see its primary role as working for those aspects of civil society that the law protected. Thus, all citizens would be protected in terms of offences against the person, and property-owning citizens would be protected against loss and damage of their property. Equally, as historical and contemporary cases have shown, where the offences against the person conflict with the protection of property it is nearly always the case that offences against the person committed while undertaking the protection of an individual's personal property are dismissed. Therefore, from a policy implementation perspective it is possible to suggest that the police primarily serve property owners simply because, in terms of working for the state, they see it as their primary role.

To whom are they accountable?

There are three approaches to answering this question: orthodox, radical and policy based. Looking at the orthodox approach, traditionally, the claim has been that, to paraphrase, the police are of the people for the people, leading to the conclusion that citizens control the police because they are simply fellow citizens in uniform. However, this needs to be quantified as even the orthodox reality is more nuanced than the above paraphrase suggests. In reality, there was a determination not to have a national, and therefore central government controlled, police force. As a result, power over the police was devolved to force level with some central oversight being retained by the creation in 1856 of HM Inspectorate of Constabulary which also enshrined the principle of central state funding of police forces. In practice, most local forces were accountable to the Chief Constable and the local watch committee, who were subsequently 'controlled' by local democratic processes.

Radical historians provide a different account. They eschew the belief that the police were accountable to, and thus controlled by, the citizens. Rather, they see the police as being controlled by the local elites who dominate local politics. Thus, in the counties and shires, police forces were controlled by the landed gentry, and in the newly emerging urban areas by the emergent industrial and financial capitalist classes. (In truth, the orthodox and radical accounts simply replicate on-going debates surrounding the control of any democratic society and a full discussion relating to accountability and criminal justice, see Barton and Johns 2012).

Turning to the policy-based explanations, at an institutional level there needs to be some form of internal accountability. This will be formal, inasmuch as there will be standard operating procedures which direct and circumscribe the actions of individual officers. Of equal import, but far less transparent, there will be informal accountability to your colleagues which as Reiner (2000) notes is a central aspect of police culture. Beyond that, large state organisations will need to be accountable to the Ministry that has responsibility for them, in this case, the Home Office. Finally, in a democratic state, state organisations will be accountable to the citizens. However, from a practical perspective, all serving officers will be acutely aware of the internal accountability because it is immediate and impacts on their day-to-day working; depending on their rank, police officers will be more or less aware of accountability to the Home Office because of the impact of directives and audits; however, it is arguable that their accountability to the citizen is viewed as abstract, obscure and tenuous and therefore may only be of peripheral concern. Though the 'attestation' or oath of allegiance sworn by officers in England and Wales makes this accountability explicit:

> I, . . . of . . . do solemnly and sincerely declare and affirm that I will well and truly serve the Queen in the office of constable, with fairness, integrity, diligence and impartiality, upholding fundamental human rights and according equal respect to all people; and that I will, to the best of my power, cause the peace to be kept and preserved and prevent all offences against people and property; and that while I continue to hold the said office I will to the best of my skill and knowledge discharge all the duties thereof faithfully according to law.
>
> *(Police Reform Act, 2002)*

Whatever perspective is adopted, it is clear that the historical development of the police has created a situation where they, in theory at least, serve three masters: themselves on an institutional and collegiate level; the state, as wielders of state power; and the citizens due both to their historical legacy of being of the people for the people and as state agents. Yet, unsurprisingly, their main locus of accountability lies in the first two with the latter coming a poor third. This is for a number of reasons that can be distilled into a simple explanation: accountability to their organisation and to the state is tangible and has a daily impact on the workings of both the force as a whole and the individual worker. It is an active two-way process that both the officer and the organisations engage in on a daily basis. Accountability to the citizen is more abstract. Even when accountability to the citizen is tangible it is done through third parties. Thus, neither the citizen nor the police, either an individual officer or the corporate entity, see citizen involvement as anything other than a theoretical occurrence. Arguably, this is not healthy especially given the role the police play in democratic societies, and successive attempts have been made to engage citizens more deeply in police accountability.

Police and Crime Commissioners: a leap in the dark?

White (2012) believes that the idea of PCCs presents a 'leap in the dark' for the criminal justice system in England and Wales and it is our intention to investigate this claim. First though we need to explain what a PCC is and what they are expected to do. As a result of the Police Reform and Social Responsibility Act (2011) on 15 November 2012 across England and Wales, 41 PCCs were elected. These individuals will be in post for four-year terms and are accountable for the manner in which crime is tackled in their areas; their key responsibilities can be summarised as follows:

- listening to and serving the public;
- providing accountability;
- providing value for money;
- working with partners;
- overseeing regional and national responsibilities.

(Police and Crime Commissioners, 2012)

The PCC will set priorities in their force area, produce an annual report to keep the public informed of progress, and appoint and remove Chief Constables where necessary. The newest Police Minister, Damien Green, appealed to candidates at a conference for the Association of Police and Crime Commissioners to truly give a voice to the communities they serve (Home Office, 2012a). This is extremely important as the role has the tag-line 'voice of the people' attached to it and individuals are expected to build relationships and foster trust between communities and their police services – something that has been steadily in decline according to aggregate opinion poll data (Seldon, 2010; Johns *et al.*, 2012).

In order to ensure that the local voices are neither lost nor distorted each PCC has to swear an Oath of Impartiality which is 'designed to provide a platform to set out publicly their commitment to tackling their new role with integrity'.[1] This, in effect, mirrors the commitment police officers make to serve with impartiality. Additionally, they are answerable to a Police and Crime Panel made up of representatives drawn from local authorities in the specific area with two or more co-opted members depending on the size of the area in question. Panels will not exceed 20 members and will contribute and monitor PCC plans, establish how much people should contribute financially (the precept) and generally hold PCCs to account (Police and Crime Commissioners, 2012).

Politically the PCCs and their watchdog panels are a signature development for the Coalition Government led by David Cameron because they seem to represent a fairly unpopular initiative by an increasingly unpopular administration. Yet, in the face of indifference and, in some cases, hostility, the Government persisted, a not insubstantial commitment as the Electoral Reform Society suggested turn-out for the elections could be as low as 18 per cent of those people eligible to vote (White, 2102). For Cameron, then, they are something of a leap of faith, but does this policy intervention – heralded as the most radical reform of police governance in the last 50 years – also constitute the 'leap in the dark' foretold by White?

As with any major policy innovation there are certainly some ambiguities to be addressed – what will this experiment in local democracy mean for the authority of the Home Secretary? The Coalition Government have been eager to pursue the Big Society at the expense of Big Government, which, simply put, requires less state action and provision and more commitment from local communities to meet their own public service needs through the principal vehicle of voluntarism (Levitas, 2012). Nevertheless, arguably what is not clear is where the line between local democracy and national strategy is to be drawn (Home Office, 2010). In a difficult situation will national priorities outweigh local demands? If recent history of police governance tells us anything, it is that, notwithstanding the frequency with which politicians have said they wish to increase local accountability, the overriding direction of travel has, nevertheless, been towards ever-increasing centralisation of control (Newburn, 2012: 44).

As policing in the UK is essentially 'national' in character (Reiner, 1991, 2000) and the funding will remain predominantly centrally allocated, this tendency seems set to continue and is a question mark that hangs over the reforms. Whether the provisions set down in the Strategic Policing Requirement (issued in July 2012 and effective from November 2012) will enable the correct balance between local and national policing priorities to be struck, it is obviously too early to say (Home Office, 2012b). Nevertheless, such questions demonstrate the implementation niggles that all new policies face and these can readily be dealt with. There are perhaps, bigger questions to be addressed about the role of PCCs in theory and practice.

One such question is the issue of PCCs coming into policing with little or no background knowledge. In a sense the idea that expertise is over-rated merely reflects the way in which professionals in public services have been regarded since the 1980s, with successive governments portraying them more as knaves than knights (Le Grand, 1997) driven more by their own selfish self-interest than by public service. This has come to reflect orthodoxy in policy making, and therefore we can link this with the orthodox perspective discussed above. Making professionals respond to the public they serve through the mediating influence of the

PCC would seem to satisfy the requirements of this approach. From a policy-based perspective there are different ways of looking at the PCC proposals. On the one hand, the independence of the police may be undermined by political influence (Newburn, 2012) while, on the other, the arrival of PCCs chimes with the 'evidence' that the public does not trust the police service or the agencies/institutions designed to monitor their work (Johns *et al.*, 2012) and so democratically elected arbiters are essential.

However, from a radical perspective, the role of PCCs could be compromised by the influx of business expertise on the one hand, which might lead to decisions driven by financial considerations rather than genuine public interest, after all ensuring value for money is central to what PCCs are being asked to provide. On the other hand, the candidature is dominated by 'authority' figures, senior individuals from political, military and other criminal justice backgrounds. This limits the range of perspectives and abilities available to the electorate. Certainly feminist and black and minority ethnic activists were disappointed at the maleness and whiteness of the candidates. The potential for extremist groups to gain influence was raised in a report by former Home Secretary David Blunkett in 2009, though the presence of one candidate does not appear to validate the strength of those concerns.

It is not just about the public trust, it is also about representativeness, which is even more important for PCCs. The diversity argument that has grown out of radical perspectives (although subsequently co-opted by business consultants, see Kandola and Fullerton, 1998) suggesting that homogeneous services cannot adequately serve a diverse society (Johns, 2006).

Conclusion

Regardless of the discussion above, the ability of the population to elect the PCC does notionally place control of the police into the hands of the electorate. Robert Reiner (2011) opines that the claim that PCCs achieve democratic governance of policing identifies democracy solely with voting and, while elections are a necessary, they are not a sufficient condition of democracy. Electing PCCs does not guarantee democratic policing. Reiner outlines several dangers:

- Tyrannies of the majority (oppression of unpopular 'police property' groups);
- Trammelling of due process: failing to respect legal and civil rights;
- Democracy becoming plutocracy, government of the rich, by the rich, for the rich;
- Unequal access to knowledge about policing and media power, frustrating evidence-based policy development.

In short, democratic citizenship requires not merely political rights but civil, and social/economic rights.

(Marshall 1950)

However, this needs to be qualified in respect of the overall fall in voter participation – put simply if only just over 61 per cent of the electorate bothered to vote in the last general election prospects for a meaningful turn-out were flagged up as a potential problem. In the event there was a 14.9 per cent turn-out which was a significant disappointment. The Electoral Commission remarked that it was 'a concern for everyone who cares about democracy' (BBC News, 2012b). While some sections of the government argued that any first time election would receive a muted response and others that the media had not 'covered itself in glory' in promoting the elections, this immediately raises questions about the authority of the PCC to 'speak for the people'. As such, citizen engagement is likely to be minimal and, again, at arm's length.

Equally, and somewhat overlooked in this debate, is the fact that engagement needs to be a two-way process. In just the same way that it is possible to argue that citizens have hitherto not been that engaged in police accountability beyond the abstract, it is equally possible to suggest that the police have done all they can to encourage this lack of citizen scrutiny. The police have operated as a closed shop with their primary accountability being internal first, with accountability to the Home Office coming second and, under previous arrangements, any accountability to the citizen a third. Even given the fact that PCCs can and will wield power it is difficult to see quite how true citizen engagement will take place.

Finally, we would point to the practicalities of accountability – how it is viewed by the police and how it directly impacts on their working life. As noted above, the primary locus of accountability and, thus, of day-to-day concern, is internal. This is what occupies the mind of all police officers with, perhaps, the exception of the very top echelons who are mindful of their accountability to the Home Office. Citizen-led, or democratic accountability is not tangible and is therefore distant from the concerns of the police. Even for the elected PCC, it is hard to see how the average officer or force will see this as anything other than another layer of internal accountability. Equally, given the low voter turn-out relatively few citizens will feel any 'ownership' of police action.

Of course, as with all new initiatives, only time will tell if the PCCs will truly engage the citizen with the police. However, from our perspective we would suggest that this initiative is flawed and unlikely to have any major impact on the manner in which the police include citizens in their day-to-day business due to the fact that the coercive nature of the police role almost defies true citizen involvement in what they do and this is exacerbated in those communities that are most heavily policed and, arguably, are most in need of accountable policing. Without stereotyping, heavily policed communities often do not have the best of relationships with the police and vice versa. It is difficult to see how the PCCs will engage those citizens in any meaningful manner.

Note

1   http://www.homeoffice.gov.uk/police/police-crime-commissioners/news/pcc-impartiality-oath.

Bibliography

Barton, A. and Johns, N. (2012) *The Policy Making Process in the Criminal Justice System*, London: Routledge.

BBC News (2012a) 'Hillsborough: Straw blames Thatcher for police "impunity"', 13/9/12, http://www.bbc.co.uk/news/uk-politics-19584313 (accessed September 2012).

BBC News (2012b) 'First police commissioners chosen amid turnout concerns', 17/11/12, http://www.bbc.co.uk/news/uk-20352539 (accessed February 2013).

Benyon, J. and Solomos, J. (1988) 'The Simmering Cities-Urban Unrest During the Thatcher Years', *Parliamentary Affairs*, 41(3): 402–422.

Blomberg, T.G. (2012) 'Continuing to Advance Criminology and Public Policy', *Criminology & Public Policy*, 11(1): 1–3.

Blunkett, D. (2009) *A People's Police Force: Police Accountability in the Modern Era*, http://davidblunkett.typepad.com/files/a-peoples-police-force-2.pdf (accessed August 2012).

Bowling, B. and Phillips, C. (2007) 'Disproportionate and Discriminatory: Reviewing the Evidence on Police Stop and Search', *The Modern Law Review*, 70(6): 936–961.

Bradford, B., Stanko, E.A. and Jackson, J. (2009) 'Using Research to Inform Policy: The Role of Public Attitude Surveys in Understanding Public Confidence and Police Contact', *Policing*, 3(2): 139–148.

Brogden, M. and Ellison, G. (2012) *Policing in an Age of Austerity: A Postcolonial Perspective*, London: Routledge.

Bullock, K. and Johnson, P. (2012) 'The Impact of the Human Rights Act 1998 on Policing in England and Wales', *British Journal of Criminology*, 52: 630–650.

Dubberley, S. (2006) 'Women Offenders: Identifying and Addressing Barriers to Employment, Training and Education', *Probation Journal*, 53: 279–280.

Fletcher, D.R. (2001) 'Ex-Offenders, the Labour Market and the New Public Administration', *Public Administration*, 79(4): 871–891.

Foucault, M. (1969/1972) *Archaeology of Knowledge*, New York: Pantheon Books.

Heilbroner, R.L. (2000) *The Worldly Philosophers: The Lives, Times, and Ideas of the Great Economic Thinkers*, London: Penguin.

Home Office (2010) *Policing in the 21st Century: Reconnecting the Police and the People*, Home Office: London.

Home Office (2012a) 'Police and Crime Commissioners', http://www.homeoffice.gov.uk/police/police-crime-commissioners/ (accessed September 2012).

Home Office (2012b) 'The Strategic Policing Requirement', https://www.gov.uk/government/uploads/system/uploads/attachment_data/file/117445/strategic-policing-requirement.pdf (accessed September 2012).

House of Lord's Constitution Commission (2012) *Judicial Appointments*, 25th Report of Session 2010–12, London: The Stationery Office Limited.

Jackson, J. and Sunshine, J. (2007) 'Public Confidence in Policing: A Neo-Durkheimian Perspective', *British Journal of Criminology*, 47(2): 214–233.

Johns, N.R. (2006) *How the British National Health Service Deals with Diversity: Professional Problems, Patient Problems*, New York: Edwin Mellen.

Johns, N.R., Green, A.J., Barton, A. and Squire, G. (2012) *Trust and Substitutes for Trust: The Case of Britain Under New Labour*, New York: Nova Science.

Kandola, P. and Fullerton, J. (1998) *Diversity in Action: Managing the Mosaic*, London: Chartered Institute of Personnel & Development.

Lea, J. (2000) 'The Macpherson Report and Question of Institutional Racism', *The Howard Journal of Criminal Justice*, 39(3): 219–233.

Le Grand, J. (1997) 'Knights, Knaves or Pawns? Human Behaviour and Social Policy', *Journal of Social Policy*, 26(2): 149–170.

Levitas, R. (2012) 'The Just's Umbrella: Austerity and the Big Society in Coalition Policy and Beyond', *Critical Social Policy*, 32(3): 320–342.

Ling, T. (1998) *The British State since 1945*, Cambridge: Polity Press.

Loveday, B. (1999) 'Government and Accountability of the Police', in R.I. Mawby (ed.) *Policing Across the World: Issues for the Twenty-First Century*, London: Routledge.

Marshall, T.H. (1950) *Citizenship and Social Class: And Other Essays*, Cambridge: Cambridge University Press.

Maxwell, P. and Mallon, D. (1997) 'Discrimination Against Ex-Offenders', *The Howard Journal of Criminal Justice*, 36(4): 352–366.

McVeigh, T. and Townsend, M. (2011) 'Michael Mansfield condemns police brutality at student demo', *The Guardian*, 6/8/11, http://www.guardian.co.uk/uk/2011/aug/06/michael-mansfield-police-brutality-student (accessed 25/9/11).

Newburn, T. (2012) 'Police and Crime Commissioners: The Americanization of Policing or a Very British Reform?', *International Journal of Law, Crime and Justice*, 40: 31–46.

Police and Crime Commissioners (2012) 'The Role of the PCC', http://www.policecrimecommissioner.co.uk/content/role-pcc (accessed September 2012).

Police Reform Act (2002) (c. 30). London/HMSO. Available from http://www.legislation.gov.uk/ukpga/2002/30/pdfs/ukpga_20020030_en.pdf (accessed 25/1/13).

Porter, L.E. and Prenzler, T. (2012) 'Police Oversight in the United Kingdom: The Balance of Independence and Collaboration', *International Journal of Law, Crime and Justice*, 40: 152–171.

Rackley, E. (2008) 'What a Difference Difference Makes: Gendered Harms and Judicial Diversity', *International Journal of the Legal Profession*, 15(1–2): 37–56.

Reiner, R. (1991) *Chief Constables*, Oxford: Oxford University Press.

Reiner, R. (1992) 'Policing a Postmodern Society', *Modern Law Review*, 55(6): 761–781.

Reiner, R. (2000) *The Politics of the Police*, 3rd ed., Oxford: Oxford University Press.

Reiner, R. (2011) *Policing, Popular Culture and Political Economy: Towards A Social Democratic Criminology*, Farnham, UK: Ashgate.

Seldon, A. (2010) *Trust*, London: Biteback.

Smith, A. (2012) *Wealth of Nations*, Hertfordshire: Wordsworth Publishing Ltd.

Smith, G. (2009) 'Why Don't More People Complain against the Police?', *European Journal of Criminology*, 6(3): 249–266.

Sullivan, R.R. (1998) 'The Politics of British Policing in the Thatcher/Major State', *The Howard Journal of Criminal Justice*, 37(3): 306–318.

The Guardian (2012) 'Police commissioner candidate withdraws over teenage £5 fine', http://www.guardian.co.uk/uk/2012/sep/14/police-commissioner-candidate-withdraws (accessed September 2012).

Travis, A. (2012) 'Simon Weston pulls out of police commissioner race', *The Guardian*, 2/7/12.

White, M. (2012) 'Police and crime commissioners: a leap in the dark for law and order', *The Guardian*, 10/9/12.

Williams, K. (2005) '"Caught Between a Rock and a Hard Place": Police Experiences with the Legitimacy of Street Watch Partnerships', *The Howard Journal of Criminal Justice*, 44(5): 527–537.

27

MAKING POLICE ACCOUNTABLE

Governance and legitimacy

Kevin Stenson and Dan Silverstone

Introduction

There was an outpouring of public support and open display of grief by public and officers in September 2012, after the murder of two popular young women police officers in Manchester. This followed a period of violent conflict over territory between organised crime networks (BBC, 2012a). It reminds us of the high levels of trust and support, the core of legitimacy, among the population achieved by the UK police over generations (Reiner, 2012: 67–114) echoed by the global reputation of the British unarmed 'Bobby' on the beat, as the archetypical symbol of democratic policing by consent. Yet trust and support is not shared by all sections of the population. This chapter will highlight key concerns expressed across the political spectrum about accountability and the ability of citizens to hold the police to account through democratic institutions and procedures. We will examine briefly the nature and institutional architecture of police accountability and legitimacy, in the light of the introduction in November 2012 of Police Crime Commissioners in England and Wales. We add to recent reviews of the literature on police accountability in highlighting salient issues for future social democratic policy and practice (Reiner, 2012: 205–238; Reiner, 2013 (forthcoming); Jones *et al.*, 2012; Rowe, 2008).

We will also examine arguments about the nature of the policing which must be held to account, including whether it can be redefined as 'security provision' that could just as well be delivered by commercial providers. We reject that redefinition, not least because security provision involves the use of legitimate force. How safely can this be outsourced to commercial players and how accountable to the public can they be? Furthermore, we see policing as an aspect of nation state sovereign governance at local level, in a context where the police and other public governmental agencies have to govern 'from above' in fast-changing demographic conditions. This is particularly important in poorer areas denuded of commercial and public institutions (Stenson, 1993). There is a pervasive tension between democracy which gives citizens (especially the majority of citizens) what they want, or are said to want, and the progressive liberal ideologies (in the broader rather than narrowly party political sense) that tend to provide a default framework of values for those working in local and national governmental agencies, NGOs and academia (Stenson and Watt, 1999). By this we mean values and practices that prioritise the worth of the individual, recognise minority rights, require checks and balances on the exercise of executive political power, and contain the use of force.

Progressives argue that police should, holistically, highlight multi-agency efforts in crime prevention, and neighbourhood policing (including police community support officers and other agents in the extended police family), and problem solving which deals with the underlying causes of recurrent crime, and efforts to help recidivists to desist from offending (Stenson and Watt, 1999; Faulkner, 2006). This will, hence, reassure the public, help rehabilitate offenders, and enable the police and other authorities to symbolise fairness in their dealings with the public and win support (Hughes, 2007). Progressive advocates of 'procedural justice', supported by an accumulation of empirical research findings internationally, claim that where the police are perceived as fair and following legal procedures, they encourage citizens to respect the law, discipline themselves, and reduce the need for intrusive policing. Public support diminishes where the police seem to be unprofessional, rude or racist, or if, for example, they appear disproportionately to use stop and search powers with particular race, age, class and gender categories, creating resentment among those targeted (Hough *et al.*, 2010 and this volume). In deeply divided societies there might be different perceptions of what is fair.

Studies of how police spend their time and resources indicate that most of their energies are devoted to maintaining order, crime reduction and dealing with crime-related reports from the public, often putting officers at considerable and unpredictable personal risk (HMIC, 2012a). The English riots in August 2011 remind us of the fragility of the public order in the face of determined collective violence, and how reliant we are on the bravery and public service ethos of the thin blue line of officers standing between chaos and order. Moreover, the crime fighting role is not at odds with the progressive focus on procedural justice, unless it leads to compromising professional standards or disproportionately targeting suspect populations without adequate warrant. While progressive, liberal themes provide admirable professional standards (Hough, this volume), the police are, at core, protectors of the public (Kinsey *et al.* 1986). If they are to protect the public, how can the police and the criminal justice agencies win the respect and support of the population *just* with procedural fairness, friendly engagement with local citizens and liberal criminal justice measures? The struggle to establish sovereign control and also procedural fairness and professionalism are intertwined. The UK police keep an uneasy balance between maintaining control in the name of sovereign law in order to protect the vulnerable from harm, through effective crime fighting and order maintenance, while also carrying the population with them by maintaining trust and the standards of procedural justice. Flagrant challenges – as in Manchester in 2012 – to public authorities by individuals and groups pursuing their goals through violence and anti-social behaviour can make the police appear weak and ineffectual. This erodes local support and respect for police and criminal justice capacity to monopolise the use of coercion, provide protection and justice. The danger is that people might look for protectors in murkier networks of power (Lea and Stenson, 2007; Stenson, 2012).

Finally, we acknowledge that public respect for, and involvement in, the institutions of representative and participatory democracy and government are under challenge internationally. So, with low voter turnout and a fast-changing population, we need other means to uncover how citizens at different points in society perceive and judge the police and how we can improve the mechanisms to hold them to account. Criminologists and other academics can help assess how the police undertake their role and how the public perceive them. This can include assisting those agencies, such as the HMIC, charged with assessing their professional effectiveness, in itself a key dimension of democratic accountability. However, policy makers must recognise that what constitutes the 'evidence base' for policing is highly contested; it is dangerous simply to leave this to those who claim to be 'experts', but who might over-rely on a particular scientific method. Well-resourced international academic lobbyists claiming the mantle of 'science' and the primacy of experimental methods, reminiscent of prestigious medical and other natural sciences, argue that their research protocols should provide the gold standard for research (Sherman, 2009).

It seems that senior British civil servants responsible for setting the benchmarks for public policy research have been receptive to these arguments, notwithstanding major misgivings among other mainstream academics (HM Treasury, 2011). We argue that these lobbies make unsustainable claims to politicians and civil servants about the 'scientific' and hence, privileged, nature of their research, which is too narrow and excluding of other forms of research. Social research about policing involves choices and values and is, like policing, inescapably political. Given that busy politicians do not always grasp these complex issues it is important that the decisions of unelected officials who play a gate-keeping role in ministries and other agencies in relation to defining research standards and allocation of public money for research should be democratically transparent to the wider academic community, and to the public who pay their salaries. We follow our analysis with policy proposals.

Problems of accountability

Multiple purported or real scandals raised by individuals and advocacy groups across the political spectrum draw attention to issues about police malpractice or incompetence. The charity Inquest claims that since 1990 in the UK there have been 1,439 deaths in police custody, or following some other contact with the police, the largest category of which involves use of restraint procedures (Inquest,

2012; Brogden and Ellison, 2012). They claim that despite this growing list of deaths few police officers are ever charged and none convicted by the courts of serious offences such as manslaughter. They claim that concerns raised by 'toothless' coroners' courts have been ignored. The death of Mark Duggan in North London in August 2011 at the hands of 'Trident' officers, and argued to have spark the London riots, is still the subject of an ongoing inquiry. For some sections of the Black community this was merely the most recent example of police brutality which has impacted disproportionally on them since the 1980s (House of Commons Home Affairs Committee, 2010).

More widely, the Lord Leveson Inquiry in 2012 into phone hacking revealed dubious relations between senior police officers and media corporations. Furthermore, an Independent Police Complaints Commission inquiry was launched after the Independent Hillsborough Panel Report released in September 2012 on the policing of a1989 football match between Liverpool and Nottingham Forest in Sheffield. During this match a crush on the terraces led to the deaths of 96 Liverpool fans. The Panel Report found police and emergency services had attempted to deflect blame for the disaster on to fans, with the altering of police statements (BBC, 2012d). Poor resourcing of the Serious Fraud Office and lack of political will to challenge financial lobbies, upon which politicians have become increasingly dependent, mean that no major players in that industry have been charged with fraud since the financial crash of 2007 and later revelations about major banks' money laundering for crime syndicates. This is despite the huge harm experienced by citizens in the aftermath of the crash (FSA, 2010). Are wealthy financiers who offend too big to prosecute; is there one law for the rich and another for ordinary citizens; and will this reinforce cynicism among the poor about the fairness of the law? (Brogden and Ellison, 2012; Whyte, 2012).

Furthermore, advocacy groups, such as feminist, anti-racist, Islamist and other social movements, claim that crime victims are often still poorly protected by police investigating domestic violence, stalking and sexual offences against women, and violence and abuse against ethnic, religious, and sexual minorities (Stern, 2010; Webster, 2007; Pantazis and Pemberton, 2009). Also, civil libertarians claim that, given what is claimed to be post-9/11 fear mongering in the war against terrorism and cybercrime, the police are being given excessive powers of surveillance (including over digital communications) and detention, which can be used to discriminate against vulnerable or unpopular minorities. This could be eroding the differences between democracies and the authoritarian societies they oppose (Ericson, 2007). In addition, the tension between democracy and progressive liberalism is manifested in claims by right wing politicians and media. They criticise the police and CPS for resisting majority public opinion, succumbing to progressive, self-serving lawyer, judicial and advocacy lobbies in being unduly hamstrung by the Human Rights Act, and for lenience towards illegal immigration, anti-social behaviour and crimes committed by minorities (Hitchens, 2004; Silverman, 2011).

Recent trials of groups of men of mainly Pakistani Muslim origin in Northern and Midlands towns for the grooming and systematic sexual abuse of young white

British girls have been accompanied by charges from investigative journalists and politicians that the police, social services and crown prosecutors had ignored reports of such endemic criminality since 2003 because of fears that acting against these offenders would lead to accusations of racism and Islamophobia (BBC, 2012b). This echoes complaints that the police and prosecutors had repeatedly failed adequately to follow up complaints by victims of sexual abuse by the late disc jockey Jimmy Saville and the late Cyril Smith MP. These all generate the familiar criticism that the police are, in effect, a closed profession, highly resistant to scrutiny or criticism, whose default position is to close ranks and protect their own. Hence, the police have acquired a serious problem in the management of their public image (Mawby, 2012), and so the agenda is how to rebuild the legitimacy of the police and improve the effectiveness of those institutions, procedures and mechanisms that try to hold police to account.

The nature of legitimacy and accountability

Yet, we should not exaggerate the unpopularity of police with the UK public, among which it retains considerable legitimacy. By legitimacy we mean the police commanding the confidence, trust, and the acceptance of their authority by citizens (Jones *et al.*, 2012; Reiner, 2012). They do this through convincing the public that they are competent crime fighters, able to contain disorder, reduce the crime that most disturbs citizens, and make people feel safe for most of the time, and are individuals who are honest and hold to ethical standards of conduct. In addition, with diminishing deference to authority, legitimacy now includes the openness and transparency of the police as an organisation, through the mass media, new social media, twitter and other channels of communication. It also includes the effectiveness of methods whereby the police communicate with the public, particularly those hardest to reach by usual methods. Media images of the police provide important frames for citizens' perceptions given that most people have little direct contact with officers.

This legitimacy could evaporate. It is not wired into the British DNA and does not result from favours graciously granted by benevolent elites. It is the product of a long history of struggles in which the labour movement played a dominant role: for the suffrage, to form trade unions, hold public demonstrations, and other rights and forms of collective security. This led to the gradual incorporation, since the nineteenth century, of working-class people into state-recognised citizenship rights, in legal, political, economic and cultural terms (Reiner, 2010: 67–114). In previous generations these citizenship rights were understood mainly in terms of the attempts to ameliorate inequality of wealth and income. When those attempts failed the police were a thin blue line managing the effects in community breakdown, disorder, protest and criminality. While protecting the law abiding majority, this inevitably brought them into conflict, disproportionately, with poorer, and more alienated sections of the population.

However, with a declining labour movement and rise, since the 1960s, of new social movements, from feminist to environmentalist, and with large-scale immigration and, hence, increasing urban ethnic diversity, the agenda for expanding rights of citizenship widened. It now includes other categories beyond class, including gender, race, ethnicity, religion, sexuality, physical disability and mental ill-health. One key indicator of newer groups' incorporation into the social mainstream is how responsive and, therefore, accountable, the police, criminal justice and other public agencies of government are to their concerns and fears: notably domestic violence against women, racist, homophobic and Islamophobic violence, and the targeting of the disabled and mentally ill. This would also include a better gender and ethnic balance among officers at every rank, so that they look more like the populations they police.

Legitimacy involves mechanisms of accountability including, at root, command and control of constables by managers. Older democratic notions of the police being accountable to the people were overshadowed under Conservative and New Labour administrations since the 1980s when the vogue of US management ideologies took root. They emphasised bureaucratic, 'tick box' mechanisms, setting targets from above and checking police performance in terms of the principles of economy, efficiency and effectiveness (McLaughlin, 2007). Since this is now unpopular and widely associated with demoralising, wasteful, managerial jargon and excess, and a related diminishing respect for professional expertise in the public services, it would be unwise to place much faith in such mechanisms as instruments of accountability (Caulkin, 2012).

Constables, like many other professional and semi-professional workers, have considerable discretion in their work. They spend much of their time beyond the purview of multiplying middle and senior managers, limiting the capacity for managerial oversight. This highlights the importance of effective police recruitment (weeding out those who lack the requisite character) and the internalisation, through initial and ongoing police education, of professional ethical standards (Waddington, 1998; Neyroud, 2001). Official mechanisms of accountability are concerned with how to keep the practice of discretion within a legal framework. The key debates are about: the judicial function – whether the rules have been breached; how to prioritise police resources; and how to manage the performance of duties effectively and efficiently (Reiner, 2010).

Until recently, the official architecture of accountability mechanisms was based on a tripartite system of accountability which, under the Police Act of 1964, distributed responsibilities between the Home Office, the local police authority (including elected councillors), and the Chief Constable of the force. That system was further endorsed by the 1994 Police and Magistrates Courts Act, the Police Act 1996, and the Police Reform Act 2002. Furthermore, the architecture includes, for example, the courts, the House of Commons Home Affairs Select Committee, Her Majesty's Inspectorate of Constabulary, the Independent Police Complaints Commission (IPCC), Public Inquiries, and reports by the National Audit Office for the House of Commons Public Accounts Committee. Much criticism has focused on the IPCC, which deals with serious issues of police malpractice. Despite improvements made in police accountability since the IPCC took over from the

Police Complaints Authority in 2004, it is now criticised for being insufficiently independent. Around a third of its investigators are ex-police officers and it lacks the powers to require serving or ex-officers to provide direct evidence to the IPCC (BBC, 2012c). The IPCC has also been criticised for not being thorough enough in its investigations, with families instead only belatedly gaining restitution from either coroner courts or the European Court of Human Rights (Panorama, 2012; BBC, 2012c). It could be replaced by a new stronger Police Standards Authority, if Labour regains power.

While broadly answerable to the requirements of law and government policy, the police, on the principle of constabulary independence, have been – until recently – shielded in their everyday operational work from interference by politicians, often driven by sectional interests and what progressives describe as populist democratic sentiment. This and cognate forms of shielding have long been held to differentiate European police and criminal justice systems from US systems, which are more directly under political control of elected mayors in the big cities and elected sheriffs in smaller settlements (Tonry, 2009). In addition, this shielding from what progressive liberals describe as populist democracy provided the space, to take the example of the Thames Valley under successive chief constables, for police and criminal justice agencies to experiment with progressive neighbourhood, community policing, crime prevention and community safety initiatives (Stenson, 2008).

Police and Crime Commissioners

The recent election, under the Police Reform and Social Responsibility Act 2011, in November 2012 of Police and Crime Commissioners (PCCs) in England and Wales has altered the landscape of police accountability and legitimacy. The new system marks a significant break with the past. The PCCs serve the 41 police force areas outside London, and in the City of London and Metropolitan Police Force areas of London the Mayor and London Assembly provide oversight. The PCC has responsibility for hiring and firing the Chief Constable and holding him/her to account, setting out a five-year Police and Crime Plan in consultation with the Chief Constable. This determines local policing priorities. The PCC sets the annual local precept and annual force budget, derived from the Home Office. He/she is also responsible for community safety grants to other organisations. The PCC is accountable to the new Police and Crime Panel (PCP) compromising a minimum of two independent members and ten councillors from the force area. The PCC has a budget which includes the policing grant from the Home Office, Drug Interventions Programme funding and other grants and funds raised through local authority precepts in the force area. Given the expense of the election campaigns, most candidates were sponsored by the major parties. Conservative candidates were more sympathetic than others to driving through government reform agendas for police institutions and practice: creating greater flexibility of labour, less generous starting salaries and pension arrangements, and fast track recruitment and promotion for the highly qualified (Home Office, 2012). These agendas also include outsourcing much of police work, where possible, to G4S and other commercial security agencies.

The creation of PCCs was prompted by concerns expressed about a deficit in democratic oversight of police officers, including an overly cosy relationship between senior officers and those charged with overseeing them. The then Policing Minister was confident that they would be a radical departure, as PCCs were meant to be high-profile local leaders with power to represent the voice of victims, the wider community and new groups becoming involved in criminal justice. Given the size of the force areas at which they are elected, they were thought to construct a large public mandate (Ministry of Justice, 2012). After the event, the chairwoman of the Electoral Commission described the record low electoral turnout as 'a concern for everyone who cares about democracy'. Analysis revealed that those PCCs who were not already established politicians were likely to be from established or closely aligned criminal justice professions, such as former police, magistrates or the military (Rogers and Burn-Murdoch, 2012). In addition, the PCC can appoint deputies on generous salaries, with no further democratic oversight. Can the accountability sought by the government for the police be the same accountability sought by different sections of the public?

Let us see how far the evolving PCC structure impacts on progressive liberal practices and culture, especially if the liberal shield, should it remain, fails to protect the weak and vulnerable. Will citizens influence *local* policy and practice? For example, the PCC for the Thames Valley force deals with three counties and over two million people. Can the PCC deal with what most people define as local issues? Furthermore, with a Conservative PCC in charge, how easily can police commanders resist political pressure to devote more resources to the patrol and defence of an image of the Thames Valley projected by the Inspector Morse TV series: dreaming Oxford spires, affluent, leafy suburbs and pretty Thames-side villages, at the expense of the politically weaker and less aesthetically appealing, troubled urban neighbourhoods of Slough, Reading, High Wycombe and Oxford (Stenson, 2002, 2008)?

Defining policing

Much of the debate about police accountability and legitimacy involves problems of definition: what are the police for, what do they, and should they, do; and how should they best deploy their resources most effectively in times of austerity; what are the instrumental professional tasks of policing entailed in maintaining order, preventing and reducing crime and funnelling offenders through to the criminal justice system (Laycock and Tilley, this volume)? This feeds into arguments paralleling those in other public services about how far policing tasks can be defined in technical professional terms as the provision of security (Wood and Shearing, 2007) and are ripe for modernisation in line with business values and practices (Savage, 2007). The claim is that much policing could be provided more cheaply and effectively by commercial providers (Evans, 2012). The counter-argument is that the police perform essential functions that cannot be easily outsourced without severely weakening the sovereignty of the nation state. Moreover, commercial firms like G4S tend to be less transparent and harder to hold to account than the state police, given their ability to hide behind the principles of commercial confidentiality and the primacy of shareholder value over the public interest (Curtis, 2011). In this regard the use of the Special Constable (someone who voluntarily provides their time but wears a police uniform and gains full police powers) is a better solution to public sector cuts than outsourcing.

For us, at the core of policing lies the exercise of sovereign powers. Sovereignty, in the expanded sense with which we use this term refers not simply to the monopolisation of the use of force in maintaining order but a range of economic, political, military and cultural practices to integrate and order territory and populations. Sovereignty refers to the meeting point, in advanced democracies, for liberal values which may have a more generic, international character, and forms of nationalism. These highlight values, histories and identities which are particular to a given nation and are embodied in its laws and dominant institutions. In addition to the struggle to maintain physical security through force by the military, security and police agencies, sovereignty involves attempts to exercise fiscal and monetary control and nation-building at local level. This includes attempts to foster cultural solidarity among increasingly diverse and pluralistic populations, often new members of the nation (Stenson, 2012). Policing is important in this respect since other agencies of national, governmental authority may often be less visible to the public.

Technical debates about police organisation, leadership and practice can narrow our understanding of police accountability and legitimacy. In conditions in which there is always likely to be a tension for police officers between crime control and (in American parlance) 'due process' (Skolnick, 1966), a narrowly technical, professional conception of policing deflects attention from the fundamental values and principles that should underpin policing and criminal justice in a democracy. If, as we argue, the police are a core nation-building institution, symbolic representatives of the hopefully unifying effect of law and the basic values of English, Welsh, Scottish, Northern Irish and United Kingdom nationhood and citizenship, then their work cannot be outsourced, like rubbish collection, to commercial providers. This is so even if the police now, as they always have done, liaise with and outsource to some private sector bodies in the margins of their work (Loader and Walker, 2007).

We see police accountability and legitimacy as inextricably involving procedural justice and securing sovereign control at local levels. This is particularly so in poor and working-class neighbourhoods. It is estimated that around 10 per cent of witnesses who get to court (and many more do not make it) are vulnerable and intimidated (Burton et al., 2006). If people are too fearful to become involved in criminal justice, this can create a vacuum of governance likely to be filled in toxic ways that can threaten the integrity of the state and its contract with citizens to provide protection and justice. So it is vital that the police and other public authorities regain sovereign control, protect the weak and vulnerable against the strong and, hence, reassure the public, important for those of modest means and dependent on the state for security (Lea and Young, 1984).

Yet there is a further significant context for understanding debates about police accountability and legitimacy. Policing is rarely concerned just with law enforcement; indeed many if not most calls for service do not clearly involve law enforcement. Policing involves a large discretionary element in whether or how to apply the law and is best seen as engaged with governance, particularly a tension and interaction between attempts to govern from above and below. Sites of governance from below can range from the family, to religious, neighbourhood-based, leisure, commercial, charitable, and social movement-based, collective groupings to less legitimate, shadowy groups involved in criminal, vigilante, terrorist, street corner gang, revolutionary and paramilitary groupings and activities, perhaps struggling to create new forms of nation state or an international Muslim Caliphate. These forms of governance can have varying relations with sovereign state government, from accommodation and incorporation through to outright, treasonable rebellion. The complexity of proliferating networks and sites of governance from below has grown with migration from poor countries and its impact on community relations (Lea and Stenson, 2007).

Increasingly police have to manage interactions and conflicts between myriad ethnic groups who originate in societies with very different modes of law and policing, and customs and practices that may be at odds with the law and dominant norms in the United Kingdom. It should be strongly emphasised that the relations between these groups and their implications for police accountability and legitimacy are irreducible to the simpler language of race and racism and agendas of lobbies that highlight those concerns. With growing ethnic complexity catch-all terms in public discourse like Black, Asian or Black and Ethnic Minority (BME) become increasingly problematic and denuded of clear meaning; new concepts are needed (Stenson et al., 1999; Stenson and Waddington, 2007; Fletcher and Stenson, 2009; Stenson 2012). Hence, alongside, and through the tasks of order maintenance (Reiner, 2012), responding to emergencies, crime prevention and reduction, the police are also – with other agencies – trying to create social cohesion, respect for law and the collective identity and solidarity of national citizenship in fast-changing conditions. This is undermined if unprofessional practice exacerbates social divisions and conflict.

Social science and accountability: evidence-based policing and the policing of evidence, from 'what works' to 'what is going on?'

Finally, let us consider how the academy can help the police to become more legitimate and accountable. One way would be to help assess the effectiveness of the most local forms of police–community liaison. After the Scarman Report, following the 1981 Brixton riots, community engagement was set up on a statutory basis with community police consultative groups, augmented now by Independent Advisory Groups (IAGs). In London, as elsewhere, IAGs and other bodies aim to represent the voices of ethnic and religious minorities. But there are often questions about whether the diversity of the voices and interests within minority populations are being properly represented by such forms of consultation, and about the dangers of such groups becoming co-opted and neutered by authorities (Fletcher and Stenson, 2009; Murji, 2011). On the one hand, for the community member, being a 'critical friend' to the police service can create suspicions among their own community about their loyalties. On the other, as the police service have tried to reach out to ever more diverse communities, especially in the attempt to implement the community engagement aspect of the Prevent (anti-terrorism) strategy, individual police officers and police units (such as the Muslim contact unit) have been subjected to critical scrutiny for engaging with politically divisive and separatist figures (Lambert and Spalek, 2010; Lambert, 2011).

Most recently community engagement in London has been encouraged across neighbourhoods in beat ward panels. Therefore, it is not uncommon within one London Borough to have a youth ward panel, a stop and search community police consultancy group, a number of neighbourhood ward panels, an Independent Advisory Group, and sometimes a community consultative group. In other boroughs and other forces, fora exist often as empty shells. Despite the plethora of guidance on how these groups ought to behave and what their membership should consist of, they remain poorly funded, evaluated or researched. Local academics, especially those deeply immersed in the area, can help with this.

Whether social science can assist democratic policing to be more effective, responsive and accountable to citizens is a timely question because of the recent institution of the Home Office-endorsed College of Policing, which will set ethical and professional standards of policing, accredit policing courses and serve as a gatekeeper of knowledge for what is claimed to be evidence-based policing. There are lobbies (predominantly academics trained in experimental psychology) which adopt the mantle of 'science', claiming, on the basis of reviews of globally drawn evidence from their own discipline, expertise on 'what works' in maintaining public order, preventing and reducing crime, policing, and punishment. This seemingly forecloses the need for tiresome academic debate involving other theoretical schools about the variable merits of theories and methods, and so, it is claimed, should determine what constitutes the evidence base for policing. According to these academics the police should be accountable to science and the evidence base as they define it. The main international experimental psychology lobby, the Campbell Collaboration Group[1] modelling itself on the prestigious Cochrane Collaboration Group for medical research, assumes human behaviour is largely determined and can be measured and predicted using the methods of experimental psychology. This involves controlling for key dependent and independent variables in causal relationships, with random controlled trials at the apex of a hierarchy of methods to assess 'what works' in policing (Sherman, 2009). However, a rival school, with different methodological preferences, but also claiming the mantle of science ('Crime

Science'), fiercely rejects the Campbellite claims for privileged status, insisting that there should be healthy, open debate and, by implication, fair competition for scarce research funding (Laycock, 2012).

Both of these schools promise analyses and policy prescriptions at the price of bypassing generations of methodological debate in history and other social sciences about the need for a science tailored for humans, and not over-relying on natural science experimental and quasi-experimental methods (Pawson and Tilley, 1997). As historians and social scientists emphasise, we are endowed with consciousness and language, have a measure of free will and, inconveniently, rarely behave in strict accordance with precise 'scientific' predictions about human action, beyond the simplest level (Bryman, 2012). Policy makers should view cautiously claims to a scientific hot line to the truth and attempts to foreclose debate. Most experienced quantitative and qualitative researchers, not just those on the radical fringes, recognise the need for humility about what we can describe, predict and explain in human conduct, and accept that we need to choose data and methods in accordance with the research question posed and varying contexts studied, not a pre-ordained hierarchy (Hope, 2009; Ekblom, 2011).

Policy makers should view with scepticism narrow conceptions of criminological science modelled *only* on experimental psychology and medical research. Police officers do not work in experimental conditions. Policing involves interaction with the public; it does not form an enclosed professional system. It is better to foster robust debate and a range of research funded from constrained budgets, including that which can help the police to understand the extreme complexity of the new, fast-changing populations and neighbourhoods that the police service has to govern and help to self-govern.

Police officers should be encouraged to seek inspiration from good practice in other jurisdictions, but because a policing method 'works' in Birmingham Alabama, does not mean it will work in Birmingham, England. To claim that many studies replicate findings, when they do not adequately describe or account for important differences in the contexts of, and subtle processes operating in, policing settings, tells us little. Off-the-shelf professional strategies borrowed from other time zones rarely work unless tailored carefully for local conditions. In trying to transfer policies and practices, researchers and police officers need tools to recognise the importance of local contexts. These contexts vary in terms of history, local economy, culture, spatiality, demography and so on (Elmsley, 2012; Neyroud, 2012: 1). And they involve evidence bases well beyond the scope of experimental psychology which skates over or simplifies the complex settings of action (Pawson and Tilley, 1997; Jones and Newburn, 2004; Stenson and Edwards, 2004). In these circumstances, precisely identifying and controlling for key variables in causal relationship with each other in myriad local settings in which policing operates – as promised by those claiming a privileged role as 'scientists' of crime and policing – is a tall order unlikely to deliver value for tax payers' money.

Another approach involves regularly taking the public temperature through questionnaire-based surveys of public response to police and other agencies involved in crime prevention and reduction. For example, the Metropolitan Police run ongoing surveys to gauge how Londoners feel about the police and their changing policies and practices. At a national level, the annual British Crime Survey (BCS) of 40,000 adult citizens includes questions about people's perceptions of and confidence in their local police and around 60 per cent of respondents reported high levels of confidence. While surveys can capture general trends, they are less good at predicting particular reactions to incidents or problematic situations, especially those involving more alienated groups, hard to reach through conventional consultative or survey instruments. Survey responses can vary with how questions are posed and reflect local myths and gossip as much as experience. Furthermore, surveys may miss nuances involved in direct and sustained engagement between police and public, or those possible between researchers and the public, using in-depth, anthropological and geographical methods to complement larger surveys (Jefferson, 1991; Innes, 2004; Stenson and Waddington, 2007).

Hence it is helpful to initiate innovative case studies, for example Foster's action research studies of neighbourhood policing, in which researchers work with officers in helping them engage with varied groups and utilise the particular qualities of individuals and local opportunities (Foster and Jones, 2010). Furthermore, much of what the police need to know (and where locally based researchers may help as critical friends) concerns not so much 'what works?' generically with hot spot, problem solving and other police strategies (much already familiar to officers), but 'what is going on?'. The key questions include, for example: who are the new groups; how do they try to govern their lives; what are their norms, values, lifestyle patterns; how do they fit with dominant English and Welsh legal and social norms; and how can lines of communication and accountability be opened up with diverse interests and needs within those populations? Much of this work would focus on unfolding, and largely unexamined, relations between the mosaic of ethnic groups, from Irish, Jewish, Vietnamese, Russian and Nigerian, to Somali, and the implications this has for policing (Stenson, 2012; Silverstone, 2010; Sampson, 2012).

Conclusion

What should a new government aiming for both criminal and social justice do? Policing in a democracy is intrinsically political; it is about the exercise of power and prioritising. It cannot simply be left to 'experts'. The question is how can a balance be drawn between different lobbies and minimise the chance that PCCs and Chief Constables become captive to sectional or only majority interests? The institutions of accountability, from the Home Office and House of Commons Home Affairs Committee, to the HMIC, mostly perform valuable roles. Root and branch change would achieve little and dismantling the new elected PCC posts may appear undemocratic but there are areas deserving improvement. First, coroner's courts need to be overhauled and given enhanced powers to investigate problematic deaths without avoidable delay and to provide some closure for the bereaved. Second, the IPCC should be replaced with a much tougher Police Standards Authority, able to require serving and ex-police officers to give evidence and with the power, along with House of Commons committees, to oversee commercial security providers with government contracts. That might require changes in company law. Full transparency and oversight is a small price for companies to pay for the easy profits that flow from government contracts. Third, PCCs' constituencies are too large to permit meaningful liaison with local people. Building on the experience of London Boroughs in the 1980s and 90s, Local Police Committees, based on borough command units, composed of elected councillors and magistrates, could provide lines of contact with local communities and, through force-wide representative bodies, could hold the PCC and Crime Panels to account, and limit the tendency towards a 'top-down' approach. These bodies would feed up the line significant local concerns and enhance the status of councillors and representative democracy, rather than over-relying on self-selected, or police-selected, community advocates. Fourth, updating Sir Robert Peel's nineteenth-century model of the police as citizens in uniform, more special constables should be recruited from every section of the population. Fifth, the College of Policing could improve the recruitment and the ethical and professional skills of officers. This would include fostering basic research skills to help officers understand the populations they serve and collaborate effectively with academics. But this needs careful stewardship to prevent capture by particular academic and other lobbies. It needs close dialogue with a range of academics in the universities. The presently shadowy role of civil servants in the Home Office and Ministry of Justice, and other gatekeepers of tax-based funding for policing research, needs the disinfectant of sunlight and oversight by House of Commons committees.

British Police as agents of the sovereign nation state at local level have to combine maintaining order and crime fighting with building the nation locally out of the crooked timber of humanity. They have to negotiate inevitable tensions between the democratic wishes of citizens, and liberal standards set by professional, including legal, civil service, and academic, elites. Whatever their failings, here, police officers contrast with those in many other countries – including a number of those whence recent waves of migrants to the UK originate – where citizens expect little of their police, or other public officials, assuming that it is normal for them to be corrupt, open to bribery, violent and unaccountable for their conduct through democratic institutions and procedures. If they maintain order it is often more through fear than through respect. Here, if the police are criticised for incompetence, unfairness or illegality it is because we have come to expect high standards and are reluctant to accept a fall from grace.

Note

1 http://www.campbellcollaboration.org/crime_and_justice/index.php

Acknowledgement

Thanks to Jennifer Brown and Robert Reiner for comments on an earlier draft.

References

BBC (2012a) 'Manchester Shootings: timeline of events', BBC News Manchester, 19 September 2012 (accessed 30/11/2012)

BBC (2012b) 'Muslim gang "white rape" claim prompts row', BBC News, 13 November. http://www.bbc.co.uk/news/uk-politics-20316934 (accessed 10/12/2012)

BBC (2012c) 'Who polices the police?', File on Four, Radio 4. http://www.bbc.co.uk/programmes/b00pxng0 (accessed 20/12/2012)

BBC (2012d) 'Hillsborough probe bill passed by Parliament', 11 December. http://www.bbc.co.uk/news/uk-politics-20681825 (accessed 20/12/2012)

Brogden, M. and Ellison, G. (2012) *Policing in the Age of Austerity*. Abingdon: Routledge

Bryman, A. (2012) *Social Research Methods*. Oxford: Oxford University Press

Burton M., Evans, R. and Sanders, A. (2006) 'Are Special Measures for Vulnerable and Intimidated Witnesses Working? Evidence From The Criminal Justice Agencies', Home Office Online Report 01/06. London: The Home Office

Caulkin, S. (2012) 'Management theory was hijacked in the 1980s. We're still suffering the fallout', *The Guardian*, 12 November

Curtis, P. (2011) 'Reforms threaten transparency and accountability, MPs Warn', *The Guardian*, 5 April

Ekblom, P. (2011) *Crime Prevention, Security and Community Safety Using the 5Is Framework (Crime Prevention and Security Management)*. London: Palgrave Macmillan

Elmsley, C. (2012) 'Marketing the Brand: Exporting British Police Models 1929–1950', *Policing, A Journal of Policy and Practice*, 6(1): 43–54

Ericson, E.V. (2007) *Crime in an Insecure World*. Cambridge: Polity

Evans, T. (2012) 'Why don't we start privatising the police?' *Evening Standard*, 17 May

Faulkner, D. (2006) *Crime, State and Citizen*. Bristol: The Policy Press

Financial Services Authority (FSA) (2010) 'The scale & impact of financial crime'. http://www.fsa.gov.uk/pages/library/research/economic/interest/crime.shtml (accessed 10/12/2012)

Fletcher, R. and Stenson, K. (2009) 'Governance and the London Metropolitan Police Service', *Policing, A Journal of Policy and Practice*, 3(1): 12–21. Special issue on policing and governance, edited by Kevin Stenson

Foster, J. and Jones, C. (2010) '"Nice to Do" and Essential: Improving Neighbourhood Policing in an English Police Force', *Policing, a Journal of Policy and Practice*, 4(1): 395–402

Hitchens, P. (2004) *The Abolition of Liberty: The Decline of Order and Justice in England* (Revised paperback ed.). London: Atlantic

HMIC (2012a) 'Taking time for crime, a study of how police officers prevent crime in the field'. London: HMIC. http://www.hmic.gov.uk/publication/taking-time-for-crime/ (accessed 20/12/2012)

HM Treasury (2011) HM Treasury's *Magenta Book: Guidance for evaluation*. London: Treasury

Home Office (2012) *Independent Review of Police Officer and Staff Remuneration and Conditions, Final Report, Volume One (The Winsor Report)*. London: The Home Office

Hope, T. (2009) 'The Illusion of Control: A Response to Professor Sherman', *Crime and Criminal Justice*, 9(2): 125–134

Hough, M., Jackson, J., Bradford, B., Myhill, A. and Quinton, P. (2010) 'Procedural Justice, Trust, and Institutional Legitimacy', *Policing, A Journal of Policy and Practice*, 4(3): 203–210

House of Commons Home Affairs Committee (2010) *The Work of the Independent Police Complaints Commission Eleventh Report of Session 2009–10. Report, together with formal minutes, oral and written evidence*. http://www.publications.parliament.uk/pa/cm200910/cmselect/cmhaff/366/366.pdf (accessed 10/12/12)

Hughes, G. (2007) *The Politics of Crime and Community*. Basingstoke: Palgrave Macmillan

Innes, M. (2004) 'Signal Crimes and Signal Disorders: Notes on Deviance as Communicative Action', *British Journal of Sociology*, 55(3): 335–355

Inquest (2012) 'BAME deaths in custody'. http://www.inquest.org.uk/ (accessed 10/12/2012)

Jefferson, T., (1991) 'Discrimination, Disadvantage and Police-Work', in E. Cashmore and E. Mclaughlin (eds) *Out of Order: Policing Black People*. London: Routledge

Jones, T. and Newburn, T. (2004) 'The Convergence of US and UK Crime Control Policy: Exploring Substance and Process', in T. Newburn and R. Sparks (eds) *Criminal Justice and Political Cultures, National and International Dimensions of Crime Control*. Cullompton: Willan

Jones, T., Newburn, T. and Smith, D.J. (2012) 'Democracy and Police Crime Commissioners', in T. Newburn and J. Peay (eds) *Policing, Politics, Culture and Control*. Oxford: Hart

Kinsey, R., Lea, J. and Young, J. (1986) *Losing the Fight Against Crime*. Oxford: Basil Blackwell

Lambert, B. (2011) *Countering al-Qaida in London: Police and Muslims in Partnership*. London: Hurst

Lambert, B. and Spalek, B. (2010) 'Policing within a Counter-Terrorism Context Post 7/7: The Importance of Partnership, Dialogue and Support when Engaging with Muslim Communities', in R. Eatwell and M. J. Goodwin (eds) *The 'New' Extremism in 21st Century Britain*. London: Routledge

Laycock, G. (2012) 'In Support of Evidence-Based Approaches: A Response to Lum and Kennedy', *Policing, A Journal of Policy and Practice*, 6(4): 324–326

Lea, J. and Young, J. (1984) *What Is To Be Done About Law and Order?* Harmondsworth: Penguin

Lea, J. and Stenson, K. (2007) 'Security, Sovereignty, and Non-State Governance "From Below"', *Canadian Journal of Law and Society*, 22(2): 9–28

Loader, I. and Walker, N. (2007) *Civilizing Security*. Cambridge: Cambridge University Press

Mawby, R. C. (2012) 'Crisis, What Crisis? Some Research Based Reflections on Police-Press Relations', *Policing, A Journal of Policy and Practice*, 6(3): 272–280

McLaughlin, E. (2007) *The New Policing*. London: Sage

Ministry of Justice (2012) *White Paper – Swift and Sure: The Government's Plans for Reform of the Criminal Justice System*. Stationery Office Limited. www.gov.uk/government/publications/swift-and-sure-justice (accessed 27/6/2013)

Murji, K. (2011) 'Working Together: Governing and Advising the Police', *The Police Journal*, 84(3): 256–271

Neyroud, P. (2012) 'Editorial', *Policing, A Journal of Policy and Practice*, 6(1): 1–3

Neyroud P. and Beckley, A. (2001) *Policing, Ethics and Human Rights*. Cullompton: Willan

Panorama (2012) 'Who's Watching the Detectives?' BBC. http://www.bbc.co.uk/programmes/b01p8r8l (accessed 10/12/2012)

Pantazis, C. and Pemberton, C. (2009) 'From the "Old" to the "New" Suspect Community: Examining the Impacts of Recent UK Counter-Terrorist Legislation', *British Journal of Criminology*, 49(5): 646–666

Pawson, R. and Tilley, N. (1997) *Realistic Evaluation*. London: Sage

Reiner, R. (2010) *The Politics of the Police* (4th edition). Oxford: Oxford University Press

Reiner, R. (2012) *In Praise of Fire Brigade Policing: Contra Common Sense Conceptions of the Police Role*. London: The Howard league for Penal Reform

Reiner, R. (2013, forthcoming) 'Who Governs? Democracy, Plutocracy, Science and Prophecy in Policing', *Criminology and Criminal Justice*

Rogers, S. and Burn-Murdoch, J. (2012) 'PCC election results 2012: what's happened in the police and crime commissioner votes'. http://www.guardian.co.uk/news/datablog/2012/nov/16/pcc-election-results-police-crime-commissioners (accessed 10/12/2012)

Rowe, M. (2008) *Introduction to Policing*. London: Sage

Sampson, R. (2012) *Great American City: Chicago and the Enduring Neighborhood Effect*. Chicago: University of Chicago Press

Savage, S. (2007) *Police Reform: Forces for Change*. Oxford: Oxford University Press

Sherman, L. (2009) 'Evidence and Liberty: The Promise of Experimental Criminology', *Criminology and Criminal Justice*, 9(1): 5–28

Silverman, J. (2011) *Crime, Policy and the Media: The Shaping of Criminal Justice, 1989–2010*. London: Routledge

Silverstone, D. (2010) 'The Policing of Vietnamese Organized Crime within the UK', *Policing, a Journal of Policy and Practice*, 4(2): 132–141

Skolnick, J. (1966) *Justice Without Trial*. New York: Wiley

Stenson, K. (1993) 'Community Policing as a Governmental Technology', *Economy and Society*. 22(3): 373–89

Stenson, K. (2002) 'Community Safety in Middle England: The Local Politics of Crime Control', in G. Hughes and A. Edwards (eds) *Crime Control and Community: The New Politics of Public Safety*. Cullompton: Willan

Stenson, K. (2008) 'Governing the Local: Sovereignty, Social Governance and Community Safety', *Social Work and Society (on line)*. 6(1): 'Special issue on De-and Re-Territorialisation of "the Social"' – commentary on the work of Kevin Stenson (www.socwork.net/2008/)

Stenson, K. (2012) 'The State, Sovereignty and Advanced Marginality in the City', in P. Squires and J. Lea (eds) *Criminalisation and Advanced Marginality: Critically Exploring the Work of Loic Wacquant*. Bristol: The Policy Press

Stenson, K. and Edwards, A. (2004) 'Policy Transfer in Local Crime Control: Beyond Naïve Emulation', in T. Newburn and R. Sparks (eds) *Criminal Justice and Political Cultures: National and International Dimensions of Crime Control*. Cullompton: Willan

Stenson, K., Travers, M. and Crowther, C. (1999) *The Police and Inter-Ethnic Conflict*. Report Commissioned by the Metropolitan Police Service

Stenson, K. and Waddington, P.A.J. (2007) 'Macpherson, Police Stops and Institutional Racism', in M. Rowe (ed.) *Policing Beyond Macpherson*. Cullompton: Willan

Stenson, K. and Watt, P. (1999) 'Governmentality and "the Death of the Social"?: A Discourse Analysis of Local Government Texts in South-east England', *Urban Studies*, 36(1): 189–201

Stern, V. (2010) *The Stern Report: a report by Baroness Vivien Stern CBE of an independent review into how rape complaints are handled by public authorities in England and Wales*. London: The Home Office, Equalities Office

Tilley, N. and Laycock, G. (this volume) 'The Police as Professional Problem Solvers'

Tonry, M. (2009) *Thinking about Punishment: Penal Policy across Space, Time and Discipline*. Farnham: Ashgate

Waddington, P.A.J. (1998) *Policing Citizens*. London: UCL Press

Webster, C. (2007) *Understanding Race and Crime*. Buckingham: Open University Press

Whyte, D. (2012) 'The Great British Summer of Corruption', *Criminal Justice Matters*, 90, December: 24–27

Wood, J. and Shearing, C. (2007) *Imagining Security*. Cullompton: Willan

28

THE RISE AND RISE OF INDEPENDENT POLICE COMPLAINTS BODIES

Anja Johansen

Introduction

Over the past fifty years, public debates about police accountability in many Western European countries have revolved around the handling of citizens' complaints against the police. While citizens' complaints procedures only constitute one aspect of police accountability mechanisms, the access of aggrieved citizens to challenge unacceptable police behaviour is the form of police accountability that most immediately affects the general public and mobilises public opinion.

Until the late twentieth century police managers were firmly in control of handling complaints, and internal police investigations of all complaints continues to be the norm worldwide. In the Western world an increasing number of jurisdictions have established independent police complaints bodies (IPCBs). It was in the UK, Australia, Canada, and certain US jurisdictions, that schemes were first introduced between the 1960s and 1980s which allowed civilian oversight of police investigations of citizens' complaints as well as police practices. In continental European jurisdictions major reforms have taken place since the 1990s, so the recent claim by Graham Smith that IPCBs are a rarity in Europe needs qualification (Smith, 2009: 262). While the process towards IPCBs has hardly begun in most of the former communist regimes of Central and Eastern Europe, today the majority of mature democratic countries in Europe have some form of independent police complaints structure, with Germany, Italy and Greece as notable exceptions. During the past decade, police complaints procedures have become a key element in European debates about police accountability and about public trust in the police. Yet, as Walker observes in relation to IPCBs in the US, there are currently no standards for assessing performance of IPCBs and no discussions of what could be regarded as acceptable levels of performance (Walker, 2001: 121; Walker, 2005: 73).

This chapter seeks to place the Independent Police Complaints Commission for England and Wales (IPCC) in the context of transnational developments towards ever greater independence from police in the handling of complaints, as well as increasing transparency and victim involvement in the procedures. Civil liberties activists, in Britain and Europe, continuously criticise existing IPCBs for poor performance, which is seen as indication of the IPCBs failing to ensure a fair and equitable process for complainants. However, such arguments are highly normative as no criteria currently exist for what constitutes good performance for IPCBs.

The argument here is that, although there is scope for improvement, the IPCC for England and Wales actually performs fairly well compared to other European IPCBs. However, the scheme needs to do more to convince complainants and the wider public that complaints are given a fair and thorough handling. The main aim of this investigation is to provide the basis for discussions about standard setting for organisational arrangements of IPCBs and for performance targets. It discusses the factors behind the rising demands in Britain and Europe for making police directly accountable to individual members of the public through fair, transparent and effective procedures. It compares eight European jurisdictions, which could all be described as progressive among police complaints arrangements within the EU: the IPCC for England and Wales (2003); the French *Comité nationale de déontologie de la sécurité* (2002) reformed to the *Défenseur des droits* (2011); the Hamburg *Polizeikommission* (1998–2001); the Belgian *Comité P.* (1991, reformed 2006); the Amsterdam *Commissie voor de Politieklachten* (1986); the Danish *Politiklagenævn* (1996, reformed 2002) followed by the *Uafhængige Politiklagemyndighed* (2012); the Swedish *Polisens Interna Utredningsgrupp* (2010); and the Norwegian *Spesialenheten for politisaker* (2002).

Accountability, efficiency and legitimacy

Opponents of IPCBs generally argue that they are costly, ineffective and even counterproductive in improving police behaviour, as they stifle internal police debates about questionable practices, and thus hinder police learning while perpetuating poor practices. That IPCBs are costly is beyond dispute. Whether IPCBs are more 'effective' than internal police investigations depends on what the IPCBs are intended to achieve. For civil liberties activists the aim is to make more complainants come forward with their grievances and to raise substantiation rates. It is assumed that by holding police directly accountable to the public, police standards will improve. Yet according to Walker, there is little empirical evidence to show that external police complaints procedures are more effective than internal police investigations in improving policing practices, while substantiation rates for complaints are only marginally improved by IPCBs (Walker, 2005: 73). Moreover, research on population satisfaction both in the US and the UK shows that a significant proportion of people with legitimate grievances do not complain, irrespective of whether the complaints procedures are controlled by the police or by IPCBs (Smith, 2009: 249; Walker, 2001: 123–127).

Both scholars and civil liberties activists increasingly analyse and justify IPCBs in terms of procedural justice (Tyler, 2006; Hough, 2013). According to this line of thinking, greater independence and transparency in the handling of complaints is claimed to enhance police legitimacy, while police-controlled complaints procedures undermine public trust in the procedures. This is based on studies showing that what matters to the public is that the process seems fair and that citizens' legitimate concerns about poor police behaviour should be investigated thoroughly and impartially (Kääriäinen & Sirén, 2012: 285; Walker, 2005: 71; Tyler, 2011: 254–255). What most complainants want is an apology and recognition that the behaviour of police was unacceptable even when it was not in breach of discipline or criminal code (McLaughlin & Johansen, 2002; Walker, 2005; Hough, 2013). While IPCBs in themselves are not sufficient to ensure public confidence (Smith, 2009: 249), evidence from many studies into public trust in the police shows that external complaints procedures are a necessary precondition for public trust. As Samuel Walker points out, with all their flaws, IPCBs should be seen as a fundamental public service, handling complaints with equity and dignity no matter how irrelevant or ludicrous the individual allegations (Walker, 2005: 79).

The dynamics of the process: factors driving the movement

The international trend towards establishment of IPCBs, which has gained considerably in strength and momentum since the turn of the millennium, can be linked to a number of factors.

Rising popular expectations

One factor that has driven the momentum towards IPCBs are significant changes in mainstream notions of police legitimacy, notably expectations of citizens being treated with dignity by public authorities. There have been continuous calls for empowerment of citizens to challenge unacceptable police behaviour and actions. This is in line with broader culture trends focusing on rights and compensation, in which complaints and litigation take an increasing role in settling disputes and conflicts between individuals and public bodies. The drive has been exacerbated by governments responding with increasing regulation and monitoring of public bodies (Smith, 2009: 258). One might also see the introduction of new schemes and recent reforms of IPCBs as a trade-off at a time when police powers have been extended and intrusive security systems have been introduced, notably since the 9/11.

Growing pressure on governments to establish IPCBs

Popular pressure and expectations have had varying success in European countries. It is perhaps not surprising that it was countries influenced by what might be described as Anglo-Saxon policing tradition (UK, US, Canada, Australia) that governments first accepted some civilian participation in the handling of complaints and opened up the possibility for further demands for independent processing of complaints. Police legitimacy rested on the idea of service to the community rather than being the strong arm of the state. When confronted with repeated incidents of serious police malpractice it was difficult in the long term to refuse external involvement in the monitoring or handling of complaints.

A second group of national jurisdictions, Denmark, Sweden, Norway, the Netherlands and Belgium, began to experiment with IPCBs in the 1980s and have gone through several reforms, gradually extending the remit and powers of IPCBs. Although Denmark, Sweden and Norway all have strong traditions for state-centred governance, this is combined with traditions for high popular expectations to responsive governance, similar to Belgium and the Netherlands. Moreover the relatively peaceful political history of these countries since the nineteenth century made it difficult for police and government authorities to brush over incidents of questionable or violent policing practices as justified by some higher interest of public security or imminent threat to the state.

Considering the eight European jurisdictions, one significant indicator that IPCBs are increasingly regarded in Western democracies as a necessary condition for legitimate policing are the developments in France and Germany. For a long time, French authorities fiercely objected to any civilian influence on police complaints. Yet during the 1980s and 1990s attempts by successive governments to modernise policing were repeatedly hampered by low levels of public trust in the police (Anderson, 2011; Berlière & Lévy, 2011).

The first French IPCB, the *Commission nationale de déontologie de la sécurité intérieure* (CNDS) was established in 2000 as a government initiative rather than caused by popular pressure. At the time of its establishment, the CNDS met what was perceived at the time to be good standards for independence and transparency, yet the resources of the CNDS were extremely limited and there were problems for many potential complainants of accessing the system as their case would have to be raised through a parliamentary deputy or a senator. Nevertheless, the very existence of such a body constituted a major shift in governance, as the French State implicitly recognised the right of individuals to have complaints heard and assessed by an independent body. A new scheme, *Le Défenseur des droits*, introduced in 2011, although far more independent, accessible and well resourced, is still woefully inadequate (see below).

In Germany, the opposition from police and government authorities both at the federal level and the level of *Länder* to relinquish any police control over complaints procedures has been even more categorical than in France. Today Germany remains – together with Italy – the only country in Western Europe where no IPCBs are in place. One German jurisdiction, the Free City of Hamburg, experimented with IPCB between 1998 and 2001 through the so-called *Polizeikommission*. It was a small but radical scheme, introduced after revelations of very serious malpractice within the Hamburg police in 1994. The scheme was highly controversial both among national police organisations and among authorities in other German federal states who feared demands for such structures would spread from Hamburg to other areas. The scheme was shut down in September 2001, when a rightwing government was voted into power, helped by the immediate shock after 9/11. Nevertheless the Hamburg *Polizeikommission* remained a reference point for German civil liberties activists, whose insistence on the illegitimacy of police investigating the police has intensified over the past decade. The continued opposition from German authorities to IPCBs has come to look increasingly unjustifiable and out of line with popular expectations.

Pressure from international bodies

Over the past decade the demands for reform from domestic critics in the investigated countries have been strengthened by an increasing number of international agencies placing pressure on governments. Until the turn of the millennium pressures on national governments to take action against police malpractice and impunity came primarily from Amnesty International (AI), the European Committee for the Prevention of Torture (CPT) and the European Commissioner for Human Rights (ECHR). Yet their reports focused primarily on individual cases, rather than institutional arrangements and systemic faults in the ability of individuals to challenge law enforcement and prison authorities.

The past decade has seen a remarkable intensification in the activities of several international bodies to promote the establishment of IPCBs. In 2001 the Council of Europe adopted a 'European Code of Police Ethics' which clearly stated that 'Public authorities shall ensure effective and impartial procedures for complaints against the police'.[1] As an increasing number of cases are brought before the European Court of Human Rights due to inadequate appeals mechanisms at the national level, the ECHR has taken a very active role in promoting IPCBs in member states, and setting international benchmarks for such institutions (ECHR, 2009). Most recently, the UN Office on Drugs and Crime issued a new handbook on police accountability which devoted an entire chapter to 'establishing independent police oversight and complaints bodies'. Eight out of seventeen recommendations of this publication directly concern independent police complaints procedures (UNDOC, 2011). The reports and recommendations on individual countries from international bodies such as ECHR and the CPT have constituted a crucial element in pushing the agenda towards IPCBs as a minimum requirement for democratic policing, and in narrowing the options for institutional arrangements around a limited number of procedural and organisational features.

The German authorities in particular have come under pressure from international bodies,[2] and their intransigence against IPCBs has come to appear increasingly untenable. Recent years have also seen increasing collaboration between civil liberties activists, IPCB practitioners and policy-makers across national boundaries. Several international conferences on IPCBs have taken place which brought together academics, civil liberties activists and representatives from national governments. In 2005 a number of IPCBs in the UK, US and Canada formed the 'International Network of Independent Oversight of Policing' with the aim of promoting greater cooperation and sharing of knowledge among practitioners. If such exchange of experience between practitioners proves useful, one can expect representatives from other countries to join.

The 'boomerang' effect

Once IPCBs have been established, no matter how weak, they constitute an implicit recognition of the principle that police should not investigate complaints against themselves, at least not serious complaints. Almost invariably, police critics and pro-IPCB activists respond with demands for the powers of IPCBs to be strengthened, their remit to be extended and resources increased. This continuous radicalisation of demands reflect the same dynamics as the increasing influence of Human Rights discourse, as described by Thomas Risse in his 'boomerang theory' (Risse, Ropp & Sikkink, 1999). According to the boomerang theory, countries that are out of line with popular expectations, which have been met by other countries, find themselves increasingly on the defensive in maintaining the status quo. This can lead to governments making some minor concessions. This might initially be notional, but in the long run it is difficult to pay lip-service while continuing practices that violate these promises, and ultimately this undermines the legitimacy of governance. Moreover if these concessions imply the institutionalisation of certain bodies and procedures, these tend to take on their own dynamics, and thereby help to define minimum standards and push for further concessions.

The effect of the internet

The arrival of the internet has strengthened the position of campaigners as well as aggrieved individuals. In the first place, the general availability of video and sound recording equipment within the public space and in the hands of individuals has undercut police control of 'what happened' in an increasing number of cases which have been recorded. At the same time the internet gives ample means for instant mass-dissemination of video and sound recordings, and has provided a forum for people who believe they have been victimised by the police to get in touch with others with similar experience. For campaigners the internet provides a wealth of knowledge about complaints cases and allows data collection independently of official bodies. Moreover the internet is of major importance in raising public awareness and creating a sense – rightly or wrongly – that existing mechanisms are inadequate in providing fair and impartial complaints procedures. The internet is also used by civil liberties activists and organisations to inform people of their rights, and explain how to complain against the police within the existing system.

Changing attitudes from within police forces

Finally, it is important to recognise significant changes in attitudes within police forces. What we observe is not the end of defensive reactions or high levels of professional solidarity when a colleague has become the subject of a complaint. Yet there seems to be increasing willingness among some police officers to blow the whistle over seriously transgressive behaviour by colleagues and to cooperate with the IPCBs. This may be linked to changing professional ethos as well as to greater heterogeneity in the recruitment. In police forces which have been completely removed from the complaints process, some officers have even expressed relief at no longer having to spend time dealing with 'obviously groundless complaints', but leave the sifting process to the IPCB (Walker, 2005: 79).

One of the most remarkable initiatives from within police ranks came from the German group *Kritische PolizistInnen* (Critical Police Officers) formed in 1987. This group made common cause with civil liberties activists in demanding more robust intervention from police managers against badly behaved police colleagues, and even had a column for whistle-blowing in their internal magazine. Although a very small group with varying intensity of activities over the years, it has been at the heart of keeping demands for IPCBs in Germany going, most recently at the Alternative Police Congress in June 2011.[3]

What we observe at the transnational level is not only intensified pressure to have complaints against the police removed from police influence, but also strong tendencies towards convergence around certain organisational features as necessary for complaints schemes to be considered acceptable.

Towards convergence and minimum standards for IPCBs

Despite considerable efforts from government authorities to reform complaints procedures in ways that empower the complainant, the power relationship between the complainant and the accused police officers remains asymmetrical. In his 2005 study on police accountability in the US, Samuel Walker concluded that the most important challenge for the future development of IPCBs was to develop national standards for the various police complaints schemes in the US (Walker, 2005: 74; Walker, 2001: 188–197).

This is equally true for European jurisdictions. In the 1980s and early 1990s, as there were few reference points and limited experience with independent police complaints procedures, reformers were experimenting with a broad range of approaches. Today the options that are considered as acceptable and credible are far more limited and demanding than what was discussed as viable only two decades ago. This movement has been reinforced in recent years by publications seeking to set international standards (ECHR, 2009; UNDOC, 2011: 49–57). Two reports from ECHR (2009) and UNDOC (2011) define a series of criteria which IPCBs should aspire to achieve: independence; adequate empowerment of IPCBs; accessibility; victim involvement; transparency; and proper resourcing (ECHR, 2009: 3). In addition, the reports both state that all cases of death or serious injury in custody should be automatically referred for investigation by the IPCB. The purpose is to guarantee protection against police impunity and enhance public confidence. For a discussion of standards setting, I have looked at how these key factors are reflected in the institutional setting and performance of the eight European IPCBs.

Independence of the complaints body

Independence is generally understood as the opposite to police control over complaints procedures and, therefore, as a precondition for impartiality in the handling of complaints. In the 1960s and 1970s the main struggle was to get some civilian participation, influence and oversight to police's handling of complaints. This gradually developed into demands for complete removal of any police involvement at any stage in the process. The most radically independent model is a specialised police ombudsman (currently only existing in Northern Ireland), or the incorporation of complaints against the police under a general ombudsman institution.

All eight schemes considered here claim organisational independence of the police. Some schemes arranged the procedures around the chief public prosecutor (Danish *Politiklagenævn*; Swedish *Polisens Interna Utredningsgrupp*; Norwegian *Spesialenheten for politisaker*). It was hoped that the authority of the public prosecutor with his experience of investigation and authority over the police would limit criticism of undue police influence over the process. This has turned out to be a vain hope, since critics have consistently maintained that the public prosecutor is structurally dependent on the police and therefore not impartial. The most recent reforms in Denmark and France operate with a vastly extended concept of organisational independence which requires IPCBs to be independent not only of the police, but of the public prosecutor as well as any governmental or parliamentary affiliation.

Organisational independence from the police is increasingly becoming a requirement for police complaints schemes to be acceptable as legitimate. Nevertheless, only the Hamburg *Polizeikommission* and the French *Défenseur des droits* can make claims to being both organisationally and functionally independent of the police.[4] All other schemes rely on the police to record the complaints submitted directly to the police, to handle minor complaints (IPCC; Belgian *Comité P.*) or at the minimum the IPCB employ former police officers as part of the investigating team (Amsterdam *Klachtenbureau*; Swedish *Polisens Interna Utredningsgrupp*; Norwegian *Spesialenheten for politisaker*). It is clear that the demand for functional independence of police involvement is going to remain at the centre of criticism and calls for future reform.

Empowerment of the IPCB

The second most important criterion for IPCBs as defined by the ECHR and the UNDOC is the empowerment of the IPCB. This covers a range of aspects including the function of the IPCB in the complaints process, as well as the powers and authorities bestowed on the IPCB in order to ensure fair and impartial procedures for the complainant as the weaker party.

1   According to the ECHR, IPCBs – even if fully independent in organisational and functional terms – cannot operate effectively if they remain weak in rela-

tion to the police. The strength of the IPCB lies not only in the powers formally vested in it, but also in the standing of senior personnel. It is therefore vital that appointments of leading personnel to the IPCB are not only apolitical and impartial, but that leading positions are occupied by people of outstanding professional credentials and with considerable personal authority in their engagement with the police. This is necessary as policemen can be reluctant to cooperate in giving evidence and engaging seriously with the investigation.

2　The IPCB needs to be in control of reception and registration of complaints. This does not exclude that police can receive complaints which are then forwarded to the IPCB for registration and processing.

3　The IPCB needs to have a broadly defined remit to deal with a range of complaints, and powers to determine for individual complaints whether or not these fall within the remit of the IPCB. The ECHR also demands that this should cover the right to consider both criminal and behavioural complaints (conduct complaints). All eight European IPCBs fulfil this requirement, although the scope could always be extended. Some critics are pushing for the remit of IPCBs to include operational complaints as well, but in all eight jurisdictions police opposition to such suggestions has so far kept the issue off reform agendas.

4　It is increasingly becoming a minimum requirement that cases of death or serious injury in police custody should be automatically referred to IPCBs for independent investigation. Such arrangements are currently in place in all the jurisdictions considered here.

5　IPCBs should also have their own investigation team with adequate resources. The majority of the investigated IPCBs have enough resources to undertake investigation of the number of cases they consider worthy of attention (Belgian *Comité P.*; Amsterdam *Klachtenbureau*; Swedish *Polisens Interna Utredningsgrupp*; Norwegian *Spesialenheten for politisaker*; Danish *Politiklagenævn*, Hamburg *Polizeikommission*). The IPCC and the French *Défenseur des droits* are set up to handle only the most serious or contentious cases, according to their own definition of this term. This inevitably leads to a lot of acrimony from complainants whose case is not considered important enough for investigation by the IPCB, and left for the police to investigate.

6　Finally the IPCB should be able to assess not only its own investigations but also police investigations. It should also be the IPCBs who determine the outcome, as well as the form of sanctions: reprimands, disciplinary action, criminal investigation, recommendations for organisational change, recommendations for legislative changes. This includes specifically the authority to transfer cases to the public prosecutor for criminal investigation.

Empowerment of the complainant

The 2009 report from the ECHR mentions as its last factor that IPCBs should ensure victim involvement, guaranteeing that the complainant's voice is heard in a respectful and impartial manner, taken seriously, and acted upon.

1   Information about the complaints procedures needs to be readily available and accessible to the public (leaflets at police stations, hospitals, citizens' advice bureaus; information on the internet that can easily be located and available in languages relevant to potential complainants).

2   The complainant needs easy access to make a complaint from multiple entry points independent of the police, even if many complainants still choose to depose their complaint at their local police station. Websites containing all relevant information about the process are increasingly seen as a basic requirement. All investigated IPCBs have very helpful websites often in multiple languages, explaining the procedures, the rights of the complainant and with a complaints form that can be sent via email or ordinary mail. Nevertheless, there is still need for reception points where complainants can make their statement orally. Potential complainants include many vulnerable people who may struggle with writing, and non-native speakers who might need support in formulating their complaint. IPCBs that cater for very small jurisdictions (Amsterdam; Hamburg) have been very proactive in facilitating direct access. The IPCC, although covering a large geographical area, has also done much to meet such needs through access points in local communities. In contrast, the IPCBs in Norway, Sweden and Denmark are centralised complaints structures that rely on people complaining in writing or going to a few national access points.

3   The complainant also needs influence over the form of processing, whether this takes the form of a formal investigation or informal resolution, rather than having the informal resolution procedures imposed by the IPCB or the police. None of the IPCBs considered here allow for such victim influence, except that complainants are supposed to consent to the complaint being settled through informal resolution, rather than a full investigation.

4   In addition, many complainants need legal aid. In 2007, the European Commission against Racism and Intolerance declared that victims of racism and discrimination ought to have guaranteed access to legal aid (ECRI, 2007: section 51). It is therefore likely that reformers and critics will use this to demand that legal aid be available for those who complain against the police.

5   Finally, adequate provision for appeal of the decision is increasingly seen as a requirement. In the Dutch, the Norwegian and the Swedish system the general Ombudsman fulfils the function for appeal of decisions by the IPCB. For England and Wales the proposed removal of the IPCC as the appeal authority for complaints handled by the police, and moving them to the elected Police and Crime Commissioner seem very much at odds with general trends in this area, and is most likely to be contested in future debates.

Transparency

Another principle identified by the ECHR concerns public scrutiny, i.e. transparency and flow of information. This implies in the first place information provided to the complainant with disclosure of all relevant information about the case and regular updating of the state of the investigation and outcome. In addition, transparency includes information to the wider public about the activities of the IPCB. All investigated schemes currently provide annual reports online with details of cases as well as figures for the number of cases received, the number of decisions made and a break-down of outcomes of investigation. This allows the public useful information about the proportion of successful complaints.

However, the figures provided follow no particular format, and it is quite difficult to establish data that allow comparison between jurisdictions. As a result the performance of individual IPCBs currently exists in a vacuum without contextualisation other than performance in previous years. There is therefore an urgent need for development of international standards for the information and figures provided in order to allow comparison of performance.

Resourcing and case load

According to the ECHR the IPCBs need to be properly resourced to handle a broad range of complaints speedily and effectively (ECHR, 2009: 3). Given the current lack of standards for what 'properly resourced' might imply, it is useful to look at how the eight European IPCBs perform on a number of key indicators as a basis for possible standard setting. For the sake of contextualisation, the figures are also provided from the Police Ombudsman for Northern Ireland.[5] Unfortunately, establishing comparable data on the basis of the figures currently provided by annual reports gives a very incomplete picture, so whatever conclusions can be drawn on this basis must be regarded as tentative. The aim of this section is to identify which data IPCBs should be expected to provide in order to facilitate comparison and meaningful quality assessment.

1   For assessment of performance we need to know the number of staff and annual budget of IPCBs. Although the indications on this point are very patchy, it appears that the IPCC for England and Wales is comparatively well resourced. In terms of the ratio of budget to the population, the IPCC is only surpassed by the Belgian *Comité P.*, and in terms of staffing it lies comfortably in line with the Belgian and Scandinavian IPCBs. The Hamburg *Polizeikommission* of 1998–2001 clearly had fewer resources than the IPCC, the Belgian *Comité P.* and the Scandinavian IPCBs. However the scheme that really stands out is the French *Défenseur des droits*. Although the budget and caseload have doubled since the establishment of the CNDS in 2000, this scheme is obviously too poorly resourced for any meaningful function.

2   Complaints rates are known to be a poor indicator of the levels of public dissatisfaction due to substantial underreporting. Nevertheless, a comparison of the number of complaints received *per annum* can help to identify a current 'norm', and constitute the basis for a discussion about standard setting. The IPCBs need to provide figures for both the number of registered complaints (with the IPCBs or a police force) as well as the number of complaints that became subject to some form

TABLE 28.1 Ratio of resources and staff to size of police forces and population

	Budget (in GBP)	Budget per 100,000 inhabitants	Number of staff	Ratio of IPCB staff to police personnel	Ratio of IPCB staff to population
England & Wales: IPCC[6]	34,300,000 (2011)	£61,140	423 (2011)[7]	1 : 570[8]	1 : 132,624
Northern Ireland Police Ombudsman	8,732,629 (2010)[9]	£482,225	144 (2011)	1 : 65	1 : 12,575
BE: Comité P.	7,967,168 (2006)	£75,161	83 (2010)	1 : 559	1 : 127,711
DK: Politiklagenævn	n.d.		25 (2012)	1 : 560	1 : 220,000
NO: Spesialenheten For Politiksaker	n.d.		31 (2011)	1 : 419	1 : 154,838
SE: Polisens Interna Utredningsgrup	3,521,866 (2011)	£38,701	53 (2011)	1 : 528	1 : 171,698
GE (Hamburg): Polizeikommission	143,920 (1998)	£8,465	5 (2001)	1 : 1,800	1 : 340,000
FR: CNDS/DdD	703,948 (2010)	£1,117	8 (2010)	1 : 32,335[10] (2008)	1 : 7,875,000

of assessment and decision, and the number of investigations. While the IPCC already provides these data, comparable figures are needed from other schemes. Nevertheless, comparison of average annual number of recorded cases for the six-year period 2006–2011 gives an indication of performance (Table 28.2).

3   The IPCBs also need to indicate the number of cases completed, thus allowing assessment of annual case load and possible developments of major backlogs which could indicate inadequate resourcing.

4   Another key indicator is substantiation rates, although we need to treat these rates with caution and not regard them as a key indicator of the success of IPCBs (Walker, 2001: 120). What levels of substantiation would be accepted as reflecting the system as fair is, of course, normative, and police and complainants tend to have very dissimilar interpretations of what substantiation rates indicate about the functioning of IPCBs. Nevertheless, comparison of substantiation rates between schemes and over time gives some indication of the norm. The figures that IPCBs should be expected to provide in their annual report should include the substantiation rates in relation to all received cases; the substantiation rates among the cases investigated by the IPCB and those investigated by the police; and finally the figures for the distribution of sanctions.

    The rate of substantiation for investigated cases in England and Wales was constant around 9–10 per cent between 1995 and 2001, then increased to

TABLE 28.2 Ratio of annual complaints to size of police forces and population

	Average annual number of recorded cases (2006–2011)	*Ratio complaints to 1,000 police personnel*	*Ratio complaints to population*
England & Wales: IPCC	31,151	129	1:1,800
Northern Ireland Police Ombudsman	3,263	347	1:555
BE: Comité P.	2,303	49	1:4,689
NL: Amsterdam Politie Klachtenbureau	529	88	1:1,701
DK: Politiklagenævn	1,012	72	1:5,435
NO: Spesialenheten for Politisaker	809	62	1:5,933
SE: Polisens Interna Utretningsgrup[11]	6,376	228	1:1,725
GE: Hamburg Polizei-kommission (1998–2001)	76	8.4	1:22,368
FR: Défenseur des droits[12]	363	1.3	1:173,554

12–13 per cent during the early years of the IPCC, but since 2006 has hovered around 10–11 per cent. The substantiation rates between police forces in England and Wales vary considerably: in 2008 the rates for Bedfordshire, Essex and Hampshire were 17 percent, but merely 4 per cent for the Metropolitan Police and Cheshire. Compared to the substantiation rates of the Amsterdam *Commissie voor Politieklachten* with an average rate of 14 per cent (2007–2010), or the Belgian *Comité P.* with annual substantiation rates at over 20 per cent since 2006, the 4 per cent substantiation rate for the London Metropolitan Police appears remarkably low.[13] It is therefore worth investigating further the reasons why some IPCBs have notably higher substantiation rates than others.

5   Another piece of information that IPCBs ought to provide is the number of cases that were transferred to the public prosecutor (or equivalent) for criminal investigation. For the IPCBs considered here the data, although very patchy, indicate considerable variation between jurisdictions (Table 28.3).

In order to properly compare the role of criminal courts as an accountability mechanism we need to know not only how many cases were transferred from the IPCBs, but the total number of prosecutions of police staff, as well as the number of convictions.

6   Finally, the IPCBs generally provide information about the average time of completion of cases, which varies considerably between the jurisdictions (Table 28.4).

While the completion time for IPCBs shows considerable variation, the overall average is a crude indicator for assessing effectiveness. An average of, for instance, 100 days might indicate effective in-depth investigation of a significant proportion of all cases, or it might just as well reflect a system that dismisses the vast majority of cases within a few days and processes a few cases extremely slowly. More detailed indicators are therefore needed. Walker's

TABLE 28.3 Cases transferred to the criminal justice authorities

	Annual number of cases transferred to the public prosecution	Ratio of cases transferred to the public prosecutor per 1,000 police staff	Annual number of prosecutions (where known)	Ratio of criminal prosecutions per 1,000 police staff
England & Wales: IPCC	444 (2008)	1.8	32[14]	0.1
Northern Ireland Police Ombudsman	1012[15] (2009–2010)	107	12	1.2
BE: Comité P.	100 (2008–2010)	2.1	n.d.	
SE: Polisens Interna Utretningsgrup[16]	102 (2011)	3.5	n.d.	
DK: Politiklagenævn	582[17] (2006–2009)	41.6	170	12.1
FR: Défenseur des droits[18]	9 (2010)	0.03	n.d.	

TABLE 28.4 Average number of days for case handling

England/Wales IPCC (2008–2010)	BE: Comité P. (2005–2007)	SE: Polisens Interna Utretning (2011)	NO: Spes.Enh. for Politisaker (2008)	FR: Défenseur des droits (2011)
210	54	40	153	377

template for a 'Model Citizen Complaint Procedure' suggests reporting of how many cases were completed within 30 days, how many within 120 days and how many in 300 days (Walker, 2001: 188–197).

Recommendations for organisational requirements and standards for performance

The transnational pressures towards more complaints being handled by IPCBs rather than the police are unlikely to diminish in coming years. The current arrangement of the IPCC for England and Wales will most likely continue to be criticised for the significant element of police involvement. Yet overall the IPCC actually performs quite well, both in terms of the standards set by ECHR and UNDOC, but also when compared to IPCBs in other European countries. Nevertheless, complainants and critics of the IPCC still need to be convinced about the equity and fairness of the scheme. The problem is more lack of trust in the procedures than lack of efficiency of the IPCC.

Improvements could be considered in the following areas:

- The IPCC needs to develop even greater transparency and detailed explanations to complainants to further their acceptance of the outcome.
- The large proportion of complaints falling into the category of 'not proven' is particularly undermining of public trust. The IPCBs need serious sanctions against police personnel for being uncooperative or 'economical with the truth', in line with the seriousness of perjury, in order to strengthen respect for the procedures.
- The secrecy of disciplinary hearings constitutes a serious problem for public trust in the system. There are good reasons for police to prefer handling disciplinary cases outside the public gaze, however the fact that the public simply have to accept the claim that the police are dealing 'robustly' with the complaint through internal disciplinary procedures is increasingly difficult to justify as legitimate in the twenty-first century.
- Finally, the IPCC could work through the 'International Network of Independent Oversight of Policing' to promote standardisation of data provided by IPCBs in their annual reports. Continuous comparison of performance with schemes abroad would provide the IPCC with strong evidence of its achievements and could help to identify realistic targets for improved efficiency.

There is an increasingly effective naming and shaming culture, mainly concentrated on the internet, which is completely outside the control of the police that police managers need to respond to in their handling of public relations. Poor or inadequate police responses to embarrassing allegations are seriously detrimental for public trust in the police, and police managers of the twenty-first century have to embrace the complaints culture to avoid undermining – and possibly to strengthen – the legitimacy of the police.

Notes

1 Council of Europe, 'European Code of Police Ethics', Recommendations Rec (2001) 10, Art.61.
2 Amnesty International (AI), 'Erneut im Focus: Vorwurfe über polizeiliche Misshandlungen und den Einsatz unverhältnismäßiger Gewalt in Deutschland', (ai-index: EU 23/001/2004), p. 86; CCPR/C/DEU/2002/5, 4 September 2002, recommendation 151; AI, 'Täter Unbekannt: Mangelnde Aufklärung von mutmaßlichen Misshandlungen durch die Polizei in Deutschland', July 2010; AI, 'Annual Report 2012 – Germany'; ECHR, *Concerning Independent and Effective Determination of Complaints against the Police*, (CommDH 2009, 4).
3 Die Grünen/EFA im Europäischen Parlament, 'Dokumentation Alternativer Polizeikongress, Universität Hamburg, 24–25 June 2011', p. 47. Almost simultaneously the political group DIE LINKE organised another conference in the Parliament of Nordrhein-Westphalen (Düsseldorf) entitled 'Democratisation of the Police' in which the question of independent police complaints mechanisms figured high on the agenda.
4 So would the Northern Ireland Police Ombudsman as the most radically independent IPCB currently in place.
5 This scheme is exceptionally well resourced, but cannot serve as a model for other IPCBs as it was designed for managing the unique context of a divided community where policing was at the heart of many conflicts.

6 IPCC, 'Report on Corruption in the Police Service in England and Wales' Part 1 (Aug. 2011) p. 8.
7 Of whom 150 are investigators, and 150 are administrative staff in charge of complaints and appeals.
8 Police staff England & Wales: 240,855. This figure includes Community support officers, civilian staff, designated officers and special constables. Home Office Statistical Bulletin 'Police Service Strength', 31 March 2012, p. 18.
9 Expenditure for the financial year ending 31 March 2011. NIPO, 'Annual Report and Accounts, 2012', p. 11.
10 258,685 police nationale, gendarmes and municipal police in 2008 (Bauer & Soullez, 2010: 4–5).
11 As a new scheme started in 2011, this is the figure for that year.
12 As the new scheme *Le Défenseur des droits* was introduced in 2011, this is the figure for that year.
13 According to Walker, the substantiation rate for IPCBs in the US is at an average of 12–13 per cent (Walker, 2001: 120).
14 Gleeson & Grace (2009: 16). While we have no figures for the number of convictions for 2008, there were between April 2010 and March 2011 a total of four criminal convictions of police personnel in England and Wales. IPCC Performance Report for September 2011 (IPCC Minutes of meeting 8.11.2011).
15 Of these only an annual average of nine cases were recommended for prosecution. PONI, 'Statistical Bulletin' April–September 2011, table 7.
16 As a new scheme started in 2011, this is the figure for that year.
17 Roughly 50 per cent of these cases concern violations of traffic regulations.
18 As the new scheme *Le Défenseur des droits* was introduced in 2011, this is the figure for that year.

References

Anderson, M. (2011) *In Thrall to Political Change: Police and Gendarmerie in France*, Oxford: OUP.
Bauer, A. & Soullez, C. (2010) 'Où sont les policiers et gendarmes?' Online publication. Available at: http://www.lagazettedescommunes.com/telechargements/etude_policiers_gendarmes_bauer_04_2010.pdf.
Berlière, J.-M. & Lévy, R. (2011) *Histoire des polices en France*, Paris: Nouveau Monde.
ECHR (European Commissioner for Human Rights) (2009) 'Opinion of the Commissioner for Human Rights concerning independent and effective determination of complaints against the police', document CommDH (2009)4, Strasbourg, 12 March 2009. Available at: https://wcd.coe.int/ViewDoc.jsp?id=1417857.
ECRI (European Commission against Racism and Intolerance) (2007) 'On Combating Racism and Racial Discrimination in Policing' Online. Available at: http://www.coe.int/t/dlapil/codexter/Source/ECRI_Recommendation_11_2007_EN.pdf.
Gleeson, E. and Grace, K. (2009) 'Police complaints: statistics for England and Wales, 2008/09', *IPCC Research and Statistics Series*: Paper 15.
Hough, M. (2013) 'Procedural justice and professional policing in times of austerity', *Policing and Society, Criminology and Criminal Justice,* 3/2, pp. 181–197.
Kääriäinen, J. & Sirén, R. (2012) 'Do the police trust civilians? European comparisons', *European Journal of Criminology*, 9/3, pp. 276–289.
McLaughlin, E. & Johansen, A. (2002) 'A force for change? The prospects for applying restorative justice to citizen complaints against the police', *British Journal of Criminology*, special issue on Restorative Justice, Summer 2002, 42/3, pp. 635–653.

Risse, T., Ropp, S. & Sikkink, K. (1999) *The Power of Human Rights: International Norms and Domestic Change*, Cambridge: Cambridge University Press.

Smith, G. (2009) 'Why don't more people complain against the police?' *European Journal of Criminology*, 6/3, pp. 249–266.

Tyler, T. R. (2006) *Why People Obey the Law*, Princeton: Princeton University Press.

Tyler, T. R. (2011) 'Trust and legitimacy: policing in the USA and Europe', *European Journal of Criminology*, 8/4, pp. 254–266.

UNDOC (2011) *Handbook on Police Accountability, Oversight and Integrity*, UN publication, June. Available at: http://www.unodc.org/documents/justice-and-prison-reform/crimeprevention/PoliceAccountability_Oversight_and_Integrity_10-57991_Ebook.pdf.

Walker, S. (2001) *Police Accountability: The Role of Citizens' Oversight*, Belmont: Wadworth.

Walker, S. (2005) *The New World of Police Accountability*, Thousand Oaks: Sage.

29

ETHICS AND POLICING

Louise Westmarland[1]

Introduction

There is general public concern about police integrity as a result of recent revelations about the behaviour of senior police officers and their relationships with the press. Lord Leveson's current inquiry is just one public arena investigating allegations of the way some police officers might have trouble maintaining acceptable standards of behaviour. Despite the Association of Chief Police Officers (ACPO) having a published Code of Conduct since 2004, some officers still seem uncertain about what is ethically acceptable in certain situations, such as receiving gifts or payments and the appropriateness of hospitality events. Recently, when senior officers were questioned by the Home Affairs Select Committee about their conduct, some revealed what appear to be overly familiar relationships with journalists, and allegations of certain activities, such as the leaking of sensitive information to the press were made. Detective Chief Inspector April Casburn from the Metropolitan Police Service (MPS) is the first to be arrested through Operation Elveden, an MPS investigation into misuse of confidential information. Several other unrelated investigations into the actions of senior officers have been conducted recently in other forces, one of which resulted in the dismissal of a Chief Constable. In addition the Independent Police Complaints Commission (IPCC) is currently running major inquiries relating to possible police corruption including the Hillsborough disaster.

The police watchdog, the IPCC, has recently published three reports on the issue of police corruption. They state that 2011 saw unprecedented levels of public concern about police integrity and corruption (2011: 4). In that first report they concluded that the 'lines between corruption, misconduct and poor judgement can sometimes be fine ones', and in their second report, published in 2012, they found that while 'corruption is not widespread, . . . where it exists it is corrosive of the public trust that is at the heart of policing by consent' (2012a: 4). The IPCC has also investigated the abuse of police powers in the perpetration of sexual violence and concluded that 'legal powers given to members of the police service, such as arrest and detention, provide status and influence as well as allowing coercive actions' (IPCC 2012b: 1).

This notion of trust in public office has also been taken up by numerous academic studies of policing recently. Three studies from the international arena have shown that the problem of non-reporting of unethical or corrupt behaviour lies with organisational systems. The 'blue code of silence' (Westmarland 2005) is preserved because officers have no confidence in their management (Huberts *et al.* 2003). In effect they are worried that, as whistle blowers, they will be blamed, stigmatised (Miller 2010) or ignored, i.e. their information will have no effect on the organisation or the individual's behaviour. Some officers believe that the violations they report might not be investigated and treated fairly and impartially (Kääriäinen *et al.* 2008). Finally, the only recent study to question a statistically significant number of serving UK police officers (n = 520) is about to report that there is uncertainty about the 'rules' of ethical behaviour, that many officers are unwilling to report colleagues' misdemeanours and that the notion of 'serious' corruption might not equate to what might be more widely viewed as harmful (Westmarland, Rowe and Hougham, forthcoming).

History of police ethics

Commentators on police ethics tend to cover topics such as corruption, professional integrity and the means by which organisations attempt to control the behaviour of their individual officers. There is also a range of literature covering more philosophical concerns such as morals and human rights and the problems encountered when high ideals meet practical needs, such as in everyday policing. In these terms police ethics tends to refer to the practical implementation of what might be more generally called 'professional morals' or what Kleinig has described as the 'moral foundations of policing' (1996). Studies have been carried out in various countries and attempts to analyse these professional 'morals in action' reveal how difficult it is to codify police behaviour. As Neyroud reports (2003), there have been attempts to develop international codes of practice but from these discussions it seems that the focus should be widened from what the police *do*, to *how* they carry out their mandate. As one international study of police integrity revealed (Klockars *et al.* 2003), many similarities can be discovered when officer behaviour and attitudes are studied, but also wide differences. For example, officers in some countries thought that accepting a bribe in return for ignoring a speeding violation was quite normal and acceptable.

There are a number of reasons that commentators across the world suggest policing and ethics should be considered a topic of concern. The legitimacy of the role as society's 'guards' relies on the confidence of the public that this will be carried out without 'fear or favour'. For this to exist there needs to be some evidence that the power the police hold, and the authority they exercise, are tempered by some form of control. Traditionally this control followed a generally militaristic model. In the past in Britain and the US for instance, officers were given 'orders' as to how to behave and disciplined if they were caught contravening the rules. However, it has been argued that police culture acted as a protective blanket for individual officers committing misdemeanours as the 'blue code' helped them avoid detection. Further, critics have suggested that if the behaviour was so serious as to be made known publicly then the institution itself would be discredited and public confidence eroded, so the organisation closes ranks to protect its own and its reputation.

In Western Europe and the US, new models of public accountability, especially in the less deferential post-Second World War period, led to a period where the authority of the professions, such as medics, politicians and, to some extent, the police, was no longer accepted uncritically. Some powerful and previously unquestioned organisations and practices were opened to public scrutiny and in Britain for instance, throughout the 1970s and early 1980s, a series of public scandals led to an unprecedented level of public distrust in the police. Abuses of police power, in the form of miscarriages of justice, were being discovered, and were found to have been caused by the police lying on oath in court. These cases 'shook public opinion' (Newburn 1999, p.66) so severely that 'a new agenda in policing' (Neyroud and Beckley 2001, p. 54) had to be developed. Invariably this involved codes of practice, which attempted to control what Reiner has described as the 'low visibility and hence inevitable discretion of much routine police work' (2000, p. 183). These ethical codes usually adopted a 'top-down' model where senior officers decided what they thought the rank and file should be encouraged to believe about their work and how they should act. Hence the level to which they might be accepted and acted upon by those that were the target of the reforms is debatable. Furthermore, the appropriateness of some of the ethical principles contained within the codes, and their ambiguity in terms of practical application, might be argued to render them useless if not damaging.

Ethical control

Ethical codes are an attempt to provide guidance in ambiguous situations for officers working in isolated and often 'heat of the moment' situations. The problem is that police discretion, the ability to make decisions in these difficult situations, is difficult to codify. In effect, as Westmarland argued in 2000, the very ambiguity of the codes leads to more difficulties rather than resolving them. In most cases, for instance, officers are asked to use their discretion ethically, to uphold the law and to behave in an honourable and professional manner. It is the interpretation of these codes that is problematic, however. As ethical codes are based on personal views of morals and principles, it is very difficult to train officers to behave in certain ways or codify what is 'right' in every situation. Policing, for the main, involves unscripted and often unpredictable encounters with a wide range of different people from classes and cultures. To codify 'morals' for each individual encounter would be impossible, and ethical behaviour is tempered by an officer's personal set of values and beliefs, overlaid to a lesser or greater extent by those relating to police occupational culture.

As an attempt to wrestle with this problem the British ACPO published a number of recommendations in the late 1990s for the development of an ethical Code of Behaviour. As the following abridged table shows, implementing ethical principles to police practice has its difficulties however.

This set of guidelines, abridged from a longer list (see Neyroud and Beckley 2001, p. 191 for a fuller discussion) is clearly aimed at front-line staff, although other attempts have been made to codify senior officers' behaviour. One example is a code developed by Alderson (1998) which was based on the premise that police officers should not carry out orders that are unlawful, even when ordered to do so by a superior officer.

TABLE 29.1 Ethical principles and practical difficulties

Ethical principles	Implementation difficulties
Acting with fairness, carrying out my duties with integrity and impartiality	Notion of 'fairness' open to interpretation
Upholding fundamental human rights, treating every person as an individual and displaying respect towards them	Everyone being treated as an individual could lead to some being treated less 'fairly' or equally than others
Support my colleagues in the performance of their lawful duties and in doing so actively oppose or draw attention to any malpractice by any person	Asking police officers to report others' misdeeds or corrupt practices might not fit easily within solidarity of cop culture
Exercise force only when justified and then only use the minimum amount necessary to any given situation to effect my legal purpose and restore peace	It is difficult to quantify the amount of force necessary in any given situation

Source: Westmarland (2000)

BOX 29.1 LEADERSHIP DECLARATION

Police Leadership: A Declaration

I will seek to inculcate high ethical humanitarian standards into carrying out of duties by officers under my command, whilst at the same time accepting their need to use force, sometimes deadly force, in the lawful performance of their duty, the need to use powers granted to us by governments so that we may protect the people, their freedoms, and their property, in accordance with the spirit of the implied social contract.

> I will not ask, demand of, or cause any officer under my command to carry out duties and actions which are contrary to the laws of my country, or to those laws of International covenants and treaties such as the Universal Declaration of Human Rights and its protocols, and the European Convention on Human Rights and Fundamental Freedoms which have been adopted by my government.
>
> All this I promise in the cause of justice, freedom and the common good.
>
> (Alderson 1998, pp. 71–72)

A version of these principles has been adopted by ACPO as part of police officers' professional standards. The level of understanding or implementation is unknown as little research has ever been conducted. It seems that knowledge of the Codes of Ethics is required and part of 'Force Orders', but only tends to be accessed by officers facing disciplinary or promotion procedures (Personal Communication, 2012).

Global policing and international ethics

The police's concern with 'clean hands', Kleinig argues, was a move which appears to have begun in America where an ethics network was instigated. According to Kleinig, who notes that as early as 1955 some police departments had published codes of ethics which had been based on earlier 'pledges' beginning in 1928 (1996: 235), this led to similar moves in Australia and New Zealand. Although Kleinig claims that the very earliest 1829 Instructions given to Robert Peel's Metropolitan Police contained 'something like a code of ethics' it was not until the early 1990s that an ethics committee was formed by ACPO in Britain. One outcome of this was an attempt to develop and then introduce a set of 'ethical principles' that could be incorporated into general police discipline codes. In terms of the behaviour the codes were aiming to eliminate, the working group who published the preliminary principles attempted to cover all possible eventualities. Excessive violence, discrimination and unfairness to those of minority groups was outlawed, while fairness and reporting on the corrupt or unethical behaviour of colleagues was encouraged.

One of the problems with this is that police officers are regularly in contact with criminals, sometimes in the most unregulated situations. The way police use informers and subsequently the intelligence they receive, for instance, begs questions about the circumstances in which officers find themselves tempted to bend the rules and how they reconcile the difficulties that arise when morals and ethics clash with 'getting results'. This is termed 'noble cause corruption', where, in the mind of the officer, the actions can be justified as 'ethical' as the ends justify the means. Indeed, a number of authors have argued that police officers occasionally use unethical, illegal or improper actions to achieve their ends (Macintyre and Prenzler, 1999; Klockars 1983). It might be argued that this is understandable in some circumstances. Problems arise, however, when such behaviour crosses acceptable boundaries. Often life and death decisions have to be made without the benefit of reflection or consultation with colleagues or managers. Sometimes these decisions are irreversible and are often investigated later when things go wrong, and so officers have to be ready to defend their actions.

Due to these difficulties it has been asked whether public servants such as police officers really need a code of ethics (Davis 1991). It has been suggested, for example, that we should exempt the police from the normal moral standards we might expect from other publicly funded professionals because 'dirty' hands are needed to catch criminals (Villiers 1987). To take this one step further, Klockars (1983) has argued that the public is quite happy for the police to bend the rules as long as it leads to the 'bad' people being arrested and punished. This seems to assume that as lawbreakers do not operate within a recognisable code of ethics, police officers should not have to do so either. As Westmarland (2000) argues, police officers see themselves as putting their lives on the line to protect the public, and sometimes have to make instant decisions that, with the benefit of hindsight, might not have been the best course of action. Their world view is coloured by the need to 'lock up the bad guys' and their moral view is reinforced and justified by those of their colleagues who also believe this to be the overriding police mandate.

Around the latter half of the 1980s particularly in the UK and US, these views began to receive an increasing amount of attention. At that time discussions about the need to eradicate corruption, including the 'noble cause' variety, seemed to gain pace, perhaps partly as a result of the growing use of electronic surveillance techniques and the increasing awareness of 'globalised' crime. This was also seen at a local level, where some cases of normally 'covert' areas of activity, e.g. infiltration of pressure groups or informer handling, became subjected to more technologically sophisticated methods of observation and recording. These techniques of surveillance varied from the mundane, such as local citizens forming themselves into local crime prevention committees to municipal closed circuit television monitoring, to the listening and recording equipment available to specialist policing groups such as those responsible for anti-terrorist operations and organised crime detection.

Technology

Although the public and the suspected criminal may be the target of such surveillance, sometimes the police are also caught by the web of recording technology. The police usually hold the means to control the technology and its output, but sometimes the availability of video recording equipment means that their misdemeanours are available as evidence. In the UK the Metropolitan Police have used hidden cameras to catch their own officers accepting bribes and to expose racist or sexist behaviour. Further, the knowledge of increased use of 'spy' technologies filters down to the public and those the police target, leading civil liberties organisations to ask questions about their use and police ethics. These discussions can be placed within traditional academic debates surrounding accountability, legitimacy, equal opportunities and ethnic diversity. In effect, how colleagues and members of the public are treated by the police has always had an ethical or moral dimension, but this has not really been explicitly stated until 'ethical policing' became an issue. The increasing availability of ever smaller and more easily hidden recording devices is another reason why ethical behaviour has emerged as a major worry for police managers. One of the ways in which recent high-profile cases have been revealed is due to the widespread use of mobile phones and the ability to record events and the facility to disseminate the evidence widely.

Attempting global parity

So it seems that senior officers tend to believe that in order to have a framework within which any training or staff development can take place there needs to be a 'policy' or statement of what is expected from employees and their managers. With regard to ethical behaviour and the police, this means that a number of problematic concepts are brought to the surface and traditional working practices might be challenged, as in the example of the ACPO recommendations for a code of ethics for their officers shown above. The five most relevant 'principles' that were selected from a list of eleven in total, which address issues such as the use of resources, self development and personal accountability show that the range of behaviour that needs to be controlled is very diverse. A recent example is a report published by the IPCC and ACPO into officers who abuse their powers for sexual exploitation. In revealing the way some police officers use their position of trust to abuse people with whom they come into contact, they produced a checklist of questions and recommendations. These included the need to work closely with organisations that have specialist knowledge of sexual exploitation and abuse and they point out that 'under-reporting may be a significant problem for the police service to address', and as a recent HMIC (Her Majesty's Inspectorate of the Con-stabulary) report noted:

> Although all forces have an anti-corruption control strategy, there is no evidence that gifts and hospitality, associations, business interests and procure-ment are considered together as a risk. All forces have a method of anony-mously and confidentially reporting integrity issues (whistle blowing), either by telephone or e-mail or both. Feedback from focus groups indicated a lack of knowledge or a level of scepticism and distrust regarding the anonymity of the systems. Five police authorities reported having their own confidential reporting system.
>
> *(HMIC 2011, p. 54)*

Given the difficulties of developing means of controlling police behaviour therefore, it is not surprising that police chiefs across the world have turned to each other for help. As Neyroud explains, in relation to the Council of Europe's European Code of Police Ethics (2001), '(t)he creation of such an international code for police ethics highlights not just the importance of the issue politically but also the growing complexity and challenge of ethics for policing Europe' (Neyroud 2003, p. 578). One of the problems with adopting an international, or even just a European, code of ethics is perhaps due to the specific cultural and socio-legal environment in which officers in individual countries have to work. As Neyroud explains later, the European Court of Human Rights makes allowances for rights to be interpreted flexibly within 'local, national traditions' (2003, p. 585). Issues such as the definition of 'discrimination' or the 'right to a fair trial', for instance, might cause discomfort for police officers in Britain because they have not been accustomed to having to consider such concepts explicitly. The introduction of the first Bill of Rights into British law, the Human Rights Act 1998, for instance introduced the idea that a number of ethical concerns, with competing values attached to various 'rights' and 'responsibilities'. In addition, the test of proportionality had now to be considered, as the 'means versus ends' argument became central to how policing was conducted. Rather than the paternalistic approach to assuming they know what is right and wrong, an extensive training programme was carried out in the UK to teach front-line police officers (among other things) the need to balance the needs of the community against the rights of the offender.

Of course, it is always going to prove difficult to arrive at an agreement about the meaning of 'philosophical' terms such as human rights, ethics and morals. As Klockars *et al.* explain (2003), integrity is a problematic concept to define and describe, but in practice many professional groups with the power to make decisions, not least of all the police, have to confront it. In an international study of integrity these authors define integrity as a summation of six concepts as illustrated in Table 29.2.

BOX 29.2 SIX CONCEPTS OF INTEGRITY

Normativeness
- A shared belief which is morally charged, combined with an inclination to behave in accordance with that belief.

The Inclination to Resist
- Attitudes are not always predictive of behaviour as people of integrity might do things that they know are wrong, although a requirement to be honest may cause the adoption of a belief in the virtues of integrity.

Police as an Individual or a Group
- Definitions of integrity may differ when describing police as individual or a group.

Temptations
- Police officers work in differing environments and police misconduct that is motivated by gain from that which is not (such as the
  excessive use of force for instance).

Abuse of Office
- Includes accepting gifts as gestures of goodwill and using legal
  discretion, such as whether or not to arrest or issue summonses
  to friends.

The Rights and Privileges of the Occupation
- An occupation ripe for misconduct with unsupervised working,
  and a 'code of silence' to protect the corrupt.

(Adapted from Klockars *et al.* 2003, pp. 2–6)

The international study of police integrity Klockars *et al.* conducted covered fourteen different countries and involved a questionnaire that was adapted in minor ways to take account of local differences in laws and regulations. Although the study was ostensibly about integrity as the typology describing their definition of the concept shows, officers were being asked about their adherence to some type of moral code. Results of the survey showed that 'the rank order in which police officers from most countries evaluated the seriousness of the misconduct in the scenarios is remarkably similar' (Klockars *et al.* 2003, p. 12). Officers from the various police departments across the world were asked about their actions in a number of increasingly serious and unlawful situations. These began with accepting a small gift at holiday time to removing large amounts of money or valuable goods from the scenes of crimes. Some questions were also about supervisors' behaviour and the use of unnecessary force.

In the UK part of the study, Westmarland discovered a similar pattern of behaviour (Klockars *et al.* 2003, ch. 5). Minor misdemeanours, such as accepting small gifts were considered less serious than the theft of the goods and money. Physical brutality was also counted as less serious than theft, and although most officers thought that covering up for a colleague who was caught drunk driving was 'serious', fewer were prepared to report it. With regards to ethical concerns, it is possible that the officers were considering proportionality in these latter two cases, however, as they considered the punishment the officer 'should' receive to be much less than they thought he or she 'would' get if reported or discovered. Similarly in another study in the UK police, Newburn (1999) argues that although there has been a history of malpractice and misconduct, many of the instances tend to be related to the 'noble cause' or practices associated with the outcome of cases rather than to those with an acquisitive motive. In comparison with the examples he cited from the United States, Australia, and other jurisdictions, British police officers appear therefore to be more 'noble' than their colleagues in other countries. Similarly, in a comprehensive examination of police integrity published by HMIC (1999), few references are made to major corruption in terms of gambling, protection rackets, or other financial gain. Rather, most of the discussion in the HMIC report regarding 'integrity' is about public perceptions of the police, the acceptance of gratuities, and the investigation and prosecution of offenders.

This is not to say that acquisitive corruption does not, or has not existed in the UK police although it has been argued by their Inspectorate that it would be 'almost impossible to achieve' (HMIC 1999, p. 8) due to the sensitive nature of the topic. A historical study conducted by Morton (1993), however, covers the period before the development of the modern police in 1829, and subsequent tracts of history until the introduction of a significant piece of legislation, the Police and Criminal Evidence Act (PACE), in 1984. These new regulations, in combination with the Prosecution of Offences Act (1985), provided 'very considerable safeguards for suspects', 'substantially curtailed the way the police throughout the country could conduct their enquiries', and 'removed opportunities for direct corruption' (Morton, 1993, p. 167). New safeguards that were developed as a result of these laws include the tape recording of interviews and the timetabling and monitoring of those in police custody. Over the 150 years of the British police before the introduction of the PACE, there was what Morton (1993) has described as a history of 'bent coppers', of police officers 'bent for self' and 'bent for the job'.

Ethical cultures

Of course the police are in a vulnerable position as a publicly accountable service because they have to appear to be upholding the highest moral and ethical standards of behaviour. Legitimate enforcers of the law have to be above subjective judgements affected by biases such as visible minority ethnicity, gender, or class. This is a matter of some concern in a number of specific areas, such as informer handling, and more generally in terms of the rights of the arrestee and bystanders' privacy. In addition, the Police Act (1997) obliged the police in the United Kingdom to develop codes of practice with respect to issues such as intrusive surveillance, the new national crime squad, information technology, and criminal records (Uglow and Telford, 1997). Reiner (2000) expressed the view that 'given the low visibility and hence inevitable discretion of much routine police work the key changes must be in the informal culture of the police, their practical working rules' (p. 183).

In quoting Wilson (1968, p. 7), Reiner (2000) argued that the police are a unique organisation, in that 'discretion increases as one moves down the hierarchy' (p. 86). In effect, therefore, those in the lowest ranks in supervisory terms have the most power in operational situations, and Waddington (1999) asks whether 'police rules made by superiors serve to insulate them from criticism by pushing responsibility *down* the hierarchy' (p. 129). Police managers and senior policy makers have drawn up codes of conduct or 'principles' for guidance in such situations, but officers may still have difficulty with adhering to a set of professional ethical standards, as the example of the police ethical principles outlined above illustrates. Furthermore, police recruits tend to be socialised by more experienced officers who teach them to be aware of a number of 'insider' cultural rules. One of the most important of these is the need to produce 'results' such as arrests. As Fielding (1988) said, new recruits are 'aware that "arrests" are one of the concrete things which serve the organization's need to assess performance' (p. 151). Even experienced officers are afforded status according to their arrest rate (Westmarland 2001, pp. 108–109).

One of the dangers of this type of 'solidaritist' behaviour, combined with the pressure to achieve targets, however, is the pressure on individual officers to conform, despite any feelings they might have that something ethically or morally dubious has occurred. Neyroud (2003) argues that in order to move 'towards' ethical policing a number of standards have to be achieved. He argues for a more professional status for the police, which go hand in hand with the 'aspiration' for a more ethical approach to policing. This can only be achieved, he argues, when the 'performance' the police are measured by is a professional rather than a quantitative target. Next, Neyroud argues, the police have to be responsive to the public they serve in order to be ethical – the challenges this provides to decision making ensures good professional standards. In terms of the challenge of covert policing, again Neyroud claims the key is about professional practice and its performance management (2003, p. 599).

Recommendations

1   It is an indication of the levels of concern that the IPCC have published three recent reports about police corruption and associated behaviour (IPCC 2011, 2012a, 2012b). However, few studies in the past have asked serving police officers about corruption, integrity or general rule bending. Two studies that have done this are Westmarland (2005) and Westmarland, Rowe and Hougham (forthcoming) although even these have concentrated on scenario-based questions about the supposed behaviour of colleagues. The problems of drawing conclusions without evidence are obvious and so the recommendation of this report is that this sort of research should be conducted to provide an evidence base for policy change.

2   As the study of police ethics comprises of a number of associated concepts such as integrity, corruption, culture, and professional codes there should be some concentrated discussion to amalgamate these concerns. At present it seems that ACPO has an Ethics Committee, but also has lead officers for Professional Standards, Corruption and so on.

3   Pressures to conform, produce results, protect and serve the community can lead to ethical decision making appearing to be a luxury the police often cannot afford. The public might not be concerned with police ethics as they may have other more immediate problems and demands. It seems, however, that given the number of codes of practice and studies of corrupt practices in place throughout the world, it is a problem that will continue to trouble police

managers, theorists, and policy makers for some time to come. The importance of ethics training, including work around the ACPO codes of practice should be investigated and, if found inadequate or inappropriate, remedies made because the threat to legitimacy, reputation and trust in the police is incalculable.

4   It would be helpful to develop a dialogue with front-line officers, and the Police Federation, to talk about ethical conduct and the seriousness of certain breaches of behaviour. This could lead to more 'bottom-up' codes of ethics that would be more meaningful to serving officers than the top-down versions in existence to date. Following this, an externally 'objective' statement could be produced, on the basis of what officers think are serious and unacceptable behaviours.

Note

1   Prepared by Louise Westmarland 25/09/2012, with assistance from Courtney Hougham, Open University.

References

Alderson, J. (1998). *Principled policing: Protecting the public with integrity.* Winchester, UK: Waterside.

Davis, M. (1991). Do cops really need a code of ethics? *Criminal Justice Ethics,* 10 (Summer/Fall), 14–28.

Fielding, N. (1988). *Joining forces: Police training, socialisation and occupational competence.* London: Routledge.

Her Majesty's Inspectorate of Constabulary (1999). *Police integrity: England, Wales and Northern Ireland. Securing and maintaining public confidence.* London: Home Office.

Her Majesty's Inspectorate of Constabulary (2011). *Without fear or favour: A review of police relationships.* London: Home Office.

Huberts, L.W.J.C., Lamboo, T. and Punch, M. (2003). Police integrity in the Netherlands and the United States: Awareness and alertness. *Police Practice and Research,* 4, 217–232.

Independent Police Complaints Commission (2011). *Corruption in the Police Service in England and Wales – First Report.* London: IPCC.

Independent Police Complaints Commission (2012a). *Corruption in the Police Service in England and Wales – Second Report – a report based on the IPCC's experience from 2008–2011.* London: IPCC.

Independent Police Complaints Commission (2012b). *The abuse of police powers to perpetrate sexual violence.* London: IPCC.

Kääriäinen, J., Lintonen, T., Laitinen, A. and Pollock, J. (2008). The 'Code of Silence': Are self-report surveys a viable means for studying police misconducts? *Journal of Scandinavian Studies in Criminology and Crime Prevention,* 9, 86–96.

Kleinig, J. (1996). *The ethics of policing.* Cambridge, UK: Cambridge University Press.

Klockars, C.B. (1983). The Dirty Harry problem. In C.B. Klockars (ed.), *Thinking about police.* New York: McGraw-Hill.

Klockars, C.B., Kutnjak Ivkovic, S. and Haberfield, M.R. (eds) (2003). *The contours of police integrity.* London: Sage.

Macintyre, S. and Prenzler, T. (1999). The influence of gratuities and personal relationships on police use of discretion. *Policing and Society,* 9(2), 181–201.

Miller, S. (2010). Integrity systems and professional reporting in police organizations. *Criminal Justice Ethics*, 29, 241–257.

Morton, J. (1993). *Bent coppers: A survey of police corruption*. London: Little, Brown.

Newburn, T. (1999). *Understanding and preventing police corruption: Lessons from the literature*. London: Home Office Policing and Reducing Crime Unit.

Neyroud, P. (2003). Policing and ethics. In T. Newburn (ed.), *Handbook of policing*. Cullompton, Devon: Willan.

Neyroud, P. and Beckley, R. (2001). *Policing, ethics and human rights*. Cullompton, Devon: Willan.

Reiner, R. (2000). *The politics of the police* (3rd ed.). Oxford: Oxford University Press.

Uglow, S. and Telford, V. (1997). *The Police Act 1997*. Bristol, UK: Jordans.

Villiers, P. (1987). *Better police ethics*. London: Kegan Paul.

Waddington, P.A.J. (1999). *Policing citizens: Authority and rights*. London: UCL Press.

Westmarland, L. (2000). Telling the truth the whole truth and nothing but the truth? Ethics and the enforcement of law. *Journal of Ethical Sciences and Services*, 2(3), 193–202.

Westmarland, L. (2001). *Gender and policing: Sex, power and police culture*. Cullompton, Devon: Willan.

Westmarland, L. (2005). Police ethics and integrity: Breaking the blue code of silence. *Policing and Society*, 15(2), 145–165.

Westmarland, L., Rowe, M. and Hougham, C. (forthcoming) Police corruption: wider issues and empirical research. In S. Lister and M. Rowe (eds), *Accountability of policing*. London: Routledge.

Wilson, J.Q. (1968). *Varieties of police behavior*. Cambridge, MA: Harvard University Press.

30

GREAT EXPECTATIONS AND COMPLEX REALITIES

The impact and implications
of the police reform process in
Northern Ireland

Aogán Mulcahy

Introduction

The police reform process in Northern Ireland is one of the most high-profile examples of institutional change in policing in recent years (Mulcahy 2006; Murphy 2013), and has been accorded the status of a 'model' for police reform generally (Ellison 2007). Analysis of any particular context must be attentive to the specificity of the issues involved, but equally it should seek to highlight developments that have a general relevance. In Northern Ireland's case, police reform was recognised as a central component of the peace process through the establishment of the Independent Commission on Policing (ICP) in Northern Ireland (the Patten Commission). The ICP specified new arrangements that could command widespread and cross-community support, and its reform programme laid the basis for an extensive transformation of policing. In this chapter I consider the reform programme outlined by the Patten Commission and assess its impact on policing in Northern Ireland. I also reflect on the wider relevance of these developments and the lessons they offer for police reform efforts elsewhere. I begin by considering the context from which the Patten Commission emerged.

Context

Although police reform was not an initial demand of the civil rights movement in the late 1960s, the Royal Ulster Constabulary's (RUC) response to the burgeoning campaign to challenge inequalities in Northern Ireland – and the disorder that emerged in an escalating cycle of protest and counter-protest – was crucial in placing policing centre stage. From then on, tied to issues of state and security, and identity and affiliation, policing was a cipher for the wider conflict, and indeed the nature of Northern Irish society more generally. Countering paramilitary violence involved a highly militarised model of policing, with an emphasis on protecting the state rather than on securing public support for the police. Attitudes towards the police were starkly divided, both on the basis of political outlook and experience, and Whyte (1990: 88) noted that Catholics and Protestants disagreed more over the 'unhealed sore' of policing and security policy than they did on constitutional matters. From the mid-1970s onwards a series of measures were introduced to increase the RUC's professionalism, enhance its capabilities, and assert its impartiality – including changes to training, public order policing strategies, and weaponry – but these proved only partially successful in securing the support of the Catholic population. Despite the huge toll in human terms – over 300 officers killed, and thousands more physically injured and mentally scarred – policing continued to be a deeply polarising issue, with seemingly intractable divisions in the views of Catholic and Protestant communities on these issues. As the peace process gathered pace through the 1993 Downing Street Declaration and the 1994 paramilitary ceasefires, it was clear that policing would have to be central to any lasting settlement, and so it was that the 1998 Belfast Agreement – the blueprint for the new political landscape in Northern Ireland – specified that an independent commission would be established to address this issue.

The Independent Commission on Policing in Northern Ireland

The Independent Commission on Policing in Northern Ireland (ICP) – commonly known as the Patten Commission – was established to bring forward proposals for future policing arrangements in Northern Ireland. Composed of a mixture of local and international members who, between them, had considerable operational and academic expertise in policing as well as in organisational change, the Patten Commission went about its business briskly. It invited submissions from interested parties, held a series of public meetings (attended by 10,000 people at which over 1,000 people spoke), met with a wide range of organisations, examined policing arrangements in other jurisdictions, and commissioned research on public attitudes to policing.

Its report was published on 1 September 1999, to huge public interest and equally huge controversy. In some respects, this response was entirely predictable, given the central role that policing had played in the dynamics of the conflict. Moreover, despite the many official inquiries that had been held into different aspects of policing during the conflict, the ICP was the first which highlighted the contested field of policing within Northern Ireland, and which linked it indelibly to issues of state:

> In one political language they are the custodians of nationhood. In its rhetorical opposite they are the symbols of oppression. Policing therefore goes right to the heart of the sense of security and identity of both communities and, because of the differences between them, this seriously hampers the effectiveness of the police service in Northern Ireland.
>
> *(ICP 1999: 2)*

The ICP's orientation was straightforward: 'By means of a fresh start for policing, our aim is to help ensure that past tragedies are not repeated in the future' (p. 4). This entailed focusing on future arrangements rather than investigating past controversies (discussed further later). In making its recommendations, the ICP sought to ensure that these were not constrained by particular political circumstances prevailing at one particular time, or that favoured one group over another, but instead that their proposals addressed 'the challenge confronting policing in any modern society' (p. 6). Thus, their recommendations were designed to be consistent with five key principles (p. 5):

1   Does this proposal promote effective and efficient policing?
2   Will it deliver fair and impartial policing, free from partisan control?
3   Does it provide for accountability, both to the law and to the community?
4   Will it make the police more representative of the society they serve?
5   Does it protect and vindicate the human rights and human dignity of all?

Key recommendations and implementation

The ICP made 175 recommendations in total, covering a wide range of issues. Some were relatively banal in content and related to the modernisation and normalisation of policing generally – recommendation 57, for instance, states that 'The word "Police" should be painted onto the sides of all Landrovers'. Other recommendations specified that: Special Branch should be merged with Crime Branch, police stations should be de-fortified, a new police training college should be constructed (the subject of much delay, with construction due to begin in late 2013, and a scheduled opening date of 2015), and while the police should remain routinely armed in light of the ongoing security threat, this should be reviewed on an ongoing basis. Shearing noted that many of the proposals were 'unremarkable' insofar as they merely 'apply principles that are routinely accepted elsewhere' (2000: 386–7). Some of the other recommendations also were relatively uncontroversial and addressed in-house matters, reflecting similar issues that had featured in other recent reviews (the RUC's own *Fundamental Review of Policing* (1996), for instance). However, while one strand of the ICP recommendations addressed the 'police' institutions, another strand sought to outline a framework for the governance of security provision that extended beyond a focus solely on the public police and, instead, encompassed the range of actors and agencies involved in 'policing' more generally (discussed further below).

Overall, the report's most prominent recommendations coalesced around a number of key themes (see Figure 30.1): to enhance accountability, oversight and governance; to work in partnership with the community and to devolve decision-making to the lowest level possible; to embed human rights within the structures of policing; to make the police more representative of the population of Northern Ireland; and to make its culture and ethos more inclusive.

Accountability, governance and oversight	Policing Board to replace the existing Police Authority
	District Policing Partnership Boards to be established at local authority level
	Police Ombudsman to be established as an independent agency to investigate police complaints
	Oversight Commissioner to monitor implementation of ICP recommendations
Human rights	New Oath
	Human Rights to be embedded within all training
Policing with the community	Policing with the community to be established as core function of the police
	Neighbourhood policing teams to be established
	Decision-making to be devolved as much as possible
Size and composition	Reduction from approximately 13,000 full-time officers to 7,500
	Introduction of 50:50 (Catholic:non-Catholic) recruitment scheme
Culture and ethos	Royal Ulster Constabulary to be renamed
	Symbols to be inclusive

FIGURE 30.1   Patten Report: selected recommendations

Accountability, governance and oversight

The ICP's most significant recommendations addressed issues of governance, accountability and oversight, through the establishment of new structures which would embed accountability in the institutional landscape of policing in Northern Ireland. In terms of governance, the ICP proposed that a *Policing Board* replace the existing Policing Authority which had largely limited itself to the role of bursar rather than serving as a robust oversight body. The function of the Policing Board was to hold the Chief Constable publicly to account, and to agree and monitor implementation of a policing plan; and the Board would be given powers to initiate inquiries, and to require the Chief Constable to report on any issue.

At local authority level, a system of *District Policing Partnership Boards* (DPPBs) was to be established, comprised of elected and independent members, and 'advisory, explanatory and consultative' in function (p. 35). Importantly, the ICP called for these to be given tax-raising powers of up to 3 per cent (similar to the powers already available to District Councils for economic development) to purchase additional policing services if required, whether 'from the police or other statutory agencies, or from the private sector' (p. 35).

The ICP endorsed the 1997 recommendation by Maurice Hayes (also a member of the ICP) that an independent police complaints system be established in the form of a *Policing Ombudsman*. This would also have the power to investigate policies or practices where there was a public interest in doing so. To ensure that the reform process itself was fully implemented, the ICP called for the appointment of an *Oversight Commissioner* with the explicit function of monitoring and reporting on the progress made in implementing the ICP recommendations. Underpinning this emphasis on oversight and accountability was an explicit commitment to embedding *human rights* within all aspects of policing, including training and appraisal. The report recommended a new oath and code of ethics, and the appointment of a human rights lawyer to advise the police.

Policing with the community

The ICP noted the complex nature of the many problems the police faced, but in seeking to address these effectively it called for a new model of *policing with the community*, a fundamental partnership between the police and the public. As it noted (p. 8):

> [I]t is not so much that the police need support and consent, but rather that policing is a matter for the whole community, not something that the community leaves to the police to do. Policing should be a collective partnership: a partnership for community safety.

It stated that 'policing with the community should be the core function of the police service and the core function of every police station' (p. 43). To realise this vision, it called for the establishment of dedicated policing teams in every neighbourhood or rural area, and for police decision-making to be devolved to the lowest level possible.

Recruitment, culture and ethos

The report also recommended that the force be *renamed* – it duly became the *Police Service of Northern Ireland* (PSNI) – and that the *force symbolism* should be neutral in terms of political affiliation.

The ICP noted the underrepresentation of Catholics/nationalists within the RUC (11 per cent in 1969, and 8 per cent in 1999), and argued that sustained efforts should be made to increase the police's representativeness of the wider population. It proposed that a new recruitment strategy should be implemented to increase Catholic representation within the police to a figure of approximately 30 per cent (which the ICP appeared to view as a 'critical mass' figure) within a 10-year period. This entailed a system of *50:50 recruitment* whereby applicants who met the entry requirements would be placed into two separate pools of Catholics and non-Catholics. Applicants would be ranked within each pool and an equal number of recruits would then be selected from each. Simultaneously, the report called for a significant reduction in the overall force size, from 13,000 officers to 7,500, which would be achieved specifically through a generous severance scheme.

Reception and implementation

In contrast to the international assessment of the Patten reforms as a model to be emulated, the local reception of the Patten Report was mixed to say the least. While it received a largely positive (if somewhat guarded) response from many nationalist commentators, within Unionism it generated dismay and outrage. The Ulster Unionist Party (UUP) leader David Trimble described it as 'the most shoddy piece of work I have seen in my entire life', and a 'Save the RUC' campaign resulted in a petition of nearly 400,000 signatures being presented to the British Prime Minister. While the Chief Constable at the time, Ronnie Flanagan, spoke persuasively of the benefits of policing arrangements that commanded widespread support, other officers were less positive. One Detective Chief Superintendent claimed that: 'The sterling service of the past and present members of the RUC is being subverted by Patten and as a matter of principle I will not be serving under his new scheme of things' (see Mulcahy 2006: 159–63, 188). Such controversies set the tone for the implementation process which was riven with emotion and intrigue. The symbolic dimensions of the reform programme – the name change in particular – encapsulated unionist fears: the loss of what many viewed as 'their' police force for its key role in defending 'their' state. The heat generated in this debate ensured – initially at least – that many of the reform measures did not receive a careful analysis (Smith 2010).

Moreover, the implementation process itself was hampered by official delay and perhaps a level of hostility also from some politicians and state officials. It seems clear that the Secretary of State for Northern Ireland, Peter Mandelson, was less than convinced of the merit of much of the Patten recommendations (perhaps due to concerns that their implementation would damage pro-agreement Union-ism), and despite his acceptance of the report 'in principle', in practice he seems to have been anxious to water down its proposals wherever possible. Certainly this was the view of the Commissioners themselves (Patten 2010; Hayes 2010), and Patten speculated that official 'squeamishness' at the prospect of relinquish-ing control which the Northern Ireland Office and British Government generally had exercised throughout the conflict led officials to 'dilute' (p. 21) many of the proposals, and a 'much weakened implementing bill had to be rewritten during its parliamentary passage in order to put back into it much of our report' (p. 23). Cer-tainly, the implementation process itself was tortuous and protracted, comprising two separate pieces of legislation and two further detailed implementation plans. Undoubtedly these delays and the political intrigue behind them eroded some of the already scarce goodwill and trust available that was necessary to shepherd the process along. In any event, political wrangling over the report ensured that its full implementation was considerably delayed (Sinn Fein, for instance, did not fully endorse the new policing arrangements until as late as 2007, at which point it took up its seats on the Policing Board and DPPs), and so any assessment of the reforms' impact must take this stuttering start into account.

Impact and assessment

As the dust settled on the immediate upheaval of the reform programme and the new institutions took root, judgement on the Patten reforms was hugely positive. The Chairperson of the Northern Ireland Policing Board lauded the reform programme as a 'blueprint for democratic policing anywhere in the world' and described the PSNI as 'the most scrutinized and accountable police service probably anywhere in the world today' (see Bayley 2008; Ellison 2007; Mulcahy 2008a, 2008b). A decade after the report was first published, the Commissioners themselves considered that the reform process was a major success. Chris Patten (2010: 25) described the PSNI as 'the best working example of how to police a divided community', while Shearing (2010: 29) noted that:

> The PSNI has positioned itself internationally as an exemplary police organisation, largely because it has become a Patten-compliant organisation . . . there is widespread support for the view that the Patten Report, and its vision of policing, provides an example of the very best thinking about contemporary policing, and that it constitutes a benchmark that policing around the world can and should look to for guidance.

Assessments of the various institutional elements of the reform programme also were largely positive.

The Policing Board assumed the high-profile role of monitoring policing, and the House of Commons Northern Ireland Affairs Committee observed that the Board had made 'solid progress in establishing its role and had developed sound mechanisms for holding the police service to account' (2005: 23), while the Oversight Commissioner described it as a 'great success' (2007: 8). However, the working of the Board was often more nuanced than this praise might suggest. Political antagonism between the various Board members (a majority were active politicians) and their party positions persisted. For example, the Democratic Unionist Party (the largest Unionist party in Northern Ireland) claimed in 2003 that its members on the Board had 'prevented many of the Patten recommendations from being realized' (p. 24). Meanwhile, in April 2008 the Chief Constable stated that he received more strategic questions from police recruits than from members of the Policing Board. Nevertheless, despite conflicts over specific issues and some party political posturing, it has come to be recognised as a robust and independent body (Rea *et al.* 2010).

The DPPBs became *District Policing Partnerships*. The recommendation that they should be given tax-raising powers was rejected, and this was probably the highest profile casualty of the implementation process. Moreover, the terrain of consultative bodies at local level was increasingly 'crowded' (Ellison and O'Rawe 2010).

A review of the criminal justice system operating in parallel with the ICP had called for the establishment of Community Safety Partnerships (CSPs) (Criminal Justice Review Group 2000), and the Northern Ireland Office appeared to throw its weight behind those, including by providing a central fund to which CSPs could apply for support towards various projects. ICP members considered this a less than subtle effort to 'nobble the emerging DPPs' (Hayes 2010: 66). Although DPPs were described as 'a genuine success story' for providing a 'forum for grassroots engagement in a way that has never happened before' (Rea et al. 2010: 137), in reality the impact of these partnerships on local policing was much more qualified. Some of this relates to the limitations of the 'public meeting' format (Brunger 2011); other concerns relate to the institutional framework within which they operated and the considerable 'role confusion' that reflected the competing and overlapping roles of DPPs, Community Safety Partnerships, Community and Police Liaison Committees, and so on (Ellison and O'Rawe 2010). Partly reflecting this ongoing criticism, DPPs and CSPs were consolidated into Police and Community Safety Partnerships in April 2012 (under the provisions of the Justice Act (Northern Ireland) 2011) with a view to streamlining and enhancing procedures for consultation and engagement with the public at a local level.

Although the Oversight Commissioner might appear peripheral to the core recommendations, it proved central to the reform process. Perhaps especially in light of the protracted implementation process, Patten described this as 'one of our best ideas' (2010: 25). Between 2000 and 2007, the Oversight Commissioner published 19 substantial reports outlining the steps taken towards the implementation of every agreed recommendation and the progress made; it also highlighted areas where further action was necessary. Although sometimes accused of operating in a tick-box fashion, its methodical and transparent approach provided a tangible record of the implementation process.

The PSNI's compliance with human rights legislation is monitored through the Policing Board, and in 2006 it noted that: 'In its commitment to human rights compliance, the PSNI continues to set the standard that other police services elsewhere in the UK should aspire to' (NIPB 2006: i). It further noted that the force's 'impressive implementation record is demonstrative of PSNI's ongoing commitment to ensure that a human rights culture exists within the organisation' (NIPB 2011: i–ii).

In terms of the size and composition of the force, while the 50:50 policy was hugely controversial – it generated fierce resistance from many Unionists, and it required the suspension of relevant employment discrimination legislation – the increase in Catholic recruitment also proceeded in tandem with other efforts to reduce the size of the police force overall. In this respect, the 'peace dividend' involved not only the prize of normalisation, but also served as an opportunity for central government to reduce its huge expenditure on policing and security generally. The reduction in force size was largely achieved through a severance programme which incentivised retirements, particularly for long-serving officers. While this served the twin goals of reducing overall personnel numbers and expediting the departure of some officers who could not countenance the new policing dispensation, it also involved the loss of considerable expertise and experience which inevitably contributed to a degree of upheaval within the organisation, as well as impacting on its service delivery generally.

The 50:50 recruitment policy was ended in 2011, by which time just under 30 per cent of PSNI officers were Catholic. Figures from 2012 indicate that the PSNI comprised 7,042 full-time and 556 part-time officers, as well as 2,383 support staff. The religious composition of the PSNI in 2012 was 67 per cent Protestant, and 30 per cent Catholic, while for the support staff it was 80 per cent Protestant and 19 per cent Catholic. In terms of gender, 27 per cent of officers were female, and 73 per cent were male. While this is a huge change from a decade previously, it is clear that greater diversity in terms of increasing the representation of 'cultural Catholics' does not necessarily produce a corresponding increase in the breadth of political outlooks evident within the organisation. For example, as Gethins (2011) notes in her research on Catholic police officers in Northern Ireland, those she interviewed were almost uniformly neutral or mildly nationalist – rather than republican – in their political outlook, despite the fact that since 2001 Sinn Fein has outpolled the more moderate Social Democratic and Labour Party in Northern Ireland elections (see http://www.ark.ac.uk/elections/gallsum.htm).

Against the backdrop of these insitutional changes, it is also appropriate to consider two other dimensions to the field of policing: crime levels, and public attitudes towards the police. In terms of crime levels, in 2000/01, a total of 119,912 offences were recorded by the police in Northern Ireland. Over the following two years this increased to 142,496 recorded offences before gradually decreasing to 103,389 in 2011/12. Taking 2000/01 figures as a base rate, this involves an increase of 19 per cent to 2002/03, and overall decline of 14 per cent by 2011/12. This crime rate is significantly lower than that for England and Wales (Ellison and Mulcahy 2009). The detection rate for offences (those 'cleared up' by the police) in 2000/01 was 27.1 per cent, dropping to 20.1 per cent the following year, and since then generally ranging from 23–30 per cent. In 2011/12 the detection rate stood at 26.3 per cent. Although the initial drop in detection rate was frequently linked with the upheaval associated with the transformation of RUC to PSNI, and the departure of many experienced officers as a result of the new policies on recruitment and composition (given the scale of these issues, it would be strange if they had *no* impact), a PSNI analysis suggests that many of the changes in detection rates are due to changes in recording practices and evidential standards. For instance, the 7 per cent drop in detection rate between 2000/01 and 2001/02 is largely attributed to the introduction of the Integrated Crime Information System, while a further 7 per cent drop between 2005/06 and 2006/07 is attributed to the introduction of a 'higher evidential standard following the establishment of the Public Prosecution Service in Northern Ireland' (PSNI 2012: 30).

Analysis of surveys of public attitudes to the police reveals a persistent difference in the views of Protestant and Catholic respondents, a pattern found throughout the conflict and up to the present day. Results from a series of surveys conducted

TABLE 30.1 Recorded crime and detection rates in Northern Ireland, 2000/01 to 2011/12

Year	2000/01	2001/02	2002/03	2003/04	2004/05	2005/06	2006/07	2007/08	2008/09	2009/10	2010/11	2011/12
Total recorded crime	119,912	139,786	142,496	127,953	118,124	123,194	121,144	108,468	110,094	109,139	105,040	103,389
Detection rate (%)	27.1	20.1	23.0	27.4	28.2	30.6	23.6	20.5	23.0	25.8	27.3	26.3

Source: PSNI (2012)

between 2001 and 2003 reveal that an average of 65 per cent of Protestants compared to 51 per cent of Catholics rated the performance of the police in their area as 'very/fairly good'. In terms of police performance across Northern Ireland as a whole, 51 per cent of Catholics rated the police as 'very/fairly good', compared to 72 per cent of Protestants (NIPB 2003: 3). The most recent figures from January 2012 suggest that while the scale of this disparity in attitudes might have reduced somewhat, it still reveals enduring differences in the perceptions of Protestants and Catholics. In this survey, 64 per cent of Protestants rated the performance of the local police as 'very/fairly good' compared to 54 per cent of Catholics. When asked about the performance of the police across Northern Ireland as a whole, similar discrepancies were evident: 73 per cent of Protestants and 63 per cent of Catholics rated the police as 'very/fairly good' (NIPB 2012: 5). The survey also found that 74 per cent of Protestants were 'very/fairly satisfied' that the 'PSNI treat members of the public fairly across Northern Ireland as a whole', compared to 62 per cent of Catholics. Overall then, we can see a clear majority of the population, and of Catholics and Protestants separately, support the policing arrangements, rate the police favourably, and express confidence in police competence and fairness. Substantial differences persist between the attitudes of Catholics and Protestants, although the scale of these differences appears to be gradually diminishing.

In many ways, therefore, the 'new beginning' for policing as outlined in the Patten Report has become a success story. One of the core achievements of the Patten reforms was the transition from a militarised model of policing to a civic-oriented one. In terms of outlining a model of policing around which the various parties could coalesce, the ICP's recommendations have been extremely successful (notwithstanding profound and enduring disagreement between the protagonists over various issues) and Northern Ireland now has an enviable reputation as being at the forefront internationally of structures of police governance and accountability. This might have involved considerable analysis of policing systems elsewhere and reflection on experiences there, but it largely involved the development of a bespoke system in line with the core principles the ICP articulated (discussed earlier). As the ICP noted: 'There is no perfect model for us, no example of a country that, to quote one European police officer, "has yet finalised the total transformation from force to service"' (ICP 1999: 3). In that sense, the success story of policing in Northern Ireland is the transition to 'normal' policing – which in turn is linked with recognising the very need for reform in the first place (Bayley 2008: 239) – and the development of robust institutions which ensure oversight and accountability (particularly the Policing Board, the Police Ombudsman, and the Oversight Commissioner). Yet, in spite of the eulogies, the Oversight Commissioner (2007: 3) noted:

> progress on policing cannot be measured solely by structures, systems and processes developed or put in place over time, but on the relationship of the police with those being policed, and the relative views and perspectives of each group toward the other.

In that respect, scepticism regarding policing in Northern Ireland relates to that same issue – the travails of 'normal' policing, and in particular translating the ethos of 'policing with the community' into an enduring reality in a context where political concern over greater levels of community involvement in the justice system remains hugely evident.

Reflections on the police reform process

In light of the reform process outlined above, several factors are worth highlighting here. First, it is important to note that controversy surrounded not only the nature of the various reform proposals, but also the very need for reform in the first place. For some sections of the public – amounting to a sizeable minority of the overall population – recognition, not reform, was what the police warranted. To 'reform' the police against an uncertain political backdrop was to accede to the demands of one's enemies, in effect, to snatch defeat from the jaws of victory. Unionists viewed the police as essential to the state's survival, and particularly as a defence against the outrages of the IRA. Therefore, to acquiesce in a far-reaching reform programme would be to cast a symbolic slur on the force's reputation while simultaneously depriving the state of a vital means of self-protection against its sworn enemies. Such political dynamics inevitably added further fuel to an already heated policing debate, and political antagonism and uncertainty across the board dragged out the reform process considerably.

Second, the political landscape within Northern Ireland has been changing in other ways which impact on the governance of policing. This includes the reconfiguration of local government boundaries and a reduction from 26 to 11 local authorities, as well as the introduction of devolution and, with it, the appointment of a Minister for Justice. The first appointee and incumbent, David Ford, represents the Alliance Party, but if it is envisaged that, in the spirit of a power-sharing executive, the position would eventually rotate between the the main unionist/loyalist and nationalist/republican parties, it is possible this would generate significant political difficulties, given the divergent views held by these parties and the level of rancour between them.

Third, while levels of paramilitary violence have plummeted since the 1998 Belfast Agreement, security concerns remain. Dissident republicans have persisted in their activities, and have been responsible for the murder of PSNI officers in 2009 and 2011, two soldiers in 2009 – and, as recently as November 2012, the murder of a prison officer – as well as several other attacks which could have resulted in loss of life. Although these various organisations are relatively small in terms of numbers of supporters and activitists, their potential to escalate their campaign – and bring with it, political destabilisation – remains. Concerns also remain about the potential for widespread disturbances to erupt surrounding the 'marching season' with a consequent impact on policing: in September 2012 over 60 officers were injured over two nights of rioting in Belfast. Further serious disturbances occurred between loyalists and the police following Belfast City Council's decision in December 2012 to reduce the number of days on which the Union flag would fly over Belfast city hall.

Fourth, legacy issues continue to cast a long shadow over the broad field of policing and justice. The ICP noted the often cathartic quality of many of the testimonies it received, but its orientation was towards future policing arrangements rather than previous policing controversies: 'We were not charged with a quasi-legal investigation of the past. If there is a case for such inquiries, it is up to government to appoint them, not for us to rewrite our terms of reference' (ICP 1999: 3). To address some of the outstanding issues, the PSNI established a Historical Enquiries Team to investigate the approximately 1,800 unsolved killings from the conflict (Lundy 2009; Orde 2006), creating specific units to review police investigations and any available evidence. While there was a possibility of individuals being charged as a result of this review, in most cases it simply provided more information which could be relayed to the victims' families and thereby provide some form of closure. Yet as Lundy (2011: 102) notes, this format is more appropriate to truth recovery in respect of individual cases, than to investigating the 'macro-truths' relating to wider practices and policies of the various protagonists around which so much of the debate on the past has focused. The focus on policing the past has, however, proven costly, both in terms of absorbing scarce financial resources as well as in diverting political focus away from the need to agree on shared priorities for the future (Oversight Commissioner 2007). The Police Ombudsman did investigate several high-profile cases, including some in which collusion between loyalist paramilitaries and the security forces was alleged. However, claims that the Northern Ireland Office sought to influence the findings in several historical enquiries by downplaying criticism of the police (and Special Branch particularly) implicated the Ombudsman in a damaging public controversy (CJI 2011; McCusker 2011), and Al Hutchinson (who succeeded Nuala O'Loan in 2007, having previously served as Oversight Commissioner) retired as Ombudsman in 2011. Whatever the circumstances of particular investigations, the wider significance of this furore is to highlight the manner in which current institutions can become enmeshed in the controversies surrounding legacy issues. This could remain the case until decisive steps are taken to embark on a society-wide process of truth recovery that provides an adequate means of resolving these issues.

Notwithstanding these factors, which extend far beyond the police institution, one crucial issue continues to dog the police reform process: realising the vision of 'policing with the community' (see generally, Byrne and Topping 2012; Ellison et al. 2012; Topping 2008a, 2008b). Since the PSNI was established, the disparity between public expectation and service delivery has been considerable. In 2001–02, Her Majesty's Inspector of Constabulary found that 'the Service, as a whole, was largely failing to deliver the community policing service articulated within the Patten Report and expected by the public' (2002: 1). Moreover, the Inspector further noted that public expectations of the PSNI were 'very high, and in many cases, wholly unrealistic', and that failure to meet these demands often led to 'robust' criticism of the police (2002: 19, 2). The Oversight Commissioner, in his final report, also noted that 'the expectations of the communities and residents of Northern Ireland . . . has not yet been reached' (2007: 3), and that:

> The reality of capacity issues such as resource restraints, call and response management, crime and clearance rates, coupled with the time it takes to build trust relationships, all point to an 'expectation gap'. Normalised policing is quite simply a complex, difficult and expensive business that can never fully satisfy client demand.
>
> *(Oversight Commissioner 2007: 212)*

These issues, in turn, reflect issues of sustainability and capacity. The Oversight Commissioner (2007) noted that for the new institutions and programmes to become sustainable in the long term they needed to become embedded in the wider policing and political environment, and their further development involved capacity issues which, in turn, were heavily dependent on resource availability (even though one of the 'peace dividends' was, ironically, a significant reduction in public spending on policing and the criminal justice system generally), while simultaneously needing to continue to 'operate at a distance' and avoid being 'captured' by the police through the development of overly comfortable relationships.

In outlining its new vision of policing for Northern Ireland, the ICP's approach extended far beyond the police organisation itself to a fundamental reconfiguration of the governance of security more generally. This framework approached policing not solely in terms of the statist model that traditionally focuses on the public police, but rather in a way that highlighted the network of agencies and actors that contribute to security provision. The views of commission member Clifford Shearing – who, with others, has long engaged with the implications of the growing diversification of policing and security provision generally (see, for example, Bayley and Shearing 1996; Wood and Shearing 2006) – appear to have been particularly influential here. While the report was silent on the issue of privatisation per se (other than in terms of specific recommendations concerning the civilianisation of some positions and contracting-out some support services), it nevertheless highlighted the possiblity of a diversity of agencies contributing to public safety, whether in terms of possessing appropriate levels of expertise and capacity, or indeed simply in terms of recognising the difficulties of delivering public safety in a context where not all sections of society fully support the public police. The emphasis on poli*cing* was fully consistent with the commission's title and mandate (Independent Commission on Poli*cing*), and was reflected in its recommendations. For example, the ICP envisaged the Poli*cing* Board's remit as going 'beyond supervision of the police service itself, extending to the wider issues of policing and the contributions that people and organizations other than the police can make towards public safety' (p. 29). A similar approach was evident in the emphasis given to 'policing with the community' in recognition of the public's role in policing and community safety, and also in the recommendation that DPPs have tax-raising powers. However, its name notwithstanding, the Policing Board has remained firmly focused on the police; 'policing with the community' might have become part and parcel of the PSNI's official ethos, but the process of translating this into a new mode of partnership and engagement between police and public appears to be limited in impact, and the DPP's proposed tax-raising powers were rejected by government. At this stage, therefore, it might be more appropriate to consider events in Northern Ireland as an example of police reform rather than a more fundamental reconfiguration of security provision. Perhaps, as Shearing suggests, the Patten Report's 'most significant contribution was the shift in thinking about policing that it introduced into the public domain' (2010: 36), and the 'nodal' model articulated within the report may have been seen as appropriate in the circumstances of 'failing states' where state agencies lacked the legitimacy or capacity to provide policing services (Dupont *et al.* 2003). In the circumstances of Northern Ireland, however, 'community' was a deeply ambivalent term, one super-saturated with meaning, particularly insofar as it remained an ongoing potential threat to state authority. In political contexts where issues of state are less entangled in social conflicts, efforts to harness the capacity of communities might meet with less resistance on the part of the state. Therefore, it could be that the full impact of this 'shift in thinking' articulated in the Patten Report is more likely to unfold not in Northern Ireland, but in other contexts where the political terrain is less volatile, or where the concept of community is not deemed as heretical as it often has been portrayed in Northern Ireland (Mulcahy 2008b).

References

Bayley, David (2008) 'Post-conflict police reform: is Northern Ireland a model?' *Policing* 2(2): 233–40.

Bayley, David, and Clifford Shearing (1996) *The New Structure of Policing: Description, Conceptualisation and Research Agenda*. Washington, DC: National Institute of Justice.

Brunger, Mark (2011) 'Governance, accountability and neighbourhood policing in Northern Ireland: analysing the role of public meetings', *Crime, Law and Social Change* 55(2–3): 105–20.

Byrne, Johnny, and John Topping (2012) *Community Safety: A Decade of Development, Delivery, Challenge and Change in Northern Ireland*. A Research Report for Belfast Conflict Resolution Consortium, University of Ulster.

Criminal Justice Inspection Northern Ireland (CJI) (2011) *An Inspection into the Independence of the Office of the Police Ombudsman for Northern Ireland*. Belfast: Criminal Justice Inspection for Northern Ireland.

Criminal Justice Review Group (2000) *Review of the Criminal Justice System in Northern Ireland*. Belfast: HMSO.

Dupont, Benoit, Peter Grabosky and Clifford Shearing (2003) 'The governance of security in weak and failing states', *Criminal Justice* 3(4): 331–49.

Ellison, Graham (2007) 'A blueprint for democratic policing anywhere in the world? Police reform, political transition, and conflict resolution in Northern Ireland', *Police Quarterly* 10(3): 243–69.

Ellison, Graham, and Aogán Mulcahy (2009) 'Crime and Criminal Justice in Northern Ireland', pp. 313–337 in Anthea Hucklesby and Azrini Wahidin (eds) *Criminal Justice*. Oxford: Oxford University Press.

Ellison, Graham, and Mary O'Rawe (2010) 'Security governance in transition: the compartmentalizing, crowding out and corralling of policing and security in Northern Ireland', *Theoretical Criminology* 14(1): 31–57.

Ellison, Graham, Pete Shirlow and Aogán Mulcahy (2012) 'Responsible participation, community engagement, and policing in transitional societies: lessons from a local crime survey in Northern Ireland', *Howard Journal of Criminal Justice* 51(5): 488–502.

Gethins, Mary (2011) *Catholic Police Officers in Northern Ireland: Voices out of Silence*. Manchester: Manchester University Press.

Hayes, Maurice (2010) 'Building Cross-Community Support for Policing', pp. 59–67 in David Doyle (ed.) *Policing the Narrow Ground: Lessons from the Transformation of Policing in Northern Ireland*. Dublin: Royal Irish Academy.

Her Majesty's Inspectorate of Constabulary (2002) *Inspection of the Police Service of Northern Ireland for 2001–2*. London: HMSO.

Independent Commission on Policing (ICP) (1999) *A New Beginning: Policing in Northern Ireland. Report of the Independent Commission on Policing for Northern Ireland*. Belfast: HMSO.

Lundy, Patricia (2009) 'Can the past be policed? Lessons from the Historical Enquiries Team Northern Ireland', *Law and Social Challenges* 11: 109–71.

Lundy, Patricia (2011) 'Paradoxes and challenges of transitional justice at the "local" level: historical enquiries in Northern Ireland', *Contemporary Social Science* 6(1): 89–105.

McCusker, Tony (2011) *Police Ombudsman Investigation Report*. Belfast: Office of the Minister for Justice.

Mulcahy, Aogán (2006) *Policing Northern Ireland*. Cullompton, Devon: Willan.

Mulcahy, Aogán (2008a) 'The Police Service of Northern Ireland', pp. 204–23 in Tim Newburn (ed.) *Handbook of Policing*, 2nd edition. Cullompton, Devon: Willan.

Mulcahy, Aogán (2008b) 'Community Policing in Contested Settings: The Patten Report and Police Reform in Northern Ireland', pp. 117–37 in Tom Williamson (ed.) *The Handbook of Knowledge-Based Policing*. Chichester: Wiley.

Murphy, Joanne (2013) *Policing for Peace in Northern Ireland: Change, Conflict and Community Confidence*. Basingstoke: Palgrave/Macmillan.

Northern Ireland Affairs Committee (2005) *The Functions of the Northern Ireland Policing Board (HC 108)*. London: HMSO.

Northern Ireland Policing Board (2003) *April 2003 Omnibus Survey*. Belfast: NIPB.

Northern Ireland Policing Board (2006) *Human Rights Annual Report 2006*. Belfast: NIPB.

Northern Ireland Policing Board (2011) *Human Rights Annual Report 2011*. Belfast: NIPB.

Northern Ireland Policing Board (2012) *Public Perceptions of the Police, DPPs and the Northern Ireland Policing Board (January 2012 Omnibus Survey)*. Belfast: NIPB.

Orde, Sir Hugh (2006) 'Policing the past to police the future', *International Review of Law, Computers & Technology* 20(1–2): 37–48.

Oversight Commissioner (2000) *Overseeing the Proposed Revisions for the Policing Services of Northern Ireland – Report 1*. Belfast: Office of the Oversight Commissioner.

Oversight Commissioner (2007) *Overseeing the Proposed Revisions for the Policing Services of Northern Ireland – Report 19 (Final Report)*. Belfast: Office of the Oversight Commissioner.

Patten, Chris (2010) 'Personal Reflections on Chairing the Commission', pp. 13–26 in David Doyle (ed.) *Policing the Narrow Ground: Lessons from the Transformation of Policing in Northern Ireland*. Dublin: Royal Irish Academy.

Police Service of Northern Ireland (2012) *Trends in Police Recorded Crime in Northern Ireland 1998/99 to 2011/12*. Belfast: PSNI.

Rea, Desmond, Denis Bradley and Barry Gilligan (2010) 'Public Accountability: The Policing Board and the District Policing Partnerships', pp. 128–44 in David Doyle (ed.)

Policing the Narrow Ground: Lessons from the Transformation of Policing in Northern Ireland. Dublin: Royal Irish Academy.

Royal Ulster Constabulary (1996) *A Fundamental Review of Policing: Summary and Key Findings.* Belfast: RUC.

Shearing, Clifford (2000) '"A new beginning" for policing', *Journal of Law and Society* 27(3): 386–93.

Shearing, Clifford (2001) 'A nodal conception of governance: thoughts on a Policing Commission', *Policing and Society* 11(3–4): 259–72.

Shearing, Clifford (2010) 'The Curious Case of the *Patten Report*', pp. 27–38 in David Doyle (ed.) *Policing the Narrow Ground: Lessons from the Transformation of Policing in Northern Ireland.* Dublin: Royal Irish Academy.

Smith, John (2010) 'Policing and Politics', pp. 68–76 in David Doyle (ed.) *Policing the Narrow Ground: Lessons from the Transformation of Policing in Northern Ireland.* Dublin: Royal Irish Academy.

Topping, John (2008a) 'Diversifying from within: community policing and the governance of security in Northern Ireland', *British Journal of Criminology* 48(6): 778–97.

Topping, John (2008b) 'Community policing in Northern Ireland: a resistance narrative', *Policing and Society* 18(4): 377–96.

Whyte, John (1990) *Interpreting Northern Ireland.* Oxford: Clarendon.

Wood, Jennifer, and Clifford Shearing (2006) *Imagining Security.* Cullompton, Devon: Willan.

31

A DIFFERENT AND DIVERGENT TRAJECTORY?

Reforming the structure, governance and narrative of policing in Scotland[1]

Nicholas R. Fyfe

Introduction: divergent trajectories

The summer of 2011 was an eventful one for policing in the UK. Many will remember it for the riots in English cities that followed the fatal shooting of a man by police in north London, but it will also be remembered for significant developments in the political landscape of policing. In September, the Police Reform and Social Responsibility Act for England and Wales became law, introducing what one government minister has described as 'the most significant democratic reform of policing in our lifetime' (quoted in Loveday, 2011: 195).

In Scotland in the same month the Justice Minister stood up in the Scottish Parliament and also announced radical reforms to policing, but these indicated a direction of travel very different to the changes south of the border. In an attempt to address significant reductions in public spending, the structure of local police forces which has existed in Scotland since the early nineteenth century is to be swept away and replaced by a new national police force, the Police Service of Scotland (PSS) from 1 April 2013. These changes will also strip local government of its traditional role in funding local policing and in calling the police to account, responsibilities that will now be exercised at a national level. These are some of the most significant changes in the history of policing in Scotland, developments that appear to herald a move towards greater centralism in contrast to the emphasis on localism in the policing of England and Wales. In this chapter the background to these changes is examined along with a consideration of the key proposals contained in the 2012 Police and Fire Reform (Scotland) Act (hereafter, the Police Reform Act). The chapter also explores the wider implications of these reforms, including what they reveal about the different drivers of police reform in the UK, the governance of policing, and changing political narratives about the role of the police in late modern society.

Context: the shifting balance of power within Scottish policing

Policing in Scotland, as in the rest of the UK, has always involved a complex inter-play between national and local interests and influences, but with many observers detecting a 'creeping centralism' over the last 20 years. The arrangements for the governance of policing which have provided the context for these developments were established in the 1967 Police (Scotland) Act which created a constitutional settlement known as the tripartite structure. Under this structure, central govern-ment had overall responsibility for policing policy in Scotland and contributed 51 per cent of the costs of policing. Before devolution this responsibility was exercised by the Secretary of State for Scotland but, with the establishment of the Scottish Parliament in 1999, policing became a devolved matter and Scottish Ministers then exercised this power and were answerable to the Scottish Parliament. Local gov-ernment interests in policing were represented through police boards made up of locally elected councillors and their responsibilities included setting the budget for their local force (and contributing 49 per cent of the costs of policing) and appoint-ing senior officers. The third element of the tripartite structure was the Chief Con-stable of the local force who, although answerable to the local police board and to Scottish Ministers, was able to exercise operational independence in relation to the management and utilisation of police officers.

Described as an 'explanatory and cooperative' model of police governance (Reiner, 2010), the balance of the relationship between the three elements of the tripartite structure has undergone significant change over the last 50 years. This is partly because the number of local police forces has declined over time as a result of a series of mergers. In the 1850s there were over 90 local police forces in Scotland but only half this number remained 100 years later. By the 1970s, the number of forces had halved again to 22 although each of Scotland's cities still had its own police force whose boundaries were broadly in line with those of the built-up urban area. As a result of local government reorganisation in 1975, however, new regional and island councils were established and the boundaries of police forces realigned to create eight new territorial forces that have existed until the current reforms. Of these, Strathclyde Police in the west of Scotland was by far the largest with a force area that encompassed almost half of Scotland's population (2.3 mil-lion), the largest city (Glasgow) and had over 7,000 officers. The remaining area of the country was the responsibility of seven other forces, which varied greatly in the size of the geographical area and population they covered and in terms of the number of officers. Northern Constabulary, for example, was responsible for a geographical area the size of Belgium; Dumfries and Galloway Constabulary in south-west Scotland had only 500 officers making it smaller than a police division within the Strathclyde force.

Along with changes in geographical boundaries, the distribution of power within the tripartite structure has also shifted significantly over the last 50 years. The Local Government etc. (Scotland) Act 1994, which replaced two-tier local government with 32 single-tier (unitary) local councils, fundamentally changed the character of police governance overnight. For Strathclyde Police, for example, this meant that rather than dealing with one regional council the police board now comprised representatives of 12 separate councils. Such fragmentation of local democratic involvement in policing was compounded by the way police boards had little capacity for carrying out independent scrutiny of their force's perform-ance and therefore typically relied on their chief constables to provide information. It is, therefore, unsurprising that some observers have concluded that '[t]he way the tripartite system works is that the key players are central government officials and chief constables with the local police board largely providing the rubber stamp' (Scott and Wilkie, 2001: 58).

The balance of power between the Scottish Government and local chief con-stables had also shifted over the last 15 years. The Scottish Government gradually acquired statutory powers that allowed it to be more interventionist, directing chief constables to include information on specific topics in their annual reports and ensuring that common services are provided where this is deemed necessary for promoting the efficiency of the police. Under the Police, Public Order and Crimi-nal Justice (Scotland) Act 2006, for example, it established the Scottish Police Serv-ices Authority (SPSA) governed by a board appointed by Scottish Ministers and with responsibility for the delivery of police training and education (via the Scottish Police College), forensic services, and the Scottish Crime and Drug Enforcement Agency. Such centralism was also evident in the increasingly prominent role played by the Association of Chief Police Officers in Scotland (ACPOS) in formulating national policing policy in ways which might limit the discretion exercised at a force level by a local chief constable. As Donnelly and Scott (2005) have observed, ACPOS's 'corporate significance may compromise the independence of individual chief constables, who may find it difficult to break ranks with an agreement reached jointly by their representatives and another party, especially the government' (p. 75). Further evidence of a centralising agenda came in 2009 when the Jus-tice Minister announced the creation of a new Scottish Policing Board to bring together central and local government partners with the police to identify strategic priorities across Scotland. This development fuelled concerns among many observ-ers that the three legs of Scotland's tripartite system of police governance (central government, local government and local chief constables) have 'a very unbalanced look about them' (Donnelly and Scott, 2005: 81) with various researchers noting a 'creeping centralism' (Fyfe, 2011: 186), a 'long centralising drift' (Walker, 2000: 191) and that 'the governance of Scottish policing appears to be moving inexorably in an ever more centralised direction' (Donnelly and Scott, 2010: 106).

Preparing the ground for reform: the search for a model of 'sustainable policing'

Although the movement towards a greater centralisation of policing in Scotland appeared to be gaining momentum by the late 2000s, few would have anticipated that this process would accelerate so quickly that a national police force would be established by 2013. The catalysts for this rapid and radical change appear to have been a combination of the economic crisis of 2008 and the resulting cuts in public spending, and a change in the politics of Scotland which gave the Scottish National Party (SNP) a majority in the Scottish Parliament. This section traces the key milestones on the road to reform between 2010 and 2011 (see, too, Fyfe and Scott, 2013).

Early in June 2010 Scotland's Justice Minister, Kenny Macaskill, spoke to Scotland's chief police officers at the ACPOS Annual Conference and made clear that the Scottish Government had no plans to merge Scottish police forces to create a national police service. In fact, his speech celebrated the achievements of Scottish policing: recorded crime was at a 35-year low, the clear-up rate for violent crime was at a 35-year high, and there were high levels of public satisfaction with policing. Within a matter of weeks, however, the Minster's message had changed. The political narrative now focused on the looming economic crisis and how the deep cuts to public spending being made by the coalition government in Westminster would impact on Scotland. It was being forecast that the decline in public spending in Scotland would mean that it would take at least 15 years (or until 2025/6) for public spending to return to 2009/10 levels. The police would need to share the burden of these cuts, with the Scottish Government estimating a reduction in police funding of £1.7 billion over the next 15 years (*The Guardian*, 17 August 2011). Against this background, work to identify what was termed a 'sustainable policing model' began. A Sustainable Policing Project team (comprising civil servants and police officers) was established within Scottish Government to explore the options for reform, focusing on three main models: a national police force; a regional structure comprising three or four forces; and continuation of the eight-force model but with enhanced collaboration. An early indication, however, that the Scottish Government was now thinking that police reform might involve a fundamental restructuring came in October 2010 when Scotland's First Minister addressed the SNP Party Conference and declared that Scotland was facing the most severe cuts in public spending in our life times and that he would put 'bobbies before boundaries' in order to ensure that police numbers were maintained despite cuts in police budgets (BBC News, 17 October 2010).

In March 2011, the Sustainable Policing Project reported to the Scottish Government. The report made clear that a single (national) force model 'provides the greatest opportunity to manage change, drive efficiency and in delivering operations when the change is complete' while the current structure (the eight-force model) 'represents the opposite' (Scottish Government, 2011a: 5). With a Scottish election only two months away, work on the options of police reform paused but the election provided an opportunity for Scotland's political parties to declare their position on the future of Scottish policing. Significantly three of the main political parties – the SNP, Labour and the Conservatives – all indicated that they would support the creation of a national force, with only the Liberal-Democratic Party continuing to argue for retaining the status quo, fearing that a national force would undermine the localism of regional forces. When the SNP were re-elected with a majority (before the election they had led a minority government) they were determined to use this political advantage to drive forward their programme of police reform.

The report of the Sustainable Policing Project also brought to the surface the deep divisions on the nature of reform among Scotland's eight chief constables. Most were in favour either of the status quo of eight forces or limited mergers to create three or four regional forces, but the Chief Constable of Scotland's largest force, Strathclyde Police, was strongly supportive of a national force. In a series of public statements, the Chief Constable, Stephen House, argued that a national force would help protect police numbers because of the savings that would be made on infrastructure (instead of eight police headquarters you would only need one) and would also allow better access to specialist expertise across Scotland (given that under the existing arrangements smaller forces did not always have the capacity to provide the same level of specialist support as larger ones). By contrast many of House's colleagues who were the chief constables of Scotland's smaller police forces argued that it was only through regional arrangements that it was possible to tailor the style of policing to the needs of very different communities, and they feared that a national force would see a drift of police resources to Scotland's most densely populated areas, leaving rural and remote areas under-provided for.

In June 2011, the month following the election, the results of the government's public consultation on the options for police reform were published. Intriguingly this revealed very limited support for a national force (less than 10 per cent of respondents preferred this option) with most respondents preferring a regional structure and a substantial minority commenting that the lack of detailed information made it difficult to make a decision (Scottish Government, 2011b). Several anxieties about a national structure were highlighted, including concerns that it would be focused on the 'central belt' (the most densely populated area of Scotland lying between Glasgow and Edinburgh) and draw resources away from more remote or rural areas. There was also a view that different approaches were required in different parts of the country and that the move to a single force would damage local accountability. Despite these results, the Scottish Government position remained that a regional structure would not deliver the level of savings required and that, following the May election in which it had campaigned for a national force, it now had an electoral mandate for reform. In another significant development, it then convened an 'international policing summit' in August 2011 at which police representatives of several European countries that had already moved or were planning to move towards a national structure spoke of their journey, including Norway, Denmark, the Netherlands and Finland. The main purpose of the summit appeared to be to provide reassurance to those involved in Scottish policing that a national structure could bring long-term benefits.

Less than two weeks after the international summit, the Justice Secretary stood up in the Scottish Parliament and announced that he would now introduce legislation to create a national police force. As the Justice Secretary explained:

The status quo was not sustainable – we cannot afford to keep doing things eight times over. To do nothing would mean going down the route south of the border where there is no alternative strategy to massive reductions in police numbers.

Moreover, the regional option was dismissed as offering 'The worst of both worlds': 'It would have been cumbersome, bureaucratic and would not have delivered the same benefits as a single service.' The government also argued that 'Communities don't care about boundaries; they want services to work effectively and efficiently' (Scottish Government, 2011c). And, echoing the themes of the international summit, the Justice Secretary declared that '[t]his Government is ambitious for Scotland. If Denmark, Finland, Ireland, Luxembourg, Northern Ireland and Norway can have successful single services, so can Scotland'.

Legislating for change: the 2012 Police and Fire Reform (Scotland) Act

In January 2012 the Scottish Government introduced the Police and Fire Reform (Scotland) Bill into the Scottish Parliament along with a 'Policy Memorandum' setting out the objectives of police reform. These objectives are:

- to protect and improve local services despite financial cuts, by stopping duplication of support services eight times over and not cutting front-line services;
- to create more equal access to specialist support and national capacity;
- to strengthen the connections between services and communities.

The Bill made its way through the Scottish Parliamentary process of scrutiny by different committees and in the summer of 2012 it received Royal Assent and became an Act. Given the relative paucity of direct police legislation and the statutory basis for the police resting primarily on the Police (Scotland) Act 1967, the new legislation is in itself a landmark in terms of establishing a foundation for twenty-first-century policing in Scotland.

The Act contains a number of important clauses. First, a national police force will be established to be called the Police Service of Scotland (PSS). The PSS will be under the direction and control of a chief constable and the responsibilities of the post are clearly stated in terms of administration, allocation and deployment of resources, and the provision of information. The overarching responsibility is to develop a national strategic plan for the service and to publish annual policing plans in order to secure continuous improvement in policing. Second, governance of the PSS will lie with a new body called the Scottish Police Authority (SPA). The Authority's main functions include resourcing the police service, promoting and supporting continuous improvement in policing, and holding the chief constable to account. An independent chair will be appointed by Scottish Ministers, and the Act provides for a membership of 'not fewer than 10 nor more than 14 other members', whose appointment must be based on possessing 'the skills and expertise relevant to the functions of the Authority'. The strategic priorities for the SPA will be set by Scottish Ministers and the SPA must produce a three-year 'strategic police plan' as well as an 'annual police plan' and involve the chief constable in the production of these documents. Another new element within the governance structure of the PSS will be a new body called the Police Investigations and Review Commissioner (PIRC) which will replace the Police Complaints Commissioner for Scotland. PIRC will have a key role in investigating serious complaints against police officers and deaths in police custody, functions which in the past would have been carried out by senior officers from another force but which is no longer possible with a single police service. Third, local policing becomes a statutory requirement and will be organised at the level of Scotland's 32 local councils. Each of these local police areas will have a local commander with responsibility for the policing of the area and the preparation of a local policing plan. Local policing plans will set out the main priorities and objectives for the policing of the local area, along with the reasons for selecting these, the arrangements for achieving these objectives, and the outcomes by which these priorities and objectives can be measured. The local council can provide feedback to the local commander, ask for reports on the policing of the area and be consulted in the preparation of the local policing plan which the local commander must submit to the local council for approval. The local commander is required to provide reports on the carrying out of police functions, statistical information on complaints about the police, and other information about the policing of its area, 'as the local authority may reasonably require'. The Act also allows the local commander to consult on police plans with other persons outwith the council. Fourth, the Act includes a set of 'policing principles' which state that:

> the main purpose of policing is to improve the safety and well-being of persons, localities and communities in Scotland, and that the Police Service, working in collaboration with others where appropriate, should seek to achieve that main purpose by policing in a way which (i) is accessible to, and engaged with, local communities, and (ii) promotes measures to prevent crime, harm and disorder'.
>
> *(para. 32)*

In line with these principles, there is also a fuller statement of the duties of a police officer which goes well beyond the 'guard, patrol and watch' of the 1967 Act. These duties include preventing and detecting crime, maintaining order, and protecting life and property, and there is an explicit requirement on officers to act with fairness, integrity and impartiality, as well as upholding fundamental human rights and according 'equal respect to all people, according to the law'.

Reflections on reform

Having sketched out the background to reform and the key changes contained within the legislation, this section attempts to step back from the specific details of the process and reflect on the wider implications of police reform in Scotland. Three themes in particular are important to address: the different drivers and divergent trajectories of police reform within Britain; the implications of reform for the governance of policing; and the emergence of a new narrative about the mission of policing.

Different drivers and divergent trajectories: Scotland's reform in a British and European context

Although it is commonplace to refer to 'British' policing as though it were a monolithic entity, there have always between important differences within Britain between the policing of England and Wales on the one hand and Scotland on the other (see Fyfe and Henry, 2012). Police reform has made those differences even starker. In terms of the main drivers of reform, the approach in Scotland that is articulated within political discourse has focused on the economic rationale for reform and the search for a financially sustainable model of policing that does not involve cuts in police officer numbers. The Outline Business Case claims that a national structure will generate savings of over £100 million a year (or 10 per cent of the annual police budget) without any reduction in what has become the 'magic number' of 17,234 police officers which the government has made a commitment to maintaining given that it is the number of officers that existed when they came into office. In England and Wales, by contrast, there will be an 11 per cent cut in police officer numbers (equivalent to over 16,000 officers) in order to address a 20 per cent reduction in police budgets over the next four years as well as expanding the process of outsourcing certain police functions to the private sector as another way to making financial savings. Interestingly the new Chief Constable of the PSS, Stephen House, has made it clear that he does not have an appetite for increasing the involvement of the private sector in Scottish policing and will seek to make any financial savings through rationalisation rather than privatisation (House, 2013). It needs to be borne in mind, however, that although the stated rationale for reform in Scotland is economic, there is almost certainly a political dimension to it as well. A referendum on Scottish independence will, in all likelihood, take place in the autumn of 2014 and the Scottish Government cannot be unaware of the symbolic associations between policing, nationhood and 'polity-building' (Walker, 2000: 133) and so the establishment of a national police organisation should be seen in this context as part of that wider state building project (Fyfe and Henry, 2012).

There are also significant differences emerging between England and Wales and Scotland in relation to the distribution of power over policing. Police reform south of the border is clearly strongly informed by a political–ideological vision focused on transferring power from 'the centre' back to local communities. The introduction of locally elected Police and Crime Commissioners (PCCs) in England and Wales builds on concerns that date back to the last Labour Government of a perceived 'democratic deficit' in policing governance because of the lack of a 'clear line of "electoral accountability" by which citizens could express their support for, or censure of, locally elected representatives charged with overseeing policing' (Sampson, 2012: 7). In Scotland, the greater involvement of Scottish Ministers in setting strategic priorities, the creation of the unelected SPA and the abolition of local police boards all suggests a much more centralised, technocratic and bureaucratic approach to police governance. The introduction of PCCs also suggests that England and Wales continue to look across the Atlantic towards the United States in terms of policy innovation in policing given some parallels with the role of locally elected officials in the running of police departments in America. Scotland, by contrast, has looked across the North Sea and engaged in a dialogue with northern and western European countries for evidence of the operation and effectiveness of national police organisations. Indeed, Scotland is following a very similar trajectory to the Netherlands in terms of police reform given the Dutch have merged their 25 regional forces to create a national police force which began operation on 1 January 2013. The Scandinavian countries, too, have all embarked on major structural reforms over the last 10–15 years which has resulted in a significant centralisation of policing by the merging of local districts to recreate larger regional territorial units. In Denmark the number of police districts has been reduced from 54 to 12; in Finland 90 districts have become 24; in Norway 54 districts have become 27; and in Sweden, 118 districts have become 21 with plans to create a single police force by 2015. While there are different drivers for these reforms in the different countries (ranging from strategic attempts to improve the capacity of the police to tackle changing patterns of criminality to political frustration at what have been seen as past police failures (see Fyfe *et al.*, 2013)), these changes underline the way in which Scotland's amalgamation of its eight forces to create a national structure is closely aligned with the pattern of police reform in many other countries in northern and western Europe.

Democratic criteria and the governance of policing in Scotland

Jones (2008) has set out a range of democratic criteria that form the basis of a series of normative claims about the governance of policing. These include issues of equity (policing services should be fairly distributed between geographical areas, groups and individuals), the distribution of power to influence policing policy (which should not be concentrated but should be distributed across a number of institutions and agencies) and participation (citizens should have the opportunity to participate in discussions about, and have influence over, policing policy). In each of these areas there are important questions to be asked about the reform of policing in Scotland (see Table 31.1) In relation to equity, for example, how will decisions about the allocation of resources between local policing areas be determined? How will conflicts between local and national views as to appropriate resourcing be resolved? How will access to specialist expertise be facilitated in an equitable manner? In relation to the distribution of power, it is clear that although the trend towards centralism pre-dates the current reforms, the 2012 Police and Fire Reform (Scotland) Act has significantly accelerated this process. Scottish Ministers will not only appoint members of the SPA but have the power to direct the SPA in relation to both general and specific matters (although

TABLE 31.1 Democratic criteria and governance of Scottish policing (based on Jones, 2008)

Democratic criteria	Questions raised by Police Reform (Scotland) Act
Equity (Policing services should be fairly distributed between geographical areas, groups and individuals)	• How, and by whom, will decisions about the allocation of resources between local policing areas be determined? • How will conflicts between local and national views as to appropriate resourcing of local areas be resolved? • How will access to specialist expertise and resources be facilitated in an equitable manner?
Service delivery (The police deliver appropriate services as efficiently and effectively as possible)	• How will the SPA determine what should be delivered nationally and locally and does consideration need to be given to an intermediate geography (i.e. regional level) for some services? • To what extent will delivery be shaped by centrally determined statistical targets and performance indicators, and what scope will there be for local democratic input in the setting of these?
Responsiveness (As long as it is consistent with equitable policing, the police should be responsive to the views of representative bodies in determining priorities, the allocation of resources between different objectives and choice of policing methods)	• Against a background of declining responsiveness to local representative bodies and growing central government influence, how responsive will policing be to local preferences expressed through local elected representatives with only limited statutory powers? • What mechanisms will be in place to respond to the perceived needs of local communities directly (i.e. other than through local councils)? • At a national level, how responsive will the SPA be to the views of external bodies when its membership is selected rather than elected?
Distribution of power (The power to influence and review policing policy should not be concentrated but should be distributed across a number of institutions and agencies)	• To what extent will the proposals address the centralisation of power that has occurred within the tripartite structure over the last 20 years? • Will the proposals around local consultation between the local commander and local authority be sufficient to address the democratic deficit that has emerged at a local level? • What powers, if any, will local councils have in relation to the local consultation proposals?
Information (There should be clear and accurate information available to relevant bodies and community groups about funding, expenditure, activities and the outputs of policing)	• Against a background of growing concerns that unrefined police performance data in the public realm might have hindered rather than enhanced sophisticated debate about policing (Jones, 2008: 717), how will the different (but overlapping) information needs of police managers, local authority members, community groups and the public be addressed?

Redress (There should be effective means of redress for the unlawful or unreasonable behaviour of individual police officers)	• What are the implications of the changes proposed for the investigation and review of complaints by the public against the police, including the replacement of the Police Complaints Commissioner for Scotland with the Police Investigation and Review Commissioner?
Participation (As far as possible, citizens from all social groups should have the opportunity to participate in discussions of policing policy and have real influence over policy choices, but participation must not compromise a commitment to equitable policing)	• Are the proposals, which focus on increasing the *quantity* of locally elected councillor involvement in local policing, likely to improve the *quality* of the engagement between police and citizens at a local level? Who will have responsibility for ensuring engagement and participation between the police and other social groups so that their views on local policing are also heard? • At a national level, how best can the membership of the SPA be constituted in such a way as to properly involve as wide a range of interests as possible in discussions of policing policy?

not in relation to specific police operations) and the power to determine strategic police priorities. The Chief Constable will also hold considerable power in relation to the direction and control of the police service and the development of strategic policing plans. At a local level, however, the Scottish Government has stripped local councils of all the powers they used to have to shape local policing. In the past locally elected councillors on the police authority had the power to set the police budget and appoint chief officers. After reform, these local councillors will have no financial responsibility for policing, their local commander will be chosen by the Chief Constable of the PSS, and their role in setting local priorities will be a consultative one in relation to a local policing plan drawn up by the local commander.

This raises some intriguing questions in relation to Jones' (2008) criteria of participation and the future relationship between 'national' and 'local' within Scotland. The 2012 Police Act makes clear the requirement on a local commander to submit a local police plan to the relevant local authority for approval. Given that such a plan must have regard to the national strategic police plan as well as priorities identified by local community planning there are areas of potential tension around the balance between a participatory 'bottom-up' approach to setting local priorities and objectives and a more 'top-down' approach led by the SPA and Scottish Ministers.

A new narrative for policing?

In Scotland, the reform programme has also been used as an opportunity to articulate a set of new 'Policing Principles' in which the emphasis on crime and disorder is subsumed within a broader statement of the policing mission: 'the main purpose of policing is to improve safety and well-being of persons, localities and communities' and that this is to be achieved in a way that engages with communities and promotes measures to prevent crime, harm and disorder. This is an important shift in emphasis away from a crime-centred definition of the purpose of policing. In England and Wales, by contrast, the Home Secretary has made it clear that the police focus must be crime reduction. 'The mission of the police', the Home Secretary contends, 'which was established by Sir Robert Peel as preventing crime and disorder has not fundamentally changed' (Home Office, 2010: 2) and expresses concern that over time the 'Police have become form writers rather than crime fighters' (Home Office, 2010: 10).

We will need to wait and see how far Scotland's policing principles are translated into practice but the Police Reform Act does place a duty on the Chief Constable to take 'due regard' of these principles. In addition, the principles embody the idea of the police working in partnership with others and the local police commanders will be under a duty to participate in community planning, a mechanism for bringing together different local agencies, including health, education and housing, as well as policing, to agree on a shared set of outcomes for improving community well-being. It remains to be seen how exactly this network of engagement with local policing will work out in practice and the degree to which there will be a consistent approach across Scotland.

Conclusions

The creation of the new PSS on 1 April 2013 marked the most radical change in the history of policing in Scotland for over 100 years. While this could be interpreted as simply the end point of a long process of 'creeping centralism', such a conclusion oversimplifies what is a more complex set of changes. On the one hand, establishing a national force under the control of a single chief constable and accountable to a new national body (the SPA) made up of members appointed by Scottish Ministers creates an unprecedented level of centralisation in relation to the operation and strategic development of policing in Scotland. Combined with stripping locally elected councillors of their traditional roles in setting local police budgets and appointing chief officers, these developments raise significant questions about the emergence of a democratic deficit in relation to police governance. On the other hand, local policing is now a statutory requirement and the new Chief Constable of Scotland, Stephen House, has made it clear that he intends that there should be a policing plan for each of the council ward areas across Scotland (of which there are over 300) as well as at the level of the 32 local authorities (House, 2013). All local councillors, rather than the handful appointed to a police board, will also have the opportunity to participate in a formal relationship with the local police commander, and councils are being given the freedom to determine what form that relationship takes. This combination of enhanced centralisation with a new localism does, however, bring with it risks of serious tensions between the national and local levels. It is unclear, for example, what would happen if a local council refused to endorse the policing plan of their local commander or if a local commander was unhappy with the allocation of resources provided to the local area by the chief constable. There also appears to be confusion around whether the process of developing local policing plans is meant to follow a 'top-down' approach which begins with national policing priorities, or a 'bottom-up' approach based around consultation with local stakeholders.

There are also significant implications for those working within the police service. The government's commitment to not reducing the numbers of officers below the figure of 17,234 that existed at the beginning of the reform process might be politically expedient but disguises important changes that will occur in roles and responsibilities as a result of reform. Civilian police staff do not have the same protection and it is likely their numbers will be reduced as budget cuts take effect. The result could be to undermine the progress on workforce modernisation over the last 10 years which has attempted to create a more flexible mix of sworn and non-sworn police personnel, so that tasks not requiring police powers were undertaken by civilian staff. It is likely therefore that some police officers will be required to return to so-called back-office functions, reducing the numbers available for 'front-line' duties. Another significant change will be the radically reduced opportunities for promotion within the new national force. There will no longer be a need for a chief police officer organisation (ACPOS) because their numbers will be reduced from over 40 to 11, and with just 32 local commanders and one national headquarters the number of senior management ranks will be significantly reduced. For those joining the new PSS, the landscape of career opportunities and promotion will look very different to what it did in the past.

Will the public notice any difference in the service provided by a national force compared with the regional model? It will take time to assess this although the evidence from other countries indicates that major restructuring of police organisations can lead to a period of declining public satisfaction. In Denmark a longitudinal study of citizen perceptions of policing revealed that perceived levels of police visibility, availability and effectiveness all fell for a few years immediately after reform before improvements began to be recognised (see Holmberg and Balvig, 2013). Looking across the public sector to the impact of structural changes on performance in other areas is also not encouraging. As Braithwaite *et al.* (2005) note in relation to health services which have experienced mergers and an 'altering of the responsibilities between central and peripheral bodies': 'The evidence for [restructuring] making a difference, let alone demonstrably improving productivity or outcomes, is surprisingly slender.' As Scotland embarks on the most radical reforms of policing for a generation, attention will now focus on whether these reforms will achieve their objectives of creating a police organisation that results in improved local services, greater equity in accessing specialist support, and enhanced connections between police and communities.

Note

1   This chapter draws on collaborative work with Alistair Henry (Fyfe and Henry, 2012) and Kenneth Scott (Fyfe and Scott, 2013) and I am very grateful for their permission to draw on this work.

References

BBC News (2010) 'Bobbies before boundaries' (17 October) Online. Available from: http://www.bbc.co.uk/news/11561160 (accessed 2 July 2012).

Braithwaite, J., Westbrook, J. and Ledema, R. (2005) 'Restructuring as gratification', *Journal of the Royal Society of Medicine*, 98(1): 542–544.

Donnelly, D. and Scott, K. (eds) (2005) *Policing Scotland* (1st edition). Cullompton: Willan Publishing.

Donnelly, D. and Scott, K. (2010) 'Governance, accountabilities and Scottish policing', in D. Donnelly and K. Scott (eds) *Policing Scotland* (2nd edition), Cullompton: Willan Publishing.

Fyfe, N.R. (2011) 'Policing, surveillance and security in contemporary Scotland', in H. Croall, G. Mooney and M. Munro (eds) *Criminal Justice in Scotland*. Cullompton: Willan, pp. 175–194.

Fyfe, N.R. and Henry, A. (2012) 'Negotiating divergent tides of police reform within the United Kingdom', *Journal of Police Studies*, 25(4): 171–190.

Fyfe, N.R. and Scott, K. (2013) 'In search of sustainable policing? Creating a national police force in Scotland', in N.R. Fyfe, J. Terpstra and P. Tops (eds) *Centralizing Forces? Police Reform in Northern and Western Europe in Comparative Perspective*. The Hague: Boom Publishing.

Fyfe, N.R., Terpstra, J. and Tops, P. (eds) (2013) *Centralizing Forces? Police Reform in Northern and Western Europe in Comparative Perspective*. The Hague: Boom Publishing.

The Guardian (2011) 'Police chief backs call for a single Scottish force' (17 August). Online. Available from: http://www.guardian.co.uk/uk/2011/aug/17/police-chief-single-scottish-force (accessed 2 July 2012).

Holmberg, L. and Balvig, F. (2013) 'Centralization in disguise: the Danish police reform 2007–2010', in N.R. Fyfe, J. Terpstra and P. Tops (eds) *Centralizing Forces? Police Reform in Northern and Western Europe in Comparative Perspective*. The Hague: Boom Publishing.

Home Office (2010) *Policing in the 21st Century: Reconnecting Police and People*. London: HMSO.

House, S. (2013) 'Future Policing in Scotland', Keynote address to the Scottish Institute for Policing Research (SIPR) International Policing Conference, Edinburgh, 22 November 2013 (see http://www.sipr.ac.uk/events/IPC2012.php).

Jones, T. (2008) 'The accountability of policing', in T. Newburn (ed.) *Handbook of Policing*. Cullompton: Willan Publishing.

Loveday, B. (2011) 'Commentary', *The Police Journal*, 84: 195–198.

Reiner, R. (2010) *The Politics of the Police* (4th edition). Oxford: Oxford University Press.

Sampson, F. (2012) 'Hail to the chief? How far does the introduction of elected police commissioners herald a US-style politicization of policing in the UK?' *Policing: A Journal of Policy and Practice*, 6(1): 4–15.

Scott, K. and Wilkie, R. (2001) 'Chief Constables: a current "crisis" in Scottish policing?' *Scottish Affairs*, 35: 54–68.

Scottish Government (2011a) *Sustainable Policing Project Phase Two Report: Options for Reform*. Edinburgh: Scottish Government.

Scottish Government (2011b) *Research Support for a Consultation on the Future of Policing in Scotland*. Edinburgh: Scottish Government.

Scottish Government (2011c) *Renewing Scotland: Scotland's Programme for Government 2011–12*. Edinburgh: Scottish Government.

Walker, N. (2000) *Policing in a Changing Constitutional Order*. London: Sweet and Maxwell.

INDEX

Note: *tab* = table; *fig* = figure; *n* = note.